THE GREAT LAND RUSH AND THE MAKING OF
THE MODERN WORLD, 1650–1900

The Great Land Rush and the Making of the Modern World, 1650–1900

JOHN C. WEAVER

McGill-Queen's University Press
Montreal & Kingston · London · Ithaca

Legal deposit second quarter 2003
Bibliothèque nationale du Québec

Printed in Canada on acid-free paper that is 100% ancient forest free
(100% post-consumer recycled), processed chlorine free.

This book has been published with the help of a grant from the
Humanities and Social Sciences Federation of Canada, using funds
provided by the Social Sciences and Humanities Research Council
of Canada.

McGill-Queen's University Press acknowledges the support of the
Canada Council for the Arts for its publishing program. It also
acknowledges the financial support of the Government of Canada
through the Book Publishing Industry Development Program (BPIDP)
for its publishing activities.

National Library of Canada Cataloguing
in Publication Data

Weaver, John C.
    The great land rush and the making of the modern world, 1650–1900 /
John C. Weaver.
    Includes bibliographical references and index.
    ISBN 0-7735-2527-0
    1. Right of property – Great Britain – Colonies--History. 2. Land
tenure – Great Britain--Colonies – History. 3. Land settlement – Great
Britain – Colonies--History. 4. United States – Territorial expansion.
5. Colonization – History. I. Title.

JV105.W42 2003   323.4'6'09171241   C2002-905705-1

Typeset in Sabon 10/12
by Caractéra inc., Quebec City

Contents

Maps and Tables

Acknowledgments

During ten years of research and writing, I have benefited from conversation and hospitality in many places. I wish to thank Patrick Troy in Canberra, who arranged the sponsorship of my first research trip to Australia, and influenced my thinking. Assistance and hospitality were extended over the years by Donald Loveridge, Peter and Maribeth Coleman, Giselle Bynes and Steve Hamilton, Richard Hill, and Matthew Trundle, all from Wellington, New Zealand (a city of book lovers); Ian Tyrrell of Sydney, Diana Kirkby and David Philips of Melbourne, and Mark Copland, Bill Kitson, and Jonathan Richards of Brisbane; Bill Baker, formerly of Lethbridge; and David and Edith Burley and Henry Trachtenburg of Winnipeg. For their suggestions on readings or their editorial advice on parts of this book, or on the several articles that I wrote which reinforce its arguments, I thank Michael Adas, Virginia Aksan, David Burley, Peter Burroughs, Carolyn Gray, Rhoda Howard-Hassmann, Stephen Heathorn, Denis Jeans, John McLaren, Jim Phillips, Joseph Powell, Evan Simpson, Frederic Vallvé, Michelle Vosburgh, Alan Ward, Ian Wards, and Adam Weaver.

I learned too from students in my graduate seminars on colonization and settlement frontiers taught from 1997 to 2001. Jim Greenlee, Jim Lemon, and Richard Rempel read early drafts of parts or all of the manuscript. Jim Greenlee's command of British imperial literature and his sense of language resulted in recommendations on almost every page; most were incorporated into the book. Jim urged me to situate this book more fully in British imperial historiography. At least a dozen anonymous reviewers read parts of the manuscript and related articles. Their suggestions and criticisms made this a much better book, although several may take issue with its arguments. I have been fortunate in having the benefit of John Parry's editorial wisdom and attention to details. Reg Woodruff and Michelle Sharp prepared the maps. Ron

Edwards wrote a fine index and raised valuable queries. Errors are my responsibility.

Many librarians have assisted me in the Chiffley and Menzies Libraries of Australian National University, the State Library of Queensland and the Oxley Library, Griffith University Library, the State Library of New South Wales and the Mitchell Library, the State Library of South Australia and the Mortlock Library, the State Library of Western Australia and the Battye Library, the State Library of Victoria, the Auckland Public Library, the National Library of New Zealand and the Turnbull Library, the National Library of South Africa (Cape Town), and the Library of Congress. The last-named is one of the world's finest institutions for leaning, as visits to its reading rooms or web page will attest. The interlibrary loan service of the Mills Memorial Library at McMaster University secured hundreds of items for me from scores of libraries around North America, although the library's British imperial holdings and those on early U.S. history were strong, on account of the efforts of Charles Johnston and David Russo. The staff at the Noel Butlin Archives Centre at Australian National University, a national historical treasure recently saved from closure, helped launch this project. The extensive business collections there diverted me from urban to colonial land history in July 1991. Also hospitable and supportive were archivists at the National Archives of New Zealand, the Victorian Public Record Office (Melbourne), the State Archives of New South Wales, of Queensland, and of South Australia, the Provincial Archives of British Columbia, of Manitoba, and of Ontario, the Glenbow Institute (Calgary), the National Archives of Canada, and the National Archives of South Africa (both the Cape Town and the Pretoria Repositories), and the American Heritage Center, University of Wyoming. The last-named institution assisted me with a visiting research fellowship (2001), as did Australian National University (1991).

At McMaster University, Emöke Szathmary and Harvey Winegarten, provosts, enabled me to conduct research trips during the summers when I was dean of graduate studies. Mark Hatton, Eva Incze, Paul Jessop, Adele Reinhartz, and John Scime arranged their work in the School of Graduate Studies so that I could plug away at this project from 1994 to 1999. Colleagues in the university community could not have been more supportive.

I also owe a major debt of gratitude to the Social Sciences and Humanities Research Council of Canada, which supported a substantial portion of the research.

Joan Tamorria Weaver assisted my research in Australia and South Africa, and helped me with editing. To her, for her love, moral support, and backing throughout our life together, I dedicate this book.

THE GREAT LAND RUSH AND THE MAKING OF
THE MODERN WORLD, 1650–1900

Arranging New Worlds

True, our system is wasteful, and fruitful of many small disputes. True, a large estate can be managed more economically than a small one. True, pasture-farming yields higher profits than tillage. Nevertheless, master steward, our wasteful husbandry feeds many households where your economical methods would feed few. In our ill-arranged fields and scrubby commons most families hold a share, though it be but a few roods. In our unenclosed village there are few rich, but there are few destitute, save when God sends a bad harvest, and we all starve together. We do not like your improvements which ruin half the honest men affected by them. (Imagined statement from a manor jury to an estate steward in R.H. Tawney, *The Agrarian Problem in the Sixteenth Century* (London: Longman, Green, and Co., 1912), 409)

Human industry works its greatest miracles only when the skill and capital of an improved society are brought to bear upon the superior lands of a new country. (Upper Canadian political reformer Dr Thomas Rolph, *Emigration and Colonization* [London: John Mortimer 1844], cited in Catharine Anne Wilson, *A New Lease on Life: Landlords, Tenants, and Immigrants in Ireland and Canada* [Montreal: McGill-Queen's University Press, 1994], 51)

What a settlement one could have in this valley! See, it is broad enough to support a large population! Fancy a church spire rising where that tamarind rears its dark crown of foliage, and think how well a score or so of pretty cottages would look instead of those thorn clumps and gum trees! Fancy this lovely valley teeming with herds of cattle and fields of corn, spreading to the right and left of this stream! How much better would such a state become this valley, rather than its wild and deserted aspect. (Henry Stanley, gazing in 1871 on country near Lake Tanganyika, quoted in David Spurr, *The Rhetoric of Empire: Colonial Discourse in Journalism, Travel Writing, and Imperial Administration* [Durham, NC: Duke University Press, 1993], 29–30)

This book tackles several questions of global magnitude by recounting a history of land taking – the great land rush – in regions of the world that became rich, food-exporting states. These Neo-Europes, as Alfred Crosby labels them, have dominated the international trade in food-stuffs, not by brute productivity but by combining technology and extensive cultivation.[1] Crosby lists as food exporting Neo-Europes the United States, Canada, Australia, New Zealand, South Africa, and Argentina; he suggests that Brazil and Uruguay may also fit the description. Many factors account for the development of food-exporting regions, not least "the superiority of the Europeans in economic and political organization."[2] Crosby's writings, however, stress other expla-nations, especially the robustness displayed by Eurasian plants and animals in new environments, where they flourished, free for a while from old-world predators and parasites. However, the organizational dexterity of Europeans relative to those of indigenous peoples, as he points out, was significant too. Capital mobilization was one charac-teristic skill of Europeans, and it hinged partly on ideas about property rights and improvements, because they braced credit. They installed an influential doctrine of individual property rights in land in a number of productive Neo-Europes. That concept advanced the modern notion that land is an article to be measured, allocated, traded, and improved; it aided the capitalization of grazing and farming – processes that contributed to the monumental outcome noted by Crosby. Describing selected episodes, my book professes that the extraction of wealth from frontiers benefited from a tension, remarkable and fateful, between defiant private initiatives and the ordered, state-backed certainties of property rights. It looks at five regions of British settlement colonies and their independent successors – the United States, Canada, Australia, New Zealand, and South Africa.

In a critique of how certain grand schemes to *improve* the human condition had failed, James C. Scott argues that centralizing states bear responsibility for causing most havoc, and he refers specifically to freehold tenure and land measurement, because they impaired local autonomy.[3] Rationalized land tenure and cadastral maps were state tools that centralized; however, in Neo-Europes, these two instruments of settlement that states installed were not enacted by governments acting in isolation.[4] In the major colonial exercises to improve new worlds, the organization of space originated in tangled processes that involved far more than heavy-handed states. Many violent episodes of colonization began with a defiance of the state by wilful individuals. Rule-breaking conduct by land-seeking individuals and consortia, in conjunction with a grudging official toleration for defiant acts of land taking, enabled landholders to raise capital on security of inchoate land-based securities. Neo-European settlement resulted from a messy convergence of private impertinence and the coercive might of the state. Sustaining both aggressive land seekers and states in uneasy associations were evolving cultural attitudes about property, social station, the market economy, popular democracy, and improvement. Acts of defiance by land takers and the nursing of property rights by governments together made possible an apportionment and organization of land in the food-exporting regions identified by Crosby.

Any account of the great land rush must consider how Neo-Europeans acquired as well as distributed land. From the sixteenth to the twentieth centuries, when colonizing Europeans encountered other civilizations, they invariably measured them by European religion, laws, science, technology, political organization, knack for warfare, and use of land.[5] These appraisals, especially those supporting land-taking where Europeans could wedge their way into an ecological niche, harmed indigenous people for generations. This book investigates their treatment and that of the lands that they occupied; it connects particular practices of land-taking to patterns of violence and intimidation – notably between colonizers and first peoples. There were conflicts among colonizers, although these confrontations resulted in nothing like the harm inflicted on indigenous peoples by colonization.

In addition to developing these points, the book suggests sources for the powerful idea of improvement and elaborates on its role in reordering property rights. Improvement and its synonyms and antonyms – terms such as betterment and advancement; negligence and waste – were intrinsic to formal and informal practices of taking and allocating land. The rationalizations and rhetoric of legislators and administrators incorporated these almighty words when they justified formal schemes to take land from indigenous peoples or drafted regulations for distributing land to settlers. The ever-present squatters also adopted the rhetoric of improvement, deploying it in petitions to underpin their claims. Loaded words often made the disregard of rules by squatters, settlers, and speculators tolerable to authorities.

On these topics, this book sheds light and shows interconnections. In accomplishing these goals, it demonstrates that comparative history, using a long time span and a search for parallels outside the framework of conventional chronological sorting, can sharpen a critical understanding of attitudes and practices about property rights, which have grown to influence the contemporary world. In the decade after the collapse of the Soviet Union and the demise of communism in eastern and central Europe, free market economists have broadcast what they regard as the elegant efficiency of individualized and transferable property rights. It is therefore worth trying to understand the background ideas and settings for actions that refined these highly praised rights. For the sake of intelligibility, I decided to concentrate on landed property, largely setting aside mineral, timber, and water rights. There is a contrast in the depiction of property rights offered by economists who refer to history in their accounts of property rights and a historian's presentation of how property rights were carved out of new worlds.[6] The great land rush that helped frame modern property rights involved moral issues, turning points in the destinies of indigenous peoples, the emergence of economics as a field of study, and an intersection of American republican democracy and self-government in British settlement colonies. Participants in the rush adapted to variations in environment and tried to alter what they found. Some complications and harmful consequences should warn against simplified prescriptions for economic ills which assume that the practices of acquisition and allocation refined during the great land rush offer an ideal model for development throughout the world today. In this book, I subscribe to James C. Scott's critique of programs that promised to improve the condition of humanity, although government actions in this regard had foundations in cultural values and non-government initiatives, both of which emerge in the following account of the great land rush.

The first part ("Scanning the Horizon") has three chapters. Chapter 1 establishes what made British and American practices of land allocation different from those practised in other land-acquiring and land-granting empires, including (in order of discussion) Spain, Portugal, France, Germany, the Netherlands, and Russia. Chapter 2 defines concepts – such as property rights and legal interests – and discusses ideas – such as improvement of land – that inform the events reported in the book. Chapter 3 also focuses on ideas; however, the particular concepts that it identifies and explains pertain mainly to the geography and tempo of the land rush.

Chapters 4–7 (part II: "An Appetite for Land") cover the acquisition of land from indigenous peoples and its redistribution mainly to white occupants according to assorted regimes of allocation. Chapter 4 considers the ways in which colonizers dealt with the common law's recognition of a possessory right due first peoples by their occupation of territory. Chapter 5 examines land grants and quasi-aristocratic arrangements. Chapter 6 presents government rules and techniques for sale and purchase of land, while chapter 7 accents the actions of landhunters, grazers, and squatters, whose unorthodox ploys for getting and holding land frequently contravened authority. This opposition of forces generates the tension between enterprise and order, creative action and orchestration, defiance and respect, populist tendencies and vested interests.

Chapter 8 (part III: "Reapportioning the Pieces") outlines some ways in which societies that seemingly exhausted their frontiers began searching for land that was passed over in the initial waves of occupation and started to invest capital in existing properties to increase production. The conclusion indicates the enduring consequences of what happened in the great land rush.

The book leans towards a conceptual organization, which allows us to uncover the shared urges, values, dilemmas, accomplishments, and tragedies that comprised a monumental installation of property rights in new worlds and in the accompanying ideology of liberal economic development. Chapters 4–8 therefore arrange sequentially the steps in land seizures, allocations, and reforms typical of colonial and frontier societies. More than the first two chapters do, they note the history and environments of the places considered.

PART ONE

Scanning the Horizon

CHAPTER ONE

Concepts:
Empires and Perspectives on Land

The ensuing chapters deal with upheavals that introduced property rights among British settlement colonies and the United States. There is a practical reason for concentrating on these Neo-Europes. It is humbling to explore the history of several jurisdictions, and there are limits to how much work a researcher can dedicate to a project. There are also reasoned justifications for an emphasis on British colonial and American settings. First, the regions selected include most of the food-exporting Neo-Europes mentioned by Alfred Crosby. They are located mainly in the mid-latitudes, where summer's extended sunlight hours provide excellent conditions for crop photosynthesis.

Second, these places were exposed to a particular cultural understanding of land. An early-modern English elite culture – laden with obsessions about landed property and the power or profits that it could convey – provided ideas about land improvement and the possibilities for increasing income through rents and greater production. Summarizing the character of the business community of seventeenth-century England, Richard Grassby wrote that "the assimilation of all potential rivals by the landed gentry created a united propertied interest which embraced business, agriculture and the professions."[1] Merchants and landed gentlemen interacted in England, and one outcome was the application of ideas of business management to some agricultural estates. A number of ideas about land apportionment and improvement arrived with colonizers in a few locales favoured by climate for the successful introduction of European settlers, domestic animals, and crops. These places include five constellations of settlement colonies: colonial America and its successor, the United States; colonial British North America and its inheritor, Canada; the Cape of Good Hope and its offspring, southern African colonies and the *boer* republics; the colonies of Australia; and New Zealand. The British preoccupation with land was important for world history. From the appetite for owning land evinced by aristocracy and gentry sprang an urge, found among some people from all classes in British and American jurisdictions, to secure tracts and legal interests. With legal interests came credit and thus leverage for supposed improvements.

Third, governments in British colonial and American locales avoided enforcing the placement of people at specific places on frontiers – slaves, convicts, and soldiers excepted. Mobility and a lack of supervision enabled free subjects and citizens to scout for prospects and to squat. Effective freedom of movement was not unique to British and American frontiers, but it was a necessary condition for the great land rush and was constrained in territories seized by the Russian empire.

Fourth, a powerful cultural ideal of improvement – a non-legal doctrine that influenced the drafting of property laws – had a British lineage. The creed that land should be improved was not exclusively British; French Enlightenment prophets of measureless progress expressed similar ideas. In Western secular thought by 1800, civilization was generally regarded less as a steady state than as a matter of continuous advance. By application of effort, societies, it seemed, could escape a cycle of decline and recovery and could progress incessantly. The British contribution to a cultural fixation on improvement emerged from schools of domestic rural practice and from fear of decline, not from continental theories.

Fifth and most distinctive, as an outcome of democratic aspirations and manhood suffrage, the United States and subsequently British settlement colonies institutionalized access to land ownership by people of modest means. These initiatives were invariably compromised, and large landholders, including favoured individuals and pampered companies, acquired and retained immense estates, sometimes contrary to the spirit, if not the letter, of laws about land allocation. Yet if codified measures to widen access were subverted, they were not erased. In the early nineteenth century, prior to other colonizers, the British and the American authorities endeavoured to distribute a substantial amount of land systematically with good titles to common people. In these jurisdictions, actual distribution of assets to ordinary folk was often undermined in practice, and railways ("railroads" in the United States) and associated land corporations benefited from major grants; however, compared to what happened in many other parts of the world, laws providing access to allotments for smallholders pointed to an effectual democratic insurgence. U.S. railway grants stopped in 1871, and in 1872 "there was not a party platform which did not condemn the whole system and insist that the public domain be held for settlers."[2] There ensued judicial and political fights to recover certain railway lands.

When applied in dry regions, concessions to smallholders were environmentally unwise, since they allowed too many people and too much livestock into fragile ecological zones. Major allocations transpired in an age of emergent Anglo–American democracy and European migrations, not in an era of prudential land management informed by science. The eastern and midwestern public domain that the United States first organized for distribution on easy terms in the early nineteenth century included extensive tracts suitable for small farms, and that accidental circumstance strengthened a trust in the viability of small land parcels. That faith coincided with populism in the United States. This alignment of an environmental circumstance and politics was momentous for the rest of the American public domain, and also for Australia, New Zealand, and Canada. The small-farm ideal would burst onto the political scene in Australia and New Zealand, thanks in part to American migrants in the 1850s and 1860s. To secure immigrants, the colony of Upper Canada and later the Dominion of Canada had to pay attention to their neighbour's land policies.

Sixth, and almost as distinctive as allocation to smallholders, landholders on British and American settlement frontiers experienced political stability and security of property during epochs of liberal land allocation. It is true that ineptitude, favouritism, corruption, and haste meant that one of the greatest distributions of resources in history was shot through with wrong-doing. Still, apart from the momentous seizure of land from first peoples – a major exception – British and American governments did not divest people of property without some due process; even the dispossession of *most* first peoples engaged legal processes, though ones manipulated by colonizers. The importance of legal packaging conjoined with good surveys should not be slighted, because the capitalization of animal husbandry and agriculture required that borrowers and lenders feel secure about the future and the solidity of assets. The legal foundations of property strengthened confidence. When security was presumed, investments could render tangible the doctrine of improvement. Metropolitan financiers and colonial administrators worked in a culture of legality that influenced events during the great land rush. Moreover, that early attention to legality has in recent times enabled indigenous people in a few places to force negotiations to rectify early land grabs.

THE CURIOUS EXAMPLE OF ARGENTINA

Below in this chapter, I analyse the anglophone world's dominant place in the great land rush, and I compare six empires in order to draw out the place in world history of the British and American frontiers' distribution of assets. However, to underscore now the role of British and American laws that promised distribution to smallholders, and to explain more cogently the historical importance of stability and pre-dictability in property rights, I say a few words about Argentina, which, of all the Spanish-American republics – perhaps of all Neo-Europes – has an environment and economic history resembling the five constellations of British settlement colonies considered in this book. Argentina provides a good contrast with them, because it was similar in many respects. Like Australia, Cape Colony, New Zealand, and the U.S. west, Argentina, through much of the nineteenth century, experienced a grazers' sprawl. In the first decades of independence, this outcome was not what the country's liberal politicians, who framed republican land laws inspired by English classical economics, would have desired. They had hoped to create a class of investing agriculturalists along English lines.

The influence of English thought was natural, for Argentina was connected by trade and by a liberal intelligentsia to western Europe, especially England. Pervasive Albion, as John Lynch called it, contrib-uted stock-raising expertise and capital to advance sheep-raising in Argentina, as it did on the other frontiers. As was also the case elsewhere, British capital flooded the country in the mid-nineteenth century with "bubble enterprises; – and of course one day the bubble burst."[3] Land booms and busts were common during the great rush.

Additional parallels and ties with other Neo-Europes were evident in the actions of land reformers in the second half of the century. They examined and copied elements of British colonial and American land-allocation laws.[4] *Los leyes de la tierra pública* of the late nineteenth century contained little that had not already appeared in the statute books of British colonies or the United States. Public land was sold both before and after survey, with and without improvement condi-tions, in large and in small parcels, and with and without credit arrangements. Land scrip was granted to soldiers, and land was sold to raise funds for public works. A land act of 1884 even introduced "en cierta forma el *homestead americano*."[5] This law came late in the history of the great land rush. Ideas for land allocation and national development typically flowed from British commentators and Ameri-can legislators to Argentina and Brazil, not the other way. Momentous events in Argentina intervened, as we see below, between independence and this late imitation of American practice.

Despite connections with the great land rush in the English-speaking world and despite the presence of liberal intellectuals and politicians, colonial Spain's generous grant practices and the freedom to occupy grazing land remained ideals for a few politicians in the immediate post-

independence decades. No Neo-Europe escaped concentrated landholding – not the United States, and definitely not Argentina. Accumulations
of freehold land, leaseholds, and grazing rights occurred around the
world; however, in Argentina, capricious presidential orders, which
were abundant and occasionally extreme, contributed to the formation
of huge estates. Major executive interventions damaged the country's
reputation as a secure place for investment. Above all, General Juan
Manuel de Rosas reversed Argentina's course of development.

After Argentina became independent, the province of Buenos Aires,
to promote investment in cattle-raising, granted land on generous
terms for *estancias*. In 1822, the modernizing politician Bernardino
Rivadavia – an admirer of British and French liberalism, of the writings
of Jeremy Bentham and Jean Charles Léonard Sismondi – instituted
enfiteusis, a form of leasehold that anticipated the land-reform pro-
posal of Henry George. Under enfiteusis, the government attempted to
calculate the intrinsic value of plots of land and to levy a tax on that
assessed value rather than on improvements.[6] Grazers opposed this
cumbersome but sophisticated experiment, and in a few years it gave
way to generous land grants to cattlemen – a practice wholly at odds
with the goals of Rivadavia. At a critical juncture in its history,
Argentina's economic development was bumped onto an unconven-
tional path during Rosas's years in power (1829–32 and 1835–57). An
estanciero, Rosas was not an improving landlord, but a grazer who
"stood for size and numbers rather than technology and quality."[7]
Favouring stock-raisers with generous terms for land purchases, sus-
pending recruitment of immigrants, and suppressing small squatters,
Rosas bound Argentina to the pastoralists, who comprised a political
force even in liberal, progressive times. Administrators on other land-
rich frontiers – notably Australia, Cape Colony, New Zealand, and the
United States – laboured at around the same time to rein in grazers in
the name of improvement, welcomed immigration, and started to come
to terms with small squatters. Rosas did more than invert Argentine
priorities and divert Argentina from practices on British and American
frontiers. He did more than accelerate land consolidation. Rosas
undermined European faith in Argentine land tenure when he expropriated his enemies' property. He allowed the provinces leeway to
distribute land, which several did by reverting to Spanish colonial
practices. In the estimation of a liberal historian, the Rosas regime
resorted to anachronisms and cronyism because enfiteusis had alienated
powerful interests in the state of Buenos Aires.[8]

Rosas and his fellow estancieros assigned the countryside a social
and economic pattern before Argentina received its waves of immigrants. "Before modernization even began, the system of landholding,

the size of the estates, and in many cases the personnel, all had been permanently fixed."[9] In the same period, the country – like many others in Latin America – was fragmented for decades by civil strife, which postponed national development until the late nineteenth century, whereas in the United States the survival of the public domain helped the national government assert a presence before and after its relatively brief, if exceedingly bloody, civil war. Jeremy Adelman argues that Argentina was not an exception to the liberal norm but that civil strife and war with neighbours "wreaked havoc in the larger political economy" and Rosas inserted cronyism.[10] The government that replaced Rosas's threw property rights into confusion by nullifying some of his grants and by freezing land distribution until the land question could be studied.[11]

In common with counterparts in southern Africa, Australia, New Zealand, and the United States, grazers in the province of Buenos Aires expanded remarkably during the early nineteenth century; like stockmen on the other frontiers, these estancieros at first appreciated the benefits of open land, held without property titles. Open access was cheap and permitted expansion as well as scouting for better pastures. However, as Hilda Sabato found when studying the pastoral age in the province, "this situation proved more and more inconvenient for large estancieros, who wished to ensure their rights to a tract of land, the possibilities to expand and improve it, and the elimination of the competition."[12] In other countries, comparable anxieties and ambitions, as we see below in chapters 7 and 8, provoked grazers into cunning acts that subverted reforms – for example, forcing station operators in Australia and ranchers in the United States into compromises with poorer people, including making payouts for their homestead entitlements. Argentine estancieros did not have to combat either a culturally significant adulation of the small farm or a purposeful administration of laws aimed at dissolving large estates.

In land-allocation practices, British colonial and American governments were more amenable to populist movements than were regimes in Argentina. Along the River Plate in the nineteenth century, the owners of livestock-raising operations – the *latifundia*, which resembled Australian stations and American ranches – realized relatively early a security of tenure, something denied initially to Australian or American counterparts, which had to buck smallholder land acts; Argentine reformers who championed U.S.-style land-allocation laws were by comparison ineffectual.[13] Estates, at least in the province of Buenos Aires, were broken up in the late nineteenth century, not by reforms but by fragmentation among heirs who sold their bequests rather than reconsolidating them. Rich families transferred their assets from countryside to city.[14] Reforms also failed to break up many large holdings in Australia and the United States, but at least a large percentage of the crown land or public domain was never alienated, and, equally important, innumerable settlers with little cash or credit participated in the great land rush and derived earnings from farming or selling out, even though many Australian selectors and North American homesteaders abandoned their entry claims. All the same, who was permitted to participate in the rush near the outset remains significant, because policies that allowed some access denoted both the political sinew of striving people who lacked wealth and grudgingly given sanction to their yearning for land.

Land allocation in Argentina was, relative to American and British regions, overwhelmed by presidential orders, which helped form extensive estates. During the half-century after independence, civil strife, wars against indigenous peoples, and a war with Paraguay advanced the militarization of political life, which supported government by executive action and rewarded the army and militias with a series of *primios* (grants of land scrip).[15] Wars and railway schemes forced land sales to cover debt obligations. Public lands were exposed to impulsive interventions, and the wealthy added to or protected their latifundia by acquiring secure tenure cheaply. There were, of course, places on American and British frontiers where landed estates were similarly organized thanks to recklessness, corruption, and environments that could best support grazing; however, in these jurisdictions, laws allowed homesteaders – whether true farmers or small speculators – to obtain benefits from the public domain or crown land. The scope for productive linkages between immigrants' expectations and initial allocation of land was not as extensive in Argentina as in the United States and Canada, or, after mid-century, in British colonies in Australasia. While there are parallels between land-taking in Argentina and its manifestation in British settlement colonies and the United States, Juan Carlos Rubenstein points out, with dramatic licence, the object of expansion: "En Estados Unidos lo realizó el *hombre*. En Argentina, la *vaca*."[16]

LAND, PROPERTY RIGHTS, AND IMPROVEMENT: THE ANGLOPHONE DYNAMIC EDGE

Rubenstein's comment evokes the buoyant nationalism of Frederick Jackson Turner's frontier thesis. However, there are "significant elements of westward expansion that received little or none of Turner's attention." Richard Hofstadter's list (1968) of these omissions included "the careless, wasteful and exploitative methods of American agriculture; ... the

desecration of natural beauty; ... the failure of free lands to produce
a society free of landless labourers and tenants ... ; the frequent
ruthlessness of the frontier mind."[17] Ruthlessness is a vague under-
statement. There was intimidation and violence among the newcomers
themselves, as well as their mistreatment of Indians. Moreover, *el
capitalismo* – not just *el hombre* – figured on the American western
frontier. The histories of settler occupation and corporate consolidation
are complicated. Jeremy Adelman and Stephen Aron propose one
pattern of transformation in the New World – namely, from borderlands to bordered states. They suggest that there were many borderlands – the Great Lakes, the Missouri valley, the Rio Grande, Florida,
Central America, the River Plate, and northeastern Brazil – where the
frontier was *not* closed, because relations among first peoples and
newcomers were fluid and the frontier was inclusive.[18] Comparable
openness existed in Aotearoa prior to and immediately after Britain
annexed it as New Zealand in 1840, and perhaps too both in the
territory occupied by the mixed-race Griquas led by Adam Kok in the
northern Cape Colony and in the Red River settlement in Canada's
Rupert's Land.

Although there were private negotiations among colonizers and first
peoples in many places discussed in this book, inclusive frontiers
seldom lasted long. If, instead of seeking the genuine inclusiveness
sought by Adelman and Aron, we can reconsider borderlands or
frontiers as areas where the colonizer's regime of property rights had
not been firmly installed, but where newcomers were already marking
out places in anticipation of that condition, then there was a multitude
of frontiers from the sixteenth to the nineteenth century. Concurrent
with this idea of a frontier as a place where a state had not yet installed
its apparatus for allocating property rights, we should pursue the idea
that British imperialism and colonization, and American manifest destiny and frontier settlement, which have usually been appraised sepa-
rately, form parallel streams. This approach is in keeping with the aim
of historians who suggested in the early 1990s that "the United States
is different but not exceptional."[19] From the standpoint of property
rights on frontier lands, there were no long-lasting, profound differences among our five constellations of colonies and states, but there
were countless variations in specific policies and practices and many
non-synchronicities in the chronology of key trends.

British Imperial Expansion

The course of American history connects deeply, extensively, and recip-
rocally with land-taking and land-allocation episodes in the histories

of British settlement colonies. For authorities, the challenges of taking and allocating land posed similar problems, for which there were a limited number of practical solutions. More generally, this book shows that "the expansionary drive of American culture" was not just American.[20] To integrate U.S. national and British imperial events against a backdrop of world history, I turned to debates about colonization and imperialism, adapting an interpretation of British imperial expansion that focused on events on so-called peripheries. Although British imperial history is not global history, it provides one broad and well-documented point of entry into the transnational. Summations of the British empire's dynamics have swung from an emphasis on events in the homeland to happenings in the colonies, and recently back again to Britain.

While intricacies in the debates over British expansion are outside this book's scope, it is reasonable to claim that they originate in the analytical anti-imperialism of J.A. Hobson and V.I. Lenin. Those writers alleged that European capitalism drove expansion, because metropolitan bankers and manufacturers required outlets for surplus products and capital.[21] C.A. Bayly wrote that Lenin got the essential argument right, but his timing was off. The great age of imperialism was indeed "a stage in the history of capitalism, when powerful and well-armed bodies of aristocrats and financiers struggled to redivide the whole world, as Lenin argued," although the Russian concentrated on events in his own lifetime and Bayly accented the period 1760–1830 as the high age of imperialism.[22] Bayly is correct about the importance of these decades; however, the plentiful literature on the growth of the British empire, while loaded with references to trade, is short on accounts of the links between unsanctioned land dealings among indigenous peoples and colonizers and the imperial authorities who attempted to stabilize such fluid relations by taking charge of them. The negotiations between individual settlers and indigenous peoples fit an alternative interpretation of imperial expansion by Ronald Robinson and John Gallagher, although Bayly was more accurate than they were on the crucial decades in Britain's imperial expansion, for they – like Hobson and Lenin – concentrate on the late Victorian era, when the great land rush had already petered out in the most promising parts of the globe.

The following chapters explain the dynamism behind the formation and, more especially, the expansion of anglophone Neo-Europes in terms compatible with Robinson and Gallagher's assertions that events away from Europe promoted imperial expansion and that indigenous collaborators and mediators often were indispensable aides and later mistreated subordinates.[23] While Robinson and Gallagher argue for an approach to imperialism that values events outside European capitals, they compile evidence from the annals of British political and administrative history and occasionally from the high politics of Europe. Their reliance on literature that covered happenings in capitals contrasts with their claims for the salience of peripheries.[24] Peter Cain and Anthony Hopkins in their analyses of the British empire, published in the early 1990s, focus on the United Kingdom, indeed on London, and dwell on the fiscal supervision of colonies and dependent states. They depict these efforts as achievements of a gentlemanly British elite. When Cain and Hopkins shift the vital narrative of imperialism from the colonies to the City of London, in contradiction to Robinson and Gallagher, they accent the period after 1850 and recount London's role in the provision of the colonial financial services required for infrastructure. They overlook the immense territorial acquisitions in settlement colonies and insist that picking up "territorial spoils" in Africa, the Far East, and the Pacific constituted an age of high imperialism.[25]

This book accents a British impetus to the great land rush, the result partly of the human and material capital of London's gentlemen, who, along with merchants and investors in the provincial cities, supported agents in the land rush, but also of two other factors. First, since a number of British and American settlement frontiers happened by chance to be environmentally agreeable to old-world crops and animals, they registered colonization successes that attracted attention among other colonizing powers. On occasion, governments in Argentina and Brazil, for example, borrowed – late and incapably – from British and American land-settlement schemes. Second, features of English culture, supplemented with ideas from the continent, stirred quests for land on distant frontiers. Ideas originating from a land-improvement culture – about how to profit from the possession of territory – roused land hunters to cross boundaries, moving from regions of close government control into areas where authority was practically absent.

Of course, in order to fathom the aims of expansionists, we need to fathom the colonizers' aims, assess the military and capital resources, determine the resolve, and recognize the administrative abilities located in metropolitan centres, whether London, Washington, New York, Chicago, or Sydney. Encroachments onto frontier zones usually proceeded faster than metropolitan government officials were prepared to condone at that moment or were capable of overseeing. The private urges – personal and corporate – to acquire resources cheaply arose from commodity markets in a hierarchy of urban places that led back to a major metropolis. William Cronon's *Nature's Metropolis: Chicago and the Great West* is instructive, demonstrating how rural and urban landscapes were connected by ingenious modes of exploitation, including commodity markets.[26] The exact force of metropolitan finance and consumption varied with place and time, and the study of metropolitan ties can inspire a slew of books. Consider several examples of the different ties binding frontiers and the urban centres – proximate and remote – discussed in the chapters below. The Cape Colony *trekboers* by the early nineteenth century sought land for a way of life that had been connected for several generations to a rustic and attenuated market economy for livestock and hides; the buyers of Maori deeds to millions of acres in New Zealand during the 1830s hoped to unload them on the Sydney land market, buoyed up by wool dealers with metropolitan connections; the cattle ranchers on the American open range by the 1870s looked to east coast bankers and British investors to finance stock purchases and strategic land buying.

Metropolitan centres unquestionably played crucial parts in the great land rush, while people on the spot – the actors who interest us greatly in this work – executed the breakouts for quick profits or a stake in a new territory. Some self-generated dynamics helped propel the land rush: frontier residents prospected for better situations; parents acquired land reserves for children; migrants attracted to populist land reforms sought an escape from poverty; grazers coping with an increase of livestock scouted for new pastures; speculators darted with the apprehension that they might lose a golden opportunity. Many people near seemingly vacant spaces acted to occupy territory, because they recognized that land was a unique item and that, if they failed to act, others would not hesitate. Formal imperialism – British or American – was often reactive; it included a multiplicity of responses by governments and masters of capital to initiatives taken by resource hunters probing and extending the frontiers of authorized settlement, and their pre-emptive exploits often launched inequalities that persisted in communities for generations.

Estates and Private Initiative

In this section we look at English estates as a model for colonial landowning and at the related development of private initiative, at the adaptation of classical economists in colonial expansion, and at the many voices of the era that inform this book.

In frontier after frontier, a major feature of imperialism consisted of wilful freebooting – privately initiated exploits – a mode of European colonization that often preceded formal acquisitions of territory, including episodes outside the scope of this book. Spanish conquistadors in Mexico and Peru, Cossack conquerors of Siberia, and adventurers

serving with the British East India Company in eighteenth-century India
are examples. They plundered resources by force of arms; official
approval for their expeditions was meagre. The parties that advanced
on frontiers in the regions examined in this volume often operated with
minimal government approval too, but they looked for land – a different
form of plunder. Those who staked claims early knew their trade well
enough to encircle land promising productive potential or strategic value,
so that ensuing colonizers encountered leftovers and either came to terms
with early claimants or moved on. Latecomers forfeited opportunities.
Fear of this eventuality fuelled the rush.[27]

Among the resources – hides and pelts, timber, minerals, and land
– hunted by British and American parties, land formed a special case.
It was not only a resource and a place, but also a keystone of British
and American culture. A longing to hold and improve land has been
associated with leading chapters in English political, economic, and
intellectual history. Holding land for quiet enjoyment was one matter,
sustained by the law; improving land was another, and ambitious
improvers sometimes changed the law to weaken the quiet enjoyment
of people whose presence seemingly obstructed efficient estate management. Between 1510 and 1640, wool and grain prices and land
rents increased appreciably in England, prompting those who could to
expand their holdings of productive terrain.[28] The Tudor break-up of
church estates, the enclosing of open fields and commons, drainage
projects to increase productive acreage, and the seventeenth-century
expansion of the English colonies in Ireland expressed a will among
the ambitious and opportunistic gentry to possess and manipulate
more land, at the expense of occupants. Entitlements were not sacro-
sanct. The craving to improve flourished into the eighteenth century,
and enclosures continued. G.E. Mingay relates that not only were the
abundant innovations in farming from 1650 to 1750 carried out by
the principal landowners, but that many landlords required tenants to
undertake up-to-date practices. Enclosures and assorted improvements
were pervasive and ongoing.[29]

Estates were esteemed not only for the prestige and influence that
they conferred on a lineage, but because of improvements and closer
management "they promised financial gains unknown to the grand-
fathers and great-grandfathers of the enclosing landlords."[30] Changing
the land's uses to increase yields, rather than maintaining a static order,
represented a socio-cultural departure in Europe; in France, by contrast, the aristocracy was drawn into court life and lost an awareness
of estate supervision. In England, there was even more cultural substance to an interest in land than the old aristocratic ideas of land and
order or the new ones about land and profits. Ann Bermingham has

suggested that "precisely in this period of accelerated enclosure (1750–1815), there fell the dramatic aesthetic and cultural discovery of the countryside on the part of the middle class."[31] The social reality of a changing, improved countryside and an idealized representation of a rustic past, though seemingly in contradiction, complemented a drive among British immigrants to acquire land in new worlds. English history set the stage for a momentous tension between, on the one hand, law and entitlements and, on the other, appeals to improvement and access. The strains and struggles were played out in settlement and plantation colonies around the world, though first and foremost in British and American settlement regions.

In another important development, government supervision of the economy, although it had increased under the Tudors, suffered during the débâcle of the civil war of the 1640s. The landowning aristocracy and gentry esteemed a weak central state. Later, when colonization accelerated, "the British government rarely played a role in determining where its citizens *ultimately* settled."[32] It did, however, attempt to direct subjects of the crown to *initial* sites. In Upper Canada, the crown gave loyalists location tickets specifying where they could enter crown land. Recipients found buyers for these commitments and were free to move and seek land elsewhere from speculators. To strengthen the colony near the projected route of the Rideau Canal, the government tried establishing settlements of disbanded soldiers. Many arrived without families, were at liberty to move, found the land poor, and departed as soon as government rations ceased.[33] Convicts in New South Wales were a notable exception to the rule of freedom of movement, although the penal colony attracted free settlers.[34] Many colonists lured in 1820 to the Albany district of the Cape Colony as a frontier security measure recognized a miserable situation and withdrew to towns. The unbound character of English colonization owed much to imperial parsimony; there was also an ascendant political culture distrustful of central authority.

Quasi-private experiments in planting compact settlement colonies – for example, South Australia (1836) and New Zealand (1840) – also failed as controlled exercises. Both were founded along lines suggested by Edward Gibbon Wakefield, who proposed that land should not be sold cheaply by governments, since that would make it difficult for employers to find inexpensive labour. Wakefield proposed that revenues from orderly land sales at a sufficient price could fund the emigration of the poor. In South Australia and New Zealand, supervision of the frontiers required to support land prices faltered for lack of resources, and the model colonies straightaway succumbed to grazers, who overran the territory granted to philanthropic companies by the imperial government. While Wakefieldian schemes faltered in these two British colonies, they inspired a major Brazilian land law in 1850. Large land plots were to be sold, revenue was to be used to sustain surveying and importing colonists, and squatting was to be crushed. Emilia Viotti da Costa contrasted this measure with the U.S. Homestead Act of 1862, which conceded that smallholder squatting could not be repressed.[35]

The frontiers of British and American settlement regularly witnessed a conquest of space by private enterprise defying government rules, followed by the phenomenon of private parties plunging into trouble and pleading for government succour in the name of civilization or improvement. Most such settlement frontiers also experienced – to a greater or lesser degree – another expression of the lust for land. Populist movements no later than the 1860s – and several decades earlier in the United States – forced enactments to limit or break up large landed estates. An incredible exception was southern Africa, where, as we see below, the only attempt to reorganize property and force a break-up of large farms came in an early, ambitious attempt (1813–22) to check *boer* landholding; this curious reform – involving a tax on the intrinsic value of plots of land – originated with crown officers, not with populist crusaders. Similar to enfiteusis in Argentina, land reform in the Cape stirred resistance from pastoralists, who, like counterparts elsewhere around the world, preferred simple, nominal grazing fees. Although it came as a top–down modernization, not as a popular measure, the rational quitrent plan installed at the Cape was consistent with a British desire to extirpate waste. Southern Africa was a variant and remained so. When white colonists in southern Africa eventually did call for land reforms in the late nineteenth and early twentieth centuries, they plotted to wrench territory from black Africans, not to act against other classes of white colonists.

The coincidence of a passion for land and an opening of opportunities for private initiative occurred as the British planted colonies in America, Australia, and New Zealand and when they assumed control over the Cape. The British empire was the first global realm in which large-scale taking and reallocation of land became *the* leading activities, activities engaging administrative attention and invention. During the years covered in these pages, an English will to possess and manipulate land travelled with colonists – rich and poor – to settlement colonies, where its carriers struggled initially to interpret new surroundings in the light of familiar values and institutions. Gaining in understanding about how to exploit their milieu, some ambitious colonists proceeded to adapt and refine the old world's ideas about landed property. Although landhunters' ideas about validating what they were doing included their slighting of first peoples as unproductive, many of these same indigenous people were essential to landhunters. Long ago, Ronald Robinson stressed the value to imperial expansion of native collaborators, and he and Gallagher describe how plans and actions of indigenous kings and religious leaders helped instigate British expansion. As we see in this book, there was also collaboration, mediation, and resistance from individuals, clans, and tribal chiefs.[36]

Adapting Classical Economics

In new settings, the English fascination with landed property as wealth led to refinements in the instruments and ideas that defined and organized property rights. Customary conduct, statutes, case law, surveying methods, and government administrative practices were often modified; however, the story is not linear, and sometimes ancient laws that inhibited conveyancing were retained, because influential colonizers saw merit in the stability of a more traditional society or could not reach agreement on new practices. All the same, the trend was towards streamlining, and there was a parallel mounting sophistication in ideas about improvement. Royal instructions from 1755 to 1774 to the governors of new crown colonies expressed a vague idea of betterment. They censured the large proprietary grants of the past. Henceforth governors were to grant land to parties in proportion to an ability to cultivate it.[37] This wish was a mere aspiration compared to conceptions of rural improvement in writings of François Quesnay – an economist's economist – who in 1759 published a prescient theory in his *Tableau économique*. He attempted to show how a government, by taxing land rather than produce, might promote investments in agricultural improvements for the benefit of the nation. In his *History of Development*, Gilbert Rist argues that, during the eighteenth century, "the philosophy of progress carried the day."[38] For Quesnay, progress towards greater abundance required astute tax policies to make the land yield a surplus, not just a living. The French nobility might be content with the latter, but, for Quesnay and other Physiocrats, progress required state measures to introduce a bourgeois spirit to the development of the soil.[39]

It took a while for theories as sophisticated as Quesnay's to develop in Britain, although during the late eighteenth century practically minded advocates of better husbandry – the agricultural patriots connected with the didactic Arthur Young – studied and reported on agricultural practices around the kingdom.[40] Then, beginning around 1815, economic theories concerning land and taxation appeared in

treatises, notably by Thomas Malthus and David Ricardo. As witnesses
to an age of war and the domestic suffering that it inflicted, these
pioneers in social science deliberated over land's worth to the kingdom
under stress.[41] More fundamental, they attempted to foster a scientific
understanding of society that precluded the maintenance of a self-
reproducing, defensive, and orthodox style of thought. Behind this
objective lay an expansionary vision. Modernizing land tenure and
land taxation could coax landlords and tenant farmers to make
improvements that would produce more; thus the kingdom could
withstand future hostile embargoes like that attempted by Napoleon
and standards of living would be lifted. By the 1830s, inquiries into
the disposal of crown land in the colonies invariably revolved around
how the government – imperial or local – could, through pricing and
taxes, weed out unimproving land buyers and put resources in the
hands of people able to increase yields.

Some eighteenth-century Enlightenment *philosophes* and English
economists of the early nineteenth century shared a common faith that
progress and national power could be achieved by applying reason to
taxation, so that landlords and farmers would commit more capital to
agriculture. Applications of economic plans, at home or in the colonies,
had to wait. After decades of war (1775–1815), the crown was intent
on rewarding loyal subjects. In the colonies, that meant that land
apportionment was not to be rationalized immediately. For a while in
the early nineteenth century, land-granting practices in British colonies
involved favouritism along with some experimentation. C.A. Bayly
describes the epoch from 1780 to 1830 as one of British overseas des-
potisms, in which autocratic generals tried to govern by executive
authority.[42] Neither the crown nor its autocratic local agents regarded
the empire's landed resources as economic assets to be carefully hus-
banded. Rather, they exploited these lands as a source of reward and
patronage for loyalty and service. Vain attempts were sometimes made
to scale free grants on the basis of grantees' declared or supposed ability
and willingness to bring land into cultivation or to make other improvements, and in the Maritime colonies of North America and in New
South Wales grants were subject to the payment of an annual quitrent
to the crown. Occasionally, the British government recognized that the
disposal of crown lands could yield revenue to sustain a colony's executive authority and relieve the treasury in London of expense, but this
impulse was spasmodic and generally ineffectual. Cronyism and
muddle flourished. There was always a basic opposition of interests
whenever governments tried to manage settlers and speculators habituated to acquiring land on easy or familiar terms. Local disputes of
this nature were exacerbated in culturally diverse communities when

British authorities sought, as they did in Quebec and the Cape, to reconcile the established land-tenure systems of conquered territories with British usages and preconceptions.

By the late 1820s and early 1830s, the writings of classical economists about land's intrinsic value informed land-dispersal discussions in London and settlement colonies, stimulating new allocation regulations for British North America and Australia and leading to the East India Company's diverse reforms of land tenure and taxation.[43] Erudite reflections on economic rent and how to advance the contributions of landed wealth to national strength were missing in the United States when the national government began the serious work of apportioning its public domain early in the nineteenth century. No citizen of the republic contributed to classical economics, which originated in British discussions about population growth, the worth of a landlord class, and worry about soil depletion. In the United States, this last problem could be tackled – or so it seemed – by expansion onto new land. Rather than concern over landlordism or depletion steering U.S. land debates, sectional politics, log-rolling, and the rhetoric of republican democracy were the motivating factors. Land disposal figured as a presumed source of revenue for national development projects, and state and national legislators quarrelled over the degree of ease to accord citizens of a democracy when they sought land on the public domain.[44] Improvement was not reviewed with the practical obsessions of an Arthur Young or the theoretical exactness of the English economists; however, this potent idea of improvement prevailed in a more general form, which maintained that entitlements to land had to be justified by improvements. It certainly affected the treatment of Indians and their land, because their usages were denigrated. It surfaced in land-allocation measures, such as the Homestead Act (1862), which allowed cash-short homesteaders to make improvements as one means of securing a title.

By mid-century, in an early example of an American influence flowing into the wider English-speaking world, democratic politics mingled with land-policy discussions in British settlement colonies, and there followed American-influenced populist campaigns to spread the wealth of land to all classes. Leaders of these movements alluded to American practices. Regardless of the system of government, administrators everywhere muddled along, and millions of acres slipped through their fingers. That was one common feature among our five constellations, no matter which authorized system of land distribution was in play at any particular moment. Improvement remained a well-used notion throughout the distribution exercises, although its meaning shifted with circumstances, serving colonizers' justifications for securing title from first peoples, advancing the claims of aspirant farmers and speculators against pastoralists, advancing the claims of some landseekers against others whom they branded mere speculators, supporting the demands of people in arid regions who lacked riparian rights, and justifying the corporate consolidation of smallholder tracts. In these and other instances, parties argued for property rights as a consequence of avowed improvements; however, there were occasions when something different was argued in the name of improvement. On a few occasions, colonizers assumed that indigenous peoples would be improved if they were granted individualized property rights.

This twist to improvement's connotations has current relevance. In the last decade of the twentieth century, the World Bank sponsored reports on economic development in former communist or developing countries; their authors proposed that, along with free-markets in agricultural commodities, well-defined and individualized property rights to land would improve standards of living.[45] Improvement and property rights have had a reciprocal association since the Enlightenment. People who improved land deserved property rights; property rights improved societies. A British-born will to possess and improve landed property, enhanced by American innovations, guided the way in which property rights developed in far-flung states, so that by the end of the twentieth century something close to a global convention about private property rights reached out and enfolded items other than land – for example, embracing assorted classes of intellectual property. Land-allocation exercises during the peak years of the great land rush, from roughly 1815 to 1870, taught legislators, bureaucrats, financial institutions, and wealth-seeking citizens to think of property rights as individualized, precisely defined, enforceable, transferable, and promoting the public good. Property rights in land on new-world frontiers had seldom originated with the clarity of these mercenary principles, but in the late twentieth century precisely those qualities of market-oriented property rights just mentioned were championed by states and agencies committed to capitalist practices for all manner of property and for exploiting any unalienated lands left *wasting* around the globe.

A Host of Voices

In the following pages, glimpses of a culture that mattered greatly in its consequences for ecologies, indigenous peoples, and practices of wealth formation appeared in peoples' worldly desires. While this study relies on information from the books and articles of many scholars, it also lets participants in the land rush speak for themselves through correspondence and recollections, in order to reveal defiance, urgency, triumph, secrecy, regret, and cunning. To get as close as possible to colonial and frontier expressions of a will to secure landed property rights, we can turn to archives and national libraries in a variety of jurisdictions. Here survive the private letters, official reports, petitions, memoirs, laws, and visual images that assert – frequently with breath-taking candour – a host of private ambitions and tactics that embodied a phenomenal culture of landed property. The tenacity of individuals in pursuing land and tackling the challenges – legal, administrative, environmental, political, financial – of exploitation is remarkable. It is a common hazard of narrative history and patriotism to become captivated by the endurance, manipulative skill, and instrumental knowledge of individuals who sought land or who discerned – so they thought – effective ways to extract more from it. In the case of Daniel Boone, a savvy U.S. frontier surveyor vaulted into national mythology.

On other frontiers, comparable patriarchs likewise looked for land and survived calamities and tragedies. Australian geographer Joseph Powell, who respected the cleverness of consummate landhunter Patsy Durack, wrote that "if Hollywood had been in Australia the Durack family's epic struggles would have been immortalized in our popular culture."[46] Follies and killings accompanied the struggles and manipulations, including those of the Boones and Duracks. Certain landhunting acts created serious problems. Whether in the form of environmental degradation, native land claims, or traditions of violence, events based in the history of the great land rush are routinely thrust into the daily news. It is a duty of historians to try to assign credit and blame, though not just to set the record straight or fashion moral myths. It is also vital for them to assess conduct – the roads taken and those not taken – in order to affirm the possibilities for change. Scrutinizing events that helped set a society moving in a particular direction may encourage change by exposing moral issues, so that people can make reasoned choices in the future about new forms of property rights, including ones that cover artistic creations and genetic information. Property rights as we know them now were shaped by culture, not by an immutable necessity.

The symbolic realities that cultures embody are absolutely necessary for human social conduct. Humans lack the inborn instincts of animals to guide them in ordinary social activities. Behaviour in groups is not established by instinct among people, and this absence of biologically conditioned patterns for conduct in groups results in a need for guidelines for social conduct, hence the presence of the created symbolic order that we know as culture. Cultures have varied widely. Local

limits and possibilities have helped condition how people have organized themselves. Nevertheless, situational constraints – ecologies, for
example – can never alone provide for cultural formation, because
reasoning by individuals facing constraints can produce unique outcomes and draw on a highly portable resource – ideas.[47] In this study,
one culture rich in ideas about landed property rights rolled across
other cultures that formerly had maintained different perceptions of
the land. Human agency is quirky, unpredictable; creative responses
to limiting conditions are often ingenious and unforeseeable. Agency
and creativity thus appear at work throughout this book, and when I
emphasize them I do so because the action or idea cited revised
blueprints for social conduct as it pertained to landed property. Cultural
systems affected the ways in which modes of production developed.
European empires embodied different cultural systems.

OTHER EMPIRES, OTHER CULTURES

The premise of this book – namely, that a particular tradition concerning land, property rights, and notions of material improvement shaped
the character of the modern world – is perilous for several reasons,
which I must confront. First, projects that explore bygone eras only
to sound a warning or to explain an injustice risk presenting anachronistic abridgements of the past, which then undermine the cause by
weakening credibility. Second, other colonial powers thrust their cultures on communities outside Europe, and I look in turn at Spain,
Portugal, France, Germany, the Netherlands, and Russia, but largely
to contrast their land-allocation philosophies and practices with those
in British colonial and American settlement frontiers. The first hazard
represents a well-known challenge for historians – they must enter
different worlds, accept and appreciate unexpected complications, and
report the anomalies as well as the trends. Therefore respect for context
is an essential part of the art of writing history; however, the struggle
to discern underlying dynamics, and to exercise moral judgment, is
crucial. At the conclusion of some reflections on the problem of how
much weight to assign context, Bernard Bailyn writes that history
should comprise "structural studies woven into narratives that explain
the long-term process of change and the short-term accidents, decisions, and encounters which together changed the world from what it
had been."[48] To accomplish that goal in this book, I assume that
colonial cultures included endeavours "that have both a directed
dimension – they come from the goals of particular historical groups
– and a dynamic existence that emerges in practice and takes on
different profiles in particular places."[49]

The second problem – the focus on regions where English ideas about property and law took hold – is important. What did our five sets of Neo-Europes share that made them unusual as a group? How does this group of European settlement colonies relate to projects of transnational history? Other empires assailed indigenous peoples, met with resistance, applied ingenuity to colonization, and implanted languages, laws, and religions. The English, however, concentrated early on a variety of landed property issues and followed up with refinements. As I have suggested above, English colonizers practised great independence of action. In England, there had emerged by the eighteenth century understandings about property suited to a society thriving on commerce, governed by families with landed estates, and favoured with political stability. An array of practical ideas for the organization of landed property rights originated and matured in the common law world, and the common law happened to privilege raw possession, while its sibling, equity, promoted flexibility and recognized diverse interests. These claims do not amount to abject praise for the common law and equity, and they should not support any narrowing of historical interest to merely these traditions, because knowledge of other understandings of property and the law protects us against an obtuse faith that everything has turned out perfectly as it should or that the British and American ways of doing things alone have been commendable. We need only be reminded that jurists who could think only in terms of the common law and equity long ignored – or condemned – the practices of indigenous peoples. Although historians considering other Neo-Europes will find intersections with trends in the common law world, there are reasons why they may not find a comprehensive set of strong parallels.

Spain

Non-English systems of thought about land and rights did not contribute so massively to the foundations for a modern-day preoccupation with individual property rights, which continues to expand beyond Neo-Europes. For example, imperial Spain in the sixteenth century, with conquest after conquest, created new colonial societies in Central and South America and in the Philippines. As the social domination of indigenous peoples proceeded, "Spaniards were busy also mastering the territory of America in various ways."[50] Expeditions collected information to acquire wealth, principally through the discovery and mining of precious metals. Mines and towns promoted commercial agriculture as well as the introduction of European crops and livestock. Many colonists preferred to oversee indigenous labour rather than toil themselves.[51] In addition to the prominence of mining and the pursuit of cheap labour, Spain put its American colonies on a distinct course respecting the handling of lands. The crown attempted to sustain central control over the empire. During the sixteenth century, Spain was the most advanced state in Europe, and what John Elliott calls its "global bureaucracy" functioned more or less effectively on a scale previously unknown in Europe.[52] Spanish America, a territory of such scale and diversity that it is dangerous to generalize about it, experienced forms of landhunting, landholding, exploitation, and speculation that diverged in four leading ways from what transpired in English colonies.

First, colonial bureaucrats, notaries, advocates, and judges arranged the benefactions of land grants; there was an elaborate bureaucratic structure engaged in distributing land to elites. Second, when these elites established landed estates in the Americas during the colonial period, they also sought official sanction for their mastery over labour and local markets. The rapid devastation of the indigenous population by introduced diseases led to the *hacienda* system, which placed survivors under the control of a landowner. Frequently, indigenous people were relocated to Spanish and *mestizo* haciendas. Therefore, even though Spain imposed laws and administrative procedures on conquered societies, the results in Latin America, and to a lesser extent in the Philippines, were sweeping new configurations of landholding and labour exploitation, although the forms derived from a feudal past. Third, the church emerged as a major proprietor of estates. As a consequence of these three factors, landholding and political power overlapped, and both were greatly concentrated. Finally, following the independence struggles in Spanish America, large landowners – including merchants who purchased estates – overcame land-redistribution reforms, doing so with greater ease than individuals and companies that consolidated landholdings on British colonial and American frontiers. Concentration, as we have seen above, was the case in Argentina, and it applied as well to other Latin American republics.[53]

Distance from Europe and the absence of mineral resources meant fewer ecological, social, and property-allocation disruptions in the Philippines than in Latin America. European livestock and crops were introduced gradually and "coexisted on a reduced scale with the indigenous flora and fauna ... Epidemic diseases did not threaten the Filipinos to the same extent as the American Indians," because they had acquired immunities from contacts with Eurasia.[54] When demand for agricultural commodities – sugar and hemp – increased in the nineteenth century, the active landowners were Chinese mestizos and Malay Filipinos, not Spaniards, who apparently lacked the entrepreneurial spirit. Dennis Roth concludes that for several reasons Spaniards were unable to make a go of it on the land. There was no large local market for agricultural estates or ranches, and the greater diversions of office holding and trade weakened interest in estate management. Both Filipinos and Spaniards donated land to religious orders, creating large estates. Friar estates replaced secular hacenderos in the seventeenth century and exercised an almost-unmolested possession of major landholdings near Manila for two hundred years. Shortly after the United States occupied the islands in 1898–99, the new colonial regime redeployed its homestead myth, purchasing the estates from religious orders and selling plots to peasant cultivators. Within a few decades, manipulation of the land laws enabled the wealthy to accumulate this land. On the grassy uplands of north-central Mindanao, Americans even created a ranching frontier to stimulate individualistic behaviour among Filipinos.[55] During the nineteenth century, visions of landscapes tamed by small farmers influenced land policies in the United States and British settlement colonies to a degree not found in former Spanish territories. The break-up of the friar estates and the promotion of ranches in the Philippines are notable precisely because they sprang from American proclivities.

More so than on British colonial frontiers, bureaucracy channelled enterprise in the Spanish empire, allegedly with notable consequences. In the opinion of economist Douglass North, the Netherlands and England permitted decentralized control of commerce, which let competition thrive, forcing efficient institutions. "In Spain, Portugal, and France, colonies were run by bureaucratic decree," so these societies lacked efficient government and "pursued a downward path that would continue for centuries."[56] Although North does not make the argument himself, his observation about bureaucracy can apply to land distribution, because British and American operations were relatively permissive. In an argument that parallels North's, Mancur Olson praises the English constitution, because it avoided bureaucracy. He assumes that the turbulence of the seventeenth century inspired compromises that "increased the security of property rights and the reliability of contract enforcement" to a greater extent than anywhere else.[57]

These opinions from economists, though congenial to arguments in *The Great Land Rush*, are suspiciously neat. Still, the idea that land ought to be distributed unencumbered to smallholders came late to Latin America; in rare cases where reforms were tried, they were inspired by U.S. economic success and by immigration – envied developments attributed to homesteading. Late in the nineteenth century, liberal economic reforms in former Spanish colonies and Brazil included "assaults on peasant (and Church) landownership as well as the alienation of vast quantities of public lands to large, politically connected landowners. Liberal regimes everywhere made formerly inalienable lands subject to private ownership and sale."[58] A few assessments of land allocations in independent Latin American states show that revenue-seeking reformist governments occasionally broke up large estates; however, major pastoralists conserved their estates by a myriad of devious practices, which, like operations in the United States and Australia, depended on small settlers or employees who would acquire interests and sell them to masters of pastoral estates.

The tactics of estate building in Latin America – including cunning manipulation of laws, political influence, bribery, and violence – have counterparts on some British and American frontiers. Even though many British colonists and American homesteaders failed to farm the acreage that they claimed under one or another generous distribution law, and even though quite a few extensive pastoral estates endured in spite of hostile legislation, many recipients of small land grants acquired transferable assets at low cost and benefited from opportunities to play a hand in the land game. They may have left their plots but accrued capital from their entitlements by selling them or their improvements. Laws to assist North American homesteaders or Australasian selectors therefore did not produce a countryside fashioned purely by smallholders. All the same, laws that placed smallholders at the centre of land distribution had weight. In Latin America, governments in every century since the arrival of Europeans more typically sanctioned large holdings straightaway, and although they sometimes made concessions to undercapitalized petty claimants, these actions were not the mainspring of land laws until late in the chronology of land allocation.[59] In Latin America, the apportionment of land during the great land rush engaged processes that differed from those used on British and American frontiers. Small aspiring freeholders were unable to exercise much influence on events. In Argentina, as I reported above, a few characteristics of a pastoral land rush resembled those on similar British and American grazing frontiers. During the initial stage of pastoral occupation, Argentine grazers occupied open land just like the *trekboers* of southern Africa, the station operators of Australia, or American ranchers. Once in possession, all, including the Argentines, tried to fortify their legal grip on the land. However, nothing like the extensive connections among smallholders' pressure, freedom to hunt land, government rules, and canny violations of rules commonly operating on British and American frontiers occurred in Spanish and Portuguese colonies, French settlement colonies, the German and Dutch empires, or Russia's conquered Asian territories that it colonized, all examined in this section.

Portugal

In Portuguese Brazil, the crown attempted at first to limit grants to avoid concentrating land in the hands of a few, for in Portugal it had been the custom of kings to allocate sparingly the limited tracts of productive land. Brazilian viceroys and governors discarded this precedent and from the 1530s forward granted lavishly. Proprietary captains (*donatários*) received huge grants along the coast. In areas of commercial value, sugar planters from the sixteenth to the eighteenth century found the means to accumulate land beyond immediate needs. Almost from the beginning of colonization, land apportionment produced large holdings, and the trend persisted to serve a plantation economy with slaves. Excess land on estates maintained tenants and sharecroppers. Land also helped establish social standing and hence a colonial plantation aristocracy. As a consequence of granting practices, "the good coastal land was quickly divided into immense sugar plantations and not many more decades elapsed before huge semarias [estates] for cattle ranches in the interior put much of the backlands under claim as well. Grants along the coast of twenty to fifty square miles of land were common, and in the interior they frequently encompassed areas of ten to twenty times that size."[60] A Brazilian attorney-general in 1810 recommended grants and loans to smallholders. These initiatives would increase the revenues of the state, he forecast, because the industry of these people would add to colonial prosperity. Royal authorities could never seriously consider such a reform, since it meant a social revolution.[61]

In areas of no commercial value, land was available to anyone able to seize it from Indians and survive. There was nothing to parallel the heed that British colonial administrators – outside Australia, a special case – generally paid to native title; there were no proclamation lines like those attempted by the British in North America and in the Cape of Good Hope to separate colonizers from indigenous people. Squatting persisted in Brazil into the nineteenth century. Immediately after independence in 1822, it expanded as the most common form of acquiring virgin land, and a number of squatters occupied large tracts to plant coffee, the latest tropical commodity to sweep the country. The 1850 land law, mentioned above, enabled plantation-scale squatters to secure legal titles. This state of affairs led one historian to claim that "Brazilian elites resembled in some ways the planters of the [American] South, with the exception that they controlled the nation alone."[62] The planters in Brazil delayed the abolition of slavery and enacted land legislation that confirmed their property. Land allocation in Brazil, like that in British and American colonies, involved squatters, although the granting of the best coastal land during the colonial era meant that squatters were active not only on public land, but also on private property.

The inadequacy of property surveys contributed to near-anarchy. When small squatters located on estates claimed by large landowners, they were not dealt with through the courts, "which implied a distasteful equality of rights. It was quicker to arm a foreman and a few tenants."[63] Adding to uncertainties as well as to consolidations, land fixers known as *grilos* – crickets – jumped from place to place "falsifying documents, trading in tenuous or fictitious titles, and befriending notaries, politicians, and judges."[64] The backing of powerful families assisted with these validation practices. In this respect, Brazil differs from the British and American settlement regions. Populist politics in the United States attempted to democratize land distribution by conceding ever-greater legal rights of occupation to squatters (1830s–40s), then formalizing a process of land granting to homesteaders (1862). The crown in Upper Canada in the early nineteenth century favoured loyalist officers and gentlemen with large grants; common settlers received access to smaller, though not insubstantial plots. On the prairies, the Dominion of Canada followed the American lead with a homestead act in 1872. In Australia and New Zealand, there were smallholder settlers; known as selectors, they were authorized by law to pick land on pastoral leaseholds (1860s on). Nineteenth-century Brazil, having countenanced land grabbers as the colonial government had done previously, could spin no myth of free land to allure immigrants.[65] During the late nineteenth century in São Paulo, the absence of public land compelled coffee planters to organize – with government help – agrarian colonies for European immigrants, in order to benefit from their labour and food production. During the early twentieth century, in the same rich province, successive attempts to define boundaries and discover the extent of public land failed because of weak governments and wretched surveying practices.[66] Just when Latin American governments began to identify immigration as complementary to economic growth and to regard land as an inducement to newcomers, Brazil's better and more accessible lands continued to be alienated to the powerful or cloaked in confusion.

Brazil's sugar plantations made Portugal's colonial venture a going concern, but the kingdom failed to establish settlements in its two major African colonies. Historical currents in Angola and Mozambique did not flow in parallel, except in general neglect, until the mid-twentieth century, when Angola started to attract European immigration. The Portuguese had first arrived in Angola in the late sixteenth century, lured down the west coast to equatorial islands to raise sugar cane. Decades earlier they had used force of arms to occupy a number of trade centres on the east coast of Africa. In the early eighteenth century, Islamic forces re-established control of many of these places, and the Portuguese retreated to Mozambique. European settlement of Angola's arid expanse and Mozambique's pestilential coast was nearly impossible. Specific events lured and pushed the Portuguese into the tropics and into two colonies that had little in common. The slave trade oriented Angola towards Brazil, while Mozambique was integrated into the ancient trade networks of the Indian Ocean. The enclave at Goa in India exercised more influence over Mozambique than did Lisbon. Except for adventurers pursuing slaves on the west coast and gold, ivory, and slaves on the east, the industrious classes of Portugal avoided Africa until the twentieth century.

In Angola, a large part of the European population consisted of *degradados*, transported criminals and exiles. Something different occurred on the east coast, because a number of merchants and soldiers penetrated inland on the Zambezi River in the late sixteenth century and carved out chiefdoms – *o regime dos prazos* – under paramount African chiefs. For two hundred years the *prazeros* held onto estates and slave labour without much notice from Lisbon. Eventually, in order to ensconce territorial sovereignty, Portugal recognized these de facto estates. The prazos and their recognition expressed the common frontier pattern of squatters achieving *some* legal interests; however, the prazados were not truly secured in property rights by Lisbon. In the mid-nineteenth century, a liberal, modernizing government in Lisbon outlawed the system along with slavery, and at the end of the century Portugal drove off the prazados with troops. The estates were then leased to large companies funded primarily by British, French, and German capitalists; the largest three concessions held two-thirds of the colony's land in 1900. The Portuguese did not oversee a broad-based land rush in Africa, but eventually followed the course of other imperial states; they attempted to refine strategies for the production of commodities to serve the metropolitan economy. Ultimately, their ability to do this depended on Britain and other major European powers.[67]

France

In the late seventeenth and early eighteenth centuries, French ideas about the role of land tenure in sustaining colonies to serve the strategic plans of the crown produced seigneurial estates in New France. In chapter 3, I show that this experiment, extending across an attenuated empire, was not broadly influential in the long run in North America.

Following the Louisiana purchase of 1803, American commissions examined French and Spanish land grants in Louisiana and converted the ones that they sanctioned into freehold tenure. In Quebec, where French property law and land grants survived the formal withdrawal of France in 1763, a legislative act abolished seigneurial tenure in 1854.[68] The demise of the French empire in North America and the modification of its land practices signify the magnitude of an English culture of landed property rights. Apart from seigneurial tenure – a practice of the *ancien régime* modified for the New World – there was another noteworthy aspect of French thought respecting land, namely unique French ideas about the place of land in society and in the generation of national wealth. The eighteenth-century Physiocratic analysis of economic development stressed the productivity of the soil and assumed that the hierarchical structure of rural France was a divinely established order. Reappraisals suggest that Physiocracy abounded in observations about the economic stimulation of peasant consumption that made it, in many respects, as interesting as the contemporary laissez-faire analysis of Adam Smith. Its influence, however, was narrow, because of the static and aristocratic social order that it envisioned.[69]

The Revolutionary and Napoleonic epoch inspired ideals of progress and improvement, and France advanced practical schemes for mapping and registering landed property. Except for parts of Algeria and New Caledonia, *la plus grande France* lacked authentic settlement colonies where the state would shape the formation or confirmation of property rights.[70] In Algeria, French armies, bureaucrats, and land speculators of the 1830s and 1840s committed mistakes and misdeeds similar to American and British counterparts. They assumed that there would be abundant unalienated land, only to learn that the conquered territories were covered in layer on layer of indigenous custom and philosophy of landholding "derived from the vicissitudes of local history, the exigencies of human ecology, the imperatives of balancing sociological reality with economic requirement."[71] To acquire a public domain, the French resorted to a combination of tools, including conquest, expropriation, investigations of traditional title, and one-sided laws that freed up inalienable land held by tribes and Muslim religious orders. After expending more military effort than they envisaged at the start, the colonizers brought some rural land under a rationalized European system of surveys and registries.[72] In New Caledonia, which France annexed in 1853, the western plains of Grande Terre attracted cattle raising, following Australian practices. Shortly after the takeover, the colonial administration bought land for nominal amounts from Melanesian clans, expropriated more land, and claimed what to the Europeans seemed unoccupied territory. The techniques of acquisition, property definition, and reallocation practised in Algeria and New Caledonia resembled those prevailing among British and American colonizers, and the system adopted for recording land titles was influenced by a scheme first used in Australia (examined in chapter 6) but owing much to British thought and measures.[73]

Germany

A late arrival to overseas colonization, imperial Germany obtained South Pacific and African territories with mostly poor potential for European exploitation. German New Guinea, its first acquisition in the Pacific, attracted few Europeans; by 1914 a handful of plantations there used indigenous labour on land purchased from tribes. In West Africa, Togo was a mere sliver of territory, and Kamerun a land of fever. In New Guinea and Africa, Bismarck's Germany at first undertook colonization by granting concessions to companies. Some firms practised Raubwirtschaft (an economy based on plunder and coercion), which depended on direct coercion of African labour, forced displacement from the land, and stealing cattle from Africans.[74] Belgium's King Leopold II directed a comparable predatory imperialism in the Congo basin, although no German, French, or British concessionary company in Africa was as rigorously exploitative as that run by the Belgians. Settlement was not an objective in Congo.[75] Major changes in the early twentieth century dissolved concessionary monopolies in German East Africa in favour of more indirect modes of exploitation, partly because exposure of abuses in Belgian Congo placed the German empire under scrutiny as well. In their two West African colonies, Germans attempted plantation agriculture and after 1907 planned a so-called West African development scheme that favoured cash-crop production by black Africans with the aid of European-built infrastructure. In arid South-West Africa, German citizens in the era of the concessions had cheated tribes through purchase agreements whose details Europeans alone designed, and authorities forced black Africans onto reserves to free up land for settlers and for a handful of grazing outfits strung along a few unreliable rivers. The new exploitation there brought a savage suppression of African dissent (1893–1907), railways, mines, bore water, but very few settlers.[76]

Germany's pearl was East Africa, comprising the mainland section (formerly Tanganyika) of modern Tanzania as well as Rwanda and Burundi and a small corner of Mozambique. In East Africa, the poor laterite soils of sub-Saharan Africa and African occupation complicated a white settlement policy bent on improvement; the Germans responded to constraints by trying to manage land for Africans and Europeans, although when settlers pushed they won and Africans suffered. After 1895, the government recognized African rights to land only if it was occupied. Further land could be set aside for Africans sufficient for future expansion; the customary amount was four times the existing cultivated area. Colonial powers, as we see in the chapters below, invariably imposed European perceptions of waste to extract more terrain for plantations or settlements reserved for Europeans. Land distribution to Europeans in East Africa turned on two alternatives to the West African scheme of African production. The Germans experimented with white settlement and with European-owned plantations using African labour. Generally, settlers could acquire freehold land only through a lease-purchase agreement, which required government inspection of improvements prior to a conversion into freehold. As in grant arrangements in British colonies and the United States that imposed settlement conditions, the objective was to preclude speculation, deemed another form of waste. In practice, however, settlers in a desirable northeast highland region near Mount Kilimanjaro could secure land titles in a district granted to concessionary firms during early colonial rule.[77]

In common with British and American settlers, German colonists thought instinctively of freehold and realized that stronger titles ensured better loan arrangements. Consequently, there was tension between clamorous settlers and a colonial governor who feared revolt if black Africans were robbed of more land. At the outbreak of the First World War, the small European population was expanding, and settlers had goaded the government on land matters. "If settlement was an experiment, it was an experiment which was steadily succeeding."[78] Plantations meanwhile had labour-supply problems and difficulty finding profitable crops. On a very small scale, late in the rush, government schemes clashed with settler initiatives in German East Africa. The government usually submitted to the pleas of settlers, and native occupants lost. Following the Treaty of Versailles, the British deported German settlers from what was now Tanganyika, took over German firms, and ostensibly introduced the West Coast policy of mainly African development. Modelled on Nigeria's land laws, Tanganyika's were intended to protect black African title, but new white settlers – British subjects this time – persuaded colonial authorities to eject black Africans from pockets of superior land.[79]

The Netherlands

As a small European country with an old empire of densely occupied islands in the East Indies, the Netherlands tread warily on land tenure, recognizing that local rulers and village elites would resist restructuring. Following the Napoleonic wars, the Dutch struggled to reoccupy territory formerly held by the Dutch East India Company, and, once they had accomplished that, they resolved to exploit the land more effectively. Just as the British East India Company balked at seizing land for settlement in India but wielded taxation, the Dutch did likewise and for comparable reasons; they were intruders among relatively rich, populous, and politically organized civilizations. From 1830 to 1870, the Dutch endeavoured to extract cash-crop surpluses for export by levying taxes on villages. In the latter year, a new agricultural act liberalized the state-run economy without truly freeing it from government management. Where land was settled, native title was recognized and land made inalienable, although with government supervision Dutch planters could lease native land for short periods. Meanwhile, the supposedly unoccupied tracts – the waste – became government property, open to long-term leasing, an arrangement useful to plantation operators. Since the East Indies in the late nineteenth century remitted substantial revenue to the Netherlands, government support poured into crop research to assist plantations that harnessed Asian labour to European capital. The Dutch not only held the idea of improvement in common with contemporary European colonizers, they were truly zealous and systematic about it. Well-planned Dutch economic designs and local conditions in the East Indies steered colonial exploitation to agrarian policies with underlying state support. This form of plantation development proceeded without free-wheeling European squatters, pastoralists, and manic land speculators.[80]

Russia

Russia in the seventeenth century and again in the nineteenth appropriated territory in blocks that exceeded even the gargantuan acquisitions of the United States. The conquest of Siberia during the sixteenth and seventeenth centuries involved a merger of traders and Cossack warriors. A weak government presence followed. Spontaneous peasant settlement played a minor role, since the distances, dangers, and hostile climate deterred all but the boldest. The region resembled the French fur-trading empire in North America. As in New France, in Russia adventurers pressed on because they rapidly depleted the stocks of furs in areas that they penetrated. Later, as a place of internal exile for criminals and dissidents, Siberia witnessed little economic growth that was not state directed.[81] In the nineteenth century, the conquest of central Asia south of the taiga of Siberia occurred as a late phase in a Russian expansion that had been under way for centuries. Among

the reasons for the vigour of this drive into central Asia, according to
Richard Pierce, "the Kazakhs occupied rich lands, as attractive for
Russian settlement as the lands of the Indians had been for settlers in
the Americas. Beyond the Kazakh Steppe lay the fabled wealth of
Turkestan, Persia, and India, offering a vision of trade which had
excited imaginations in Russia from early times."[82] There were super-
ficial parallels with the development of the American west. Boom
towns grew with "American rapidity." Land allocation in central Asia
became a studied question as imperial administrators in the 1890s
grappled with assigning land to several million Slav settlers in the midst
of the Kazakh stock-raising economy. The dispossession of indigenous
peoples undermined their way of life and provoked a Kazakh uprising
in 1916.[83]

Tsarist officials thought that they were civilizing Asia and invoked
the familiar doctrine of improvement. In his history of Russia,
Dominic Lieven describes the European terms in which Russian impe-
rialists thought about the Asian territories. "Natural resources wasted
by the natives must be efficiently exploited, the slothful Asiatic converted to the industrious."[84] Despite parallels with European settlement colonies, Russian colonization was different. Several factors
guaranteed that nothing like the tension between individual initiative
and state regulations, common on British and American frontiers,
erupted in Russia's new territories. There were obstacles to private
initiative. Siberia, colder than the Canadian prairies, could not sustain a commercial, land-extensive pastoral economy, while the peoples of central Asia, who practised grazing, possessed their own land-
tenure practices and were not exposed to any novel disease vectors or
threats to livelihood that opened the door for an influx of colonizers.
Where there was Russian colonization, it involved state planning. It
is unlikely that determined squatters and speculators could have loosened government scrutiny, added to which there was the prospect of
indigenous resistance.

Colonization was organized, and the Russian colonists accepted
state management, because Russian social organization discouraged
outbreaks of individual or collective defiance. Until the emancipation
of the serfs in 1861, rural life was structured around manorial
farming, and after emancipation socio-political organization still
accented membership in state-prescribed status groups.[85] In many
regions, the post-emancipation peasantry preferred communal landholding to the increased productivity of a minority who held land
individually. Thus privatization and enclosure moved slowly.[86] Yet
until the revolutions of 1917, the Westernizing governments of imperial Russia tried to individualize land title in European Russia and

across its Asian territories. In the southeast corner of Manitoba in the late nineteenth century, the traditional Russian approach to land tenure had a rare external influence. Mennonite immigrants from Russia organized colonies where they agreed to community management of Russian-style open field strips. These practices were not intrinsic to their faith, for Mennonites who emigrated from Pennsylvania to Upper Canada in the early nineteenth century practised an individual management of land.[87]

CONCLUSION

How specific settler groups, such as the Russian Mennonites, interpreted landscape and nature and applied cultural traditions, labour, and capital to change what they found is a boundless topic, which has inspired stellar accounts by generations of historians and geographers. The ensuing pages set aside the sort of high magnification applied in those studies – not because of any lack of enthusiasm for the art of describing the interactions of people and local habitats, but to allow investigations of a wider world. Without the labour and genius of generations of scholars dedicated to the study of local history and ecology, this synthesis could not have been contemplated. The book describes the technologies – including legal instruments – employed on frontiers to convert land into private property. In many of the attitudes that underpinned the long, widespread land rush, it is possible to detect the heritage of an aggressive will to possess and alter land that flourished first in England. Planted earliest and strongest in British settlement colonies, this spirit propelled innovations in organizing the material world into tidy assets, elbowed aside indigenous peoples, fostered rule-breaking aggression, led to debates about the distribution of land to smallholders, and helped found today's preoccupation with property rights. As this chapter shows, bits and pieces of this array showed up in several colonial empires, yet the whole package first emerged in the ample and mainly environmentally agreeable territories of the British empire and the United States (Table 1.1).

In several empires, British and American ideas and practices influenced innovations near the end of the great land rush. Admirers and imitators worked with imperfect knowledge of what they respected from the English-speaking world. Seeking order and prosperity, they saw only what they wanted to, not the whole picture. As the next chapter explains, components of the British and American property regime were fraught with conflict, imprecision, impossible administrative burdens, economic risks, unfulfilled expectations, unintended consolidations, and corruption.

Table 1.1
Colonization and land-allocation practices, by colony, before and after 1800

Colony	Salient features of land allocation
BEGINNINGS TO LATE EIGHTEENTH CENTURY	
Colonial Spanish America	Large grants by crown Consolidation of landholding and power Church estates
Colonial Brazil	Large grants for sugar plantations Smallholder squatting dealt with violently by estate owners
Angola	Little European settlement Slave-trade economy
Mozambique	De facto crude estates formed along Zambezi without security of tenure Slave trade
New Netherland (New York from 1664)	Large estates authorized in principle for Hudson valley
Dutch Cape Colony	Some land grants Explosion of grazing by squatting on large tracts
Dutch East Indies	Trade, pillage, and plunder Little colonization of land
New France	Organized and regulated settlement for strategic reasons Exploration by fur traders
Russian Siberia	Expansion by fur traders and Cossacks Trade and mine outposts Little colonization
British American colonies	Assorted schemes for allocating land to smallholders, planters, estate builders, and speculators Land distribution a complex political issue across and within individual colonies
NINETEENTH CENTURY	
United States; Ohio and Mississippi valley public domain	Organized land sales with goal of enabling smallholders to secure land Easy terms developing into acceptance of squatting
Upper Canada	Grants to loyalists and others who petitioned and could demonstrate utility Sales introduced Allocation designed for smallholders but also supports politically influential speculators
Australia	Penal colony Grants of land ostensibly for improvers By 1830s, large-scale squatting By 1860s, populist reactions against large pastoralists and rise of farming selectors and small pastoralists

Table 1.1 (continued)

Colony	Salient features of land allocation
Argentina	Land allocation affected by General Rosas, who favours large estates for cattle Land consolidated swiftly
Brazil	Squatting on plantation-sized tracts legitimized Planters consolidate land without challenge, and slavery persists until late in the century
Angola	Little European settlement until twentieth century
Mozambique	Country divided late in 1890s among several companies Sugar plantations prominent
Dutch East Indies	Exploitation by taxation, followed in 1870 by earnest state management of land for plantation economy
Cape Colony	British confirm Dutch squatting with land titles but try to enforce rational allocation and improvement.
Boer Republics	Grazing farms generously allocated until land shortage in 1880s Landholders resemble smallholders more than large estate owners but hold large acreage.
New Zealand	Smallholder farms intended Large pastoral estates emerge in 1840s and 1850s. By 1860s, populist reactions against squatters and rise of farming selectors and small pastoralists
French Algeria	Attempts at European agricultural colonization complicated by pre-existing landholding arrangements
New Caledonia	Penal colony for Europeans Cattle estates in some locales
United States: high plains	Range ranching with land controlled by freehold tracts acquired through Homestead Act (1862), other land acts, and railway land grants Some opportunities for smallholders
Russian Siberia	Penal colonies for internal exile
Russian central Asia	Organized state colonization efforts Not spontaneous
Canadian prairies	Organized for smallholder occupation Also substantial acreage held for sale to immigrant smallholders by Canadian Pacific Railway and many land companies
German East Africa (Tanganyika) and Kenya	German and British administrators claim to protect Africans, but settlers push and get choice land. Highland plantations

CHAPTER TWO

Property Rights:
Origins, Organization, and Rationales

Old-world ideas accompanied European migrants, and a few changed the globe. An English obsession with landed property was implanted in settlement colonies, and the East India Company in the early nineteenth century even attempted to introduce features of private property into the Bengal and Madras presidencies[1]. Between the late seventeenth century and the late nineteenth century, in the settlement colonies, private initiatives clashed with official designs for land acquisition and allocation. The interaction of private parties and governments determined the property rights to extensive regions. Encounters among private ambition, first peoples' interests, and government authority influenced civil society in Australia, Canada, New Zealand, southern Africa, and the United States. Part of it, however, embodied order, because law codes, surveys, and bureaucracies defined and enforced property rights. Part of the civil society, though, embodied defiance, because, before state control was firm, individuals frequently seized property. In some areas, they founded traditions of direct action and even violence along the way. The clash and mix of order and initiative varied from place to place, but common ingredients can be identified, as I show in this and subsequent chapters.

The confrontations between individuals and sovereign authority happened on resource-rich lands in temperate zones. Chance thus helped identify individualized property rights with generation of wealth. A particular doctrine therefore found fortunate springboards. And spring it did. Following the Second World War, individualized and transferable property rights became explicit core values in a "free world" ideology; free-market international agencies and the United States promoted their extension to developing countries and advanced their resurrection in central and eastern Europe after the demise of the Soviet empire. In recent times too, property rights have fostered new industries, in software and genetically modified biota. They have changed traditional activities such as art and entertainment. The objects affected by refinements to property rights on frontiers were *in situ* – land, water, and minerals – while the objects of recent attention are mobile products of grey matter. Nevertheless, the intellectual and the applied history of property rights is of one piece. To help explain how this fruit of the English world spread and ripened through colonization, I show in this chapter how the British settler colonies and the United States derived, organized, and rationalized property rights and interests in the lands they took from indigenous peoples.

DERIVING PROPERTY RIGHTS AND INTERESTS

On the high plains of Wyoming in 1889, a rancher and farmer debate doctrines of property rights. They race through arguments. Like multitudes of land seekers on countless frontiers, these parties know their roles and hurry. Frontiers were places of haste and confrontation.

Shane [Paramount Pictures, 1953][2]

First encounter:

Richer: I came to inform you I got that beef contract for the reservation ... I'm goin'a need all my range.
Stark: Now that you've warned me, would you mind getting off my place.
Richer: Your place? ... You and the other squatters ...
Stark: Homesteaders you mean don't ya?

Second encounter:

Stark: You've made things hard on us, and us in the right all the time.
Richer: You, in the right? Look Stark, when I come to this country, you weren't much older than your boy there. We had *rough* times, me and other men that are mostly dead now. I got a bad shoulder yet from a Cheyenne arra'head. We *made* this country. *Found* it and we *made* it. Worth blood and empty bellies. Cattle we brought in were hazed off, by Indians and rustlers. Don't bother you much anymore, because we handled 'em. Made a safe range out of this. Some of us died doin' it. We made it. Then people move in who never held a rawhide through the old days. Fenced off my range. Fenced me off from water. Some of them like you paw ditches, and take out irrigation water, and so the creek runs dry sometimes, and I got to move my stock because of it. And you say we have no rights to the range. The men who did

the work and ran the risks, have no rights? I take you for a fair man, Stark.

Stark: I'm not belittlin' what you and the others did. But at the same time, you didn't find this country. There were trappers here and Indian traders long before you showed up and they tamed this land more than you did.

Richer: They weren't ranchers.

Stark: You talk about rights. You think you got the right to say that nobody else has got any. Well, that ain't the way the government looks at it.

The protagonists in *Shane* telescope settlement history. Events flash by in an elegy of European occupation. Cast as villain, the rancher still makes a plausible stand. He *improved* the plains, but in a hierarchy of land uses grazing was vulnerable, and besides the homesteader ploughed with the law on his side. The Homestead Act of 1862, which legitimized Stark's occupation, stipulated that free land could be earned by making improvements. On all frontiers, pastoralists encountered criticisms that they were unimproving nomads or greedy land barons. By claiming to have done his part for civilization, Richer starts an argument that he cannot win. It is an argument that engages only white occupants. Neither Richer nor Stark associates indigenous peoples with rights to the land.[3] They dismiss native Americans as vanquished adversaries who obstructed improvement and now ate Uncle Sam's beef; white people tamed the land, and the time of savage conflict had passed. As a technicolour fable about newcomers, *Shane* captures a limited reality about frontier struggles for property rights. As self-conscious cinematic art, it transports this truth about specific conflicts over a backdrop of melting snow on the Grand Teton Mountains to audiences in the world beyond. On the pastures of Victoria's Riverina (1830s) and Queensland's Darling Downs (1840s), by Natal's rivers below the Drakensberg Mountains (1840s), and in the resplendent Wairarapa valley of New Zealand (1840s), both men would have been understood. Descendants of settlers know that Richer (the rich man) and Stark (the morally strong), the grazer and the farmer, clashed on more than one frontier during the long land rush. If they listened carefully, they might have detected a slight reference to native resistance. This too they would have understood, though in debased terms as native outrages.

Several organizing concepts guide this book.[4] Scenes from Hollywood's most reverently artistic western introduce two principal ideas: property rights and frontiers. Related concepts include occupation and improvement. At least four groups of real actors not cast in *Shane* – speculators, landhunters, stock growers' associations, and first peoples – figured prominently in the script of real land rushes. Because they constitute an essential concept for deliberations in philosophy, law, and the social sciences, property rights can be discussed from several angles. The perspective taken in this study is that a property right is a relationship between a person and other persons respecting access to material resources.[5] Political economist C.B. Macpherson expressed this idea in a more active form, describing a property right as "an enforceable claim to some use or benefit of something."[6] An absolute property right in something – a patented invention, an original work of art, computer software, a broadcast frequency, access to water, a mineral deposit, a plot of land – vests in someone exclusive use of that property. The idea of a simple and exclusive right has been embedded in popular and theoretical understandings of property. So expressed, it is a misleading guide for many historical situations. Less-than-absolute rights proliferated on frontiers, and there were always struggles to increase them. When that becomes clear, it makes deep comparisons of frontiers achievable, because campaigns to capture more complete rights figured at the crux of strife and innovation. An absolute property right to land would mean a right to use and manage it; to derive income by letting others use it; to transfer it to another by gift or bequest; to capture the capital value of the land by sale; to claim immunity against expropriation of the property; and to operate without a term limiting the possession of these rights.[7]

Frequently, people on frontiers clutched just a few sticks from this bundle of rights. Certain of these sticks constituted assets – a stake of some kind in the land – that could be held more cheaply than outlays needed to secure a full bundle. Capital scarcity on frontiers made discounts attractive, but there were hazards to resting content with a cheap set of incomplete rights. They permitted confusion, conflict, litigation, and frustration. Hear the exasperation of a New York official who in 1765 inquired into a deed for 500,000–600,000 acres secured from the Iroquois by speculators. "There will be much Labour as well to collect all the Materials & Instructions necessary for a true understanding of this Affair, so much perplexed as it is."[8] The initial transaction in this infamous Kayaderosseras patent occurred sixty years earlier.[9] Legions of frontier speculators – like the Kayaderosseras proprietors – manipulated interests to try to add more sticks to an initial weak bundle. The great land rush precipitated quests everywhere for workable balances between cheap access and marketable interests.

We must not underestimate tenacity and defiance. In British colonies, a licence to use crown land as a commons at the government's pleasure was a well-known weak interest. The Dutch East India Company started a comparable practice at Cape Colony in the early eighteenth century. It cropped up in Australia during the wool boom of the early nineteenth.[10] Grazing licences had official sanction, but they assigned no specific places to their holders and gave no guarantees against government removal. It was less than a lease, although by the 1780s Dutch grazers at the Cape "by assertiveness on their part and resignation on the part of the government" established firm locations and bought and sold these loan farms (*lening plaatsen*).[11] To increase their rights, Australian licencees in the late 1830s and early 1840s petitioned to become leaseholders or freeholders, insisting on little cost to themselves. To justify an economical upgrading of their rights, they complained about the un-Britishness of exposure to officialdom's whims and hailed their own productive efforts as remarkably useful to civilization.[12] For a while in the 1820s, the *estancieros* of Argentina who wanted entitlements could only lease public land; then General Rosas transferred freehold title through sales, gifts, and pensions.[13]

In the late nineteenth century, many ranchers on the American public domain fashioned their own remedy to the insecurity of grazing. For a few, leasing, which implied fixed boundaries, was undesirable, because they sensed advantages – water and winter pasture – in access to an open range.[14] Regional associations therefore protected ranchers' interests and deterred interlopers. Other grazers by the 1880s were stringing barbed wire on public land without government consent.[15] The pattern of colonizers pushing ever to increase their interests in the land – and usually succeeding – surfaced repeatedly, even in British East Africa in the early twentieth century. Despite London's disapproval of large holdings and condemnation of racial discrimination in land allocations in Kenya, a sweeping land ordinance approved in 1915 gave white settlers almost all they had hoped to gain. They had wanted nothing less than freehold title to as much land as they could buy, for that was what they saw was available in Australia, Canada, and New Zealand. Their victory showed the inability of the Colonial Office to impose an unpopular policy on an unwilling European population. The Devonshire Declaration of 1923, which stated that in Kenya the interests of the black Africans must be paramount, was honoured more often in the breach than otherwise. However, settlers' influence in London ebbed in the 1920s.[16] Nevertheless, across the centuries, around the globe, the assertiveness and influence of individual and corporate colonizers generally forced governments to retreat when they tried to preclude or restrict settlers' property interests in order to protect indigenous people or to manage frontiers.

In English and colonial law, there were interests that arose from circumstances in which strict enforcement could bring about unfair outcomes. Squatters' labour or capital, applied to land unlawfully occupied, created equitable interests, because to eject occupants for valid legal reasons could exact hardship and loss. Wherever newcomers got ahead of government surveys, lawyers argued that the following comprised interests: evidence of a private purchase of native title; a government promise of land even if the terms of occupation were not executed by the recipient and no patent had been granted; a government acknowledgment that it would study a request for land; a homestead entry; squatting without permission on a tract; evidence of a transfer of any of these interests. Squatting was a prevalent interest, and sales of interests proliferated, because they could be defended in court and by intimidation. Where farmers held land in leasehold, the custom of a tenant's right – the ability to sell the remaining duration of the lease and capture the difference between the contractual rent and the current rental value of land – constituted an informal interest.[17] The custom of the tenant's right amounted to an interest.

Individuals with squatters' interests bolstered their position by admonishing other parties, face to face or in public notices and newspapers. To protect land that he occupied, a resident of Van Diemen's Land (Tasmania) published in 1818 a notice "warning off all people."[18] A Montana ranchers' association advised readers in an 1883 issue of the *Rocky Mountain Husbandman* that "we positively decline any outside party, or any party's herd upon the range."[19] They were trying to close the open range. Newspaper announcements about improvements helped to secure tracts for squatters by signalling their will to fight for compensation if late-comers holding government-issued rights attempted to displace them. Feuding New Zealand pastoralists in Canterbury province, during a heated land rush in the early 1860s, paid a newspaper to print notices to intimidate rivals.[20] Bluff played a part in tactics to hold interests. When colonial governments began to accept squatting grazers' attachments to specific locales, notices began to appear in *Government Gazettes* as part of a licensing process.

In our definition of property rights, *relationship* stands out, because it underlines the social and political character of property rights. From starting points like our definition, philosophers, legal theorists, and economists have analysed how societies *should* allocate resources, how they *should* identify and correct unjust distributions, and how they *should* settle disputes. Theorists have tackled such essential questions with formal arguments, but also with historical evidence. For example, when Robert Ellickson argues in *Order without Law* that people commonly establish rules of conduct that are not codified in statute books, he recounts an informal rule observed by nineteenth-century whalers.[21] The harpoon in the whale established a right that whalers respected. Douglass North, who usually stresses government's "major role in the performance of an economy" by its reduction of the transactions cost, also explains why informal normative codes sometimes work. Repetitive activities may promote them, because they open possibilities for retribution in a "tit-for-tat" sequence.[22] Whaling captains were going to encounter one another often; taking someone else's whale could initiate an outbreak of chaotic seizures that injured the original transgressor. Self-interest recommended prudence. Ellickson and North have picked examples from history. As a rule, historians are not as interested in formal concepts and abstraction as social theorists are with history. Although historians debate theoretical matters, they also document untidiness in human endeavour. Returning to the chaos of evidence, they find it as confusing as contemporaries did. For two good reasons, the essential subject here – the formation of property rights in new-world situations – can only benefit from attention to theory. First, any urge to discover common meaning in the histories of several countries needs a decent chart. Second, property rights offer a common – in fact, paramount – theme in colonization.

Comparison of how British imperial and American frontiers were occupied requires an engagement with theory. Property rights in the English-speaking world have long been the subject of elaborate discussion. Commentators over the centuries have identified basic questions regarding property rights. John Locke – and recent commentators on Locke – have raised exactly the issues that can organize a study of colonization. Where do property rights originate? How complete should they be? Are they just? These questions about the concepts and parameters that underlay the great land rush (chapters 1–3) can guide comparisons of settlement frontiers, and they frame the structure of this book, for it then proceeds from an account of acquisitions (chapter 4), through systems of allocation and the refinement of property rights (chapters 5–7), to projects of reformation (chapter 8). The purpose of noting these questions, then, is not to attempt answers through formal argument, but to use them later to probe events.

ORGANIZING PROPERTY RIGHTS AND INTERESTS

Norms

Where do property rights in society originate? A relationship between persons regarding property can emerge in at least four ways – the exercise of norms or personal ethics that people understand and accept, the arranging of contracts, the setting up of organizations of people with like interests, and government activities and legislation. In this section I examine each mode in turn and then suggest how their regional variations help provide the basis for a comparative study in what follows. Those who have argued that there can be order without law stress that norms can maintain relationships over property. They do not dwell on famously contentious situations, yet frontier history concerns bitter inaugural contests for resources where initial rounds of acquisition and allocation were thought to be once-in-a-lifetime opportunities. The antiquity, scale, and complexity of the Kayaderosseras claim in colonial New York suggest that landjobbers pursued immense profits from a few campaigns, whereas we know that whalers had many encounters with their quarry. The landjobbers acted accordingly, trying to haul in as much as they could by hook or crook, because comparable chances might not occur often. Hence, frontiers teemed with defiance, secrecy, and deception. These attitudes were directed not just at governments, but at other individuals as well. If enduring property rights were to emerge from frontiers, they could not flow from normative conduct.[23] Only after governments had confirmed entitlements could occupants cultivate ties that supported parochial norms. Minor boundary disputes and the disposition of wandering livestock could be handled in close-knit communities once larger resource issues had been settled.[24]

On many frontiers, indigenous peoples were anything but compliant when newcomers roughed out property rights for themselves and planted settlements that disturbed habitat. Resistance checked "plantations" from the start. Friction over territory prompted an Indian attack on the colony of Virginia in 1622.[25] Frontier wars had assorted immediate causes, but most involved territory and use of habitat. Where first peoples were pastorialists, as in southern Africa, they clashed with settlers over both grazing boundaries and stock ownership.[26] In western Cape Colony during the late seventeenth and early eighteenth centuries (1680s–1720s), the Khoikhoi raided white stockmen who occupied valleys and springs north of Cape Town, in order to defend environments that supported them.[27] Khoikhoi herdsmen next resisted the northeastward advance of white grazers in the late eighteenth century (1750s–90s).[28] On the eastern frontiers of the Cape Colony, large-scale stock raiding back and forth between white colonizers and African grazers proliferated during interludes that separated a string of frontier wars between the Great Fish and Great Keiskamma rivers (1770s-1850s) and along the Caledon River (1850s–60s).[29] Like the intermittent wars between American settlers and first peoples, these conflicts flared up over control of habitat and incursions into buffer territories. Violence accompanied the occupation of numerous locales, particularly from the 1780s to the 1880s.[30]

When Australian squatter Edward Curr reminisced wistfully about his eighty-square-mile tract of grazing runs, he remembered extensive marshlands, filled with fish and ducks, and "a great stronghold of the Banderang Blacks, whom ... my brother found troublesome."[31] He let slip a dirty little secret. Australian Aboriginal people in several south-eastern locales in the 1830s and 1840s maimed sheep that overran traditional hunting and fishing areas. Many – not all – grazers drove Aboriginal people off sheep runs, and their tactics extended to murder. The sequence continued to century's end as stockmen expanded counter-clockwise, north, then west, through the better-watered parts of the driest continent. Writing about family members who partici-pated in that movement, Mary Durack courageously admitted that "first-footers had made no pretence of coming to 'an understanding' or forming a sort of 'treaty' with the Aborigines."[32] Across the Tasman Sea, in the 1840s and 1850s, Maori cultivators drove away European stock that trampled their plantings.[33] Stock raiding was a staple of conflicts over habitat in the United States and southern Africa. Horses were valued for use in later attacks, oxen shunned on account of their slow pace during an escape. Dealings with indigenous peoples were accompanied everywhere by misunderstanding and duplicity, episodes of collaboration, selective borrowings by peoples on both sides of the frontier, ecological change, and violence.

We do not have to seek only the conspicuous inter-cultural struggles over habitat to recognize that live-and-let-live arrangements were uncommon when newcomers hewed out property interests. It may be, as Ellickson proposes, that norms obtain in how some people sort out workaday lives with one another; however, harmony and restraint were rare during the serious business of initial allocations of property rights. In Mancur Olson's words, "just as individuals can often serve their interests through voluntary associations, some of them can sometimes also serve their interests through the threat of – and sometimes the use of – force."[34] White grazers feuded among themselves. In Cape Colony beginning in the early eighteenth century, and in Australia and New Zealand a century later, officials mediated and prevented violence, although a few grazers struck low blows at a neighbour's assets. Driving diseased stock over a disputed boundary was a standard tactic.[35] During the range conflicts of the 1880s, some Texas cattlemen likewise turned scabby sheep loose among the flocks of sheepmen who dared to fence pastures.[36]

Direct personal brutality among white newcomers was common in the United States. No British colony experienced anything like the bedlam that accompanied disputes over land claims in Missouri (1807–12), where "men were pursued into their own homes and butchered

on the spot" and where assailants fired cannon balls into Moses
Austin's parlour.[37] The approximately 120 violent raids and skirmishes
between cattlemen and sheepmen from 1880 to 1920 in Arizona,
Texas, and Wyoming originated in struggles over access to grass and
water. Colorado sheepmen reported that cattlemen employed Texas
desperadoes to destroy flocks.[38] In the cattle country of Oregon, a jury
of settlers freed the killer of a resident cattle baron who had been
harassing later settlers with litigation.[39] Examples of murder over land
are plentiful, and more are likely to be found in local court records
and newspapers. A search for normative conduct in frontier history
will return scant evidence that individuals can sort out significant
original rights without major initial intervention by governments and
courts or without intimidation or worse.[40]

Contracts

In both theory and history, a relationship that delimits property rights
may also originate in a contract between parties or an agreement
among members of an organization. Contracts, compacts, and mutual-
protection organizations that dispensed resources appeared on frontiers; however, they pose complications for theories that look for
examples of order without law. Consider direct contractual land dealings between indigenous peoples and private individuals. In colonial
America, the United States, southern Africa, Australia, and New
Zealand, individuals rushing to tie up land either for exclusive use or
for gain from sales attempted to lease or purchase it directly from
indigenous peoples. British colonial governments by the late seventeenth century normally prohibited these dealings.[41] So too did a
successor government, the United States.[42] However, it was not easy
to overturn such arrangements or to prevent further violations. Land
speculators artfully exploited leniency and exceptions. Nevertheless, a
doctrine was consistently applied to British colonial and American
frontiers: no direct negotiations for land without prior approval by
government.[43] This was an unreasonable imposition on first peoples.
   It was paternalistic and arrogant. It was also damaging, because it
designated first peoples as political inferiors, and this status left them
exposed to the erratic integrity of colonizing governments. Nevertheless, frontier affairs were complicated and brimming with dilemmas for
distant governments. Eventually, settlers wanted a full bundle of rights
to a well-defined tract. As North puts it, "not only must the rights be
measurable; they must also be enforceable."[44] The question of whether
a land system based on direct negotiations between settlers and first
peoples could have served a market economy on North's terms is a

thorny one. British and American colonizers hungered after real property and caused endless disputes. Establishing rudimentary land surveys and dispute-resolution systems would have strained native vendors and speculative buyers, just as it exhausted and embarrassed colonizing governments. To transform tribal rights that served a particular way of life into private rights that served another could be accomplished in several ways. None was facile and free of trouble.[45] Therefore we should be sceptical about the durability of direct contracts. It is unlikely that they could have provided a precise, effectual system of land registration. Contracts seem a recognition of the political rights of first peoples, but their devotees were sharp land dealers. In colonial America, the United States, and New Zealand, lawyers for several large land jobbers argued without success that first peoples had a natural right to sell. It was a prescient modern argument with shady backers.

In classical liberal theories of property rights, a legitimate contract that appropriates a resource must, as a minimum condition, originate in fair procedures. Direct dealings between newcomers and first peoples took place on frontiers from the Ohio valley to the coast of New Zealand, from the 1750s to the 1850s, and they present no obvious instances of fair conduct in large-scale direct sales between private individuals and first peoples. Governments recognized this problem and cancelled most private agreements, except those pre-authorized by government licence or free from taint of speculation. To have done otherwise would have thrown away any thought of peace. I reconsider direct dealings from time to time below, to witness their hazards and how their illegality affected the status of indigenous peoples.

Organizations

Because of bans on direct dealing, we must turn to other processes when searching for relationships that underpinned property rights on nineteenth-century frontiers. There is no shortage of examples of organizations that regulated relationships with regard to resources. Plentiful they were, but these agencies – what one historian financed by a meat-packing company graciously called a "cattleman's commonwealth" – functioned as flawed architects of property rights and poor managers of magnificent grasslands.[46] In an influential article, Kermit Hall argues that "the entire movement of land law in the Great Plains at the end of the nineteenth century was from communal to exclusive ownership."[47] I show in chapter 7 that the trend in landuse ran from open access, available briefly to frontier stockmen, through exclusive usage at minimal cost by parties who sustained cattlemen's associations, to individual, exclusive use at increased cost – a phase that occurred when ranchers set about controlling strategic sections of freehold.

Throughout these stages, cattlemen's associations were not agents of communalism, but rapacious cabals, some more powerful than others. Montana rancher Granville Stuart wrote "that to be successful the entire range business must be run as one outfit."[48] A few associations tried to run a range and to mediate among members who clashed over their presumed range rights. Mostly, cattlemen's associations let individual ranchers sort out specific territorial conflicts, although they commanded the range by determining if ranchers should have the benefit of association-managed round-ups and theft-control measures. In effect, the big ranchers' attention to the co-ordination alluded to by Stuart extended mainly to combatting rustling. No county, state, or territorial association paid attention to judicious management of the range resource. Depletion of the native grasses – rawhiding the land – advanced during the cattle boom of the mid-1880s. In his history of the U.S. west (1859–1900), Rodman Paul claimed that the pressure on the land allowed noxious weeds to replace native grasses, turned springs to mudholes, and advanced erosion. What he described was recognized as early as 1898 when a U.S. government report remarked that, compared with the start of the cattle boom, it now took more land to support stock, because the tall buffalo grasses were disappearing.[49] The spread of small farmers, especially in Kansas and Nebraska, and the severe winter of 1886–87 compelled winter feeding on confined pastures and summer grazing on the open range. In the 1930s, a host of state and federal studies of ranching denounced overstocking on public land, especially on summer ranges and stock trails and around waterholes.[50]

For legitimacy, ranchers could claim – as Stark did – prior occupation. In several exceptional instances – most notably, the six million acres of the Cherokee Strip – ranchers also claimed authority through illicit leases from first peoples.[51] Where did prior occupation and exclusive organizations leave slightly later influxes of newcomers who alleged that they could increase productivity on specific tracts? The forecast of improvement, based on core tenets of European – especially English – culture, was an instrumental idea on frontiers, and it challenged the standing of indigenous peoples and pioneer occupants – particularly of grazers, who in British colonies at first held licences or on the American open range carved out interests enforced by protective associations. Later, in some locales, farming challenged stock raising. "The legal culture of the Great Plains," Hall proposed, "resonated far more to the economic pressures associated with a shift ... from the nineteenth-century economics of pastoral stockraising to the twentieth-century practice of farming."[52]

A troubling feature of private regulatory associations was their recourse to threats and violence, practices injurious to the formation of civil societies and contrary to ideas of communalism.[53] One set of organizations that arranged resources on behalf of members in these troubling ways consisted of cattlemen's associations. Since they managed relationships to benefit current members across a public domain, they had no wish to institute rules that managed access to resources by consent from all parties who might claim an interest. They acted as clubs – complete with black listing – to keep non-members off the land. However, they could not prevent their members from overstocking the range. Any arrangement of property rights that places no burden on first-comers to consider the impact of their unlawful appropriation on late arrivals and on the environment is problematic.[54] Unlawful occupations occurred often in the United States, beginning long before the occupation of the high plains. In their early years (1870s–80s), ranchers' associations resembled squatters' claims clubs in the midwest (1830s and 1840s) and California (1850s). Employing intimidation, these agencies barred late-comers, including legitimate buyers of public land – among them, aspiring farmers.[55]

The self-reliance of the clubs and their acts of intimidation constituted a single, ambiguous package, a bundle of both organizational genius and intimidation. Those bodies have been described as agencies that "secured land for yeomen, and induced feelings of justice and empowerment."[56] In contrast to that gloss, an 1835 report illustrates how some functioned. Forty families on a lovely prairie in northern Illinois settled on lands surveyed into townships, but not yet sectioned for sale. A Methodist circuit rider asked them about "what security they had." "The reply was, that there was an understanding in the country equivolent [sic] to a law of the land, that the settlers should sustain each other against the speculator, & no settler should bid on anothers land. If a speculator should bid on a settlers farm, he was knocked down & dragged out of the place, & if the strikers was prosecuted & fined, the settlers paid the expense by common consent among themselves. But before a fine could be assessed, the case must come before a jury, which of course must be selected among the settlers ... And if these means could not protect the settler, the last resort would be to 'burn powder in their faces.'"[57] In Missouri, around the same time, a traveller reported that land-buying speculators were intimidated by squatters dressed as Indians.[58] But who was a speculator, and who only a late arrival entitled by law to buy? Were the clubs really defending frontier hearths? Allan Bogue, who examined a number of clubs in Iowa active in the 1840s, finds that they harboured speculators who profited from "a cunning mixture of brute force and Virgin land."[59]

Mob attacks on the Mormons in Missouri (1838) – a repulsive episode of midwest collective violence – had many causes, but pre-emption rights to land played a part. The Rev. Sashel Woods, a militia officer, reportedly told his men that "if they could get the Mormons driven out, they could get all the lands entitled to preemptions."[60] Looking backward in time, one can perhaps make a better case for private enforcement of property interests by inspecting the co-operating groups of small American squatters who, in the 1780s and 1790s, attempted frontier social revolutions by occupation.[61] Collective defiance sometimes represented struggles by poorer citizens to win self-sufficiency. These squatters' communities acted at a time when influential merchants, speculators, and planters seemed poised to reap fortunes through their commitments to purchase large tracts carved out of the public domain at knocked-down prices, something explored below in chapter 5.[62] If some early squatters' organizations display a Robin Hood image – casting federalists as the sheriff of Nottingham – that gloss can never be applied to ranchers' associations.[63] But mentioning impoverished toiling agrarians and heavily capitalized ranchers in the same breath is no mistake. Private organizations that thrust themselves into processes for initial distributions shared defects. Authorities in charge of formal allocation processes may not always have served the public well, but irregular groups were not necessarily any better and practised coercive illegalities. Defiance of law can be a means with many agents and ends. Repeated episodes of defiance in matters of property rights helped nurture a culture of direct action that advanced lawlessness as a too-prominent feature of American life and as an ingredient in its history of bloodshed.[64]

Other frontiers witnessed an avoidance of government regulations in varying degrees and arguably suffered for it. By the mid-eighteenth century, the Dutch East India Company, the agency that established the Cape Colony in 1652, proclaimed restraints on colonists' treatment of the Khoikhoi. The company lacked the will to intervene in frontier conflicts, and the trekboers, left to their own devices, began in 1774 to deploy *kommandos* to protect livestock and homes. These raids also led to the slaughter and enslavement of the Khoikhoi; defence slipped easily into offence.[65] The defiant practices shaped during the eighteenth century on the northern frontier of Cape Colony influenced white settlers' activities on other Cape frontiers.[66] Following tentative migrations in the 1820s, thousands of pastoralists crossed the Orange River and established autonomous states in southern Africa (1835–42). These republics originated in the departure of people determined to shake themselves free from British laws that restricted access both to land and to cheap native labour. Bold, purposeful expeditions, organized by unofficial, loose-knit associations, the *treks* initiated a cycle of inter-racial raids and wars. Unofficial organizations that tried to govern people's relationships with respect to land merit critical scrutiny. In certain instances, an appraisal of their actions fosters sympathy for squatters, because they had been marginalized and faced further manipulation. Buenos Aires civil servant Pedro Andrés Garcia reached this conclusion in a 1813 report, after investigating the complaints of an estate owner who wanted to expel roughly 250 people or absorb them as tenants. Garcia could not bring himself to recommend that the government ruin these citizens by allowing the rights of a proprietor to be placed ahead of the people.[67] Groups that seized land posed dilemmas for governments and now challenge historians.

During the nineteenth century, the United States practised an exceedingly loose administration of its unalienated land, and that encouraged the formation of claims clubs. Such looseness evaporated early in the twentieth century, particularly in the west. "Uncle Sam," wrote Carl Abbott in the early 1990s, "is now more active and omnipresent than nineteenth-century pioneers could have imagined."[68] In contrast to nineteenth-century American permissiveness, British authorities responsible for frontiers attempted, early in comparison to the United States, to administer public (crown) lands. A tradition of management over royal estates and forests enabled in a philosophical, not in an applied, sense the British administration at the Cape to direct Dutch colonial officers – the inspector of lands and woods and the *landdrosts* and *veldkornets* (roughly speaking, magistrates and constables) – to try to constrain land taking. It is almost certain that these institutions and their role in land allocation influenced the governor of New South Wales, Sir Richard Bourke, who arranged in 1833 that commissioners of crown lands should superintend his colony's crown land. Bourke had served as lieutenant-governor in Cape Colony.[69] The use of crown commissioners to manage grazing licences, to prevent unauthorized timber cutting, and to oversee land sales was next applied in New Zealand.

Even on several British frontiers that were supposedly being supervised, squatters became features of early settlement. Except in Upper Canada and on the Canadian prairies, unauthorized occupants also played rough with late-comers and indigenous peoples. Supervision by the home government on most British frontiers was ludicrously thin, because after the Napoleonic wars Britain reduced its army and for several decades confined strategic imperial aims in order to economize. In the absence of diligent and even-handed policing, some frontier colonizers committed atrocities. In Australia, in the 1830s and 1840s, a few squatters poisoned and shot Aboriginals and drove them off waterholes in droughts. Nothing like this happened in Upper Canada during the same years. Besides being essentially a peninsula with a fairly thin band of prime land, this colony's climate and forests made it unsuitable for land-extensive grazing; it therefore escaped swift-moving outbreaks of aggressive land taking, and the absence of "Indian troubles" was one of its attractions for land-seeking U.S. migrants in the early nineteenth century. The pattern of organized settler violence towards first peoples was also comparatively modest on one vast frontier – the Canadian prairies.[70] Isolation delayed massive occupation of land in western Canada – a remote, interior empire, lying mostly in a climatic zone that made grazing risky. These environmental conditions presented an opportunity rare for frontier governments. Untroubled by numerous and well-stocked advance parties of pastoralists occupying extensive territory, Canada uniquely could organize settlement by procedures on the prairies that accentuated order. After an interlude of "free grass" (1874–81), cattle ranches established south of the Red Deer River in the Districts of Alberta and Assiniboia followed Australian practice and leased crownland. Upper Canadian and prairie settlers retained unbloodied hands. In the United States, southern Africa, and Australia, however, unauthorized group action to govern people's relationships over resources descended into raids and killings.

Governments

Norms, contracts, and organizations could not foster relationships to convert frontiers into lasting private assets through a series of just steps. Violence and threats tarnished the foundations. Agreements administered by organizations fell when exposed to government challenge, and uncertainty about government intentions discounted their market value. Individuals who seized resources eventually had recourse to government institutions, because private arrangements could not serve them adequately in financial markets.[71] At critical junctures, as they engaged with a market economy, squatters or those who purchased their interests treated with lenders. The capitalist economy rewarded better security with better credit. Australian squatter Henry Dangar assumed in 1844 that leasehold for grazers would provide "ample security for the English capitalist."[72] Some people who held interests sought capital to increase the carrying capacity of land through improved livestock, fencing, wells, irrigation, or drainage. Imperfectly defined and loosely held assets were deficient for leveraging costly projects.[73] Governments universally skimped on land-distribution mechanisms and earned the scorn of people in a hurry. Subjects or citizens who obeyed the letter of the law were left sadly behind. Administrators' inability to keep pace with people's movements, and their failure realize how to associate environment and land grants, allowed squatters to charge authorities with incompetence.[74] Paradoxically, frontier dwellers, aware of the cost of public services, wished to keep them down. The great land rush is replete with tensions between enforcement and access, discipline and immediacy, costly order and frugal tumult.[75]

Many popular and formal arguments have rationalized the actions of impatient individuals who seized frontier lands. A widely heard one was that hustling occupants, not bungling governments, made frontier land valuable. Petitions for an upgrading of rights usually listed changes to the landscape, including the introduction of domesticated European plants and livestock. Pleas for further property rights on account of improvements already achieved paralleled a formal theoretical argument. The most persistently stimulating theory about how individuals legitimately acquire property rights by their own actions originates with John Locke (1632–1704), who proposed that people could, by adding labour to things found in a state of nature, exercise a maker's right that entitled them to articles, including fields.[76] This argument – or something very close to it – often materialized in real-life situations, because land takers tried to firm up interests by asserting improvement. If Locke is associated with a maker's right to property, Thomas Hobbes (1588–1679) is identified with theories of a strong state. Legal centralism imposes a dark judgment on human nature.[77] Locke's full argument also places severe moral limits on a party's property rights because of unease about what individuals might do out of self-interest, but it omits mechanisms of scrutiny and management of limits.[78] Hobbesian legal centralism contemplates limits and is more frankly distrustful about what a person or group may attempt to secure when acquiring from a position of strength. Douglass North asks a pertinent question: "under what conditions can voluntary cooperation exist without the Hobbesian solution of the imposition of a coercive state to create cooperative solutions?"[79] Only a strong state, Hobbes's modern followers would argue, can prevent an extreme appropriation of material resources that would subvert general welfare.[80] It is not within the scope of this book to make a general case for legal centralism; however, a Hobbesian perspective accords with what occurred on frontiers in several continents. I make no greater claim, because frontiers existed, by definition, as exceptional places. They approximated a Hobbesian realm of near-chaos, where governments were feckless and disputes over rights to property, especially land – and often the related water rights – escalated into sly dodges, corrupt dealings, and even raids and wars. Although people seeking land on frontiers had recourse to a variety of ploys for holding onto it, the requirements of an evolving economy were such that, sooner or later, government approval leading to confirmation of title was essential.

Governments that claimed sovereignty over frontiers were conclusive agents for preparing, legitimizing, and administering rules that managed relationships among people with respect to resources. They were the third-party enforcers of the relations that *made* property rights. How well did they do? One school of interpretation insists that they lacked the heroic qualities needed for just acquisitions from first peoples and likewise for just allocations among newcomers. American land-policy historian Paul Gates devoted his career to chronicling "the malfunctioning of an intended democratic system of land disposal."[81] Thomas Abernethy, in a study of land speculation prior to the American Revolution, lamented a failure of governments to allocate land suitably for the benefit of actual settlers.[82] Echoes from American progressivism, these older studies were joined by later ones that documented chaos and corruption. Critics blamed poorly devised land-sale practices for helping speculators, whom, they alleged, held land off the market, thereby slowing settlement and bleeding farmers' capital. In-depth studies of land speculation challenged these critics and showed that speculators tended to sell quickly and accepted financial risks. The presence of freewheeling agents has also been commended as an element in marketplace efficiency and as a necessity, given the limited state that characterized American frontiers.[83]

These upbeat analyses do not touch other grounds for criticism, "including environmental damage, over investment (in unproductive land speculation), and the human toll from foreclosures or relocation."[84] We must add dishonesty, intimidation, and violence to the debit columns. Failure stands as a reasonable verdict overall.[85] Were finer practices and better outcomes feasible? Greater wisdom, fairness, honesty, and peace in managing resources would have required substantial commitments of state resources very early. That would have entailed three conditions: ample state coffers, acceptance of big government, and social consensus. Consensus was absent everywhere, at home and in the colonies. Even small, remote colonies – New Zealand, for example – were splintered by class and regional interests. Conflicting schemes to bring people of disparate means onto virgin lands were plentiful, because the concept of colonization inspired plans that addressed contemporary issues of poverty and aspirations for national or imperial development.[86] Competing designs for frontier land – to improve labourers' conditions, to combine settlement with protection of indigenous peoples, or to increase state wealth – were well-expressed in phrases familiar to Europeans. Richer and Stark propose contrasting visions of land use but speak a common language of rights and improvements. For them, consensus on details is impossible, and so it was for real-life adversaries. States, moreover, were unaccustomed to large peacetime undertakings. No matter which resource-allocation plans faraway governments adopted, administrative support pulled up short. Throughout *Reluctant Empire*, John S. Galbraith emphasizes chaos on the Cape Colony's frontiers, where economy-minded governments sent administrators "to battle cosmic forces."[87] In land matters, around the globe, disarray was in the cards.

We can open wide Gate's thesis of failure to encompass more regions of the world. He dwells on an American tragedy – as he sees it, a betrayal of U.S. democratic values. Aspects of what he reports, however, formed part of a wider, more intricate medley of events. Many systems, not just the American, malfunctioned in the nineteenth century.[88] Gates believes that the basic U.S. system of land allocation had been fashioned to realize democratic goals; however, it was not quite a social or political program, certainly not one guided by a neat, enduring charter. A report of the Public Land Commission in 1880 codified the nearly 3,000 acts of Congress that affected the public domain. The compendium was once reputed to have been "referred to more than any other public document."[89] Additionally, a number of states with public lands developed their own allocation laws. In concert with distribution arrangements elsewhere, therefore, the United States's allocation system stumbled along as a complicated, diversified, much-amended work in process. In that condition, it disbursed an empire. Similarly, British colonial administrators, working with an outpouring of statutes and executive rules, parcelled out another, more scattered empire. The effort was enormous. By 1900, New South Wales had nearly 100 acts that dealt with land transactions, and a stately Italian Renaissance–style Lands Department building graced Sydney's business district.[90] Legislation and administrative practices everywhere grew in particulars; land and registry offices expanded apace. A New Zealand land ordinance of 1849 contained 46 sections; its 1877 successor, 172.[91] The statutes and administrative offices that guided allocation are artifacts of huge undertakings that could not keep pace with cosmic forces.

Throughout the nineteenth century, the most complex legislation in settlement colonies concerned lands. In all jurisdictions, authorities responded to administrative problems, shifting ideals, pressure groups, bribery, new environments, and evolving modes of exploitation. Therefore the democratic, independent yeomanry that Gates feels was intrinsic to the American land system – though significant – was not an all-commanding principle that allocated the U.S. public domain. Democratic rhetoric gilded American schemes, but vitally active landhunters and ingenious speculators adopted democratic language and subverted land regulations. How could that happen? Many regulations were undermined by slick manœuvring lubricated with bribes. Additionally, entrenched British and American doctrines about legal entitlements sustained the activities of squatters and speculators. The linked notions of occupation and improvement unlocked many frontiers for speculators; these substantial tenets rivalled and interacted with democracy on American frontiers. They influenced the formation of property rights on the frontiers of Australia, New Zealand, southern Africa, and, to a lesser extent, Canada.

A question opened this extended discussion. Where do property rights originate? Given what we have seen, it is reasonable to claim that the relationships that ultimately defined property rights on frontiers had to originate in statutes and the common law. Organizations played an interim part in installing crude property rights, in some places, by helping individuals maintain raw possession, which they could parlay into more comprehensive rights. What, from the perspective of social history, are the consequences of direct action to seize resources for founding civil societies? And on behalf of economists, for whom moral questions belong in other disciplines, we should ask whether the tensions and fluctuations concerning property rights formed a mix of stability and freedom that lowered the transactions cost without sacrificing creative opportunities. If so, a weakly controlled initial formation of property rights bears responsibility for malevolent cruelty and prosperity. Karl Marx and Joseph Schumpeter urged people to think of major economic change as destructive and liberating simultaneously. The great land rush was such an episode.

Another question can be posed. Theorists interested in entitlements and the maximization of welfare ask how complete property rights should be. From the historical perspective, we can ask how complete property rights *were*. Different social systems have described property rights in singular ways. Until the early modern era in western Europe, feudeliam constrained property rights in many locales. In England, these constraints accompanied the Norman conquest in 1066. Prior to then, land in England could be *allodial*, meaning not subject to any rent, service, or exercise of authority from an overlord. After the conquest, land was subject to a doctrine of *tenures*. As a result of conquest, all land belonged to the crown and subjects held it directly or indirectly from the crown. The crown parcelled out land to tenants-in-chief (*in capite*), who paid service to the crown. Tenants-in-chief could subgrant the land and require a service from tenants. Some land was granted for communal usage, but again a service was required. This scheme of tenures continued as an active arrangement for several centuries. Bit by bit, services to be performed were commuted to money payments. The crown, for example, received quit rents rather than military service.

A Variety of Tenures: Elements for a Comparative History

The variety of tenures in England was reduced, and the Statute of Tenures (1660) essentially individualized title; however, in England and the settlement colonies of the British empire, there was no reversion to allodial tenure. Subjects could not own the land itself; technically, all land was held from the crown. English colonies applied the term "crown land" for unalienated territory. Subjects could own an estate in land, and that estate entitled them to enjoy the land as fully as if they owned it; lawyers had liberated much of English real estate from the dead hand of feudalism, although several royal favourites who were granted proprietorships in the colonies may have wished to re-establish feudalism.[92] Proprietary colonies, of course, did not sustain feudalism, and the American Revolution disposed of the crown and installed allodial tenure. Land held by the U.S. national government was henceforth the public domain. Both reformed English title and allodial title went a considerable distance towards providing extensive individual rights that ran with the land, although allodial title went further. Some American historians, to underline the supposed radicalism of the revolution, include property law reforms – especially the abolition of primogeniture and entail – in lists of significant departures.[93]

These were symbolic changes affecting few Americans, while practical ideas about land – the doctrine of improvement, squatters' possession, the marketability of interests, and the quest for a complete but cheap bundle of rights – pervaded frontiers in both the United States and the British empire for a long, long time. The revolutionary colonial governments that seized millions of acres from Tories, mostly in New York, enabled other rich men to accumulate them.[94] Nevertheless, the revolution made a difference in the United States and eventually in British settlement colonies; the largely symbolic distinction between public domain and crown land must not be entirely slighted, because republican advocates of free land passionately invoked the term "public land" as if it were a material benefit embedded in the constitution. New York reformer George Henry Evans, who in 1844 organized the National Land Association, which influenced Horace Greeley ("Go West, young man, and grow up with the country"), insisted that the public domain should benefit working people. The Free Soil Party adopted some of his ideas, and in 1860 its offspring, the Republican Party, approved of free land.[95] Distinctions between crown and public land did not mean that smallholders were kept off the land in British colonies; rhetoric helped to strengthen the ideal of free land for all in the United States, but that concept also entered Canada and Australia without benefit of the term "public land."

A few restraints on property rights remained even in the United States. Allodial title did not sweep away complicating entitlements, interests, and non-market measures. Women retained dower rights; where usury laws lingered, lending was convoluted; mortgagors and mortgagees had rights in law that varied in details with each colonial or state jurisdiction. Generally rights that accompanied ownership of land, or an estate in land, essentially included free and exclusive enjoyment and the right of transfer, but until legislative reforms abolished them, residual obligations or interests endured. Streamlining took time throughout the English-speaking world, and a long time in England, where the influential legal profession combated statutory changes in Parliament.[96] Speculators and settlers alike aimed to secure the maximum rights for the lowest outlay. They abjured some rights, in return for reduced outlays, and, although many of them would have denied it, they were squatting. Cotton growers in southern Mississippi during the early nineteenth century, for example, used capital first for slaves and buildings and delayed payments to government land offices, perhaps hoping for Congress to waive their obligations.[97] In the meantime, their occupation would not be challenged. Many petitioners in Upper Canada who received location tickets for crown lands postponed paying fees required for a crown patent, using scarce specie to buy stock or to pay labourers to clear trees. Canadians are not conditioned to thinking of illegality as natural to their nation-building saga, but strictly speaking it was. For most of their history, Australians have been more forthright. Thus, concerning formal applications to graze in remote areas, squatter Edward Curr suggested that grazers fancied that these could be "put off for a century or two."[98] Stalling was bound to be temporary, however, because occupants without title were vulnerable. Douglass North describes this situation well. "The more easily others can affect the income flow from someone's assets without bearing the full costs of their action, the lower is the value of that asset."[99]

Fortifying rights – hence income flow and collateral value – when squatters could afford to do so was a customary practice. They could not expect to enjoy quiet use of the land or transfer quiet use. Still, they routinely relinquished strong legal rights in return for a low-cost position on the land.[100] Getting a bargain foothold and then adding to the legal interests became a strategy from at least the early eighteenth century in America; rich and poor alike practised it, although the precise tactics and ultimate goals of wealthy and subsistence land hunters – to take extreme examples – differed. The wealthy, the influential, and the wisely opportunistic garnered documents that conveyed rights in crown or public land. Land warrants, scrip, compensation rights, and deeds of grant were government-issued face cards in a game of land poker.[101] I discuss the usefulness of these paper instruments in chapters below. During the first decades of the nineteenth century in New South Wales, for example, a promise of grant at a future date was "known to pass current with as much confidence in the public market as a Spanish Dollar."[102] It was the same elsewhere. Even with drawers stuffed with helpful paper, richer players often worked with incomplete rights because they contracted mortgages, pledged the same land as security many times over for additional purchases, attempted purchases by devious means that incited court challenges, struck careless bargains that left clouded titles, neglected to pay taxes, and fell flat when land booms collapsed.[103] In one settlement frontier after another, however, the distilled result was that profits – though often elusive – were private, and the costs of enforcing property rights were socialized.

Private gains in the great land rush were possibly more often dreamed of than realized. In the Swan River Colony in western Australia, where the crown granted land in the late 1820s to applicants from the English gentry, some grantees falsified declarations of assets in order to inflate entitlements.[104] This conduct was not unusual. Neither was disappointment. Many petitioners failed to satisfy the settlement conditions exacted by the crown, which then denied them patents. Often the great land speculators were neither as rich nor as secure as their posturing suggested. Defending a portfolio of interests soaked up capital, and often a boom came too late to rescue speculators. Buoyant markets could not wait for clear titles, so people sold what they did not own, and other people tried to prevent such transactions from ruining their own interests. In 1794, after forty years of experience with speculation and estate management, George Washington professed, "I have found distant property in land more pregnant of perplexities than profit."[105] Almost fifty years later, the Sydney whaler, merchant, and speculator in Maori deeds Joseph Weller confided that "land which I always looked upon as a resource in case of pressure and calculated on a sale or to raise money on Mortgage, may be considered as valueless from the deficiency of capital to invest."[106] There were failures among speculators; however, it often was other speculators who picked up the pieces. Tax sales provided one mechanism for Upper Canadian speculators to obtain land cheaply.[107] Similar prospects beckoned in other places. Washington, DC, banker William W. Corcoran, for example, purchased treasury department lands in

Illinois, land that the department had accumulated from defaulting federal officials.[108] The Corcoran Gallery of Art in Washington, built around his collection, was established to encourage American genius. Many of the nineteenth-century artists represented there raised the conquest and occupation of the public domain to the level of romance – a decided contrast with Corcoran's desk-based feats. Chapter 8 below looks at particular land-rush services of metropolitan capitalists such as Corcoran.

The interests in land secured by the rich often amounted to less than a full bundle, but what they held subtracted from someone else's bundle of interests, and that could force a compromise or buyout. Meanwhile, frontier folk who lacked powerful backers or easy credit relied on raw occupation and sweat-equity improvements. As well, from time to time, affluent and poor go-getters co-operated on landhunting projects. Whatever the social origins of frontier speculators, there were among them risk takers in the land trade who took positions early and accepted – for an interlude – something less than full rights. The diversity of interests in the land – sticks in that metaphorical bundle of rights or interests – complicated land speculation everywhere. Understandably, interests in property became objects of reform. On frontiers, mere interests were traded and marshalled in legal battles. As frontiers congealed into settler societies, reform of property laws in ways designed to decrease this litigation was much desired, but contentious on details. No speculator relished costly lawsuits. The prospect of seeing interests bled white in courtrooms was unnerving. Thus reformation of property rights transpired amid debate and compromise. Turning points were not synchronous; details were unique to jurisdictions. Consequently, when searching for parallels, we cannot expect exact duplication of measures. It is to deep trends formed outside a lock-step chronology that comparative history must look.

RATIONALIZING PROPERTY

Determining What Is Just

It is natural to ask whether property rights, found at a particular place and time, are just. This question connects to the first one raised in this chapter – about how rights originated – because "chains of transfers must end in acquisitions which are themselves not transfers but sources of original title."[109] How, for example, did governments acquire frontier lands from first peoples? How did the government that Stark mentions as the source for his homestead secure its transcendent claims to the public domain? The adversaries in *Shane* neglected an important party to all discussion of property rights on frontiers. Native interests in the land were a fundamental issue on all frontiers.

Robert Nozick, in a provocative contribution to theories of property rights, which stirred great interest in the subject, wished to frame a theory of entitlements that avoids a priori aims or subjective end states. A modernization of Locke, Nozick's system of acquisitions would involve a scrutiny of transactions that appropriated resources to see if they had been characterized by just steps.[110] If just steps were followed, then the entitlement so created may be considered legitimate. That way, as he sees it, it would be possible to dispute the claims of socialism, which sought end-state arrangements without taking into account the history of how entitlements were derived. To the proposition of just steps, Nozick attaches a modified Lockean proviso. Locke realized that any appropriation of resources or goods through the means of labour or contractual agreements might leave one party far worse off than before. Therefore he proposed that after the appropriation there should be "enough and as good left in common for others."[111] For appropriators, this could impose a stiff condition. Happily for them, an escape beckons. It may be, argues Nozick, that the complete appropriation of a property still could provide countervailing benefits that would answer a weak, not a firm and literal, understanding of the Lockean proviso. What is important, he suggests, is that those who yield a resource should not be left worse off than before its surrender. That modified Lockean proviso compels a search for countervailing benefits. If the new owners of the property rights can generate greater benefits for themselves as well as for those who ceded the rights – if the pie has grown and all parties share in the increase – then perhaps the proviso has been satisfied.[112]

Nozick seems uncomfortable with his argument, because he realizes that it would be no simple matter to estimate how things might have developed without the appropriation. "Lockean appropriation makes people no worse off than they would be *how*?"[113] What is the imagined baseline? Nozick's dilemmas about the basis of property rights have arisen recently in the successor states to colonial frontiers. During the 1980s and 1990s, there were heated public arguments and litigation about whether appropriation from first peoples involved just steps and whether they gained indirectly from land cessions to colonizing governments. Benefits, so called, seem inconspicuous, ambiguous at best. What is the baseline? To answer this difficult question would require a separate work that applied the insights of anthropologists, demographers, economists, historians, and first peoples to each case of a land cession. Some of this complicated work has been under way in New Zealand and has started in Canada and South Africa. Determining how white settler governments harmed indigenous peoples was a prospect that frightened an Australian government into denial and prompted the passage of legislation in 1998 prejudicial to Aboriginal land claims. In the United States in recent years, Indian land claims have been off national agendas, although a legal battle initiated by Indians may recover funds improperly held in trust by the federal government and promote a reformation of relations between Washington and the first peoples that it bullied, patronized, and defrauded.[114]

In addition to the caveat of the Lockean proviso – literal and demanding or amended and relaxed – there is the major test of just steps, which requires that an acquisition of resources must be carried out fairly. When describing, from a historical perspective, the legal precepts and actual practices by which states secured land from first peoples, the simple idea of just steps has an illuminating quality, as far as it goes. Nozick admits that *rectification* must be part of a theory of entitlements: "Past injustices might be so great as to make necessary in the short run a more extensive state in order to rectify them."[115] Rectification has started to move beyond theory and into practice, and it has proven complicated – for example, in New Zealand, where property rights have been part of national politics since the mid-1980s. In Australia and Canada, too, court decisions confirming first peoples' claims during the 1990s have ignited political crises, because of the complex interests affected by rectification. Governments have been unprepared for the discussions that court rulings necessitated.[116] South Africa is reviewing land claims arising from the displacements of apartheid. Whether the examination of white appropriations will stop there is anyone's guess. Displacements originating in the colonial era have long been recognized as economically damaging to Africans.[117]

How can people today evaluate eighteenth- and nineteenth-century negotiations that resulted in appropriation to determine if they followed just steps? How should an educated public begin to understand acquisitions from first peoples? For a start, everyone can pay attention to the advice of economist John Roemer. In his estimation, theories of justice that originate in ideal bargaining outcomes are "sterilized of real-world aspects," including differential bargaining skills, unequal states of knowledge about the resources' potential, deprivations that lower a bargainer's expectations, and different time preferences (people with shorter life spans may bargain away rights for short-term gains).[118] I apply Roemer's perspective to the discussion of native title and government acquisition of land in chapter 4. An assortment of complications can be gathered from the histories of all settlement frontiers, and jurists have outlined the intricate legal issues at stake. Working out any program of rectification will not be easy intellectually or politically.[119] Property rights – in philosophy and economics – will generate debates for ages. As a resource for additional understanding, history can illustrate how some experiments in so-called bargaining worked out. Comparative history can show the widespread rationalizations of power by indicating how colonizers acclaimed land acquisitions as fair negotiations, presented them as opportunities for native improvement, or described them as acts of protection.

Something else pertains to just steps. When some governments negotiated to acquire land from first peoples, they hampered private individuals from direct purchasing on their own account, and they occasionally justified this monopsony on the grounds that only governments possessed the detachment, resources, and ideals to conduct upright and careful negotiations. Self-interested individuals, in contrast, would be prone to haste, incomplete consultation, and duplicity. On many other occasions, the supreme standing of government negotiators was asserted bluntly as a sovereign act. From these two justifications, obligations fall on governments' shoulders. When claiming moral scruples and exercising paternalism in dealings with first peoples, they signified a responsibility. If governments claimed greater integrity than self-interested individuals when treating with first peoples, they had (and have) obligations to live up to their posturing. Instead, land-managing and land-purchasing exercises marginalized first peoples economically, and paternalism subordinated their cultures. In southern Africa, a white settler government (Transvaal) defended trusteeship over African tribal lands in words that American legislators and British colonial administrators could have embraced at various time in the nineteenth century. "I do not think," wrote H.C. Shepstone in 1879, "that as yet the natives are sufficiently advanced in civilization to be allowed to hold land by individual title; if it should be allowed to hold land by individual title, they will fall prey to land jobbers and speculators."[120] A government's exclusive right to manage or purchase land, in the name of the crown or people, placed a duty on governments. By closing off freedom of action or competition, they took on obligations to attend to the needs of those whom they claimed to be helping. Many acquisitions were patently fraudulent, unjust even without reference to monopsony and assessments of fiduciary responsibility. Three elements discussed in this section intermixed in the five regions under study to produce the new forms of landholding – frontier conditions, landhunters and their needs, and the doctrine of improvement.

Frontiers

A lot has been written about the frontier in history, and for many decades Frederick Jackson Turner's triumphal themes about the American frontier predominated. For our purposes, a frontier is a region pervaded by legal conflicts and assorted forms of intimidation.[121] In our restricted designation, frontiers occurred when migratory Europeans entered a region where a government that claimed sovereignty had scarcely any practical authority. Seeing this fragility, yet having faith in the inevitability of order, some risk-takers – a spectrum of operators ranging from the impoverished to the rich – moved beyond "the limits." Frontiers were never wildernesses. They were landscapes occupied first by indigenous peoples. In frontier zones, therefore, it was common to find what Leonard Thompson calls "a medley of peoples."[122] Indigenous peoples and newcomers often made accommodations in the ways that they had formerly lived; they influenced one another for a while.[123] As I suggested in the introduction, that interlude was the frontier's moment, the time before borderlands became border states.

Frontiers have been regions of interaction where "no one has an enduring monopoly on violence" – or put another way, transitory societies that exist at the edge of more stable political systems.[124] In the absence of a dominant authority, people on frontiers were apt to take direct action, provoking distant authorities to intervene when they could, in order to defend citizens or prevent additional bloodshed. Yet, aware of the costs of intervention, governments sometimes hesitated or retreated and thereby discomfited newcomers in frontier areas. In many regions – notably northern Cape Colony (1720s–90s), the old (U.S.) Northwest (1750s–1790s), the Orange River Sovereignty in southern Africa (1840s–50s), and parts of the North Island of New Zealand (1840s–60s) – colonizers put themselves at risk, encountered heroic, organized, protracted resistance from indigenous peoples, and participated in "the slaughter ... of tribesmen and the subjugation of the survivors."[125] Once government authority became sufficiently established in a region to the extent that it could grant land, the area ceased being a frontier. Private parties profited from the transformation, because the costs of securing and organizing resources had been socialized.

We can classify frontiers by their primary economic activity, always recognizing that several pursuits may take place concurrently.[126] There were North American fur-trading frontiers, as well as timber-cutting and mining frontiers in many parts of the world. The latter two forms involved extensive conflicts over property rights (mineral rights, water rights for hydraulic mining, and timber rights). They are not the express concerns of this study; grazing and farming colonies are. A number of migrants to these subsets of frontiers often steeled themselves to endure the absence of resolute government supervision and protection, because they entered unorganized regions in order to squeeze gains from the meagre government control. They knew the

risks full well. Petitions for help ran as torrents when the predictable
disasters happened. When British explorer Dr Andrew Smith encountered trekboers living beyond the limits of Cape Colony, he heard their
complaints that the government should protect them in their illegal
occupation. "They even maintain that the outrages which were from
time to time committed by the natives ought to be avenged merely that
they might live in security and peace."[127]

The bonds of race and culture, as well as ideas about improving the
land, many times rescued European interlopers, because government
agents were loath to abandon or eject people whose habits of thought
they shared, even when these people shunned laws restricting occupation. Besides sharing faith in a common providential mission to civilize,
regulators and truculent squatters – often the most genial of adversaries
– cherished a common ideology of improvement and operated in political systems that claimed to reward industry. Charles Buller, in his 1838
report on British North American land disposal commissioned by Lord
Durham, alleged that squatting was widespread in Nova Scotia, involving possibly half the population of Cape Breton. The interlopers
escaped a blanket condemnation from him because the colony's
progress in agriculture "appears, from the evidence, to be attributable
almost entirely to the squatters."[128] Some illegal occupants on frontiers,
moreover, had powerful friends and sponsors at distant centres of
power, and regulators seldom ignored these connections. Thus, perhaps
only beyond the Orange River frontier of Cape Colony – where ferocious African counter-strokes made imperial support of settler occupation costly – did a government repudiate (1854) a large-scale
annexation (the Orange Sovereignty in 1848), born in land hunger.[129]

Based on their conjectures about when and how government would
install order, newcomers assumed that they could secure advantage by
seizing early positions on the land. Once launched on their improvements, they never ceased to demand protection so that "things can go
forward." By a pre-emptive occupation, they believed that they could
establish interests at little cost and make them pay, through sales or
exploitation. Relatively poor and self-reliant American frontiersmen
played the game, and so too trekboers, who by the 1820s had some
connections with the market through sales of livestock, hides, and wool
and through purchases of gunpowder and household articles.[130]
Expanding herds and flocks required additional pastures. More affluent
landhunters – parties willing to lay out capital – believed that they
could acquire title at a time when near-anarchy discounted the price.
Regardless of their exact tactics, people keenly interested in securing
property rights – at bargain prices – pressed onto frontiers. A few put
their lives at risk and lost. What seemed cheap came dear.

While a lack of authority may have served upstarts for a while, many of them prayed for order and technical support – troops, land offices, cadastral maps, courthouses, and banks – to advance marketable interests in landed property. For economists, this urge shows wealth-maximizing individuals seeking to reduce a transactions cost – the expense of defending property.[131] The frontier promised rewarding consummations when the frontier itself would be extinguished. The trick was to seize interests, hang onto them, and keep one's skin. Governments obstructed these adventurers, but rarely with sustained force, and most reconciled themselves to squatter occupation. Governments had reasons for initially limiting or even prohibiting access to frontier territory. First, in some instances – the old Northwest (1763–75) and unceded territory in southern Africa (1835–43) and New Zealand (1840–55) – imperial officials worried about costly confrontations between their encroaching citizens and first peoples.[132] Interlopers staked out plots or stock runs to build interests and destroyed political and demographic balances that sustained frontier peace. Second, on public and crown land in settlement colonies people thrust ahead of authorized occupation to extract use value (grazing) or to strip assets (cutting timber illegally). Governments decried the loss of revenue. Third, if illegal occupants intended to stay on the land that they were stripping, then bans or restrictions originated in government concern about land-sale trouble ahead. Squatters' interests could never defeat the crown or the U.S. government, but once people cleared fields, planted crops, and erected shanties it was uncomfortable for governments to sell the land from under them.

A squatter's outpost on choice acres could pre-empt late arrivals, notwithstanding government title. To eradicate this possibility, American soldiers burned out squatters in the Ohio country in late 1785, but during the next decades federal authorities balked at enforcing anti-squatting laws.[133] In Missouri in 1816, the territorial militia refused to march against squatters, and the governor conceded their right of occupation.[134] In 1884, black troops – less likely to identify with the white squatters – were ordered to remove white squatters encroaching on the Indian lands of Oklahoma.[135] During his administration in New South Wales (1806–8), Governor William Bligh, late captain of the *Bounty*, ordered the destruction of private buildings on government ground. Despised for these acts and his seizure of smuggled goods, the governor was arrested by his senior officers.[136] Some authorities in other jurisdictions, to avoid politically dangerous confrontations when soldiers removed frontier occupants, tried first to attenuate squatters' interests. In 1825, the landdrost of Graaff-Reinet, Adries Stockenström, required grazers who "temporarily" drove flocks

beyond Cape Colony to "promise not to set on foot or build anything
of a permanent nature, nor to cultivate the least portion of land there,
being fully impressed with the conviction that we have not the least
claim or title to any inch of said land, and cannot consider this
indulgence as a precedent for the future."[137] New South Wales in 1833
made it an offence to squat on land available for sale.[138] Like some
American counterparts, these measures never curbed squatters for long.

Landhunters: Squatters and Speculators

In this study, a squatter is someone who violates formal rules to occupy
land in order to originate an interest. A complication arises with
Australia. After early squatters there succeeded in fortifying their
interests, through the crown's concession of leasehold in 1846, they
retained the "squatter" label and elevated it to respectability. Except
in that special circumstance, the term means an unlawful occupant,
irrespective of financial standing. Like the squatter, the speculator
needs to be explained. Technically, speculation involves holding a
commodity off the market in an attempt to drive up the price for a
windfall profit. More generally and flexibly, it can mean a business
dealing that assumes a great risk for the promise of a huge gain.
Speculators worked and hoped for quick turnovers. Turning profits by
sundry practices, not the actual magnitude of a supposed profit, char-
acterizes land speculation. Thus I treat a pre-eminent financier with
millions of acres in prospect as a speculator, and so too the dabbler
in scrub acres.[139] Robert D. Mitchell describes how a small "lokator"
in the Shenandoah valley in 1746 profited from land sales. Overshad-
owed by large speculators, but "adept at land negotiations and selling
land and real property to newcomers, and then moving on to new
locations,"[140] these individuals played a part in the occupation of all
frontiers. Assumptions of risk and the expectation of reward characterized speculation, not the scale of the operation. But we must not
forget the differences between wealthy and threadbare speculators –
they danced to the same music, but attended different balls.[141]

Influential speculators contrived fantastically complicated dealings.
Some made friends or partners of officials who could grant land; others
brought capital to unsettled tracts, bid on acreage, and also made use
of connections to discover the best tracts and secure good terms.
Speculators became active wherever a frontier had just closed or was
on the verge of doing so. Many of their contemporaries employed the
term "speculation" in contradistinction to "improvement" and thereby
insinuated misconduct; they did not regard speculators as improvers,
and both American frontiersmen and some class-sensitive British colonial

administrators denounced those who would not improve land. The censure expressed by Governor Bligh is representative of an outlook among pompous officers and gentlemen. Writing about land policy in 1807, he drew a common distinction. "Classes of plain sensible farming Men, of moderate expectations, are most valuable to come here; such as the Blaxlands, who lately came out, become so speculative as to care for nothing but making money; they endeavour to monopolize under a principle of buying cheap as they can and selling dear."[142] The label "speculator" was applied in many circumstances to prompt or condone punitive action. When squatters ran off land buyers, they could more easily justify the deed if they maligned the latter as rapacious speculators, claim-jumping vermin, or "invidious wolves in human form."[143] Sometimes they were, and local small speculators occasionally sent them packing. When New York–backed speculators descended on Green Bay, Michigan, for land sales in 1835, they were driven away. One agent wrote that "upward of a million of money was taken back from here which could not find investment."[144] Deterrence of accumulations by capitalists through direct actions by smaller operators was unlikely to have been as successful in Latin America as it was in Green Bay and at numerous other public sales.

Upper Canada experienced both accumulation by powerful speculators and acquisition by smallholders.[145] When land reformers throughout the British and American world promoted the break-up of large estates, they counted speculators among their targets. A firm distinction between wholesome homesteading and greedy speculating, however, was now and then a rhetorical feint made by modestly capitalized, fleet-footed squatters in their contests to thwart impending sales to modest legal buyers. Both groups may have intended to sell. During the global land rush, manipulations were always intricate, the players diverse; the range of people who might be thought of as speculators was broad. Distinctions between investors who increased production and speculators who sought capital gains blur in practice when "the investor must often assume risks of changing values and the speculator may have to engage as a producer in the development of a property as a condition of ownership or to promote the increase of value sought."[146] While critics of speculation appealed to usefulness and betterment, such ideas were often intrinsic to the practices of so-called speculators (Table 2.1).

Landhunters and landhunting are also important concepts, and there were landhunters among speculators or working for them. Their defining characteristics appear in their practices. Landhunters – "land lookers," one Michigan surveyor called them – searched for good land and marked it, for themselves, their partners, or their backers.[147] Among

Table 2.1
Categories of land speculators, by scale, location, and time-frame

Scale	Location	Time-frame	Land acquisition practices
Large scale	Frontiers	Long: holding land for later development and eventual sales	Attempted purchases from indigenous peoples Squatting beyond limits of settlement Grants from weak governments lacking firm authority Filibuster raids
Large scale	Organized territories	Short: planning prompt sales	Grants from friends in government Buying discounted land scrip issued by governments Buying at sales for tax- or land-payment arrears Land auctions Contracting with governments to settle Buying and partitioning estates of indebted landlords
Small scale	Frontiers	Varying	Squatting Joining squatter communities Working as landhunters for large-scale speculators
Small scale	Organized territories	Varying	Squatting Joining claims clubs Filing entry documents for homesteads Assisting large-scale speculators Working as surveyors

the traits associated with their specialty were the following: an ability to read the landscape for productive and strategic purposes; frontier survival skills learned perhaps while hunting, trapping, and trading; a bag of tricks for marking and holding a tract against rivals; and a restlessness and a delight in journeys of exploration. Among their number were western Virginia scouts in the pay of land-speculation companies (1750s–80s), Australian stockmen driving mobs of sheep or cattle (1820s–30s), voortrekkers (pioneers) crossing the Orange River boundary (1830s–40s), pre-emptive homesteaders in the U.S. midwest (1840s–50s), and Great Basin ranchers (1870s–80s). This list is merely suggestive. Once landhunters settled on a tract and stopped looking for additional or better land, they ceased being landhunters. Landhunters pursued interests aggressively. In some frontier situations, where the state had installed land regulations, they worked with (but not always within) the rules. They collaborated with and manipulated nearby officials, who provided a boundary-dispute service and issued the licences of occupation that could act as a wedge for broadening a person's legal interests or yield a marketable asset. Even in locales lacking land commissioners, a principle of law extended the means for landhunters to hold territory against other individuals. With acts of occupation, landhunters evolved into squatters. Landhunters and squatters settling on the public domain, or crown land, or land beyond any organized sovereignty could bar entry to other individuals. Although occupation might defy a government regulation, authorities hesitated to remove landhunters and squatters. Occupation therefore deflected rival squatters and impending settlers. To paraphrase Abraham Lincoln's comment on his policy towards the Mormon occupation of Utah, it was easier to plough around a stump than to remove it.

No one relished confronting landhunters and squatters. If a potential challenger with a putative legal title or interests arrived, the prior party, with benefit of occupation, could usually insist on compensation for improvements or try to discourage the title holder by threatening a financial penalty. Trespass was not normally a crime, but rather a tort or wrong, whose remedy required a civil action, with possible costs. Threats of litigation helped squatters convince late rivals to move along. For some earnest settlers, the squatters' occupation was a hurdle across paths to lawful tenure. Some squatters played the game as a holdup for a payoff, accepting money or entering into partnerships with parties who held land scrip or other government promises. Squatting was not always a game for an extorted profit. Hardworking but poor arrivals on the Illinois prairie in the 1830s seldom persisted for long, because, as John Mack Faragher discovered, squatters among them sold their improvements to "strong-handed farmers" who came with enough capital to buy them out.[148] In Upper Canada, claims John Clarke, squatting was tolerated because it was seen as a social good and recognized as advantageous to speculators, "especially if a cordial arrangement could be arrived at to compensate the improvements. because such improvements made the property more desirable."[149]

Complicated dynamics among people with designs on land – some lacking capital and others with it – were the essence of settlement history. Occupation, however, could never defeat a government's root title to crown or public land, yet governments found it awkward to punish or oust squatters. For political, economic, and even humanitarian reasons, officials avoided ejection, either because occupation probably involved economic and settlement activity that the state believed furthered its presumed civilizing mission or because drought and insect infestations made pleas by distraught squatters compelling. But legal interests conceded out of compassion could snowball; what began as an expedient ended as an interest. Drought-stricken trekboers in the mid-1820s secured temporary permits for grazing beyond the Cape Colony's boundaries.[150] Soon these passes were trading among grazers as if they embodied property rights, and trekboers pressured the Griquas – an important community of mixed Khoikhoi and European origin living just beyond the colony's borders – to grant them formal leases to Griqua land.[151]

Governments frequently capitulated to squatters, awarding them part of the territory in question; other times they made compensatory grants elsewhere or distributed certificates redeemable in land. When squatting occurred on land held by indigenous peoples, governments commonly secured title and legalized white occupation. The demise of the (Cherokee) Indian Territory in the United States illustrates this recurrent trend. In 1881, cattlemen were forbidden to lease land directly from the Cherokees, but they continued to do so until the Department of the Interior began a series of purchases from the Cherokees in 1890 to redistribute the land according to congressionally sanctioned practices.[152]

To obstruct or combat occupation, yet avoid a political backlash, some governments sold or granted substantial blocks of land to companies or group-colonization promoters. Then these entities had to cope with squatters.[153] For many reasons, in the 1780s and 1790s, the United States and those state governments that retained public land endeavoured to sell huge tracts at discounted prices. A contributing factor was an urge to reduce overhead for securing, protecting, and selling parcels of land. One of the most notorious sales in American history occurred when the Georgia state legislature – bribed into compliance by land agents – disposed of 20 million acres to a few companies in 1795. A history of the affair concluded that "if it was a corrupt bargain, it was not essentially a bad one ... Was it really such a bad trade for Georgia to sell land which was in many places clouded by three sets of conflicting claims – those of Spain, the federal government, and the Indian tribes?"[154] In Upper Canada, some escape from the squatter and overhead problems occurred when the crown disposed of roughly 1.3 million acres to the Canada Company in 1826, and much more in later years. In Indiana and Illinois, during the 1840s, the U.S. government allowed settlers and speculators "to encroach upon the grazing commons of the squatting cattlemen," forcing them to buy or move.[155] Australian colonies and New Zealand handled occupation by allowing licenced occupation and then leasehold. Subsequently, governments were elected there in the 1860s to effect land reforms, and they passed laws that encouraged prospective farmers to enter leased grazing land and to pluck freehold farm tracts.[156] Schemes that used a cat's-paw approach to the threat of squatters had obvious appeal.

Arrangements to sell or lease large tracts to individuals or companies erected lightning rods for populist dissent, since they handed estates to a select few. Governments tried to shift the burdens of resource allocation by selling large tracts to companies or by empowering selectors; however, they could never entirely slip responsibility for distribution. Therefore allocation of land – the first business of frontier governments – complicated public life in all new societies and figured in regional protest movements in the United States and in demands for self-government in British colonies.[157] On every frontier, disgruntled claimants insisted that a local government would do a better job. In New Zealand, devolution of power went to extremes, and the small colony fragmented into provinces (1854–76). Several provinces retained control of land administration.[158] One consequence of devolution was that policy makers drawn from frontiers could not be neutral in arbitrations between first peoples and Europeans, because "they were dealing with matters that intensely affected their own lives."[159]

The Doctrine of Improvement

Improvement or betterment lies at the heart of Locke's notion of property rights. It is linked to landhunting, squatting, and speculation; often it was also the basis for government acquisition of land from indigenous peoples and a principle guiding how governments reallocated it. Improvement in a broad sense was common ground for informal and formal processes of occupation. To improve the land meant to apply labour and capital, so as to boost the land's carrying capacity and hence its market value. As I pointed out above, squatters could attempt to improve title holders out of their estate. Cultural bonds joined improvement and squatting. In a famous argument, Locke proposed that when people mixed labour with something else, "that [mixing] excludes the common right of other Men."[160] Comparable beliefs were on the lips on frontiersmen everywhere. Governments, whether under a crown colony constitution or a more democratic form, could not dismiss improving claimants without paying a political price. In *Shane*, the rancher shares an improving European heritage with the homesteader; as a consequence, the latter could not "belittle" what ranchers had done. In an embedded cultural sense, improvement meant humankind's duty to tame wilderness, rescue wasteland[161] – even more, to deliver itself from want and indolence.

Around the world, colonizers who pleaded for access to territory or enhanced property rights articulated common arguments, ones like those depicted in *Shane*; they suggested that, if only they could have greater control of the land, then the territory in question would flourish. Nicholas Canny finds expressions of this aggressive stance among seventeenth-century Englishmen who wanted to dislodge the traditional leaders of Gaelic society in Ireland in order to "make room for the appointment of a new ruling elite who would establish the existing society on a new foundation and would introduce a leaven of enterprising Englishmen."[162] Something like this attitude cropped up regularly in later periods, and it expressed a cultural arrogance fused with ideas about social and economic advancement. On the occasion of an anniversary of the Sons of the Pilgrims, in December 1802 John Quincy Adams questioned bombastically whether "the lordly savage" should "forbid the wilderness to bloom like roses? Shall he forbid the oaks of the forest to fall before the ax of industry and rise again transformed into the habitations of ease and elegance?"[163] A pamphlet defending South Australian grazers in 1864 outlined the mission of improvement more prosaically. What did lands produce as they were? Nothing. "The lands owe their value principally to us, not only because we explored and rendered them available, but because, as every old settler will bear me out, we have by our stock, by our cultivation, and by importing European grasses, rendered them worth double what they were when we first came upon them."[164] The author defended grazers against government land reforms favourable to small farmers. The rancher in *Shane* had precursors and champions.

Richer and Stark argue about which group of newcomers had done more for improvement – trappers and traders, or ranchers. However, they agree that land had to be domesticated. A dispute over improvement in a narrow or tactical sense animates these archetypes. The two barely mention a conflict over improvement in the wider meaning, as a conflict between a European-based Christian culture and the cultures of first peoples. The film reduces this significant clash of cultures to a painful artifact – an "arra'head" in Richer's shoulder. In history the clash between a doctrine of improvement and the status quo, between newcomers and first peoples, was profound. This means not that indigenous peoples were inactive and peaceful prior to contact with Europeans but that the newcomers – particularly the English – carried an ideology that insisted on making the land bountiful, even if that required the confiscation of land, which is what the English government practised on several occasions in Ireland before and after the 1641 uprising. The idea of material improvement motivated and informed the legal and political processes that colonizers used to evaluate the colonized. In the colonies, the dispossession of a number of first peoples – and sometimes the uprooting of white grazers – advanced under that most revered regimental pennant of colonizers, "Improvement."

While first peoples were adept cultivators and grazers, where biota and climate permitted, colonizers still thought that they stood in the way of improvement, because they appeared – to different degrees – less dedicated than Europeans to imposing a purposeful, regular pattern on the wilderness.[165] The idea of organizing a landscape so that nature might better serve human needs was long embedded in Western thought. The concept may originate in part in popular Christianity, which has been, of all religions, "the most insistently anti-natural."[166] In an interpretive history of ecological ideas, *Nature's Economy*, Donald Worster contends that some thinkers through the ages could admire nature as the handiwork of God, but in the eighteenth and nineteenth centuries "this arcadian mood was often swept away in the rush for man's empire over nature."[167] From the end of the seventeenth century on, writes Gilbert Rist, "the intellectual landscape suddenly shifted, and the ideology of progress acquired a dominant position."[168] He exaggerates. Boyd Hilton has recounted evangelicalism's moderating influence on economic and social thought in early-nineteenth-century England, and he alleges that its pessimism, uncertainty, and moral philosophy promoted a static view of society, though one lacking the confidence of medieval Schoolmen; by mid-century it had given way to the idea of progress.[169]

Evangelicals and Tories feared the consequences of yielding to the seductive prophesies of ceaseless growth, but the idea of increase already had secured a place in philosophy and politics. There were as well religious grounds, if not for faith in increase, then for a duty to strive. In early-modern European thought, governments had "the task of ensuring proper conformance with God's demand for the thriving of the human species as far as possible."[170] Locke's theory of property insisted on a theological connection between people and resource usage. Gopal Sreenivasan's summary of one of Locke's tenets is apposite: "[One] should only appropriate as much as one can use before it spoils, and [this] is imposed by the law of nature. It obtains, more precisely, in virtue of God's intention that the earth should serve the preservation of mankind and so not be wasted."[171]

Christianity alone does not fully explain the rise of the idea of improvement, because, along with inculcating God's command to be fruitful, the church promoted the idea of natural limitations – humanity's fate after the fall from grace. Other cultural fountainheads, including the Enlightenment, must help explain the force of the improvement doctrine on British and American frontiers. There was an English stimulus to the rise of a culture dedicated to material improvement. Joan Thirsk points out, respecting changes in English agriculture (1660–1750) that "as the government retreated from compulsion, it

silently gave encouragement to the use of private acts. Landowners
took the hint, and cast their aspirations in local terms."[172] Freedom
was given to individuals to seize estate-based opportunities, and they
became more confident and individualistic than their peasant predecessors.[173] That freedom had become a national necessity by the late
eighteenth century.

The diffusion of the improvement doctrine within the English-speaking
world, from the late eighteenth century to at least the mid-nineteenth,
began with Arthur Young, the untiring apostle for the agricultural revolution in England. His *Annals of Agriculture* (1784–1815), published
in forty-six volumes, encompassed folk wisdom and agricultural science.
George Washington and Thomas Jefferson corresponded with him.
These Americans pointed out, among other things, differences between
farming in England and farming in the United States, where land was
inexpensive. The correspondence was so cordial that Washington
approached Young to sound out tenants for Mount Vernon.[174] Young's
stream of advice for husbandry was the principal way he promoted the
idea of improvement, but he also nagged about the scandal of waste
and defended enclosures as saving squandered land. Progress could not
be taken for granted.

Young's tract *An Inquiry into the Propriety of Applying Wastes to
the Better Maintenance and Support of the Poor* (1800) connected
enclosures to a scheme of reducing poverty. Consistent with his conviction that good practices could extract greater produce, he proposed that
the rural poor should be granted waste lands and parish loans for farm
improvements. His commission as secretary to the new, government-
appointed Board of Agriculture in 1793 denoted the state's serious interest in agricultural affairs. Agriculture was seen as complementary to
building national strength in wartime.[175] The mobilization of land for
national purposes – what C.A. Bayly calls "agricultural patriotism" –
would remain topical in Britain throughout the wars with revolutionary
and Napoleonic France.[176] By the end of that period, Young no longer
figured centrally in ongoing, refined debates about how the state might
induce improvement and avoid backsliding.

By 1815, discussions about land and national strength embraced partisan polemics and sophisticated analysis over which tax systems might
best encourage, or even compel, more thorough exploitation of land.
Young maintained for decades that any taxation of landowners deprived
these useful people of the capital necessary for increasing their productivity. In his introduction to the *Report on Enclosures* (1808), however,
he took the contrary position – that the higher tax burden carried
recently by landowners spurred them on to greater improvements.[177]

Thomas Malthus and David Ricardo carried this discussion of taxation and improvement further than Young. Intrinsic to this new branch of the formal debate about improvement – one of the foundations of economics – were moral-efficiency judgments about landowners: were they merely siphoning off the land's wealth, or were they applying capital to the land? Young's abhorrence of waste was an established attitude in England before he put it into print, which he did again, and again, and again. His promotional zeal advanced the concept of improvement, which became a commonplace of British imperial ideology. At the same time, he helped initiate an important theoretical discussion.

War and peacetime adjustments caused parliamentarians and political economists to wonder whether the kingdom had the right balance of manufacturing and agriculture and, if so, what measures could sustain it. Some wondered too about how the landowning elite's wealth could be justified. Did it serve a national or social purpose, as Young unquestioningly asserted? Waste, lethargy, inefficiency, and unearned profits weakened the kingdom's moral capital and capacity to mobilize for a struggle; capital accumulation, investment, helpful taxation measures, and vigorous husbandry strengthened it. The associated political controversies – for example, over the Corn Laws (tariff protection for grain) – persisted though the first four decades of the nineteenth century. Educated colonists and public officials participated in the ferment of ideas and experiments, because starting about 1815 land allocation and land use became topics for broad, sometimes-vehement polemics. In 1815, Thomas Malthus, David Ricardo, Robert Torrens, and Edward West each published a work that dealt with economic rent – "the premium which can be charged for the use of land more fertile than the least fertile land being used."[178] It was a short step from this concept to Ricardo's argument that economic rent was a premium that accrued to landholders after they paid for labour and improvements. Therefore it followed that rising food prices meant higher, windfall incomes for rural property owners.

In Ricardo's hands, this analysis made landowners a pariah class, especially if they benefited from other economic privileges, such as tariff protection in England. Ricardo would have disapproved of low usufructuary fees or cheap land on settlement frontiers – the objectives of so many landhunters.[179] There were people in the colonies who thought as he did. The inspector of lands and woods for the Cape Colony, Charles D'Escury, attempted to implement a land reform that would force improvement by taxing economic rent. He initiated his experiment in 1813, before Ricardo had published a theory of economic rent. In 1820, the Scottish-born Upper Canadian reformer Robert Gourlay, a reader of political economy, vilified the colony's land system because it had "gifted away [land] to drones."[180] His choice of invective, not the truth or falsehood of the assessment, should interest us. Gourlay had recently compiled statistics and reports gathered from correspondents around the colony. His objectives were to expose incompetent administrators and deficient policies and thus to speed efficient exploitation. When Charles Buller submitted a report (1838) to the imperial Parliament on the disposal of crown land in British North America, the idea that land should be priced sufficiently high and be appropriately taxed to discourage idle speculators was well established.[181]

Humanity's empire over nature was a cultural touchstone that made appeals to improvement irrepressible. In the estimation of governments in charge of frontiers, invocations of improvement absolved landhunters, squatters, and speculators. But only until someone detected possibilities for even greater improvements! There was no end to hypothetical betterment, and no lack of alleged laggards – white colonizers and indigenous people alike. Donald Moodie, a British fortune seeker in Cape Colony, ascribed the hardships of many of its white people to nomadic grazing. In 1834, on the banks of the Orange River, he asked Piet Botha why trekboers trapped their children in an inferior way of life. "We are stupid," Botha allegedly answered. "But we see that; but tell me, who will employ our children, if we teach them trades? Not the Boers, for they are Jacks of all trades … we must keep sheep, and seek pasture, as far as the government will allow – or starve."[182] Botha joined the Great Trek and may have been the Piet Botha killed at Veg Kop during a N'debele attack in October 1836. The boer and the Englishman met at a historic crossing, then separated over degrees of improvement. In other pastoral regions, some land dealers honoured improvements for practical reasons. Early in the twentieth century, a major Winnipeg speculator instructed an Alberta realtor to spurn sales to ranchers. "Placing a few Ranche buildings in a section does not improve it in the same way that mixed farming does." Grazers could steal away with stock, but "a mixed farmer's improvements as a rule must remain on the land" and made better collateral.[183] That was a practical consideration, but the great importance of a hierarchy of improvers crowned by farmers rested with its inordinate cultural significance. Moodie and Botha perceived that. The idea of farming as an estimable way of life would have political repercussions in several movements for land reform that appear below in this book. When divorced from the pragmatism of Arthur Young or the Winnipeg land agent, the farming ideal contributed to the assignment of subsidies and water rights in the twentieth century. Farming became a sanctified, though hard way of life, and some practitioners acquired entitlements that would have scandalized Ricardo.

CONCLUSION

British and American newcomers on frontiers applied a web of complicated worldly ideas about property rights.[184] That web consisted of informal and formal steps for taking land: occupation, the recognition and sale of interests, the ban on direct dealing, and the doctrine of improvement, with its succession of higher uses. Powerful commonplace British and American ideas and practices contributed to a universal story. What happened next, as people exploited resources and shaped the landscape, was mediated by climate, geology, the ecology of flora and fauna, and first peoples. But imported ideas associated with the law and economics of land had been influential. The conversion of frontiers into assets involved collisions between firmly held, insistent, widespread habits of thought and a staggering diversity of habitats that indigenous peoples used with varying intensities. We may measure the power of ideas about entitlements to property rights by citing lists of endangered species, by chronicling incidents of native dispossession, and by witnessing the rival claims of grazing, intensive agriculture, and irrigation farming.[185]

CHAPTER THREE

Parameters:
Places, Shapes, Scale, and Velocity

Competition pervaded the land rush and promoted an urgency that had incalculable consequences. Astute landhunters knew that if they failed to seize land quickly others would scoop it up. Urgency attended every outbreak of landhunting. In a famous letter of 1767, George Washington explained this situation to his agent, William Crawford. "Any person ... who neglects the present opportunity of hunting out good lands, and in some measure marking them for his own, in order to keep others from settling them, will never regain it."[1] Washington expressed perfectly the mood of the rush. It was all about possession and beating out rivals. One hundred years later, a New Zealand land agent, negotiating grazing rights from Maori, informed his client about rival syndicates and advised him "that there is no time to lose."[2] Wyoming rancher John B. Thomas sent a scout to the Little Missouri River in 1885 to locate open range; finding space among several existing ranches, he provoked a reaction from a nearby rancher, "who suspected he was coming in there and hastened to gobble it."[3] An agent working for a ranching syndicate in 1902 predicted that the South Dakota railway land that they desired would go fast. "We will hafta get a hustle on our selves [sic] or that RR land will be sold on the Little Cannonball. They have been buying like everything."[4] Exigency and expediency ruled almost everywhere.

Landhunters introduced a particular tree of knowledge into many Edens – knowledge, in the form of European laws about possessory rights, individualized titles, transferability of title, and – most important – an insistence on improvement. From 1750 to 1900, approximately 1.5 billion to 2 billion acres of the world's most arable land and productive pastures was newly exploited.[5] To get some perspective on dimensions, consider that Australia and New Zealand together comprise an area roughly equal to that of western Europe, including

Table 3.1
Examples of territory occupied and main usage, 1650–1914

Approximate dates	Region	Latitude	Main usage in period
1690–1830	Cape Colony	30–34° S	Grazing Pockets of viticulture
1750–1820	Old (U.S.) Northwest	38–41° N	Grazing Grain
1750–1850	Buenos Aires province	35–40° S	Grazing
1785–1860	U.S. public domain east of Great Plains and north of Tennessee River	37–42° N	Mixed farming Grazing
1785–1840	U.S. federal and state public domain in the south	30–34° N	Cotton Mixed farming
1785–1850	Upper Canada	42–45° N	Timber Mixed farming
1803–30	Van Dieman's Land (Tasmania)	41–43° S	Grazing
1788–1840	Southeastern Australia	27–38° S	Grazing
1820–50	Texas	26–32° N	Grazing Cotton
1836–60	Boer republics Natal	23–30° S	Grazing Grain
1865–90	U.S. west: high plains Great Basin	32–49° N	Grazing
1846–90	California	32–42° N	Grazing Gain
1840–60	New Zealand	36–46° S	Grazing
1870–1914	Canadian prairies	49–54° N	Grain Minor grazing
1890–1900	Zimbabwe (Southern Rhodesia)	15–22° S	Grazing Tobacco Cotton
1900–14	Highlands of Kenya	Equatorial	Grazing Coffee

Russia west of the Ural Mountains; they cover an area as large as the continental United States. Together the grain lands of the American midwest and the Canadian prairies are approximately the size of France and Italy combined. Newly-settled regions in the Americas, Australia, New Zealand, and southern Africa emerged as leading producers of wool, red meat, and grain (Table 3.1). Within three generations, during the nineteenth century, some of the best land in these locales was secured, surveyed, apportioned, registered, and drawn into finance capitalism. This unrepeatable opening and closing of access to enormous resources challenges the idea that a uniformly thriving global economy, free of barriers to labour migration, will soon emerge in the future. Paul Hirst and Grahame Thompson argue that the world's underprivileged have little choice but to endure poverty. "The equivalent of the 'empty lands' available to European and other settlers in the USA and Canada, South America, Southern Africa, and Australia and New Zealand just do not exist today, with a concomitant loss of 'freedom' for the world's poor."[6]

Late in life a few early settlers could reminisce and even reflect about the ecological damage their efforts to improve had brought. Some old pioneers were nostalgic about the worlds that they had encountered and had worked to seize and change in a short time. They and their children were the last to know lakes, forests, marshes, and grasslands before all was "improved." Upper Canadian Charles Durand remembered in 1897 the "beautiful sea salmon" in Burlington Bay – gone by the 1830s.[7] South African William Collins listed the splendid birds that he knew at Bloemfontein in the 1850s. "Where are they now?"[8] "I may as well out with the truth," admitted Australian grazer Edward Curr, "it is to regret the [passing of the] primitive scene, the Black with his fishing canoe, the silence, the gum trees." "Blacks, reeds, and bellbirds are gone."[9] When E.D. Swan left Missouri in 1860 to prospect for gold near Pikes Peak, he encountered buffalo herds along the Arkansas River. He had described them to his daughter. "Oh my, oh my, you don't have no idea."[10] Ten years later, he had discovered that they had been thinned out. Worse was to come.

However great the natural history enthusiasms and aesthetic sensibilities of observers, these values could not compete with fierce campaigns to hold and change the land. Whether pursuing raw possession or legal grants, land seekers had little time at the height of their abilities and ambitions for long reflection or for assessing the worth of an unimproved world. To fulfil ambitions, they drove forward with support from the persuasive doctrine of improvement, often with the backing of metropolitan capital. Europeans' convictions about improvement and waste, their assumptions about supposedly advanced and less-advanced peoples, helped make the land rush unstoppable. Europeans on frontiers shared rudimentary beliefs about history and their own privileged place in it. When the diseases, plants, and domesticated animals of Eurasia accompanied these convictions into other continents or onto islands, colonization intruded forcefully.[11] Australian Henry Haygarth in 1864 described feminine Nature affronted by a virile will to improve. "While Anglo-Saxon energy at last triumphs over every obstacle ... Nature, as if offended, withdraws her beauty from the land; some of the rivers and lakes run low, others become wholly dry."[12] He was right about the application of energy to the wilderness and its consequences. Of course, the energy that he mentioned expressed not the unique dynamism of a race, but the capital, labour, and knowledge that colonizers transmitted onto frontiers.

The four sections in this chapter look at occupation in terms of place, shape, scale, and velocity – specifically, at improvement (places and scales), the vexed model of Virginia (shapes and scales), the second British empire (shapes), and the velocity and tempo of occupation.

PLACES AND SCALES:
IMPROVEMENT IN VARIOUS GUISES

Precepts about betterment enabled governments to rationalize their acquisitions of land from first peoples and abetted individuals who seized land. Administrators charged by their governments with stewardship of land clashed time and again with persons anxious to get on that land. All the same, throughout the great land rush, these responsible officers spoke the same language of improvement as the people whom they were ordered to restrain and police. A common royal instruction for governors of new British colonies, mentioned above in chapter 1, provided an abridged statement of a creed of betterment, one introduced belatedly by the crown to America. Starting with Georgia in 1755, the instruction condemned the large grants of the past. "Whereas great inconveniences have arisen in many of our colonies in America from the granting excessive quantities of land to particular parties who have never cultivated or settled it and have thereby prevented others more industrious from improving the same ... you are to take especial care in all grants to be made by you." Grantees were to obtain land "in proportion to their ability to cultivate it."[13]

"In proportion to their ability to cultivate." That phrase goes straight to a complication. Squatters might show improvement. As a Pennsylvania tenant farmer put it in 1765, "in newsettled Colonies Possession and Improvement is the best Title any man can have."[14] How could other people, seeking legal sanction, show ability to cultivate or improve before they held that land? In British crown colonies, until the early 1830s, a forthright social hierarchy guided land grants. It is possible that the revolutionary wars (1775–1815) strengthened a British inclination to grant land according to a person's station or declared capital, because the era of political upheavals entrenched reactionary parties in England.[15] For many years in British colonies, social standing, services to the crown, or evidence of capital determined the acreage of land grants. Meanwhile the United States weeded out overt partiality in land-granting practices, founded on class. Like the British empire, however, the republic rewarded soldiers with grants graduated by rank. That remained a formal, enduring exception to a levelling approach. Once land-distribution practices introduced sales with generous terms, as happened early in the United States, social station in itself lost its utility as a guide to peoples' ability to improve. However, competence determined by cash and credit-worthiness contracted its own problems. In the republic and certainly elsewhere, lawmakers argued about who could best improve the land: capital or labour, large ranchers or small farmers, absentee title holders or local squatters? Was labour or title "the soul of new property?"[16]

Controversies erupted about how far particular tracts of land could be improved, although they were contained by a shared culture that valued improvement. A communal outlook about historical evolution made it difficult for the stewards of crown land reserves or the pubic domain to withstand pressure from squatters. Despite unlawful conduct, the latter could usually be embraced as improvers by officials and definitely so by elected politicians. But where did a religion of improvement leave the property rights of settlers with an imperfect title when someone arrived in their midst with a scheme that proposed greater yields? The law surely sided with agriculture, but did that mean grazing, smallholder farming, or capital-intensive irrigation? A doctrine of improvement led to complexities that I consider below in chapters 7 and 8, where I describe battles between farm "selectors" and sheep grazers throughout Australia and between farmers and ranchers across the American west. And, if the law was on the side of agriculture, it was also on the side of possessory occupation – a fact that both worried and spurred on George Washington, as well as frontier counterparts around the world. Competition for occupation marked relations among landhunters.

The global land rush was a stunning finale to "the expansion of Europe" that had distant roots in the late fifteenth century. The surface of the planet was changed during this closing phase of that expansion. Today, on a cloudless flight across habitable regions in many countries, fields express the survey systems used to define land parcels. Other improvements are visible: roads, railways, irrigation systems, and urban centres. Everywhere, land companies featured in each type of development. What these living graphics cannot express is the cultural encapsulation of the land, the way beliefs and technologies started a reconstruction of the world. Land was measured and marked, but landed property rights were then abstracted into statements on documents, reduced to ciphers, and these texts or codes travelled, enabling interests in land to be traded or pledged for security against loans. Many times during the great land rush, investors and speculators handled these distillations of property without bothering to examine the terrain behind them. By an astonishing conceptual revolution, worked out in both old- and new-world settings, the most tangible and non-moveable property conceivable was organized into interests and condensed into paper assets that, in good market conditions, could be cycled quickly from person to person, person to corporation, corporation to corporation, corporation to person, and so on. This European-derived facility to move titles enabled landholders to borrow capital to refashion the land itself. Both the physical and abstract treatment of land developed along similar lines in the United States, southern Africa, Australia, New Zealand, and Canada. The representation of land on documents participated in a metaphysical revolution by which words and numbers could stand in for something larger and concrete. Maps represented estates, countries, and empires; books represented history; deeds represented land.

There are good reasons why an almost-concurrent transformation of frontiers into assets in a variety of distant places shared general features and a few specific details. Of course, there were singular traits in the transformation of each frontier. Local, regional, and national events played roles. For decades, historical geographers and environmental historians have described new-world habitations with a sensitivity to climate, flora and fauna, and the cultures of first peoples and newcomers. This approach has been brilliantly executed, rewarding for students and scholars. However, it is no less constructive to suggest a loose unity to an English-speaking assault on new-world frontiers, because this proposition elicits a reconsideration of the history of settlement colonies. Besides, the problem facing any student of local history and regional history is that, no matter how carefully bounded these studies are, they involve processes that originate in and involve far larger areas. Donald Worster asks his readers to "forget for a while the broader tides of imperialism and Christendom ... and the market-place," in order to concentrate on how people in a specific locale "tried to wrest their food, their income from the specific land in question."[17] The request is commendable, although by stating it he enunciates the very themes – capitalism and imperialism – that he feels threaten to cloud an appreciation of human interaction with local environments.

Refined local studies and global comparative ones contribute to knowledge at different scales. It is advisable to try to look past national concerns and propose similarities and connections among several jurisdictions. The U.S. government established momentous innovations early in the land rush. As well, democratic politics in the republic, the sequence of huge territorial acquisitions (Table 3.2), and the sheer magnitude of the public domain led to standardized measures intended to be simple and efficient. Not all innovations in landed property rights emerged in that country. During the nineteenth century, Australian colonies made an ingenious contribution to registration of land title – Torrens title – that influenced U.S. jurisdictions. Furthermore, as significant as

Table 3.2
Acquisitions to the U.S. public domain (excluding Alaska), 1781–1853

Territorial area	Year(s) acquired	Area in acres	% of total
Cessions by states	1781–1802	236,826,000	16.2
Louisiana Purchase	1803	529,403,000	36.2
Red River basin	–	29,602,000	2.0
Cession from Spain	1819	46,082,000	3.2
Oregon Treaty (from Britain)	1846	182,771,000	12.5
Cession from War against Mexico	1848	338,571,000	23.2
Purchase from Texas	1850	78,927,000	5.4
Gadsden Purchase from Mexico	1853	18,970,000	1.3
Total		1,461,152,000	100.0

U.S. innovations were, they applied to a series of opportunities and challenges that presently broke out in other parts of the world. Thus, even though the idea of a public domain was original to the republic, the settlement colonies of the British empire witnessed political movements for land reform that equated crown land with public land. As myth, the prospect of becoming a yeoman farmer spread far and promised independence and property. It is plausible, moreover, that the migration of Americans helped advance these ideas about public land and freedom.[18]

The American Revolution and republican ideals undeniably influenced the language of that nation's land rush; republican convictions prompted several innovations in land policy and law that were picked up elsewhere. Additionally, the idea of selling land to finance state projects in the name of a common good originated in the new republic and flourished there first in the 1820s.[19] Sales or grants of land to finance public works eventually ensued in settlement colonies. As an articulated republican policy linked to democracy, the shift at mid-century from land sales to free grants for homesteaders arguably began in the United States. However, the underlying concept for homestead grants – the completion of settlement conditions that tied legal title to a settler's undertaking to make improvements – was stipulated earlier on frontiers in the British empire.

Studies of legislation and case law show local variations in the evolution of property rights. For example, the property rights to water on western American lands – a well-studied area – comprise a complicated tale of local and regional experimentation.[20] However, just as significant for our story as the reporting of particular events is the delineation of underlying cultural values, of common technologies, and of fundamental dilemmas and faultlines of conflict. In the making of the modern world, the land rush was a foundation event. Afrikaners, Americans, Australians, Canadians, and New Zealanders participated in comparable ways. The three common denominators just mentioned deserve clarification.

First, there was the force of shared cultural traits. As routine as work and worship, these characteristics materialized in three sets of Anglo–American attitudes: ideas about private landed property that were supported in the law; a popular and correct belief that privately held land was a source of freedom and power; and the juxtaposition of improvement and wilderness.[21] These attitudes – discussed in the pervious chapter – equipped colonizers of all stations with a familiar language that was so ingrained in their thoughts, so persistently stated in letters, petitions, treaties, court judgments, and statutes, that even the most enlightened colonizers could engage only in narrow discussions about land with first peoples, because they were culturally bound and in a hurry. The convergence of robust ideas about land and property rights in the eighteenth and nineteenth centuries reverberates into recent times. It extends to recent negotiations about native title in many jurisdictions. Successor states to nineteenth-century frontiers retained a great deal of colonial language and thought.

Second, in addition to the influence of cultural values, particular technologies advanced the conversion of frontiers into assets. Surveying, cartography, and bureaucracy made possible the creation of land parcels. Surveying and map making were obviously helpful, although in the absence of the administrative order of bureaucracy – even as under-staffed as it was – the land rush could never have achieved revolutionary outcomes. Without the legions of government clerks – and private agents – the abstraction of property rights that promoted real estate markets would have collapsed under the weight of impending transactions. Paul Gates, a meticulous pioneer in the study of the American public domain, judges that from the 1830s to the 1850s the registrars and receivers of the land offices, along with private land agents, were "among the most important people on the frontier."[22] Even so, bureaucrats stumbled from overwork. Matters were no different on British frontiers.[23] Tasks and temptations overwhelmed emergent public services everywhere.

Third, the great land rush was the scene of intense controversies, which we can express in terms of questions repeatedly asked by those who administered frontiers. How should land be allocated? If it was sold to settlers, what mechanisms should determine the price? How were squatters to be treated? What should be done to thwart land speculation? Was the formation of great landed estates to be welcomed or resisted? These problems were intrinsic to putting "vacant" land into the hands of parties "in proportion to their ability." Some remedies were communicated around the world when governments – and their critics – traded information. The exchanges among governments and reformers augmented the universality of the great land rush.

SHAPES AND SCALES OF OCCUPATION: A TROUBLING MODEL

The Would-be Empire of Virginia

Examples ground and illuminate concepts. An initial illustration – more accurately, a mighty harbinger – occurs in Virginia, from the 1720s to the 1790s. This Virginia is not the *post-bellum* truncated state, but a colonizing commonwealth that had immense territorial cravings and generous, even profligate land-granting practices. Virginia's loose practices appear in subsections on the Ohio Company, on Daniel Boone, on land markers and tract shapes used by colonizers, and on what the new republic learned from Virginia's mistakes.

Virginia today covers a fraction of the area once claimed. Until the Old Dominion surrendered to Congress its interests in the Ohio valley in 1784, it had designs on an area approximately six times its current size. A substantial part of the western territory that it retained after 1784 became the state of Kentucky in 1792. During the U.S. Civil War, another section broke away to form West Virginia. Today Virginia embraces only 40 per cent of the area that it controlled prior to the formation of these two states. The territory vacated by Virginia in 1784, the lands surrendered for Kentucky in 1792, and the future state of West Virginia are of more than passing interest, because they experienced intense land speculation. Out of Virginia, moreover, came legendary landhunters. Some reached Spanish Louisiana in the 1790s by way of Kentucky. Virginians and Kentuckians were arriving in Texas by the 1820s.

There was potential for an empire of Virginia. Other colonies disputed Virginia's claims, and, from the Royal Proclamation of 1763 until the demise of the first British American empire in 1783, London generally prohibited the alienation of land west of the Allegheny Mountains. There were a few exceptions to this policy: frontier forts needed food, and thus land could be assigned around these outposts; Virginia military warrants could be applied to land over the king's line. On Virginia's frontier, as on others that followed, governmental prohibitions never fully obstructed scheming. Enough schemers acquired interests in land to keep defiance alive. Virginia's claims on western territory gave just enough colour of promise to encourage expansive speculative dealings and provocative surveying expeditions. On all the British Colonial and American frontiers that followed, proficient landhunters ignored government rules intended to contain or delay occupation of the land. The limit set in 1763 was applied by British imperial authorities, who created an Indian territory after the conquest of New France. Comparable limits were applied in New South Wales in the 1820s and 1830s. In the late eighteenth and early nineteenth centuries, both Dutch and British administrations at the Cape of Good Hope tried to confine European occupation to a zone of authorized settlement. Virginians led a parade of people who defied British imperial limits of occupation.[24]

Tidewater Virginia by the 1720s was home to an elite that esteemed landed property. Newcomers to America from the United Kingdom had departed a society that revered landholding; the great land rush coincided with the last phases of commons enclosures at home and of English estate building in colonized Ireland. Measures of enclosure had sensitized victims and beneficiaries, tenants and landlords, to the importance of property rights. Prospects for landowning were restricted in the United Kingdom, but possession of landed property endured as a symbol of social pre-eminence. Landed property also continued in the eighteenth century – and much of the nineteenth – to play a major part in the life of the state, for appointment to office in England was still based largely on property. In Virginia, colonial leadership by 1720 had formed an aristocratic culture that imitated country society in England. Planters managed estates, bought and sold land, and held public office. Unlike English aristocrats, however, they directly exploited slaves and could look for speculative projects on hinterland frontiers.

In time, a number of aspiring Virginia landholders roamed the interior Piedmont region.[25] These parties soon looked to unalienated lands further west, across the Allegheny Mountains, as sources of profit for themselves, as opportunities for their extended families, or as a means of dealing with the soil depletion that accompanied tobacco growing. The craving for land, and a keen understanding of how to speculate in it, derived from the colony's economy. Lacking a great port city and the associated mercantile openings, Virginia's investment opportunities focused on tobacco, land, and slaves. There was, moreover, a particularly influential estate enterprise. One highly successful venture – the Fairfax Proprietary – inspired others. This estate, which bridged English property holding and new-world speculations, originated in a grant made by King Charles II. America had proprietary colonies

(Maryland, 1632; Carolina, 1663; New Jersey, 1664; Pennsylvania, 1681) and large landed estates (for example, the Van Rensselaer estate in New York), but the Fairfax estate presented planters with a nearby model of a large estate with manors. It was managed at mid-century by individuals who settled among the Virginia oligarchy on the lower Potomac River. In 1729, an agent for the Fairfax heirs protested the colony's grants of land to settlers in the Shenandoah valley. The dispute concluded in 1746, when the Fairfax claim was largely upheld. The heirs were entitled to quit rents from approximately 6 million acres (Map 3.1). Some of this territory extended across northern Virginia and into parts of what became West Virginia.[26]

Virginia had also granted hundreds of thousands of acres south of the Fairfax estate to a handful of individuals in the late 1730s.[27] These grants and the Fairfax holdings were situated along migration lines. The expansion of settlement into colonial frontiers proceeded swiftly, because land in New England, New York, and Pennsylvania was becoming less readily available after 1750. As well, pioneer life in western Virginia "was predicated upon generous land grants that encompassed individual owner-occupied farms arranged in initial self-sufficient, open-country neighbourhoods."[28] This arrangement, fanning westward for the next hundred years, comprised an element in the cultural thrust of the mid-Atlantic colonies and the south beyond the Mississippi. Reaching back further in time for an explanation of the dynamic character of "backwoods" settlement, Terry Jordan and Matti Kaups propose that the Pennsylvania pioneers, learning from the Scandinavian colonists in mid seventeenth century Delaware (New Sweden), "gravitated to a long-fallow slash-and-burn cropping system and dispersed-settlement pattern." This approach brought about highly extensive use of land.[29]

Access to western land from the 1750s to the 1790s was organized mainly from two directions. From the east, Virginians could move up the Potomac River and its tributaries, the Shenandoah and the South Branch of the Potomac. The Potomac not only pointed to the interior, its estuary connected the residences of men who coveted western lands. From the north, a line of settler movement into the western territories claimed by Virginia ran southwest out of Pennsylvania and into Virginia.[30] Lines of movement from east and north merged at Potomac ferry crossings; parties could continue southwestward between the Blue Ridge and Allegheny mountains. Long used by the Iroquois of New York, this warriors' route became the Philadelphia Wagon Road by mid-century.[31] Colonizers, landhunters, and backwoods pioneers who wanted to go over the mountains left this trail and cut westward, ascending valleys, crossing the height of land, and descending the

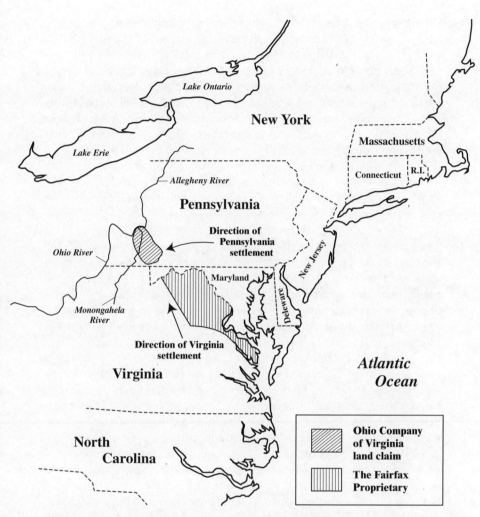

Map 3.1
The Fairfax Proprietary and the Ohio Company of Virginia land claim
Sources: Kenneth T. Jackson and James Truslow Adams, *Atlas of American History*
(New York: Charles Scribner's Sons, 1978), 81; Bryce Jordan et al., *The Atlas of Pennsylvania*
(Philadelphia: Temple University Press, 1989), 82.

valleys of tributaries to the Kanawha River, finally entering the Ohio valley.[32] Or they could shift northwestward and reach the upper Ohio valley through the tributaries of the Monongahela River, a route that took them into Philadelphia's hinterland. Some Pennsylvanians coveted the Ohio territory, while more pacific Philadelphia merchants dominated thinking about its exploitation and looked to the Indian trade. That meant discouraging colonization schemes that upset Indian nations.[33] There was a major exception, however. Pennsylvania landhunter, merchant, and deputy superintendent of the northern Indian department George Croghan negotiated with first peoples. Still, he knew the value of peace on the frontier and at times lived among its inhabitants.[34] Virginians, however, entered the west audaciously to survey the land.

The Fairfax Proprietary embraced land in the Shenandoah valley – the popular access point for routes into the interior. Fairfax agents managed to extract revenue from agrarian immigrants.[35] In early 1748, the family planned surveys on land beyond the Shenandoah. George Washington, then sixteen and learning the arts of surveying, joined the party. From that expedition and subsequent missions on behalf of the Fairfax interests, Washington acquired a full set of surveying skills. To survey land was to do more than measure it, mark it, and describe it; it was also to read its potential. Good surveyors on all frontiers enjoyed reputations for skill in assessing the ease of clearing land, the value of timber, the availability of water, and the strategic importance of particular locations. By 1750, Washington, now a complete surveyor, took the measure of land for his own account.

Surveying, as Washington knew it, and as it came to be practised years later in much of southern Africa, Australia, New Zealand, and parts of British Columbia, rested on a free selection process that authorized a plucking of the best land. It also permitted selections that could have environmental coherence, such as consistency in soil quality, a matching of water sources and land, or mountain valleys. From the standpoint of squatting or holding more than that to which one was entitled, free selection licensed a serious game of strategic claims.[36] Land grants in colonial Virginia involved the following process. In the name of the crown, the colonial administration granted a certain acreage – usually 100 to 1,000 acres – to an individual. There was no spatial framework for the individual grants. The grantee received the privilege of selecting the land to be patented. Tracts were neither required to be contiguous to cleared land nor laid out in a regular shape.[37] The grant amounted to a hunting licence. Recipients could proceed to the frontier, mark out a plot that contained the specified acreage, return to register their claim, and secure a title patent after fulfilling certain conditions. What counted above all else was marking the claim. Even without the patent that confirmed title, a grantee had a marketable asset once the boundaries were marked. Free selection is a crucial concept, because it surfaced on other frontiers, though in different contexts in different periods; however, everywhere it was practised around the world, it betrayed the same characteristics. The granting government assumed minimal responsibility for the survey and avoided initial expenses.

Free selection only postponed costs, because eventually a survey had to be conducted to tie in the disconnected pieces and clarify who possessed what, so as to minimize uncertainty in maturing land markets. Working on behalf of grantees, landhunters and professional surveyors used crude devices to mark the boundaries of their selections. They blazed trees, piled rocks, constructed beacons, and noted natural boundaries such as streams or ridges. This was the method used in western Virginia in the 1750s; it was the way things were done in southern Africa at least as early as the 1750s, in Australia in the 1830s and 1840s, and in New Zealand in the 1840s and 1850s. Usually, Virginia's surveyors delineated spaces within straight, though not necessarily parallel, lines. Typically, too, they delimited more land than granted. In the territory that became Kentucky, free selection was invigorated by a post-revolutionary outpouring of Virginia land warrants, issued to finance the war of independence and to reward potentially mutinous revolutionary soldiers. These land rights allowed a welter of shingled claims.[38]

The scale of Virginia's territorial claims and the character of its land-granting system assured work for generations of lawyers and thereby inspired early law reforms to reduce litigation.[39] Free selection admitted governments' weakness. They could not cope with the speed and scale of landhunting; they could not block an activity that was intrinsic to the strategic and economic welfare of the frontier; they could not resist temptations to discharge debts with torrents of grants. On frontiers where governments pursued orderly processes with some success from the outset, there were special environmental and political circumstances at work. The Canadian prairies, surveyed and allocated in the late nineteenth and early twentieth centuries, exemplified a more methodical – but not perfect – arrangement. The prairies were the last, most inaccessible, and coldest grand region opened during the rush.

The Ohio Company

Virginia's colonial administrators assisted land speculators. The helpful participation of its eighteenth-century royal governors contrasts with the conduct of a few royal governors in the British empire after the

Napoleonic wars; although some of these men plundered their colonies and favoured cronies, many were stiff-necked defenders of the crown's interests. Whatever their personal inclinations respecting participation in the land rush, governors in every colony could advance or obstruct land grabs. A succession of Virginia's governors – especially William Gooch (1727–49), Robert Dinwiddie (1751–58), and John Murray, Earl Dunmore (1771–76) – assisted land speculators and would-be estate builders. Gooch countenanced several large personal grants and sought advice from the Board of Trade in London respecting a petition for a land company partly inspired by the Fairfax Proprietary. London consented to the plans of this Ohio Company (1748), whose organizers included George Fairfax and George Washington's two older brothers.[40] The Ohio Company received a right to select 200,000 acres along the Ohio River and another 300,000 if it maintained a fort and one hundred inhabitants (Map 3.1). Although it struggled and died, it managed to sell some property. In comparison to a number of other colonial land companies, it requested modest acreage. Another British venture promoted by a neighbour of Thomas Jefferson's, Thomas Walker, the Loyal Company (1749) petitioned for access to 800,000 acres, mainly in what became Kentucky. Whereas the Ohio Company had a settlement condition imposed on it, the Loyal had none.

The exploratory operations of the Ohio Company were of international significance, for they aroused the French to strengthen their presence in the Ohio valley. The French move provoked a combined colonial and British counter-stroke that commandeered company facilities. The Ohio Company championed colonial criticism of British efforts to restrict settlement west of the Appalachian Mountains, and it helped draw Virginians into conflict with indigenous peoples. Governor Dinwiddie, an investor in the company, had London's sanction to remove the French from the Ohio valley, by threat or force. The French defeated a Virginian force in 1754 and also a larger British and Virginian expedition in 1755. However, French withdrawal in 1758 seemed to secure the valley for Virginia, for its land speculators and squatters. Yet the collapse of the French empire did not open the territory as Virginians hoped. For an indefinite time and for a variety of reasons, the British established an Indian territory beyond the Allegheny Mountains. This was explained in the Royal Proclamation of 1763, which inconvenienced speculators, but failed to stop them. Circumvention was second nature, as we see in the next chapter.

The occupation of the western Virginia frontier, between roughly 1765 and 1775, witnessed a feature seen later on other frontiers. Risk-taking frontiersmen took positions beyond the limits of legitimate occupation, on the "King's side" of the mountains. Speculators who hesitated, because of a wish to move with the legal protection that accompanied official authorization, watched good locations being surveyed by squatters. George Washington wrung his hands: "Every good, and fertile spot will be engrossed and occupied by others."[41] Some daring land scouts and squatters risked their lives in moving beyond the line. A number of Indian villages in the forbidden territory opposed encroachment. English policy and vigilant Indians had replaced the French to complicate land grabbing. The Shawnees and Mingoes stood in the way of the Virginians' land schemes. The northern allies of these tribes, the Iroquois, betrayed them in September 1768 and ceded hunting lands – mostly in present-day West Virginia – that the Shawnees in particular claimed. Adroit British agents – Sir William Johnson, for the northern department of the Indian territory, and John Stuart, for the southern department – isolated the Shawnees from other tribes by diplomacy.[42] When they had done so, Governor Dunmore drew the Shawnees into a brief war. The Battle of Point Pleasant, fought on 10 October 1774 at the confluence of the Ohio and the Great Kanawha rivers, was "the climactic event in the history of colonial western Virginia."[43] Both sides at Point Pleasant were surprised by the other's tenacity. In the end, however, the Shawnees withdrew and signed a treaty that kept them north and west of the Ohio River.

During the first years of the American Revolution, the western frontier of Virginia was quiet, and surveyors went about their business.[44] One of them, George Rogers Clarke, a son of lesser gentry, was a rough Virginia gentleman. After the Shawnees withdrew, Clarke and others like him occupied the bluegrass region of central Kentucky. Clarke rhapsodized about the new region. "A richer and more Beautiful Cuntry than this I have never seen in America yet."[45] He engrossed all the land he could and during the revolution led a campaign against the British and their Indian allies. In 1786, he commanded an unsuccessful expedition to stop Indian raids on western colonizers. In common with Virginia's process of free selection, Clarke and his men signified colonization by audacity without plan or patience.[46]

The Ohio Company, with claims in western Virginia, assisted in the removal of the French and the Indians. Its influence penetrated deeper. By calling attention to western lands, by sponsoring surveyors, it gave a fillip to private landhunting. Both the colonists who bought the company's land and the agents whom it employed discovered opportunities to freelance. George Washington's moves are instructive. He had traversed the Ohio Company's tract and in 1755, under the command of General Edward Braddock, moved troops and supplies over its colonization road. He liked what he saw, coveted land in the area, and subsequently instigated a scheme for a speculation. Soldiers who had campaigned in the French and Indian wars (1754–63) received bonuses in the form of warrants – land scrip – that could be converted into land through free selection. Similar land warrants went to veterans of the War of 1812 and the Mexican War. By 1880, the U.S. government had distributed warrants convertible to over 61 million acres[47]. The issue of scrip – to soldiers, Indians, Métis, and recipients of government compensation – would be practised far and wide on several continents. Invariably speculators everywhere bought scrip at discounts from recipients and marshalled it astutely to assemble or defend major estates or to put together plots for resale.

Washington and a network of fellow officers formed a syndicate in 1769 for the purpose of accumulating warrants to secure choice land in the Ohio valley. To survey the land in the fullest sense, for another venture, he turned in 1767 to a brother officer, a surveyor with Ohio Company experience, William Crawford. In a 1771 report to Washington, Crawford described a state of affairs repeated countless times around the world during the great land rush. Truculent rivals had already positioned themselves on the land that Crawford intended for his employer. "I do not much like running [surveying] any land in Tygart's Valley, as the people in general are very contentious there."[48] All frontiers attracted squatters, whose possessory occupation was difficult to supplant. In law, some had a shallow claim, yet just enough to delay ejectment. They occasionally united for mutual protection. Along the Monongahela River in 1771, a number of recent arrivals entered "into a bond or article of agreement to join and keep off all officers of the law."[49] Late-coming landhunters on all frontiers – even when outfitted with official paper, in the form of scrip, grants, or location tickets – tended to sidestep these troublesome people to reach accommodation. Washington and his associates yielded ground to some squatters and tackled others. If he judged a claimant weak, Washington set up a rival claim.[50] It took time to perfect titles. His agents commenced removing squatters from his selections at Chartiers Creek in 1773 and completed the operation by 1794. The general point is that land companies in western Virginia introduced clever private landhunters to a frontier. That would become a pattern. In the early 1840s in New Zealand, a major land and colonization body – the New Zealand Company – failed in most of its objectives but put canny landhunters on the ground.[51] Frontier land companies were important, though less for enduring power and huge profits and more for their surveys, their capacity for complicating frontier politics and diplomacy, and their introduction of determined landhunters and colonists on frontiers. See Table 3.3.

Table 3.3
Examples of colonial land companies: America, 1748–75; other colonies, 1820–40

Year formed	Company	Region covered	Acres granted or sold by crown
1748	Ohio Company	Company to select in Ohio valley	200,000 initial
1749–50	Loyal Company	Western Virginia (Kentucky)	800,000
1768–72	Vandalia Colony	South of Ohio River from near Pittsburgh to Kentucky River	20 million–30 million
1775	Transylvania Company	South of Ohio from Great Kanawha River to Tennessee River	20 million
1824–25	Australian Agricultural Company	Near Hunter River in New South Wales	1 million
1824–25	Van Diemen's Land Company	Northwest Van Diemen's Land (Tasmania)	250,000
1824–26	Canada Company	Upper Canada	Purchased roughly 1 million in Huron Tract; over 2,360,000 altogether
1834–36	South Australia Company	South Australia	(Land between 132° E and 141° E)
1839	New Zealand Company	Mainly around Cook Strait and parts of South Island	20 million, reduced to 1.3 million by 1845

Sources: Daniel Freidenberg, *Life, Liberty, and the Pursuit of Land: The Plunder of Early America* (Buffalo: Prometheus Books, 1992), passim; Jan Kociumbas, *The Oxford History of Australia: Possessions, 1770–1860* (Melbourne: Oxford University Press, 1992), 122–3, 139–41; Roger Hall, "The Canada Company," (PhD dissertation, Cambridge University, 1973), 414, 422; Waitangi Tribunal, *The Taranaki Report* (Wellington: Waitangi Tribunal, 1996), 22–3; "Land and Sovereignty," Plate 31, in Malcolm McKinnon, ed., *New Zealand Historical Atlas* (Wellington: David Bateman in Association with Historical Branch, Department of Internal Affairs, 1997).

The Odyssey of Daniel Boone

Washington's conflicts with rival claimants and squatters revives an important issue from the previous chapter. Who was a speculator? Between the chartered land companies and so-called pioneer settlers there were many shades of land jobbing. Companies or syndicates such as Washington's aspired frankly to profit from land sales. At the other extreme, there were settlers who wanted simply land to live on, although they might later take advantage of a rise in property values, sell out, and move. All landholders were potential land producers – that was axiomatic on frontiers. Although few speculators had Washington's connections, there were always individuals whose contacts assisted with their amassing large grants. In many places, however, the majority of speculators consisted of rugged and resourceful personalities, relatively poor scrappers and seekers. As "cuckoo squatters," they ran sheep onto large Australian grazing stations during the 1830s. Defying British authorities in Cape Colony, stockmen drove cattle and sheep over the Orange River boundary during the same years.[52] Many of these pastoralists hunted for game as well as grazing land. In *The Empire of Nature*, John MacKenzie writes that "hunting added impetus to frontier expansion, since hunting was, of course, exceptionally land extensive."[53] Serious game hunters acquired knowledge about the capacity of particular locales to support livestock. When John B. Thomas's scout went probing for open range in Montana in 1885, "he got two old Buffalo Hunters to show him the place. They have hunted in there for four years and say the snow never has bothered them, going off quickly and not having a heavy fall."[54] Now that we have connected frontier hunters and land seekers, let us turn back to colonial America and consider the archetypal hunter-surveyor, Daniel Boone. Early American frontiersmen pursued game hunting, trapping, and land speculation. Boone blended them into a perilous way of life and became an American legend. In the assessment of one biographer, Boone was a good surveyor, not in the technical sense, but in being an able woodsman and landhunter.[55]

Boone's career as an ardent landhunter began in 1769, when Judge Richard Henderson hired him to scout for land in southwestern Virginia, west of the present state. Originally from Virginia, Henderson had moved to North Carolina. His Transylvania Company ignored the prohibition in the Royal Proclamation of 1763 against direct land dealings between colonizers and first peoples. Henderson and his partners defied this ban on the basis of a flimsy legal opinion (discussed in the next chapter), and they purchased an enormous tract from Cherokee chiefs.[56] The Transylvania Company claimed nearly twenty million acres lying south of the Ohio River between the mouths of the Great Kanawha and Tennessee rivers. Like Washington, Henderson found himself beset by squatters who "stubbornly held to the land."[57] His company was not the last to attempt a frontier purchase directly from an indigenous people. It happened in southern Africa, Australia, and New Zealand. A brazen stroke, the Transylvania undertaking attracted resilient frontier folk. Washington learned the craft of landhunting from

the Fairfax Proprietary; Daniel Boone gained experience in the Transylvania's employ. Although he may have been informing parties about
western lands before then, the company put him on a trail to fame and
sorrow. He was one of the first to locate and file a claim with the
Transylvania. One of his sons was killed on its claim in 1773, in a
prelude to what Boone admitted was a "war of intrusion" against the
Shawnees for control of the lower Ohio valley.[58]

Landhunters mixed activities. In 1774, when it was apparent that
Virginia was about to go to war with the Shawnees, Governor Dunmore
sent Boone to warn other land surveyors – that is, other landhunters
– about an impending Indian war. Boone took advantage of this official
mission to mark land for a number of clients.[59] In the years immediately following the revolution, when the outpouring of Virginia land
warrants sent surveyors swarming over western Virginia, Boone functioned as a surveyor, tavern keeper, merchant, and horse trader. These
enterprises, according to biographer John Mack Faragher, were but a
means to allow him to play in the biggest economic game – real estate
speculation.[60] By 1783, Virginia had distributed grants for almost
2 million acres to several land companies, 5 million to revolutionary
soldiers, and 38 million to promote investment in the treasury warrants
that backed Virginia's debt.[61] Enough free selection rights had been
distributed to cover the Kentucky region four times over.[62] Kentucky
land became a byword for sharp, crooked dealings. Boone's speculations failed. Like most land agents in Kentucky, he sold *entries* or
claims to land; rarely did he patent tracts. Often, claims to Kentucky
land overlapped. Boone bonded his claims. He pledged to defend them
against challenges when he sold them.[63]

A form of vender-issued insurance against the eventuality of clouded
titles, such frontier guarantees were plied by desperate speculators with
slender interests, as inducements to secure settlers who would construct
a possessory interest through improvements.[64] The game was to put
people on the land, commit them to payments at a later date, and
count on their labour to help protect what had been sold to them.
Buying entries was a gamble all around, and Boone lost heavily. His
bonds dragged him into ruinous litigation in the late 1780s. In various
jurisdictions, different remedies for buyers' anxieties about uncertain
land titles would emerge during the great land rush, with an influential
solution – a government guarantee called Torrens title – originating in
South Australia in 1849. Twenty-one U.S. states adopted the Torrens
system by the early twentieth century, although a number of U.S.
jurisdictions opted for private title insurance. Land markets honed
procedures to neutralize the risks of imperfect titles.[65] A lack of trust
in claims forced price discounts. By the early nineteenth century,

immigrants were avoiding Kentucky, although it may have contained some of the finest land in the United States.[66] For those who located and stayed, "horses and law-suits comprise[d] the usual topic of their conversation."[67] Squire Boone not only had to give up his best Kentucky bottom lands, he forfeited public esteem when he became an expert witness in litigation over "shingled" claims.[68] Opponents accused him of being a "chimney corner" surveyor who sat by his fireplace and set down boundaries from memory or fancy.[69] Making a final play for a landed estate in 1799, Boone resettled his clan to Spanish Louisiana. His land grant from Spanish authorities along the Missouri River – one of many investigated by the U.S. government after it purchased Louisiana in 1803 – was not completely confirmed, because of suspicions that many concessions granted in the last days of Spanish sovereignty evaded regulations to benefit favoured speculators and thus were believed illegal under Spanish law.[70]

At the time of Boone's legal troubles, in the 1790s, a new system of allocating land – involving survey before settlement – had displaced free selection on the U.S. public domain. As a barrier to squatting and muddled claims, it proved an incomplete remedy. If free selection was an admission of government's frailty, survey before settlement was an act of hubris. A legislated formality could never eliminate landhunting squatters. Events across the public domain demonstrated that the scarcity of government land agents incited squatting. Squatters were, in theory, improvers and, in fact, potential voters. They were not easily budged. Not far from Boone's Missouri colony, around the time of his death in 1820, near the confluence of the Mississippi and the Ohio, on the Missouri side, squatters cut timber for the New Orleans market and fattened herds of cattle.[71] About this Ste Geneviève district, it was reported there could be no "country in the world where cattle and hogs can be raised with so little trouble ... no country better adapted to the raising and keeping of large flocks of sheep."[72] The hyperbole and illicit practices would soon become commonplace. In Australia, New Zealand, and Upper Canada, unauthorized timber getting supported early settlers. Justices of the peace were loath to fine them. Asset strippers – sawyers and grazers – blamed the government for its failure to prepare the frontier for exploitation. From their standpoint, the absence of authority incited them to disobedience, because to wait was to lose. Once ensconced, frontier folk looked to government to define and protect their property rights. Nevertheless, out of episodes of initial and illicit seizure emerged anti-government folklore common to frontiers and successor cultures.

In 1819, about three hundred miles south of Boone's Missouri colony, across the Ozark Mountains, Thomas Nuttall, a naturalist collecting plant specimens, met two keel boats heading up the Arkansas River, one heavily laden with whisky and the other belonging to two elderly men "out on a land speculation"[73] – whisky, land speculators, and science. Americans were heading to the west. As William H. Goetzmann stresses in his history of U.S. exploration of the region, "men appear to have gone out West to reconstitute the society they had known on countless frontiers to the East – only of course with themselves at the top instead of the bottom of the social and economic ladder."[74] Nuttall had joined a company of soldiers sent to remove white squatters from land between the Canadian and Red rivers, territory claimed by the Osage. The area in dispute was four hundred miles west of the Mississippi and close to the border with Spanish Mexico (Texas). As many as three thousand squatters had journeyed overland from the north and east.[75] Nuttall watched the exodus of uprooted squatters, watched them abandon their fields of planted corn and cotton. Cursing the U.S. government, cursing the law, they withdrew to San Antonio.[76]

English-speaking landhunters, some with Virginia and Kentucky connections, would wrest Texas away from Mexico in 1836. Had Nuttall encountered one of the parties that would locate in the Texas colony just being established by Virginians Moses and Stephen Austin? On his 1856 anti-slavery fact-finding tour of the southwest, Frederick Law Olmsted visited "a first-class Texas grazier" near the Gulf of Mexico and the Trinity River. His host – "originally a Kentuckian" – possessed a herd that increased by five hundred head a year. In Olmsted's estimation, isolation and the ease of the cattle trade permitted the family to slide into indolence – a conventional criticism of grazers.[77] In the 1880s, it could still be said that Kentuckians were a prominent and clannish population in the west. "Let two meet who never saw each other before, and inside a half an hour they'll be chewing tobacco from the same plug and trying to loan each other money."[78]

Land Markers and Tract Shapes

I mentioned above that squatters at the mouth of the Ohio grazed cattle. Hogs, horses, and cattle assisted land occupation. Squatters depended on occupation. They laboured to signify it by blazing trees, raising cabins, clearing fields, and warning off newcomers. Cattle provided food, a source of revenue, and mobile land markers. In explaining the Europeans' ability to thrive on many frontiers, Alfred Crosby and Jared Diamond remark on the hardiness of domesticated Eurasian animals.[79] Hogs, cattle, and sheep underpinned squatting. On the North America prairies, an undomesticated rival to cattle affected the timing of the conversion of frontiers into assets, and that rival –

the buffalo – could not readily be domesticated. The great herds of
the west could have impeded settlement, except that millions of the
animals were shot during the 1870s and 1880s for the buffalo robe
market. The eastern variant of the species imposed no delays on eastern
land occupation. The wagon road between the Blue Ridge and Allegheny
mountains may once have been a buffalo track, and migrants and
government surveyors used similar tracks in territory just east of the
Mississippi. More thinly established than the plains buffalo, however,
the eastern buffalo posed no challenge to grazing.[80] Apart from assisting settlers with establishing occupation on small holdings, cattle were
soon over the Allegheny Mountains in large enough numbers to set
up a thriving cattle trade.[81] As early as 1784, drovers moved cattle
from the South Branch of the Potomac River, across the Alleghenies,
and into the Kentucky bluegrass district. By the 1790s, several of
Daniel Boone's fellow adventurers from Boonesboro surveyed land
grants in Kentucky that developed into cattle estates. From Kentucky,
herdsmen moved stock north into Ohio and west into Missouri. Cattle
were by 1800 on the lower Mississippi, and by 1820 on the prairies
of northwest Louisiana and in the Red River district of Arkansas.[82]

Grazing was intrinsic to landhunting in southern Africa, Australia,
New Zealand, Texas, and the U.S. high plains. Wherever grazing could
thrive, so too could expansive squatting. Cape Governor Sir George
Napier, writing in 1839 about the nature and consequences of the
Great Trek, depicted something larger – the phenomenon of grazers
taking a lead. "They [the Dutch grazers] idolize their flocks, they will
brave hardships and death to procure the means of supporting these
flocks, therefore if we follow them in all their wanderings & take
possession as a colony of every foot of land which they seize the colony
must extend to the very verge of the habitable ground."[83] In races
between government officials – magistrates, surveyors, land agents –
and stockmen, the latter usually won. Stockmen moved faster than
survey crews. There were environmental limits to grazing, and brutal
winters, like those that gripped the Canadian prairies, checked drovers.
In Canada, ranching was confined to southern Alberta and the arid
valleys of central British Columbia.[84] Because of its harsh climate and
isolation, the Canadian prairies were spared the pastoral squatting that
often sped frontier occupation.

A Virginia compass has directed us through historic river valleys into
the centre of the United States. The expansionary colony of Virginia
gave way to a substantive American empire. Virginians and colonists
ranging through the Old Dominion had precipitated a vigorous, more
or less continuous, land rush. Many tricks and risks of the trade

surfaced in Virginia and its western territories. In the global land rush, unruly and ingenious players emerged early and fast in western Virginia. Early and fast is what landhunters aimed to be. Yet there was a counter-stream of events in the American colonies – one that stressed order. It is common practice in surveys of U.S. history to contrast the land-distribution practices and landscapes of the colonies of New England with those in southern colonies. The generalization is sound. An early New England ideal of village, village common, and surrounding fields persisted. At first, committees apportioned land and managed the commons. However, "as the Revolution neared, stewardship of common land evolved into improvement of private property."[85] A relatively compact and tidy landscape endured. In contrast, an abundance of land in southern colonies enabled farmers to run their livestock with some freedom. Neat, well-cleared farms were less common there. Squatter occupation and disputed land titles discouraged initial investment on southern frontiers. In New England, a colder environment – hostile to casual grazing – and great community control over land allocation – especially in Massachusetts – contributed to cadastral and legal order. Avoidance of free selection and a confined hinterland reduced the opportunities for shingled claims and thus for confrontation, anger, and litigation.

The Maine district of Massachusetts (a state only from 1820 on) presents an instructive exception to the New England paradigm of reasonably well-ordered land distribution. Before the revolution and for years afterwards, parts of eastern Maine were ensnared in bitter and occasionally violent land disputes. Major land claims originated in letters patent from Charles I and in Indian deeds. Heirs and agents pressed several claims, as had been the case with the Fairfax estate. For migrants to Maine, there was no salubrious hinterland, no nearby attractions such as the Kentucky lands that pulled people over the Allegheny Mountains. Farmers and timber cutters held their ground as squatters on Maine's proprietary estates from the mid-eighteenth century until the early nineteenth century.[86]

Similar confrontations between alleged landowners and squatters materialized on many unalienated acres in the United States, because from the mid-1780s to the mid-1790s large-scale land speculators initiated complex schemes with millions of acres of national and state land in the Northwest Territory, western New York, Pennsylvania, North and South Carolina, and Georgia.[87] This first American land bubble left a mound of legal debris.[88] Clouded titles and squatters' activities led to locally legislated compromises. Something had to be done to resolve economically the conflicts between equitable interests (including improvements) and legal interests (grants) that applied to the same tracts of land. The compromises between those who occupied the land and those who claimed title borrowed from the doctrine of improvement. Occupants who had imperfect titles could secure absolute ownership through newly legislated mediation procedures. Their improvements – buildings, fences, wells, and the like – would be appraised, and the resulting figure set against the land's assessed value. The difference between the two estimates could be paid as compensation to other claimants or landlords.[89] Reconciliations of occupants' improvements and the interests of parties with deeds were sought on frontiers around the world. Litigation or out-of-court arbitration valued and evaluated improvement. In effect, this "threw the risk of bad title entirely on the innocent nonoccupying owner."[90]

A republican discourse accompanied campaigns to settle land disputes in favour of the people who lived on the land. Republican politicians called on state legislatures to recognize betterment. They were able to achieve compromise, not victory, because conservative state leaders defended the legal claimants. The underlying concept of equitable interests built up through improvements was not unique to republican politics. However, because of political campaigns to recognize the value added to a property by squatters or delinquent tenants, legislatures made an important contribution to property law. They codified equitable practices rather than entrusting them to protracted resolution in the courts. Elsewhere, simplified rules to compensate improvements became features of land regulations in Australia and New Zealand by the mid-nineteenth century.[91] Meanwhile, the Northwest Ordinance of 1785 was "specifically designed to preclude ... trouble from combines of squatters and opportunists."[92] It set a fixed price of one dollar per acre and established a national land system of grid surveys. Subsequent national measures established land offices and modified sale conditions. The genius of the American innovations in land matters between the 1780s and the 1840s was that they simplified affairs by standardization. The independent Republic of Texas, however, retained free selection, and when it joined the United States it kept its public lands and the old allocation system.[93]

The Old Dominion's approach to land allocation came to a halt in southwestern Ohio around 1790. Free selection and grid survey before settlement collided in Ohio. When states such as Virginia ceded their western land claims after the revolution, they retained some tracts for special purposes. To discharge revolutionary war losses, Connecticut sold the block of land that it had preserved in Ohio to New Englanders who aspired to found an orderly colony.[94] Settlement of this reserve was slow until after 1825, but in 1800 it had been incorporated into the national grid system of land allocation.[95] Meanwhile, Virginia held onto a region of Ohio that would encompass twenty-three counties in the south of the state. Land in the Virginia Military District was supposed to compensate revolutionary war veterans. Parties with land warrants located their plots without reference to a public survey. As in Kentucky, a long course of litigation followed. Irregular polygons still describe plots of land in southern Ohio. They demarcate the northern limit of Virginia's reach.[96] Westwards, across the Mississippi, in Missouri, the freely selected tracts granted by Spain, covering a tier of counties fifty miles back of the river, blanketed the country "with a jumble of surveyed holdings" whose "depths were jagged and irregular."[97]

In a discussion of early American cultural regions, historical geographer Robert D. Mitchell traces the influence of the Chesapeake–Potomac area on western Virginia, that of western Virginia on central Kentucky, and that of this tertiary area on southwestern Ohio. North Carolina and Tennessee, he proposes, were also influenced by the cultural hearth of the Chesapeake.[98] Others have argued that the cultural complex of the Virginia backcountry simply was "exported intact to the edges of the Great Plains."[99] Specialists may disagree over the scope and completeness of Virginia's cultural impact, though not over its existence. It is even possible to glimpse, in the lives of grazers, the reach of western Virginia's culture south into eastern Texas and ultimately west to California and Oregon.[100] How cultural regions are defined and mapped is a specialized topic. We have not considered some relevant clues: religious affiliation, family names, adoption of slavery, law codes, vernacular architecture, crops, and crop-rotation practices.[101] We have, however, accomplished two things by studying Virginia's reach. We have seen how far and fast several landhunters carried their manœuvres. We have identified practices in landhunting that flourished in greater Virginia, and I have proposed that they occurred in other places. A list of these practices includes a defiance of regulations, scheming to remove first peoples, the free selection of allotments, the force of possessory occupation, the strength of the doctrine of improvement, the use of livestock to register both possession and improvement, the presence of different interests in the same plot of land, and the scourge of extensive and prolonged litigation.

Learning from Virginia's Mistakes

A benchmark event in comparative frontier history, the (U.S.) Northwest Ordinance of 1785 and subsequent enactments were supposed to prevent a repetition elsewhere of Virginia's land-granting mess. Before the start of the revolution, an imperial instruction ordered a reformation.

The British government in 1775 sent new instructions about land distribution to the governors of East Florida, Georgia, New Hampshire,
New York, North Carolina, Nova Scotia, South Carolina, Virginia, and
West Florida. The crown ordered them to have surveys made of the
tracts not already granted, to assess the quality of the remaining lands,
and to sell the land by auction.[102] Suppressing rebellion immediately
engrossed colonial governments. It would have been interesting to see
how the royal governors would have implemented the vague new recommendations for overhauling land distribution. The experience that
the United States soon had with its public domain and that Australia
had with its crown land suggests that the stillborn guidelines of 1775
were naive. Surveys were expensive, the size of land parcels was controversial, and pricing was an intricate affair engaging frontier politics.

Prior to the revolution, London had reacted belatedly to confusion
in colonial land matters and to settlers' avoidance of land fees –
namely, the quit rents due the crown. The new republic turned to
comparable problems of order and payment and tackled order through
an ordinance whose main enduring feature – the U.S. national land
system – mandated a rectangular template for much of the public
domain. U.S. public lands eventually comprised an area of approximately 2.8 million square miles, or nearly 2 billion acres; in mountain
regions, a trigonometric survey was used, so the grid did not apply to
all public lands. Several British colonial governments eventually considered adopting the grid, and, except for Canada, most opted for the
greater precision of the trigonometric system. Although the grid is a
renowned instrument of American colonization, a review is in order.
The U.S. survey grid started with two lines that intersected at right
angles. A north–south line of the scheme was called a principal meridian; the east–west line was the principal base or parallel. Meridians
and baselines were not laid out uniformly across the republic, but
established on acquisition of new areas by cession from states, sales
by other countries, conquests after war, and cessions by indigenous
peoples. The survey progressed in instalments, and not all of them
meshed with one another logically. In contrast, the Canadian prairies
– leaving aside the important issue of native title – were purchased in
a single transaction from the Hudson's Bay Company in 1869. As a
result, a unified plan of meridians and baselines was announced. The
American survey, however, was not as coherent, and it eventually
produced thirty-four principal meridians. From each of them at ninety
degrees, range lines were surveyed east–west at intervals of six miles.
Along the baselines and at ninety degree to them, township lines were
surveyed north and south, also at intervals of six miles. Ideally, the
U.S. system created a grid with squares called townships that contained

thirty-six square miles. Each square (640 acres – one square mile) was known as a section.[103]

The scale of the grid subdivision created logistical and mathematical problems. It was no small matter to supply survey crews, and there were always demands from speculators and desperate settlers to complete the job faster. The mathematical challenge derived from the convergence of the meridians. They could not be parallel because, as they extended towards a polar north, they drew closer together. By 1855, a standard remedy was to run a new east–west baseline after every four townships, or twenty four miles; from the new baseline township lines were run north.[104] The grid encountered another problem of its own making. Once the survey extended past 100° W and into the arid shadow of the Rocky Mountains, the standard blocks of land were not readily integrated with available water sources. Free selection had at least allowed landhunters to shape their entitlements according to how they read the landscape and its economic potential.[105] Standardization had great benefits and a few limitations.

The grid survey aimed at a speedy and reasonably accurate partitioning of the land. Its survey monuments had legal standing as true corners, even though they may not have been exactly where professional care or astronomically based observation would have put them. European travellers in the United States during the first half of the nineteenth century remarked on untidy haste in many things, which they attributed to the cost of labour.[106] In an 1825 letter from Missouri, German migrant Gottfried Duden related that nearby farmers wasted little care on crops and allowed weeds to flourish. Because of an abundance of space, "European perfection would be a waste here."[107] So it was with the grid survey. Perfection was a waste when there was so much land. British traveller (1818–20) James Flint remarked about the grid that "there can be no necessity for giving names to farms or estates, as the designation of the particular township, and the number of the section is sufficient, and has, besides, the singular convenience of conveying accurate information as to where it is situated."[108]

The grid accomplished a certain deceptive homogeneity. Land came in uniform parcel sizes, each distinguished only by the township and range number. Ideal for initial location purposes and for later transactions, it was a colourless departure from named estates, such as those of colonial Virginia. The grid's ordinariness deflected attention from the land itself and objectified plane areas ranged across maps of squares. It adapted awkwardly to sharply varying landscapes, and, in some arid parts of the American west, squares climbed watered valleys zigzag fashion. Despite its authors' hopes, moreover, the grid failed to banish litigation over property rights. Paul Gates concludes that

"controversies between conflicting claimants reached heights of excite-
ment and open warfare in Iowa, Kansas, and California that exceeded
anything witnessed in Kentucky."[109]

THE SHAPES OF OCCUPATION:
BRITISH EMPIRE II

Having lost the thirteen American colonies, the British forfeited the
challenge of dealing creatively with frontier lands in a major way until
after 1815. Following the Napoleonic wars, the British empire
responded immediately to major issues of land allocation in Upper
Canada, the Cape of Good Hope, and New South Wales, which
included Van Diemen's Land (Tasmania). European imperialism in the
nineteenth century involved different sorts of colonies. There were
exploitation colonies that extracted wealth by pulling out resources or
levying taxes. The Dutch East Indies, British India, and French Indochina
are examples. There were also maritime enclaves that permitted the
commercial penetration of hinterlands. Hong Kong and Singapore
served the British. Then there were the settlement colonies, where
resident farmers and planters made use of cheap land and, in some
cases, the cheap labour of an indigenous population.[110] Their governments devoted attention to land affairs, although the unique beginnings
of Upper Canada, the Cape, and New South Wales furnish unlikely
candidates for comparisons with each other or the United States. Not
only were their socio-political origins distinctive, but Upper Canada's
cooler climate and tree cover constrained the occupation of land.
Grazing exploded on the warm and relatively open frontiers of the
Cape Colony, in New South Wales, and also the Argentine provinces
of Buenos Aires and Pampa. Winter and forests kept grazing estates
out of Upper Canada; speculators and settlers understood this to be a
country of small farms.[111]

In Upper Canada, imperial authorities first planned a colony for
loyalist refugees from America. Preliminary surveying and settling of
loyalists transpired in the 1780s and 1790s. The colony would shortly
experience commonplace property issues as newcomers without loyalist credentials entered for the cheap land. New South Wales was
founded in 1788 as a penal colony. At the Cape, the British arrived to
stay in 1806 because of the route to India. In these last two colonies,
attempts to contain occupation within organized districts fell afoul of
mobile grazers. At the three disparate places – Upper Canada, New
South Wales, and the Cape Colony – and in the satellite colonies of
New South Wales, administrators addressed standard predicaments,
ones like those encountered in the thirteen colonies and early republic:

the presence of first peoples on frontiers; the operations of squatters and their disregard for government rules; the importance of occupation; the accumulation of land by speculators; the costs of mapping and organizing the land; and the challenge of extracting revenues from settlers. The particular remedies were the unique outcomes of local politics and natural environments. At the same time, however, the shaping of property rights in roughly standard ways was a global phenomenon. Tract shapes in Australia and New Zealand expressed the shrewd analysis of landhunters and grazers as they interpreted local circumstances and occupied odd shapes that reached out to enfold desired resources; meanwhile, government countered with a succession of regulations insisting on straight lines and rectangles "as far as is practicable."[112] There was, however, no fixed imperial standard.

Rectangles and squares were the usual shapes of land parcels, although the river lots in New France, granted in the seventeenth and eighteenth centuries, were narrow, deep strips to allow occupants access to the water. French settlers at outposts along the Mississippi applied the same practice, and so too did the colonists in the Red River settlement of Rupert's Land. There was also a more unusual variation in shape. It first appeared at the Cape and spread across southern Africa. Starting in the early eighteenth century, the Dutch East India Company allowed squatters near Cape Town annual usufructuary licences. Known as loan farms (*lening plaatsen*), they provided revenue for the company and extended formal interests to grazers. By the late eighteenth century, loan farms meant certain things to their possessors. Farms were moored to an identifiable pivot point (*ordinnatie*), a supposedly fixed centre, such as a spring, a house, or a marker beacon.[113] From their beacons, farms ranged outward, taking the shape of a huge circle, customarily to a radius of a half-hour walk, or 1,500 to 2,000 paces. Generally, this provided 3,000 morgen, or slightly over 6,000 acres.[114] Where the ordinnatie consisted of a spring (*fontein*), it furnished the farm's name and represented the essential property that the parties spoke of when transferring grazing rights.[115] Out of these loose, yet well-understood arrangements, abundant problems tumbled into the courts. Centre points were notoriously mobile. Farmers shifted them so that their farm circumferences could encompass better land and more water, and springs were unstable. What constituted a walking pace was nebulous.

Aggressive neighbours, spiteful family members, and grasping executors put boundary disputes before the Court of Justice. Where encroachment was proven, the Dutch East India Company and successor governments cancelled the new loan farm, forcing the occupant to scramble for another place. Petitioners often occupied the land before

securing approval. Inexpensive in the short term, because it did not
require a cadastral survey, the loan-farm setup eventually entailed costs
for the government and for a number of farmers driven to litigation
or relocation. Inconvenient transactions costs were not inevitable for
all farmers, because some occupants located in ways that left buffers
among them. Thus, for many, the arrangement's imperfections were
not threatening, while its flexibility and cheapness were plain. By the
time of the reform-minded Batavian government (1803–6), some occupants assumed that loan-farm occupation carried more property rights
than mere licenced usage. This presumption worried the Batavian
authorities and their British successors, because, if they conceded it,
the colony stood at risk of losing title to almost all of its usable land.
The unceded Cape lands were an enormous untapped asset, although
they were occupied.

There was another feature to loan farms. A countryside quilted with
circles jeopardized the realization of a countryside of snug-fitting,
adjacent farms. The circles left isolated, unassigned tracts, inaccessible
to all except abutting farms. This feature led to charges early in the
second British occupation that farmers squatted on crown land – they
were "using the land beyond the limits of their Diagrams."[116] After
1814, no new farms were to be granted in customary circles, and
farmers were encouraged to convert from loan-farm tenure to permanent quit-rent tenure. The double-barrelled attack on custom enraged
Cape *boers*, and both the land reform and the enmity that it stirred
contributed to the Great Trek. When *voortrekkers* bolted across the
Orange River, they took along the idea of circular farms. The 3,000-
morgen farm with its ordinnatie and boundary beacons at the end of
radii became a fixture of colonization in the Orange Free State and
Transvaal. The archetypal loan farm may have been circular, but
boers, locating water sources and reading soil conditions, also pushed
out in certain directions and pulled back in others. Circular layouts,
though rare, appeared temporarily on at least two other frontiers. In
New South Wales the initial form of licenced grazing (roughly 1810–
27) allowed the occupation of a circle around a stockyard.[117] The
Métis buffalo hunters and white descendants of Selkirk's Red River
settlers (in present-day Manitoba) wintered stock along sheltered river
banks and cut hay in a common behind their river lots. Each year, on
1 September, anyone could cut the hay there. Parties staked their right
by cutting a circle around the field that they wanted. A rectangular
survey followed by homesteaders swept over this hay privilege in the
early 1870s. For several years, a few old settlers attempted unsuccessfully to exercise customary access. The law backed the homesteaders
on their rectangles, while the dispossessed received land scrip and

assimilated to sedentary farming or sold their scrip to land agents and moved west.[118]

THE VELOCITY OF OCCUPATION:
ROUTES, RESISTANCE, LAND QUALITY,
AND PAPER

We have had an opportunity to consider scale – both the global scale of this study and the scale of the frontier lands under the jurisdiction of particular governments. I say more in chapters below about scale in reference to individual estates and to sizes of land parcels in relation to ranching, farming, or irrigating. I have introduced places – states and colonies – and so too a discussion balancing the histories of local places with the pursuit of universal themes. Of the organizing concepts mentioned in this chapter's title, velocity remains. It defines a rush. To participants, it seemed that land was taken up very quickly. While this is true, it did not happen with spatial or temporal uniformity. There was no evenly advancing front. Landhunters probed opportunistically, seeking points of little resistance and occupying well-watered tracts in arid regions. Not all advances were enduring. When parties of voortrekkers descended from the dry highveld onto the wet lowlands of eastern Transvaal, the *anopheles* mosquito (the carrier of malaria) and the tsetse fly afflicted the migrants and their cattle, driving the newcomers back up onto the central plateau of southern Africa.[119]

As we see in this section, a number of factors – routes and barriers, first people's resistance, the quality of land, and the availability of paper documents – profoundly affected the pace of land rushes.

Sometimes landhunters leapfrogged barriers or barrens to establish a new foothold and, from these nodes, moved out again in new directions. Once routes had been discovered over the Alleghenies in the mid-eighteenth century, the Ohio valley lands beckoned. Most remarkable in the western trek of Americans were the residents of the Mississippi valley who caught Oregon fever in the early 1840s, joined wagon trains in Missouri, and crossed the Great Plains, Rocky Mountains, and Great Basin. They wound their way to the Willamette valley, covering two thousand miles in five months. Some sought improvements in their livelihood, others speculative gains; some fled from debts, justice, floods, and malaria along the Mississippi.[120] In Oregon, they practised selection before survey and ran their boundaries as they saw fit, so that when a surveyor-general was appointed for the territory, his office found overlapping claims – a "medley of tangled lines and queerly-shaped tracts of land."[121] These transcontinental migrants – and contemporaries who went to Utah and California – passed over the plains that later fortune seekers – frequently grazers – were to occupy.

In the trans-Mississippi west, from the late 1860s to the mid-1880s, grazing spread from a number of core areas in a variety of directions: from Missouri west, from Texas north, from California north, from Oregon east, from Dakota west. Second-generation Mormons spread concurrently north into Idaho and Alberta and south into Arizona.[122] In New South Wales, the forbidding valleys of the Blue Mountains curbed westward migratory moves until in 1813 landhunters found a track used by Aboriginal people.[123] After that, the puzzle for decades was to secure reliable water sources. T.M. Perry's observation about Australia's first frontier in New South Wales holds true for frontier occupation in many other places around the world. "The spread was not a simple continuous movement, the extension of a single nucleus of settlement; it was a series of movements producing new nuclei often widely separated from the already existing settlements."[124] Rugged mountains on the South Island of New Zealand confronted expanding pastoralists who in the 1850s drove sheep over barren ridges into mountain valleys.[125]

In North America, landhunters travelled on rivers when that was possible and along valley trails when it was not. On no other frontier was there anything like the heavily travelled migrant tracks – the Oregon, California, and Mormon trails – each of which followed the North Platte River around mountain ranges and over plains. In southern Africa and Australia, the river systems did not compare in length and navigability with the Mississippi and its tributaries, and so those regions saw nothing like the fleets of rough-built boats that carried American landhunters and their supplies between the 1780s and the 1820s.[126] But southern Africa, Australia, and New Zealand had the sea. By a combination of overland expeditions following water courses and by coastal shipping, pastoralists in Australia and southern Africa moved the livestock so essential for outbreaks of landhunting. Sea-borne transport in the 1830s was critical to the spread of sheep stations in what became the colony of Victoria. In the same decade, shipping served wool farmers around Grahamstown in Cape Colony, while voortrekkers on landhunting missions searched for access to ports on the Indian Ocean.[127] In New Zealand during the early 1840s, adventurous grazers chartered vessels and inspected the east coast of the South Island for pastures, setting up stations at Otago Harbour, near present-day Christchurch, and on the Banks Peninsula.[128]

The resolve and power of authorities – who often opposed dispersal – influenced the timing of occupation. During the late seventeenth century, Dutch East India Company officials at the Cape routinely forbade free access to the northern frontier regions, but late in the century defiance prevailed handily. By 1730, most watered land within roughly 100 miles of Cape Town had been occupied.[129] On a number of frontiers around the world, during the first half of the nineteenth century, when the export of pastoral and agricultural staples prospered, occupation burst ahead, as well-positioned and politically astute land seekers anticipated the removal of administrative barriers or native title.

Resistance by first peoples also affected the speed and direction of landhunting. We saw above how Indian antagonism towards European settlement steered landhunting in western Virginia. Repeatedly, as Americans reconnoitred the continent for occupation, they met with outright resistance or the stalling tactic of a conciliatory sale.

Raid-induced panics blasted innumerable U.S. speculations. Writing about skirmishes in the Ohio territory in the late 1780s, land agent John Cleve Symmes described how they reversed a land rush. "One family fleeing from the purchase causes more detriment to the settlement than fifty staying away."[130] Ohio valley Indian village "republics," as Richard White depicts them, frustrated land speculation in the region from the early 1780s until their defeat at the Battle of Fallen Timbers in 1794.[131] In the U.S. south, the Cherokees, Chickasaws, and Choctaws ceded land in the early nineteenth century, to 1830, in the hope of holding onto a tribal heartland.[132] From the 1860s to the 1880s, on the Great Plains north of the Platte River, a multi-sided struggle for control of habitat included inter-tribal conflict that assisted white settlement by fragmenting and demoralizing Indian tribes. The Dakotas, or Sioux, in the 1840s and 1850s were pushed ever further northwest of the Missouri River and into collision with numerous smaller tribes, including the Blackfeet, Bloods, Crows, Piegans, and Shoshonis. The restrained inter-tribal raiding was not directly responsible for a great loss of life; however, it added to the other disruptions caused by white settlement, contributed to pressure on dwindling buffalo herds, and added further cause to the government's campaign to confine Indians to reservations. Therefore, although the chaotic raiding only briefly disturbed settler occupation, the dislocations suffered by first peoples opened the plains to white settler culture.[133]

First peoples checked European colonization in locales outside North America. In the Cape Colony, beginning soon after 1700, white *trekboers*, taking cattle from the indigenous people, by trade or raids or driving stock up the west coast, provoked sporadic raids by the Khoikhoi, whose water sources, cattle, and game habitat they expropriated.[134] From the 1770s to the 1790s, the conflicts intensified into a frontier war that caused the temporary abandonment of outposts on

the northern boundary region of the Cape.[135] During the early nineteenth century, influenced by the war with the Khoikhoi and seeking
better-watered pastures, trekboers and companies of "Cape coloured,"
who had been expanding fairly rapidly in a northeasterly direction,
"encountered Bantu-speaking frontiersmen … continuing their centuries-
old movement in the opposite direction."[136] Southern Africa "was
becoming partitioned into two types of societies, colonial in the west
and African in the east."[137] From the early nineteenth century to the
1850s, colonists and Africans clashed along an eastern frontier that did
not bend quickly in the Europeans' favour. Stiff resistance to land-
acquisition missions also occurred in New Zealand, where some Maori
took up arms to prevent further land sales to white settlers on the North
Island. Their resistance largely succeeded from the late 1850s until the
late 1880s. Pastoral landhunters reacted to the war and the subsequent
standoff in land acquisition by initiating land-seeking operations on the
less densely populated South Island.[138]

In Australia, resistance, though prevalent, only disturbed pockets of
occupation. On Van Diemen's Land (Tasmania), the government
planned a ruthless campaign that killed or drove Aboriginal people
from the island during the late 1820s and the 1830s.[139] In the early
1840s, the Aboriginal people in the western district of Victoria and in
territory west of Moreton Bay temporarily forced squatters to abandon
sheep stations.[140] Aboriginal people, like the Khoikhoi in southwestern
Africa, lacked the warrior-based leadership of the Bantu-speaking
tribes or of New Zealand's Maori. Officially organized or sanctioned
territories for first peoples also redirected the thrusts of landhunting.
The short-lived Oklahoma Indian Territory is an example, and so too
the enduring southern African state of Basutoland (now Lesotho),
formed in war and diplomacy by the masterful King Moshoeshoe in
the mid-nineteenth century. The general point is that first peoples
everywhere influenced the speed and direction of European land occupation. When the resistance stopped and treaties ceded land, land
buyers swept in, and vast territories were alienated within months.

Canada is missing from this sketch of resistance by first peoples. The
reason is not idyllic Indian–white relations, but rather the grave plight
of many indigenous peoples before large-scale migrations of white land
seekers spread around them. Before the advance of settlement in Upper
Canada (1780s–1850s), dislocations caused by wars in the seventeenth
and eighteenth centuries – wars among tribes as well as against Europeans – appear to have reduced and dispersed the indigenous population. Clustered mainly in villages in American territory south of the
Great Lakes, the affected clans endured as a formidable force in the
Ohio country into the 1790s. Meanwhile, in the region that was to be

carved out of Quebec to form Upper Canada in 1783, this retreat of Iroquoian people was accompanied by an influx of the Mississauga, whom early settlers met in relatively small numbers.[141] On the prairies, a flash of resistance in 1885 arose from desperation. Isolation had preserved the prairies as "the last best west" and postponed settler pressure until famine weakened first peoples. An opening of a different type assisted the Boers in their Great Trek across the Orange and Vaal rivers in 1835–37. A series of dislocating tribal wars on the highveld in the 1820s – the *Mfecane* – permitted voortrekkers, who crossed the Orange in several expeditions, to gain African allies and locate grazing lands.[142] First peoples influenced settlement everywhere because of their familiarity with the terrain. Landhunters required guides, translators, and allies. They *always* found them.[143] The cliché "Divide and conquer" was all too true here, because inter-tribal hostility and inducements to join white expeditions or punitive raids assisted with the process of bringing land into the private hands of colonizers.

In the great land rush, the quality of the land, grass, and climate, the availability of water, and proximity to navigation combined with the state of commodity markets to draw speculators and settlers unevenly across public domain or crown lands. Some districts were more immediately enticing than others. Lush plains, perhaps the product of a rare wet year, might trick grazers who, once drawn forward and caught by drought, had to move again. There could be no turning back, because land left behind fell to new occupants. During a series of droughts in the early nineteenth century, Dutch grazers near the Cape and at the distant interior base of Graaff-Reinet greatly extended their operations northeastward, looking for springs and rivers.[144] Demand for cotton pulled land jobbers in the early nineteenth century to rich bottom lands along the Mississippi – acreage later sold quickly and dramatically in Alabama and Mississippi. Because corn and wheat promised slower returns than the easy wealth of cotton, demand for tracts in Ohio, Indiana, and Illinois was merely strong and steady.[145] The great rush into the centre of the United States waited until the 1830s, after sales in the south.[146] English demand for wool in the 1820s and 1830s incited land rushes in Cape Colony and New South Wales and initiated a Sydney-based speculation in Maori deeds.[147]

Participants in the great land rush chased off rivals, precipitating a sequence of explorations to find suitable land that could also be defended against encroachment. Anxiety about competition animated folk on many frontiers. An example from 1885 illustrates a commonplace uneasiness, plus its basis in a well-understood consequence of unregulated occupation. When Samuel Gibson, a horse and cattle raiser from central Utah, addressed the U.S. Public Lands Commission, he described a chain reaction: "Very few herds can occupy any range for a long period, because as soon as it is known that good grass is found there herds from other ranges which may have been eaten out are driven upon it, crowding it beyond its capacity. The newly arrived herds have themselves been driven away by the same cause."[148] These remarks echoed complaints made by grazers in Australia and New Zealand between the 1830s and the 1850s. Sometimes, however, rivals for grass rose up from nature. The sheep grazers of southern Africa pressed onward in the 1820s because of concurrent natural hazards. *Landdrost* Andries Stockenstrom reported in June 1827 from Graaff-Reinet on "the distressed state to which the locusts, drought, and Trek Bokken [springboks] have reduced this district."[149] His neighbours pleaded for permission to drive flocks out of the colony. Usually the competition that pushed pastoralists further out came from other grazers. Competition likewise affected those farming frontiers where, prior to land sales, settlers staked claims and forced prospective buyers to move further out.

Velocity applies to unseen transactions as well as to land staking. All sorts of paper resting on various interests in land moved through frontier economies, including acknowledgments of petitions for bringing occupied land under freehold (southern Africa in the 1820s), grazing licences (colonial Australia and New Zealand), warrants (colonial America), scrip (the United States, Canada, and New Zealand), deeds, registered mortgages, unregistered mortgages, and in some places entitlements such as dower rights and the equity of redemption (second mortgages). To expand or improve land, grazers, farmers, and speculators sought capital through mortgages. It was not only Americans who "devised a mechanism for pulling themselves up by their economic bootstraps, raising capital for productive investments by hypothecating, often extravagantly, the future productivity of the investments themselves."[150] Loans backed by the collateral of land shored up purely speculative activities on frontiers around the world. Laws that controlled lending were loosened everywhere, until the land bubbles burst and revulsion set in.

During booms, land-backed paper of various kinds moved rapidly. In depressions, one great imperfection with landed property and its derivatives was universal – namely, inadequate liquidity. When speculation in land faltered, costly litigation accelerated. In many colonial and U.S. state jurisdictions during the first half of the nineteenth century, legislators introduced laws aimed essentially at increasing the velocity of transactions. Specifically, they tried to improve the quality of landed assets by establishing offices for the registration of documents, eliminating interest-rate restrictions on mortgages, facilitating mortgage foreclosures, and abolishing a wife's dower rights in a husband's property. Reforms to land title were calculated especially to smooth transactions, although liquidity remained a problem.[151] Land booms and busts persisted, and legislators could not guarantee a steady velocity to transactions. Nevertheless, reforms unclogged markets in important technical ways that involved adjustments to traditional English property law. Throughout the acquisition and allocation phases of the great land rush, speed, impatience, and short-term goals usually triumphed over the interests of first peoples, order, and assessments of natural environments. What traverses the topics that organize the next chapters – apart from references back to organizing concepts such as property interests, improvements, place, shape, scale, and velocity – is a theme of confrontation, between individuals, individuals and governments, order and turmoil, fairness and rapacity, labour and capital. Frontiers in their closing days were places where colonizers acting in haste grabbed at property rights and marginalized indigenous people when doing so.

Dr Andrew Smith's expedition towards the Tropic of Capricorn in 1834–36 increased interest in regions across the Orange River, helped inspire the Great Trek, and thus contributed to the fateful expansion of white colonization in southern Africa. *Voortrekkers* used similar wagons. Watercolour by Charles Bell, c. 1834. Courtesy Old Mutual Life Assurance Company, Cape Town, South Africa.

The first party of "overlanders" from Melbourne to Adelaide left on 1 January 1838. This depiction of the Hamilton party about 1840 suggests a well-equipped commercial stock drive. Hand-coloured lithograph by George Hamilton, NK3399/6, Rex Nan Kivell Collection. Courtesy National Library of Australia.

On the Orgeon Trail. "A view from the Summit of Independence Rock exhibiting the Sweet-water river and Mountains, and the Washington City Company corralled, at noon, July 26, 1849," by J. Goldsborough Bruff. Courtesy Henry E. Huntington Library and Art Gallery, San Marino, California.

Landhunters – members of the Horrocks party in 1846 – study a map as they look for grazing land in South Australia north of Spencer's Gulf. S.T. Gill, "Country North-west of Tableland," c. 1846. Courtesy National Library of Australia.

Indigenous people had encounters with surveyors that were more
confrontational than Samuel Charles Brees's depiction of a meeting
at Porirua Bush. Brees was a former principal engineer and surveyor
to the New Zealand Company. Engraved by Henry Melville, London,
1847. PUBL-0020–01. Courtesy Alexander Turnbull Library,
National Library of New Zealand, Te Puna Mātauranga o Aotearoa.

Group of Maori sitting outside a shop in the Wanganui area, possibly waiting for a land-court hearing. 1/1-000013 G. Courtesy Alexander Turnbull Library, National Library of New Zealand, Te Puna Mātauranga o Aotearoa.

Colonization involved visible changes to the landscape but also surveying and registering to serve a land market. The town and part of the harbour of Nelson, New Zealand, in 1842, about a year after its foundation. Drawn by John Saxton; Day and Haghe lithrs, London, 1845. PUBL-0011-06-2. Courtesy Alexander Turnbull Library, National Library of New Zealand, Te Puna Mātauranga o Aotearoa.

Hunting and landhunting were often concurrent activities. Squatters quickly occupied the prime pastoral lands of the Plain of Ruamahanga near Wellington, New Zealand. Drawn by Samuel Charles Brees, Day and Haghe lithrs, London, 1845. PUBL-0011-08-2. Courtesy Alexander Turnbull Library, National Library of New Zealand, Te Puna Mātauranga o Aotearoa.

PART TWO

An Appetite for Land

CHAPTER FOUR

Acquisition: Uprooting Native Title

Misdeeds by European colonizers expedited frontier land acquisitions during four hundred years beginning in the early sixteenth century. Colonizers took and held territory by force. Immense experience with warfare often gave them enormous advantages in tactics, weapons, fortifications, and organization. As Geoffrey Parker put it, "white men ... fought dirty and (what was worse) they fought to kill."[1] What is more, some went to stay, not just to plunder and run.

At the same time, European empires articulated legal forms when acquiring subject people or territory. The legal status of first peoples engaged administrators, jurists, and clerics in every European empire.[2] From the sixteenth to the eighteenth centuries, Spanish, Portuguese, and French authorities paid attention to indigenous peoples as potential religious converts and allies. The Spanish empire, committed to legal form, produced abundant government and court decrees that ostensibly restrained the colonizers' freedoms and most assuredly those of indigenous people. Within the Hispanic colonial world, few influential individuals favoured accepting unconverted Indians as people with personal rights or with interests in the land. The *reconquista* of Spain – concluded in 1492 with the surrender of Granada, the last Islamic state on the Iberian peninsula – conditioned Spain and Portugal to equate rights with religious conversion. Caution or scruples about the treatment of indigenous peoples emanated from a few clerics, not from secular jurists. Possibly because of the English obsession with estates and productive uses of land, Britain's empire, as well as its successor states, with several notable exceptions, accorded indigenous peoples legal interests in land. British recognition of entitlements originated from secular ideals adapted from a humanism of high culture that venerated the rule of law. In the nineteenth century, French and German colonial authorities acknowledged the legal interests of indigenous peoples and acquired land much as British colonial authorities had been doing all along – namely, by purchasing it or by claiming terrain alleged to have been underused.[3]

Since resource exploitation figured centrally in all colonial empires, rudimentary recognition of native personal and property rights was universally eroded. Exactly how that occurred in British and American jurisdictions is a tale that points to the doctrine of improvement, which privileged productivity rather than religious conversion and cultural assimilation. Variations among imperial systems in how they situated indigenous people in their worldview contributed to the distinctions between the English-speaking new world and the colonies of the Spanish, Portuguese, and at first the French. British colonial administrators and local legislators narrowed and manipulated a recognition of legal interests, aiming to efface the property rights that they acknowledged existed among true occupants of the land.[4] In essence, British and American governments normally accepted the theory of native property interests but set about assessing how much was occupied in terms of standards of usage and improvement familiar to the colonizers. Then governments exerted power through sovereign acts to acquire or expunge whatever native title had been conceded to the indigenous people.[5]

Attention to a particular legal form when seizing land was a trait often – not always – expressed in British colonization and American expansion. Governments and private landhunters alike shared a remarkable attachment to process and form, and that produced documents which occasionally exposed their deeds to questioning by scrupulous people and subsequent generations. Selected episodes in the uprooting of native title can show trends in the common law world. Moreover, the transition from the customary uses of territory by indigenous peoples to the introduced customs of newcomers expresses a more universal transformation. Often it was effected by European empires, although some parts of the world free from colonizers experienced transitions from subsistence to commercial land uses and, accompanying that shift, refinements in the means for defining, valuing, and transferring property rights. Changes in land tenure are part of a global socioeconomic transformation. In the regions represented in this study, however, that evolution occurred because of shocks from outside.[6] As this chapter shows, these jolts included first, imposed legal doctrines; second, an emphasis on speed; third, Eurocentric assessments of first peoples; fourth, sly practices by private landhunters and government favouritism; and, fifth, the application of military force.

LAND LAW AS TECHNOLOGY

The common law constrained colonial proprietors, the crown, and the people of the United States. Until the rights of antecedent inhabitants – first peoples – were purchased or otherwise extinguished, sovereign entities held an imperfect root title to the land over which they claimed the right to rule and thus could not grant a perfect title to subjects looking for *waste land* to *improve*. Colonial proclamations and acts affirmed this precept many times over (Table 4.1). Admittedly, in Australia and several other places, the theory of native interests was applied with a twist that degraded first peoples. Governors in New South Wales during the early nineteenth century – by silences on acquisition and by their land-granting actions – denied that Aboriginal people had interests in the land. Courts later sustained that denial by alleging that Aboriginals were "wandering tribes" whose allegedly nomadic ways meant that they "were never in the situation of a conquered people [such people retained their property rights]."[7] Prejudicial theories about human development, erroneous beliefs about a weak relationship of tribes to regions, and distorted convictions about proper land use led to imperial assumptions of *terra nullius* in Australia. It was presumed – in land-granting actions and later court rulings, rather than by any decree – that the continent of Australia belonged to no one. Imperial authorities upheld a theory that indigenous peoples could enjoy interests in particular tracts, but the theory imposed a Eurocentric requirement that they had to occupy the territory in ways that colonizing newcomers recognized.[8] This monopoly on evaluation allowed colonizers to trim or deny meaningful *interests* to first peoples.

Except where *terra nullius* seemingly cleared the legal slate for settlement projects, colonizing authorities faced tactical predicaments when clearing native interests. Exactly which territory was at stake? Who was empowered to purchase the interests? Who among indigenous peoples could surrender them? What was to be done if indigenous peoples refused to alienate their interests voluntarily? Could fraudulent agreements involving first peoples be nullified? Although colonizing governments conceded that first peoples theoretically held interests in land, they appropriated absolute sovereignty by one of three mechanisms: the right of discovery, the right of conquest, or the surrender of sovereignty by treaty.[9] These rationalizations for sovereignty originated from convictions of cultural superiority – only one authority could govern, and it would be European. With sovereignty in colonizers' hands, native interests in property rights were vulnerable. For example, by the sovereign act of barring the transfer of property interests from

Table 4.1
Effective sovereignty in property rights: assertions of the government right to exercise an exclusive right to purchase: America, 1629–1783; other colonies, 1761–1840

Place	Year	Measure
New Netherland	1629	Dutch West India Company practice to inspect sales in keeping with Roman–Dutch law, which after 1580 required all land sales to be reviewed by a magistrate
Massachusetts	1633	Act
	1637	Act
Plymouth	1643	Act
Connecticut	1640	Act
	1717	Act
	1722	Act
	1750	Act
Rhode Island	1663	Act
New Jersey	1672–76	Agreements of Proprietors
	1703	Act
Virginia	1655	Act
	1658	Act
	1705	Act
	1779	Act
Maryland	1676	Act
	1711	Act
Pennsylvania	1681	Proprietor's Instructions
	1700	Act
	·1729	Act
New York	1697	Royal instruction
	1777	State constitution
North Carolina	1669	John Locke's "Fundamental Constitution"
	1715	Act
	1748	Act
South Carolina	1680s (?)	Unclear
Georgia	1757–58	Act
Northwest and Canada	1761–63	Local orders
		Royal Proclamation of 1763
United States:		
Articles of Confederation	1783	Act
Southern Africa	1836	Proclamation
New Zealand	1840	Treaty of Waitangi

Sources: for American colonies: Cyrus Thomas, "Introduction," in Charles C. Royce and Cyrus Thomas, eds., Indian Land Cessions in the United States: Eighteenth Annual Report of the Bureau of Ethnology (Washington, DC: Government Printing Office, 1899), 549–644; House of Representatives, 21st Congress, Laws of the Colonial and State Governments Relating to the Indian Inhabitants, in Loring B. Priest, ed., The American State Papers: Indian Affairs (Wilmington, Del.: Reprint by Scholarly Resources, 1972), vol. 1, 217–68.

indigenous occupants to individual settlers, British and American governments could press their sale to the crown or state. This so-called pre-emptive right bared the very sharp edge of sovereignty.[10]

Most American colonies banned private sales unless they had the prior approval of a government body. Not all colonizers abided by the rules. Rhode Island's nonconformist founder, Roger Williams, a notable dissident in the history of colonization, made a private purchase from two Narragansett tribal chiefs in 1637 and ignored the King's pre-emptive right.[11] Williams acted as a principled radical with good intentions towards Indian neighbours. Defiant private buyers on many other frontiers in later years, however, sought personal gain from comparable direct dealings. Many speculators, cut off from crown support for their grasping designs, embraced doctrines of native sovereignty as legal cover to continue their schemes. On several frontiers, especially during busy decades of frontier expansion – the 1750s to the 1850s – speculators proclaimed, with references to international law and natural rights, first peoples' right to cede land directly. In a great irony of frontier history, canny lawyers, working on behalf of speculators, prepared briefs that foreshadowed human rights declarations in the late twentieth century.[12]

The first of these land-grabbing theories, however, was baldly unsophisticated. The so-called *Camden–Yorke* opinion (1757) supplied a narrow, dubious justification for direct dealing; it allowed a handful of major American speculators in the southern colonies later, in 1775, to feel honourable in their enterprise. The crown law officers who drafted this opinion alleged that grants of property from Moghul princes to the East India Company did not require royal letters patent, for these potentates possessed full sovereign authority. An edited version of this opinion circulated in the southern colonies; it claimed that individuals could negotiate directly with Indians for land, and that assertion intensified local disgust with London. Prominent southern speculators spoke of seeking independence if the crown failed to let them buy land directly from the Indians. In early 1775, a North Carolinian syndicate negotiated a purchase of 20 million acres from the Cherokees in western Virginia. Virginia's royal governor declared the transaction illegal and chose that awkward moment to publicize London's instructions (1775) that colonies with land should begin to sell it by auction. On western Virginia's frontier that spring, landhunters scouted as never before; word about land auctions incited a number of them to align themselves with direct buyers of Indian territory and thereby to defy the crown. It seemed to them a question of either hurrying ahead on these lines or accepting an end to cheap land. Irony was thick when Virginia's revolutionary government and the U.S.

government reaffirmed the crown prohibition on direct transactions. But in the post-revolution United States a shadow of populism survived; people who bought from direct-dealing syndicates could still establish squatters' interests.[13]

Marriages of convenience between speculators and theories of native sovereignty recurred. Later briefs dispensed with the inappropriate and recycled *Camden–Yorke* opinion. In *Johnson v. McIntosh* (1823), Daniel Webster, taking the side of lessees who occupied land purchased privately from Indians, advanced a natural rights argument. As proprietors of the soil, Indians had a natural right to sell. The U.S. Supreme Court ruled otherwise, upholding the exclusivity of state sovereignty.[14] Comparable arguments for and against allowing direct transactions resurfaced in Australia and New Zealand, where the American cases were dissected. In the late 1820s, John Batman, a grazer in Van Diemen's Land, considered expanding by crossing the Bass Strait and establishing sheep runs in the Port Phillip District of New South Wales. With partners from Hobart and Launceston, he became serious about the move in 1833. His syndicate petitioned for government approval; none came, so in early 1835 Batman "negotiated" with Port Phillip Bay Aboriginals for a concession. The partners claimed title to 600,000 acres, but Governor Richard Bourke declared them trespassers on crown land.[15] This may have been the sole instance of an attempted large-scale purchase in New South Wales.

Speculators in Sydney, however, were soon dealing with New Zealand's Maori. By late 1839, aware that the government of New South Wales intended to quash their deeds, they prepared an argument to support a case for private dealings with indigenous peoples. The government, too, prepared.[16] In mid-1840, the parties clashed head-on in debate. Citing U.S. case law, New York Chancellor James Kent's *Commentaries*, and reports from the crown's law officers, Governor George Gipps introduced, for the approval of the colony's legislative council, an ordinance to nullify private transactions in New Zealand. William Charles Wentworth, Sydney lawyer and member of the council, defended the Maori's right to sell. He had been snapping up Maori deeds. Like Daniel Webster, he appealed to international law and argued without hope of upsetting entrenched practice.[17] Land-hungry newcomers to New Zealand subsequently persisted in buying directly from Maori. In *Regina v. Symonds*, New Zealand's Supreme Court in 1847, after reviewing American colonial history and the republic's recent case law, concluded that a direct sale was good against Maori vendors – but not against the crown. Deemed important because it "involves principles of universal rights of the crown, the aboriginal natives, and the European subjects of the Queen," the decision was printed in the *New Zealand Government Gazette*.[18] The fabric of property rights, spun exclusively from crown titles, was not to be unravelled by speculators.

Quarrels between the crown and a few subjects over contracts with indigenous peoples played out to radically different outcomes in southern Africa. Dutch-speaking migrant grazers, leaving Cape Colony for frontier territories in the mid- and late 1830s, cracked the sovereignty constraint exactly as Americans had. They asserted independence from the crown. On their exodus from the colony, *voortrekkers* negotiated – at first – with African chiefs and soon abandoned that path and declared root title by conquest. They executed the most successful filibustering raids of the nineteenth century.[19] Bravado backed by legions of colonists showed that direct action could penetrate thin patches in the crown's shell of authority; however, courtroom arguments never cracked sovereignty by alleging indigenous peoples' sovereignty or their natural right to their land. Argument alone never prevailed, although sometimes, by virtue of capital invested and principles of equity, direct buyers secured a slice of what they bargained for. Obliged to appear fair to useful subjects, the crown, by grace and equity, could grant tracts of land to parties who bought from first peoples. If the territories claimed were immense, the granted tracts were substantially smaller; if they were small farms, the whole acreage might be granted. The validation process avoided any hint of indigenous sovereignty, and the concern over scale demonstrated a disapproval of holding land back for speculation.

There is a distinction between property interests and sovereignty that is critical to all efforts to understand British and American frontier history. Property interests pertain to private law, and its subject matter is *interests*; sovereignty, in contrast, relates to public law, and its subject matter is the arrogation of power to make rules. Sovereignty became one culture's mechanism for perfecting the conquest of another culture.[20] Sovereignty permitted acts that defined and enforced property rights and authorized the decrees, ordinances, and statutes that helped pry first people loose from their interests in land by curtailing their ability to do with a territory whatever they pleased. Public law affected private law. Private law and public law together constituted a technology of occupation, for, like engineering, they encapsulated knowledge with practical ends. State and judicial hierarchies wielded and refined this technology for centuries, to construct property rights first at home, later in colonies. Private and public law formed the refined countenance of Europeans' well-armed selfishness. Once governments concluded that trade connections or strategic alliances with first peoples should give way to a different relationship, one based on improvements to the land as envisioned by colonizers, they stepped up their projects of acquisition.[21] Colonizing governments punctiliously conceded property interests to first peoples on most frontiers, but then monopolized sovereignty. From that ascendant position, they insisted on their exclusive right to purchase from indigenous peoples. This was the right of crown or state pre-emption.[22] Beyond the raw instrumentality of the law, British and American attention to legality supported the colonizers' assumptions that "what was legal – for example, as defined in treaties written in their own complex terms – was also just or moral." That attitude was one of several cultural props that in the newcomers' minds authorized acquisition.[23]

When introduced to frontiers, property rights had behind them layers of historical incidents and meanings. Unlike trade and military conventions between first peoples and Europeans, negotiations over property rights were not born of mutual need and not founded on the translatable and more-or-less mutually familiar ideas of exchange and alliance. Rules flowed from one group, whose members could orchestrate to advantage an eccentric lexicon. The technology of law that colonizers introduced through sovereignty over frontiers excluded the habitat and social practices of first peoples, although those peoples had resolved conflicts and determined relations with respect to territory prior to contacts with Europeans. A one-way flow of concepts meant that when first peoples were approached about ceding property rights, even by scrupulous, sympathetic, and linguistically adept colonial agents, the parties bargained across a cultural abyss. Legal arguments benefit from nuance, and that made matters one-sided enough. The appropriation of sovereign power proved detrimental, because governments could establish rules that made indigenous peoples suffer if they failed to cede their interests.

Nasty surprises arising from land agreements generally affected first peoples because it was not their technology that framed property rights. First peoples, however, were not above tricky dealing. On occasion, they deceived white agents during land negotiations, but victims sometimes included other native peoples, and ideas of a united opposition to white advances were known to fail on account of intertribal enmity over land dealings. Hoodwinked colonizers (if we assume that they were fooled, not just devious) were not necessarily going to lose an advantage by accepting a tainted sale.[24] Some white negotiators accepted defective legal cover to secure a document to wave at white rivals. During vigorous quests for interests on a frontier, a tainted deed or treaty of cession was better than none. Legal challenges to illicit deeds could drag on for decades. In the end, what counted was that speculators and settlers would act on the strength of putative deeds and find in these documents enough hope to occupy the land.

When he learned of a 1754 sale of Delaware Indian land to a Connecticut company by the Iroquois confederacy, Pennsylvania Indian interpreter Conrad Weiser, who had witnessed plenty of land fraud, foresaw a tragedy.[25] Settlers would come, blood would be shed, and "the Indian would then be oblidge [sic] to move away."[26] No matter that this deed was tainted. In the late 1830s, the Weller brothers of Sydney bought land from several Maori chiefs near Molyneaux Harbour in New Zealand. Suspecting that they held weak titles, they plotted to sell regardless, because "parties buying will be obliged to support us to make their own claim good."[27] Cunning white agents and first peoples alike practised deceptions; however, illegitimate tactics served colonizers far, far better, because the technology for acquisition arose solely from their history. The colonizers' technology supplied ideas for agreements that were at worst unfairly forced. It also put discussions on a materialistic plane, when materialism was a highly esteemed British and American manner of thought. Only the colonizing culture organized the land for individualized allocation, and it also placed peoples on a hierarchical scale that devalued groups not dedicated to increasing production by the application of technology. During the eighteenth century and for most of the nineteenth, Europeans thought themselves superior on what they determined were cultural attainments – especially technology – rather than on physical traits.[28]

THE PRESSING QUESTION OF TIME

Occasionally, mitigation trickled towards indigenous peoples, when some decent authorities laboured to apply an imposed technology of acquisition with what they understood to be even-handed goodness, whose application took time and showed acquisition. During a brief stay (1682–84) in his proprietary colony, William Penn went about extinguishing native interests according to principles. The first two representatives of the crown in New Zealand, William Hobson (1840–42) and Robert FitzRoy (1842–44) pledged fairness. Periodically, to assist a fair process, authorities suspended major acquisitions to slow matters down, establish control, and prepare for honourable negotiations. Sorting out the conflicting claims among first peoples to their land required time. Claims overlapped, were in dispute, were in pockets surrounded by the holdings of other tribes, and were held on a temporary basis from another tribe with a previous claim. These complexities were incomprehensible to outsiders who hurried to install their own vision.

A famous instance of a government's seeking time, not yielding to the rush, was the Royal Proclamation of 1763. A terse decree issued after the fall of New France, it figured in many later discussions of Indian status, as well as in historical debates about the character of the American Revolution. Those who stress that that revolutionary upheaval accomplished nothing for slaves or Indians point to links between land grabbing and criticism of the proclamation. Robert Williams notes that Thomas Jefferson's *Summary View of the Rights of British America* "harmonized the colonists' resistance to royal authority and their self-interested pursuit of frontier lands."[29] Historians of the revolution have wondered, however, if the proclamation was a one-time action, not part of "fixed English land policy."[30] If the proclamation was exceptional, then condemnation by revolutionaries would appear a principled blow against an arbitrary deed. In fact, the proclamation embodied previous and enduring policies; it elaborated the crown's long-established recognition of Indians' interests in the land. The crown followed, albeit much later, with a series of declarations to close frontiers in southern Africa, Australia, and New Zealand (Table 4.1).

In these places, as in America in 1763, interdiction originated less from humanitarian sensitivities than from economy and pragmatism. The establishment of boundaries caught governments in an impossible situation. Frontier authorities were ever desperate to check unauthorized incursions, but simultaneously reluctant to smother enterprise. Thus the crown's servants in North America administered the proclamation loosely enough to allow some speculation. Some was never enough. That was the rub, around the globe. Distant imperial authorities clutched at the idea of impermeable – but temporary – boundaries that might assure peace and rein in the expenses of colonial defence until first peoples were ready for cessions, or could be overwhelmed without great cost, or were prepared to assimilate to what was presumed an improving culture.[31] This interest in a boundary of convenience was true for the British in North America (1760s), in New South Wales (the Limits of Occupation in the 1820s and 1830s), and in New Zealand (1840s–65). It was also true for the Dutch at the Cape, who nevertheless understood quite early the rapacious conduct of landhunters. In 1786, the landdrost for Graaff-Reinet, then described as a distant colony, was warned by his superiors to enforce the boundary with the Xhosas, although "it is further presumable that, in spite of the express prohibition, one or other of the residents has settled beyond the Great Fish River."[32] Rules and prohibitions riled settlers and speculators. Still, had they known it, time favoured acquisition, because limits to occupation existed purely to be rolled back.

The reasons for prohibiting colonization and proscribing private trans-actions were provisional. Although boundaries between native lands and colonies were conceived as transitory, speculators and settlers plotted in the here and now and insisted on benefits *pronto*. Timing mattered greatly. Policies respecting indigenous peoples fed landhunters' impatience, and the alacrity and audacity of individualism complicated frontier affairs. Some examples show what I mean.

Important commercial and diplomatic relationships existed between the Dutch – later the English – and the Iroquois in New York. When Dutch colonists wished to buy Indian land, the transactions required the gov-ernor's approval. The purchase was initiated by a white buyer who found a native vendor; the parties presented their contract to the gov-ernor for approval. In fact, this was nothing more than a requirement in Roman–Dutch law that all land transactions be confirmed before a magistrate. With relatively small tracts involved, the sovereign author-ity licensed individuals to buy native interests, subject to this standard review. The Dutch and English successors attempted to supervise pri-vate dealings to preclude misunderstanding that could unsettle the fron-tier, jeopardizing the fur trade and throwing diplomatic advantage to New France.[33] With appointment in 1692 of an astonishingly venal governor of New York, Benjamin Fletcher, controls on private pur-chases collapsed, and speculators and estate builders assembled exten-sive tracts. Delegation by licence was one model for purchasing from first peoples; another was government monopsony. Evidence of corrup-tion led to a phasing out of the former practice in colonial America by the mid-eighteenth century. Strategic considerations influenced this decision. The Board of Trade in London, during part of the eighteenth century (1735–75), worried about the swindling sprees in New York, because the excesses undermined frontier stability. It took seriously the military capabilities of the Iroquois confederacy in western New York, because the French, until the collapse of their empire in 1759–60, made capital of British slights towards first peoples.[34] Respect for the Iroquois waned somewhat following the American Revolution. Government land acquisitions in northern New York escalated accordingly.

In southern Africa, privately arranged deeds of cession were banned, but also attempted. Defying a direct instruction not to buy land, British traders at Port Natal negotiated a cession of roughly 2,500 square miles in 1824 from Shaka, the Zulu paramount chief.[35] Great Trek leaders negotiated usufructuary arrangements and territorial conces-sions from the chiefs.[36] Most famous, in late 1837, Piet Retief believed that the Zulu chief Dingane would grant *voortrekkers*[37] land in Natal, in return for executing a stock-recovery raid against another chief.

Dingane appraised how these newcomers handled his mission. From their success, he deduced that they were crafty and dangerous, and he ordered the destruction of Retief's party. Dingane's concession remained important to voortrekkers, who found the deed of cession in a leather sack near Retief's remains. "This precious document survives to today," reported nationalist writer Johannes Meintjes in 1973.[38] It seems to have disappeared, however, and is currently unavailable for appraisal. I say more below about voortrekker incursions onto southern African frontiers.

Military vulnerability and the tactics of land acquisition were connected in New Zealand, where administrators in the early 1840s recognized their colony's reliance on Maori goodwill and took pains to purchase land carefully. The superintendent of New Zealand's Southern District warned subordinates in 1845 to behave well. "The state of the Country consequent on the disturbances at the Bay of Islands renders it more than ever incumbent to see that every transaction with the Natives is conducted upon the most equitable terms."[39] A more recklessly assertive government in 1854 pushed through a flawed purchased in the Taranaki district. A perceived balance of power affected frontier land acquisitions, and newcomers seeking to build up interests in land regularly pressed New Zealand government agents to dispose of indigenous peoples' interests quickly and cheaply. Always there were landhunters asking *when*? Impatient ones acted directly, despite prohibitions.

Christian reformers who prodded Parliament and the Colonial Office in the 1830s insisted on fair treatment for first peoples. Idealists could nudge a few administrators, but well-meaning London guardians were too remote to superintend frontiers, and several of their projects caused unintended results that upset good intentions. Tragic was the fate of the Protectors of Aborigines, an office created in New South Wales in 1838; the experiment disclosed the impossibility of protecting indigenous people on vast frontiers by commissioning a handful of blithe spirits. There was little that native protectors could do to rescue Aboriginal people from white murderers, disease, and loss of habitat.[40] The reserves selected by protectors were dismantled a decade later. Aboriginal people who returned to tribal regions found them "disfigured by fences, homesteads, roads and towns."[41] In South Australia, protectors served colonization, warning Aboriginal people about the grief that they would suffer should they resist inrushing squatters.[42] The protector for New Zealand in 1840, George Rogers Clarke, was expected to be the government's main negotiator for land purchases. When his incongruous duties were separated, in 1846, land acquisition – not Maori protection – was the government's prime objective.[43]

Humanitarian reforms introduced at the Cape Colony, especially the protection of the "Cape coloured" in 1828 and the abolition of slavery in 1832–33, contributed to an estrangement of frontier grazers, whose flight from British rule precipitated decades of armed struggles on the highveld from the Orange River to the Limpopo. British humanitarians exercised sufficient clout only to effect negative measures – abolitions, prohibitions, and retreats – that committed the home government to moral stands with minimal sacrifice. Thus the Colonial Office in 1835 rebuked Governor Benjamin D'Urban for annexing territory on the Cape's eastern frontier and ordered a retreat. But what would happen when civilian colonizers accepted the risks and costs of incursions despite official censure? Armed with flimsy proclamations, Cape authorities tried but failed to control voortrekkers in the late 1830s. Frustrated Cape administrators, following in D'Urban's footsteps, announced annexations in the 1840s, only to have the Colonial Office disown them.[44] The military costs of sustaining the annexations, not just the lack of fairness to indigenous peoples, troubled London. Humanitarian influence on imperial policy was waning at mid-century, and the proof was in the handling of New Zealand.

Annexed to the empire at the height of evangelical influence on the Colonial Office, New Zealand was supposed to exemplify humane colonization. Within fifteen years, the government's aggressive missions of land acquisition tainted its relations with Maori. The slide from protection and good intentions, through negotiations, to deceptions, and finally to the use of force showed that frontier avarice throttled principle. A fragile restraining influence on territorial acquisitions in the 1830s and 1840s, humanitarianism exercised negligible influence on British imperial policies by the 1860s.[45] Still, a requirement that indigenous peoples' interests in the land be cleared by formal acts became entrenched in the ideology of legality that survived on British colonial and American frontiers. Humanitarians would come and go; lawyers went on forever. Ordinarily, documented concessions – treaties and deeds of cession – were necessities. This firm idea explains the many exertions of private individuals and government agents to obtain signed documents. Legal cover – even if improperly obtained – was thought important; so too, in a practical way, was the goodwill of the people whose land was about to be occupied. More often than not, of course, fairness in negotiated concessions was negligible, for reasons explained above in chapter 2.

In the United States, the federal government, particularly after 1830, discarded fair treatment in order to clear title expeditiously. As a basic operating condition, fairness required diligence and patience, because indigenous peoples, whose political arrangements typically depended on personal relationships, needed to consult widely and reach consensus. However, the timetables of restless colonizers drove acquisitions. On American frontiers in the early nineteenth century, roughing things out and making speedy progress achieved renown as celebrated Yankee talents. Immigration, democratic politics, and speculation contributed to urgency, and so the clearing of native interests in the United States from 1820 to 1835 degenerated, really for the first extended period on any British or American frontier, into openly sanctioned and praised expulsions and land swaps, authorized by legislation and backed with military force. For the remainder of the century, when first peoples resisted ceding land or intimidated white squatters, the government threatened or applied force. The army coerced removals in a multitude of confrontations, although government expenditures for purchasing Indian occupancy started to rise appreciably in the mid-1820s. By 1880, the total direct revenues from public domain were far less than what had been spent on quieting native title since 1776. The government subsidized settler colonization.[46]

Indian hostility to occupation throughout the Great Plains in the 1850s almost presented a barrier of opposition to settlement from Canada to Mexico. U.S. army policy, which initially centred on police actions that responded to individual acts of violent opposition, escalated into offensive campaigns against whole tribes.[47] From the end of the Civil War until the closing of the American frontier (1891), there were 800 recorded clashes between the army and indigenous peoples.[48] In Robert Utley's assessment of continental occupation, however, the army did not conquer Indians; rather the great westward migration, depriving them of subsistence resources, accomplished that result.[49] This observation invites comparisons with British settlement colonies, but before indicating parallels I would record that there were an unknown number of killings of Indians by white migrants and fortune seekers. That the deprivation caused by buffalo hunting was catastrophic there is no doubt, but the leading white attitude towards Indians throughout the period was casual hatefulness, and many Indians died as a result. Frontier killings flourished on account of a dehumanization of Indians. Prospector, high plains wagon freighter, and rancher E.G. Swan recalled that after an attack on one of his wagon trains "we wasted no time looking for dead Indians."[50] Peppered through his memoir without evidence of regret are killings by firearms and noose. Swan reported that around 1884 several men with his wagon outfit hanged a pair of Indians, presuming that they had killed a white woman. A sheriff from Helena heard of it, interrogated him, "bit his lip ... and said I think you done right."[51]

In Australia in the early 1840s, Aboriginal people resisted newcomers' incursions in countless small actions, which, though alarming to isolated squatters, did not amount to a war. On the Canadian prairies, the destruction of the plains buffalo (1865–85) inflicted a catastrophic blow on indigenous peoples and gave the Dominion possession of the west without protracted conflict. A war of resistance was fought in New Zealand, and many were joined in southern Africa. On the conflict-riddled eastern frontier of Cape Colony, the War of the Axe in 1847 was distinguished by three things: the flimsy pretext for an invasion of Xhosa lands, the viciousness of the attack, and the decision of the government to annex western Xhosaland, which D'Urban had attempted to do earlier (1835).[52] In New Zealand in 1860, an army marched into a region where Maori protested hastily conducted land-purchasing missions and assertions of crown sovereignty. The ensuing New Zealand wars continued for almost a decade and provided flimsy legal cover for the confiscation of land, some of it from people who had not lifted a finger against British forces.

SIZING UP FIRST PEOPLES

Misdeeds by land-seeking colonizers expedited frontier land acquisitions from at least the early eighteenth century to the late 1890s. Two historical legacies, however, have reopened the books on a number of improperly executed agreements. First, deceived parties passed on their lore about the inequitable concessions; indigenous peoples retold their histories. Second, the legal theory that first peoples had interests in the land was too fundamental to be trifled with. Law was harnessed as a lopsided technology by colonizers, but it was not an utter sham, not purely an expedient. True, where the idea of native interests was initially excluded, as in Australia, it has proven more difficult for first peoples to initiate claims involving specific tracts, for there are no treaties of cession to revisit, no dishonoured contracts to expose before the courts. However, the original basis for this voiding of interests – namely, the claim of *terra nullius* – violates contemporary human rights, for it rests on a repugnant doctrine of cultural inferiority. When we learn more about the universality of shoddy acquisition practices, past misdeeds may yet be exposed and corrected. That will require political nerve, knowledge about the history of acquisition, and concern for the well-being of indigenous peoples.

The technology of acquisition had a materialistic nature. When applied scrupulously, or at least when implemented according to its own standards, it required an evaluation of native entitlements – a materialistic

assessment applying the moral and political yardsticks of the colonizers, which were gauged to notions of improvement. When invoking
these measurement standards, colonizers might ask several questions.
How much land did a particular indigenous people control? How
fully? Could a map be drafted to show what was used and what was
waste? By the late eighteenth century, the acceptance of first peoples'
interests in land rested on a crude perception that they currently
occupied a territory more or less convincingly. However, the next
thought was decisive. If they occupied the land in a political and
military sense, there remained some questions about how fully they
exploited the soil's potential. To calibrate the scope and strength of
native occupation, governments implicitly calculated the costs and
benefits of expansionary conflicts. Colonizing governments rated the
military potential of indigenous peoples in terms of their numbers,
political organization, and strategic importance. The British empire
and the American republic established different thresholds for deciding
whether acquisition could repay the costs of war, because the American
public domain was a national asset; in whatever manner it was allocated, it was intrinsic to nation building. However, what London
fought for on the distant frontiers of settlement colonies was hazy. For
the ambitions of distant colonists? Which colonists? The grazers and
planters, or the working poor? Were frontier lands to give relief to the
kingdom's destitute? Were seized lands to benefit current or future
generations of emigrants? London had less proximate reasons for
aggression than Washington and withdrew support for wars in New
Zealand and southern Africa.[53]

In two critical decades of frontier expansion, from about 1830 to
1850, war-shy British governments required colonial governors to
restrict settlement to prevent provocative encounters between
landhunters and indigenous peoples. During these years, the United
States directed a policy of mandatory cessions and forced removals.
As it turned out, British authorities could not stop frontier occupations
and were dragged into annexations. Command from a distance cut
two ways: while it made acquisition seem unrewarding, it also allowed
fait accompl is. Landhunters and speculators precipitated the annexation of New Zealand (1840); voortrekker landhunting brought about
the annexation of Natal to Cape Colony (1843) and the Cape's brief
sovereignty over the Orange River colony (1848–54).

Prowess in combat often earned first peoples credit as noble occu-
piers of the soil who had to be treated carefully, but, when the frontier
was closing and settler governments ruled, warrior resistance played
into allegations of savagery, thus confirming unfitness for tribal or
individual land title. In the opening phases of frontier occupation,

sensible landhunters and grazers purchased goodwill and tried to placate tribes whose land they occupied. There was another material-istic calculation, one related to government perceptions of what a particular group of first peoples might accomplish as improving occu-pants. Administrators judged white squatters against a hierarchy of land uses, in order to refine allocations, so it is not surprising to realize that they also classed first peoples, making presumptions about their capacity to improve the land and conducting this appraisal in concert with assessments about the character of the land itself. They underes-timated the former and overestimated the latter. This imputed discrep-ancy furnished moral and practical scope for putting low values on such legal interests of first peoples as the colonizers would grant.

Some first peoples were assumed to make better use of the land than others; they were classified as more deserving. Such pseudo-moral arguments, connected with the doctrine of improvement, are unaccept-able in the light of modern human rights, because they are discrimi-natory.[54] Offensive representations need to be noted, however, for landhunters and governments made facile judgments that harmed gen-erations of indigenous peoples. In his 1917 sketch of squatting in north Queensland, Cuthbert Fetherstonhaugh averred that squatters assumed that Aboriginal people had fallen below a threshold of civilization; whites therefore felt justified in taking possession of the continent.[55] Colonizers might rely on indigenous peoples' skills, recruit native troopers, and negotiate alliances. Ultimately, however, they reproached these indigenous partners for failing to be European cultivators or for neglecting to occupy all of the seemingly unused terrain. In *The Rhetoric of Empire*, David Spurr writes perceptively that colonizers sought "to dominate by inclusion and domestication rather than by a confrontation which recognized the identity of the Other."[56] There was a corollary to the ideal of assimilation. Indigenous people could not be expected to make the leap forward immediately. From the earliest years of American colonization, settlers proclaimed a gap between the land's supposed optimal potential and its current usage and manage-ment by indigenous peoples. Conceivably, the most repeated justifica-tion for occupying frontier lands turned on a single word – *waste*: the waste of land, the waste of water, the waste of native labour. In *Changes in the Land*, William Cronon cites early-seventeenth-century New England commentaries that claimed that Indians lacked industry because they lacked the advanced arts of cultivation.[57] That attitude circulated on frontiers for at least two hundred years.

Colonizers' encounters with first peoples, from the 1620s to the 1820s, presented for their attention a multiplicity of indigenous cultures: Iroquiosian hunters and cultivators, Maori hunters and cultivators,

Khoikhoi and Bantu grazers, Great Plains buffalo hunters, and Australian Aboriginals' adaptation to many ecologies. Instead of respecting diversity as evidence of a skilful use of available flora and fauna, colonizers, driven to multiply their introduced and domesticated plants and animals, scrutinized and graded imputed discrepancies between indigenous usage and an expected climax of fecund settler exploitation. By the late eighteenth century a theory of historical development served these appraisals. A model of human development, such as Adam Smith proposed in his 1766 lectures on property rights and private law, had become a common and influential theory of history and social organization that "classified different societies according to their mode of subsistence, and accredited them, on the basis of that ranking with different degrees of sovereignty and proprietary rights over the territory they inhabited."[58] The theory treated property rights as variable according to whether a society was based on hunting, pasturage, farming, or commerce. Jared Diamond explains in *Guns, Germs, and Steel* that the indigenous peoples of southern Africa, the Americas, and Australia lacked Eurasia's diversity of animals and plants capable of domestication.[59] Colonizers' interpretations of people and habitat overlooked this elemental difference and centred on a premise of settler industry, hence validating a claim to wasted resources. Ignored in this rationalistic – but mistaken – understanding was the fact that for many indigenous people land was imbedded in social arrangements, sometimes through complicated overlapping entitlements to use. Land formations, moreover, often abided in myths and belief systems.

Classification of first peoples was brusque, coarse-grained, inaccurate, and expedient. It served the interests of colonial administrators and landhunting parties. Administrators took an interest in classification, because it could help them plan tactics of negotiation or provide reasons for shunning contracts.[60] Reports from frontiers upheld, in key words, notions about how a particular people supposedly underappreciated a territory's potential. A few exceptional statements by newcomers show that not everyone was prejudiced or blinkered. Nevertheless, more commonly than not, the ways of indigenous people, as well as of peoples of mixed heritage, were branded indolent and wasteful. Indigenous peoples could not win in a game of appeals to improvement, because arrogant landhunters and governments could always peg their productive capacity lower than fanciful projections of what a territory might yield in the hands of improvers. If the lands sought by Europeans were superior to reserves simultaneously being planned for indigenous occupants of the coveted tracts, that did not matter to colonizing governments, because the idea of improvement was not that Europeans should apply their vaunted skills to uplift poor territories, but that they should manipulate the best places, which would have been squandered if they were not in European hands. By this logic, it was indigenous people who had to accept poor land; by this logic, the Lockean caveat was pushed aside.

Moreover, when some indigenous peoples adapted to the improving ways of colonizers, they still remained subject to adverse evaluations – a circumstance illustrated by the U.S. removal of the Cherokees.[61] Indian agents in the republic promoted an assimilationist policy; however, around 1808 the War Department decided to downplay these efforts and to propose a land exchange that would place the Cherokees west of the Mississippi and protect their presumed traditional ways.[62] In the 1820s, the Cherokees were prospering by adapting to white society; despite these circumstances, proponents of the land trade characterized them as hunters and gatherers, whose native ways were to be conserved by a forced eviction. Their removal still required invocations of improvement.[63]

Characterizations of indigenous people as less than thorough exploiters of the land's full potential were loaded with incongruities. Walter Mantell, the crown's agent at Otago, New Zealand, in 1852 reduced Maori reserves, because he felt that occupants should not be allowed to live as idle, rent-collecting landlords. This would be a radical proposition if he had applied it – as David Ricardo and Karl Marx did – to rural England's landowning families.[64] Of course, the key word was *idle*. Who was judged idle was a matter of politics and power.

Law and culture – embracing the appropriation of sovereignty, the exercise of government pre-emption, a weighing of military costs, a model of civilization that put European agriculture at its pinnacle, and ideals of material improvement – fashioned the cognitive framework for acquisition. What transpired in the minds of colonizers affected indigenous cultures. Iniquitous landhunters supplemented the leading materialistic ideas of land entitlement with devious land-grabbing tactics. Systemic biases and crass tricks can be seen in selected purchases in the mid-Atlantic colonies (1680s–1770s), in the enforcement of the 1763 Royal Proclamation, in the dealings between white voortrekkers and African chiefs, and in crown purchases from Maori in New Zealand (1840s–60s). I note acquisition by forced displacement and conquest in remarks about U.S. Indian policy (1830s–90s) and the formation of southern African republics and Natal–Zululand (1837–1900). I describe *terra nullius* with reference to the early Cape of Good Hope, Australia, and British Columbia. There is one final set of land-acquisition practices. With the dissolution of any shade of respect for indigenous peoples' autonomy, colonizing governments in the United

States, New Zealand, and southern Africa empowered special courts and commissions to convert *surplus* native territory into crown land and public domain.

THE TACTICS OF PRIVATE ACQUISITION

Landhunters attempted to manipulate governments, and they appealed to the doctrine of improvement. As well, they plied sharp practices to swindle first peoples. Even the more decent colonizers undermined indigenous people. The land-acquisition practices of William Penn in Pennsylvania suggest fair and just steps. To sell land to colonists, estate builders, and speculators, Penn recognized, he had to remove native interests and secure absolute title. He sent his cousin William Markham as purchasing agent. Markham consulted with Captain Lasse Cock, an experienced settler fluent in the Delaware dialect.[65] Markham and Cock summoned a meeting of the Delawares, following the sound principle that a number of members of first peoples should be present when deeds of cession were signed. Compared to other land buyers, Markham was generous. Largesse stimulated a chain of sales. When Penn arrived, he participated in the negotiations and stressed that cessions *permanently* conveyed all rights. On many frontiers in later years, first peoples, when familiar with the distinctions between selling use rights for a limited period and parting with all rights forever, preferred the former, to the distress of official land buyers. There is no record of the Delawares' thoughts about Penn's strict condition. A relatively fair buyer such as Penn still pursued exact ends that fell far outside the vendors' cosmos.

Another drawback to Penn's contracts concerned their vague rendering of space, which was not necessarily a deliberate act of bad faith – more likely a consequence of haste and economy. Many deeds described an ambiguous boundary, such as the distance that a horse and rider or a man walking could travel in a day or two. Thus, although Penn worked methodically to purchase Indian interests, consulted Indians in groups, paid with relatively decent goods, was a cordial host, and had no wish to displace Indian villages, he kept a keen watch on his affairs and left behind uncertain boundaries.[66] The latter nicely served his sons and their agent, James Logan, in a notorious affair.

In 1735, Logan assembled a number of Delawares and showed a *copy* of a purported deed made by Penn in 1685. It appeared to cede land north of a certain creek, although the Delawares disputed the authority of the chiefs who allegedly signed. Time and again, around the world, similar complaints would be heard: the chiefs had no authority in that area, had usurped it, or had not consulted all interested

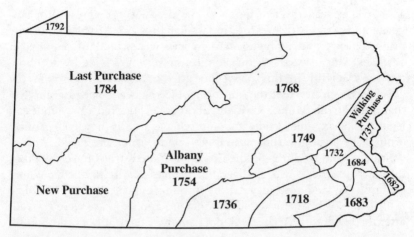

Map 4.1
Pennsylvania land purchased from the Indians, 1682–1792
Source: Bryce Jordan et al., *The Atlas of Pennsylvania* (Philadelphia: Temple University Press, 1989), 82.

clans. Logan smothered protests by getting ten chiefs from the Iroquois, erstwhile allies of the Delawares, to vouch for the 1685 deed. A meeting was held to settle the Delaware matter in 1737. The Delawares were tricked into signing a confirmation of a written description that they could not read and whereby they ceded the disputed territory. They also agreed to a determination of the boundary that had been described only as a day and a half's walk. Logan had already prepared to exploit the loose term by clearing a trail and hiring three men to undertake a fast walk. Two walkers dropped out from exhaustion, while a third one covered fifty-five miles in eighteen hours. With its length so determined, the tract comprised over 750,000 acres (Map 4.1).[67]

The Iroquois knew the stings of sharp dealings. A number of tainted private purchases in New York had been approved in the 1690s. Of all the tribes in the Iroquois confederacy, the Mohawks, located near Albany, experienced the most trouble because landhunters and speculators could see the potential for settlement up the Hudson River. Indian vendors, bribed and pretending to be great men, sold without tribal consent. In 1710, a vigilant sachem of the Mohawks, asked the governor to assure that future purchases were made in public with members of all clans present. For a while, speculators who obtained deeds by fraud did not press their claims. Indian complaints, however, resumed in the mid-1730s, when surveyors arrived to measure large speculative tracts. An astounded surveyor-general encountered

Mohawk grievances. The terms of the deeds were expressed in language and systems of measure unfamiliar to them. Missing boundary measurements and ambiguous references were standard features in swindles. Was a tract six square miles or six miles wide by an undetermined length? In this particular attempt at deceit in 1736, the governor suspected that the improper objective was to get a grant "on that side of the Mohawks River about one hundred thirty miles in length and six miles wide."[68] This scheme to slip a vague petition around the local government and get London's consent failed. Abuses continued, and by 1761–62 the Board of Trade warned the crown that dishonest dealings with indigenous peoples' lands harmed colonial welfare. The land grabs against the Iroquois influenced imperial policy in British North America.[69] The principles applied there were revived, after the revolution, in the remaining and new territories of the empire.

The crown's plans for eastern North America by the early 1760s combined an intolerance for egregiously corrupt land speculation with designs for the territory acquired by the surrender of New France. Civil governments were to be set up in Nova Scotia and Florida, which were to encourage settlement and relieve pressure on newly secured western lands. The Royal Proclamation of 1763 dealt directly with this pressure by prohibiting settlement in the territory west of watersheds that discharged into the Atlantic. As well, when indigenous peoples wished voluntarily to relinquish any of these reserved lands, they could sell them only to the crown. For the next hundred years, wherever British settlement colonies encountered substantial numbers of well-organized indigenous peoples, integral features of this proclamation resurfaced. In southern Africa, Australia, and New Zealand, the crown cordoned off organized colonies, which were open for approved settlement. What were the penalties and benefits of entering regions where landhunting was prohibited? In the United States, the answer was complicated, but by the late 1850s, a few land jobbers in Kansas directly bought Indian lands with impunity.[70]

Almost a century before this brazen defiance of the ban in Kansas, loopholes kept alive speculation and incited settler impatience. Loopholes allowed landhunters to continue surveying in the Ohio valley after the Royal Proclamation. Their activities outraged some indigenous peoples and persuaded others to consider selling. Although new patents could not be issued in the region reserved by the crown, legitimate claims for land – military warrants, for example – would have to be honoured when and where indigenous peoples ceded their interests to the crown, when and where the Indian line was rolled back. Speculators gambled, with favourable odds, that in the fulness of time the crown would secure land for colonization, and when that happened illegally occupied tracts covered with warrants would have good titles. In 1767, George Washington knew that this process was about to engulf a portion of the Indian territory. He had thousands of acres marked "to secure some of the most valuable Lands in the King's part which I think may be accomplished after a while not withstanding the proclamation that restrains it at present and prohibits the settling of Them at all for I can never look upon that Proclamation in any other light (but this I say between ourselves) than as a temporary expedient to quiet the Minds of the Indians and must fall of course in a few years especially when those Indians are consenting to our Occupying the Lands."[71] Washington had been informed that the crown was likely to purchase a block of Indian territory, and he appreciated that surveys and warrants could secure the best of the imminent crown lands.[72] Evidence of possession and surveys deflected competing speculators, while warrants secured title once an area became crown land. This sort of one–two salvo from an astute and well-equipped speculator would be tried by others in other places. For example, west of the Mississippi, after the purchase of Louisiana, speculators combined occupation with French and Spanish land grants.

Squatting and old military warrants equipped speculators, but the British also considered fresh commitments for land grants in the Indian territory. General Thomas Gage "had it in view" – once his forces had suppressed the Indian uprising led by Pontiac – "to make a strong settlement about or near Fort Pitt, to accomplish this the King should have a large tract there be granted out in small Lotts."[73] Gage's vision exposed a willingness to permit exceptions to the proclamation. Later, he did allow occupation by settlers along trails and near forts where their farms could help victual an army. He promised occupants a right to a title in fee simple when the land was purchased from the first peoples and opened to settlement.[74] The licensing of white settler occupation before native interests had been cleared, accompanied by an understanding or commitment that full rights would eventually follow, was an expedient resorted to as early as 1734, along the Pennsylvania–Maryland border.[75] A similar practice broke out in the Hawkes Bay district of New Zealand in the early 1850s, where crown agents promised crown grazing licences to pastoralists once Maori sold their interests. Common drives, hypocrisies, and consequences characterized these hasty and irregular frontier arrangements. The licences were squeezed into existence by some first peoples' resistance to land cessions, the government's fear of widening hostility, and the fact that landhunters could not be restrained. From official standpoints, the

informal understandings put *productive* people on the land, induced
them to back official acquisition missions, and allowed pious assertions
that the crown still recognized a territory as Indian or Maori land.
Licences hedged with enticing assurances failed to answer the landhunters' all-important questions. When and where were indigenous interests
going to be removed? The answers sorted out winners and losers.

Something basic subverted the Royal Proclamation of 1763, as well as
comparable decrees on other frontiers. Prohibitions were troublesome
to enforce. Frontier officials and soldiers – too few, too merciful to
their compatriots, or too compromised – could not chase out people
who merely ignored the law. The United States in 1793 and New
Zealand in 1846 codified fines for defiance of bans on direct transactions for native lands, but these punitive measures were unevenly
applied. At heart, the Proclamation of 1763 refined an older recognition of first peoples' legal interests, identified that they applied to
western lands, and attempted to standardize how they should be
cleared in future.[76] Defiant landhunters counted on government for-
bearance. Events in the Juniata valley – eventually part of Pennsylvania
– exemplify how raw occupation and official empathy could undermine
prohibitions. Since the early 1740s, the Iroquois had protested about
squatters in this region east of the Allegheny Mountains. On one
occasion in 1742, Pennsylvania directed magistrates to remove them,
only to hear from the Iroquois that these men proceeded with their
own surveys. To repair relations in 1750, when the French were
courting the Iroquois, Pennsylvania sent its unofficial Indian agent,
George Croghan, to do something about squatting. Croghan, with
other justices of the peace, encountered about sixty squatters in the
Juniata valley. After deliberations, authorities decided to appease the
Iroquois by burning a few log cabins, of a type that could be rebuilt
in a day or two. Today the town of Burnt Cabins, just west of the
Tuscarora Tunnel on the Pennsylvania Turnpike, marks the spot where
the ease of re-establishing crude possession was conspicuously demonstrated. Four years after the incident, the Penn family arranged to
purchase the Iroquois interests to the land in question.[77] The next
procedure was absolutely crucial for speculators.

As a matter of policy, the Penns conceded squatters a pre-emptive
right of purchase. Those in possession at Juniata thereby secured an
interest that they could hold onto or sell. The episode is instructive.
Short of incapacitating criminal fines or bloodshed – both unlikely –
bans on squatting invited scorn. Nothing ventured, nothing gained.
For the Juniata speculators and settlers, and for counterparts who
operated west of the proclamation line, there were two preconditions

for a successful land grab: possession and the willingness of officials – the Penns in this case – to accord them an enforceable interest. The only feasible weapon against squatting and speculating in Indian territory was a flat, unequivocal refusal to issue any enforceable interest. At some point, vendors would try to assure buyers about the legal interests protecting their investment. Military warrants, the Penn's stated practice on squatters' rights, and occupation licences with a promise of fee simple all endowed land jobbers with a legal path to a proper title. Without these tools of the trade, land speculators who worked with raw possession alone – or with Indian deeds and possession – could find their backs to the wall, as George Croghan did. Croghan, whose career cuts across frontier diplomacy and speculations, emigrated to America from Dublin in 1741. Backed by Philadelphia merchants, he developed a successful fur-trading operation in the upper Ohio region. Business was good during the late 1740s, because during King George's War (1744–48) the British had cut off the supply of French trade goods. During these years, he constructed his base of knowledge and alliances. He learned to speak Iroquois and Delaware and had a daughter by a Mohawk. Solid mercantile backing from Philadelphia made him a curse to French fur traders, for he could supply superior goods. In 1749, he negotiated a private land transaction with the Iroquois for 200,000 acres near Fort Pitt and embarked on his path to become – in the words of Alan Taylor – "the most avid, indeed manic, land speculator in colonial North America."[78]

Croghan's private arrangement lacked prior official sanction. Year after year, the crown refused to confirm title to a single acre. There were limits to how far the crown would bend to help a subject, and Croghan's Indian deed overreached. It was too blatantly a speculative bid. The proclamation put his claim beyond the proclamation line, making it precarious. Still, illegalities never deterred Croghan from trying to sell *locations*. In 1767, Washington turned down a contract when he sensed Croghan's vulnerability.[79] The Indian trader lacked the legal capital – warrants, for example – to convert his "Indian deed" into a title, so his claimed acres merely inconvenienced others. Washington worried that, if he showed Croghan where he was staking land, the wily frontier trader would shift a few acres from the undefined land of his Indian purchase to form a nuisance survey. Croghan's unconfirmed floating tract complicated other speculators' preparations. There was more to Croghan's impact on the frontier than his nettlesome personal claim. He helped to influence western land speculation through service as a government negotiator.

To clear a few matters left unresolved by the Royal Proclamation of 1763, delegations from New York, Pennsylvania, and New Jersey and

3,000–4,000 first people assembled at Fort Stanwix in September
1768. To co-ordinate colonial Indian policy, northern and southern
Indian departments had been established in 1756. The northern superintendent, Sir William Johnson, made Croghan his deputy in the Ohio
region.[80] Johnson convened the Fort Stanwix gathering. Croghan
attended on behalf of the northern department, the colony of Pennsylvania, the Penn family, various merchants with claims, and himself. At
Fort Stanwix, the major imperial and colonial objectives were, first, to
clear the interests of indigenous peoples in a vast tract of land so that
the crown could grant titles, and, second, to do this in a manner that
helped establish the Pennsylvania–Virginia boundary. Beyond these
official aims, influential parties schemed to embed their private claims
to western land in the treaty. Croghan wanted his Indian deed acknowledged. Identical practices and aspirations cropped up west of the
Mississippi from as early as the 1790s to the 1830s. Traders put
Indians on credit books and pressed for settlement when treaties of
cession were negotiated.[81]

The Iroquois ceded interests in the region between the Appalachian
Mountains and the Ohio River for £10,000. Concerning the southern
territory of this cession, they presumed to speak for the Shawnees, who
were directly concerned and unwilling to surrender interests. As we
saw in the last chapter, this tainted cession led to war between the
Shawnees and Virginia. At Fort Stanwix, the Iroquois ceded about
15 million acres and hoped that this might divert the Europeans from
their own lands.[82] Speculators and settlers immediately grabbed the
spoils released at Fort Stanwix (Map 4.2). In 1769, with native interests lifted from their section of the ceded region, the Penns opened it
for sale and almost immediately took in 2,790 applications, each for
300 acres. They sold 1 million acres in four months. In western
Virginia, 6 million acres were granted or petitioned for.[83] The Iroquois
cession also covered land that was effectively under Cherokee control
and technically in the crown's hands. This double bind drove landhunters
there to shoulder risks.

Illicit private dealings with the Cherokees commenced. At this moment,
for obvious reasons, the *Camden–Yorke* opinion made the rounds
among irate southern speculators. Their northern counterparts, it
seemed, had all the luck with Indian policy. A passel of squatters along
the West Branch valley of the Susquehanna River, however, found themselves outside the new purchase, and lacking legal cover. Their solution
was the classic remedy of squatters aiming to hold land until they could
build legal interests. They formed the "Fair Play Territory" and
appointed a tribunal to confirm claims and adjudicate boundary disputes

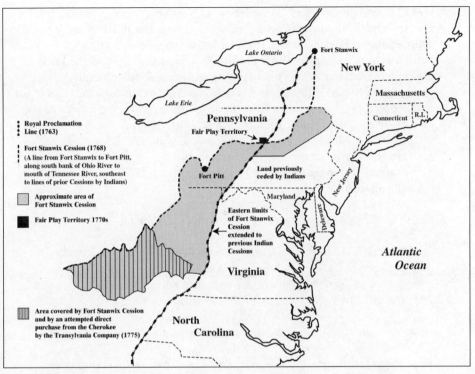

Map 4.2
The Proclamation Line (1763) and the Fort Stanwix Cession (1768), American
colonies
Source: National Geographic, *Historical Atlas of the United States* (Washington, DC: National
Geographic, 1988), 68; Kenneth T. Jackson and James Truslow Adams, *Atlas of American History*
(New York: Charles Scribner's Son's, 1978), 70; George O. Wolf, *The Fair Play Settlers of the
West Branch Valley, 1769–1784: A Study of Frontier Ethnography* (Harrisburg: Pennsylvania
Historical and Museum Commission 1969), 3–15.

(Map 4.2). In 1774, the British assignment of the territories beyond the
proclamation line to Quebec appeared to solidify the status of the unceded territories. Granting Quebec jurisdiction threatened to delay the
acquisition of Indian territory for settlement. "Fair Play settlers"
embraced the revolution, and, when the Iroquois ceded the territory in
question in 1784, established occupants filed for pre-emption rights.[84]

A number of Indian villages opposed the Treaty of Fort Stanwix.
Raids and killings in the Ohio country, from the early 1770s to the
early 1790s, followed from the Fort Stanwix example of a mundane
frontier practice – namely, a purchase from an indigenous people that
lacked approval from all interested parties. Worse practices were forth-
coming. To place a legal cover over more land acquisitions, the American

republic initially pursued a tactlessly aggressive doctrine; it claimed
title to land in the northwest by right of conquest from Indians who
supported the British during the revolution. A grand council of dissenting tribes, meeting at Fort Detroit in December 1786, repudiated
the territorial cessions of Fort Stanwix and several other treaties. The
victory of the U.S. army over dissidents at Fallen Timbers in August
1794 forced them to confirm these treaties and to surrender additional
land.[85] The United States thereby cleared title to land well into the
Indiana territory. In the judgment of Dorothy Jones, whose *License
for Empire* is a judicious guide to treaty history (1763–96), warfare
had drained the Indians so "they were reduced to colonial status on
land that had once been theirs."[86]

ACQUISITION AND CONQUEST

In this section we look at southern Africa's experience, particularly in
the years around 1840; at New Zealand's in the same period; and at
the concept of *terra nullius* and its role in southern Africa, Australia,
and British North America.

Southern Africa

The Great Trek (1836–46) in southern Africa had far-reaching consequences for Africa and the British empire. Guided by a handful of
patriarchs, family bands of Dutch-speaking colonists from along the
eastern and northeastern frontiers of Cape Colony streamed north to
an assembly point at Thaba Nchu. Thence groups shifted in two
directions: east into the future colony of Natal and north over the Vaal
River. In both areas, migrants organized short-lived republics. Their
forays led to the British annexation of Natal (1843), the organization
of a succession of states that became the Orange Free State (1852), a
federation of republics that formed the South African Republic or
Transvaal (1844), the seizure of other territories, including Southern
Rhodesia later in the century, and local law-making that minimized
the property interests of black Africans. After an initial decade of
turmoil, a handful of landhunting expeditions, backed by a few thousand migrants, decreed white sovereignty over a region the size of
California (Map 4.3).

When thrusting northward, *voortrekkers* revealed an acquaintance
with property law, native legal interests in particular. They had dealt
with it before. In the 1820s, droughts coupled with expanding flocks
and herds compelled *trekboers* to seek pastures over the colony's
boundaries, where some negotiated contracts with resident chiefs.
Some dealings were bold. Eighteen-year-old Carolus Trichardt had

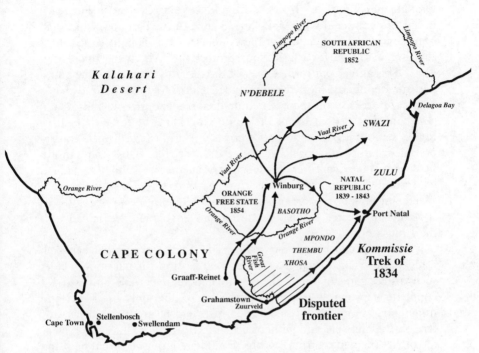

Map 4.3
Cape Colony and the routes of the Great Trek, 1836–40
Sources: T.R.H. Davenport, *South Africa: A Modern History* (London: MacMillan, 1987), 51;
Leonard Thompson, *A History of South Africa* (New Haven, Conn.: Yale University Press, 1995), 89.

been instructed in 1829 by his father, Louis, to drive 1,300 oxen and
8,000 sheep far across the dangerous eastern frontier to Tsomo Mountain, where the family leased 12,000 morgen (about 20,000 acres) from
the Xhosa chief Hintsa.[88] Meanwhile other grazers attempted, with
mixed results, to lease land just outside the colony, north of the Orange
River, from the Griqua captain Adam Kok. Kok, a reluctant landlord,
correctly feared trekboers as harbingers of white occupation. Robert
Ross concluded that by 1870 "the Griquas were already an anachro-
nism, as the whites were already in the process of gaining control of
almost all of southern Africa."[89] When the boers applied pressure to
Griqualand, they were concurrently attempting to purchase land
directly from the Khoikhoi in the same general region.[90] In their direct
dealings, the boers resembled Ohio valley squatters and speculators
defying the Royal Proclamation of 1763.

As they migrated, the voortrekkers sought permission from local
chiefs to graze their stock en route. Apart from temporary arrangements, they craved enduring rights to land and water between the

Orange and Limpopo rivers.[91] In mid-1836, trek leader Hendrick Potgieter contracted with Makwana, a chief of the Bataung, which had been harried by the Zulu and the N'debele. "If it is land you want, I can give it to you for I need your protection," Makwana told Potgieter.[92] This agreement formed part of the cessions claimed by the South African Republic. Another commander, Piet Retief, recognized that a secure future for his people required a trade outlet at Port Natal (Durban) and consent from the Zulu King Dingane to settle nearby. Retief set out to gain both objectives in late 1837. British traders preceded him to the coast by more than a decade. In 1824 a handful of Port Natal adventurers visited the *kraal* of the Zulu King Shaka, who granted a cession of territory. The white traders did not secure sovereignty under this arrangement or subsequent ones, only status as sub-chiefs protected by Shaka's authority.[93] Sovereignty remained with the Zulu king.

It is impossible to pin down precisely what transpired when trek leaders approached each chief about land cessions. A paramount chief such as Dingane of the Zulu – who had many kraals and warrior regiments – probably believed that he was ceding only use rights and trade concessions. Makwana, in contrast, had been uprooted by warfare on the highveld and perhaps ceded territory as well as sovereignty to voortrekkers in return for protection. He relinquished what he could not hold alone. From the late 1830s to the late 1840s, the colonizers north of the Vaal River met with many chiefs to negotiate agreements and alliances; land cessions lacked precision, and, as ever, there were complications about which chiefs had authority. Trek patriarchs, early republican leaders, and later Afrikaner historians invested the resulting treaties of cession with sweeping political and moral significance. Since the British government proclaimed at first that voortrekkers were subjects of the crown who had stolen into forbidden territory, trek leaders looked for ways to legitimize sovereignty as well as title to the land. Negotiated treaties of cession and forced treaties recognizing a right of conquest served political objectives. Did colonizers expect something else from these formalities? What were the goals of the trek?

Patriarchs rationalized the trek, decrying how British ordinances in the 1820s and 1830s changed race relations by ameliorating the conditions of slavery and then abolishing it altogether. For some Cape grazers, British humanitarian policies, along with censure of the boers' search for grazing lands on the borders of the colony, appeared intrusive and unhelpful. As Robert Shell puts it, "geography was to be the epic, heroic, but not final solution for the preservation of their way of life."[94] Added to their scrapes with the government, trekboers on the eastern frontier clashed with the Xhosa tribes, who bitterly resisted encroachment. Trekboers were hemmed in. To thrive as augmenting pastoralists, they needed new country.[95] How far were participants in the Great Trek drawn into commerce? Were they expecting to amass more than growing flocks and herds, expecting to stake out land enough for personal use, children, and sales? Were any of them speculators? Voortrekkers measured wealth in livestock. Dealings with cattle, hides, and ivory buyers were routine in Cape Colony, and itinerate traders *(smous)* followed migrants when they left the colony.[96] Louis Trichardt and Piet Retief's expeditions sought locations near coastal trading posts at Lourenço Marques and Port Natal, respectively. Gerit Maritz, leader of a major trek into Natal from Graaff-Reinet, was a wealthy wagon builder with investments in Cape farms.[97] These principals were attuned to rural commerce and were not mere subsistence farmers. Although expedition heads may not have speculated on a large scale, followers did.

In the short-lived Republic of Natalia (1839–43) – encompassing territory praised by Martiz as "a land overflowing with milk and honey, the air and country healthy for man and beast" – early occupants sold portions of their claims to migrants coming behind them.[98] To the west, in the Caledon valley, land was occupied in the late 1830s and early 1840s by boers who settled there with the permission of the Sotho chief, Moshoeshoe. While the chief believed that the white grazers would contribute to his security from attacks by his enemies, he and his French missionary adviser became alarmed in the mid-1840s at the signs of long-term investments and the informal sale of land to new arrivals from the Cape Colony. During the 1840s and early 1850s, in the adjacent territory of the Orange River Sovereignty, land speculation concentrated large holdings. By 1853, 139 proprietors held 2.5 million acres, and only about 40 lived on the land. Across the Vaal River, up-and-coming men soon manipulated public offices connected with land allocation to profit from private dealings in the 1850s and 1860s.[99] Unlike expeditions into the Ohio valley from the 1740s to the 1780s, it seems that no virtuoso land speculators led the Great Trek, although new lands offered opportunities to profit from buying cheap and selling dear. The frontier republics of southern Africa wasted no time in establishing loose methods of land allocation and a registry system.[100]

When their people were few and their military position weak, Afrikaner patriarchs negotiated with African counterparts for land concessions, but the *maatschappy* – the corporate political body formed by trekkers – soon justified their acquisitions through conquests and a doctrine of underusage akin to *terra nullius*. They portrayed black Africans in Natal as miserable wretches grubbing for roots in a country waiting for the labour of white husbandmen. Claims that Natal was

largely vacant were common and figured in a motion for its annexation
passed at a Cape Town meeting in January 1834. In support of
colonization, the attorney who moved the resolution argued that he
could not support "an aggression on the aborigines," but "the country
had been visited by the tyrant Chaka, who, like a typhoon, had swept
away the inhabitants, leaving it entirely depopulated and in a state of
nature. It is thus a country *derelict*" (emphasis added).[101] This assertion
applied to a limited region, whereas later rationalizations for taking
much of the land between the Orange and the Limpopo depended on
arguments of voluntary cession or conquest. By one "justification" or
another, white Africans took the best land from black Africans; mostly
they relied on conquest. Complex and fluid inter-tribal relations north
of the Orange, the imposition of voortrekker military power into tribal
politics and wars, and imprecise land cessions by first peoples to trek
leaders set the stage in the 1830s and 1840s for battles and land grabs
that punctuated the next fifty years.

Following Dingane's slaughter of Retief and his men in February
1838, the Zulus attacked voortrekker encampments in Natal. They
raided to advantage until Andries Pretorius took command and
reformed the invaders' discipline and tactics. Pretorius insisted that
wagons accompany all *kommandos*, to form a temporary bulwark
against Zulu infantry. On 16 December 1838, a well-planned defence
checked Zulu regiments at the Battle of Blood River. The victors
chiselled details, along with their right of conquest, onto a flat
stone.[102] At Blood River, Dingane's people took appalling losses, and
his brother, Mpande, subsequently conspired with the voortrekkers to
overthrow him. After Dingane's army had been dispersed in early
1840, by allied forces of black and white Africans, Pretorius, on
behalf of the settlers' Volksraad, declared Mpande "Regerende Prins
van die geemigreende Zulus (the ruling prince of the emigrant Zulus)"
– an act that professed settlers' sovereignty and depicted the Zulus as
newcomers [geemigreende].[103] Not stopping there, Pretorius blamed
the Zulus for an unprovoked war that incurred expenses, and as
compensation he seized extensive coastal territory, apart from the land
in Retief's deed. By deed cession and conquest, settlers in Natal cut
into Zululand from the south and emphasized their rights to "our
dearly-purchased and lawfully-acquired new country."[104] From the
1860s to the 1880s, the South African Republic – a union of trekker
settlements between the Vaal and Limpopo rivers – pressed in from
the northwest. Conflicts and further seizures followed the end of
Mpande's long rule (1840–72). In 1897 Natal annexed the remaining
areas of Zululand, and in 1905 it put on sale 2.6 million of the
remaining 6.5 million acres.[105]

There was another voortrekker expedition whose land-taking exploits show again the combination of conquest and negotiation and an outward show of legality. While several expeditions turned east into Natal, Hendrick Potgieter proceeded north, inciting resistance from the N'debele chief Mzilikazi, whose kraals lay nearby. To stop N'debele raids, Potgieter in 1837 directed two kommandos with the aid of native auxiliaries. Mzilikazi fled across the Limpopo, and a trek leader tersely but eloquently expressed the consequences. "That which had been his became ours."[106] Mzilikazi remained a power, and Potgieter's colony concluded treaties with him in 1847 and 1853.[107] Shortly after his flight, Potgieter laid a foundation for land appropriation by putting the Cape government on notice about his purchases and conquests. "We bought a part of the country" from vendors who came of "their own free will." As for Mzilikazi, "we are definitely occupying [his] country until he returns our cattle to us, though he has fled so far away that we do not know where he is."[108]

Potgieter appreciated the technical niceties of land taking. Since the crown insisted on a pre-emptive right to purchase native land, he countered that his people constituted a free nation, not bound by this rule. He successfully dared Cape authorities to demonstrate sovereignty. Potgieter's influence continued. He established another community, towards Delagoa Bay in late 1844, to be nearer a port and to escape British attempts to regulate frontiers. At the start of the Great Trek, the Colonial Office proclaimed (1836) that only the crown could conclude treaties, and in Africa this interdiction was to apply as far north as 25°S latitude. Annexation of Natal (1842–43) brought the British closer to Potgieter, who crossed the line at 25°S towards the coast. Malaria soon drove his people off this well-watered, fertile land, back onto the veld and into a complicated situation. They occupied a region claimed by two tribes. In 1845, Potgieter concluded an agreement with the Pedi under chief Sekwati. In mid-1846, a *volksraad* countermanded this agreement and insisted that land should be purchased from the Swazi, led by Mswati. This sale – like many on frontiers – may not have been sanctioned by the rightful occupants, and it is doubtful that the Swazi appreciated that, although they were willing to allow white settlement, the newcomers would claim that the Swazi had alienated the land. The transactions gave colonists legal interests and a bridgehead. For the next fifty years, they exploited rifts among the Zulu, Pedi, and Swazi. By intimidation (1860s–80s), and later via land inquiries, white farmers and grazers acquired the bulk of Swaziland.[109]

In seven years (1836–43), approximately ten thousand voortrekkers had wrested control of major portions of territory between the Orange and Limpopo rivers. Their republics drove wedges into both tribal regions and politics. A cycle of encroachment, conflict, expropriation, encroachment and conflict churned for decades. The initial expeditions made possible this turbulent course, because the primary inroads of occupation attracted white settlers and inspired additional filibusters. Unlike the inconclusive wars on the Cape's eastern frontier, thrusts northward extracted land enough to form pocket states. Defeating N'debele and Zulu regiments, voortrekkers claimed sovereignty and property by right of conquest. In their footsteps, freebooting mercenaries from the 1860s to the 1880s attached themselves to African chiefs in return for promises of land to be stripped from the chiefs' enemies. Stellaland, a short-lived robber republic of 5,000 square miles, originated in such a pact.[110] Aggression did not stop there. In 1893–94, Cecil Rhodes's British South Africa Company paid mercenaries with promises of land in today's south-central Zimbabwe. London banned grants, pending an investigation of land use in Matabeleland, but the company registered the grants surreptitiously on its books, and in 1894 imperial land commissioners upheld the conquest and confirmed these allocations.[111] Mayhem and the impoverishment of black Africans in southern Africa originated from a white lust for property and from voortrekker successes. When the dust settled after 1900, many black Africans had to pay rent or taxes for the right to live on formerly black land seized by white colonizers.

The emigrating Cape Dutch took land away from a much larger population by force. Concurrently in New Zealand, relatively small numbers of Maori checked British regulars and colonials for nearly a decade, suggesting that the voortrekkers were strikingly well-suited for seizing their chosen fields of operation. After initial setbacks, the voortrekkers came to respect Zulu bravery, refined their own defensive techniques, and launched surprise attacks.[112] Regular army commanders in New Zealand, by comparison, underestimated Maori ingenuity in crafting traps that bled attackers.[113] British troops fought a plodding offensive war on behalf of New Zealand colonists, while boer combatants battled for their own expansionary mission and often could depend on African allies. Tribal conflicts prior to and during the Great Trek permitted divide-and-conquer stratagems. Terrain was unlike that in New Zealand. Although there are alpine-like regions in southern Africa, the grazing lands of the highveld lacked cover. Trek leaders knew, from experience on the eastern frontier, to avoid ponderous moves against mountain positions. In New Zealand, prevalent valleys and mountain ranges restricted colonists' mobility.

In addition to having clear objectives, commitment to a struggle, black African allies, and appropriate tactics, voortrekkers possessed horses and had firepower that swept over the veld. Their Zulu opponents – unlike the defensively minded Maori – clung to light infantry attacks and close combat. This preference was disastrous for the Zulus, given the emigrants' firepower. Embargoes on the sale of gunpowder and of muskets to indigenous peoples, moreover, may have been more effective in southern African than elsewhere. Maori had used muskets since the 1820s, and Europeans in New Zealand sold weapons and powder for decades before the wars (probably during the wars too), despite bans. In America, prohibitions on gunpowder had been tried on the Ohio valley frontier in the early 1760s and provoked distrust.[114] In any event, by their successful military actions, the voortrekkers appropriated substantial regions. During the next half-century, they severed piecemeal many remaining blocks of land by opportunistic wars and so-called sovereign acts.[115]

The Annexation of Aotearoa

In climate, topography, and wildlife, southern Africa and New Zealand were studies in contrasts; however, speculators and governments in both locations introduced similar ideas. Speculators scanning the coasts of New Zealand during the 1830s shared an appetite for land with patriarchs on the Great Trek and appreciated the value of assembling some legal interests through direct dealings with first peoples. Sydney land speculators were playing the same game as the vootrekkers at the same instant: negotiating private land treaties with indigenous peoples. Such dealings forced the formal expansions of empire, for only by assuming sovereign authority could imperial officers try to choke off further transactions and investigate the equity of previous sales. Parallels existed between New Zealand and southern Africa, although land affairs on the North Island from 1840 to 1855 more strongly resembled manœuvring in the Ohio territory from 1750 to 1775. The speculative urges were comparable, the landhunters' ploys alike, imperial reactions analogous, and outcomes similar. Though comprising only a sliver of the territory in the great land rush, the "land of the long white cloud" was transformed by ideas and practices much like those seen in the territory "protected" by the Royal Proclamation of 1763.

New Zealand had been for a handful of Australians and Britons – and for several Americans – a field of frontier mercantile activity until, in the 1830s, whalers, timber cutters, missionaries, colonizers, and outright speculators became ambitious Croghans and Retiefs. They negotiated huge, unsanctioned land acquisitions. From the imperial viewpoint, Maori were akin to Indians beyond the boundaries of the American coastal colonies, prior to the Peace of Paris and the Proclamation of 1763, or like African peoples beyond the Orange River limit of the Cape Colony in 1836. They were not yet subjects, but they were engaging in land sales with British subjects. Maori legal status and social organization, antecedent to the series of acts in 1840 by which the British asserted sovereignty, deserve comment. Possibly New Zealand's colonization was on the British agenda, and anxieties about law and order merely gave the pretext for intervention. In the late 1830s, trade, land use, and labour relations between outsiders and Maori were relatively harmonious, despite the absence of a European form of government.[116] Perhaps things had to change quickly. Perhaps worry about violent encounters was a reasonable forecast, not a hallow excuse for a planned colonization.

Property rights were at the heart of potential trouble in Aotearoa. Without realizing what they had done – how could they, without divining the colonial mind's obsessions with land, improvement, and the market economy's capacity to trade in deeds – Maori vendors obliterated any possibility of living in peace without a European-style government. Private land buyers eventually needed measurement and dispute resolution. Seen in the light of the practical requirements of property rights, a history of inter-tribal conflict sunk prospects for Maori sovereignty. This deterministic proposition – that freewheeling land jobbing doomed Maori sovereignty – has a glaring imperfection, since one official British action accelerated land speculation. Parliament in 1839 chartered a New Zealand colonization company, thus advancing a probable land and native-affairs mess that the Colonial Office, too familiar with recent border wars in Cape Colony, wished to nip in the bud. What were the choices: an uncontrolled land grab with possibilities for frontier wars and filibustering, as in southern Africa, or an undertaking to control and restrain landhunters?[117] The Colonial Office and the government of New South Wales were perplexed as to how to stop what they correctly viewed as peace-endangering enterprises. In 1833, New South Wales sent a British Resident to the Bay of Islands but arranged no extra-territorial authority. In southern Africa, a comparably ineffectual procedure had been shoved into the breach. The Cape of Good Hope Punishment Act, 1836, declared that British subjects who left the colony in pursuit of outside land remained subject to British law.[118] Sovereignty without effective control over a territory proved ridiculous, as the boers so capably demonstrated by their occupation of the highveld.

In a next step towards acquiring sovereignty over New Zealand, Governor Bourke of New South Wales sent Captain William Hobson to protect British subjects in the Bay of Islands during a Maori conflict in 1837. On his return, Hobson submitted a plan that called for the crown to purchase enclaves where British subjects would be concentrated. The scheme left a gapping defect, for landhunting would inevitably spread from the enclaves, like the one established privately by the Weller Brothers in the early 1830s. Claiming to be worried about being caught in inter-tribal raids in 1835, they asked the government of New South Wales to provide "a howitzer and shot" to protect Europeans at Otago.[119] Hobson presently learned more about the irrepressible lust for land. By late 1839, Sydney land jobbers and the New Zealand Company filed with their lawyers impressive-looking parchment contracts for millions of acres. Neither they nor Maori vendors carried out meticulous surveys. Buyers loved vague descriptions, so much the better to devour country later. Maori could manage disputes on use rights among themselves. Coping with feuds over boundaries and use rights among newcomers, and between newcomers and themselves, was another matter. Law and order were not conjured excuses for colonization.[120]

A decision to intervene left puzzles. How should the empire go about establishing sovereignty over New Zealand? By right of discovery? The British claimed a right to govern colonies in Australia because of Captain James Cook's 1770 expedition. By treaty? In the Indian territory of British America (1763–83), victory over the French empire was the means; in southern Africa, the voortrekkers often claimed land by conquest. After annexation, what would be the status of pre-annexation transactions? Would Maori, prior to having ceded sovereignty, have had a perfect right to sell their land to whomever they wished? Would that safeguard speculators? Messy answers were arranged on the fly. As usual, disarray originated from haste. Hobson, a resolute enemy of speculators, was sent back to New Zealand in early 1840, to suppress land dealing and to bring New Zealand under British authority as an appendage of New South Wales.

The Colonial Office required Hobson to treat with Maori for their recognition of the Queen's sovereignty "over the whole or any parts of those islands which they may be willing to place under Her Majesty's dominion." He could, at his discretion, decide to annex the South Island by right of discovery, based on Cook's expedition of 1769. This was a flimsy claim. At Waitangi, in early February 1840, Hobson negotiated a treaty accepted by a number of northern chiefs. Faulty translations and less-than-unanimous approval were imperfections.

Hobson delegated missions to take copies of the treaty to communities of Maori around the islands for their assent. Not all chiefs approved. Yet, as Claudia Orange points out, after the initial signing, "it was inconsequential whether Maori signed the treaty or not. Hobson's intention, of which Maori were unaware, was to assume British sovereignty anyway."[121] Hobson and Major Thomas Bunbury issued several declarations of sovereignty and more or less relied on the right of discovery – plus a very few treaty signatures – for extending sovereignty to the South Island. London accepted that these steps established sovereignty, and the government of New South Wales now formally nullified Maori land sales. The Treaty of Waitangi itself stipulated the crown's pre-emptive right.

A number of New Zealand landhunters, Hobson discovered, now switched from buying to renting Maori land. That too promised enforcement problems similar to direct land sales, and it jeopardized crown land-purchasing activities. Hobson responded with an ordinance that made all direct land transactions illegal in civil law. His successor, Robert FitzRoy (1843–45), convinced that a strict defence of the crown's pre-emptive right poisoned the government's relations with its powerful new subjects, relaxed the ban and allowed direct sales if buyers secured licences. Commanding a skeleton military force, FitzRoy vacillated and temporized while speculative landhunting proceeded. Governors were expected to rule, not innovate, and, for deviating from home government advice on land policy and other matters, FitzRoy lost his post to George Grey. Shortly after his arrival, Grey introduced the Native Land Purchase Ordinance (1846), which made it a criminal offence, subject to a fine, to engage in any land dealings with Maori.[122]

This measure resembled the strongest in a series of U.S. Non-Intercourse Acts (1790–1834), which likewise placed direct land buying under criminal law.[123] Together with appointments of purchasing agents, the ordinance attested to Grey's ambition to buy cheaply from Maori vendors. For the next ten years, agents backed by the ordinance wrested land loose from Maori. The ordinance played a nasty part, because crown buyers could tell Maori chiefs that they no longer could hope for rental or sale revenue, for this was now illegal. Violators, already on the land, were told privately that if they helped persuade Maori to sell to the crown, they would be treated well after the purchase. The most effective crown land buyer to ply this tool was Donald McLean, from 1848 to 1858. In 1838, young McLean emigrated from Scotland's west coast to a sheep station in New South Wales. Drought in 1840 led him to Sydney, where he was hired by a partnership that cut timber in New Zealand. Operating from the

Hauraki Gulf, he learned Maori language and customs. Requiring interpreters, the colonial government hired McLean and in 1844 placed him in charge of native affairs for a substantial part of the west side of North Island.

By 1848, the government was dispatching "Te Makarini" as a trouble-shooting emissary to Maori and roving agent to buy their land. A composite of Sir William Johnson and George Croghan, McLean possessed the former's political authority and diplomatic polish and the latter's linguistic skills, wilderness prowess, and cupidity. At his decent best, McLean bought land for the crown through a consultative process that involved open discussion with village assemblies. He knew enough to distrust eager vendors as probably lacking extensive interests; chiefs with real authority would be cautious and would take their time. The best practices in New Zealand were exactly what they had been in colonial America, but some of McLean's purchases fell short of standards. Moreover, in the Wairarapa valley in the early 1850s, McLean started to work too closely with local pastoralists, manipulating Maori out of their land. In nearby Hawke's Bay, a clique of squatters drew him into their schemes and arranged sheep runs on his behalf.[124]

Maori opposition slowed crown purchasing on the North Island in the mid-1850s. The perpetual question – when? – was now the colony's great topic. One attempted purchase from this period shows the type of hurry-up pressure that McLean encountered. John Munro arrived in the Bay of Islands in early 1857 to establish a colony of fellow Nova Scotians on 75,000 acres at Whangarei. He may have bought the land directly from a pro-settler chief, or he may have furnished money for the crown to buy it, on the understanding that he would get the title. Either way, he needed the area proclaimed as crown land, and to this end he pressured McLean. On this occasion, McLean worried about the breadth of Maori consent. A furious Munro felt that, if there were additional Maori claimants, they could petition the chief who sold. That vendor then would have to handle disputes, although the crown should, in Munro's opinion, proclaim the land soon to flush extra claimants out into the open before the chief had disbursed the purchase money.[125] Everywhere on British and American settlement frontiers, there were cries for expediency and a willingness to let others clean up the mess later.

Terra Nullius *and Dereliction*

There was an absence of treaties of purchase or cession on several frontiers. In western Cape Colony, Dutch occupation in the seventeenth and eighteenth centuries proceeded via sporadic land dealings between the Dutch East India Company and Khoikhoi. In 1672, the company hoped "to make a bargain with some Hottentots [sic]" in order that "these should declare us the true and lawful possessors of this Cape district"; however, five years later the Council on Policy ruled out peace treaties with the Khoikhoi who, they judged, "cannot enter into contracts after our manner." Yet in 1679, when permitting colonists to select land, the council insisted that they come to agreement with the Khoikhoi who also grazed there, "so as to prevent any ill feeling between us."[126] Over many decades, the western Cape's territory was acquired by conquest, informal purchases, and absence of formality. Some grazers made arrangements to placate indigenous peoples. Augusta de Mist recorded in 1802 that remote stockmen paid the Khoikhoi "a sort of tribute in sheep from time to time."[127]

Acquisition was a nebulous affair, and the British claimed the Dutch rights by conquest. Nineteenth-century boer republics, as we saw above, asserted sovereignty by conquest and justified land title by treaties of cession and convenient "histories" of tribal warfare and movement that undergirded the doctrine of *terra nullius* for segments of the highveld.[128] The South African Republic (Transvaal) in the 1850s articulated a blunt policy on land. By conquest and *terra nullius*, the whole of the unalienated domain belonged to the state, although tribal peoples could use land and water "so long as they behaved peacefully."[129] In neighbouring Natal, the British in 1846 established native areas by fiat and contemplated a trusteeship for these regions.[130] To separate the races, Natal proclaimed that removal of some blacks – "by force, if necessary" – was "essential to their welfare."[131] The neighbouring Afrikaner republics denied Africans freehold tenure even when they attempted to buy plots from white settlers. Land was held in trusteeship, and transaction approved by the government. In sum, British and Afrikaner governments similarly dismissed native title outside Cape Colony.

Britain claimed sovereignty over Australia on the basis of discovery and assumed title to the land on the basis of *terra nullius*.[132] The crown avoided dealing with native title, although squatters occasionally recognized Aboriginal entitlement in order to secure their runs, not against government title or one another, but against attacks from Aboriginal people. Widespread Aboriginal resistance to grazers' encroachment not only bears witness to struggles over habitat, but elicited rare testimony that a few squatters understood Aboriginal rights to land and water. The purchase of good relations was practised on stations in New South Wales as early as the 1820s.[133] When John Stieglitz crossed from Van Diemen's Land to Port Phillip Bay in 1836, he wrote to Governor

Bourke that, in addition to taking 1,000 ewes, he brought "sundry articles for conciliating the natives."[134] Queensland Commissioner of Crown Lands William Wiseman, in the mid-1850s, censured white violence as "wild and foolish." For their part, Aboriginal people were "not so utterly devoid of courage and pride as to yield without struggle that country which he claims as his own on which he is obtaining his food and to which he is undoubtedly attached."[135] Simultaneously, Wiseman underwrote assumptions about Australia as an open territory. Amid abductions and killings, he wrote: "destiny proclaims the certainty of the future of the white race and the final extirpation of the aborigines."[136] In central Queensland, where conflict was bitter, a few squatters negotiated arrangements with local first peoples and let them stay on the runs, as reserves of unwaged labour.[137]

A fatal decline in the population of indigenous peoples was a common forecast by colonizers everywhere except in Africa. Demographic predictions served the politics of land taking, since they also forecast an expanded range of wasted land. Meanwhile, pragmatic newcomers who had no stomach for war or murder acknowledged that, until first peoples disappeared, first peoples retained an attachment to the land. By reaching accommodations, squatters admitted that indigenous populations possessed habitat or entertained feelings for land. Squatters on Australian frontiers, from the 1830s to the 1890s, disputed among themselves whether to kill Aboriginal people or make arrangements. Considered in terms of squatter expansion, not legal theory, *terra nullius* was an illusion, for pioneering grazers knew that their operations displaced Aboriginal people and directly or indirectly killed many of them. Until the Australian High Court's decision in *Mabo* in 1991, there had been no formal acknowledgment of native title in any Australian jurisdiction, because of an official stance, first by the British and then by the Australian authorities, that Aboriginal people lacked the appropriate attachments to places that would have given them legal interests.

Across the Pacific, in British Columbia, most Indians also lacked treaties, until *Delgamuukw v. British Columbia* forced a reversal in the late 1990s.[138] Explanations for a failure to implement a well-known doctrine earlier are not clear-cut. When the colony was established in 1849, Governor James Douglas arranged fourteen treaties on Vancouver Island, but he later suspended the activity, and no one resumed the practice on the island or mainland. There is conjecture about why Douglas stopped. The British government refused to pay for clearing title, and Douglas, governing on behalf of the Hudson's Bay Company, was unwilling to draw further on the local treasury. It

Table 4.2
Areas and means of acquisition, 1600s–1894

Years	Colony or country	Acres (approximate) or other description	General means of acquisition
To 1664	New Netherland	Parts of New York	Private purchase approved by Dutch West India Company
To 1763	New France	Unclear, but extensive claims	Essentially *terra nullius*
Before 1775	East Texas and Louisiana under Spanish authority	150 million	Spanish sometimes recognized native interests, particularly in villages.
To 1775	Thirteen American colonies	300 million	Purchase or treaties of cession
1775–87	United States	65 million	Treaties of cession and treatment of Indians as defeated allies of the British
1783–1850	Upper Canada/ Ontario	50 million	Treaties of purchase and cession
1788–1991	Australia	1.9 billion	Terra nullius
1788–1804	United States	40 million	Purchase or treaties of cession
1805–19	United States	155 million	Same
To 1806	Cape of Good Hope	60 million	No treaties Dutch East India Company made a few shoddy purchases. Colonists paid slight tribute.
1820–34	United States	175 million	Purchase or treaties of cession
1838	Natal	22 million	Purchased from Zulu Chief Dingane Crown grants settlers title for improvements.
1835–49	United States	115 million	Purchase or treaty of cession
1838–45	Southern Africa, between Orange and Limpopo rivers, excluding Natal	Uncertain acreage; complex mix of peoples and land	Claimed mainly by conquest Some acquired as price of alliance
1840–65	New Zealand, North Island	8 million	Purchases by crown agents
1840–65	New Zealand, South Island	38 million	Same
1840s–90s	Pieces added to Southern African republics and British colony of Natal	Parts of territory from Orange to Limpopo rivers	War Treaties Government boundary adjustments Trusteeship manipulation

Table 4.2 (continued)

Years	Colony or country	Acres (approximate) or other description	General means of acquisition
1850–64	United States	300 million	Purchase in the east War in the west
1864–79	United States	450 million	After March 1871 by executive orders and acts of Congress
1865–1900	New Zealand, North Island	11 million	Crown purchases Land courts Confiscation
1871–99	Canadian prairies	485 million	Purchase of European claim from Hudson's Bay Company Native interests stilled by a series of treaties
1880–94	United States	150 million	Executive orders and acts of Congress

Sources: Charles C. Royce and Cyrus Thomas, *Indian Land Cessions in the United States; Eighteenth Annual Report of the Bureau of American Ethnology* (Washington, DC: Government Printing Office, 1899), maps 1–67; Arrell M. Gibson, "Indian Land Transfers," in *History of Indian–White Relations*, vol. 4, 211–29; Paul Stuart, *Nations within Nations: Historical Statistics of American Indians* (New York: Greenwood, 1987), 78; Robert J. Surtees, "Canadian Indian Treaties," in Stuart, *Nations within Nations*, 202–10; Tom Brooking, "'Busting Up' the Greatest Estate of All: Liberal Maori Land Policy, 1891–1911," *New Zealand Journal of History* 26 (April 1992), 78–9; T.R.H. Davenport and K.S. Hunt, eds., *The Right to the Land* (Cape Town: David Philip, 1974), 9–11; John Bird, ed., *The Annals of Natal* (Cape Town: C. Struik, 1965; facsimile reprint), vol. 2, 203. For the United States, territorial estimates are crude and dates somewhat arbitrary, because treaties and sales were often renegotiated. As well, tribes originally neglected received compensation for their interests after an initial sale to the U.S. government by another tribe.

has also been argued that he wished Indians to claim land grants and assimilate.[139] After the colony joined Canada in 1871, the question of land cessions was complicated by federal–provincial disagreements over who should absorb the cost of treaty settlements. Besides, mountainous territory on the mainland did not attract landhunters in numbers that provoked a stream of confrontations. Indigenous people were even forbearing in the face of trespassing on reserve land set aside for them.[140] No explicit doctrine of *terra nullius* rationalized the absence of treaties; rather, a false (second) step by Douglas put the colony on a path that later governments followed, and for a long time there was no incentive for the self-governing colony and nation to correct its deviation from imperial policy.

On Canada's east coast, the Indians of what are now the Maritimes provinces never concluded land treaties. A series of treaties, beginning with the Treaty of Boston in 1725, dealt with peace and friendship, and several later treaties recognized Indians as occupying particular districts. Hazy treaty language and nebulous grants for reserves created chaotic title histories, where the search for undisputed titles through the courts "may never end."[141] Restitution will undoubtedly take a long time.

EPILOGUE

In the second half of the nineteenth century, wherever desirable land remained with indigenous peoples and under British or American rule, governments supplemented or replaced with new tools the traditional legal technology for securing land. New Zealand established a land court (1865) empowered to individualize title and partition Maori land, so that holdings could be more readily sold to white buyers. The crown also retained authority to buy tribal land, and it did so vigorously. The United States terminated (1871) its treaty practices and dealt with tribes by executive decrees and acts of Congress.[142] In 1887, Congress passed the General Allotment Act (Dawes Act), which initiated a process for apportioning tribal lands to individuals and selling tracts to satisfy settlers' "land hunger." By the time the policy was cancelled in 1934, the Indian estate in the United States had shrunk from 138 million to 52 million acres.[143] Meanwhile, Natal and the boer republics of southern Africa placed tribal land under white trusteeship; the executive branch of government then exercised authority to buy, sell, and lease out tribal land. However, Cape Colony – where colonists had already secured much land – allowed individual African title and did not force the pace of change in African communities.[144]

A global transition from negotiated purchases to other instruments of acquisition signalled two things about the great land rush. First, it designated an end to frontier conditions; firm, unilateral, overpowering, subordinating, and anger-provoking applications of sovereign power now prevailed. Second, it attested to the fact that the doctrine of improvement continued to serve land speculators. Late Victorian innovations in land seizures rested on the familiar conviction that first peoples wasted natural resources by underutilization. By the late nineteenth century, the search for waste turned from landhunting on frontiers towards land reforms that insisted on breaking up great estates. Investigation and reformation targeted pastoral stations, cattle ranches, speculators' tracts, railway-company blocks, and, of course, reserves earlier set aside for first peoples. Governments also reviewed humanitarian legislation meant to protect indigenous people from further land grabs. In jurisdiction after jurisdiction, from the late nineteenth century to the mid-twentieth, when colonial regimes and Neo-European governments announced hearings to settle *once and for all* the land question, it was a sign that they were embarking on another round of promise breaking.

CHAPTER FIVE

Allocation by Rank:
Landed Estates
and Citizen Speculators

Power is the capacity to structure the possible fields of action of others[1]. In new worlds, one way in which European sovereign authorities exercised power over fellow Europeans was through the allocation of property rights. What was conveyed and why it was bestowed expressed prerogatives. There were remnants of feudal arrangements on British seventeenth-century frontiers. Aristocratic aspirations – and a few aristocratic practices – persisted into the late eighteenth century, longer in British colonies than in the U.S. republic. When a shift in power towards democracy occurred, sovereign bodies debated in similar terms the disposal of the public domain and of crown lands, discussing prices, credit, citizens' subjects' entitlements, and public welfare. Some new land-distribution operations in the United States during the nineteenth century borrowed practices from commerce, while others resembled pre-revolutionary procedures. These latter, retrogressive tendencies included programs that threw big allotments towards companies that promised public benefit and small ones to individuals who completed settlement conditions. The underlying premise of giving property rights on the basis of relative ability to improve the land was not at all innovative, but public discussion about land granting was novel. In both the United States and British colonies, debates about who should get land flourished from the 1820s to the 1890s. Land allocation mirrored shifts in the loci of power.

Early-seventeenth-century European colonization schemes installed feudal property rights in new worlds. The traditions lingered. Long after the English abolition of feudal tenure by 1660, the practice of favouring certain petitioners with crown grants in the colonies persisted. "One's ownership of acres was ... a public measure of one's proximity to the throne."[2] Well-placed individuals in the American republic – merchants, public officials, revolutionary army officers –

could accumulate large tracts. They did what elites had done in pre-revolutionary times – they petitioned for favours. However, they also embarked on commercial land schemes that required capital. After the revolution, land policies in the United States evolved under the aegis of a market economy, whereas, for approximately another forty years, British settlement colonies in southern Africa, North America, and Australia disposed of land mainly through grants that expressed government design or favour. For a while, pre-modern or at least early-modern values – social rank and loyalty – rebuffed market allocation in the British empire.

During the age of revolutions (1775–1815), the cultures of power in the United States and the British empire began to separate, and land allocation featured centrally among the distinctions. By the 1830s, democracy and capitalism finally came to bear in British colonial land policies. However, before any changes in British allocation measures, landhunters and speculators in the colonies, like those in the United States, assessed the dangers and possibilities of immediate occupation, imagined forms of improvement, looked for capital, and acted to frame legal interests. After I trace the surviving feudal and aristocratic elements in our five new worlds, I look at the creation of the U.S. public domain after the revolution and at two citizen speculators in particular. Finally, I consider aristocratic values and several colonizing schemes in the British empire in the early nineteenth century.

FEUDAL TRACES IN NEW WORLDS

There are at least four themes to recognize in early-modern allocation systems. A review of colonization, beginning in the early seventeenth century, highlights three – *colonial diversity*; personal, and thus idio-syncratic influences on *types of land tenure*; and *charter changes and ill-defined boundaries* separating colonial territories. These conditions contrast with early- and mid-nineteenth-century plans for sales and grants of land which often attempted to spread property rights broadly and to attach them to relatively compact and precisely defined land parcels. From *diversity, imprecision*, and *disorder*, allocation systems evolved, in outward appearances at least, towards homogeneity, order, and efficient exploitation. I briefly review these three themes.

Historical comparison of English, French, and Dutch settlement colonies then yields a fourth theme. It indicates a relatively early recognition of land as a source of private wealth in the English colonies of the eastern American seaboard. The crown had granted ill-defined colonies – Maryland (1632) and Pennsylvania (1681) to individuals who hoped for income from a tenantry, plantation crops, and land sales; Virginia soon had an estate-holding elite. Land-based schemes for riches were unusual for the time, although a few colonists and officials in several non-British colonies similarly appreciated opportunities for landed wealth. In the Dutch and French empires, these exceptional individuals succeeded in obtaining consent for landed estates and settlements in what home governments and trading companies valued essentially as strategic and commercial colonies.

By 1750, arrangements for land allocation in the colonial forerunners of the United States, South Africa, and Canada were *strikingly diverse*, because of unique founding objectives. Established by the Dutch East India Company in 1652, the colony at the Cape of Good Hope remained until 1795 an adjunct to a miserly trading enterprise, which "did not expect the Cape station to make a profit on its own [and] tried to keep the costs of its administration to a minimum."[3] Concurrently, the French in North America installed a quasi-feudal system of tenure suited to a thinly populated, spacious colony, where frontier warfare often threatened. Each English-American colony pursued distinctive arrangements for allocating land. This was partly because revolutions and dynastic changes at home affected colonization and schemes of land tenure. As well, in the light of changing opportunities, English colonizers revised their expectations, and hence the charters that empowered them. For most of the seventeenth century, the British crown devolved responsibility for local colonial government onto chartered companies or highly favoured individual proprietors. In the first decades of the seventeenth century, several English companies adjusted their emphasis, moving from commerce to landed revenue. During the first half of the seventeenth century, colonists, associated with chartered companies, clustered in culturally distinctive communities – Virginia, Plymouth, Massachusett's Bay, Maryland, Rhode Island, Connecticut, and New Haven (all established before 1660) – whose existence contributed to variety in colonial arrangements for land distribution.

Seventeenth-century English colonial charters were drafted against a background of struggles over the *type of tenure* that should prevail within the kingdom. The concepts of tenure being debated from roughly 1600 to 1660 pivoted on two timeless issues for governments: sources of revenue and the power to create or curtail property rights. These debates were well-known to privileged individuals who petitioned for company charters and colonial grants; therefore domestic controversy about land tenure spilled over into the design of colonial charters. Petitioners for charters weighed the advantages and disadvantages of two available forms of tenure. Under *in capite* (an estate held directly from the sovereign), parties holding land were liable to an assortment of feudal dues, but they could establish landed estates with tenant farmers, and they could exercise certain judicial powers. *Ut de manore* (an estate held through a royal manor) restricted duties to the crown but also constrained the scope for government and landed estates. Early English colonial ventures set trade as their objective. Consequently, a right to extract rents from tenants initially seemed unimportant, and so tenure *ut de manore* was favoured. Under charters with this tenure, land could be granted to colonists whose value to the company was not rent, but rather ability to produce supplies for trading posts and vessels. The charters of the Virginia Company of London (1609), the Virginia Company of Plymouth (1609), the New-foundland Company (1610), and the Bermuda Company (1615) took this form. All American colonization schemes originating in a company charter followed this type of tenure.[4]

By the 1620s, new-world companies formed in England were failing to make their merchant sponsors rich. Wealth came from raising tobacco, not from the hoped-for discoveries of minerals or from the trade in furs. The frontiers of seventeenth-century America, as English colonizers realized, could best be converted into assets through plantations.[5] Land-based enterprise now garnered attention, and this circumstance required altered property rights for the proprietors of colonies. Consequently, the next series of charters incorporated *in capite* tenure. The king granted favoured petitioners, if they wished, the right to operate new-world estates with tenants. To varying degrees, the crown granted the proprietors of these colonies nearly vice-regal power, including certain powers of government. In return, grantees accepted feudal obligations to the crown. The crown made similar arrangements for the English grantees of Irish estates. Proprietary grants in America arose alongside English plantations in Ireland, and D.B. Quinn and Nicholas Canny point out the "regular appearance of similar actors who were alternately engaged in the conquest or settlement of Ireland and in the exploration or colonization in the New World."[6] With their ambitions fixed on land, on plantations in the old and new worlds, the English colonizers of Ireland and America used the legal models that they had at hand, and these followed feudal forms until the English revolution and law reforms at mid-century.

During a revival of *in capite* tenure, George Calvert, Lord Baltimore, asked for and received, in 1635, a grant to an estate in America that he named Maryland. The crown gave him specific powers with respect to forming agricultural manors. The grant for the colony of Maine, to Sir Ferdinando Gorges in 1639, was slightly less generous in conferring this authority. In 1620, the Virginia Company of Plymouth successfully applied to have an old commercial charter cancelled in favour of a fresh one that established investors as proprietors of a colony in New England, although these partners in what was known as the Council of New England did not immediately ask for tenure *in capite*.[7] In 1623, however, some proprietors occupied territory granted under that tenure.[8] The Council of New England and other grantees in the region provided legal titles for the Plymouth Colony.[9] The Massachusetts Bay Company was granted a royal charter in 1629 and received lands initially given to the Council of New England.

There were frequent charter changes and vague boundaries in the first decades of the seventeenth century. The preliminary distribution of property rights mirrored English politics. The early Stuart kings, who granted this mosaic of charters, were jealous of royal prerogatives, and *in capite* tenure fit their expectations about prerogatives and revenue. The significant fact is that a series of early charters – except those enabling religious communities to colonize in New England – concentrated on extracting wealth from land. That made English colonization different. Moreover, no authority enacted a standard law for social organization or land distribution. In fact, as William Cronon observes, the towns of seventeenth-century New England "acted differently at first in relation to their common lands depending on the land practices of the regions of England from which their inhabitants came." Some adopted open-field systems, others, closed fields.[10] Many English colonizers judged land rents and sales as promising sources of wealth – an outlook not shared by contemporary French and Dutch colonizers. The holders of shares in new or converted English charters for American colonies tended to be country men.[11] Much earlier than anywhere else, land in America replaced commerce as the centrepiece of initial colonization. When Charles II granted William Penn proprietorship of an ill-defined colony in 1680, the idea of colonies as great landed estates reached its pinnacle.[12] The Penn family managed Pennsylvania profitably as a land business but had to cede its rights after the American Revolution. Commerce established great fortunes in American port cities, but land speculation retained a solid footing. Its prominence, in conjunction with the proliferation of charters for ill-defined territories, assured that the occupation of the western frontier – land beyond the Allegheny Mountains – was tied up in jurisdictional controversies from the 1750s to the 1790s.

English attention to landed property rights differed from that of other colonial powers. This can be seen in colonies that passed into British hands in the seventeenth and eighteenth centuries. The Dutch colonies of New Netherland (now New York) and Cape of Good

Hope originated as outposts of the Dutch West India Company and Dutch East India Company, respectively. Quasi-public organizations, chartered in the early seventeenth century, the companies received government aid to further the state's strategic goal of making trouble for Spain. "The Dutch initially thought of colonization in terms of war or commerce rather than emigration and settlement," and as a result they governed these two colonies as limited estates where occupants would have limited rights.[13] Soon there were exceptions, mildly favourable to landed estates.[14] Shortly after the Dutch West India Company organized a colony on the Hudson River, one faction of directors pressed for settlements, while another accented fur trading and privateering.[15] As a concession to the former group, the company in 1629 allowed two types of settlement: lordly estates granted to members of the company (patroons), and smaller grants to less wealthy individuals. Patroonships were open to company members who agreed to settle a specified number of families. Those members looking towards manorial rents were convinced, like their English counterparts, that with feudal tenure they could better control estates and extract rents.

Kiliaen van Rensselaer, a company proponent of manors, adopted the model of lordships found in the rural Netherlands. His patroonship initiative "never extensively took root," although the English who seized the colony in 1664 "succeeded in erecting an imposing manorial structure upon it."[16] Van Rensselaer and partners registered a patroonship for themselves in 1629. An English patent of 1685 described the estate's limits as extending 24 by 48 miles, an area of almost 750,000 acres. Rensselaerswyck became a prototype for English manors along the Hudson River, and it retained a tenantry until farmers bought out the landlord's rights in the 1850s.[17] Although the company also made smaller grants and allowed local governments to issue land titles, company taxes and controls over manufactures proclaimed its mercantilist designs. In August 1664, the colony capitulated to an English expedition.

At Cape Colony, which began as a strategic garden for victualling ships, the Dutch East India Company experimented modestly with agricultural settlement. Impressed with the potential for intensive agriculture, Governor Jan van Riebeck planted trial fields in 1656. A year later the company released a number of employees from their contracts, granted them plots, and encouraged these freeburghers to raise livestock and crops. Implanting white farmers "was probably the most significant event in the history of modern South Africa."[18] The company's control of markets, a shortage of farm labour, unco-operative slaves, a lack of capital, and the arid climate limited the scope for intensive agriculture, although in the Cape district the company continued to grant small freehold farms. To provide for the natural increase in population, it organized the settlement of the Stellenbosch (1679) and Drakenstein (1687) districts, not far from Cape Town. To allow for expansion while protecting its interests in the land, it permitted the leasing of terrain adjacent to or surrounding the freehold plots.[19] Within the organized territory, grazers located freehold plots strategically to control access to water. The tracts were far apart, "ensuring the continued success of extensive agriculture."[20] The company's attempts at control were consistent with its preference for intensive agriculture, which facilitated its regulation of economic and social relations from its local headquarters at the Castle of Good Hope. But by the early eighteenth century, grazing stretched beyond the districts where the company could manage orderly settlement.

"The slow moving and centrally directed farming frontier" – Richard Elphick's evocative description – "began to crumble as it moved away from Cape Town. In its place there arose an expansive pastoral frontier which would one day be responsible for the dispersal of white men over much of the future Cape Province"[21] – and beyond, during the Great Trek in the late 1830s. Thus, in addition to grantees who had legal title and leases for farm lands close to Cape Town, there were fugitives, runaways, and *trekboers* (hunter grazers); these frontier people formed a pastoral vanguard that ignored company authority altogether and moved stock until they were checked by raids from indigenous peoples (the Khoikhoi) or encountered semi-deserts. As would occur on many frontiers – the Ohio valley, Texas, New South Wales, New Zealand, and the American high plains – the pasturing of livestock drew settlers away from intensive agriculture and across extensive acreage. By the 1770s, trekboers encountered vigorous Khoikhoi resistance as they moved north, up the west coast. Trekboer squatters supplied beef and mutton for a limited market that catered to visiting ships, but a gradual shift from mutton sheep (African fat tail) to wool sheep (merino) began in the 1820s, and squatting within the colony assumed a more commercial character. Security of tenure and access to capital assumed greater significance, and by the early 1840s speculation in frontier lands across the Orange River and in Natal was under way.[22]

Historical Comparisons: English, French, Dutch

While a global land rush with common elements can be traced through a number of frontiers, significant differences appeared among the English, French, and Dutch settlement colonies, especially in distribution of land. The mix of classes on frontiers differed, even among

English colonies. While landhunting in colonial America was enlivened by individuals of great wealth and influence, and somewhat similar circumstances occurred on the frontiers of Australia and New Zealand, most landhunters of southern Africa were poor. Many, at least from 1700 to the early nineteenth century, pursued a subsistence existence, because the Dutch East India Company denied free commerce and constrained artisan employment, and slavery undercut the labour market.[23] The inferior quality of tracks within the colony compounded trekboers' poverty, for rough trails curtailed the haulage of their bulky produce to the very few market towns. By the late eighteenth century, there was, despite impediments to rural commerce, a budding market in land, because attacks from the Khoikhoi and water shortages pinched pastoralists. In a few cases, pastoralists withdrew to privately purchased tracts. In common with other frontiers, some land there was purchased that had not yet been granted by the government. Vendors sold improvements and, occasionally, the goodwill of harmonious relations with the Khoikhoi. It was all quite irregular and insecure. Wool exports by the 1820s stimulated a more lively land market. Pending confirmation by the British government, which took over the colony in 1806, land claims had been traded with confidence for years, in the expectation of their being recognized.[24] But of all frontiers under review, those in Cape Colony, among the longest occupied, were the slowest to develop lively, extensive land markets.[25] Unreliable rainfall affected most of southern Africa; speculation concentrated in better-watered pockets.[26]

Land policy at Cape Colony was tied at first into supplying the Dutch East India Company's trading fleets; hence the attempts to initiate intensive agriculture adjacent to Cape Town. For most of the eighteenth century, the company's habit that had most bearing on land allocation was its frugality. The company discouraged rapid occupation of territory on its northern and eastern flanks, because of the expense of warfare with first peoples. By the 1770s, it had more or less adopted a laissez-faire attitude with respect to trekboers. Closer to Cape Town, it behaved like the manager of a landed estate, renting out farms and collecting revenue, but its control diminished further up the coast and to the east, and it let trekboers organize their own defences. The company devoted little sustained energy to colonization, although late in the eighteenth century land rents from loan farms formed an essential source of its revenue. It lacked the vigour to change the willy-nilly distribution of land, but its successors tried to install a more studied and regulated system. The Batavian Republic (1803–6) and the British after their second conquest of the colony put allocation on a more orderly footing.[27]

Trading companies also figured in the early years of New France. With its core along the St Lawrence River, the French colony originated in shaky attempts to found year-round fishing and fur-trading posts, first at Île de Sable (1598) and Tadoussac (1600). In 1608, Samuel de Champlain built a base at the narrows of the St Lawrence, the site of Quebec City, about 150 miles upstream from Tadoussac. For the next quarter-century, New France was a trading factory and warehouse for furs and European goods. A light-weight, high-value staple, fur proved a successful article of trade, and the merchants who financed the colony showed no interest in the land. In 1627, the French cardinal-minister, the duc de Richelieu, an architect of French aggrandizement in Europe and abroad, established the Company of New France with title to the colony and a trade monopoly; the crown charged the company with establishing settlers, but it failed to live up to this obligation. New France's expansion followed the fortunes and routes of fur trading, although there was a departure from the rule. An outpost upstream, at the current site of Montreal, was undertaken by a religious society in 1642. By 1660, New France was a subsidized and thinly populated colony; in the estimation of the crown, the company made insufficient progress.[28] Thus, a new organization – the Company of the West Indies – ran New France from 1664 to 1674. The crown assumed full command in 1674. During both the company and crown-colony eras, land granting proceeded by means of *seigneurial tenure*.[29]

From the 1630s to 1663, the Company of New France attempted to discharge some of its settlement duties by granting land in substantial blocks to individuals – *seigneurs* – who agreed to introduce settlers. Uninterested in managing the landed estate of the colony, the company prepared no plans for allocating land to potential seigneurs. "As a general rule," it appears from retrospective study, "the more important the individual, the larger the grant he could expect to get, but there was probably almost the same degree of correlation with the ability to argue a good case."[30] The crown, in the person of the dynamic French minister of marine, Jean-Baptiste Colbert, kept a watch on the Company of the West Indies, and in 1672 he ordered a reduction in the size of the grants.[31] A great number of seigneuries – forty-six – were granted that year. Several along the Richelieu River went to officers of a French regiment sent in 1665 to bolster the colony's defence. Some four hundred soldiers settled as their officers' *censitaires*. The hope was that military settlement would complement two forts and help block a route used by Iroquois war parties.[32] Although this episode in colonization underscores links between strategy and land apportionment, the seigneurs were not part of a truly feudal arrangement based on military service.

Settlers – the censitaires – owed military service not to the seigneurs but to the crown through local militias, whose officers came from the settlers' own ranks. They performed service labour not for the estate, but for the crown. However, they did owe dues – *cens et rentes* – to their seigneur.[33] It remains a matter of interpretation whether obligations borne by the censitaires comprised a burden that approximated a feudal relationship.[34] In several respects, seigneurs were unlike landlords found in English colonies. The crown had not granted them land as a reward or recompense that they could dispose of as they wished. Instead, it entrusted them with duties in a project of colonization. From time to time it could insist on a progress report. A colonial official – the *intendant* – superintended the system. Families that settled on the seigneuries had a right to expect good management of the estate, local justice, fair distribution of lands and forests, and the presence of a mill. They could report shortcomings to the intendant. Many seigneurs from the 1670s to the 1740s transferred portions of their estates to discharge obligations, form family alliances, arrange inheritances, or endow religious orders. Far from the supervision of Quebec, in the settlements established on the alluvial soil of the Illinois country during the eighteenth century, inhabitants ignored the seigneurial system and adapted the open fields and nuclear villages common to the northern European plain. Settlement along the St Lawrence, in contrast, expressed state design, not European peasant traditions.[35] However, within French law and élite values there was scope for the use of estates in private economic plans. Yet transactions – for example, the creation of *les arrière-fiefs* – should not be seen as evidence of a land market where participants sought capital appreciation. Seigneurial obligations and status remained considerations. The transfer of New France to the British crown in 1763 included a guarantee to conserve the land-tenure arrangement, but no office like that of intendant survived the conquest, and new investors discovered that, with the aid of lawyers, they could evade obligations and exploit this tenure system for commercial rents.[36] In 1854, an act of the legislature of the United Province of Canada converted the system of land tenure to freehold, reducing complexity in property rights so that legal instruments could trade more readily.

Dutch and French authorities, for separate reasons, showed little interest in allowing – let alone fostering – a commercial attitude towards landed property rights. The limited nature of their resources prevented the Dutch from managing frontiers at the Cape and at New Netherland.[37] By the end of the seventeenth century, at the Cape, the Dutch East India Company started a lackadaisical, incomplete allocation of property rights. Concurrently, seigneurial tenure in New France enjoined mutual obligations on seigneur and censitaire. Neither Dutch nor French authorities esteemed land as a commodity that individuals could trade on their own initiative and independent of official review. Apart from a shared aversion to land as a trade good, the Dutch and French had absolutely nothing in common in allocation practices. In New France, allocation was regulated, and *habitants* adapted to a structured arrangement of rural society. Opportunity, necessity, and wanderlust led some to participate in arduous fur-trading expeditions, but New France witnessed nothing like the defiant, roving trekboers who moved with cattle and sheep.[38]

Voyageurs journeyed far and penetrated frontiers, while trekboers spread across frontiers encumbered with family and cattle. Contrasts in political and military commitment and in natural environment explain this distinction. By the 1660s, the crown had determined that New France would be resolutely defended and closely governed. "Imperial success was seen as the necessary adjunct of monarchical glory."[39] Climate co-operated to perfection with the French strategy of concentrating population and of affiliating occupation with crown institutions, for frigid winters precluded any eruption of extensive pastoral squatting and stock raising, the only way that substantial numbers of people could quickly occupy frontier tracts and place themselves beyond regulation. A maritime people, the early-modern Dutch never marshalled a comparably elaborate effort to colonize the Cape. Eventually the Dutch East India Company could do no more than caution people, help them fend for themselves, register the fact that they occupied a loan farm, and plead with them to avoid excessive bloodshed in dealings with the Khoikhoi.

Meanwhile England liberalized land tenure laws by the mid-seventeenth century. Parliament passed acts between 1646 and 1660 that abolished the feudal obligations of tenure *in capite*. Certain obligations remained in the colonies – for example, quit rents due the crown. Yet property law had been simplified in settlement colonies, as it would continue to be during the next two hundred years. In the mid-seventeenth century, however, an English reformation in landed property rights came from a central government, not from an innovative periphery. The American colonies experienced rivalry and territorial disputes that would continue until the formation of the republic. In summary, land-distribution arrangements seen in the settlement colonies of the Netherlands, France, and England during the seventeenth century present kaleidoscopic patterns comprised of trading companies, charters, and distinctive environments. Home governments occasionally shook the pieces into new patterns. Importantly, only in English colonies had landed property rights seized the attention of leading colonizers and colonists.

One English company falls outside this pattern. Operating under a charter granted by Charles II in 1670, the Hudson's Bay Company directed fur-trading factories over the vast domain of Rupert's Land. For almost 150 years, it traded and discharged government responsibilities but took no interest in land revenues or permanent colonization. In common with seventeenth-century chartered companies and proprietary colonies, the company's boundaries were imprecisely defined. The territory claimed turned out to be immense, and a substantial portion consisted of grassland. Granted the territory drained by rivers flowing into Hudson Bay, the company's extensive prairie domain derived from the reach of the Assiniboine and the North and South Saskatchewan rivers. Isolated in the middle of the continent, the extensive grasslands escaped organized colonization until 1812 and serious attention from eastern speculators until the late 1850s. The obstacles to reaching Rupert's Land delayed its participation in the rush.

I proposed above that looking into property rights might allow us to learn about power and community organization. Now the material just presented can elucidate this claim. Indicative of the mercantile character of their companies' directors, Dutch colonies skimped when settling the land. In the Dutch colonial world, trade articles and vessels comprised valuable property. In New France, the crown capitalized on an opportunity through land grants to instate direct ties with its subjects and to do so without the rivalry of a regional nobility. In the charters for English colonies, there was evidence of the political turmoil at home, but also, where climate and geography permitted, of the idea of an estate-holding gentry and aristocracy. Commencing in the late seventeenth century, the crown took a more direct interest in new colonies than it had when granting charters and proprietary colonies, and it also tried to influence colonies operating under the older charters and grants. "The increased influence of the crown in the colonies in the eighteenth century is represented by the rise of the royal province replacing in importance the feudal colony of the seventeenth century."[40] All the same, the crown exercised but slight control over detailed land issues in the American colonies. Virginia, which on the default of the Virginia Company's charter had become the first American crown colony in 1623, evolved its own system of allocation. The Penn family maintained independence with respect to land allocation. Massachusetts initiated a methodical system, enabling groups of settlers to found new townships. As colonial clearings expanded towards one another, especially near the western lands claimed by both Pennsylvania and Virginia, diversity and rivalry complicated allocation in an uncharted region. London could not enforce effective control over the actual land distributions.

THE AMERICAN EXPERIENCE, 1775–1800

A National Political Culture and the Public Domain

In one area of land policy, however, London in the 1760s attempted enforced coherence. With respect to land and first peoples, it removed the negotiations with Indian tribes from the hands of individual American colonies and created an Indian department with northern and southern divisions. It endeavoured to control settlement, as we saw above, by creating an Indian territory in 1763, although there was little that an imperial government could do to enforce compliance with restrictions on settlement in that region. The Royal Proclamation of 1763 still hampered speculators, at least until the 1768 cession of Indian lands on the southern end of the Allegheny Plateau arranged by the Treaty of Fort Stanwix.

In Stanwix's wake, cliques of speculators convened in inns and coffee-houses to capitalize and manage new land companies. Their frontier pawns hustled to survey prime tracts. A few had jumped the gun and now were well placed. The rushes for interests degenerated within months into a tangle of conflicting legal claims on overlapping tracts. Speculators mortgaged and sold interests, guaranteeing clouded titles for decades. Since Virginia and Pennsylvania disputed sovereignty over part of the ceded terrain, partners and shareholders in rival ventures journeyed to Philadelphia and Williamsburg to solicit consent. A word from a governor or a resolution from an assembly added premiums to the imperfect interests that speculators hastened to sell. Intrigues crossed the Atlantic, for the Board of Trade and the King in Council could bless or ruin a scheme.[41]

The American Revolution eventually forced comprehensive changes in a state of affairs that had degenerated into frontier bedlam. Machinations to keep interests in land alive consumed money and time. As speculators discovered, a defence of shaky interests required vigilance, ceaseless conniving, and improvements. Burgeoning conflicts over interests in frontier lands – a consequence of divided government authority and free selection – inflated the transactions cost of land speculation. Speculators wondered whether the skirmishing in the courts, the lobbying in assemblies, and the jostling in frontier clearings could be lessened.

In four steps, between 1775 and 1785, revolutionary American governments attempted to rationalize the allocation of frontier lands. Step one – independence – eliminated dealing with London. Severing the connection by warfare was costly and forced the fledgling states to nurse their assets. Thus, just as London had recognized – too late –

that land auctions might provide greater revenue than the troublesome Stamp Act, the states and national government turned to unalienated acres as a way to discharge the war's obligations. In step two, as a consequence of the war, Virginia – profligate disseminator of land warrants – turned the screws on pre-revolutionary land companies, syndicates, and especially people who claimed interests under private arrangements with first peoples. In step three, extensive negotiations over the regions where the states disputed jurisdiction led to boundary settlements and the transfer of an enormous land bank to the national government. Leaving aside territory that New York and Massachusetts disputed, the public domain in 1790 consisted of about 228 million acres. In step four, the national government enacted an ordinance of 1785 that framed a cadastral template for this immense patrimony.

In principle, the crown had unified allocation, because all titles originated in crown grants. In practice, chartered companies, proprietors, or governments in crown colonies drafted and administered distinctive practices with respect to allocation. After 150 years of division and diversity, a new republic clarified authority, established a national estate, and seemingly eliminated free selection. Ostensibly, reform curtailed landhunters – large or small – by ending free selection without reference to cadastral maps. But, as happened often during the rush, the doctrines of occupation and improvement sustained squatting. Confusion and litigation persisted. As if these doctrines were not cause for trouble enough, additional complexities touched the public domain, and they explain why its management would often be judged a shameful failure. A single remarkable accomplishment, however, must be stressed. As an instrument for entrenching, extending, and defining a national identity, the public domain was a peerless asset. Out of its creation and expansion flowed explorations, survey teams, army detachments, and land office officials; the existence of the public domain, with its democratic label, also assured debates about national purpose. The land bank created by the states' cessions helped the United States to create itself.

Although squatting upset the planned disposal of the public domain, six additional factors also splintered any neatness of design – the complexity of the task, the circulation of securities, pervasive corruption, the inadequate bureaucracy relative to the scale of the domain, the hasty actions of this bureaucracy, and the existence of French and Spanish land grants. First, establishing terms and conditions was exceedingly controversial in a republic. While the British, often at war in the late eighteenth and early nineteenth centuries, turned from flirtation with the idea of land auctions and embraced grants as rewards to individuals for service to the crown, early republican politicians continuously revised policies on land sales. Conflicting national and sectional dreams inevitably led to change. A policy of cheap land and easy credit dovetailed with the ideal of an Arcadian democracy and also with the calculation that land enough, and cheap enough, might make urban labour scarce and keep workingmen's wages decent. In contrast, a policy of higher prices and tighter credit supported designs for national expenditures on public works and could help strand the toiling classes in towns and cities, thus driving down wages.

A second cause of complexity derived from the circulation of state and national securities, many convertible into land. Issued first during the revolutionary war, these commitments gave speculators splendid new instruments with which to play, and their manipulations compounded allocation. In later years, other forms of convertible paper went into circulation, and they too enticed sharp operators to the land games. A third factor that disturbed a tidy evolution of allocation was corruption at every level, from local office clerks to state and federal legislators. A fourth consideration – namely, the initial size and intermittent expansion of the public domain – made tight central control impractical, especially since the administrative staff was never sufficient for an orderly, peaceful distribution. Magnitude fostered a spendthrift outlook. Americans took abundance for granted, accepted plenty as their reference point, and let a moving frontier absorb errors committed in the administration of the public domain. In southern Africa and Australia, land was abundant, but not water; in New Zealand, water cascaded plentifully, but land was rugged, and level plains were generally of modest extent; in Canada, land and water were plentiful, but winters severe. Despite extensive mountains and drylands in the west, the United States embraced a bounty of good land, and so the subject of shortages seldom arose. After the purchase of Louisiana in 1803, the domain looked limitless. War with Mexico in 1846 added millions of acres, and the Oregon cession from Britain added millions more (see Table 1.2). As the bounty increased, it slipped away. That is ever the case.

Fifth, the velocity and tactics of land occupation on American frontiers, as on others, were beyond the management skills of limited governments. Moreover, the scale of entitlements – rights to land granted generously to individuals or companies – came as a bit of a surprise to some administrators and politicians who were chagrined to discover what their predecessors or deputies had done. Finally, diverse and extensive claims to land in territories newly acquired by the republic – French and Spanish land grants, for example – precipitated courtroom battles for control of huge estates that eventually claimed parts of the public domain before they officially became part of it. Now you see it, now you don't. A national accounting of the public domain awaited late-nineteenth-century inquiries and historical accounts, by which time the domain had slipped through the republic's fingers. Its economic legacy was considerable, and so too its cultural importance. An abundance of land – partly real and available, partly imagined and inaccessible – helped shape Americans' belief in themselves as a people of plenty.[42]

The real history of the domain was not an uplifting tale in every respect. Nevertheless, the early speculative adventures depict vitality and ingenuity. The republican era was packed with contrasts: democracy and elitism; sectional and national interests; rural dissent and mercantile ambition. Land allocation figured in the ferment and contradictions. The revolution, as I suggested, led to reforms to organize and simplify land allocation. However, it also rejuvenated land speculation remarkably, because it blasted away the legal-administrative barrier of the Royal Proclamation of 1763, and it generated a medley of government securities convertible into land. In the early 1780s, grand speculations re-emerged and, with them, the familiar complications of clouded titles and litigation.

Finance Capital and Citizen Speculators

After the revolution, the Royal Proclamation of 1763 had no force, although native title endured and governments remained mindful of a legal necessity to eliminate this obstacle to a clear title. The Northwest, where speculative parties could now probe at will, remained effectively in the hands of Indian villages hostile to colonization. The hostile confederated villages north of the Ohio River remained a deterrent until the U.S. army defeated them at the Battle of Fallen Timbers in 1794, during which engagement British allies of the Indians remained neutral.[43] Even before that decisive action, Americans assumed the opening of the territory to be only a matter of time, and that prospect helped – along with the new federal constitution – to support the republic's credit with its European bankers in the late 1780s.[44] Another matter entirely was the domestically held debt, which had been heavily discounted throughout most of the 1780s, and that slump – an inconvenience to affluent investors who held the paper – caused innovations in debt funding that directly rejuvenated large speculations.

Under the Articles of Confederation (1779–89), the central government and the states issued a multiplicity of securities. Wary of the central government, states shouldered part of the military debt to protect their autonomy and began paying soldiers in so-called military warrants. Another set of commitments originated in the debt incurred by the central loan office, which sold federal debt certificates to local investors. Congress lacked the authority to generate independently the revenue to meet interest payments. Politicians who favoured a strong central government exploited this crisis in 1782–83, in an unsuccessful bid to legislate a national revenue system. Opposed to channelling funds through the capital at Philadelphia, to the benefit of that city's merchants and financiers, a number of states covered interest payments on the federal certificates with their own special paper – namely, state indentures, known to contemporaries as *indents*. The ad hoc treatment of the debt in the early 1780s led to a slide in the market value of state and national paper.[45] The handling of this problem varied from state to state. Some tackled their rising obligations with taxation; others made state paper convertible into public land.[46] Speculators pounced on the opportunities. An eruption of large-scale American land schemes, linked to financial manipulations, happened prior to comparable ventures on other frontiers. These new, vast land dealings required links between financial and land markets; they also needed tracts of unalienated land, a substantial number of individuals pre-pared to take risks, and prospects of immigration and migration, or the likelihood of some agricultural commodity production. In the late eighteenth century, these conditions came together in the republic. City-based merchants, already an impressive source of enterprise, ven-tured into land speculation. Other regions of the world had experi-enced a mix of metropolitan capital and agrarian estates – for example, the sugar plantations of Brazil and the Caribbean. When the English woollen industry boosted sheep grazing in southern Africa, Australia, and New Zealand, metropolitan enterprise and land speculation were again connected.

American speculative enterprise in the 1780s built on solid prospects with zeal and optimism, but the new land ventures pushed the limits of capitalization and management capability. The scale and complexity of the undertakings outstripped the capacity of the founders' management arrangements; engaged in heady gambles, large speculators of the late 1780s and early 1790s adopted dangerously short time-horizons for funding their debts and arranging their sales. Immediacy – intrinsic to the great land rush – marked their thinking. They functioned with thin organizations. What they as colonizers and promoters envisioned required internal specialization and the staying power of a corporation. All that they had was themselves, and that proved inadequate for the long-term projects that land selling became. In terms of business history, these early speculations were transitional. They resembled the land com-panies of the 1750s and 1760s and even somewhat the chartered com-panies of the seventeenth century, because handfuls of individuals again attempted major undertakings. Yet, unlike earlier ventures, they involved more elaborate financial dealings and greater promotional and sales efforts. However, they were not full-fledged corporations. The maturation of land companies occurred late in the nineteenth century, when a number of corporations – the land departments of North American railway companies, a few commission agencies that took over Australian pastoral estates, and Canada's Hudson's Bay Company – acquired landed estates and developed some of the management skills, prudence, and assets absolutely necessary for protracted development schemes.

Overreaching caught up with the large American speculators of the 1780s and 1790s, and in this failing they shared something with forerunners and successors alike. In the midst of all land booms, lessons from the past tend to be ignored. The activities of two land speculators in the early republic – Robert Morris and John Cleve Symmes – could have been instructive to later generations. In addition to illustrating the risks that could beset this type of business, they also elucidate the outbreak of confusion in land markets at the inception of the public domain and suggest comparisons with individuals who held large estates in British settlement colonies.

Respectful biographers designate Robert Morris "the Financier of the United States" – a tribute to his accomplishments on behalf of the revolution.[47] Morris emigrated from Liverpool in 1747. Robert senior, a tobacco agent for an English trading house, apprenticed his son to a Philadelphia mercantile firm that traded in the West Indies and Europe. Robert junior became a partner in 1757 and enlarged the firm's activities until, at the beginning of the revolution, it was one of Philadelphia's leading houses.[48] From 1776 to 1778, the firm prospered from blockade running and privateering. Morris entangled his partners in the affairs of a new government, whose agents and credit he used freely for private business. Morris "was of a class and generation that made no distinctions between private and public interest."[49] By the skin of his teeth, he survived charges of dishonesty and rose to be superintendent of finance for the Continental Congress.

A revolutionary leader who improved the federation's finances and credit, he nevertheless behaved too recklessly for his cautious original business partners, and after 1778 he acquired new associates.[50] Morris transferred habits from commerce and applied them inappropriately to land speculation. As a trader, he imported European goods on credit, bought flour and timber to send as remittances, and ran these transactions on short-term credit and quick turn-arounds. For dealing with readily liquidated assets such as European trade goods or rural consumables, short-term credit worked. However, advice that Morris offered as superintendent of finance suggests that he strayed into sly practices to postpone payments. On the basis of personal knowledge, he proposed *note kiting*, or sending out bills of exchange drawn in ways that slowed their return for settlement.[51] When he began speculating in land, Morris again drew on his commercial experience. He looked to a network of agents in Europe to dispose of his land, just as commission agents sold American commodities. Mixing public and private business conceivably left him with an exaggerated sense of his relationship with European bankers.[52] His business knowledge derived from either mercantile practices or war finances. Land was different, and a failure to appreciate the distinctions contributed to a crash of his massive land operations. Character traits also contributed to his fall. He relished risk and took on more business than he could track. "Why," asked one critic, "did you engage in so much more business than you were competent to?"[53]

Morris left his position as superintendent in November 1784 and embarked a year later on a complicated speculation. He contracted to supply the French tobacco monopoly at a set price. Although the American market price for tobacco dropped, giving Morris a profit margin, he had used his dominant position in this trade to manipulate exchange rates. Merchants needed bills of exchange drawn on European trading houses, and the French paid Morris in these promissory notes. Therefore he calculated that he had enough bills coming in to oblige merchants to buy their bills from him. He offered his French bills for gold or paper securities – a move that he believed would drive up the value of the paper securities that he held – but the squeeze failed[54]. Retaining grandiose ambitions, he withdrew into real estate.

Morris was not alone in plunging desperately into an alien business. Land speculation spread among American merchants in the 1780s and early 1790s, because of commercial adversity, the lack of hard currency and bills of exchange, and poor relations with English merchants. His first venture in land went well. It originated in one of the post–revolutionary war settlements over state lands. When New York and Massachusetts settled their conflicting claims to land in western New York, a syndicate was formed, in 1788, to purchase from Massachusetts the 4 million acres that it took as compensation for ceding sovereignty to New York. In the years just after the revolution, syndicates, companies, and individual investors resolved problems for governments with unalienated territory. For the new republic and those states that retained unalienated acres, the asset tantalized them as a way to discharge obligations to creditors and soldiers. As always with real estate, the tricky part was liquidating it if the market soured.

As we saw in chapter 3, in 1775 London had naïvely instructed some governors to survey and sell lands by auction.[55] By then, experienced speculators – many of whom now flourished in American public life – knew that sales to agriculturalists would be laborious, slow, complicated by native title, and frustrated by squatters. Therefore large block sales to investors willing to accept risks and management costs made sense until the public domain was sufficiently organized to allow sales to a yeomanry. Thus several states and the national government dumped millions of acres. Nominal prices seem low in retrospect, and the real prices were often deflated further because governments accepted payment in state securities, whose market price had been depressed for several years. Not all fluctuations were downward; in the case of the western New York syndicate, a rise in market price of Massachusetts securities undermined the group. Morris joined the western New York syndicate in 1790 and soon acquired its total acreage. He sold mostly to Dutch investors. Typical of Morris, before he had completed the transactions, he embarked on another immense undertaking, this time involving Pennsylvania lands.

At the end of the war, the Continental Congress had asked the states to improve the condition of the army by making up some of the difference between soldiers' nominal pay and the depreciated market value of the currency that they had received. Pennsylvania responded by issuing depreciation certificates and setting aside western counties with depreciation lands. Also, the state promised donation lands for officers and soldiers, according to rank. Speculators accrued the land-backed paper, and several state officials manipulated power and information to assemble rustic principalities for themselves. John Nicholson, the state's officer responsible for supervising the conversion of paper into land, speculated notoriously. Learning of good sites, he delayed approving their alienation until he could buy them; if he needed funds, he would sometimes issue certificates using the names of ineligible people. Around 1793, Nicholson was, on paper, the largest landowner in the state, with interests in about 4 million acres. Overextended, he turned to Morris and an influential New Englander, James Greenleaf.

Rather than putting existing ventures in order, the trio hurried into additional speculations, purchasing over 7,000 building lots in Washington, DC. They used their landed assets – many times over – as security for loans to sustain old and new speculations. By 1795, crushed between faltering sales and insistent creditors, they resorted to a desperate measure and organized the North American Land Company, which claimed to hold 7 million acres in a number of states. Perhaps the largest land syndicate until the era of railway land grants after the Civil War, the company floated securities to fend off creditors.[56] The manœuvre failed to rescue Nicholson and Morris, who were imprisoned as debtors. Familiar with consumables and securities,

Morris was a stranger to the liquidity risks common in real property dealings, and he never acquired a first-hand knowledge of the land that he hoped to sell. He was a shifty and tricky specimen of the genus of land speculator who sought to reap where he had not sown.

Unlike the dealings of Morris, those of another of the period's large speculators, John Cleve Symmes, depict a sincere effort to colonize coupled with the profit motive. Symmes contracted to purchase approximately one million acres along the Ohio and Miami rivers. Speculation kindled his interest. The national government paid attention to Symmes. He was an officer with important friends, and his plan involved taking in the government's paper securities and assuming the chore of colonizing in the Northwest, where Indian villages remained hostile to white settlement. Speculators squatting along the Ohio River in the early 1790s cut across Indian tracks that led into Kentucky; a procession of armed stations into the Northwest threatened the autonomy of the Indian villages. Practical problems awaited government agents and speculators alike. Surveying was going to be costly and slow. Small buyers required credit; some were bound to default. Squatters already occupied public land. Further, the sheer abundance of land that could be placed on the market threatened to make it a buyer's commodity. Notwithstanding these perils, speculators such as Symme calculated that the discounted domestic debt and its convertibility into land presented opportunities that outweighed these genuine risks.

Symmes, a resident of New Jersey and a teacher and surveyor before the war, had proven himself a competent officer during the revolution. His vocations provided him with friends and connections. He followed the debates on debt conversion and listened to reports about the Northwest. An acquaintance took him on a landhunting tour down the Ohio in the spring and summer of 1787. On his return, Symmes, an impetuous optimist, approached the treasury board with a conversion scheme that hinged on his personal contract to buy public land north of the Ohio. He ultimately arranged for one million acres on a tract that today includes the cities of Cincinnati and Dayton (Map 5.1). By the terms of the agreement, he would pay 66 2/3 cents per acre in federal treasury certificates and military warrants. He had the freedom to set the price on the land, and he accepted government securities for payment.

For Symmes to transform government paper into land, and land into wealth, he had to present himself to the public as a more proficient colonizer than the government. He had to command confidence, because he would not only sell land, he – and others who played similar games – depended on a panicky public to dispose of paper cheaply to the speculators' agents, who in turn resold them at a higher price to

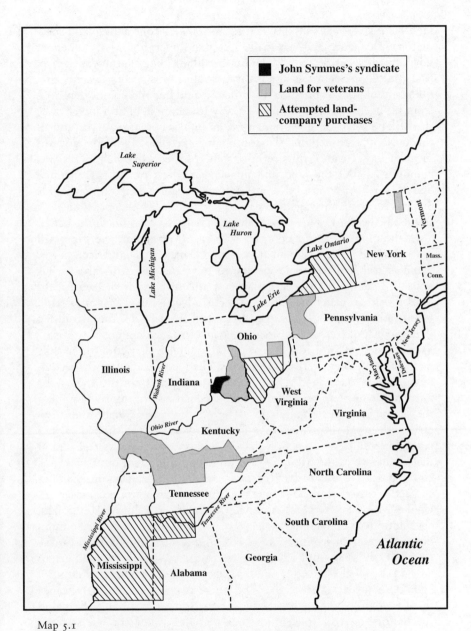

Map 5.1
Land reserved for Revolutionary War veterans and attempted land-company acquisitions, 1775–90
Source: Lester J. Cappon et al., *Atlas of Early American History: The Revolutionary Era, 1760–1790* (Princeton, NJ: Princeton University Press, 1976), 61.

land-buying colonists or speculators. As a major contracting land speculator with agents, Symmes made a double wager: first, that holders of
government securities would continue to think the government ineffectual and sell its securities at a great discount to his agents; second, that
other speculators or prospective settlers would buy these same securities
from his agents at a mark-up, as a way to secure land at a lower price
than that set by the government on its public domain. At the end of
this cycle of transactions, the contracting speculator paid the government in its securities, thus retiring some of the public debt. This was
complicated, but the land and financial markets of the early United
States were brimming with ingenuity and risk takers. In order for
Symmes's particular wagers to pay, he had to instil confidence and show
results. If the market for paper remained depressed, so much the better.

At the moment of his contract with the government, the depressed
market value of government paper gave scope for a handsome profit.
Symmes still had to induce people to buy land and to deal with his
approved agents for paper. To accomplish these goals, he worked to
inspire trust in his choice of a tract. His advertisement was masterful.
It not only painted a landscape of rich soil free of rocks but promised
that "no dispute respecting titles in the first instance can possibly arise."
Symmes pledged immediate surveys in the Ohio valley, and for a while
this exceeded the government's pace.[57] His record as an officer recommended him as a leader. From New Jersey and the northeast, he
attracted a nucleus of colonists and speculators willing to buy what
they assumed were bargain lands, selected by a clever officer, and deliv-
ered with good root titles. Significant profits, Symmes hoped, would
come from sales on a section that he and several partners reserved at
the confluence of the Miami and Ohio rivers. The Miami purchase was
equal parts frontier adventure and financial speculation; Symmes
showed a passion for the former and little comprehension of the latter.
Unlike Morris, a remote, conniving financier who moved into land
speculation as if dealing in tobacco or bills of exchange, Symmes
directed on site a frontier estate. His strategy, from his arrival on the
tract in early 1789 until 1795, was to require colonizers to build defensive *stations* – the term for small settlements used earlier in Kentucky
and subsequently in Australia – of ten or twelve men and to advance
these ever deeper into the tract.[58] At the same time that settlers and
speculators moved into Kentucky and the Ohio valley, trekboers on the
northern frontier of Cape Colony clustered in groups of no fewer than
four families as security against the attacks of the Khoikhoi.[59]

Symmes personally furnished rations when these were needed, but
his efforts were not enough, and the risks turned against him. A series
of Indian victories over the U.S. army through the early 1790s drove

away settlers and prospective buyers. Kentucky land jobbers attempted
to squat on his tract; when resisted by Symmes, they spread rumours
that his Miami tract was a slaughterhouse, where Indians killed settlers
with impunity.[60] On the finance side, he confronted rising prices for
the government paper that he or his agents bought, sold, accepted for
payment, and deposited with the treasury. Faith in the new U.S.
constitution, and the paper-to-land conversion process itself, drove up
demand for the securities. The earlier price spread evaporated, and
eastern investors turned away from land speculation. Jonathan Dayton,
one of Symmes's partners in reserved lands, warned him in September
1788 that "the rise in Certificates makes the people here less eager to
engage in land speculations than when you left."[61] Symmes shared bad
luck on this front with scores of individuals throughout the republic.
They had contracted for acres to be paid with public securities. By late
1790, the secretary of the treasury, Alexander Hamilton, had reformed
national finances and announced that holders of securities should not
sell them, but should wait until they reached their true value.[62]

   Problems multiplied. Rumours in the mid-1790s that the U.S. government would open its own land offices undercut demand for Miami
plots. "Hundreds," Symmes lamented, were "locating and making
elections of land. They almost laugh me full in the face when I ask
them one dollar per acre."[63] Pre-emptive squatting also helped to
knock the bottom out of the Ohio land market. Symmes caused trouble
for himself too. Energetic and shrewd, he nevertheless "lacked the
faculty of organization and with entirely too wide a sphere of action,
he neglected the most important field."[64] Careless about property
boundaries, he sold land outside his tract. Legal and political disputes
reduced his property; Dayton, his partner in the reserve lands, was
Speaker of the House of Representatives (1795–99) and did what he
could in Congress to help, but Symmes made enemies.[65] He eventually
defaulted on payments to the treasury. In 1811, a fire – started possibly
by tenants or debtors – destroyed his estate, "North Bend," and most
of his land records.[66] His family's saga continued. His daughter Ann
married a frontier army officer, Captain William Henry Harrison, who
rose to fame in the War of 1812 and became the ninth president of
the United States. Benjamin Harrison, Symmes's great-grandson, was
the twenty-third president. The Harrisons' family home at North Bend
stood on Symmes's old estate.

By the late 1790s, the republic was on the verge of organizing the sale
of public-domain land in small, well-defined parcels to agriculturalists
or speculators. Symmes experienced the ruinous impact that rumours
of a government land office visited on private land contractors. From

that point forward to the age of large grants to railway companies, the public domain was not again distributed though a subcontractor system that involved large tracts. While allocation in British colonies would remain for years an affair of grants to deserving individuals – with the ambiguities and abuses that this nebulous concept allowed – the first major disposals of the American public domain came in a surge of speculation and innovation. Political influence and cronyism thrived, as they would under British colonial grant systems. The truly noteworthy fact, however, is that commercial and financial intricacies marked early American land allocation.

Simultaneously, in the upper Hudson River valley, landed estates, authorized by the Dutch and added to greatly by English governors, experienced a burst of expansion. An expanding tenantry sustained a handful of landlords, who had retained their estates because, unlike counterparts nearer New York, they backed the revolution. In the first several decades after peace, they felt politically secure and set about pursuing delinquent accounts and accepting more tenants. Often, the new arrivals were migrants leaving land-poor New England. The landlords' eventual downfall, according to Reeve Huston, was a consequence of a republicanism that affected them and their tenants. The latter frequently had perpetual or multiple-generation leases. Security of tenure therefore was not a volatile issue. However, by the late 1830s, resentment over paying rents to men who did not till the soil developed into a political movement. Some landlords had already broken up their estates and sold to settlers, although the manors of Rensselaerswyck, Claverack, and Livingston remained consolidated estates with a tenantry into the 1820s or later. Landlords who supported the revolution "were as anxious as their fellow patriots to eradicate hereditary aristocracy," even if that meant "abolishing a wide range of legal and familial practices – including primogeniture and entail."[67] They also abandoned alliance marriages. Such conduct is unimaginable among Argentinian and Brazilian contemporaries. The Hudson manor owners ceased behaving like aristocrats; however, as grand-bourgeois republicans, they expected property rights to be upheld and insisted on compensation.

LANDED ESTATES IN THE BRITISH COLONIES, TO THE 1830S

In the British empire, well-connected individuals, or those who had performed special service, were meant to be beneficiaries of grants. Until the early 1830s, the Colonial Office promoted the idea that land should be administered locally to foster economic growth and simultaneously to reward the crown's friends and servants. London imposed no standardized land-grant regulations for settlement colonies. A shift from free grants to sales in the early 1830s split the history of imperial land codes into two epochs: first, a prolonged, reactionary, pre-modern phase (1750–1831), during which the imperial government rebuffed a market approach to allocation but allowed favouritism and a secondary market in property interests; second, the market phase (1832–50).

The importance of class and rank – though restrained when compared to seventeenth-century proprietary grants – was nevertheless exemplified by the apportionment of the Island of St John (Prince Edward Island) after France ceded sovereignty in 1763. The Earl of Egmont, described by J.M. Bumsted as "a staunch advocate of the reinstitution of feudal tenures and traditional ways," petitioned the crown in conjunction with distinguished officers, merchants, and politicians for a proprietary colony under the rule of a company.[68] The Board of Trade and the Privy Council rejected Egmont's schemes and determined instead to apportion the territory to individual gentlemen, not to a ruling company. Sixty-seven applicants for crown largesse were selected in 1767 to participate in the assignment by lottery of sixty-seven lots of approximately 20,000 acres each. There would be no lord high paramount, which Egmont had proposed; most of England's laws would be in force. The grantees received title on the condition that they would settle the island, pay quit rents, and develop the fishery. There were expectations of betterment. In subsequent years, titleholders attempted to establish a tenantry for their estates, but their accomplishments as improving colonizers were uneven, and in the early nineteenth century some tenants wanted the crown to reclaim its estate. The allocation of Prince Edward Isand depicted several themes in the emergent British pattern of colonization. Grantees could sell their interests, and many did so. The crown favoured an initial distribution to loyal servants, expected the application of industry and capital, and allowed the land to be alienated to others who undertook the actual settlement.[69]

In the empire's first era of colonization, as described above, there were before the 1830s market-oriented experiments, such as land sales in Upper Canada and New South Wales; however, grants continued to be the dominant mode of allocation. During this grant phase, the Colonial Office permitted governors flexibility with administrative details; however, recipients of the crown's bounty were expected to be loyal, worthy, and productive. A senior officer or board in each settlement colony screened applicants for character and recommended approval or rejection of petitions for land. Particular local matters influenced these deliberations. In Upper Canada, loyalty was a recurrent concern, because of proximity to the United States. In New South Wales, after 1818, an emancipated convict could apply for a small grant, but the government worried about allowing former convicts on grazing frontiers. Racial outlooks were apparent in Cape Colony. Its governor in 1809 reviewed applications by *Bastaards* (people of white and Khoikhoi parentage) for land with reference to their standing in the community. Individual Khoikhoi received plots only in unusual instances. Land was granted, for example, to "250 Coloured and Khoikhoi families at the Kat River settlement founded in 1829, but preference went to men with property or those who had served with the Cape Corps."[70]

In the British empire generally, once character requirements had been satisfied, the crown made a grant to people who claimed to be bona fide settlers and promised to make the land productive. There was more to the actual allocation than just putting land into resourceful hands. Governors discriminated with terms and conditions, and grants varied in size, according to social rank or favouritism. Influential people usually did not have to wait long for a grant, and they could secure additional ones. In Van Diemen's Land, Sharon Morgan finds, 407 people received additional grants, and 38 per cent of these grantees held some public office.[71] In Lower and Upper Canada, a build-up of land grants in the hands of office holders – the so-called Château Clique and Family Compact, respectively – presented reform politicians with a celebrated grievance.[72] Favoured British officers in the Cape Colony secured enlarged tracts in preferred locations, and the land grant officer (1814–27) insisted on evidence of wealth as a qualification.[73]

An approved grant allowed a petitioner to select the specified amount of acreage, by free selection or, in the case of Upper Canada, from surveyed plots – or at least frontage points – on a grid. Proof of improvements was required within a specified period, before a patent could be issued. Fees for handling documents at each step leading to the patent provided functionaries with their emoluments of office. Even when the process worked smoothly, it was cumbersome and put people to expense and trouble. From a government's perspective, the system broke down when grantees located their land and failed to go to the expense of securing patents. Grantees often traded their interests in land, and markets for their interests flourished wherever financial conditions favoured speculation or wherever there was pressure on the land. In the early nineteenth century, although the great land rush moved decisively towards a system that included initial allocations influenced by democratic politics, demands for freehold tenure, and land speculation, in British North America a conservative political interlude aided a handful of Scottish and Irish gentlemen who wished to procure estates and settle a tenantry in order to leave a patrimony to their sons or to resettle dispossessed countrymen.[74]

Four Grand Projects

The existence of a landed estate (Lord Mount Cashel's until 1856) on Amherst Island in Upper Canada from 1835 to the end of the century leads Catharine Anne Wilson to affirm a point that, though made by several American historians, is easily overlooked because of the appeal that freehold held for settlers from many backgrounds. "Tenancy was common on the frontier, precisely because it had economic relevance."[75] Consolidated estates – as opposed to a few scattered farms owned for rental income – were unusual, but not absent from newly opened lands in nineteenth-century North America. Paul Gates finds estate-building schemes in U.S. prairie regions in the 1830s, when credit was easy. Despite political rhetoric to the effect that tenancy was un-American, when wealthy easterners bought land for development by tenants, local boosters were jubilant. Besides bringing desirable capital, these landlords attracted praise because they were not necessarily going to hold onto the land. They were improving speculators. Their idea was to make use of tenant labour to increase the property's value, compensate tenants for the improvements, and sell either to them or to other settlers.[76] In British North America during the first several decades of the century, two landed estates examined below – Lord Selkirk's several settlements and Thomas Talbot's colonization efforts along the shore of Lake Erie – as well as Lord Mount Cashel's venture on Amherst Island, retained more aristocratic ingredients. This section also explores colonization projects in the Cape Colony and New South Wales.

Thomas Douglas, 5th Earl Selkirk, inherited a title and fortune in 1799 before he was thirty. His ideals defied a market attitude towards land. In the Scottish Highlands, the rationalization of estates dispossessed tenant farmers and created a serious social crisis; concurrently, Ireland was in economic and political turmoil. Douglas, a paternalistic aristocrat sensitive to the plight of the United Kingdom's rural poor, proposed an immigration scheme to the Colonial Office as a cure for the ills of Ireland, but it was rejected. He turned next to alleviating the distress of Highlanders and secured an estate on Prince Edward Island in early 1803. A few months later, he selected land at Baldoon in Upper Canada, under one of that colony's many allocation schemes.[77] Selkirk was hostile to the American levelling spirit and favoured large grants to install a new-world landed aristocracy.[78] His Baldoon colony faltered because of high mortality, but the Prince Edward Island colony took root. In 1809, Selkirk bought an interest in the Hudson's Bay Company (HBC). To combat incursions by a rival fur-trading company,

the HBC considered planting a colony, and Selkirk submitted a pro-
posal.[79] His plan came as the first formal design for occupying land
on what eventually became the Canadian prairies. The HBC, which
had ignored settlement and concentrated on the fur trade, now acceded
to Selkirk's colonization venture in 1811. A prospectus – *Ossiniboia*
– combined a speculator's embellishments with an idealist's plan to
help dispossessed Highlanders.[80]

With a 116,000-acre grant from the HBC, Selkirk founded a proprietary colony at the junction of the Red and Assiniboine rivers. His
colonists joined other people along the Red River. Employees of the
HBC and its rival, the North West Company, were already present.
Selkirk's hand-picked governor for the colony, Miles Macdonnell,
aggravated hostility between newcomers and the established population of fur traders and descendants. To strengthen his colony, Selkirk
recruited former Swiss mercenaries in 1815. Tit-for-tat raiding cli-
maxed on 19 June 1816, when twenty colonists and a new governor
died in a shoot-out with a party from the hunting and trapping
population. Order was re-established, and Selkirk signed a treaty with
the local Assiniboines, Crees, and Ojibwas to extinguish native interests in the soil. The fairness of that transaction was questionable,
although the facts that Selkirk entered into an arrangement and that
the HBC continued to pay a quit rent to the Indians testify to a sense
of legalism that included native interests in the land. The status of the
rest of the prairies was uncertain at the time of Canada's purchase of
HBC interests in Rupert's Land in 1869–70. Consequently, the HBC
specified that the government assumed responsibility for clearing
Indian interests. As for Selkirk's people, a few persisted beyond the
1820s, but hostilities, floods, and locusts drove others out. The Selkirk
estate surrendered its title to the colony to the HBC in 1836.[81]

When Selkirk arranged his Baldoon colony in 1803, he had applied
under a local provision. In Upper Canada, where Thomas Talbot was
to be active, it had been possible since 1803 for approved gentlemen
to claim 1,200 acres and to have an additional 200 for each family
settled – 50 of the 200 acres went to the family. A pyramid scheme to
people a colony quickly, the plan was one of a multitude tried in Upper
Canada. One distinctive grant condition pertained to loyalists and their
descendants. The home government designated Upper Canada as a
haven for colonial refugees who had supported the crown during the
American Revolution. Townships were expressly laid out to receive
people from refugee camps in Lower Canada, and the crown gave
native allies land for a colony within the province. Sir Guy Carleton,
Lord Dorchester, the governor-in-chief of the British North American
colonies, bestowed a mark of distinction on loyalists who fled before

1783 by allowing their children land grants. A clause in his proclamation mentioned that "to that end their posterity may be discriminated from future settlers." That salute to fidelity was interpreted – by those who stood to gain – as an entitlement that allowed the children of loyalists and their children to claim grants.[82]

Other grant practices discriminated too, by applying sliding scales of military rank and social hierarchy. Disbanded soldiers were entitled to land on the basis of rank, and administrators made grants that favoured magistrates, merchants, and government servants. Adding to a mix of allocation procedures, the crown instructed Lieutenant-Governor John Graves Simcoe in 1791 to lay out land in Upper Canada equal to one-seventh of its value for the support of a Protestant clergy and other lands equal to the clergy reserves for the support of the government.[83] Attempts to fashion a little England in America stopped short of ensconcing a titled nobility. There were, however, several colonizers with aristocratic attachments and designs. A former Anglo-Irish army officer, Thomas Talbot, directed a vast, irregular colonization system (1807–38) by which he appropriated local authority and assembled a personal estate of more than 65,000 acres. He started in 1803 with a field officer's grant of 5,000 acres, which he located along the shore of Lake Erie in Middlesex County. Then he availed himself of Upper Canada's generous regulations that had enabled Lord Selkirk to start his ill-fated Baldoon colony. From his original grant, Talbot would give 50-acre plots to family heads, and for his trouble the government would allow him to claim from nearby townships 200 acres for each family settled.

In 1807, Talbot deviated from regulations and placed settlers on 50-acre plots outside his original 5,000-acre estate. Remarkably, the government ceded control of title registration, and until 1815 it had no idea what Talbot had done. In reply to a request from the lieutenant-governor, he reported the settlement of 350 families; two years later, the number was 804. In 1828, the government stopped his personal land acquisitions, although his colonization efforts continued. By 1836, his colonists occupied over 500,000 acres. The majority of alienations had never been reported to the surveyor-general, and only a quarter were patented. Talbot, who retained the essential maps and records until his death in 1851, operated beyond review in rustic isolation. The product of an aristocratic upbringing and the army, he could turn to the highest authorities in the colony and at home for support.[84] If there were any North American parallels to the Talbot tract, they were located in the Republic of Texas, where an 1841 ordinance established an empresario system that gave land contractors sections as bonuses for locating families on public land.[85] The colonizing and road-building activities of the unofficial baron of Lake Erie should also be seen against the backdrop of an era of hostilities, for they enacted a strategic policy of settling Upper Canada. There was no enduring Talbot estate.

What happened on Amherst Island was a clearer instance of aristocratic estate building. Lord Mount Cashel's farms passed into the hands of another owner in 1856, and, much like landlords on the American prairies, this proprietor set to work to sell the land. In North America, tenantry proved for landlords and farmers to be a means, not an end.[86]

Like Thomas Talbot, only in southern Africa, Lord Charles Somerset was affected by an epoch of wars. He, however, was no ordinary estate-managing colonizer, no scion – as Talbot and Mount Cashel were – of minor Irish aristocratic families. Somerset, the autocratic governor of Cape Colony (1814–26) and a descendant of England's Plantagenet kings, was the second son of the fifth Duke of Beaufort and had received every benefit that a duke's second son could expect: a public school and university education, purchased military commissions, and royal connections.[87] At the Cape, Somerset administered by decree without benefit of an advisory council. He resembled a marcher lord charged with stabilizing a border region. The war-drained imperial government yearned for an economical management of the Cape's frontiers, not for further expansion. The problem on the northeastern boundary, a region of fluid movement, was to control the trekboers and to prevent extensions of the colony; given the scope of the region and the grazing economy of the white population, this mission was hopeless. The challenge on the east, where ferocious conflicts had recently checked settlers' advances, was to stop border raids by and against the Xhosa. At the same time, Somerset had to watch for disloyalty from the Dutch colonists. To achieve these ends, he pursued several related schemes. He rewarded military officers with land grants and local public offices in border districts. The career of one favoured grantee, Colonel Jacob Glen Cuyler, portrays the far reach and persistence of the eighteenth-century landed-estate ideal.

Born in Albany, New York, in the year of the Declaration of Independence, Cuyler descended from wealthy land-owning families long established in the Hudson valley. His grandfather and father served as mayors of New York, and the latter's estate was seized because he remained a loyalist during the revolution. In 1799 Jacob joined the British army, and in 1806 he participated in the British invasion of the Cape. Almost immediately, he was appointed *landdrost* for the frontier district of Uitenhage. In that capacity, he helped organize the 1817

hanging of boer conspirators whose list of grievances included opposition to the introduction of quit-rent tenure for loan farms. Power
was certainly being expressed through land policies in southern Africa,
as we see in more detail in chapter 6. Landdrosts received land as
partial compensation for discharging public duties, many of which
dealt with land allocation. Cuyler manipulated his knowledge of local
topography and his authority to acquire Khoikhoi labour, obstruct
justice, and accumulate land until he owned an estate that encompassed 12,000 acres. *Dornkraal* (Thorn Enclosure), the core farm, he
renamed Cuyler Manor, an invocation of the family's lost Hudson
estate. A new frontier district was named Albany after his birthplace.[88]

In 1819, Somerset revived a plan originally proposed in 1809. With
support from the home government, he would colonize a buffer zone.
British colonists would be implanted on a vital wedge of territory. The
plan incorporated features of current British predispositions about land
and society and about production of exports, as well as Somerset's
own ideas about frontier stabilization. Parliament allocated £50,000
to assist the transportation of approximately five thousand immigrants.
Arthur Keppel-Jones summarized a deception. "A scheme was then
devised, the attractions of the Cape advertised, and the applications
called for – but the applicants were given no hint of the military rôle
they were expected to play."[89] They were being sent to occupy Xhosa
land, overrun by whites in 1811–12 and 1817–19.[90]

Only two and a half months before settlers disembarked at Algoa
Bay, a Xhosa force nearly drove the British out of Grahamstown, the
main regional centre.[91] Perhaps half the new colonists were poverty-
stricken artisans and labourers. Another group consisted of rural
workers and smallholders. A third was made up of gentry who faced
declining fortunes at home because of a depression and the rationalization of an agrarian economy, which limited opportunities for the
less competitive members of this rural class. The great majority of
settlers came in sixty parties with leaders; many of the latter, more
affluent colonists, expected to establish landed estates with a tenantry.
Cuyler escorted the first parties to their locations. Poorer immigrants,
it was supposed, would toil as farm labourers or tenants. Instead, a
good number rejected old-country rural deference and moved to the
towns. Colonists with resources who persisted in dreaming of country
manors shifted about, abandoning sites, petitioning for better locations, adjusting boundaries, and naming their farms with care.[92]

The new arrivals from England included liberals who succumbed
immediately to contradictions. They complained about Somerset's
autocratic rule but looked for favours; they despised slavery but desired
cheap labour. Somerset's military colony, in the administrative district

of Somerset, with his son's estate of Oatlands as social hub at Grahamstown, evolved in the 1830s and 1840s into a stronghold of the Cape's
wool trade, whose well-capitalized grazers installed repressive measures
to dispossessed Africans and their livestock. A guiding idea – improvement – was interpreted by capitalized stockmen to sanction a margin-
alization of various African peoples, who were vilified as adversaries
of progress. The Plantagenet aristocrat had introduced the nucleus for
a mode of agrarian capitalism, for which control of land was essential.[93] The concept of strategic frontier settlements persisted at the Cape
and was adopted by the boer republics from the 1860s to the 1880s.
More than on contemporary frontiers in North America and Australasia, quasi-military colonies played a part – though still only a small
one – in the allocation of land in southern Africa.[94]

Just as Symmes's Ohio dreams dissolved in courtrooms, as Selkirk's
remote prairie colony foundered in violence, as Talbot's settlement
took on its independent character, and as Somerset's immigrants
inspected land on the Zuurfeld, another adventurer with privileged
access to government looked for an estate, this time in New South
Wales. Alexander Berry had attended St Andrews and the University
of Edinburgh and for a time served as a surgeon's mate and surgeon
on East India Company vessels. In 1807, he outfitted a merchant ship
for trade between India and New South Wales, and he followed that
with an expedition to New Zealand and Fiji, looking for sandalwood
among the latter islands and for spars in New Zealand's island-flecked
northern bays. He returned to the United Kingdom for a while, but
in 1819 he embarked for New South Wales, this time with a partner,
Edward Wollstonecraft, nephew of feminist Mary Wollstonecraft.
Seeking land grants, the pair came with letters of introduction from
the secretary of state for the colonies. Over the next few years, they
worked hand-in-glove with the colonial government. In 1822, a
commissary vessel carried them down the coast, south of Sydney, on
a successful landhunting expedition.[95] Berry found the situation that
he wanted at the mouth of the Shoalhaven River and contracted for
a 10,000-acre grant. Berry and Wollstonecraft agreed to assist the
government in order to acquire land. Certain land grants to free
colonists in New South Wales required the maintenance of convicts.
By agreement, the government promised the acreage to the Shoalhaven estate builders if they would take one hundred life-term convicts. Not all hundred were transferred, so instead the partners were
allowed to buy 4,000 acres each. Governor Thomas Brisbane in 1822
implemented an experiment to sell land at five shillings an acre. Berry
and Wollstonecraft seized the opportunity.

In colonies without a constitutional provision for a local legislative body to oversee the disposal of crown land, governors could dispense it through their executive authority on behalf of the crown. Granting, not selling it, was the common practice in these crown colonies, and during the 1820s the basis for distribution could be crown favour, status as an emancipated convict, the number of convicts taken off crown hands, personal merit, service to the local government, or possession of capital. Building a mill seat or exploring the country was an example of worthy service. The three landhunters who followed Aboriginal trails over the Blue Mountains escarpment in May 1813 each received 1,000 acres. William Charles Wentworth – years later a speculator in Maori deeds – was one of the trio whose adventure "marked a turning-point in land exploration and the invasion of the continent."[96] In 1831, Governor Ralph Darling exercised his executive authority idiosyncratically to grant up to 1,280 acres to women as marriage portions and to provide land for the children of the clergy. In the last stages of the granting regime, £500 of capital conveyed into New South Wales entitled an applicant to consideration for 640 acres.[97] A land board could insist on an interview, and grants could be denied for "lack of character."[98]

In New South Wales, Berry and Wollstonecraft assembled a landed estate. With consigned convicts and contract labour, they cut cedar for shipment to Sydney and drained marshes. The partners methodically accumulated land from crown grants and purchases from neighbours.[99] One of their practices involved buying land from other crown grantees, keeping it if it served their plans, and exchanging it for crown land elsewhere if it was not what they needed. Colonial Secretary Alexander Macleay informed them in 1829 that this practice, tantamount to securing a floating grant, was "contrary to the general regulations that Land once taken possession of shall afterward be surrendered." But the governor saw "no objection in this case."[100] The government treated these improvers generously. Wollstonecraft died suddenly in 1832 and left his estate to Berry, who continued to amass a landed domain. By 1840, Berry held over twenty square miles, which he managed from Coolangatta, his manor overlooking Shoalhaven Heads.[101]

As laird of the Shoalhaven, Berry managed his lands like an English estate peopled with tenant farmers, and he embarked on a land-development project in 1845 when he laid out the townsite for Berry. Its grid plan with courthouse square, he reminisced, had been inspired by Roman *municipia*. A half-century after its founding, at the time of Berry's death in 1873, the Coolangatta Estate embraced 15,000 acres with 270 tenant farmers and additional grazing land. At the main homestead at Coolangatta, Berry assembled a tiny village with estate workshops.[102] In later decades, Australian sheep and cattle stations would achieve comparable self-sufficiency. Berry's experiment with a tenantry was unusual for Australia, although in the late 1820s and early 1830s the small, struggling colony along the Swan River in western Australia attracted a handful of colonists – gentry and half-pay officers – who intended to introduce landed estates with indentured labour.[103]

CONCLUSION

As we have seen in this chapter, governmental designs steered the occupation of frontiers in the old (U.S.) Northwest, the Red River, Upper Canada, eastern Cape Colony, and New South Wales. Portraits of determined colonizers have shown how individuals, applying political leverage or promises of a public good, obtained or distributed property rights. Personality and influence, character and power, mixed with government rules to produce distinctive experiments in colonization. Several grantees aspired mainly to private wealth; several wished to manage estates because that conformed with traditional marks of rank, refinement, and independence. At the turn of the century, land allocation remained personalized, a circumstance true even in the young American republic. Governments persisted in favouring privileged individuals.

Symmes, Selkirk, Talbot, Somerset, Cuyler, and Berry advanced frontier occupation by taking a direct hand in colonization or estate management. Each was motivated to colonize. These participants in government allocation schemes also identified with a tradition of landed elites. Symmes maintained a fascination with estate building that went beyond a mere assignment of unseen sections to unknown buyers; he was interested in the character of the people whom he hoped to entice. The self-awareness of these colonizers, who conceived of themselves as improvers, included historical comprehension. Parallels with Roman colonization appeared explicitly in the labours of Symmes and Berry, who imagined themselves new Romans. Selkirk spent a fortune on a philanthropic vision, and whether or not he considered himself a new Roman, his Red River colony, with its Swiss mercenaries, made him one. Somerset planted the English colony along the Great Fish River boundary for a strategic purpose, and the devious loyalist Cuyler assembled his manor to restore an estate seized in a revolutionary war. Talbot, an aristocrat with connections, went his own way and personally superintended a frontier estate near the border with an expansionist United States.

This list of similarities has limits. Symmes, the American colonizer who resembled colonial aristocrats, was part of a vital branch of

English culture, but his participation in a financial manipulation and his drafting of enthusiastic advertising copy marked him as a clever Yankee. Colonists for Cape Colony were recruited through advertising, but trickery in this case serviced a penny-pinching defence policy. As for Robert Morris, who was no colonizer, he epitomized outrageous greed and nerve. Selkirk evinced a contrasting, philanthropic intensity. The old-country elite phantasm of anchoring social order with landed estates certainly persisted with greater authenticity in Canada, South Africa, and Australia than in the United States, but it had not vanished altogether from the republic, although Morris brought to land acquisition and allocation an appetite and genius that linked land to finance and speculation.

The aristocratic ambition faded eventually on all frontiers, but vestiges survived even in the United States. Suggesting what made colonial America unusual, Gordon Wood describes it as a truncated society because it lacked a true aristocracy. This condition was not unique to America; British settlement colonies had ephemeral, would-be aristocrats, but no enduring, institutionalized aristocratic class. However, in the British settlement colonies attenuated remnants lingered.[104] Importantly, the market idea had been sidetracked there by revolutions and wars. Entrenched during a long, conservative reaction, land granting as a matter of grace and favour rendered tangible Tory constitutional values at odds with aspirations unleashed in a land-selling democracy. The profiles of large operators embodied these differences, although in one regard the United States and the British settlement colonies were alike. A will to possess real property gripped the public. Landed estates with tenants were attempted everywhere, but they seldom persisted as significant establishments for long, and they never achieved political or social roles comparable to the domains of the English aristocracy. Land availability and the will to possess were solvents that jeopardized new-world estates that had tenants. Manors along the Hudson River were attacked by tenants in the 1840s. In Prince Edward Island, landlords and tenants clashed from the late eighteenth century on, until the Dominion of Canada pledged to finance buy-outs in 1874. The government purchased the last estate in 1895.[105]

EPILOGUE:
A NEW METHOD OF ALLOCATING LAND

Eventually, as the colonies turned from land grants to land sales, distinctions between British and American settlement frontiers in the important function of land allocation consisted principally of instrumental details; no longer did they express a fundamental divergence in convictions about land, social order, and power. The distinctions started to pale when British imperial authorities began to encourage land sales in settlement colonies. In Upper Canada, this inclination started piecemeal in 1819, when crown land in settled townships was now to be alienated only by sale.[106] Then in 1824, the Colonial Office recommended that Upper Canada consider adopting regulations tried in New South Wales and Van Diemen's Land that permitted both large sales to parties with capital and small grants with quit-rent arrangements to poorer colonists. The Tory administration of Upper Canada accepted sales in principle, because generous grants had served to populate the colony, and now it was time to secure "some permanent advantage to the Colony, if possible, derived from what remains."[107] One challenge to the operation of this sale system was its requirement that upset, or floor prices be based on a crude assessment, which ultimately entailed guesswork. Additionally, the actual transition to land sales in 1826 did not eliminate loyalist and militia claims for grants. From 1826 to 1838, the crown "disposed of forty times as much land by grant as by sale, exclusive of the sale to the Canada Company."[108] Eligible individuals could as loyalists claim land scrip until legislation cancelled that extraordinary right in 1853, by which time the best farm lands of the colony were in private hands.[109]

A large step was taken towards a regime of land sales in 1831–32, when the British government instructed that unalienated lands in crown-administered settlement colonies should be sold by auction. These so-called Ripon regulations did not apply to Upper Canada. Accorded a degree of independence in land affairs, the legislature in 1837 passed an act for land disposal that codified a complex system of grants that extracted fees, auctions, and sales at a fixed valuation to squatters.[110] In Cape Colony, the government delayed introducing auction sales because the conversion of Dutch loan-farm tenure to quit-rent tenure involved much of the colony's useful land; meanwhile, consultations with London concentrated on avoiding or concluding frontier wars. Only by 1844 did this colony implement the Colonial Office's instructions.[111] The regulations were applied in Australia and in New Zealand when it was annexed. The introduction of land sales permits us to compare strategies, problems, and remedies found on the frontiers of the United States and those of British colonies, as I do in chapter 6.

By the mid-nineteenth century, American and British colonial governments alike worked to improve the character of land as a traded commodity, and they conceded that land distribution rated public debate. When the British colonies followed the American practice of apportionment by sales, the republic was well advanced with liberalizing terms and conditions, a trend that promptly influenced debates and policies on the pricing question in British colonies. The British and American frontiers eventually formed a network of related societies competing for immigrants and access to capital, aiming for economic development, and deploying land in that cause. British colonials in Australia and Canada watched what was happening in the United States; reformers insisted on duplicating American initiatives, and they often succeeded. Liberal reformers in Argentina and Brazil, who also observed the United States, faced greater challenges. British colonies involved in the great land rush, like the American republic, could not level the topography of the land that they controlled, but they could – and did – level access by rank, equalize fees charged for titles to land, and provide a reasonable amount of title security. Similar developments neither reached as far nor moved as fast in the Neo-Europes of Latin America.

CHAPTER SIX

Allocation by Market: The Geometry and Ledgers of Assurance

During the first three-quarters of the nineteenth century, each colony, province, or state considered in this book prepared land for the marketplace. Each continuously adjusted the terms for disposal of crown or public land, attempted to improve surveys on meagre budgets, and worked with varying degrees of success to reduce the vestigial complexities of property law, which obstructed the treatment of land as a marketable good or security. Features of property laws helped preserve the landed wealth of the English country elite and were ill-suited for dynamic land markets in newly acquired territories. The early-modern development of estate management in England, however, was affected by the desire for improvement. Stewardship required a little general knowledge of surveying and law. This knowledge was in the service of a few powerful families.[1] Although the doctrine of improvement thrived in rural England, market-oriented practices for the measurement and transfer of land were not ascendant there in the seventeenth and eighteenth centuries. Innovations often occurred instead on settlement frontiers, where the old-country aristocracy and legal establishment could not blunt reformation. The American republic and British settlement colonies innovated in terms of arranging and apportioning territory and of firming up the boundaries of land parcels, perfecting these objects of desire whose immobility made them fine pledges of security. In mapping and defining the landscape, colonizing governments improved the flow of capital.

In this chapter, I discuss changes in the colonies and the United States in two pairs. First, there were those innovations that applied to the sale of crown or public land; these included advances in providing certainty of title through land offices and in surveying. Second, there were those that pertained to property sales once land was in private hands; these included public registries for documents and refinements to mortgage law. Administrators and legislators in assorted jurisdictions contacted one another, so that many market-friendly alterations to the law in the nineteenth century resembled one another. When the government of Manitoba, for example, contemplated establishing a new system for land titles in 1884, it consulted Australian colonies, which had tried a major revision; I outline western Canada's distinctive and epoch-closing experience in the last section of this chapter. Common law jurisdictions consulted one another about measures to render real estate as negotiable as any other property.[2]

Common trends are strong, but there was variation because of chance elements. "There is no reason," writes economist Carl Dahlman, "why we should presume two countries with similar resource endowments, identical technologies of production, and the same preferences to have a historical process that turns out identical products." Unique historical events "will inevitably make the two societies pass through different evolutionary schemes since the structure of transaction costs will differ between them."[3] The details of property reforms did not jibe across all jurisdictions, but a tendency towards economic efficiency appears wherever we look. During the nineteenth century, jurisdictions in the English-speaking world revised conditions so that land transactions that had required weeks – and had left lingering doubts about the scope of the interests that changed hands – could be struck and completed in half an hour. Before considering this development, however, we must look at another subject. The previous chapter indicated that market values displaced aristocratic ideas of worthiness. A prominent issue for the United States and the British colonies therefore became how to allocate land in market-oriented societies. After slavery and racial discrimination, the disposal of the public domain was the dominant domestic issue in the United States. In southern Africa, frontier security, land, and the exploitation of cheap labour were interconnected as leading issues among the white colonizers. For Canada, land questions were surpassed in political importance only by the assorted cultural questions, which, when drawn into the political arena, split English- and French-speaking populations. No subject, however, eclipsed land policy in Australia and New Zealand.

PUBLIC SALES

Land Offices: Six Systems, Three Continents

Enveloped in perpetual controversy, land-disposal practices from the 1780s to the 1880s present a bewildering surface of changing regulations. The confession of G.S. Wright, secretary to the Crown Lands Department in South Australia, warns us against attempting a wearisome review. Asked if he was aware of the land laws of neighbouring

New South Wales, he said that "as a matter of fact I have difficulty keeping pace with the legislation of this province."[4] Diversity is deceptive. When legislators, editors, and lobbyists debated, around and around, they really disputed only a handful of goals and techniques for attaining them. Furthermore, arguments made in one part of the world resurfaced elsewhere, because governments shared information on schemes, though not identical environments. However, the impact of environment on official land-allocation practices and prices was negligible, because other interests – for example, the expenditure of land revenues and the political costs of supporting attentive land offices – preoccupied authorities. As a variable for the pricing of land, environment had at best a marginal influence, because the appraisal of land was both costly in itself and bound to initiate rounds of appeals.

When aristocratic values had first been shed, schemes for disposal were driven by economic purpose. A revenue model of disposal was common. In many instances, the justification was to raise funds for a grand purpose: retiring a war debt (the United States under the Articles of Confederation; Upper Canada after the War of 1812; Argentina after its Indian wars in the 1870s), public works (the United States after the War of 1812; the Australian colonies after 1850), or creating an emigration fund to rescue the poor of the United Kingdom (the initial plan for both South Australia and parts of New Zealand). The lingering entitlements of people with claims under prior schemes added complexity. Because of the ongoing rights of loyalists and their heirs, and land endowments for the established churches in Upper Canada, that colony maintained a bewildering set of regulations and entitlements. Only in the mid-nineteenth century did the government of Canada close out the loyalist rights and convert its clergy reserves to crown land. Meanwhile, special commissions and courts cleaned up grants made by displaced foreign regimes – in the case of the United States, the grants of Spain, France, and Mexico; in the case of Cape Colony, the loan farms of the Dutch East India Company.[5] Unpatented promises of land in Upper Canada and New South Wales forced later administrations to scrutinize claims and to convert interests into titles. Upper Canada / Ontario's Heir and Divisee Commissions functioned from 1797 to 1896. In New Zealand, a special commission determined the merits of private land transactions between Maori and newcomers.[6] Notwithstanding these and other exceptional instances, for a while revenue was a pole star for government land disposal.

In time, however, the revenue model drew criticism. One line of attack stressed individual entitlements, justified on the grounds either that individuals' improvements invested land with its real value or that citizens and subjects had a right of access to public resources. So long as there was unalienated land, people asked what good they might derive from it. Critics of the revenue approach scrutinized developments in other jurisdictions and concluded that their colony, to build a hive of activity, simply had to distribute land at nominal prices to stimulate growth. When a South Australian commentator compared his colony to New South Wales, Queensland, Victoria, Canada, New Zealand, and the United States in 1888, he claimed that these rivals for immigrants possessed better land and apportioned it at lower cost than officials in Adelaide. The Americans "distributed their broad acres with lavish hands to all who will use them, and they are covered with people and products."⁷ In the land-allocation frenzy of the nineteenth century, the variety of concessions available allowed landhunters and speculators to point to the most generous terms and forecast a local slump unless comparable measures were adopted.

Democratic politics, the doctrine of improvement, and competition among jurisdictions gradually shunted aside the revenue model around mid-century. The United States (1862), Canada (1872), and British Columbia (1875) instituted free homestead grants; Texas (1869–79) subscribed to these efforts to keep its public lands accessible to real settlers on small plots; several Australian colonies and New Zealand provinces pursued comparable measures from the 1860s through to the 1880s that allowed prospective farmers to select freehold farms on pastoral stations.⁸ Argentina's arrival on this scene was overdue, and when it determined on drawing in European immigrants late in the century it relaxed its entry requirements, but it could not hold out the same vision of abundant land for smallholders as had the United States or Canada.

Recurrent modifications to land sales complicate accounts of the revenue model; however, in the United States from the 1780s on, and elsewhere later, six basic systems were put into operation – first, large sales to individuals or companies so that, ideally, a great deal of money could pour quickly into treasuries, sparing governments headaches caused by squatters and defaulters; second, the sale of special survey areas or land orders at a flat rate per acre; third, public auctions with upset prices; fourth, sales by sealed tenders with upset prices; fifth, sales by flat charge per acre, usually established as the auction upset price; and sixth, sales based on a valuation of individual tracts.

First, large sales kept government overhead to a minimum. It was championed by the U.S. secretary of the treasury, Alexander Hamilton, and something like it had enabled Symmes to make his Ohio purchase, but the moment of the big buyer was a fleeting interlude in the republic and rare elsewhere too. The sale of over 1.3 million acres in Upper

Canada in 1826 to the Canada Company occurred because the colony pledged to indemnify civilians for property losses in the War of 1812. In Lower Canada, the British American Land Company purchased crown reserves and lots in the eastern townships to the extent of nearly 850,000 acres.[9] In South Australia, opportunities for so-called special surveys, permitting investors to buy blocks of 4,000 and 20,000 acres, were extended soon after the founding of the colony, because small-holders had not stepped forward in hoped-for numbers.[10] Popular with administrators in charge of lands, wholesale disposals entailed lower overhead costs than the sale of the same area in smaller units. However, large special surveys appeared to entrench privilege. Public touchiness about schemes that could *lock up the land* restrained governments.

Second, allotment by special survey and allotment by land orders shared characteristics. Both aimed to attract people with capital, and, for that reason, sales were negotiated in metropolitan centres remote from the land in question. Alexander Hamilton's doomed recommendation (1790) that Congress institutionalize large-block sales proposed that the land office should be at the seat of the national government so that "the principal purchasers, whether citizens or foreigners, can most easily find proper agents and that contracts for large purchases can be best adjusted."[11] Sponsors of the South Australian colonization scheme (1836) and the directors of the New Zealand Company (1839) sold land orders in London. Special surveys covered huge areas and involved a process of selection before sale, whereas the holders of land orders bought floating rights, and problems ensued with the assignment of tracts. The surveys were seldom ready, and lotteries or meetings of order-holders were required to perform the distribution.[12] After rejection of a special survey scheme, the United States in 1800 enacted a law for public auctions near regions recently surveyed. Not all governments assisted frontier occupants by holding sales nearby. New South Wales, at least into the late 1840s, auctioned grazing licences at Sydney, forcing grazers to travel or to employ agents.[13]

Third, there were the auctions. One of the earliest American auctions – a direct threat to Symmes's scheme – took place at Chillicothe in April and early May 1801. The crier called out the description of the allotments and received bids near this Shawnee village, which had figured in the Indian resistance to white settlement in the 1770s and 1780s.[14] When the number of surveyed tracts ready for sale increased in the early nineteenth century, so did the land offices. To manage a far-flung system, Secretary of the Treasury Albert Gallatin circulated rules in 1807 to enable "a good sober crier and an accurate clerk" to auction off 160,000 acres in ten days. Knocking down millions of acres in the shortest possible time was the objective, although several problems erupted during these early years. Combinations formed to prevent competitive bidding, and sales created an enormous amount of clerical work. Granting credit to buyers, moreover, put the system under immense administrative and political stress.[15] Years later, in 1836, near the end of a boom, the treasury department estimated that processing land patents would occupy fifty clerks for a year.[16] Government land sales helped school the modern state in managing large undertakings through regulations, forms, office routines, and annual reports.

In theory, public auctions should have maximized revenue for the republic in a timely and transparent way, yet defects arose, essentially because Washington in the early nineteenth century could hardly control frontiers any more effectively than London had in the 1760s. If squatters sitting on good tracts went to auctions to buy what they occupied, they were likely to experience disappointment unless they resorted to collusion or coercion. In some regions, a substantial number of parties – members of claims clubs – refused to bid against squatters. Allan Bogue believed that claims clubs in Iowa existed to defeat the public auction.[17] Intimidation occurred at government land sales, as well as at later auctions held under writs to recover land from buyers who failed to complete treasury payments on time. The final payments for initial sales of the public domain fell due in 1805, and from that year onward, until after its abolition in 1820, the credit provision – attended by a string of relief acts – created administrative nightmares.

The provision of credit placed the government in the unpleasant role of collecting on delinquent accounts, and its actions revealed people's boldness when they wished to possess land cheaply. During his western rambles in 1819, William Faux heard that a debtor's son had arrived at a sale of land in arrears. Brandishing a club, the lad threatened that "the land is mine and if any buyer takes anything away, he shall have me on his back."[18] When agitated debtors appeared at auctions, few contested their right to the land, and the majority were permitted to re-enter.[19] The 1800 act that established disposal by auction also allowed for purchase at a land office for a flat fee of two dollars per acre for land that failed to attract bids. Charles Buller's report to the crown on land distribution in British North America recommended in 1838 a flat rate, not only because he felt that a common price would encourage industrious settlers and discourage purchasers unable to develop the land, but because he recognized that U.S. auctions had become auctions in name only, for squatters could obstruct buyers and then secure a title by paying the two dollars per acre. Since actual occupants could "take from under the operation of this system (auctions) nearly all the lots which would be likely to excite competition," the British colonies, Buller explained, should simply adopt a standard price and forget about the pretence of auctions.[20]

Washington's administration of land sales to fatten the treasury, the status of squatters as trespassers on the public domain, and the upset price aroused American reform crusades from the end of the War of 1812 to the early 1840s. They led inexorably to the idea of free homestead grants. Some petitions and state resolutions favoured a drop in the floor price on unsold land, recommending that it should continue to fall, the longer it remained unsold. This was known as *graduation*. Western states demanded that more of the public domain be placed under their control *(cession)*. Eastern states wanted a portion of the revenue *(distribution)*.[21] The revocation of the credit provision in 1820 created a crisis for squatting settlers who intended to buy their lands when they came up for sale. So they launched campaigns for a right to purchase – at a future date – if they proved their occupancy *(pre-emption)*.[22] Proponents of these concepts justified them by insisting that the public domain belonged to the people, and all but distribution originated in western regions. When a faction in the eastern labour movement in the mid-1830s considered free western land as a means of slashing a labour surplus, thus possibly increasing urban wages and security, the slogan that "all men have a natural right to the soil" acquired political force.[23]

What the cry meant was that all who subscribed to improvement claimed a right to the soil, and that was the premise of concessions that culminated in the Homestead Act of 1862. An early step came with the recognition of a type of squatters' pre-emptive right. Legislation in 1830 allowed them to enter and occupy tracts on the public domain, with an understanding that they would redeem their technical trespass by bidding for the land at a future date. The act stipulated that this consideration would expire in ten years. Due for renewal in 1840, pre-emption became an election issue. In a contest of log cabins against palaces, the cabins won. An 1841 act of Congress did more than allow a continuation of pre-emption, for it erased the occupants' status as trespassers who retroactively redeemed themselves by purchasing the land at auction. Instead, they could stream onto the public domain with a legal right and stake claims to the exclusion of others. They lacked a perfect title until they purchased at the floor price, but that did not squelch a market in interests. Occupants or those to whom they sold their rights could not be dislodged as squatters by the government, because they held a right of legal entry. This change essentially terminated the revenue model in the republic.

A comparable demand for pre-emptive rights, along with compensation for improvements if an occupant was ousted, came from grazers in New South Wales and Western Australia during the 1840s. The Australian Lands Act of 1846, passed at Westminster, granted leases to grazers and pre-emptive rights to them to purchase parts of their stations.[24] After reviewing the process of land distribution in Upper Canada, Buller recommended logically that the local and imperial governments should treat the colony's squatters generously, granting title if they were improvers, because prosecution would "add this great practical grievance to those causes of disaffection which already exist."[25] The province's surveyors and land agents were careful in later years to recommend title for industrious squatters.

Intimidation at American public auctions might have been dealt with by requiring sealed bids. This method of allocation, the fourth in the list that I mentioned above, was rarely practised, because the political discourse about allocation – moving quickly through frontier booms, busts, and credit emergencies – favoured a populist tenderness that dictated the direction of legislative experimentation.[26] In fact, on no British or American frontier were sealed bids common, perhaps too because of a distrust of public officials. As an experiment in 1826–27, New South Wales allowed the purchase of land by selection. Petitioners chose the land that they desired to a maximum of 9,600 acres, and the colonial government imposed an upset price and invited sealed bids.[27] It was this trial auction system that inspired the Upper Canadian attempt to assess land values. In the late 1840s, the leases for vacated grazing lands in New South Wales were bid for by sealed tender, but this system too was short-lived.[28] Peter Burroughs concludes that "the auction system of the United States was widely discussed and admired in the 1820s by individuals interested in colonies or emigration," and it influenced the Colonial Office's regulations of 1831, intended mainly for Australia. London thought that by abandoning grants with a quit-rent obligation it could rid the colonies of blatant patronage, the troublesome chore of collecting quit rents, and the pretence of demanding settlement conditions that everyone knew were seldom enforced.[29] For the next two decades, public auctions with an upset price – adjusted several times – guided Australian apportionments. Some tracts were surveyed in advance of sales, but generally parties selected their land and had it surveyed, and the colony's *Government Gazette* announced an auction date.

Fifth, flat rates emerged de facto in the United States, when the Distribution–Pre-emption Act (1841) privileged settlement over revenue and fixed the levy for unsold land at the legislated upset price for auctions. The trend occurred elsewhere. New Zealand during the 1840s auctioned off crown land, but by the early 1850s the colony's provinces allowed purchases of land that went unsold at auctions for the upset price or gave people a choice of purchase methods. Buyers could opt for an auction with a modest upset price per acre and chance hostile bidding, or they could pay a higher flat price per acre. Competition to reduce upset prices broke out among the provinces, although in Canterbury province pastoral interests procured a price increase – a poison pill for potential buyers – to protect leaseholds against raids by sharp investors.[30] The details of pricing debates revolved around a limited number of plans, and almost everywhere – notwithstanding exceptions such as Canterbury – self-governing colonies eased purchase conditions. A common dilemma followed official discounting. In some locales, the relaxed terms permitted speculators to engross holdings. Meanwhile, scrip redeemable in land, bought by speculators at discounts of from 25 to 50 per cent, complemented land jobbing in the United States, Australia, New Zealand, and western Canada.

Sheer simplicity recommended holding auctions or charging uniform prices. However, there was another, more complicated system – the sixth in our series. Critics of the simple practices recommended finding the real value of the land. But there were problems. Private surveyors working for landhunters could assess carefully the utility of specific tracts, but government surveyors, forever straggling behind demand, wanted no part of assessing land to determine local upset prices or of valuations for grazing leases. In early 1831, for example, the government of New South Wales contemplated a careful appraisal in order to calculate upset prices parish by parish; however, exasperated Surveyor General T.L. Mitchell advised superiors that his staff could not keep up even using simpler processes.[31] After the fall from office of General Rosas in 1852, the province of Buenos Aires stopped granting land lavishly and cheaply to pastoralists, and the new regime aspired to set minimum prices or to fix upset valuations for auctions. One price was set for unalienated land within settled regions, another for land in the wilder districts; the former price also took into account a tract's distance from market centres. "Both methods were strongly criticized at the time because they made no distinction regarding the quality of the soil."[32] That was a common flaw of most rough-and-ready valuation schemes. Across the Canadian prairies in the 1880s, Dominion land surveyors reported each section's agricultural value, but "they were scarcely soil scientists," and in some districts land agents spurned their classification.[33] Valuations seemed sensible, but everywhere they were tried they encountered insuperable challenges.

In an attempt to adapt an experiment from New South Wales, Upper Canada's executive council required local officials to assess unalienated land in 1825–26, so as to provide upset prices preparatory to introducing land auctions alongside the colony's complicated grant system. Soon, however, the council judged that the valuations "are found in some instances to vary so much, and without any apparent reason, and in others to fall so far short of the known value of the Land that the Council have felt obliged to exert its own judgement."[34] Valuation burned the fingers of all who touched it. The government in South Australia opened controversy in the 1860s when it attempted to place a real valuation on land leased to grazers. Was real value equal to the gross annual return plus the value of improvements, or was it the grazing value averaged over a given number of years? Who would conduct the valuations?[35]

Despite the practical and political bother connected to any government assessment of land value, Cape Colony attempted a massive, refined appraisal between 1813 and 1822. It was unique. The project's roots can be traced back to a reform administration sent to the Cape by the Batavian Republic (1803–6). It insisted that applicants for loan farms and local officials collaborate to define boundaries carefully. The British adopted the same course after their capture of the colony in 1806. With advice from former Batavian officials, Governors Alexander du Pré, Earl Caledon (1806–11), and Sir John Cradock (1812–14) determined to solidify farm boundaries and place tenure on a permanent basis for a price. An 1813 ordinance granted permanent tenure in return for an annual quit rent. Although conversion was voluntary, no new terrain would be granted to petitioners unless they adopted permanent quit-rent tenure for all their holdings.

There were astonishing elements to the Cape land reform. Charles D'Escury, the administrator chosen to initiate change, was a Dutch refugee from the French Revolution and a keen political economist who grasped the concept of *economic rent* just then being worked out by Thomas Malthus and David Ricardo. He applied the idea in a grand design to value Cape Colony land as a prelude to determining quit rents. Some British reformers in India years later advocated a similar measure, and Eric Stokes's description of their notion of economic rent is apposite here. It embodied, writes Stokes, "the differential advantage enjoyed by all soils of a higher quality than the last taken into cultivation. On the last quality of land, at the margin of cultivation, the capital merely replaced itself and yielded the ordinary prevailing rate of profit. But all other soils yielded a surplus or rent beyond this."[36] This rent could thus be determined by subtracting labour and capital costs from the gross product of the land. D'Escury attempted to determine the rent for thousands of properties by designing and refining forms that local officials had to fill out after examining occupants in their localities; then he recommended his own assessments to the governor. Disputes over valuations rocked the colony, exacerbated friction between the government and boers, and almost certainly contributed to many boers' abandoning the colony during the Great Trek. Unsympathetic with D'Escury's utilitarian project, Governor Lord Charles Somerset nullified it in 1822 by accepting only the valuations of local officials, who tended to protect their neighbours. Quit rents remained a part of Cape tenure into the twentieth century, but local valuations watered it down.[37] In Argentina, Rivadavia's introduction of *enfiteusis* in 1822 similarly inflamed opposition because the guidelines instructing local juries on how to determine the intrinsic value of land lacked clarity. Occupants contested the valuations.[38]

Land evaluation and sale practices were, however, just one source of landhunters' grievances and government anxiety. Land surveys seldom were completed in time to satisfy fast-moving colonizers or to protect a government's interests. Among the more important crafts on frontiers, surveying was subject to innovations intended to accelerate the production of land parcels while maintaining just enough accuracy to support the faith in property descriptions that a real-estate market required. Surveyors were forward agents of capitalism and the state, and, when soldiers were not close at hand, they often had to negotiate temporary relationships with first peoples, who understood the power symbolized by chains and stakes.

ENCAPSULATING THE LAND

Surveyors and Their Instruments, Crews, and Perils

Technology is the art of transforming things found in nature to serve human ends. Property law and land surveying, essential to recasting land for the economic ends of colonizers, evolved during the great land rush. Some advances in surveying had already started in an improving rural England. The major land adjustments in early-modern England – the enclosures, the draining of the fens, and the break-up of church property – created a demand for surveyors and for surveyor's manuals and a need to simplify calculations based on English measurement's unwieldy units. Handbooks with titles such as *The Exact Surveyor*, *The Faithful Surveyor*, and *The Country Survey Book* rendered service. Published in 1682, the last heralded a shift towards simplicity by promoting actual measurement of *metes and bounds* rather than calculation of them through triangulation. By the latter system a surveyor would stake the corners of a property, measure the quantity of land (*metes*), and determine its boundaries (*bounds*) – all from observations made at divers staked points (*stations*). From known distances and the angles between sight-lines radiating from stations to other staked points, it was possible to calculate missing distances. This Pythagorean process required a higher degree of mathematical learning than what early-modern surveyors acquired through apprenticeship.[39]

One difficulty with the alternative method – measuring every boundary and calculating an area – was that the wire, cord, or chain marked distances in English measurement. Converting these into areal units required mathematical skill too. Consider the grotesque units. For linear measurement they were 12 inches to 1 foot, 3 feet to 1 yard, 5 1/2 yards to the rod, 40 rods to 1 furlong. For area, they were 1 square rod to a land perch, 40 perches to 1 rood, 4 roods to the acre. The seventeenth-century mathematician and astronomer Edmund Gunter – inventor of Gunter's chain (1620) – simplified the tortuous conversion of calculations. His device was not only ingenious in the sense that it could render English measure into decimal form, but it could be used with either end forward, since the units of measure were marked not as sequential numerals, but as brass rings denoted ten links. The lead chainman could drag the chain ahead and resume measuring, and the possibility of errors when reading parts of the chain was reduced because there were no numbers. The chain consisted of 100 links and extended for 66 feet. Ten square chains, or 100,000 square links, constituted an acre. Full acres and decimal fractions of acres could readily be derived by lopping off five decimal places from the number of square links.[40]

Whether surveyors chained all distances or resorted to triangulation, they needed sighting instruments. When measuring an area, they had to guide chainmen between stations to determine the lengths of sides; if using trigonometry to calculate the area, they had to view – and draw – straight lines between stations. If marking off a given distance, they needed to pilot chainmen along a line. A *plane table*, a *compass* or *circumferenter*, and a *theodolite* or *transit* were the standard instruments of alignment. On British and American frontiers, the *plane table* was the most accurate instrument readily available until the late eighteenth century, and it remained in use in some situations into the twentieth century. A simple version of the table consisted of a board about two feet square with a sight rule and off-white paper that minimized glare. Since freely selected tracts in the eighteenth and early nineteenth centuries stood on their own, typically without reference to other tracts or to a master map, surveyors walked around the chosen area, logged prominent natural features, staked a number of stations, and placed the table's supporting tripod over the latter in a sequence. They sighted landmarks or stakes along the rule and drew corresponding rays on the paper. They would move the table to other stations, to secure further lines and angles. They would carefully chain a few baseline distances. From plane table diagrams, trigonometric calculations yielded missing distances.[41] In England, surveyed properties could be tied into landmarks such as churches, bridges, and other historical structures. In the colonies, blazed trees and so-called monuments in wood, stone, or sod had to suffice.

Developed in the late eighteenth century, the modern *theodolite* or *transit* consisted essentially of a sighting telescope and compass card with degrees inscribed on it. The whole delicate apparatus sat on a tripod. The telescope could be flipped end to end (180 degrees), so that a back-sighting on a known point could steer a forward continuation on an identical line. This principle of reversal, *transit* of the telescope on the vertical plane, gave the device its alternate name. Rotation on the horizontal plane enabled angular measurements. Deflection lines could be run off this axis by reading degrees from the compass card, although bumps suffered on trails decreased reliability. The theodolite was a fixture on frontiers by the early nineteenth century.[42] Surveyors also ran straight lines with a hand-held compass or a *circumferenter* – a compass fitted with sights and mounted on a staff. The method of sighting a course referenced to north guided chainmen on the desired line. The problem with alignment by compass was that the deviation of magnetic north to true north varied from place to place and changed over time. Exact boundaries for a freely selected tract could not be nailed down by compass and chain, but they were used to survey grants selected in New South Wales until the late 1830s.[43]

The composition of survey crews, and division of labour, remained consistent during the nineteenth century and afterwards. A surveyor carried his instrument, directed the running of line, scribbled the all-important field notes, and later used these to draft maps, describe properties for deeds, or guide landhunters to prime tracts. As a minimum, a crew chief took along two labourers, who, apart from hauling the chain and hoisting it taut to a level position for accurate measurements (not an easy chore), carried ten or eleven iron pins, sometimes called arrow markers, that kept track of the chains measured. On relatively flat ground, a crew could chain five to eight miles a day, although Canadian chain draggers near Medicine Hat in 1882 boasted of once running 53 1/2 miles in 3 1/2 days.[44] Parties on long expeditions might include a cook and, in forested areas, at least one axeman. When surveying in Kansas in 1830, Isaac McCoy took his two sons, as well as "two white men as chain-carriers, and a black man as cook."[45] A Queensland squatter who wanted his station on the Upper Burdekin River surveyed in 1868 hired four men and a cook for three months.[46] It was not unusual to find first peoples in the United States, Canada, southern Africa, and New Zealand joining crews to interpret and to handle chains, axes, canoes, and pack animals, typically working for lower wages than white labourers.[47] Gustav Baumann, an Orange Free State surveyor, reminisced that his only companions were "simple farmers, or my native boy, and the only topics of conversation were beacons, cattle, and sheep."[48] In some instances in the United States and New Zealand, first peoples participated to oversee the layout of their reserves. Intending settlers joined crews too, for there was no better way to become an informed landhunter.

And there were few more likely ways to meet a violent death. In 1789, Symmes's surveyors on his Ohio tract encountered hostile Indians, supply shortages, and the hazards of wildness travel. One surveyor died when a canoe upset.[49] New Zealand surveyor John Turnbull Thomas wrote in his diary that "surveyors are made to be killed."[50] So it must have seemed. It certainly was a risky business. Some first peoples disrupted surveys on frontiers, because they correctly distrusted crews as harbingers of a new order or because crews encroached without permission or backing of a treaty or found themselves in the midst of inter-tribal disputes about land cessions. Settlers blamed Indians for some of the shingled claims in Kentucky, because ambushes obliged surveyors "frequently to suspend their business."[51] Following the Treaty of Fort Wayne in 1809, surveyors swarmed onto newly ceded lands in the old Northwest and emblazed 250,000 trees. This resounding announcement of white advance contributed to the ill-feelings behind Tecumseh's uprising.[52]

Crews surveying southern portions of the U.S. public domain during 1812–14 were impeded by swamps, pirates, the War of 1812, and the uprising of the Creek Indians.[53] Some first peoples recognized that surveyors heralded white colonization and reservations, and they contested the pending upheavals by intimidating survey crews. In 1828, the Osage of the Arkansas River raided a party marking off their reserve. They rode into camp and "in a solid phalanx dashed through, trampling down tents and camp fixtures." The episode ended with an impromptu war dance and an emphatic demand for the crew to depart. The survey recommenced only in 1836.[54] The crew laying out township sections in California's Owen's valley in 1856 temporarily suspended work out of fear of Indians who killed several of their mules.[55] In India, where the goals of early-nineteenth-century surveying included defining the boundaries of principalities and extracting taxes, resistance "crossed all social and economic groups, from rajas to peasants."[56] British-trained surveyors in Siam found their work impeded by nobles who feared confiscation, and local people killed at least one crew member.[57] On settlement frontiers as well as in other areas of the world where European ideas about boundaries were being introduced, surveyors experienced acts of resentment, some symbolic, others deadly.

When Aboriginal people living in the Port Phillip District of New South Wales killed two members of a contract survey party in 1840, the surveyor-general issued a circular letter, advising all crews to advance in a flank formation with flintlocks at-the-ready.[58] Not long after the Treaty of Waitangi, it dawned on the British in New Zealand that Maoris – like all first peoples – resented seeing surveyors marking the land before negotiations were concluded. The burning of surveyors' huts near Nelson in 1843 provoked a rash white response that escalated into an affray at Wairau that left four Maori and twenty-two Europeans dead. Shortly after that débâcle, the government warned the New Zealand Company against showing survey instruments before the completion of land sales.[59] Caution waxed and waned. In 1866, Maori impounded the equipment of a crew subdividing land seized at Tauranga. The surveyors returned to work with an armed escort, something that American surveyors frequently requested decade after decade. Invariably, Maori gave ample warning that a survey should not proceed, and surveyors stopped for a while.[60] Maori interruptions to survey operations between Mount Taranaki and Wanganui Town in early 1867 were preludes to Titokowaru's War, which began the following year.[61] Elsewhere on the North Island two surveyors who continued to run line were shot and killed in 1869–70.[62]

In October 1869, on the other side of the world, where the Precambrian Shield abruptly ends and black prairie chernozem begins, a party of Métis led by Louis Riel stepped on the chain and stopped Canadian surveyors running a base line. By this symbolic act, they contested Canada's right to Rupert's Land before Indian and Métis interests in the land and government of the colony had been settled. The tension culminated in the Red River Rebellion of 1869–70, which forced the federal government to establish the province of Manitoba and to issue compensatory land scrip to residents who lost customary land-use rights.[63] According to Canadian surveyor Aeneas Shaw, plains Indians west of Winnipeg resented entry on their land but never resorted to violence and rarely removed survey markers. Instead, they sometimes "defecated upon the top of every available stake."[64]

Local hostilities, foul weather, insects, bad water, low rations, a poor cook, plus sundry other demoralizing inconveniences caused sagging chains and careless instrument set-ups. These lapses and surveyors' generosity towards landhunters contributed to inaccurate surveys.[65] Some surveyors added a link to Gunter's chain to assist landhunters and settlers. In Cape Colony and Australia, there was also confusion over systems of measurement. Former surveyor – turned pastoral squatter – Henry Dangar recalled that in the early 1820s surveyors in Australia used English, Scottish, and Irish miles. At the Cape, Rhineland and English measurement clashed, but truly serious problems originated from the Dutch East India Company's apportionment of loan farms without benefit of surveyors. Claimants and local officials fixed farm limits by means of half-hour walks.[66] This extensively used approach to apportionment in southern Africa contrasted with the *nonvarying grid* and *trigonometric* (hereafter *trig*, a common expression) systems, and it left a mess to be resolved eventually by a trig survey. Inexpensive in the short term, because it did not require a survey, the loan-farm setup eventually entailed costs for the government and likewise for farmers driven to litigation or relocation. Inconveniences, however, were not inevitable for all farmers. Thus, so far as many were concerned, the arrangement's imperfections were not threatening, while its flexibility and cheapness were plainly advantageous. By the time of the Batavian government, some boers assumed that loan-farm occupation carried more property rights than mere licenced usage. That presumption worried some Batavian officials and their British successors. As we saw above, the scheme to rectify boundaries was merged with an extremely unpopular exercise in land valuation.

Marking Better Rectangles Faster: Grids, Trig Surveys, Verified Co-ordinates

On all frontiers, the surveyors' terms of employment contributed to problems. Free selection – whether in American colonies or later in Australia or New Zealand – put them in the field alongside people whose future estates they measured, and that connection blurred lines between public and private service. For a consideration, some surveyors would demarcate boundaries that enclosed more land than grants specified. American and Canadian grids, starting as early as the 1790s, reduced opportunities for huge falsifications or errors; trigonometrical surveys (from the 1830s on) and international verification of co-ordinates (beginning in the 1880s), both techniques also examined in this section, further enhanced acuracy and certainty.

The non-varying grid's capability for enforcement of reasonable accuracy originated from the fact that it consisted of standard units, not singular rectangles. Yet non-varying grid systems in Canada and

the United States differed. In Upper Canada, starting in 1791, surveyors laid out most townships in grids of uniform allotments; however,
these townships were not integrated within a master grid composed of
pre-established meridians of longitude and baselines of latitude. The
township grids often stood alone, and the government experimented
with several sizes and configurations of allotments. By contrast, in the
Indiana Territory the township grids nested in a larger grid of meridians and baselines, although the scope of these master grids was
contained by the piecemeal clearing of native title on the public
domain. West of the Mississippi, the spacing of the meridians and
baselines also embodied the history of Indian–white relations, as well
as topography. On the relatively flat Canadian prairies – that enormous
latecomer to the great land rush – the township grids, fitted into a
grand design of evenly spaced meridians and baselines, was unrolled
at one pronouncement for the entire region. In North America, the
grid prevailed; however, exact characteristics diverged.[67]

If a specified number of grid allotments – for instance, thirty-six for
a township – were to be laid out, the distance of line run would be
known in advance. At the end of the survey, the accuracy of the work
could be verified by noting how close the calculated distance came to
the actual chained distance that tied into a monument established
earlier by a trig-check survey or a prior, adjacent township survey.
Township surveys on the non-varying grid buttressed each other inexpensively, but imperfectly. In early Upper Canada, moreover, a shortage
of capable surveyors meant that lot boundaries in the grid were run
hastily and without uniform care regarding tie-ins with other elements
of the survey. Errors showed up as jogs in road allowances or as
wandering lines at the backs of adjoining allotments. However, when
conducted carefully and systematically, the non-varying grid permitted
an inspection of accuracy. Although the grid allowed checks on surveyors' honesty and ability, it was imperfect, because governments
often employed surveyors as private contractors, not as public servants.[68] Abuses arose from contract arrangements, because, as Malcolm
Rohrbough relates, most surveyors, knowing as much as they did
about the wilderness, "connected themselves in one way or another
with the buying and selling of lands."[69]

The American midwest frontier was not unique in this respect. A
number of Upper Canadian surveyors received payment in land.
Among the busiest, Mahon Burwell accumulated over 40,000 acres,
some allocated by ballot, but selection was allowed if the balloted land
proved unsatisfactory. Several contractors, paid in blocks that they sold
quickly, never ran surveys themselves, but hired others.[70] There were
other opportunities. Government land agents in Upper Canada/Canada

West in the 1850s used their authority to ignore squatters' legal interests in favour of sales to business associates. Sealey Brothers of Timaru, New Zealand, who surveyed for that colony's government in the early 1870s, shared an office with the government's land agent, and snooped into public records on behalf of clients.[71] The team of John B. Thomas and Henry G. Hay surveyed on contract roughly 150 townships in southeastern Wyoming in the early 1870s; at the same time they advised ranchers on purchasing land judiciously so as to hold extensive grazing ranges and the pair also embarked on their own sheep and cattle enterprises.[72] Rancher G.B. Goodell advised his manager to make use of the surveyors when they showed up on his outfit's range. "If those surveyors go to work before I come up I wish you would keep track of them and have them make entries in their field notes of any claims we want to make, even if we have no improvements up now – the springs above the ranch for instance towards Spencers – and any places you think of that we don't want anyone else on – also get the number of the land so we can make our own entries."[73]

Surveyors were tempted to "double dip," getting paid for learning about locations through government contracts, picking up earnings from private work on the same terrain, or taking good land on their own account.[74] The other problem with contracting out was that it paid by length of line run – an arrangement that rewarded haste. When Upper Canada adopted contracting, surveyors hurried through townships, creating "instances in which scarcely a single lot is of the dimensions or in the position assigned to it in the diagram."[75] Pressure to rush intensified when things went wrong in the field. Crews lost time fumbling to locate the corner monument whence they had to run their line. The surveyor occasionally had to return to a base with damaged equipment and wait for a replacement instrument.[76]

In addition to enabling checks on the size of the tracts that surveyors laid out, the non-varying grid absorbed errors by a simple expedient. Ideally, surveyors of the thirty-six square miles that comprised a standard American township ran its outside boundaries first, setting corner monuments to anchor the next set of westward townships and to provide reference points for later surveys of the thirty-six component sections. With the township monuments in place, a crew – often not the one that installed the township – started at the township's southeast corner and worked to the northwest, roughing in the sections and finally tying into the northwest township monument. Time lags between township and section surveys invited direct action by squatters and claims clubs and pressed governments into corner-cutting practices. In order to minimize the number of miles run for the sections, without sacrificing much accuracy, a number of expedients were tried.

In some cases, only lines for the east and west sides of sections were laid out. Errors tended to accumulate on the northwest sections, the last ones surveyed in a township. The United States ingeniously made the ground bounded by surveyors' monuments – not the acreage specified in deeds or depicted on plats – the legal grant. Sections or quarter-sections thus comprised more or less than the statutory 640 or 160 acres. The rule worked minor hardships, giving one party a smaller area than another, but buyers had to accept a shortfall as a condition of purchase.[77] A compromise between accuracy and speed was achieved. The idea that it was the ground marked, not the acreage granted, that comprised the legally sanctioned parcels was clever. Priority for pegs in the ground, not for plans in the registry office, gained acceptance elsewhere, except at the Cape.[78] There, by the late 1870s, if a resurvey disagreed with original beacons (in other jurisdictions, known also as monuments and picquets), diagrams were to show old lines in black and new ones in red. There could be two definitions of a single property. Understandably, this solution worsened confusion.[79]

The non-varying grid fabricated parcels that depended on a township's corner monuments and later monuments for sections (640 acres) and quarter-sections (160 acres). Surveyors had to scrounge local wood or stone, and in Kansas, Nebraska, and Dakota and on the Canadian prairies such material was scarce. Earth mounds, used instead, were easily destroyed by the elements. Settlers in some areas removed wooden posts for fuel or shelter.[80] Survey monuments were vulnerable, and "evil-disposed persons" on several frontiers moved them for an advantage. In southern Africa, where boundary markers regularly walked away, cunning surveyors- in addition to tying in a monument with measurements to nearby trees or rocks – buried articles (gin bottles, for example) below monuments. The practice furnished evidence at inquiries. On other frontiers, surveyors likewise tied in with measurements and buried enduring articles, noting these steps in field books that could be introduced in court. A crew running line in Kansas in 1830 deposited pieces of granite, flint, chert, and iron ore; another, conducting a resurvey in Ontario around 1873, buried broken crockery or glass, then planted the monument post.[81] Governments answered the destruction of monuments with punitive fines, commissions to reestablish monuments, meetings with witnesses to the original partitions, and the erection of durable beacons. Official countermeasures ran up expenses. The work of replacing missing beacons in southern Africa exasperated local officials and witnesses and sometimes left matters in doubt, because of confusion so great that, as one commissioner said, "when it is a matter of beacons, I can't believe myself."[82] The Cape Colony attempted to stabilize land parcels with whitewashed stone and cement beacons at least six feet high, but neighbouring colonies thought them too extravagant.[83] The Cape's beacons still stand out.

Equipment and crew configurations changed slightly over two centuries. Adaptations responded to different circumstances. In all likelihood, English surveyors from the late seventeenth century could have adjusted quickly to field operations in the colonies or America in later centuries. It was mainly conceptual changes, rather than technological improvements, that enabled surveyors to strive to achieve three linked goals essential for reliable land titles. At some point, the system of measurement and description had to increase the landholders' certainty that they occupied a particular amount of territory at a definite place; it had to enable governments to avert anarchy in their management of allotment; and it had to move quickly and inexpensively to fulfil both public and private demands. As far as conceptual changes to landed property go, the non-varying grid – even with its flaws – was stunningly ingenious. The rival system – free selection – met the velocity and budget requirement (although cost avoidance was temporary), and it possessed one further quality alluded to in chapter 3. It was responsive to environmental conditions.

When grazers in the three constellations of Southern Hemisphere British colonies eventually needed to define their places and register precise descriptions – to satisfy creditors, protect against encroachment, or conform to new government regulations – they realized that selection without formal survey, though fast and cheap, was the bane of certainty. Some hill or gully or line of trees that had constituted a boundary was mistaken for another; because of rising property values, a neighbour suddenly disputed an informal border line. Survey costs in these circumstances could no longer be deferred.[84] Usually, when governments prescribed a finer definition of places, occupants had to straighten boundaries, if rectangular tracts had not already been demanded as a condition of occupancy. Either initially or retroactively, ordinances compelled rectangles to be aligned if possible along the cardinal points of the compass. In some cases, the regulations imposed limits to the ratio of depth to breadth.[85] Survey fees made simplification desirable too, because kinks translated into larger bills. Over time, these considerations forced an ordering of landscapes in southern Africa, Australia, and New Zealand – not into North American checkerboards of ostensibly equal squares, but into quilts of unequal rectangles.

Troubles with free selection persisted, even when surveyors laid out boundaries and reconfigured individual properties, because, although lines were now legally determined, straight, and fewer in number, separate parcels still benefited from connections to a larger system that

referenced places to one another or – far better – to longitude and
latitude. Land departments also believed that they needed reliable
monuments, so that they could check on the work of their contract
surveyors to discover incompetence or corruption. Grid surveys generated abundant reference monuments installed by different crews, and
when a crew finished a township it would have to see how close it
came to dropping a plummet atop another party's monument. This
helped guarantee that actual farm sizes were more or less what they
purported to be in documents. Trig surveys could assure that too.

By the late nineteenth century, when governments everywhere began
to dedicate adequate budgets, survey departments undertook trig surveys. The first step was to lay out an accurate baseline of two to three
miles, which served as the foundation for a network of triangles with
stations of known longitude and latitude at their apex. Typical were
operations in Van Diemen's Land, which began in 1832, when surveyors went to work on muddy plains near Hobart.[86] In preparation for
settlement near present-day Brisbane, Queensland, a surveyor, two
assistants, and twenty-one convict labourers found a suitably flat place
and ran the base line.[87] It was one thing to initiate a trig survey, another
to complete it in a timely way. In New South Wales, Victoria, New
Zealand, and southern Africa, the benefits and costs of triangulation
were debated for decades, while impatient settlers, squatters, and gold
prospectors forced suspension of trig work in favour of fast, messy
surveys. Senior surveyors revered the trig survey's precision, but
landhunters, settlers, and governments wanted mere functional parcels
and wanted them completed at their convenience. As was the case with
clearing native title, peoples' impatience had a telling impact. The
erection of trig stations was habitually postponed, until later in the
century. Town planner and surveyor Colonel William Light, who laid
out the townsite of Adelaide in 1836, resigned as surveyor-general of
South Australia because of his dislike for a running survey as opposed
to a trigonometric one. Contemptuous of fast, shoddy methods and
their champions, he scorned his successor as "the booby."[88]
   Trig surveys produced their own problems. In New Zealand, they
started at different times in each province. During the 1860s and 1870s,
they advanced independently, and by 1875 they covered a third of the
islands. Many were essentially worthless, a fact that complicated
attempts to reform the colony's land titles, because without reliable
surveys, the indefeasible titles that New Zealand aspired to provide
could not be granted.[89] In India, as Matthew Edney argues, the trig
survey entailed an effort to make state control more effective, and
behind that exertion lay the promise of greater land tax revenues. In

areas of the world where colonizers believed that they could establish European-style settlement societies, state control undergirded individual property rights. Believing that southern Africa would bear colonies of Europeans, British colonial authorities began to work on trig surveys at the Cape in the early 1840s. In 1904, the surveyors-general of southern African colonies met to co-ordinate standards and baselines – work that they regarded as a step towards South African confederation.[90] When Canada's Department of the Interior devised its Dominion Lands system in 1870–71, it applied the non-varying grid to the prairies in conjunction with a controlling trig survey.[91] Established communities, more securely financed than fledgling colonies, superimposed trig webs over both the quilt pieces of free selection and the non-varying grid. Once places were accessible by telegraph, longitude could be established with considerable precision for a number of trig stations.

In the 1880s, the verification of co-ordinates engaged national and international agencies. The globe was being overlaid with rectangles, squares, and triangles.[92] This geometry of assurance underpinned land markets with the certainty of place. Recent historians of cartography propose that maps defined the empire's nature – transforming the exotic to the knowable, implementing science, dominance, and separation, – but that view may privilege mapping per se to an untenable degree that by-passes immediate practical purposes, such as revenue and property rights.[93] Maps figured in the extraction of revenue in India and in the advancement of property rights in the United States and in British settlement colonies. They were part and parcel of a nineteenth-century European export of technology and of the accompanying idea of rigid precision; in this instance, the application of Western techniques explained national boundaries and private estates in inflexible forms. Surveys and maps helped install European imperialism by replacing indigenous concepts of territories and boundaries, which could entail ambiguities. In their place, Europeans introduced ways of envisioning space that originated in the geographical sciences, which aspired to create the new supposed realities of nations and plots of land. The technology of measurement and the language of improvement were connected to form realms of order that reduced multiple interests and, potentially, litigation; these new renderings of locales enabled capital markets to catalogue property with development potential.[94]

From the perspective of colonizers, the improved survey systems reduced cheating and gave people a good idea of their domains. Countless nineteenth-century plat maps served local planning activities and real-estate markets. Maps and property descriptions originating in the non-varying grid aided expeditious transactions, because they were

precisely condensed portraits of the land. There were no nebulous
estate names, no error-prone descriptions of *metes* and *bounds*, no jogs
and bends to report, merely numbers that led logically through a
nesting of units whose numbers and letters occupied little space in
advertisements, letters, and telegrams. Examples show the advantages
for dealings at a distance. It was easy for agents, buyers, and vendors
to correspond with exactness. A North Carolina deed, representing the
old system, was held void because it could have applied to two or
more properties: "a tract of land containing one hundred and seventy-
three acres, lying and being in our county of Wilkes, on a big branch
of Luke Lee's Creek, beginning at or near the path that crosses the
said branch, that goes from Crane's to Sutton's on a stake, running
west 28 chains 50 links to a white oak, on Miller's line, then south
60 chains to a stake, then south 60 chains to the beginning."

In contrast, we can look to a Missouri deed that described a comparable quantity of land on the grid of the public domain: "the
southwest quarter of section eleven, township fifty-three, range sixteen."[95] Advertisements for lots in an unvarying grid could convey vital
information in a single line, as this example from Manitoba in 1890
illustrates: "NW qr Sec 3 Tp 13 Range 2E, 160 acres, $5.00 per acre,
Torrens Title, Easy Terms."[96] In this relatively succinct form, instructions by telegram could effect deals. The standardized inscription of
land, like the grading of flour, grain, and lumber, broke the bonds of
distance and served market expansion.[97] In the range-ranching regions
of the American west, the grid also served those cattlemen who wished
to consolidate and monopolize the public domain that made up the
bulk of their ranches. Astute cattlemen, as well as their agents and
surveyors, kept printed template grids at hand, sketched on them
depictions of streams and waterholes, and used these simple maps to
determine which quarter-sections or forty-acre blocks they should
claim by formal entry in order to hold the surrounding territory.[98]

Stored near the survey maps in registry offices, another set of records
was the object of changes that advanced certainty in land markets, not
in regard to place but with respect to certainty of ownership. Plat maps
guided conveyancers into land registry documents, which either permitted a reconstruction of a property's legal history or led to a certificate that guaranteed an owner's title. Other documents showed liens,
mortgages, and easements. Like the non-varying grid and the simple,
connected idea that official surveys marked on the ground conveyed
the legal property, a registry open to public inspection was an innovation that expedited private markets in real property and advanced the
formation of credit arrangements. Registries reduced uncertainties

about property title and allowed land, when presented as collateral for loans, to act as a lever in its own transformation.

PRIVATE SALES

Enhancing Certainty: Registry Offices and Torrens Title

Registration of documents and Torrens title narrowed significantly the range of fraudulent land transactions and credit deceptions on frontiers in the nineteenth century. One set of helpful measures – registration – built on registry procedures in Europe. One can begin an analysis of registration systems by asking whether they were voluntary or mandatory; broad or narrow in the scope of documents held; limited to a few local jurisdictions or extensive; established to serve primarily the state, the courts, or commerce; accessible and well indexed or obscure. The purpose of registration of property instruments, however, was the same everywhere: it simply put information at the disposal of buyers and lenders. If parties to conveyancing wished, they could employ specialists to investigate the registered documents in a bid to reduce uncertainty. Registration did not guarantee titles. However, two methods for limiting risk developed. First, South Australia created a state guarantee of title in 1840. Known universally as Torrens title, it spread to many jurisdictions; its advocates alleged that it added market value to a property, and I examine it extensively after considering the varying modes of registration that developed and evolved in our five regions. Second, private title insurance, popular in the United States, was another approach to managing title risk, but one not discussed in this study.[99]

Profiles of three registration arrangements in Scotland, England, and Ireland help explain issues in registration. First, the oldest registries – in existence since at least the early sixteenth century – were in Scotland, because Scottish law required litigants to file documents. By contrast, the English common law relied on oral testimony. For that reason, and because the English rural land market, serving mainly the aristocracy and gentry, was stable, England had no registries until the beginning of the eighteenth century. Second, a registry of deeds opened in the west riding of Yorkshire in 1704, in the east riding in 1708, in Middlesex in 1709, and in the north riding of Yorkshire in 1736. The reasons for their creation are broadly similar. Parliamentarians wished to eradicate frauds and suspected that secret transactions in mercantile communities allowed swindles that could ruin whole families. Yorkshire's freeholding cloth merchants often needed credit. The security of their property helped, and a registry aided arrangements. Third, in Ireland, the British government established a registry of deeds in 1708 in order to reduce

frauds, but also to complement laws intended to divest Catholics of
landed property. Unlike English measures, the Irish law applied to the
whole country and covered a wider range of documents.[100]

A cursory review of New England evidence suggests that, to accom-
modate land granting, colonies established registries quite early, several
before the mid-seventeenth century; however, they were "astonishingly
sloppy in the beginning, because there was little English precedent for
them."[101] By the late eighteenth century, as new counties were incorporated, registries appeared in the courthouses of former frontier
districts. In a series of steps between the 1820s and the 1890s, courts
and legislatures in states and territories bestowed ever-greater authority
on registered documents, so that the act of recording a conveyance in
a local registry office operated as notice to third parties who might
have an interest in the estate. Recorded deeds and mortgages received
higher standing in courts than those left unregistered.[102]

    The law in British settlement colonies moved along a path from occa-
sional registrations to routine, prudential practices. South Australia took
the next step and introduced government-guaranteed land titles. Two
conquered colonies – Quebec and the Cape of Good Hope – possessed
registration practices at the time of their capture. French and Dutch law
placed premiums on registered documents, as did other colonial empires.
Whereas the registration of documents was not a feature of the common
law, it was common on the European continent and in Spanish, Portuguese, French, and Dutch colonies. When British and American governments formally annexed settled territories, they had to determine which
laws to retain. Criminal law – charged with symbolism – was changed
straightaway. Civil law was different. Its principles and operating details
regulated ongoing commerce and estate management. A root-and-
branch displacement was out of the question. Criticism and evolutionary
change, however, were feasible. Merchants and investors familiar with
the common law trickled into new territories and appraised the merits
of either pulling local law into line with the common law or adapting
themselves to the existing legal processes. In Quebec, rival estimations
of the civil law held by modernizers and traditionalists agitated political
life for almost a century after the conquest.[103]

    In Cape Colony, a more cordial evolution occurred. Explanations
are not hard to find. The contentious features of Quebec civil law
related to *seigneurial* land tenure, which, in the eyes of its critics, stifled
an active property market, or at least required considerable – costly –
legal manipulation. When New France became a royal colony, the
administration of the land system precluded speculation. Contracts and
deeds were supposed to be examined by notaries, and copies sent to

the capital, but there was no public registry until 1841.[104] At the Cape, the Dutch East India Company pursued no sophisticated plan to mesh land, social order, and strategic settlement. Moreover, Roman-Dutch law – logical, codified, and honed by a commercial society – had the capacity to serve land transactions. The law required the registration of an extensive list of transactions and obligations.

In Roman–Dutch law any deed or mortgage for immoveable property that had not been reviewed by a notary public and registered at the court in the locality in which it was negotiated was vulnerable in the event of litigation. Registration was a fine idea for a small, flat European country, but impractical on the Cape's frontiers. The Dutch East India Company in 1714 required the registration of all obligations at the Castle of Good Hope. By the late eighteenth century, land dealings occurred many days away from the centre of government, and that disrupted registration. Nevertheless, registration was intrinsic to the law, and anyone could examine the registry – a circumstance that helped protect buyers and mortgagees against clandestine sales, undisclosed partitions, or secret pledges of properties for security. Fraud was not eliminated, because vendors and debtors could present misleading descriptions of property for registration, and the government gave no guarantee of accuracy.[105] In England and in new societies, a number of commentators and inquiries by the mid-nineteenth century specified that an ideal conveyancing system should inspire *trust* in the *security* of land titles.

Mere registries for documents were in disarray everywhere at least into the mid-nineteenth century, and they harboured misleading or imperfect documents as readily as sound ones. They contained the shingled claims of Kentucky, for example. Even in South Australia, whose founders professed rational settlement ideals, land titles degenerated into a mess. Overcome by grazers who raced ahead of a grid survey, the South Australian experiment wobbled off course within a few years. It was said in 1857, as background to reform, that of 40,000 titles, 30,000 had been misplaced, 5,000 were seriously defective, and a number were in the hands of absentees who could not be located.[106] In Canterbury and Otago, the pastoral land rush, with its array of landholding tactics, created such confusion that a member of the New Zealand Parliament believed that there "was scarcely such a thing as a marketable title."[107] Faulty property descriptions made by inept frontier surveyors entered registry offices. Not only did surveyors have to know how to run accurate line, but they had to prepare property descriptions that could stand up in court. Critics of traditional conveyancing practices believed that a rigorous review of documents associated with registration could add premiums to subdivided properties, which would inspire speculators to insist on proper surveys.

In addition to improving security, the proposed conveyancing and registration reforms of the mid-nineteenth century promised simplicity, accuracy, economy, and quickness. Registration alone merely allowed the recording of property documents and combined secure storage with facilities for public access. Anyone could examine the documents and find the essential chapters in the transaction story of particular properties, but registration itself failed to cure defects in the documents. Transactions were slow in older jurisdictions where free selection and poor surveys prevailed, because cautious buyers engaged surveyors to resurvey lines and retained lawyers to check for defects and to determine if there were other parties with interests. Predicated on suspicion, conveyancing that relied on a traditional deeds registry was not as simple, accurate, cheap, and speedy as possible.

Credit for the breakthrough in thinking about land titles went to a zealot. Robert Torrens of Adelaide did not single-handedly devise Torrens title; however, building on the ideas of others, he assembled its components, helped implement a trial in South Australia, and embarked on a crusade to transform conveyancing from a stodgy craft into a streamlined business, to reduce the work of days into a few pen strokes.

To understand Torrens title and Robert Torrens's mission to convert the common law world, it is helpful to know that his father, Robert Torrens, Sr, had – along with James Mill and David Ricardo – founded the London Political Economy Club. An intellectual and a member of Parliament, he kept radical company.[108] The classical economists and politicians with whom the elder Torrens consorted aspired to make England home to an efficient economy. To that patriotic end, they censured a miscellany of antiquated laws and practices, which, though benefiting particular classes and professions, seemed bereft of general utility. In his campaign to spread the good news about a better – as he saw it, a perfect – title system, the younger Torrens, like his father's acquaintances, flayed the bizarre features of property law and skewered the lawyers who profited from esoteric legalese. Astute critics of tradition and privilege, his father's friends were the century's leading exponents of utility and progenitors of modern economics. The son had the opportunity to champion practical relief for people who wanted to make capital improvements to their property.

In 1840, through his father's influence as chairman of the colonization committee for South Australia, Robert Torrens became the colony's collector of customs. He advanced through a series of senior administrative positions, culminating in appointment to the colony's executive council in 1855. As a member of the colony's executive, he introduced the scheme that eventually would bear his name, although the measure itself gathered the musings of many individuals.[109] All lands alienated from the crown in South Australia henceforth came under the legislation's provisions, and lands granted prior to that date could be absorbed by voluntary applications from proprietors. In the latter circumstance, applicants brought in deeds, surveyors' plans, and statements from lawyers qualified as "examiners of titles." These professionals reviewed the documents precisely as they would have done for an intending purchaser under the old system; however, once a recorder of titles approved the application, no lawyers were required again to search that title.

All allotments accorded a Torrens title became registered estates whose owners possessed a copy of the title, while the registry retained another. Title was indefeasible, which meant that if, by error or fraud, it had been granted incorrectly, it remained good, and victims received cash compensation. For this purpose, an insurance fund was created by a small levy charged when land was first brought under the system.[110] Torrens title reduced friction in property markets. First, because parties who held the registered title kept the land in the event of error or fraud, capitalists who were innocent of any wrongdoing retained their investments in improvements. This mandatory definition of the rightful owner encouraged improvements, because property developers did not have to worry about losing capital. Second, the compression of title to a single document eliminated an accumulation of records and extensive indices and, with that, excuses for search fees and delays. Third, Torrens title promised, in its early years, to clean up mortgage law, since it abolished the old fiction that a mortgage transferred the legal estate to the mortgagee and eliminated a costly gambolling about with complex traditional operations.

Torrens title spread to colonial and American jurisdictions in concentrated bursts of legislative activity. While the unvarying grid was the U.S. contribution to conceptualizing real property during the global land rush, Torrens title was Australia's. During the 1860s and 1870s, Australian colonies and New Zealand provinces embraced the essential plan. Next, in the 1880s came several Canadian provinces and territories, and finally, from the 1890s to 1920, a score of American states. From the 1880s to the First World War, Torrens title was installed too in British crown colonies and British African protectorates. The French adopted it for *le régime de l'immatriculation* in its African colonies; American colonialism in the Philippines advanced legal clarity by introducing the Torrens system these in 1902.[111] Torrens title was a favoured instrument of rational colonialism.

Legislators altered particulars to fit circumstances or deal with quibbles. New Zealand made registration mandatory. Several jurisdictions gave recorders the power to correct title errors. When that idea was proposed in New Zealand in 1860, the crown law officers in London hesitated to recommend the idea, and the colony's attorney-general, Henry Sewell, replied that the convoluted ways of the old country should not apply. "Facility of dealing with and transmitting property is material to the development of a new country."[112] Wherever Torrens title was introduced it was accompanied by deviations in mortgage law.[113] Whereas Torrens title attempted to streamline mortgage law, a number of jurisdictions, especially in the United States, jettisoned this feature. Torrens title attempted to eradicate litigation, and jurists remained wary of statutes that could deprive someone of property without due process. Court rulings thus reintroduced old principles of mortgage law and made conveyancing once more a mystery to lay people.[114]

Not all common law jurisdictions adopted Torrens title. In several that did, voluntary enrolment was popular mainly in urban areas, where it facilitated suburban tract sales. By 1907, twenty-one American states had adopted Torrens title, but others decided that the unvarying grid and traditional documentary registration furnished enough protection or concluded that title insurance companies sold an effective alternative.[115] Registration assisted land markets, and Torrens title especially facilitated urban property transactions; however, certain documents, safely lodged in registry offices, could clog transactions, because Torrens title by itself left unimpaired many complexities. The basis of the law in British colonies under Torrens title remained feudal, not allodial – that is to say, land was not an object of absolute ownership, but an estate in the land derived from the crown.[116] Courts of common law and equity made that estate anything but simple. Allodial title in the United States, meanwhile, could not guarantee clarity and security because, as we saw above, squatters complicated matters with their improvements. Inasmuch as records represent the law's complexities, a reformation of registration alone could not modernize conveyancing. Much more than just a good registry system, Torrens title, or title insurance was needed to increase fluidity in land markets.

Unleashing the Market: Reforming Mortgage Law

In the eighteenth-century English countryside, where aristocrats and gentry had manipulated property relations for generations, the ruling classes made the law support a society in which landed estates should remain intact, secure, and attached to heirs in ways meant to guarantee a family's power in future generations. Several things could unravel the fabric of ruling families and country estates. The days were past when royal displeasure could result in an escheat of an estate; however, imprudent expenditures and errant heirs threatened patrimonies. Trust arrangements helped protect large country estates against one generation's folly, but the safeguard that concerns us was intrinsic to mortgages and spread to the colonies.[117] The wonderful term for it was "the equity of redemption." The expression captured the idea that mortgagors had a right to redeem their mortgaged property. The issues involved with its rise and modification suggest a protracted dialectic between the interests of lenders and those of borrowers.

English law in early modern times protected debtors against the loss of their land for failure to pay an ordinary debt. Where an estate in land had been pledged as security, the situation became far more involved, although borrowers were safeguarded. To use land as security, borrowers and lenders resorted to a manipulation of the common law known as a mortgage. A debtor – the mortgagor – conveyed the land in fee simple. *Mortgage* in old court French, introduced into England after the Norman conquest, meant a dead pledge, because mortgagors pledged that estates in land became dead to them if they failed to meet the conditions required by mortgagees. The transfer in fee simple technically made it dead once the mortgage was contracted, but mortgagors attached a covenant that entrenched their right to resecure the land if they could satisfy that covenant's conditions. A mortgage therefore contained two agreements: the debtor's sale to a lender and the lender's agreement to sell back the land to the debtor.

English common law courts appraised these transactions strictly as far as the mortgagor was concerned. However, in the mid-fifteenth century the lord chancellor began to intervene to protect debtors against shameful abuses of strict enforcement of contracts. A branch of law, known as equity and conducted by a court of chancery, interfered with the strictures of the common law in the name of moral scruples. About 1625, more or less as a matter of course, chancery began granting relief against unconscionable enforcement of forfeitures. The exercise of leniency was elevated to an estate in the land by the eighteenth century. In no branch of law was the sanctity of law less regarded than in equity.[118] For example, mortgagors and their heirs owned a perpetual right to redeem mortgaged land by discharging the debt. This estate in land comprised the equity of redemption, and, by creating it, the law of chancery maintained that a mortgage merely served as security for a loan, whatever its outward appearances as a conveyance.

In theory, chancery's intervention favoured the landowning classes; however, chancery evolved techniques for balancing the rights of borrowers and of lenders. Mortgagees could initiate an action in a court of chancery to foreclose the equity of redemption. Precisely at the moment of vigorous colonization, English mortgage law expressed a

tension of interests; it no longer conclusively favoured landed borrowers or secured lenders, for it made debt recovery cumbersome. Lenders'
potential expenses for litigation to foreclose translated into premiums
charged for the use of money and into efforts to simplify the foreclo-
sure process. The see-saw that characterized mortgagor–mortgagee
interests in England entered the colonies and the young republic.

A few examples can illustrate the issues and show the direction of
change. For a while in Upper Canada, the ruling elite conveniently
ignored chancery. The colony received all of the laws of England in
1792, but successive governments neglected to establish a court of
chancery. New South Wales lacked an equity court until 1814, and
after that all later Australian colonies took in the full body of English
property law.[119] However, in Upper Canada, the failure to establish a
court with a jurisdiction in equity banished the equity of redemption
from the colony for decades, so that lenders who accepted land as
security, as well as speculators who sold land on credit, could exercise
simple and direct common-law recovery practices. They could repossess
the pledged land with mortgagors' improvements, because there was
no protection for mortgagors. An English chancery expert appointed
to the Upper Canadian bench exposed the omission in 1827–28. Political reformers, who tended to represent debtor interests, succeeded in
passing two acts in 1834 that enabled mortgagors to redeem their property up to twenty years after its seizure. That jolted the elite into action.

In 1837, the government introduced an act to create a court of chancery and limited the life of the equity of redemption to ten years. The
legislated limits to a mortgagor's actions presaged the future of mortgage law in this colony and elsewhere too. From the early nineteenth
century forward, mortgage law in British colonies and the United States
would be refined by legislation, not just by court decisions. Moreover,
the acts that modified the relations between mortgagors and mortgagees
appear to have increased creditors' advantage, or at least they made
mortgagors' interests in landed security more explicit, more certain.[120]
When Upper Canadian jurists and legislators tinkered with mortgage
law in the 1830s, a few looked to the United States for guidance. One
judge advised legislators to pay less attention to the type of court that
would exercise an equitable jurisdiction and consider instead a codification of equity along the lines of New York state, where James Kent
had just reformed mortgage law. In the assessment of Morton Horwitz,
Kent "contributed to the subversion of the long-standing regulatory
role of Equity."[121] That had been Torrens's objective too. Codification
forced an analytical dissection of mortgage law; its principles and practices had to be described in a comprehensible fashion, and that helped
to open it up to legislative initiatives.

Once exposed, mortgage law could be assessed by parties who made lending their business; they could see how the law served them and recommend changes. In most jurisdictions between the 1820s and 1890s, therefore, jurists and legislators co-operated to fuse equity and common law in an effort to simplify mortgage lending, increase trust, and consequently reduce the price of money. Two main areas of reform invited attention: first, the life expectancy of the equity of redemption; second, the means by which mortgagees could secure what was due them. From the 1830s to the 1860s, many jurisdictions pared back the period allowed mortgagors to redeem, unless foreclosed, although there seems to have been no commonly accepted time limit. Upper Canadians in the 1830s, for example, set it at twenty years, and then at ten. Meanwhile, the government of New Zealand in 1842 fixed the period at six months, provided that the debtor had been given a warning.[122]

The remaining major question – by what means mortgagees should be allowed to secure satisfaction when mortgagors defaulted – engaged judges and legislators in quests for reasonable settlements. In common law, the mortgage was a conveyance, so traditional instruments seized the pledged property, but this practice deprived indebted occupants of compensation for any of their work that increased the property's market value. In some circumstances, a creditor might not want property, but desire liquid assets to cover the outstanding debt. Therefore, by the mid-nineteenth century, mortgagees in some places could sue for the outstanding debt and force a sheriff's sale of the mortgaged property. Their right to do so did not derive from common law or from equity, but from powers of sale written into mortgages or provided by statute law.[123] Legislators adjusted the character of sheriffs' sales. Mortgagees, who theoretically could conspire to fix an auction and secure properties for low sums – and still be due the balance of debts owing – were sometimes barred from participating in auctions when this path to debt recovery was first formalized. However, by the second half of the nineteenth century, legislators presumed that mortgagees and mortgagors had a common interest in seeing to it that a sheriff's auction yielded a good return. Therefore the prohibition was lifted in jurisdiction after jurisdiction.[124] Detailed treatises on mortgage law disclose continuous housekeeping changes achieved through court decisions and statutes. The alterations condense to a principle enjoining mortgagors and mortgagees to treat the property with care and to respect each other's interests; as well, the acts and court rulings depict a flexibility that ministered to market forces, not simply to a dominant landed class. Mortgagees certainly gained a great deal, including several options for proceeding against debtors. Meanwhile, mortgagors, other things being equal, found it easier to borrow money at less-than-usurious interests rates, because lenders felt secure enough to relinquish some of the risk premium.

The equity of redemption privileged land over capital, while ensuing changes modified that bias. Roman–Dutch law nearly inverted this condition to produce an early-modern legal system that animated capital. The great wealth of the Netherlands flowed from seaborne trade directed by an exclusive class in Europe's quintessential commercial society. Dominant merchants desired from the law levers to force the speedy settlement of accounts. Interlocked procedures accomplished this splendidly. Using a Dutch law from 1580, the Cape courts could render what was termed a provisional sentence. This decree in favour of a creditor on a clear, definite, written undertaking of debt signed by the debtor gave a swift judgment. However, the process was not so lopsided as to deter borrowing. The decree was not final, and the plaintiff gave a bond, to cover the eventuality of a further action.[125] When a committee of the Cape assembly investigated mortgage law in 1843, it praised what it called a summary process for debt recovery.[126] It was typical of Roman–Dutch law's logical compartmentalization that it exposed mortgages to rational subdivision. *Tacit* mortgages derived from one's obligations as a government officer or executor of an estate; *judicial* mortgages resulted from a court ruling; *express* mortgages were agreements among parties. Following an elegantly logical path of discussion, the law identified many things that could be mortgaged and divided them into *incorporeal* items such as shares and licences and *corporeal* objects such as moveable and immoveable property.[127] The treatment of mortgages by Roman–Dutch law anticipated reforms that other jurisdictions struggled with during the nineteenth century. This was surely paradoxical in the Cape Colony, where tidy property laws perched atop a ramshackle land-allocation setup and where adherence to the requirements of Roman–Dutch law was hit and miss. Still, the Cape's market-friendly property laws contrasted with the elaborate dance of common law and equity.

In most respects, the English obsession with land brought enormous changes to frontiers; however, the character of English property law – illogical from the perspective of bourgeois capitalism – occasionally clogged the mechanisms of enterprise. Two impediments – the right of dower and usury laws – deserve mention. I do not discuss either obstacle at length; however, elaborate controversies over both arose in a multitude of jurisdictions. Proposals to eliminate dower or usury initiated profound debates about the nature of society. Dower rights guaranteed a widow a right to a portion of her husband's estate; if his land was to be sold, her rights had to be cleared. In effect, neither husband nor wife could sell without the consent of the other, and widows retained an interest in their husbands' estates. Astute widows and careless conveyancing created headaches for speculators. When Washington, DC, banker William Corcoran tried to unload land in the 1850s – parcels in Illinois acquired from the U.S. government – he discovered that federal authorities had not cleared the dower rights of the defaulting grantees from whom the government reacquired the land. So many title disputes arose that Corcoran claimed that he would never recover costs and interest.[128] His experience was not unusual, but many jurisdictions eliminated dower rights, though not always swiftly. Their removal began in the early nineteenth century and continued in some places until the mid-twentieth. Careful research on dower in Canada suggests that, although it was an irritant to conveyancing, some communities preserved it because it was appropriate for rural economies, where the contribution of women to a family-based economy was a recognized fact.[129]

The disposal of usury presents a related, elaborate tale. Roman–Dutch and English legal systems shared one archaic feature that complicated mortgage lending. In the early nineteenth century, the colonies and the U.S. republic clung unrealistically, though unenthusiastically, to usury laws that prohibited charging interest at rates higher than 5 or 6 per cent per annum. A medieval fusion of canon and civil law, usury measures held it unlawful for Christians to take any kind of excessive interest on loans. English enactments from the thirteenth to the early nineteenth centuries attempted to fix ceilings on interest rates; British colonies and American states followed and officially held interest rates at 5 or 6 per cent.[130] New South Wales was one of the first jurisdictions to void English usury law. Matters came to a head in *Macdonald v. Levy* (1833), a case heard by the Supreme Court at Sydney.

In a two-to-one decision, the court upheld 8 per cent interest, even though this contravened an English statute. The majority ruled that 8 per cent was customary in the colony and that "the laws of England are our birthright where they apply to our condition, and can be administered to us with advantage." Because the 5 per cent allowed by the English statute either deterred investment or led to illicit practices, it was not to the colony's advantage.[131] Uncomfortable with a judgment that slighted an English statute and nearly asserted autonomy, the governor and the legislative council conducted an inquiry. Witnesses debated the pros and cons of a usury law, but the council concluded that money would always regulate its own value, so usurers would prevail one way or another. In colonies and American states, lenders evaded usury laws by placing the nominal value of the debt above the actual sum; the difference represented the spread between the amount of interest due at market and at official rates. An act of the council set, interest rates in New South Wales at 8 per cent, and the crown gave its assent.[132]

Lobbying by Canadian institutional lenders in 1850–52 precipitated a repeal of an 1811 usury law by a single vote in a mainly regional vote in 1853. Members of the assembly from Lower Canada – mostly French-speaking and basically anti-commerce – upheld the existing law against usury; members from Upper Canada – English and pro-commerce – successfully argued for nearly unfettered lending. The repeal abolished penalties for usury but established that interest charged in excess of 6 per cent was unenforceable. Further legislation relaxed this control and special restrictions on financial institutions.[133] At the Cape, the British government accepted Dutch usury law and briefly attempted to enforce it. By the 1820s, authorities looked the other way, because anything less than 8 per cent interest would not attract outside capital. A very few desperate debtors, however, continued into the 1840s to sue successfully for relief from usurious contracts.[134] In the United States, for the first half of the nineteenth century, pro-commerce judges were inclined to disapprove of laws that made usuary a crime, but since such laws were legislative creations they acted cautiously, accepting what the politicians created while making their usury measures unenforceable.[135] State legislatures continued to support usury laws. At the outbreak of the Civil War, every state except California regulated a legal rate of interest, although few supposed that penalties could deter the practice.[136]

Usury laws – a moral restraint on lenders who could abuse their negotiating power – represented a world fast fading. Courts and legislatures gradually withdrew firm statutory protection for mortgagors, who increasingly were expected to negotiate their own terms. In the words of Gregory Alexander, "the issue of marketability of property was established as the dominant background issue in property law [in the United States]."[137] Alexander affirms, however, that there remained an important American legal discourse about property, and it involved a dialectic between liberality and technicality, between dynamism and stability. Mortgage and usury law captured this tension, and comparable debates took place in settlement societies besides the United States.

A VAST, FRIGID, ORDERLY FINALE:
THE CANADIAN WEST

Isolated and bone-chillingly frigid in winter, the Canadian prairies were long spared the presence of extensive landhunting operations. The region was the last great frontier absorbed into the processes of the great land rush. In the late 1850s, the government of the United Province of

Canada took a formal interest in the Rupert's Land territory of the Hudson's Bay Company, but a purchase was postponed until 1870. Major settlement commenced with a land boom in the late 1870s and early 1880s, ebbed during a crash, and swelled in an incredible era of sod-busting after 1900. While the great land rush slowed everywhere else in the 1880s, it was only just beginning on the prairies.

Late development favoured the region with a relatively orderly occupation. Ottawa's imposition of a territorial government without consulting inhabitants – a grave lapse in judgment – provoked the first of two western rebellions (1869–70 and 1885). Those French and English residents who seized power in the first rebellion demanded several political rights, followed by an insistance on "a free Homestead and pre-emption Land Law."[138] Leaving aside Ottawa's initial blunder, neglecting for a moment the controversial grants to railways and colonization companies, and ignoring the confusion regarding the land entitlements of the Métis, the Dominion of Canada achieved a grand, rationalizing plan. The mistakes cannot be slighted, but neither can the accomplishments. Partly through dumb luck, partly because of able civil servants, a sparsely populated colony successfully organized a vast territorial acquisition with relatively few murderous conflicts, no extended warfare, minimal pastoral landhunting, modest squatting, and sound land titles.

The ease of occupation experienced by the government of Canada and white colonizers stemmed really from a cataclysm that struck the Indians of the Great Plains. The catastrophes on the prairies started when American railways built lines across the great plains in the 1860s and 1870s and facilitated a commercial slaughter of buffalo for hides. The startling disappearance of the great herds poses problems of explanation, although the commercial buffalo hunt remains the leading suspect.[139] As heirs of a specialized culture attached to the buffalo, the Plains Indians, within one generation, suffered extreme privation through no fault of their own. Worse still, an ecological disaster precipitated warfare among themselves. The Crees, dislocated by the dwindling buffalo herds, moved into the game-rich Cypress Hills and encroached on the Blackfeet. A destructive war (1869–70) ensued, and it weakened an afflicted people.[140] Excepting the brief flash of the second rebellion (1885), Canada remained free from warfare with the first peoples of the prairies, because the region's first great ecological disaster laid them low.

Chance of an odd kind also favoured colonizers with a winter curse that stymied range grazers. The isothermal lines for North America followed latitude imperfectly, for east of the Rocky Mountains cold fronts plunged southward, except in southern Alberta, where occasional warm Chinook winds melted the crust of snow. There the

foothills offered livestock cover and some winter grazing, but protective valleys were less abundant on the Canadian prairies than on the
American open range. Environment thus constrained range grazing. A
critical inducement to cattle ranching – an urban market – certainly
beckoned in Canada's west, since Chicago and Minneapolis claimed
Rupert's Land/Manitoba as hinterland during the 1860s and 1870s.
This promising connection appealed to at least one British capitalist
with a roving eye for opportunities. His reasoning is worth citing,
because it depicts the global pursuit of opportunities during the latter
stages of the great land rush. In 1876, W.F. Wesley Fitz Gerald wrote
Manitoba land jobber and politician John Schultz, looking for a
ranching opportunity. Seeking places for his son, Fitz Gerald investigated Ceylon coffee plantations (not much future there, he wrote),
Texas cattle raising (too lawless, he thought), and Australian grazing
(good speculative prospects). Cattle raising in Manitoba, he believed,
had the advantage of a nearby American market, and a ranch could
later be broken up into farms for a profit. He wanted his son to juggle
ranching and real estate because, "of course, Real Estate Agency is one
of the best things to attend to in North America."[141] British investors
put money into grazing in the United States, Australia, and southern
Alberta. They always found local agents like Schultz.

The interconnections among Indians, wagon trains, army posts, gold
prospectors, government beef contractors, and cattle drovers that initially excited landhunting in the western United States from the late
1840s to the Civil War were absent north of the border, and the climate
did not generally support the extensive commercial ranching that arose
in the American west from about 1870 to 1885. Canadian authorities
were relieved from reconciling the competing interests faced by American officials, who struggled ineffectually to install law and order
among rival parties squatting on the public domain and Indian lands.
By and large, the Dominion enjoyed the unique luxury of marking and
safeguarding its western frontier land prior to colonization. There was
some squatting on the prairies prior to the arrival of surveyors, but
settlers who preceded the platting of the land lived only near river
valleys, where they hunted, fished, and cultivated modest acreage.[142]

The delay in extensive prairie occupation meant that Canadians
benefited from a breathing space when they could learn and apply
lessons from other jurisdictions. Ottawa adopted the unvarying grid
but instituted a control trig survey and a plan for routine corrections
to cope with the narrowing expanse between meridians as lines were
run north. Whereas the United States surveyed piecemeal, using
assorted baselines and many meridians, the Dominion executed a
uniform and integrated survey across a quarter of the continent.[143]
American surveys occurred after Indian lands had been ceded; however,

the government of Canada – under no threat of an Indian war and free from an invasion of clamorous settlers – negotiated treaties of cession only *after* it announced its settlement plans. The policy of clearing native title by treaty drew on established practice in Upper Canada, but in the west, as J.R. Miller expresses it, "initiation of the treaty-making process was at least as much the work of the Indians resisting Euro-Canadian incursions as it was the prescient preparations of the government."[144] Indians warned but did not raid, and their warnings prompted negotiations.

Canada's acquisition of the last major frontier from a fur-trading enterprise, the Hudson's Bay Company (HBC), took place for a number of reasons, including campaigns for annexation spurred on by empire-building Upper Canadians and a Canadian party resident around Fort Garry. Canadian and British worry about American expansionism helped too.[145] Annexationists claimed that the HBC could not manage a settlement colony – a sensible judgment shared by a majority of HBC shareholders. Mindful of both the potential market value of the company's fertile lands on the southern fringe of Rupert's Land and the cost of running a proprietary colony, shareholders in 1866 considered whether land development would pay. Their discussions drew on knowledge that colonial land investments – for example, in Australia – had not always paid. A majority rejected colonization, and protracted negotiations with Canada commenced.[146] An ultimatum from the imperial government forced a settlement whereby the company got £300,000 and retention of 5 per cent of a fertile belt across the prairies. This residual estate of over 7 million acres stocked the company's land department, free of debt and without the duties of a government.

The history of land registration for Métis and Selkirk settlers suggested that management of a speculative colony could have overwhelmed the HBC. In the early 1820s, Selkirk's executors let the HBC manage its interests at Red River, and one consequence was that the company opened a registry for the settlers' grants and invited other occupants who lacked title deeds to apply for them from the company's governor.[147] By 1850, the culturally diverse colony with its own customs of land use had little recourse to the company register. Selkirk's settlers applied the land-tenure practices of Scotland, using a cultivated infield and an outfield pasture; many Métis adopted a similar arrangement. Roughly 5,000 inhabitants spread along the banks of the Red and Assiniboine in an arrangement that replicated the river-lot system of Lower Canada. The English-speaking settlements adapted the agrarian practices of "a Scottish valley-side, spread flat on a North American plain, within the framework of a French-Canadian survey."[148] Parties

to land transfers occasionally requested entries on the register, but registration was not mandatory, and transactions were loose. Besides,
some Métis squatted and challenged the company's authority to make
grants.[149] Adam Thom, a university-educated Scot who prepared the
settlement's first law code in 1841, recalled that, when sitting as a judge
for Assiniboia, he witnessed two cases where the absence of documents
meant that "while the one party contemplated only the sale of houses
and fences, the other thought he was buying the land as well."[150] To
Thom and other fault-finding and modernizing outsiders, squatting,
verbal agreements, and transactions scrawled on scraps of paper
betrayed backwardness by inhabitants and company alike.[151] Canada's
annexation cast a legalistic commercial order over a fragmented traditional society. Some inhabitants of the Red River colony resisted, were
overwhelmed, and moved west. Ottawa surveyed the west and determined the major allocations, but the territorial and provincial governments legislated property law. They learned about security of title and
simplicity in transactions from other jurisdictions. To make dealings
less expensive, they opted for the Torrens system and associated
reforms that tried to simplify conveyancing and mortgaging.[152]

Canada followed the general path of the United States and disposed of
millions of acres in homestead grants, railway bonuses, and school
lands. In Australia, colonial revenues typically built government-owned
railways, although Western Australia followed North American plans
and offered land grants to stimulate private railway construction.[153] As
we see further in chapter 8, on American, Australian, New Zealand,
and Canadian settlement frontiers in the second half of the nineteenth
century a variety of corporations either received land-grant empires or
started to consolidate landholdings. In Canada and the United States,
several huge corporate accumulations originated as grants in aid of railway development. Unlike the generous land grants in Argentina or
Brazil, the intention here was not to create ranching empires or plantations, but to put thousands of farmers on the land. The Canadian Pacific
Railway (CPR) garnered 25 million acres on specifically numbered sections along its line and was empowered by an indemnification clause to
select replacement lands if some assigned sections were of poor quality.
These terms mirrored those offered railways in the United States.
    Allegedly, the CPR ran an astute land department, although ample
records have not surfaced. It is certain that the directors relied on
political influence. So tightly connected were their fortunes meshed
with the ruling federal Conservative Party, and visa versa, that the
company successfully pressed the Department of the Interior into a
world record for land surveying. Forever in a hurry to reassure creditors, the CPR pushed Ottawa to complete the survey of its sections

in 1883. Ten surveyors of baselines, twenty-one of township bound-aries, eighty-two contractors for section surveys, and four examiners of contract surveys ran line for 27 million acres of CPR, HBC, and crown land.[154] In the history of colonization, only on the Canadian prairies was a surveyor-general given the resources needed to stay ahead of occupation. The blistering pace of surveying would not have supported orderly settlement if the territory had attracted range graz-ing and seen the formation of property interests and extensive political power by ranchers.

To get a sense of how a modern land company functioned, and to detect contrasts with those in colonial America and the early republic, it is necessary to turn to the HBC by default because of its wealth of doc-uments and the scarcity of records for other land and colonization com-panies. This imbalance in documentation is unfortunate, because the HBC was no hustling enterprise. There were slight deviations from iner-tia between 1872 and 1914, but usually the directors instructed the land department to wait for business. Fur trading remained profitable, the company owned its acres debt free, and unlike the CPR, which needed rail traffic, it had no overpowering interest in hastening colonization. It could wait and allow improvements near its sections to drive up their value. Shareholders expected good returns from the department, so there was one interlude when the HBC's land department behaved like a vigorous land company. The company hired "a great administrative juggernaut" as head of the department in 1879. Charles Brydges had been a managing director of Canada's Great Western and Grand Trunk Railways.[155] As the first modern corporations to require a rigorous com-mand structure, railways schooled corporate managers. The land departments of railways and the more serious colonization companies engaged specialists in advertising, law, and accounting on an ongoing basis. The administrative hierarchy and division of labour contrasted with an enterprise such as Symmes's Ohio project of the 1790s.

Brydges wanted the HBC to "act like any merchant with wares to sell," and he envied the resources of Yankee competitors.[156] The Minneapolis, St. Paul, and Manitoba Railroad, he moaned in 1880, was "buttonholing … everyone passing St. Paul who wants to settle on land, and have their people on every train, talking up the advantages of their lands amongst the passengers, especially those going to Manitoba."[157] Scrambling to beat rivals in 1880–82, Brydges pumped allotments into a land bubble that burst in late 1882. From that moment until the HBC dispensed with his services in 1889, he pressed for payments and recov-ered land from defaulters. Orderly retreats were rare among the spec-ulative land companies, for they simply failed. Some credit for a determined salvage operation goes to Brydges, a modern manager, but the fact that the HBC owned its lands debt free gave it time to recover. After the 1882 collapse, the company reined in Brydges and waited for the west to grow up around its holdings, which, after all, had cost it nothing.[158] In contrast, the CPR behaved like a major land developer, especially – as we see in the final chapter – when it created an irrigation colony in southern Alberta. Peculiar conditions allowed the HBC to be a passive and enduring land company.

Unique conditions also bestowed on the Canadian prairies a relatively peaceful colonization history, punctuated by exceptional clashes. The two fleeting rebellions (1870 and 1885) led by the charismatic Louis Riel – important in the history of Canada's west – cannot overturn a conclusion that western settlement passed without protracted warfare against the region's first peoples. Indian wars like those executed by a succession of armies in Argentina and the U.S. army, or like the wars of colonial expansion carried out by the boers north of the Orange River and by British colonists in Cape Colony, Natal, and New Zealand, never occurred in western Canada. The North West Mounted Police helped maintain law and order and furnished relief in emergencies; however, they were never severely tested in dealings with first peoples or squatters, nor was the Canadian state tested year after year by hostilities arising from Indian resentment over its acquisition of territory.[159] Constable Winter enforced order and checked pastoral squatting, while trooper Starvation weakened the first peoples, whose civilization centred on the buffalo. The comparative calm awaiting white settlers in western Canada owed much to ecological factors. Severe winters and isolation – forests and the rock of the Canadian Shield on the east and mountains on the west – preserved this region for a late European occupation. The collapse of the buffalo herds rendered that movement uncontested except for the Riel rebellions. Uncommonly pacific when compared to other colonization events in the great land rush, the settlement of the Canadian prairies helped foster a myth of Canada as the peaceable kingdom, with a consensual respect for law and order. While the myth is misleading as history, it is benign and venerates non-violence.

As a foil to an array of government actions covered in this chapter, we see in the next one various operations of privatism. Feisty individualism and corporate land grabbing were at work in assorted blends on frontiers in southern Africa, the United States, Australia, New Zealand, and Canada. The scope for white settlers' action free of government and corporate involvement was greatest in the boer republics of southern Africa, while government and corporate control was tightest in western Canada, followed closely by the United States, then Australia and New Zealand.

In the last stages of the great land rush, reserves for indigenous people were subjected to schemes to individualize title and severe land for allocation to white settlers and speculators. An allotment crew ready to divide land at Pine Ridge Reservation, South Dakota, 1891. X-31493, Western History Collection. Courtesy Denver Public Library.

Some drylands west of the 100th meridian were the object of irrigation
efforts at the turn of the twentieth century. Grand Valley, Colorado,
GB-7921, George Beam Collection, Western History Collection. Courtesy
Denver Public Library.

Begun as private land-development schemes, the Australian irrigation
colonies at Renmark and Mildura eventually involved substantial
government support. Apricot orchard, Renmark, 1893. B53444.
Courtesy State Library of South Australia.

In South Australia, as in many dryland regions around the world, bore water provided salvation in the 1880s and 1890s. The Coward Bore, 1892. B30167. Courtesy State Library of South Australia.

The challenge with some bore-water sources and irrigation canals was to raise water to the surface or, in the case of irrigation, to the bench level of farms. Windmills, common landmarks by 1900, provided cheap lifting power, but seldom enough to sustain irrigation farming. B34397. Courtesy State Library of South Australia.

Progressive historians deemed the distribution of public land a failure.
Laws were manipulated by speculators, ranchers, and railway companies.
However, homesteaders included a variety of people. The Jerry Shores
family (facing, top), the John Curry home (facing, bottom), and the
Chrisman sisters (above), photographed by S.D. Butcher, Collection R62608,
items 1231, 1053, and 1048, respectively. Courtesy Nebraska State
Historical Society.

The settlement of the Canadian prairies took off after a series of shocks
to the first peoples of the Great Plains. A Cree encampment south of
Vermilion, 1871. C5181. Photographer Charles Horetzky. Courtesy National
Archives of Canada.

Manitoba real-estate agents await prospective settlers, 1915. PA119426.
Courtesy National Archives of Canada.

An expedition of American farmers looking for land near Scott, Saskatchewan, c. 1910. C005402. Photographer John R. Woodruff. Courtesy National Archives of Canada.

CHAPTER SEVEN

Allocation by Initiative:
Landhunters, Squatters, Grazers

Previous chapters showed administrators and legislators, bureaucrats and surveyors, doing their best to extinguish frontiers and, as economies became more sophisticated, to perfect the asset quality of land parcels. Aristocratic systems of acquisition and allocation (chapters 3–5) collapsed into those of a market economy (chapter 6), which in turn diversified, prompting improvements to surveying, property registration, and mortgage finance (also chapter 6). Official actions effected these changes; however, landhunters, grazers, and squatters by the thousands executed common moves that advanced private property rights in the face of governments' hostility, caution, overwork, and sluggishness. Even when authorities responsible for frontiers accommodated private individuals, the latter pressed for further concessions. Where squatters lacked government-backed security, they arranged expedients to protect what they deemed were their places. The framing of property rights occurred amid robust private initiatives. By chapter sequence, I have placed official actions ahead of individual ones, even though they interacted. In Cape Colony beginning around 1700 and in New South Wales starting in the 1820s, early squatting by pastoralists compelled governments to come to terms with uncontrolled property-forming initiatives. It was grazers who forced authorities, grudgingly or inadvertently, to grant incremental property interests. Small cadres of officials administered the evolving systems of land allocation. On American frontiers, as we saw above, state legislatures and Congress recognized squatters' pre-emptive interests. Squatting on the public domain attained legitimacy as an approved step towards securing title to land, and land offices were scarce in the midwest and on the high plains. Slow acceptance of squatters' interests in crown land and the ineffectual American administration of the public domain led to private parties' making their own arrangements.

In Virginia's empire, in parts of southern Africa and Australia, and in the regions of the American public domain open to grazing, early property diagrams and maps depict non-uniform cadastral allotments. Irregular allotments – circles and polygons – allude to private acts of possession, recourse to natural boundaries, serious attention to water sources, strife between newcomers and governments, and jostling among individuals. The grid survey that covers most of the United States and Canada, by contrast, connotes order; however, not even in historically sedate Canada was design monotonously triumphant. Squatting and illicit timber stripping flourished in parts of Upper and Lower Canada.[1] Encounters with hostile, inept, or inconveniently placed authorities provoked protests from landhunters, grazers, and squatters on many frontiers.[2] The very idea of a pre-emptive occupation prior to petitioning for a grant or in advance of an organized sale was dismissive of central authority. But the character of dissent against authority varied. In the United States, it seems undeniable that "untrammeled individualism and competition without interference were the accepted standards of the frontier."[3] On British colonial frontiers, squatters were slightly more accepting of government's role than were American counterparts, although sheep grazers in the United States, who usually wanted security of tenure, welcomed authority more generally than did cattlemen. As we see in this chapter, scrimmages for land expressed grazers' calculations about just how many legal interests they required for their operations (Table 7.1). The contests for interests also indicated their tactical readings of local environments. On the government side, only land surveyors had an appreciation equal to theirs for the strategic and economic potential of specific places.

Individualism and competition on frontiers amounted to more than landhunters, grazers, and squatters challenging and bending crown and state regulations. Individualism and competition also meant whipping rivals, sometimes literally. By the 1780s, farmers near Cape Town complained about neighbours and transients who treated the commons as their own property. Reporting in 1823 on a century of tenure at the Cape, the inspector of government lands wrote that grazers "go on asking for more and more, and in very many instances only in order to insulate themselves and to keep others at a distance."[4] An encroaching grazer near Queanbeyan, New South Wales, in 1837, intended "to obtain possession of the country and drive away all others." "The strongest and boldest," he asserted, "shall retain the country."[5] Niel Black, a squatter on Port Phillip Bay, vexed by rivals in 1840, was kept busy "flying from one part to another to keep off the enemy, civilized man. He is much more troublesome to me than the native."[6]

Table 7.1
Examples of growing property interests: grazing frontiers, 1700–1900

Generalized summary of property interests	Examples of places and times
Open commons, with government hostility to pastoral squatters: no legal interests to a place	Cape Colony (1650s–early eighteenth century) New South Wales (1828–36)
Open commons, government licensing, unofficial boundaries, no government aid to sort out boundary disputes: no legal interests to a place, but occupation legal and regulated	Cape Colony (1700s–perhaps 1750s) New South Wales (1836–39) U.S. high plains (1860s–1900s)
Licensed usage with boundaries, government aid to sort out boundaries, compensation for improvements if land sold to other parties, interests compromised by government right to cancel licence and right of sale: legal interests building	New South Wales (1839–late 1840s) New Zealand (1840–50) U.S. national forests grazing lands (1899 on)
As entry above, but with renewal and rights of transfer accepted by government	Cape Colony (1750s–1830s)
Leasehold for defined areas: substantial property interests	Australian colonies / states (1850s–present)

Individualism and competition were not just American traits, nor was the corporate consolidation of landholding that could be found during both the landhunting phase of occupation and the capital improvements phase. This chapter looks first at landhunters – mainly stockmen – and their need for land. It then describes the tactics they used in their search. Its next theme is the growing importance of place and how it affected the process of occupation. It considers finally how squatters sought to improve their legal interests.

DRIVING STOCK TO THE ENDS OF THE EARTH

Who were the landhunters who challenged one another as well as governments? It is tempting to accept a colourful depiction from an 1859 issue of the *Nelson Examiner*. Inland from this port established by the New Zealand Company on Tasman Bay, a reporter saw "long-legged, long-headed, long-pursed individuals who are striding over the land in all directions, keenly noting its capabilities, marking its natural advantages, fixing on its pleasant places."[7] Long purses or deep pockets were not universal accoutrements, because landhunters constituted a very mixed society. Personal wealth or depth of backing from partners and financiers varied; objectives in life diverged. But by definition

all landhunters explored, observed, marked, and worked to retain
ground. A few apprenticed as land surveyors. Others acquired experience as boundary riders on Australian and New Zealand sheep stations
or as cowboys on American cattle ranches. A few joined landhunting
expeditions, stock drives, or grazing operations as "cadets," to learn
about land rushes and to work in locales where they could initiate
their own landhunting on the side.[8] Of the first thirty-seven squatters
into the verdant Wairarapa valley of New Zealand, six were land
surveyors and eleven had been shepherds.[9] Elsewhere, there were also
adventurer-amateurs such as author Samuel Butler. Sale of his South
Island, New Zealand, sheep station, Mesopotamia, doubled his capital
and provided him with leisure to write. Once they staked a claim,
successful landhunters crowed about how they "eyed the country,"
"looked for country," "shifted for country," "took country," "picked
country." What types of country had they "prospected"?

We need a global backdrop, lest this chapter's accent on the common
attitudes and practices of landhunters and squatters evoke a flat-earth
chessboard with sheep and cattle played as pieces. Part of this chapter
focuses on land occupation associated with grazing – a leading,
dynamic, and confrontational activity shaping property rights; however, after initial occupation, agricultural experimentation and capitalist consolidation were prompt, and areas went through trials and
adjustments. By 1900, landholders in parts of the world that concern
us had tested crops and production methods that promised high
returns. In the colonial American south, rice and indigo had been tried
by 1750, while cotton growing exploded after the Napoleonic wars.
Vineyards flourished near Cape Town as early as the 1750s; they were
planted in the Hunter valley of New South Wales in the 1820s and in
South Australia and California in the 1850s. Sugar cane plantations
were up and running in Queensland and Natal by the 1870s. In the
1860s, wheat farming in California expanded at the expense of ranching.[10] Railways in the American midwest fostered grain production in
the 1860s and 1870s. Wheat too became a major staple in South
Australia by the 1880s and served as a foundation for Canadian prairie
settlement from the mid-1880s to the early 1910s.[11] In the late nineteenth and early twentieth centuries, irrigation colonies were championed with missionary-like zeal by governments and companies in the
American west, Victoria and South Australia, southern Alberta and
interior British Columbia, and southern Africa.

Experimentation and capitalist organization of agriculture started
immediately after property rights were firm enough to draw in capital;
this was true too of areas where grazing endured, because fencing and
artesian bore water were standard pastoral improvements by the

1880s. Of concern here, however, are events that installed the first vital property interests. Where private action played a major part in framing property rights, the indispensable agents were often grazers, especially from about 1820 to 1880. There were exceptions, of course. Where government control of territory was loose, and soil and climate were suitable for mixed farming, though hard on sheep and cattle, squatting farmers, perhaps with timber-cutting sidelines and speculative intentions, exerted a formative presence. Mixed-farming squatters operated on Virginia's western frontiers, on the public domain west of the Mississippi (north of Texas and roughly east of the 100th meridian), on crown lands and clergy reserves in Upper Canada, and even amid pastoralists in New South Wales. There are gaps in knowledge about small squatters on frontiers everywhere, although accounts of colonization in all Neo-Europes point to interactions among small squatters, first peoples, and large landholders, whether speculators, ranchers, or plantation operators.

Accounts of early-republican settlement in the Ohio valley, contemporary protests in New England, and colonization in Upper Canada and New South Wales have added details to an understanding of class relations among colonizers. Moreover, administrative histories of the public domain have situated squatters (1820s–1850s) in core political events of the *ante-bellum* republic. Starting in 1813–16, Congress and several state legislatures surrendered practical control of the public domain to squatters. Congress in 1816 conceded that squatters could stay, if they applied for that right, until the land they occupied was sold. Counting on government leniency, squatters concentrated on deflecting other landhunters and, to save time and expense, neglected filing for these pre-emption rights.[12] The legitimacy granted squatters in the midwest prepared the way for the toleration of grazing squatters on the public domain further west.

Administrative histories of crown land and public domain describe what happened when squatters correctly surmised their government's resignation towards squatting. Official unwillingness to enforce rigorously crown or state legal interests almost simplified the land game, because, once governments cleared native title, landhunters were left mainly to worry about – and resist – each other. Though commonplace, this struggle was complicated. When squatters operated without government approval for their use of a particular place, what they lacked was an unassailable means for establishing, against others, their interests in a particular plot of land. The solution in the U.S. midwest – as I intimated above – involved claims clubs, which flourished at the end of the Black Hawk war in 1832. After the United States cleared native title to a tract of prairie lands west of Chicago, following that war of

Indian resistance to removal, competitive landhunters fanned out. By 1836, an estimated 10,000 squatters occupied land in eastern Iowa, and more than a hundred "extralegal" squatters' organizations protected parties who ostensibly occupied the land first. Functioning like government land offices, clubs maintained records on members' pre-emption claims. Pre-emptive squatters dashed ahead of government surveyors, used rods at high noon to find true north, paced off distances, and sketched their tracts for insertion on the clubs' township plats.[13] More fine-grained information about the interaction of small-scale squatters everywhere with private land agents on crown land and public domain would be welcome.[14]

Knowledge about landhunting grazers is extensive, because by the mid-nineteenth century their sweeps through large tracts inflamed populist indictments of allocation systems. Grazers' occupation of large areas incited allegations that they monopolized land, and the grazers' and their city agents countered with justifications. In fighting for cheap tenure, against latecomers and reformers, pastoralists slipped histories of occupation into their petitions and lawsuits. Although the capital that grazers dedicated to land was initially not great, their investment in stock was often considerable, and this walking capital linked them to centres of finance and politics. There administrators, publicists, and legislators debated the pros and cons of squatting. It was impossible for politicians and journalists to remain neutral about grazers as frontiers closed and their recourse to finance capital increased. While a tight union of commercial grazing and metropolitan finance was not quite the case for the many non-commercial pastoralists roaming the northeastern Cape Colony and the early southern African republics, *trekboers* in the eighteenth century nevertheless filed reports on their occupation of the land, and *voortrekker* republics formed in the mid-nineteenth century memorialized white occupation of the highveld as an astonishing deed, even a providential achievement. Grazers everywhere assured themselves of prominence in local settlement histories, because they supplied a past in order to build property interests (Table 7.2).

So great was grazing's sweep that, excluding the major anomaly of Canada, pastoralism on its own could bind an abridged comparative history of frontier occupation, because four of the world's five great grazing regions (the interior of central Asia, southern Africa, the plains of South America, Australia, the trans-Mississippi U.S. west) were opened mainly in the nineteenth century. In the United States, livestock was important to the taking and holding of land in Kentucky, southern Ohio, Missouri, and Arkansas (1790s–1820s).[15] Next, cattle centres on the Iowa wet prairie, in Missouri, and in northwestern Texas became staging bases for a diffusion of grazing onto the Great Plains

Table 7.2
Trends in landhunting, 1700–1900

Notable types of landhunters	Period	Location	Comments	Examples in this book
Family grazers (*trekboers*)	1700–1835	Cape Colony	Largely non-commercial, driven by drought and family increase	Piet Botha Louis Trichardt
Professional scouts working for speculators Frontier squatters	1750–90	Western Virginia Ohio valley Kentucky	Major speculation expeditions and small-scale squatting	Daniel Boone William Crawford
Professional scouts Frontier squatters Family parties	1800–30	Missouri Arkansas Texas	Squatters and organized colonies	Daniel Boone Moses Austin
Professional sheep overseers working for backers and speculators "Overstraiters" and "overlanders" Some small operators	1830–40	New South Wales Port Phillip Bay	Commercial and often well-financed sheep grazers	John Batman William Brodribb Niel Black
Family grazers Some speculators	1834–45	Natal Orange to Limpopo rivers	The Great Trek Well-organized and -equipped scouting expeditions followed by emigration	Gerit Maritz Piet Uys
Stockmen and speculators	1835–55	New Zealand: North Island and east coast South Island	Same	Ben Boyd George Duppa Rhodes brothers

Table 7.2 (continued)

Notable types of landhunters	Period	Location	Comments	Examples in this book
Professional sheepmen on overland drives	1838–45	From New South Wales into South Australia and into future Queensland	Same	Evelyn Sturt Patrick Leslie
Scouts working with well-supported sheepmen	1845–60	Into interior South Island, New Zealand	Often well financed Considerable speculation	Thomas Henry Potts
Organized colonization	1847–50	Utah	Religious colony squatting on public domain	Brigham Young
Cattlemen	1850–75	From Texas into Arizona, New Mexico, and Dakotas	Established cattlemen following gold rushes and U.S. army	
Cattlemen	1850–75	From U.S. midwest across U.S. west	Mixed land use in support of cattle Capitalized	Richard King
Cattlemen "Queensland Overlanders"	1860–90	Counter-clockwise north and west from Queensland around "top end"	Established cattlemen moving into tropics	Patsy Durack
Cattlemen	1870–75	From California into Oregon	Leaving California because of pressure from farmers	Peter French

in the 1850s and 1860s, and slightly later into the Great Basin. Also in the 1860s and 1870s, grazers who had expanded in California during the gold-rush population boom moved north and east into the Great Basin, Transcascadia, north as far as Kamloops, British Columbia.[16] In Australia during the 1870s and 1880s, overlanders drove cattle in an arc northward in Queensland, west of coastal mountains, and across the top end into the Kimberley Districts of Western Australia. Cattle tolerated tropical heat, sheep did not. A British wool boom supported landhunting outside the tropics in southeastern Australia from the 1810s to the 1830s (Map 7.1). The search for pasture in southern Africa produced the treks of the 1830s. Sheep raising spread in the 1840s from Australia to New Zealand, where it incited a South Island land rush during the mid- and late 1850s (Map 7.2).

Inner dynamics spread pastoral expansion. Frontier grazers multiplied when migrant farmers discovered that intensive agriculture on frontiers was laborious and that markets were difficult to reach. Livestock increased and moved – it seemed – with comparatively little fuss.[17] Union Army veteran Andrew J. Robertson of Illinois searched for prospects after the Civil War. This rolling-stone took a business course, tried farming in Illinois, attempted growing cotton in Mississippi (1869), journeyed to Utah to prospect for gold (1871), and joined a squatters' league along the Beaver Creek in Indian Territory (1872). On Christmas Day 1872, he expected "the soldiers here to drive us off every day." Robertson sojourned in Texas and New Mexico (1873) and finally settled in Wyoming, earning a reputation as an astute ranch manager. Throughout his quest, Robertson recorded assessments of soil, water, and timber. At the Stinking Waters Station in Utah, he spied "a splendid place for rasing stock. Don't have to feed at all in winter." Later, "I think this part of Texas (near New Braunfels) beats the world."[18] Rob, as his Wyoming cowboys knew him, guided the expansion of the Sturgis and Goodell Ranch, one of the most important in the Territory. In late 1874, he sent Shorty, a trusted hand, to the North Platte River, to camp in the cold and hold a new range. Shorty reported both success and anxiety to Rob. "I have got the S&G men and all horses over on Lightning Creek holding South side. I have been riding everyday since we came here ... The cattle are doing very well *indeed*. The best cow Country on Earth. Except None. Of course, we must keep this to Ourselves until our folks gets all there Camps maid [*sic*]."[19]

Two Texans can represent a legion of converts from farming to ranching. In the early 1850s, John Hittson felled trees and pulled stumps, all to grow a little corn and wheat, but he did not fancy "the doom of hard labour for life." Starting with sixty cows, he began a ranching career, a business that attained an apogee of notoriety when,

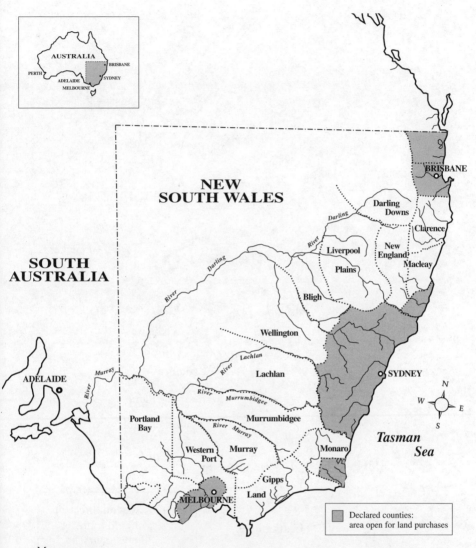

Map 7.1
New South Wales in 1844: declared counties and pastoral squatting districts
Source: John C. Weaver, "Beyond the Fatal Shore: Pastoral Squatting and the Occupation of
Australia, 1826–1852," *American Historical Review*, 101 (Oct. 1996), 980.

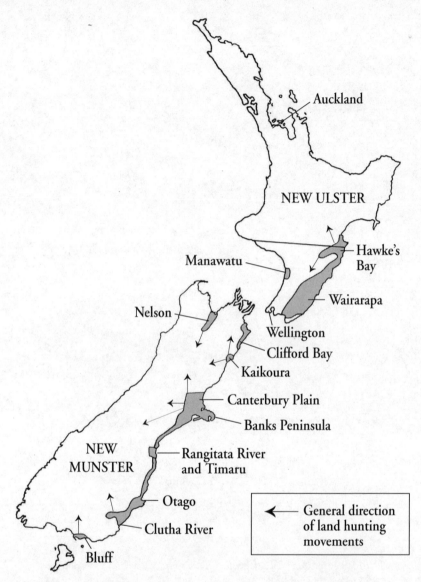

Map 7.2
Colonial provinces and approximate boundaries of squatting regions, New Zealand, 1845–51
Source: John C. Weaver, "Frontiers into Assets: The Social Construction of Property in New Zealand, 1840–65," *Journal of Imperial and Commonwealth History*, 27 (Sept. 1999), 21.

in 1872, he led at least ninety gunmen on a murderous raid into New Mexico to recover stolen livestock.[20] Steamboat captain Richard King, a builder of the legendary King Ranch, turned away from the Rio Grande in the early 1850s: "cattle and horses, sheep and goats, will reproduce themselves into value. But boats – they have a way of wrecking, decaying, falling apart, decreasing in value and increasing in cost of operation."[21] Frederick Law Olmsted observed the practices of east Texas grazers and reported that their cows were seldom sold, "so the herd enlarges in compound ratio."[22] Eventually, pastoral operations became costly, but not until the idea that they paid handsomely lured ranchers and flock masters onto an open range or other forms of cheap land (Map 7.3).

On frontier after frontier, plans for compact agrarian settlement crumbled under hooves. Families on pastoral frontiers propagated too, and that required strategies for inheritance, particularly in southern Africa. On the grazing frontiers there, fruitfulness – of stock and people – stirred European pastoral expansion by the late seventeenth century, because grazing permeated the soul of the colony's culture.[23] A German traveller in the 1780s observed how younger sons of Cape grazers managed farms on shares, and after building sufficient stock they "move[d] to a different part of the country ... But those sons, who can find no such opportunity for their maintenance and wish to marry, are soon compelled to travel about the country looking for a decent place to settle, if possible next to a Hottentot [sic] kraal."[24] Historian Robert Ross finds that often sons waited until the death of the father to leave, "but the point is that these new starts were possible."[25] A century later, natural increase – and now the attraction of supplying meat to diamond mine camps – drew pastoralists to remaining open lands. Colonel C.J. Moysey, directed to arbitrate land claims near the Cape–Transvaal border in 1882, ignored the petitions of squatters "moving about the country in search of pasturage or water. Of these I noticed not a few."[26]

Hawke's Bay squatter Donald Gollan – a former New Zealand Company surveyor – implored Donald McLean in 1857 to hurry with purchasing Maori land, because "between Napier and Castlepoint, there are already upwards of 50,000 ewes producing annually from 30,000 to 35,000 lambs, which with the growing compound increases will be sufficient to stock all the available country between Napier and Auckland in a very few years."[27] The explosion in the number of sheep in California in the 1870s and 1880s vaulted it ahead of Ohio as the largest wool-producing state by 1890, before a decline.[28] A Judaeo–Christian celebration of fertility endorsed the grazers' outreach for land. God ordained that pastoralists needed more land. "Can man fight

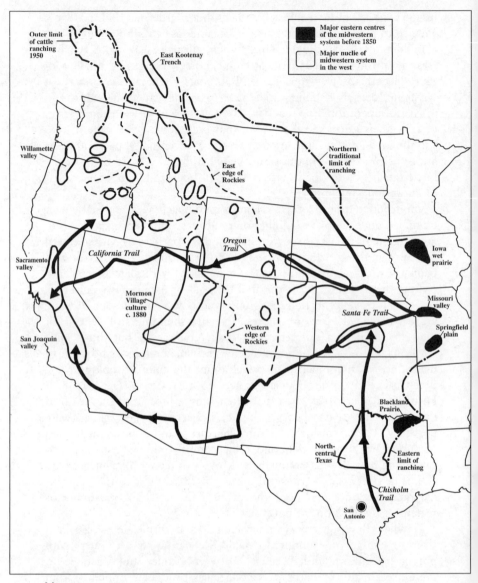

Map 7.3
The diffusion of ranching in North America, 1840s–80s
Source: Terry G. Jordan, *North American Cattle-Ranching Frontiers: Origins, Diffusion, and Differentiation* (Albuquerque: University of New Mexico Press, 1993), figure 54.

against nature, against the will of God? He maketh our flocks and herds to prosper, or not, as seemeth best to his Providential mission." And His mission was theirs.[29] Donald Akenson has shown in *God's People* that this belief in a covenant strengthened into a national tenet in the boer republics, particularly when the British empire isolated boer political ambitions in the late nineteenth century.[30]

Overstocking – making one blade of grass grow where two had been – did not inevitably compel occupation of new territory. There were retreats. Close management of stock was another solution, but it was uncommon until land became scarce in the mid-1880s. Apart from retreats, there were other drastic emergency measures. During a serious commercial depression in Australia during the early 1840s, cash-strapped grazers boiled sheep for tallow.[31] Suffering this same crisis, the Rhodes brothers of New Zealand drove 5,000 sheep off a cliff into the sea.[32] Argentine grazers sent sheep to the tallow plants as a means of disposing of surplus stock in the early 1840s, and again in the mid-1860s.[33] Ranchers on California's overstocked pastures, in the early 1860s, carried out voluntary slaughters to preserve native grasslands.[34] Advocates of stock improvement felt that thinning could be helpful. The greatest killing-off of livestock, however, occurred through natural causes in 1886–87, when a severe winter on the American Great Plains left herds drifting without food or water. The ranchers' organizations, established to enforce property rights, experienced a corresponding decline. From 1886 to 1889, membership in the Wyoming Stock Grower's Association plummeted from 416 to 183, and its Montana counterpart likewise went into a temporary decline.[35]

In prosperous times, grazers split flocks and herds, sold livestock and good will to the land that they used, and sought new pastures. At the Cape throughout the eighteenth century, *trekboers* on long, drawn-out game-hunting expeditions kept a look-out for additional grazing lands.[36] The disruption of the U.S. Civil War allowed Texas longhorns to multiply, sending ranchers up trails in the 1870s to secure northern urban markets and, soon, northwestern open-range pastures.[37] Sometimes, however, grazers stocked the land superficially so that they could sell out to a later squatter or to a city syndicate. In the booming mid-1830s, Australian landhunters lost no time in founding new stations and selling the old. When exploring the limits of a new run in that period, Edward Curr spied, "from the top of a range, far to the north, a large tract of open country."[38] He sold out and moved. While William Wyse was pursuing stray cattle in 1835 along the Murray River, he came on rich flats and could not resist forming a second station.[39] "Each took all he could get, and each kept all he could," recalled a squatter about the 1840s on the Darling Downs.[40] "This is

the way to make money," boasted Queenslander Colin Archer about
grazing in the Fitzroy and Leichhardt districts in the early 1860s.
"Stock and sell."[41] California sheepmen, who had been forced to buy
land in order to compete for it with cattle ranchers, began selling their
appreciating asset to agriculturalists in the 1870s and 1880s and
dispatching flocks to Montana, Wyoming, Utah, Colorado, Nevada,
Oregon, and Washington.[42]

Non-speculative grazers spread out because they insisted at first on
high ratios of acreage to stock, demanded reserves for increase, contemplated selling stock and good will to late-comers, and set aside
specialized territory – emergency water-holes, buffers against neighbours, winter pastures, lambing grounds, fields for diseased sheep, and
the like. Frontier grazing systems for sheep and cattle varied by environment, tradition, and commitment to stock improvement, but they
were land extensive, even when grazers practised close management
that restricted livestock. So long as cheap occupation remained feasible
and labour dear, grazers rarely confined sheep or cattle to what would
be merely sufficient pasturage. When open range became tight and
there were thriving markets for livestock, hides, and wool, there was
a temptation to overstock.[43] Exigencies consumed territory, and opportunities degraded it. Grazers, blaming stock diseases on pasturage,
bolted from districts with poor reputations. To save animals and thus
wealth, drought-stricken grazers pressed onward. In Cape Colony,
failed rains repeatedly drove trekboers beyond the colony's northern
limits and back again during the 1820s. A decade later, Natal enticed
grazers such as these because the region was within range of monsoons
that built up over the Indian Ocean. Sheep farmers in New South Wales
during the early 1830s ranged beyond the counties officially opened
for settlement, because of drought around Bathurst and Mudgee and
an overstocking of the Hunter valley. Severe droughts in 1862–65
started California ranchers dispersing east of the Sierra Nevada.[44]

Grazers often miscalculated or lacked sufficient information when
selecting ranges and runs; yet, so long as open territory remained
somewhere, trekboers, Australian squatters, and American ranchers
could remedy erroneous first estimates of water-supply, land quality,
and climatic severity by moving on.[45] Complaining to the government
of New South Wales in 1832, Edward Parry, Arctic explorer turned
manager of the Australian Agricultural Company's million-acre block
near Newcastle, identified a disadvantage of freehold grants. A fixed
location paralysed the venture's grazing operations before Parry could
determine the reliability of water sources. By contrast, neighbouring
squatters roamed at will.[46]

On many frontiers, aridity pushed landhunting, but in New Zealand poor drainage and cold winters in the mountains forced pastoralists to move for the good of their sheep. Frederick Weld, who made his fortune in New Zealand grazing and went on to serve as governor in Western Australia, discovered after one season that his first station in the Wairarapa valley in 1842–44 was too wet. Maori resistance and stock increases contributed to his search for new runs on the South Island, where his explorations for interior stock routes won acclaim.[47] On every pastoral frontier, grazers assessed trade-offs among security of tenure, its costs, and freedom to test by roaming. Individual decisions reflected both local ecologies and the extent of land believed freely available. From the important perspectives of the law and European cultural values, livestock established possession and signalled improvement. About conservation, there was not a word. Grazing devoured territory, more so than labour-intensive forms of landhunting associated with felling trees, pulling stumps, ploughing, and planting.

Affluent landhunters shifted for land around the world, in Cape Colony's Albany settlement (1820s), southeastern Australia (1830s and 1840s), and New Zealand (1840s and 1850s). Albany colonist Thomas Philipps, trained as a barrister at Gray's Inn, London, presented Cape governor Lord Charles Somerset with letters from influential people at home and successfully pleaded for more and better land.[48] "Mighty Ben Boyd," a legendary land seeker in eastern Australia, a latecomer who raised £1 million in England, arrived on his yacht *Wanderer* in 1842 and purchased squatters' grazing rights to over 2.5 million acres. True to form as a cheap land taker, Boyd skimped on licence fees but pressed the government for greater security of tenure.[49] Among richly supported characters, George Duppa arrived at New Zealand in 1840 equipped with company land orders and a portable house. Unable to select desired tracts at Wellington, he collected stock and sailed for the South Island, where in 1842–43 he began his vocation as a bullying pastoralist. Those whom he could neither intimidate nor bluff he bought out.[50] In tenacity, awareness of competition, control of serviceable paper, and knowledge of land-taking tactics, he resembled an earlier, astute, and powerful landhunter, George Washington, although Duppa was a grazer and speculator, not a slave-holding plantation owner and speculator.

THE METHODS OF THE LANDHUNTERS

For a sharp social contrast to elite and commercially attuned landhunters, we can point to the Cape's farmers who sought grazing areas outside the colony by at least soon after 1700. Descendants fashioned a frontier life with minimal commercial links to Cape Town. By the time young Washington eyed western Virginia, trekboers had spied pastures beyond their colony's limits and gauged wealth by tallying sheep and cattle. Dr Andrew Smith in 1834 believed that on the Orange River frontier "nearly every inhabitant [was] wandering in quest of subsistence for their flocks and herds."[51] In fact, while Boyd assembled licences for runs in the Monaro and Riverina districts in the early 1840s, and while Duppa was consolidating a South Island grazing estate in the 1850s, trekboers extended grazing operations beyond Cape Colony, testing the carrying capacity of the highveld from the Orange River to the Limpopo. Measured against the Virginian's schemes, and Boyd or Duppa's manipulations, the Afrikaner pursuit of terrain and water was not emphatically commercial. But it was unequivocally expansionist, and hunting elephants for ivory by some trekboers was decidedly commercial.[52] Commercial or not, Dutch grazers in Cape Colony asserted property interests early in the history of frontier occupations.[53]

The size and sophistication of landhunting expeditions diverged, and variations in scale were sometimes independent of social background and wealth. A core of trekboers organized the large, well-conceived, well-equipped expeditions of the Great Trek. There were assorted ways to grip land legally. Washington employed surveys, cabins, and clearings, supplemented with land warrants. For the next hundred years, other shrewd landhunters around the world had recourse to a nearly identical array of devices, including land warrants by other names. In Canada these included loyalist and militia scrip (Upper Canada), military-service land scrip, indemnity scrip, Indian scrip, Métis land scrip (Canada), and road labour scrip (British Columbia). In Australasia there were British officers' remission certificates (all Australian colonies), volunteer land orders (New South Wales, Victoria, and Queensland), and company land orders (South Australia and parts of New Zealand). Americans could receive land notes (Texas), French land grants (eastern Missouri), Spanish land grants (parts of the Louisiana Purchase, New Mexico, Arizona, and California), and agricultural college scrip (issued so that some eastern states could share in the public domain). Argentina had *los boletos de premios* (the abundant tickets to land rights issued by Rosas in Buenos Aires).[54]

After undertaking expeditions beyond San Francisco Bay in 1840–41, John Wolfskill secured ranch lands by a grant procured through an American brother-in-law of the Mexican *comandante* there.[55] In the mid-1860s, Queensland attempted to lure immigrants with cheap land orders, which "land jobbers" predictably scooped up at discounts. "The way one man *did* the Government with land orders," recalled

Queensland squatter Charles Eden, "was worthy of a down-east Yankee."[56] More accurately, a down-east Virginian! Anyone could be a landhunter, but it helped enormously to have powerful friends and some of the abundant convertible paper issued by governments.

While well-connected or well-financed landhunters could enlist documents to hold land, pastoralists dispersed livestock brilliantly to defend legal interests. Despite social contrasts, differences in scale of outfit, and distinctive props for holding territory, landhunters shared a trade. They operated in advance of government authority on unsettled territory, and this circumstance influenced their conduct. They went onto frontiers and applied common strategies: limited, conditional co-operation among expeditions; a substantial measure of stealth and deceit; and speedy movement at critical moments. These were hallmarks of an international phenomenon. Adversity, family expansion, unfulfilled ambitions, an urge to repair fortunes, and greed kept landhunters on the trail. Some nineteenth-century practitioners mixed these ambitions with the romance of exploration. Cape grazer John Moodie enjoyed a separation from society; "I had always been an enthusiastic admirer of Nature, and I delighted in following her through her wildest haunts."[57] Scenery and natural curiosities enchanted them, and adventure invigorated them. Donald McLean's reports about his purchasing expeditions on behalf of the crown in New Zealand leave no doubt that he enjoyed ascending rivers, packing over ridges, visiting Maori villages, and seeing plains "clothed with the richest and most luxuriant natural grasses."[58]

Rugby-educated Oscar de Satgé emigrated to Victoria's goldfields in 1853 and left them for Queensland's pastoral frontiers. His reminiscences rhapsodize about mountain-peak panoramas and the behaviour of indigenous fauna – the whir of bronze-winged pigeons and mobs of inquisitive emu.[59] It is impossible to be conclusive about the pull of human curiosity and aesthetic sensibilities, but landhunting opened remarkable possibilities for adventure and scenic delights. Keith Hancock, the outstanding pioneer of Australian environmental history, found a Monaro settler's recollections vivid but confusing: "he manages to be at one and the same time in love with primaeval nature, with 'improvement,' with 'sport.'"[60] Hancock captured a Victorian masculine disposition. But one impulse – improvement – must be stressed, for landhunters never forgot the material goal. Although de Satge paused to gaze in wonder, he generally found the pursuit of land "very tedious." What kept him going was "a kind of 'greed of country' that comes over the pioneer, which spurs him up to great efforts if the reward is a good slice of sheep country."[61] For a time, there was no sense of limits.

Landhunters bobbed and weaved through co-operation and competition, transparency and secrecy. Adversity and prudence threw some together.[62] From time to time, competitors joined forces, agreeing to divide the spoils on site. Dutch grazers on the Great Trek attempted to co-ordinate their expeditions at councils: some for *kommandos*, others for making civil law. Factionalism caused expeditions to splinter, but the amount of planning and co-ordination by boers was perhaps equalled only by the Mormon exodus from Missouri to Utah. During the height of a rush for pastoral land in New South Wales (1834–37), rival expeditions advanced a day's journey or less apart, close enough to help one another across river fords, share supplies in emergencies, or draw together for protection.[63] Sometimes the trails were congested. In late 1839, near the peak of the grazers' land rush in New South Wales, Alexander Hunter found temporary stops crowded. "The yard was occupied by another mob of cattle bound for the port [the Port Phillip Bay district]. We had to camp ours. Take water and watch."[64] Cowboy Andy Adams, reminiscing about a cattle drive out of Texas in 1882, remembered a dusty cavalcade. Five herds were ahead of his, and two were probably "pushing out west to new ranges."[65] Adams's drive, like many others, punched cattle to a railhead for market; however, as Adams intimated, there were concurrent drives to find open grazing land, which must have been scarce by then.

As landhunters passed through freshly occupied territory, they normally enjoyed settlers' hospitality, although around the tables moods were unpredictable – from invitations to settle nearby, through probing inquiries, to deceit. William Brodribb took up his first station near the Australian Alps in 1834–35. The station managers and shepherds whom he encountered extended kindness and shared information. This cooler region – not ideal for raising sheep – was thinly occupied, and local squatters embraced him as a respectable neighbour.[66] When feeling comfortable about the abundance of land around them, squatters might agree to absorb one more seeker, but Thomas Potts, on returning from a successful trip into the Southern Alps of New Zealand in 1857, faced a different situation. Stopping to accept hospitality, he was besieged with questions. "Many were the enquiries as to what we had seen and where we had come from, to which we gave as judicious answers as we could." With a South Island land rush in full swing, Potts remained tight-lipped, for he had resolved to hold 20,000–30,000 acres by squatting without a government licence.[67] Silence could conserve his capital.

Resistance by indigenous peoples, or simply a raw fear of their hostility, could galvanize rival expeditions into co-operation. At times, landhunters collected for protection. Symmes, the Ohio colonizer, instructed his settlers to cluster in groups of ten or twelve. Even when not in allied expeditions, landhunters shared news about dangers and concentrated at fortified stations during hostilities.[68] There were rare exceptions when they fired on one another, even while occupying areas under the sway of hostile indigenous peoples. In late 1773, an infamous conflict between Virginia and Pennsylvania over jurisdiction in contemporary western Pennsylvania escalated into armed confrontation. This struggle for authority and rumours of a frontier Indian war led squatter Michael Cresap to participate with Indian allies in murderous attacks during the spring of 1774.[69] Intricate relations among landhunters, traders, rival authorities, and indigenous tribes in the Ohio valley (1750–90) were matched during struggles for territory in Natal (1838–42). Although the tiny British trading community at Port Natal shared information about Zulu movements with *voortrekkers* in 1838, the two sets of newcomers soon feuded over sovereignty. In May 1842, the Cape government sent a military contingent under Captain T.C. Smith to occupy Port Natal. In short order, a boer force besieged Smith and nearly compelled his surrender.[70] Violent conflicts among white newcomers in the Ohio valley and in Natal originated from jurisdictional rivalries. Land and property rights were unquestionably involved; however, an unusual feature of these particular clashes was the loss of life, as Europeans fought one another amid hostile indigenous people. Extreme turmoil did not occur in Australia or New Zealand. Where no highly fractious jurisdictional disputes applied, landhunters suppressed internecine violence when wrenching habitat from the control of indigenous peoples, although complete openness and full co-operation were not guiding instincts among strangers.

Keeping one's counsel persisted as the golden rule of landhunting. Well-known for his extensive speculations in western Virginia, Patrick Henry in June 1767 instructed a scout, Captain William Fleming, to explore quietly near the confluence of the Ohio and Mississippi. Henry and his partner trusted Fleming's prudence.[71] A short time later, in September 1767, Washington prepared comparable instructions for his scout, Colonel William Crawford. "I recommend," wrote Washington, "that you keep this whole matter a secret, or trust in only those in whom you can confide, and who can assist you in bringing it to bear by their discoveries in land."[72] Fleming and Crawford not only plotted to defy official policy by operating over the proclamation line; they were going to encounter competitors. The Cape Dutch grazers who contemplated a breakout in large numbers across the colony's frontier in 1834–35 were initially free of competition among themselves but quite certain that British authorities would object. They had been allowed to pasture north of the Orange River, but only by agreeing not to occupy these lands permanently. A wealthy young voortrekker explained that this understanding was why "the proceedings for stimulating and organizing the emigration were kept very secret."[73]

If secrecy in landhunting was universal, then equally so was the itch to pry out information. Drafting directions analogous to Henry and Washington's, the Australian landhunter Charles Hotson Ebden impressed on his scout the importance of "a temporary silence on the subject, that no other party may be before us in the field."[74] To know how to protect the pastures that he occupied, Port Phillip Bay squatter Niel Black wanted to interrogate stockmen camping near his station, so he invited them for a breakfast. They declined.[75] New Zealand surveyor John Holland Baker went landhunting on his holidays in 1860 and found "some wonderful country," comprising about 15,000 acres at the head of the Ashburton River. Returning to file an application for a grazing lease, he stopped for a night at a sheep station. "We were careful not to talk of what we had discovered for fear that anyone might forestall us in applying to the Land Board."[76] Indiscretion could frustrate plans altogether. The ideal was an unobserved reconnaissance. When contact and exposure were unavoidable, all disguise came off, and the races began. Henry Haygarth told of the squatter who located a well-watered area. Not wishing to share it, he faked illness, retired from a combined exploration party, and doubled back with sufficient stock to hold the desired run against his former chums.[77] Night stock drives and twenty-hour shifts were undertaken.[78]

On his first expedition, William Brodribb encountered generosity near the Australian Alps. This happy situation did not yield a location that met his expectations, so he moved. During his squatting career, this rolling stone occupied at least seven stations, illustrating how one landhunter's initiatives pushed occupation. After selling his fifth station for a nice profit about 1840, he plunged into an ambitious scheme that brought home to him – if early trips had failed to – secrecy's worth. Eight partners chartered a vessel from Melbourne and sailed eastward on a landhunting trip to Gippsland. Part of their speculation involved a search for pastoral land, but this syndicate also intended to found a town. Word reached Sydney, and a rival pastoralist chartered his own ship, carrying government land orders that countermanded the town scheme and allowing access for his stock. It took Brodribb years to recoup his losses.[79]

Avoidance of loose palaver served landhunting in the United States. In his letters from that country (1818–20), James Flint alerted prospective settlers to the prevalent secrecy and trickery. Established settlers would avoid direct, honest discourse with a newcomer "but on the contrary, tell him with the greatest effrontery, that every quarter section is already taken up."[80] To cope with unco-operative people, hunters of public land had to buy the best information available, securing maps and making inquiries about people and where they lived, so that they would not be fooled. Land dealers, Flint related, practiced diligence. "It is not uncommon for reconnoitring parties of them to lodge in the woods for a whole week. By such means much of the best land, mill-seats, and other local advantages, are withdrawn from the market at the first public sales."[81] To dissuade rivals, landhunters in Cape Colony, Australia, and New Zealand hinted at danger, bluffed that all land was taken, or professed better prospects waiting further up the trail. When Donald and John Moodie about 1825 asked a boer directions so that they could locate a 5,000-acre grant, the fellow tried to frighten them. They would be entering "the elephant's nest" and following a trail so poor that "a baboon could hardly keep its feet." This farmer coveted the land for his sons.[82] Queensland squatter John Campbell remembered that in the early 1840s "it became the rule on the [Darling] Downs to recommend to all parties in search of runs to go over the Range."[83] At Coal Creek in Otago, New Zealand, a stockman named Jones told a party of landhunters to "go back and go further up," and when they did he applied for the land himself.[84] How could new landhunters survive reticence and chicanery? Join the game and accept its rules. "Polite and obliging behaviour with circumspection in every transaction, become him in this new situation."[85]

Landhunters operated in many configurations: alone on horse or foot; in well-equipped, rapidly moving expeditions; with or without livestock. Poorly capitalized amateur adventurers, such as the worldly young New Zealand surveyor John Baker – noted above – scrounged for land and, after finding their destiny, hustled the means to retain it. Professional scouts, such as the militia officers employed by Virginia speculators, searched for land on behalf of clients who owned livestock or documents that could eventually retain some of what was located on their behalf. Expeditions financed by communities of settlers – the Great Trek and the migration of the Mormons are examples – explored for space and followed up with livestock, colonists, and improvements. Expanding grazers searched while driving livestock, travelling "like patriarchs of old with flocks and herds and servants."[86] In 1834, several expeditions left Cape Colony to gather intelligence for colonization. Grazers from the districts of Uitenhage, Somerset, and Tarka supplied three parties of riders who went forth "to spy the land." The key mission, the *kommissie trek* headed by Piet Uys and consisting of twenty men, well-supplied with gunpowder, shot, and good riding horses, followed a route taken in 1832 by Dr Andrew Smith, a government-supported explorer. Hermanus Berry, a member of Smith's expedition, had allegedly repeated over and over as they traversed Natal: "Almighty! I have never in my life seen such a fine place. I shall never reside in the Colony (Cape Colony) if the English Government make this a drosty [i.e., annex it]."[87]

On his return to the Cape, Berry enthused about this territory among Dutch neighbours and relatives. Balancing the aesthetic and the practical, Smith declared it a "beautiful country," "a more healthy country for cattle could not be found."[88] Thus it happened that a government initiative located a wonderland, and reports of its bounty inspired grazers used to taking land ahead of authority. The Uys party rode through Xhosa territory with permission from the paramount chief, Hintsa, and from the Pondo chief, Faku, both of whom may have welcomed white grazers as a buffer between themselves and the Zulus led by Dingane. Uys entered what later became Natal and met with Dingane but rushed back on news that Cape Colony was again at war with the Xhosa on its eastern frontier.[89] Thanks to the kommissie trek, Natal became the Great Trek's primary destination.

New pastoral stations in Australia and New Zealand, as well as American ranches, were routinely formed by grazers. Expanding pastoralists sent outriders ahead to search for pastures and to alert established stations that they were coming through. An expedition of this kind travelled only as fast as the slowest stock permitted. Alfred Duncan, an adventurer who planted coffee in Ceylon and slaughtered kangaroos for Australian squatters, learned a lesson about stock and speed when he joined a New Zealand landhunting party outfitted with thirteen pack horses and 3,000 sheep. Despite assurances otherwise, a number of ewes were in lamb, which slowed progress. In Australia and New Zealand rains hit and bogged down the drays; rounding up strays delayed expeditions; supplies ran out and had to be brought up. These and other common frustrations of the trail were long remembered.[90] Australian grazers overlanded stock but also scattered flocks along the southeast coast by vessel. Starting in earnest during 1836, and continuing for several years, they sailed from Van Diemen's Land (Tasmania) to Port Phillip Bay, but during the early 1840s, as this district became stocked, grazers landed in the surf at coves along the craggy coastline from Geelong to Portland.[91] From the late 1830s to the early 1850s, Australians appropriated "the levels" as they cruised the east coast of New Zealand's South Island. Starting in June 1851, Charles Hazelwood, in company with two other Australian outfits, shuttled "sheep, cattle, and horses" across the Tasman Sea from Port Phillip. For the first trip, they chartered the *Sir Harry Smith*, a vessel appropriately honouring a flamboyant imperial expansionist, then governor of Cape Colony. The three parties settled on the Hurunui Plains and immediately petitioned for official acknowledgment of their boundaries.[92]

THE EVOLVING IMPORTANCE OF PLACE

Hazelwood's quest for recognition of a definite place with property lines stemmed from his seasoning as an Australian squatter who knew at first hand about squatters' interests. He recognized that he was entering a relatively small colony where access would soon tighten. Boundary-making exercises by private parties erupted on all frontiers at some point; however, during certain early phases of occupation, grazers did not bother immediately to mark limits. Well-defined places with exact boundaries were not essential while freedom of movement remained feasible and was believed advantageous. In time, government encouragement to farmers promoted a land scarcity that restricted options for pastoralists, and they had to think about defending territory that they currently occupied against other grazers. Even when blessed with a relative abundance of open land and prospects for mobility, grazers assumed that they had an entitlement to a specific base of operations – a place where they concentrated their improvements, a site for buildings and gardens. Among the earliest frontier grazers, there were those who developed an attachment to ill-defined territories. Usually they worked on a crudely framed, non-geometrical tract centred on a main station.

Not content with access merely to a commons, grazers at the Cape (eighteenth century) and New South Wales (1820s–38), for example, formed places, despite government insistence that licenced grazing occurred on a common devoid of places. Although the will to possess a place was strong and widespread, the scale of the immobile property required was not uniform. Some American cattlemen preferred a small range near an open range – a grand commons that they controlled. On the open range, branding established stock ownership, and the mobile property was sorted out at biannual round-ups: one to sort and brand calves and one to collect beef for market. Nevertheless, there were range ranchers who evinced a proprietary sense of *their* range. By the 1870s, portions of range were known by the name of a cattle brand, and sale of the branding iron was assumed to convey a right to use a more or less established territory.[93] By at least the early 1880s, a few outfits in Colorado, Dakota, Montana, Nebraska, and Wyoming designated their range on ranch letterheads, typically in terms of rivers or creeks.[94] In the early 1880s across southwest Kansas and quite probably other regions as well, it was reported as customary to hold one's cattle on a particular range and to turn back those of a neighbour. "This custom has been as closely lived up to as if it were the law, and each stockman respected the range of the other as strictly as one farmer in the east respects the pastures of his neighbor." That respect may have existed in certain localities, but a number of ranchers resorted to fencing illegally the public domain rather than hiring line riders to separate stock.[95]

Good fences made better neighbours, and at less cost than line riders. Other customs also suggest that ranchers treated the public domain as if it consisted of discrete parcels belonging to specific outfits. When some vendors sold their ranches, they agreed not to return to that part of the range; however, parties who bought a ranch and failed to keep it stocked could find their claim to range challenged by neighbours.[96] Kentucky-born Pete Kitchen, who founded several Arizona ranches from the 1850s to the 1880s, asserted the principle of occupation by stock when he sold out in 1886. When a buyer asked how much land Kitchen owned, he replied, "wherever my cattle graze."[97] As an old-timer, Kitchen lived in the past, since the idea that a rancher could spread stock onto public land without strategic freehold sections was fast becoming outmoded.

Cattlemen applied sundry degrees of care in stock management, and the importance of place to individual grazers intensified when a rancher determined to replace Texas longhorns with eastern blood stock. At one extreme, especially in the early years of range ranching, stockmen with scrawny mossyhorns from Texas were content with access to an open range and a homestead with a corral. Kitchen was an anachronistic example. When well-capitalized, improving ranchers practised breeding and close winter supervision, they wanted to separate their cattle from their neighbours' and from herds with diseased stock. This reinforced a preference for boundaries. Cattlemen diverged regarding the urgency of holding defined places, and their attitudes changed with the times. It became much harder by the 1880s for American cattlemen to use an open range without holding more and more cornerstone land on lease or freehold to shield *their* range from other cattlemen or from sheep raisers also looking for grazing.

If many cattlemen accepted a hypothetically open range, modified by customary but vague boundaries, and joined round-ups administered by an association, sheepmen really preferred holding specific places, even when practising transhumance, because any mixing of flocks was always recognized as undesirable. Sheep could not be branded, although sometimes station managers in Australia earmarked or ruddled (stained) them, and Wyoming shepherds tried to stamp flock numbers on them. Station shepherds supervised flocks, moving them out early in the morning and bringing them together in the evening. This monotonous protective labour traditionally took place on defined places and built on the cheap labour of indigenous or "mixed-race" peoples. Lambing, sheering, keeping flocks away from diseased stock, and rotating pastures required a close management of labour, livestock, and locales.[98]

During the range wars of the 1880s and 1890s in the Rocky Mountains region, cattlemen, knowing the needs of sheepmen, drove flocks together to create confusion.[99] The Aztec Cattle Company, which in the mid-1880s had invested in artesian wells and water tanks on its New Mexico range, hired gunman John Paine to drive off shepherds. Cattlemen using the Bighorn Basin did more than harass shepherd Billy Minnick, who ignored their warning. In the winter of 1893–94, they executed an example, scattering his sheep, burning his camp outfit, and murdering him. Cattlemen resorted to intimidation more readily when dealing with encroaching sheepmen than with their own kind.[100] In arid regions, all grazers – whether managing sheep or cattle – worried about water, and thus they inevitably contested the control of specific places with springs, water-holes, and river frontage; however, they usually operated by the peaceful manipulation of land-allocation laws, practices that I explain shortly when considering how grazers in the American west sought to retain control of *their* places. Now, however, our attention must turn to the sense of place nursed by grazers on several frontiers outside North America.

In Cape Colony and New South Wales, authorities – especially far-off metropolitan governments – worried about conceding property interests to squatters and forfeiting revenue. When first alerted to squatting, they tried to control it and to render grazers' interests in discrete tracts as precarious in law as possible. The Dutch East India Company's starting position, for example, was one of absolute opposition to squatters having security of place, for the company desired concentrated settlement and intensive agriculture at the Cape to serve fleets and strategic interests. In the 1680s, it granted licences for frontier game hunting, and the same register contained copies of permits for seasonal grazing. By the late seventeenth century, the company's recognition that farmers could supply livestock as readily as the indigenous Khoikhoi, helped expand settlers' grazing, despite official consternation about pastoral squatting. The company accelerated stock raising, while it rated grazing an inferior activity. The last governor to persecute squatting grazers, Simon van der Stel, believed that pastoralists shunned the arts of ploughing and planting and lived "lazy and indolent lives."[101] In the 1680s, he tried to fine stockmen who owned no land. Not even by threatening corporal punishment could he suppress their migration. Grazers were reluctant to report on one another.[102]

Van der Stal's son, who succeeded him in 1699, relaxed the Dutch East India Company's anti-squatting regulations. Starting in 1703, the company became more generous with grazing licences for freeholders who wanted to expand. Non-owners simply continued to move about on frontiers without benefit of official acknowledgment. Eventually they too were allowed licences. While it was not the company's intention to grant private rights on demarcated tracts, stock raisers erected marker beacons and constructed homesteads. On their own initiative, as I reported above in chapter 2, Cape grazers organized somewhat circular tracts in remote districts and identified themselves with these *loan farms*.[103] Bit by bit, during the eighteenth century the company extended grazers' interests without relinquishing its right to resume the land. Yet the company accepted de facto boundaries as early as 1708. In the 1720s, it granted grazing licences for loan farms for twelve-month periods, and then for two years, rather than for three or four months, thus recognizing more-than-seasonal occupation. By the 1770s, pragmatic administrators fortified the boers' sense of security of tenure by appointing commissions to adjudicate boundary and water disputes, accepting that licenced grazers should have adequate space, allowing sales of improvements, permitting transfers of loan farms, and neglecting to press for fees in arrears.[104] Neighbours could not always resolve boundary conflicts privately. When the Batavian commissary-general, Jacob de Mist, inspected the Cape in 1802, "avowed enemies" assembled wherever he stayed "to lay their differences over boundaries or other matters."[105] Governmental concessions or acts of assistance advanced squatters' interests in the land. A comparable progression occurred later, but much faster, in New South Wales.

In 1743, the Dutch East India Company again modified its policy on squatting grazers by offering them an opportunity to convert the 400 or so loan farms into freehold *for a fee*. Few grazers found this offer advantageous, for occupants could not afford it. They already struggled with modest loan-farm licence fees, and they scraped by with insecurity of tenure well enough. Still, the conversion plan suggests a softening of the company's attitude vis-à-vis loan-farm grazers and its desire to generate greater land revenues. By the end of the century, land revenues were essential to the company's operations at the Cape. Squatters meanwhile were spreading and diversifying their pastoral operations. Grazers who practiced transhumance, driving stock onto the Karoo plains in winter and to higher elevations in summer, wanted to move between the same fixed places each year, particularly when they had erected huts. Augusta de Mist thought that they resembled "shepherds of the Alps or Pyrenees [descending] the plains with their entire households at the onset of winter."[106] Established places were not desired by every grazer, because in dry regions water-holes and rainfall were irregular and a communal open range improved chances for stock survival. The variety of grazing practices, with their relationships to environments and fixed places, presaged by more than a century the intricate arrangements of open ranges, grazing rights, and property interests in the arid quarter of the United States east of the Rocky Mountains and west of the 100th meridian.[107]

Early Cape grazing licences made no mention of the quantity of land covered, let alone boundaries, so grazers disputed access to pastures. For years, the Dutch East India Company did little to avert conflict; however, about the 1770s, it required farmers to state in licence applications that they had located far enough from neighbours to be innocuous. In certain instances, the company investigated areas where a grazer requested a new loan farm or where complaints had arisen from apprehensive loan farmers established in the vicinity. Occasionally, it sent an officer to investigate complaints about encroachments, to examine the competition for water, and even to withdraw licences. By the 1780s, custom sanctioned abundant interests in delimited tracts, but, since the company warned that it could grant the land to others, the rights of loan-farm grazers remained imperfect.[108]

British rule did not immediately transform arrangements at the Cape, although the new regime, as we saw in chapter 4, wanted to regularize land tenure. An important series of land grants showed Dutch grazers the vulnerability of loan-farm tenure. The Albany colonists of 1820 found – like many settlers everywhere – that grazing was easier than tilling. But they needed larger tracts. Many received improved grants at the expense of loan farms. Massive changes, however, were held up by the expense of surveying allotments, the complexity of appraising land values preparatory to confirming quit-rent tenure, and the force of local traditions. The British inherited a functioning – though very litigious – system for managing the inevitable expansion of grazing lands and resolving boundary disputes. The Dutch system adopted by the British relied on a local official, the *landdrost*. Applicants for loan farms contacted the landdrost, who might inspect to see that enough land was truly available to countenance a licence. The governor had a right of final approval, and if the applicant received a licence, copies were retained in Cape Town and with the landdrost.[109] Local reforms in land tenure, related changes to local government administration, and the imperial government's emphasis on land sales revised the Dutch land-allocation system and changed the appearances of land allocation. Actual practices changed little. The loan-farm system re-emerged in the 1830s and 1840s as "request tenure."[110] Streams of regulations chattered over a bedrock of tradition. When they formed their republics in the 1840s and 1850s, the boers looked to the inexpensive land-taking practices that they had known for generations.[111] Muddled boundaries, mentioned in the last chapter, derived from traditional free-selection practices blessed by settler-dominated governments.

The building of grazers' interests in unalienated land happened early but slowly in the Cape Colony. In New South Wales, commercial grazing forced a sequence of debates and government concessions within a relatively short period (1820–50). It transpired before those managing the American public domain reviewed the prospects for grazing on arid lands west of the 100th meridian – an occupation under way only in the 1860s. The timing meant that the Australian model of pastoral-land management was known to Americans and discussed as a possibility, notably during an 1880 congressional review of land policy. Timing also meant that some grazers in the American west could defend places on the range with barbed wire, whereas in British colonies a more-or-less-orderly leasing system was by then in place. Depending on calculations appropriate to a variety of specific circumstances, American ranchers split into wiremen and fence cutters once this cheap means of protecting interests became available after 1874.[112] I say more about fencing below.

Another tool for securing ground and water was uniquely accessible to American grazers. They could buy or lease tracts on the sections that had been granted to railway companies to pump up their assets, and assist with stock flotation. National land grants to railways amounted to substantial portions of the public domain in Michigan, Illinois, Iowa, Wisconsin, the Dakotas, Missouri, Arizona, Utah, Nevada, and California.[113] Grazers who wanted some security of tenure for their buildings and water sources, or secure access to an open range, often approached the railways' land departments.[114] Railway lands came in alternate sections, and buying or leasing these suited some ranchers, because securing legal interests in the red squares on the check- erboard allowed them to control the black squares, which remained public domain. By the mid-1880s, a number of ranchers strung fence around the circumference of an entire board. Railways could juggle the lands to which they were entitled, and this helped grazers, since they could collaborate with the land department's agents to select strategi- cally worthwhile leaseholds. Ordinarily, railway companies received bonus land in alternate sections for a specified distance on either side of the planned route. However, because designated land might be already occupied, or because the land grant could not be determined until the precise line of the railway was surveyed, territory exceeding the company's true entitlement was withdrawn from the public domain. Even if a railway defaulted on its commitment to build a line, the reservations were not immediately forfeited and returned to the domain. Some reservations set aside in the 1850s endured into the 1880s.[115] The occupation of grazing land in the American west involved an assortment of tactics that embraced the interpretation of local conditions and then leaned on corporate enterprise, whether in the manufacture of wire or in the purchase and leasing of railway lands. Western American grazers functioned with relatively slight government supervision, but with supports originating in industry and finance.

The evolution of the New South Wales system deserves attention, because it influenced other British pastoral frontiers and contrasted with the American approach. When New South Wales experienced a wool boom in the early 1830s, colonial administrators and private individuals extracted lessons from their knowledge of the Cape's history; they made connections between distant frontiers. Governor Richard Bourke "had already seen at the Cape the way in which this occupation [squatting] could so easily be converted into a form of prescriptive property rights that deprived the crown of its rights."[116] Among the aggressive squatting grazers in New South Wales during the 1830s, a handful had emigrated from the Cape. Charles Hotson Ebden, son of a Cape banker, put capital into Van Diemen's Land in 1832, and in 1835 he backed a cattle station on the banks of the Murray River.[117] Because of prior knowledge about how property interests could originate and grow through squatting, and because squatting in eastern Australia was commercially dynamic, the policy shifts – from the familiar stand that denied squatters any connection with places to a recognition of their boundaries – proceeded swiftly, and the concessions did not stop there. Squatters' interests in eastern Australian lands multiplied, and the interplay of squatters and administrators spread to other colonies. Battles to secure official recognition of place featured centrally in the politics of New South Wales (1835–50), and the foundation colony then implanted its system for pastoral occupation in its satellites: Van Diemen's Land (Tasmania), Port Phillip Bay (Victoria), Moreton Bay (Queensland), and New Zealand.

Initially, New South Wales permitted licencing arrangements comparable to those that sanctioned loan farms at the Cape. Its earliest authorizations for land use, apart from grants, were tickets of location.

Until 1827, recipients could depasture stock free of charge on a circular tract around their stockyards.[118] Tickets of location conferred legal interests in a specific location. The home government predicted problems should a governor some day try to grant the land in question. Therefore, to dilute the squatters' interests on land not yet organized for sale, the government forced eastern Australian pastoralists from 1827 to 1838 to operate under a system that discouraged any attachment to place. In 1836, a licencing system was put in place to collect revenue from grazing on crown land, and commissioners of crown lands were legislated into existence to collect licence fees and to check on the character of squatters. Commissioners were at first prohibited from sorting out boundary disputes – for the government, no boundaries for private property existed beyond the limits of occupation.[119] Ebden, the South African emigrant, recognized how licencing impaired Australian grazers. The "license does not even reserve to you the right of bringing an action against trespassers but, on the contrary, may be granted to any number of people for one and the same spot." That expressed the squatters' disapproval with the commons. As for commissioners, Ebden believed that they were sent to the frontier "to watch the squatters with a jealous eye and retard progress."[120] In fact, the commissioners in Australia and New Zealand, and landdrosts in southern Africa, were a diverse group – some reduced grazers' runs, others accommodated the government's tenants, and a few joined a local clique and, with its help, also ran stock.[121]

In varying degrees, grazers had developed attachments to place and space, to resources and boundaries. The squatting grazers' attachment to place in Cape Colony (soon after 1700 to 1770s) and New South Wales (1827–38), in the face of government reluctance to concede interests, was understandable, because locations with improvements had market value. Flocks and herds brought good prices if transferred with pastures, and even better prices if stations included enough land for two or three years' increase in stock.[122] Consummate squatter Niel Black rephrased this proposition: "it is an easy matter to get sheep without the run."[123] The urge for private possession of land encountered resistance from rivals and governments. Governments kept alive the commons model of grazing, because this property paradigm ostensibly kept the subject land free for grants or sales to smallholders; that ambition, which frequently made little environmental sense, still guided policy and distinguished the British colonial and American experience from most practices in Argentina or Brazil. Tension between the private formation of places and government denial of the same, through its insistence on a commons to serve later settlers, occurred in parts of southern Africa, Australia, New Zealand, and the United States, in that sequence. How did jostling grazers manage to define and defend space against one another when governments insisted on measures intended to dilute their interests in expectation that someday the land would be sold?

HOLDING ON TO WHAT YOU GOT

Self-imposed isolation was a tactic for evading encroachment, where and when it was feasible. Grazers prowled for land "sufficiently extensive, and secure from intrusion."[124] George Leslie felt secure on his 25 square miles of the Darling Downs in 1847, because a mountain range lay between him and Brisbane, and there was no good road.[125] Voortrekkers put as much distance as possible between themselves and British authority, although a few found – as Leslie would – that isolation strained trade.[126] Concerning the cattlemen of the Texas gulf coast, Frederick Law Olmsted wrote, "they cannot well be near one another without the adoption of some different system of living, and are generally squatters."[127] The renowned "King of the Pecos," rancher John Chisum, a descendant of landhunting Virginians, first went looking for cattle country in northwest Texas in 1852 and found it. Influxes of settlers in 1862 and again in 1865 drove him further and further west, until his brother located a well-watered, remote range on the Pecos River in New Mexico.[128] After nine years as a drover, another celebrated cattleman, Charles Goodnight, looked for a settled life as a rancher and made a start in Colorado, then shifted to a part of the Texas Panhandle where no ranches existed yet because of the Indian danger and the fact that the land was 250 miles from a railway. A history of ranchers in the Dakota territory went so far as to suggest that cattlemen cherished isolation.[129] American sheep herder Archer Butler Gilfillan, active in South Dakota around 1910, remarked that "a sheepman ain't got no friends." The retort was "a sheepman don't want no friends."[130] It was easier, Gilfillan believed, to be on good terms with people at a distance whose occupation posed no threat. For undercapitalized ranchers, railway construction jeopardized cheap grazing on the public domain. E.D. Swan, who fled Idaho's Lemhi River valley in 1875 because it was "getting so settled up, so there was no place to raise cattle," remembered more fondly his next destination, the Big Piney country in Wyoming, where his nearest neighbours were 40 miles down the Green River. It was perfect, "because there were no Railroads close and ample feed on the range."[131]

Grazers found abundant ways to deflect encroachment. When the government of New South Wales treated squatters as if they shared a commons, it prevented them from taking trespass actions against their

neighbours, but grazers found a surrogate measure. They could prosecute a neighbour for putting "scabby sheep" on the supposed commons.[132] Pastoralists also arranged sheep and cattle to give an
impression that they occupied more land more completely than was
the case. On occasion, this required borrowing stock on shares; other
times, moving flocks around for effect. Discovering the "most princely
place I ever saw," Niel Black immediately plotted how to distribute
stock and shepherds until increases in sheep and cattle established his
presence.[133] During the years when squatters in New South Wales
grazed on what was technically a massive common like the American
open range, a few attempted to deflect encroachment by buying land
just inside the colony's practical boundaries, inside the limits of occupation. From these boundary stations, they ran stock across the line
to where the government had yet to organize land sales. Rival grazers
heading for unorganized land would have to cross these freehold strips
and expose themselves to prosecution. Along the Murray River, grazers
outside the limits built shepherds' huts every three or four miles,
starting on the east side of their runs. They hoped to deflect mobs of
sheep moving westward from the Sydney side.[134]

   Another common practice was the occupation of land at the head
of streams, which reduced the ground to be patrolled yet affirmed
practical control over a much larger region.[135] Something similar happened in the United States when barbed wire became readily available.
The open ranges left grazers exposed to the disadvantages of the
commons that Australian stockmen deplored in the 1830s. In hilly
areas, Dakota and Montana grazers fenced off the mouths to valleys,
sometimes forming enclosures of 25 to 50 square miles.[136] Supported
by the boundary-shaping aids of wire and natural formations, large
ranchers who wanted to defend a place on the open range could allege
that they held definite portions of land "by common consent."[137]
Tactical holding actions sufficed for a while, allowing occupants
enough security to make slight improvements, but when other parties
started to encroach, or when more investment was contemplated,
squatters appealed for official recognition to fortify their legal interests.
Exactly this formal acknowledgment of a right to occupy a place was
impossible during the initial years of occupation, when governments
tried to safeguard future land revenues.

   Sluggish management of the public domain was a different problem,
but one that threw squatters into the similar predicament of lacking
formal recognition of their occupation of particular places. In the
midwest, a scarcity of land offices where pre-emptive rights could be
lodged was one reason why private parties formed claims clubs. Squatting grazers in New South Wales under the 1836 licencing arrangement

endeavoured to establish control of places, and a few of the runs that
they defined included curved boundaries that suggest measurement by
a timed journey like grazing stations in Cape Colony and in New South
Wales under the location-ticket system; other irregular boundaries
embodied natural features.[138] In 1839, a New South Wales ordinance
acknowledged a grazer's right to a place on crown land by instructing
the commissioners for crown lands to judge if there were encroachments and to use this and other information to decide whether to
renew a squatter's grazing licence. On annexation of New Zealand to
New South Wales, this licencing of sheep and cattle stations on specific
tracts extended across the Tasman Sea. From the late 1830s to the late
1840s, the crown insisted on formalities that allowed grazers to protect
specific places with government collaboration. With boundaries legitimized, squatters and commissioners of crown lands started to file
property descriptions. In the early nineteenth century, several land laws
of Buenos Aires similarly required occupants to form boundaries and
measure their estates.[139]

Henceforth, the tactics for landhunting and squatting in Australia and
New Zealand became more intricate. Added now to outward races to
get on the land in Australia and New Zealand, there were bracing
competitions to lodge licence applications for specific runs. It is not
clear what happened with respect to landhunting in Argentina, but on
British colonial frontiers protective steps required a journey that signalled intentions and alerted adversaries. An Australian or New Zealand
squatter might be lucky, encounter a commissioner of crown lands
making his inspection rounds, and apply on the trail, but otherwise a
dash into an administrative town was prudent.[140] Discovering a challenger who built a hut on one of his Canterbury runs, Samuel Butler
resolved to defend his station by riding all night to the land office. A
flooded river checked his dash and allowed the rival to catch up. In a
weird epitome of landhunting's polite circumspection, the competitors
rode together without mentioning their missions. Near town, they
parted and resumed the race. Had they entered the land office at the
same time, the issue would have been settled by the drawing of lots.
As it happened, the rival managed to put his name down after the
Christchurch office had closed, but Butler successfully challenged this
illegal application.[141]

Parties moved quickly and usually by horseback, although some
hunters in New Zealand could not secure horses. The 1859 description
from Nelson of landhunters as "long-legged" was more than a figura-
tive description for a few expeditions. During the colony's earliest
years, horses were scarce. Impatient landhunters struck out on foot,

and there were those who believed that they could best assay land on foot.[142] Rough terrain, dense growth, and short distances between coast and inland plains may also have made treks by "shank's mare" expedient. In 1851, Alfred Chapman, on a three-month quest, walked from Wellington to the east coast; to hold the land that he found, he took sheep on shares from a more established grazer.[143] Not all walkers succeeded. In 1857, Donald Hay reached Lake Wakatipu, crossed it by raft, jotted down a description of the land that he wanted, and walked to Dunedin to apply for a grazing licence, only to discover that someone had registered a prior claim.[144]

To form boundaries that were then described for licencing purposes, and for subsequent struggles to confirm occupation, squatting grazers in Australia and New Zealand blazed trees; in the arid Australian interior, rocks, dry creek beds, and even imposing ant hills marked boundaries.[145] To make perimeters as enduring as possible, grazers worked among themselves to realize informal agreements. Near Mount Macedon in Victoria, John Riddell and a neighbour named Brock negotiated agreements. Neither would run scabby sheep near the other, and in October 1845 they walked their boundary together. Where there were no obvious natural features, Riddell "drew a Plough furrow along boundary with Brock." Other squatters trusted Riddell to act as an arbitrator in boundary disputes.[146] Through a government concession and by their own actions, grazers advanced property interests. They still had demands. Australian grazers lobbied for and were granted the right to compensation for improvements if the government sold the crown land; and they demanded and received the right to transfer the licence to a station, thus legitimizing sales. Each enlargement of property interests increased the market value of stations, and that made grazers conscious of boundaries and acreage. When it became clear, about 1846, that the British government would shortly allow Australian colonies to grant leases, squatters scrambled to have their perimeters confirmed. Appreciating that leases conveyed added market value, squatters refined property lines.[147] Where once a mountain range divided stations, a plough line was barely adequate ten years later. Governments directed squatters to prepare properly mapped perimeters, and that meant rectangular formations, except where natural features rendered this impossible. Curves and ambiguities in pastoral land packages were eliminated.

At every stage of landhunting, government officers, if present, could be helpful. Single squatters and land syndicates alike scouted territories where they anticipated that government authority would soon be established and settlement allowed. Anticipatory scouting was what Washington and Crawford had been up to in 1767–71. American syndicates in the 1830s sent surveyors onto Indian concessions or into regions about to be ceded by Indians. When finished reconnoitring and with notebooks crammed with descriptions, they returned to meet backers, to draw maps, and to prepare for upcoming land sales. They indulged in another universal practice – extracting as much information as possible from government employees. New Zealand's crown land buyers seldom lacked travelling companions, because keen hunters wanted to know exactly what was going to be opened, and they hoped to coax promises of use rights from their influential trail mates.[148]

When the governor of New South Wales steamed north in 1842 to proclaim an end to the convict system at Moreton Bay, he was accompanied by at least one speculator, who, aware of prospects for non-convict settlement, came to explore.[149] In the same colony, a speculative landhunter rode with Commissioner of Crown Lands William Wiseman, in a region between the Dawson and Fitzroy rivers. Marking trees, he tendered for "the right of run" as they went.[150] As governments prepared to bring territory under greater formal control, to extinguish a frontier, landhunters dashed to the scene to negotiate advantageous agreements with officials or to learn enough from them to jump on prime sites when the government opened the region. Government almost served as the squatter's friend. But the alliance was imperfect. Wiseman, for example, rejected his companion's applications when it was clear that his shadow – a non-improving speculator – would apply little labour to the land.

In New South Wales and its satellites, from 1839 to dates when leases were finally adopted, grazers could still not drop their guard. Once the government conceded boundaries, grazing squatters had three additional demands: security of tenure against the crown, the right to sell improvements, and a pre-emptive right to buy parts of their stations. Grazing licences were not leases; the crown could eject pastoralists at any time and demanded performance conditions for an annual licence renewal. For example, the land in question had to be adequately stocked, not idle or held for expansion or speculation. Grazers were loath to tell anyone about the estimated acreage of their runs or the number of animals on the station. Squatter Christopher Hodgson, writing in 1846, sketched an illustrative dialogue between two pastoralists. One party asks, "how much land do you consider your own?" The other replies, "that is a secret – I have not yet any I can call my own; however, I have not enough, and yet I have, at present; but the Government wishes to curtail the extent, so I must be careful what I say."[151]

Many land takers (it is impossible to be precise about numbers)
relied on government, not just in eliminating – by one means or
another – first peoples' interests and enforcing property rights, but in
carrying forward private landhunting expeditions. The government
commissariat in New South Wales assisted the trips of Alexander Berry
and the Leslie brothers. Decades later, in the 1880s, landhunters
followed the mounted police of Western Australia out of pearling ports
into the interior to claim grazing land. In southern Africa, one of three
exploration parties that prepared the way for the Great Trek knew of
Dr Andrew Smith's report for the government. For assistance, American landhunters in the midwest, and later on the high plains, turned
to obliging land-office clerks and surveyors.[152] In New Zealand,
landhunters travelled with crown land buyer Donald McLean and
South Island Commissioner of Crown Lands Walter Mantell. In American territories along migrant trails across the high plains, the U.S.
army acquired a string of forts in the late 1840s and the 1850s to
assist and protect travellers. Clerks and traders at these establishments
were among the first opportunists to start ranching on public land.[153]
During the early 1870s, Texas cattlemen contracted to provide beef
for army posts and Indian reservations. While driving stock or waiting
with herds, they became acquainted with ranges in Arizona, Kansas,
Nebraska, and Dakota. Ironically, aid for first peoples increased
landhunters' pressure on their territory.[154]

Ironies abounded. Landhunters and settlers benefited from the assistance of indigenous peoples, learning practical knowledge of food,
shelter, transportation, and agriculture.[155] Specific instances of aid are
present among several landhunting expeditions that we have followed
in this book. When Colonel William Crawford scouted on Washington's behalf, Indians showed him an ideal site with fertile, flat bottom
lands. The Moodie brothers at the Cape sought African guides and
preferred Khoikhoi stockmen to Europeans, "from their being more
accustomed to the management of cattle."[156] When Piet Retief contemplated leaving Cape Colony, he interrogated his Mozambican slaves
about their homeland.[157] In 1837, Australian squatter Alexander Mollison, heading thirty men, 5,000 sheep, 600 head of cattle, 40 bullocks,
and "an infinite number and variety of dogs," included three Aboriginals in his party. Another Aboriginal, who joined them at the Murray
River, guided him to land for a lambing station.[158] In early 1840, Niel
Black encountered the "son of Cameron Cluny who had been out
8 days riding the bush with a civilized native from the Sydney side
looking for a run."[159] A consortium of grazers on the Darling Downs
in 1841, anticipating overstocking, dispatched a white landhunter and
an Aboriginal to claim the northern part of the Downs.[160]

Frederick Weld's reputation as a New Zealand explorer soared when he "discovered" an overland stock route from Cape Campbell to Lyttelton. A Ngai Tahu chief told him about a critical mountain pass.[161] South Island landhunter Alex Petrie in 1858 used the huts erected by Maori for trapping eels on the rivers, and counterparts in Queensland seized bark from Aboriginal "humpies" to build their huts.[162] On the North Island, Weld judged the Maori "the keenest hands in the world at a bargain," because of their shrewd dealings as boat operators ferrying livestock and supplies.[163] In the southern African republics, the build-up in livestock with which white occupants confirmed their presence drew on African herds through trade and raids. Purchases of foodstuff grown by Maori of New Zealand and the Zulu and Sotho of southern Africa permitted colonists to concentrate on grazing.[164] The *caudillo* of Argentina, General Rosas, relied on Indian allies to secure the frontier of Pampa against the hostile Araucanians, rewarded loyal *caciques*, provisioned friendly Indians, and deployed Indian troops against opponents.[165] A few American cattlemen near Indian territories in the Oklahoma and Dakota territories benefited in the 1880s from marriage to Indian women, whose influence helped them briefly procure grazing rights on tribal lands.[166] As these anecdotes suggest, individuals among first peoples sought advantages from landhunters, who gained from their assistance.

The landhunters even benefited from the names given by indigenous peoples to landmarks, because newcomers could not fully trust in agreements among themselves that applied European names. As the land commissioners for Griqualand West put it, "such a name as 'Vaal Kop' (yellow hill), or 'Buschduiven Rand' (Bush Doves' Ridge) is as easily conferred upon one spot as another."[167] A comparable uncertainty led the government of South Australia in 1839 to order settlers to record Aboriginal names "as most consistent with propriety and beauty of appellation."[168] Enriching and individualizing locales, place names used by indigenous peoples assisted the newcomers' occupation, although there were restrictions. The surveyor-general of New South Wales instructed his surveyors in 1829 to reduce the number of letters in Aboriginal place names to a maximum of nine.[169] Naming by first peoples was to be assimilated to the service of newcomers. The great land rush involved enormous European naming exercises. Intriguingly, plenty of indigenous names endured, some because they assisted newcomers to define boundaries.

The occupation of frontiers by landhunters, squatters, and grazers involved a sparring among private parties and between these outfits and governments. On British colonial frontiers, this grappling over property interests generated a progression: squatting without authority; squatting with licences on the hypothetical crown commons without the assignment of boundaries; licences that acknowledged boundaries; licences that acknowledged boundaries but also conceded the right to compensation and the right to sell; finally, grazing on land leased from the crown. The United States was slow to provide administrative stability for western grazers on the open range. An 1879 law enabled states to lease their sections of the public domain; however, only in 1899 was there any federally regulated grazing, and that only on national forest reserves. By 1885 – perhaps earlier – many if not most American stockmen had faced some form of encroachment, and a few desired secure – though cheap – tenure.[170] Why for so long had the United States avoided acting as a responsible landlord, particularly when there were land-management models from British colonies? For one thing, legislators, bureaucrats, and ranchers were divided among themselves when it came to devising an alternative. The subject's multidimensional character invited confusion and diversity. Debate stymied official action, and during the prolonged indecision, finance capital assisted ranchers and speculators with strategic landholding ploys.

During the critical period of grazers' occupation (1865–85), Washington treated the arid plains west of the 100th meridian as if they comprised potential farm lands to be allocated as agricultural homesteads. Settlement duties – a vestige of the urge to promote improvement – made it impractical for grazers to acquire titles to the extensive tracts that they used. Advocates of other land allocation possibilities – the selling or leasing of large tracts cheaply – encountered resistance. Uncertain about the market worth of land, key federal and state administrators and legislators resisted endorsing sales of grazing land at low prices; they recoiled at the thought of speculators reaping windfall gains. At the same time, the spirit of government was "to keep aloof from meddling with private affairs as much as possible."[171] Laissez-faire was not so much a well-conceived ideology as a default position taken to avoid alienating land too cheaply to large ranching or speculator outfits. As for leasing, the public domain had not been closely assessed for appropriate land uses, and there was suspicion that leasing could undervalue sections of good farm land. Grazers, moreover, could not agree about leasing and also split on whether or not to endorse proposals to sell off large blocks at rock-bottom prices. Australian counterparts had been more enthusiastic about leasing.

A few politicians and ranchers claimed that leasing from Uncle Sam meant bowing to tyranny. Grazers were unlikely to have embraced such republican patriotic puffery without practical motives. Economic explanations for the rejection of leasehold are plausible, and they surfaced in 1879–80 when a federal commission investigated the disposal of public land in the arid west. The commissioner of the General Land Office asked ranchers' associations what they thought of four alternatives: unrestricted sales of western land at five cents an acre, unrestricted sales but with stepped reductions in price the longer the land remained unsold, the leasing of public land at 10 per cent of its valuation per annum, no change. The deliberations of the Laramie County Stock Association – soon to become the highly influential Wyoming Stock Growers Association – reveal what stockmen pondered when confronted with choices about land tenure. Members overwhelmingly favoured the status quo, because open sales or leases introduced the spectre of outsiders bumping them off the range.

Like members of earlier midwest claims clubs, Wyoming ranchers wanted to hold what they currently occupied against interlopers who could pay for titles. If Congress decided on leases or sales, then these ranchers wanted a pre-emptive right that would first offer secure tenure to actual occupants – namely, themselves. This was merely then fall-back position. Many of them supposed that their costs for sustaining private arrangements with neighbours – or for intimidating neighbours, farmers, and sheepmen to stay off *their* part of the public domain – would amount to less than either lease fees or outlays for purchases. Until encroachments absolutely threatened their cattle kingdoms (see Table 7.3), they thought that legal security of tenure was an unnecessary expense.[172] As it turned out, Congress failed to act, and land laws remained unrevised. Not long after 1880, the day came when many ranchers found their situation so threatened by other cattlemen, sheepmen, speculators, and the granger movement (organized farmers) that, even without new legislation, they had to acquire title to choice tracts to hold their range (Map 7.4).

American cattlemen who aspired to hold specific places could, as I noted above, hire line riders to patrol the boundaries of a ranch or join a clique of stockmen who informally managed a range. At times, range management for self-interest included intimidation. When they detected a herd heading in their direction, the established ranchers on the Texas Panhandle delegated a welcoming committee. "We told him we were going to try moral persuasion and good humour and if it did not work we had an injunction coming in the district court (a friendly judge rode with the committee), and if we could not get that, then we had two wagons back of us with men with winchesters and six shooters."[173] In the southern counties of Texas, however, ranchers could acquire titles to Spanish grants. In other parts of the state, they accumulated public lands at low prices. Texas was unusual in this respect. Some cattlemen in other territories, like Australians before

Table 7.3
Examples of grazing lands and ranches, U.S. west, at peak of ranching, 1885

Description of area	Estimated acreage
Grazing lands in thirteen western states	870 million (44 per cent of continental U.S. surface area)
Northwestern grazing lands	740 million (37 per cent)
The "park country" of Colorado	130 million (6.5 per cent)
Cherokee Strip Live Stock Association	5–6 million
Aztec Cattle Company, New Mexico	2 million
S.W. Dorsey's Chico Ranch, Arizona	1.8 million
Prairie Cattle Company Ranch, southeastern Colorado	1 million (200,000–300,000 fenced)
Arkansas Valley Cattle Company, southeastern Colorado	1 million
The Cheyenne and Arapahoe Cattle Company (illicit Indian lease)	1 million
King Ranch, southeastern Texas	500,000
Todhunter outfit, Oregon	200,000

Sources: Joseph Nimmo, *Report in Regard to the Range and Ranch Cattle Business of the United States*, first pub. 1885 (New York: Arno Press, 1972), 1–5; Ernest Staples Osgood, *The Day of the Cattleman* (Minneapolis: University of Minnesota Press, 1929), 190–1; David Montejano, *Anglos and Mexicanos in the Making of Texas, 1836–1986* (Austin: University of Texas, 1987), 63–70; J. Orin Oliphant, *On the Cattle Ranges of the Oregon Country* (Seattle: University of Washington Press, 1968), 209; William W. Savage, *Cherokee Strip Live Stock Association* (Columbia: University of Missouri Press, 1973), 17; Melvin Harrel, "Oklahoma's Million Acre Ranch," *Chronicles of Oklahoma* 29 (1951), 70–8; Entry on Aztec Cattle Company in the New Mexico volume and entry on Chico Ranch in the Arizona volume of ranch histories complied by Lamar Moore, box 9, Lamar Moore Collection, accession 675, American Heritage Center, University of Wyoming.

them, marked territory at the natural boundaries of individual ranches by erecting line camps. Well-defined natural boundaries in the hills and mountains of the U.S. west served to make the informal allocation of ranges by stockgrowers' associations easier than it was on the plains.[174]

Cherokee Strip stockmen in the early 1880s found line riders and camps a costly option.[175] Thus they, and many cattlemen elsewhere, resorted to other landholding tools – namely wire fencing and the leasing of land outside the public domain. Fencing had been unavailable to grazers in southern Africa, Australia, and New Zealand during the major periods of landhunting and squatting in those colonies. Fencing on Australian stations was rare, costly, and at first fashioned from

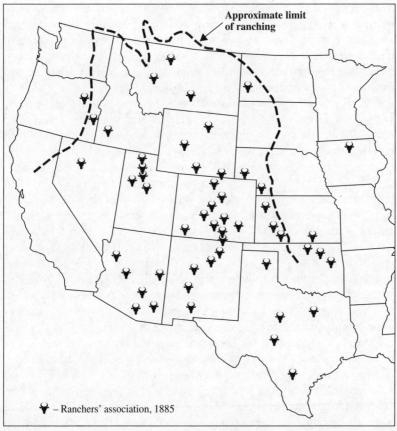

Map 7.4

Range ranching at its peak, U.S. west, 1885: location of ranchers' associations
Source: Terry G. Jordan, *North American Cattle-Ranching Frontiers: Origins, Diffusion, and Differentiation* (Albuquerque: University of New Mexico Press, 1993), figure 54; List of Associations [1884–5], box 43, accession 14, Wyoming Stock Growers Association, American Heritage Center, University of Wyoming.

saplings. Fences appeared only in the 1850s and 1860s, when security of tenure by leasing made investment feasible.[176] Queenslanders imported the prickly pear to enclose paddocks cheaply and precipitated an ecological disaster. On the American prairies in the 1850s and 1860s, some ranchers and settlers used mud fences and hardy *bois d'arc* (osage orange) hedges. In southern Africa, living fences were also tried.[177] American ranchers, however, occupied the prairies and high plains at a time when they could buy miles of relatively cheap fencing. As Ora Peake puts it in a history of Colorado ranching, "why not just fence a few hundred thousand or a million acres and say nothing about it?"[178] For a few years this worked. A decade after the first sales of barbed wire in 1874, tens of thousands of tons were manufactured annually. Barbed wire – an industrial product addressing the puzzle of boundaries on a commons – was a fitting emblem for the American west. It encompassed invention, technology, private initiative, and litigation. It served a scramble for resources.

Wire illegally ringed millions of acres of public domain in the early 1880s. For several reasons, well-capitalized cattle ranchers resorted to barbed wire. Those who intended to improve their herds could breed blooded stock free from worry about its mingling with inferior stock. Fences excluded the inferior stock of small ranchers, and it barred cattle drovers and homesteaders from the unsold tracts of the range, enabling large ranchers to attempt to control public land that they did not own. In regions exposed to severe winters, the fences – especially after the killing winter of 1887–88 – contained livestock near stored feed over winter.[179] Some ranchers who used fences also controlled range by other means, typically – as we saw above in this chapter – securing strategic freehold or leases of railway land. Not all big ranchers, however, wished to lay out capital for fencing. There were ranchers who aimed to avoid fencing costs and simultaneously dodge paying for damages done by their cattle straying over the range and trampling homesteaders' crops. They lobbied for laws that required farmers to erect fences to keep out cattle. The gist of the issue – who would pay for damages or prevention – was common on other frontiers.

Kermit Hall is correct when he observes that fencing-out laws that favoured large ranchers were "hardly unique to the Plains."[180] There were also fencing-in laws sponsored by farmers. From the 1840s to the 1860s, writes Alan Ward, "endless variations on the theme of fencing, cattle, trespass and theft, were the stock-in-trade of lawsuits on the New Zealand frontier." Maori made use of magistrates and courts to recover damages from the intruding white colonists.[181] Where cattle interests prevailed in state politics in the American west, legislatures released ranchers from responsibility, forcing farmers to bear the costs of fencing; in Nebraska and Kansas, farmer-political movements in the 1870s imposed herd laws that made cattlemen liable for crop damages, and these measures pushed stockmen out of many counties.[182] Major W. Shephard of the Royal Engineers encountered the complexities of fencing politics on travels through the U.S. west. "If stock-owners are in power, they say to the small rancher, 'Fence your fields;' if the farmers are more numerous, they turn to the stockman and say, 'Herd your cattle,' while all combine against the stranger within their bounds."[183] Fencing in the American west precipitated additional landhunting, since those grazers who were shut out of the range and kept away from water by fences moved to marginal lands.[184]

In 1885, federal authorities ordered the removal of illegal fences – about 2,640,000 acres was surrounded in Colorado. They realized what Cape Colony administrators had recognized two hundred years earlier. Squatting grazers stole into presumptive interests. The show of federal hostility to squatting inspired no unanimity about the advantages of leasing, as government's response to grazing squatters had in Australia. Fencing persisted as an option on federal land, because enforcement of anti-fencing orders proved difficult in a society where money and political influence swayed law officers. Struggles over fencing laws for *state* lands, allocated to states by Washington, were positively labyrinthine. When pressure on the open range began to intensify, in the early 1880s, the better-capitalized cattlemen started to collect clear titles to grazing lands. Although they still could not take leaseholds on the public domain itself, there were swathes of territory under the control of other agencies. Stock raisers discovered how to shield themselves against encroachment by securing interests on acreage not technically part of the domain. They rented railway lands, leased or purchased state lands, and illicitly leased Indian reservation lands – an expedient that the Department of the Interior refused to authorize, but grudgingly permitted in the early 1880s. Like generations of landhunters before them, grazers could buy discounted land scrip from speculators.[185] W.C. Hill, a land agent based in Washington, DC, notified western ranchers in 1885 that he still had on hand a stock of "additional Homestead claims, and Sioux Half Breed Scrip, the popular scrips, respectively for taking up surveyed and unsurveyed lands, without settlement [improvement duties]." His pitch explained the obvious. "With these it will pay you to take up such water holes as are in your range, and perhaps also, to avoid probable trouble in the future from settlers, such lands as are irrigable."[186]

Railway companies pulled huge blocks of land out of the public domain. To bolster the companies' assets when they floated stock, the U.S. government assigned land as development bonuses. With the exception of the Union Pacific, railways could set aside land in two bands. In the inner one, they were entitled to alternate sections of the grid for a stated distance on both sides of the surveyed line. In the outer, they could select sections to compensate for those in the inner band that had been pre-empted by early occupants. They tried to withdraw all the land within the limits of their grants, and, even if they failed to construct the road, they could keep the land out of the public domain for years, in some instances from the 1850s to the 1880s. Tens of millions of acres were withdrawn, and many sections, when leased by stockmen, controlled neighbouring sections of the public domain.[187]

American grazers secured freehold title to strategic portions of the public domain – water-holes or the openings to valleys – by manipulating federal homestead, desert, and swamp land, timber acts, and state public land laws.[188] New Mexico rancher S.W. Dorsey, secretary of the National Republican Party in 1880, reassured a partner several years later that they controlled roughly a million acres, much of it fenced, by owning land around the springs. If homesteaders appeared, he would turn off the "cock of the pipe." Dorsey had obtained the freehold in a variety of ways that would withstand the reach of any investigation "with but few exceptions."[189] Strategic land-control schemes assisted counterparts in Australia and New Zealand whose leaseholds came under pressure from land-reform legislation between the 1860s and the 1890s. New rules for the allocation of property rights in the colonies ensured that elaborate contests for the control of land were fought for decades. A tense interaction of governments and landhunters respecting property rights was repeated on a number of frontiers. The state and individuals influenced one another in a continuous process in which, again and again, a new balance was found. Each short-lived equilibrium represented an advance in the property rights of well-capitalized or credit-worthy private parties. Concurrently, governments brought new frontiers under control and marginalized the first peoples; landhunters and grazers moved on until they encountered mountains, seas, or an early-frost line. The land rush struck these barriers in the 1880s. Land agents and governments turned next to freeing up native reserves and intensifying the carrying capacity of marginal land.

PART THREE

Reapportioning the Pieces

CHAPTER EIGHT

Reallocation:
Breaking Up Big Estates
and Squeezing Margins

In the second half of the nineteenth century, landhunters and grazers were rapidly depleting the fund of fresh territory in temperate zones. By the 1850s, after nearly thirty years of zealous landhunting, Australian grazers occupied extensive territory in New South Wales, Victoria, and South Australia. In a span of twenty years, grazers took control of the acceptable pastures on the South Island of New Zealand, closing the rush there by the 1860s. Much the same occurred on the North Island, except for its centre, over which Maori retained control following the New Zealand wars. The probes for new pastoral districts in Queensland and Western Australia continued for several more decades. Following twenty years of range ranching, western American grazers ran out of desirable land during the 1880s and were overstocking the open range. Buenos Aires, initially the foremost pastoral province in Argentina, had nearly exhausted its public land reserves by the 1880s. In the same decade, the *boer* republics discovered that they could no longer grant generous allocations. When the Dominion of Canada and private land companies promoted the Canadian prairies as "the last best west," early in the twentieth century, there was substance to the slogan.[1]

As they encountered limits, societies habituated to expansion scrambled for solutions and rationalized good fortune or ill. Periods of unusually good rainfall induced a few farmers in South Australia (1875–81) and on the American high plains (1878–87) to move onto marginal land. Cattle ranchers spread over the high plains during this wet cycle. In the same years, Canadian prairie boosters promoted settlement of the southern drylands. In all three areas, science supplied the happy thought that rain followed the plough.[2] Thus optimism was a response to limits. So too was purposeful curiosity about foreign places. A few grazers from the United States, Australia, and New

Zealand considered migrating to newly opened tracts in the Patagonia Austral regions of Argentina, and thousands of Americans entered western Canada.³ In the last best west, at Pincher Creek in southern Alberta, where prairies end and mountains begin, land agent Arthur Cox received inquiries from the United Kingdom, Nova Scotia, Ontario, New York, Illinois, Michigan, Wisconsin, Minnesota, Kansas, Nebraska, Iowa, Oklahoma, the Dakotas, Montana, Idaho, Washington, and New Zealand.⁴

Perceiving an end to the rush, colonizers of all types – grazers, prospective farmers, speculators, property industry specialists – inspected their surroundings to pinpoint wasted terrain, to see if perchance a separate property could be sandwiched between existing ones. The spread onto marginal lands had many implications for grazers and farmers. As progressively less productive land was called into use, higher capital outlays were tried; agrarians experimented with ways to intensify land's carrying capacity. Some initiatives involved acclimatization of exotic flora, breeding for a better carcass or fleece, and hybridization for higher crop yields, while others pertained to engineering the landscape. Dryland farming techniques enabled some marginal lands to come into production, and from the 1880s to 1910s irrigation projects fired optimism about an improvement to eradicate the *waste* of glorious sunshine and to defeat drought. Common law precepts linked water rights to adjacent land, and because this attachment was of little help to labour-intensive farms located away from stream beds, governments in semi-arid and arid regions legislated a variety of new arrangements respecting water rights.

Other adjustments in law and property materialized in the late nineteenth century, all driven by a land-rush mentality. Indigenous peoples were exceedingly vulnerable during this hunt for pockets of waste, as they had been in earlier times. Without credit, counsel, and influence, many could not safeguard reserve acreage against raids authorized by sovereign authorities. Large-scale stockmen who frequently lacked freehold tracts found their interests exposed by the doctrine of improvement, which now helped advance a wave of new laws favourable to would-be small farmers. However, unlike beleaguered first peoples, grazers could tap capital to defend property interests. As strong men armed, like Richer in *Shane*, they confronted homesteaders with cash and occasionally weapons in the United States. How grazers reacted to homesteaders as individuals is one thing, and bound to have varied, but as a class of colonizer they universally encountered a momentous business threshold. They had to spend more than ever before to cling to their interests. Grazers in the United States,

Australia, and New Zealand found themselves in trouble, because of environmental degradation, droughts or hard winters, disease, and insecure tenure. They were not powerless vis-à-vis the last challenge, but it put them through trials. To finance protective actions they intensified their management of land and livestock. The situation in southern Africa was different, because the British land reforms of 1813 initiated a tenure-conversion process that offered permanent property rights for Cape boers, ultimately on reasonable terms. Later, in the republics, Afrikaner governments extended secure tenure to white occupants. Argentina's *estancieros* of the early nineteenth century, and later the country's well-financed sheep grazers, benefited too from government generosity.

In addition to private and government actions that coped with the perceived loss of settlement frontiers, assorted reform movements embraced land nationalization or a single tax on land's intrinsic value, with the purpose of wresting territory from alleged entrapment by speculators. Land valuation, which stimulated political economists early in the nineteenth century – but unnerved governments when they set out to allocate land – suffused debates about social justice at the end of the century. American social critic Henry George, who inspired followings in England, Ireland, Australia, and New Zealand, attributed poverty to a crisis in access to land. History, he insisted, proclaimed a universal law. "Conceive any kind of world your imagination will permit. Conceive of heaven itself, which, from the very necessities of our minds, we cannot otherwise think of than having an expanse of space – what would be the result in heaven itself, if the people who should first get to heaven were to parcel it out in big tracts among themselves? Oh, the wickedness of it; oh, the blasphemy of it!"[5] This chapter explores what happened when societies, conditioned to access and the right of first occupation, began to confront scarcity. As we are about to see, conventional politicians, and even insurgents such as Henry George, did not face up to limits, but rather searched for overlooked acres and ways to reclaim marginal territory. We look at five methods – land reform, exploitation of legal loopholes, seizure of indigenous lands, tax reform, and grand irrigation schemes.

LAND REFORM: RESUMPTION AND FORFEITURE

Like sheets of paper pinioned between scissor blades, American range ranches as well as Australian and New Zealand stations risked being cut up once access to unalienated lands tightened. The moving blade of demands for intensive land use progressed towards stockmen trapped against a finite supply of suitable terrain. Ranchers on the American public domain found themselves exposed to settlers and speculators, because they lacked leases, whereas Australian grazers in 1847 acquired the right to lease crown land for terms of fourteen or eight years, depending on the remoteness of the region.[6] In the early 1850s, when the necessary surveys became available, Australian squatters with grazing licences shifted in earnest to leasing. In 1853, London denied New Zealand grazers leasing rights, because of its belief that the islands contained rich land capable of attracting buyers. This position softened in the 1860s.[7] The variations in legal interests meant that Australian grazers in particular enjoyed access to short-term security, while American range ranchers were legally open to intrusions by homesteaders and speculators at any time. New Zealand sheep stations were more or less at the disposal of land buyers too, depending on which provincial land regulations governed the grazers' runs.

By a twist of fate, the leasehold advantage conceded to Australian squatters afforded no lasting protection, because the rights that they so assiduously wrested from reluctant British officials, combined with the sheer magnitude of many stations, roused a populist condemnation that poured into the political mainstream by way of land leagues and reform conventions. Here again a politically distinctive land-allocation history for British colonies and the United States surfaced; in Australia there was remarkably durable bottom–up insistence on giving common folks a plot of land. The outcry began immediately after the British government conceded squatters the right to lease crown land. John Dunmore Lang, a member of the legislative council of New South Wales, published a pamphlet with the incendiary title *Repeal or Revolution: A Glimpse of the Irish Future* (1848). Either repeal leasing, he warned the home government, or expect another Ireland, a society burdened with idle, unimproving landlords. Grazers deserved no boon, because they were "neither cultivating the land, nor improving the country in any way."[8] In Canada's ranching region in southern Alberta, the introduction of leasing in 1881–82 excited an identical warning that a new Ireland was in the making.[9] As a cautionary example and rallying cry for less advantaged colonizers everywhere, Ireland was peerless. Its history entered allocation disputes among colonizers who had no apparent awareness of – not to mention empathy for – other colonized peoples, the indigenous occupants. We do not have to go far to find an explanation for this paradox. European culture, including its class tensions and theories of political economy, provided reference points for resource allocation once frontiers were secured. In this section, we look at Australian land reform, starting in the late 1850s, and then at American experience in the 1860s and 1870s.

Selectors Confront Grazers in Australia and New Zealand, 1850s to 1880s

By the mid-1850s, if not earlier, pastoralists in New South Wales and Victoria worried about the durability of their equitable rights, because they realized that governments, bending under populist pressure, might refuse to renew their leases.[10] Squatters fretted and fumed about the possibility of government *resumption* of crown land, something that their enemies acclaimed as *unlocking* a public asset. Victoria squatter Edward Curr summarized the abrupt turn of events. "Going back to the days of its [Victoria's] founders, we find that they had hardly got their tents pitched, and the local quarrels properly established, when they raised a hue and cry and insisted on the Government of New South Wales unlocking the lands."[11] Pastoralists found themselves in jeopardy because, almost concurrent with the concession of leasehold tenure, Britain granted local self-government; the colonial legislatures adopted universal male suffrage, and the continent experienced the first of many gold rushes. Thousands of immigrants, many from the United States, arrived in Victoria during the early 1850s. Capitalist consolidation turned the Ballarat goldfields into a hazardous quarter for insecure wage labour, no more pleasing than sheep sheering, the building trades, industrial toil, or dockside work. Many rural and urban labourers alike fastened hopes onto crown lands, believing that this impounded treasure might yet be liquidated to finance public works, thus stimulating employment and simultaneously allowing common folks an opportunity for a rural idyll. There were memories of rural Ireland's expropriation by mainly Protestant landowners. During recessions, moreover, the colonies were short of funds, and land sales offered a solution. Thus, although pastoralists won leases by furious lobbying in the 1840s, they soon struggled in legislatures and in rural districts to maintain their runs.[12]

In mid-1857, a land-reform convention met for several weeks at Melbourne to organize against grazers who had been pressing the government for leases on easier terms for protracted periods. In successive confrontations and compromises, land-league adherents and pastoral protectionists formulated "the greatest social theme in nineteenth-century Australian history."[13] Played out in colonial capitals and on stations, contests over control of the land lasted decades and cost grazers dearly. When they battled to maintain control of their runs, they resorted to cunning manipulations. American range ranchers turned to comparable methods a few years later; the United States did not always lead with innovations in the great land rush. Except for the brisk traffic in legislation (made necessary by the Australian

squatters' right to leasehold), the separate colonial jurisdictions managing crown land, and the absence of a methodical survey system, the
onslaughts against large Australian grazers were quite analogous to
threats challenging range ranchers in the western United States.

William Wingfield, a former American surveyor who ran baselines
from Minnesota to Utah in the early 1850s, now an emigrant to
Victoria, attended the 1857 convention and spoke about pre-emption
rights on the American public domain. To secure legal entry, Wingfield
related, landhunters went unobstructed wherever they liked and forced
the government to accelerate surveys in that direction. He suggested
that the U.S. government could have acquired a huge sum by leasing
to grazers, but that would have stopped settlement. "In a word, it
would produce what we have in Victoria."[14] The convention resolved
that small farmers be allowed the right of free selection before survey
on crown lands and pastoral stations when their leases fell open and
that selectors should have the benefit of deferred payments, as well as
access to commonage for small-scale grazing. Responding to reform
pressure, a Victoria government in 1860 passed an act permitting a
limited amount of free selection.[15] Embraced by many reformers as the
best way to attack big estates, and condemned by conservatives who
saw it as tantamount to claim jumping in a gold rush, free selection
unfolded in Australia and New Zealand as a slogan with all the divisive
power of pre-emption in the United States during the 1830s.[16] When
the 1860 act failed to free up much acreage, partly because of the high
upset prices that protected pastoralists, the government of Victoria
introduced a scheme drafted by Charles Gavan Duffy.[17] An Irish
nationalist who had assisted with the formation of a tenants' league
at home, Duffy arrived in Melbourne in 1856. "He was by training a
lawyer, by temperament scholarly, and an excellent speaker. With his
experience in Britain and his particular interest in land reform, he
believed he was a real catch for such a young Colony."[18]

Support from Victoria's Irish settlers enabled Duffy to advance
populist causes and land reforms. Because of his efforts, the survey
department started to classify land quality on tracts before holding
sales. Duffy examined maps in mid-1862 to find promising territory
for small farmers on large stations that could be opened when leases
ended. With this information at hand, he drafted a bill that carved
agricultural areas out of sheep runs, identifying over 10 million acres
from the 35 million occupied by grazers.[19] Small grazers and farmers
were permitted to buy land on these reserved places under generous
terms; however, Duffy's act, which passed two weeks after Abraham
Lincoln signed the Homestead Act, also replaced free selection with
survey before settlement. Designated agricultural areas were supposed

to organize settlement like American townships, although they lacked the latters' uniformity and thus a capacity to generate land parcels described by grid co-ordinates.[20] Moreover, in the maturing Australian land game, surveys unintentionally forewarned grazers when land was about to be organized for sale. Grazers could plot defensive measures, visit bankers or commission agents, line up allies, and negotiate with loyal employees who, as potential selectors, became important players.[21] With sound information, borrowed money, and trustworthy associates, squatters could acquire strategically placed freehold land to shield their runs from incursions. Some reformers therefore believed that free selection could ambush grazers, although others disputed that claim. For example, the reform-minded commissioner of crown lands for South Australia, H.B.T. Strangeways, insisted that selection was actually a boon to grazers, who picked land "in such a way that suited them, and gave them command of the water."[22]

Beginning in the 1860s and continuing for the next thirty years, Australian and New Zealand pastoralists encountered more measures like the Duffy act, because land-allocation problems now centred on assisting close settlement, aiding smallholders, and lessening the influence of prominent grazers. One of Arthur Davis's humorous rural yarns collected in *Sandy's Selection* (1904) satirized the routine of land reform. "The Minister for Lands rose to introduce 'A Land Settlement Bill.' And made a long speech ... There was never a Minister of Lands yet born who hadn't a new scheme for settling people somewhere or other." When the minister finished speaking, a member with "a strong Irish accent said 'Hear! hear!'"[23] Judging from their rhetoric, colonial radicals "would have the shepherd kings squeezed periodically in their own wool-presses."[24] At the same time, the Australian colonies could not risk pressing the life out of pastoral estates, because sheep grew the golden fleece of colonial prosperity. Therefore legislators tested procedures that sometimes had three aims. Besides raising revenue, they were intended to put people lacking capital on land parcels sufficiently large to support them, while endeavouring to offer some stability for large grazers.

The ensuing debates invariably ran in circles around four common questions. First, as I have intimated, there was controversy on the relative merits of survey before settlement and free selection. Second, although payment schemes varied, the awkward ideal was to make land accessible without completely sacrificing revenue needed for ambitious public works projects. Third, exposés about the ability of pastoralists to subvert reform laws led to revisions that tried to impose settlement conditions and inspections, in order to reward only bona fide settlers, not grazers or speculators. Fourth, to allow a modicum of security for wool producers, the land acts often specified several classes of territory; at a minimum, they delineated settled and unsettled areas and furnished separate regulations for each, so that grazers could expect longer tenure on second-class land. Concurrent American legislation belatedly began to recognize differences in carrying capacity too; however, U.S. acts that extended special arrangements for the settlement of swamp and desert lands did not have to juggle leasehold and freehold tenure. That specific complication, with all its legal interests, was pivotal in Australia and New Zealand and present to a degree in Canada's restricted ranching area.

If initial measures faltered, anti-pastoral land reformers tried again. New South Wales in 1861 followed Victoria with land legislation that set short time periods for new pastoral leases and opened crown lands to free selection.[25] In Victoria, a more radical land reformer supplanted Duffy. The squatter-hating James Macpherson Grant, a miner with goldfield experience in California and New Zealand, introduced land laws that aspired to block grazers from manipulating friendly selectors. His 1865 act tackled fraudulent selection by initially distributing inexpensive land through conditional leases, which required lessees to make improvements at specified levels. Once the outlays had been verified, occupants could apply to buy the land at auction. To bar squatters' involvement, the act stipulated that leaseholds could not be assigned. Survey before settlement under this plan applied to designated agricultural areas that contained almost 4 million acres.[26] Grant's safeguards failed, "and just as before much of this selection was made by squatters and speculators."[27] In an 1869 act, Victoria took another stab at accelerating smallholders' acquisition of the land, but this time by restoring free selection. Buyers could select before surveying any land that was not alienated, leased, licenced, or reserved. By 1884, Victoria's land acts resulted in sales of over 6 million acres.[28]

While New South Wales and Victoria initiated early changes to their laws on land distribution, Queensland revised its legislation cautiously at first, because pastoralists dominated the assembly. Thus, although the land act of 1860 set aside tracts for farmers, it established them in places that would not greatly disturb grazers. The Darling Downs squattocracy, however, could not long control the northern colony, because organized labour in Brisbane pressed for resumption and expenditures on public works. During a depression in 1866, riots broke out in the city. Over the next several years, following elections that reduced the influence of pastoralists, new acts introduced resumption in southeast Queensland but simultaneously granted the more remote grazers longer leases, along with the right to buy large areas at low, fixed prices.[29] By these push–pull measures, land reformers in the three eastern colonies relocated many grazers from inside to outside territories. Remoteness, increasingly the fate of pastoral stations, contributed to the Australian bush myth. The selections meanwhile reared the *backblock* character – a soul whose earthy wit inspired Arthur Davis's humorous books about life *On Our Selection* and derivative silver-screen farces. Not only were land reforms a great social theme, they endured in popular culture.[30]

In South Australia, many squatters thwarted the push to the outside. In the central hill country, wary grazers in the 1840s and 1850s started assembling freehold land, especially along rivers. They triumphed at land auctions, because they defined land parcels in such large blocks that small farmers could not compete. In the auction rooms, they conspired with agents to ensure negligible competition.[31] In succeeding decades, this colony caught "the infection from her neighbours" and attempted a variety of intricate reform measures. Looking back in 1888 on dozens of enactments, one critic decried the "mental and physical energy that has been expended in the compilation and destruction of these works of art." His laissez-faire solution espoused the abiding doctrine of improvement and intimated frustration with a presumed imprisonment of resources. "Do what you will with our waste lands. Mine, graze, garden, irrigate; only use them."[32]

Of all the legislative tinkerings with land, none was more novel than Queensland's experiment enacted in 1884. Influenced by American land and tax reformer Henry George, Samuel Griffith's government believed that, despite prior reforms, land disposal still benefited grazers and recently established sugar cane planters. Griffith did not wish to see cane growers become an influential class like American cotton planters. He could do what governments in Brazil and Argentina could not – namely, tackle large estates. To secure to every member of the community participation in some share of land's increasing value, Queensland abolished land alienation and substituted leasing.[33] Technically, it debarred grazers from tendering on leases to lands resumed from their runs. The act entailed elaborate civil service participation. To arrive at a just rent, land boards held court; bailiffs and land rangers collected rents and adjusted boundaries; clerks handled scores of forms. The bar against alienation was not absolute, for farmers could buy agricultural land after a residence of five years.[34] In 1891 the government broke from the pattern of laws that slowed alienation by auctioning land to retire some of Queensland's debt; however, leasing retained a prominent place in an exceedingly complicated set of land regulations.[35]

Queensland's 1884 act cushioned slightly the blow of resumption for grazers, because a few leaseholders who voluntarily conceded resumption could swap land for security. Grazers who consented to surrender half their lands, held by leases about to expire, could secure a renewal for twenty years on what remained or, for a surrender of a third, ten years.[36] A similar practice had been informally worked out in parts of New Zealand. The usual process for achieving closer settlement there, in regions with large stations operating under grazing licences, was to proclaim a settlement district, called a hundred. That action opened land to selection. South Australia in the 1840s and 1850s employed the same terms and methods. To reduce strife and litigation when people resumed land in the hundreds, the government of Otago in the late 1860s granted pastoralists protection if they agreed to the sale of some of the land that they used under licence.[37] This practice made explicit the negotiations found wherever reformers squeezed grazers. Compromise of this sort was also evident in southern Alberta in the 1890s, when ranchers, under pressure from settlers' rights associations, "were compelled to abandon closed-lease tenure in favour of more subtle means of control."[38] Ottawa allowed leases to lapse but permitted ranchers to buy one-tenth of the leasehold, use government stock-watering reserves, and informally discourage settlers.[39]

The United States, 1860s and 1870s

In Australian and New Zealand jurisdictions, the pressures for resumption, along with resistance by pastoralists, drew governments into programs of surveying, managing the selection of agricultural lands, resuming crown land, and organizing sales. At the same time, they assumed responsibility for selecting and surveying crown reserves for public transportation and access to water, for the use of Aboriginal inhabitants, for schools and recreation, and for the conservation of timber. A mix of government and private actions constructed property parcels with assorted attached rights.[40] A few paragraphs above, I stated that the absence of leasing on the American public domain helps explain why there was nothing in the United States exactly like the Australian political movements directed against vested interests to help smallholders. In the United States, there had been, of course, an earlier string of pro-settler enactments. There had also been several commissions determining the relative rights of squatters and grantees holding French, Spanish, and Mexican documents; these bodies were not simply one-sided supporters of grantees. Judges were also about to start sorting out property conflicts between the federal government and railways. The latter had been granted over 100 million acres in one form or another. Precisely how the railways held lands was a problem that begat considerable litigation. It is wise to consider the chief opposing property interests in the American west, so that parallels with populists in Australia and New Zealand are clear. Unless they held a Spanish or Mexican grant or had purchased strategically useful free-hold plots or homesteads, ranchers lacked protection against government arrangements for the settlement of the public domain; however, luckily for some ranchers, railways held certain legal interests in large tracts of land that were considerably stronger than what ranchers could secure by mere occupation of the open range.

When former American surveyor William Wingfield described for the Victoria convention the ease of obtaining land on the public domain in the United States, that country had as yet no homestead act. It was pre-emption that rendered entry as uncomplicated as he claimed. As we know from a discussion above, pre-emption amounted to a decla-ration of intention to acquire title to a block of land and protected entrymen against intrusion by other settlers, but as against the gov-ernment their rights were inchoate. The Homestead Act of 1862 made the next step – securing a title – less expensive and less uncertain – less uncertain because it created alternatives to auction sales, a chancy affair dreaded by settlers and speculators alike. Title could now be acquired by continuous residence for five years, proof of improve-ments, and payment of a fee. Claimants could also commute the homestead entry into a full title by paying a $1.25 an acre.[41] Like Australian counterparts, American land reformers in the 1860s sought to restrain large businesses from accumulating massive holdings of land. If they held nothing better than flimsy equitable interests in the public domain, then range ranchers presented no legal roadblocks to settlers. However, the practice of endowing railway companies with massive amounts of public land permitted these corporations – which advanced colonization by their haulage business and land department efforts – to inhibit homesteading and, as we saw in the previous chapter, to collaborate with a few prescient cattle and sheep ranchers. Not only were the railways made powerful by their land grants, but railway land departments stretched their entitlements.

Grants to assist most major railways contained a homestead provi-sion, known as a *contingent right of pre-emption,* whose terms varied. Typically they specified that, if all the lands were not sold three or five years after the completion of the line, then the remaining territory would be subject to settler pre-emption, at a price not exceeding $1.25 an acre payable to the company. The companies believed that these stipulations would never be enforced, and in the short term they were not.[42] Grazers leased portions of this land until the contingent right was exercised or until the federal government recovered its conditional grants. In the 1880s, as scarcity threatened, up went the cries to unlock these railway lands. When the federal government attempted to do exactly that, companies resisted. The fact that the federal government created a class of property interests by giving railways conditional rights allowed these enterprises to resist speedy forfeiture. A U.S. Supreme Court decision in 1874 held that forfeiture clauses did not take effect instantaneously but rather could be made operative only by judicial decree or act of Congress.[43] To further complicate matters, some railways had mortgaged their grants, and the Supreme Court ruled in 1879 that mortgagees possessed interests superior to the settlers' contingent right of pre-emption.[44] Eventually, because the railways were blamed for the exhaustion of free lands, a general forfeiture act became law in 1890. After 1890, therefore, "the closing out of all but a few of the grants had become simply a matter of administrative routine."[45]

In conclusion, legal battles to free up land in Australia and the United States differed only in form, not in substance. The surface pattern of events diverged mainly because of the staggered timing of the great outbreaks of grazing in Australia (1830s and 1840s) and the United States (1860s and 1870s). Oceans too influenced the struggle for land. Landhunters, as I observed in chapter 3, could get at Australia and New Zealand's choice regions by sea, while staking claims at the centre of North America was more exacting. In chapter 7, we saw the role of industrial technology in presenting American ranchers with the means to protect the range that they used, while Australians faced the predicaments of squatting before barbed wire was invented. That deficiency precipitated the Australian complication – leasehold. The different timing and character of the grazing outbreaks in Australia and the United States had another consequence. Rail transportation in Australian colonies ensued *after* the occupation of the land in most regions, largely precluding supportive land grants to railway companies; in contrast, because the U.S. public domain remained entirely unencumbered by pastoral leaseholds, bands of railway grants girdled the American west. They caught the eye of reformers. A map of California's railway lands "first turned Mr. [Henry] George's attention to our land policy."[46] Legislative reforms targeted Australian grazing leases and American railway grants – a fact that illustrates similarities as well as differences. On the Argentine *pampas*, by contrast, pastoralists exploited a law (1884) that allowed occupants to file for the title of land that they used. "It was *estancieros* and not agricultural settlers who queued up to claim titles on the public domain."[47] The reader will recall from chapter 1 that concentration too was the pattern in Brazil after its 1850 land law. The importance of the difference between these South American situations and those found in Australia, New Zealand, and the United States is apparent in the fact that, despite considerable consolidation of landholding in the English-speaking regions, those areas also saw distributions to smaller operators and vigorous attacks on consolidation.

COCKIES, DUMMIES, AND BANKERS

Under the auspices of legislative encouragement, farmers and speculators infiltrated large holdings in British colonial and American grazing regions, using, as we see in this section, both loopholes in land laws and tricks of surveying. City speculators in Australia employed agents to spy out the countryside and to provide reliable information as to where to pluck important tracts.[48] Sometimes these agents were small farmers – "cockatoos" or "cockies."[49] Ensconced pastoralists and ranchers, whom newcomers threatened, either had initially snatched their territory by astute moves or had purchased stock and interests from landhunters who understood how to take and hold land. Prior stages of occupation therefore prepared grazers mentally for a defence of runs and ranges. Indeed, to protect themselves against rival stockmen, some already had acquired freehold title to strategically valuable plots.[50] While there was continuity to the grazers' tussles with selectors, homesteaders, speculators, and other grazers, the tempo of the conflicts increased in the 1860s. In Australia and New Zealand, the politics of land allocation stepped up the intensity of defensive land purchases, and so did the insistent interventions of banks, wool brokers, and mortgage companies. Alarmed that the fragmentation of runs by selectors would impair security for loans, creditors persuaded clients to purchase. In the United States too, populism was not the sole force pressing range ranchers; the completion of railways and a rising price for beef put more stock onto the public domain and inspired British speculation in American cattle companies.[51]

Protection of range land required freehold acreage, which could be purchased only under constraints. First, the proclaimed objective of many land laws was to unlock territory for common folks, not to hand the keys to grazers. Enactments were designed to hinder so-called land monopolists. Obstructions and limitations compelled grazers and their agents to exploit loopholes. Second, unable to afford entire ranches or stations, stockmen engaged in strategic purchases. Relying on their wits, agents, and lines of credit, some Australian squatters and American ranchers rallied to protect the land that they occupied; others quit, and so too did many settlers and speculators who had filed entries for land on ranches and stations. At the same time as pastorialists and settlers sorted out their legal rights, they tested what the ground could carry or grow. Grazers slipped past most restrictions on their acquisition of freehold – constraints that normally confined them to acreage around head stations. They exploited other openings to buy greater acreage. Despite the hostile intentions of most – not all – sections in crown land acts, they easily found loopholes.

In Victoria, where the legislative crusade began in earnest, poorly framed clauses in the first enactment allowed squatters to secure extensive tracts of freehold by enlisting dummies – parties who selected on behalf of squatters.[52] Victoria's pastorialists next accumulated freehold bastions thanks to the Duffy act. To compensate selectors who recently paid more at auction than Duffy's charitable fixed price, Victoria issued certificates in units of 320 acres. This scrip traded briskly at discounts.[53] In New South Wales, an 1862 regulation permitted the auctioning of land when there were competing selectors or when selectors forfeited their entry; squatters arranged for these enabling circumstances to happen. Volunteers for the colony's defence force, empowered each to select fifty acres free of charge, could transfer their land orders. Capable land agents kept supplies at hand.[54] In Alberta, the 180,000-acre (1884) Walrond Ranche went after strategic freeholds with "Half-Breed scrip" and by using payments to induce homesteaders to declare abandonment, so that the ranch could buy the vacated quarter-sections.[55]

The best instrument was a homestead or selection, since all family members could select a specified number of acres. The generally low prices, set by land reform acts in order to benefit selectors, actually tempted squatters and speculators.[56] A New South Wales squatter "could go into the free selection business under both his own name and under the names of his sisters and cousins and aunts and toddling children and submissive servants."[57] Not all employees enlisted to make dummy acquisitions. Monaro pastoralist Edward Pratt confided to his diary in 1876 that "good employees select for me, bad employees select against me."[58] A comparable sentiment ripened among many American ranchers. Good ranch hands selected homesteads to assist employers' property-acquisition schemes, particularly during the beef bonanza from about 1880 to 1886. After prices slumped at the Omaha and Chicago stockyards and following the disastrous winter of 1886–87 – setbacks that lingered into the late 1890s – big stockmen disdained and distrusted former cowboys who had established range ranches, on account of their reputation for starting herds with unbranded mavericks. Ranchers' associations blacklisted upstarts, cutting off their employment and blocking round-up benefits.[59] At roughly the same time, New Zealand squatters attempted to stop the declaration

of the hundreds – the step preparatory to opening an area to settlement. When that failed, they orchestrated the land-selection laws and
lined up dummies to protect their runs. Queensland's 1884 lease law,
meant to combat dummying, was ineffectual, because large squatters
found small grazing farmers who would lease out parts of their runs
to them.[60] The land may not have been used as intended, but small
operators derived a benefit.

In the United States, when range ranchers were prospering, battling
farmers, and deflecting rivals, they exploited distinctive legal opportunities arising from national and state legislation. Nevertheless, the
nitty-gritty ways to beat laws framed for small settlers were indistin-
guishable from the ploys adopted a few years earlier in Australia and
New Zealand. Everywhere, an essential aspect of the struggles over
land consisted of land agents discovering how to contort legislation to
allow strategic land buying by major grazers, even though purchases
and grants were intended for another class of settler. Moreton Frewen,
the British manager of the Powder River Cattle Company, confided in
1884 that he knew "a firm of land sharks in Colorado who seem to
have undue influence with the land department," and they could help
him hold his range. As for the interloper or the small stockman, his
advice was: "split him like a rail ... pull out his fences all over the
place."[61] Depending on environmental circumstances, grazers with or
without the aid of land sharks could pervert the goals of the Swamp
Lands Act (1850), the Homestead Act (1862), the Timber Culture Act
(1873), and the Desert Land Act (1877) by claiming land under their
provisions and arranging entries to hold huge ranges.

Once legal entry had been permitted under the provisions of one of
these acts, and improvements made, it was hard to oust grazers – even
though they might never perform the conditions of settlement, they
could deflect settlers and amass equitable interests, all the while keeping down the costs of control. A western surveyor recommended legal
entries to a client in the following terms: "A declaration or filing at
the land office will hold good for several years unless the tract is so
desirable as to originate a contract, otherwise the property is considered to be under control of the party holding the claim." He did not
think that the 2,896 acres already held in freehold was sufficient to
retain all the range, so he recommended perfecting control by filing
for one more forty-acre tract on Little Horse Creek – the key to a huge
range.[62] If title rather than mere legal entry was necessary, American
ranchers could buy freehold through dummies – friends, parents,
uncles and aunts, brothers and sisters. For this reason and the utility
of having a nearby pool of reserve labour, some large ranchers –
certainly not all, and certainly not in bad times – maintained cordial

relations with neighbours, helping them out in crises.[63] The possibilities of holding spacious ranches with strategic purchases extended to Canada. Starting in 1902, Canadian ranchers could buy stock-watering reserves, an option that they disliked at first, because previously a friendly government agent had located ample strategic reserves for their use.[64]

By crafty manipulation of allocation laws, grazers seized the tools to improve their tenure, although the scale of their exposed operations, combined with more than token upset prices, prevented them from trying to convert their total acreage into freehold at the upset price.[65] Some pastoralists in Australia and New Zealand, as I noted above, had to negotiate terms and surrender portions of their claims. Others, to maximize the efficiency of defensive buying, rolled out maps. Leaning on knowledge of local ecology, they considered how, where, and in what shapes and sizes to acquire acreage. Strategic buying informed by local wisdom was apparent, for example, in the narrow valleys of Otago, New Zealand, during the 1870s. Potential farm land lay alongside streams and rivers, while summer pasture could be found at elevations of from 1,500 to 5,000 feet above sea level. Higher land was good only in summer, so grazers needed the valleys in winter. Thus, at around the same time as Montana ranchers worked to command their valleys with barbed wire, Otago grazers tried to buy the valleys that controlled the higher pastures. Back runs needed front runs.[66]

Controlling access to water was a standard means of holding onto Australian back runs and American range ranches.[67] John W. Iliff, reputed to be the most successful Colorado rancher of his day, ran stock across the arid range from the eastern border of the state for a hundred miles west and for fifty to sixty from south to north. At his death in 1878, he owned merely 15,558 acres in 105 small parcels, some bought with military scrip, and most containing water sources.[68] Years later, about 1900, a Montana cattleman dispatched a survey team to locate "all the Circle C cowpunchers on the choice bottomlands along the creeks ... within a twenty-five mile radius on all sides of the home ranch."[69] There was a continuity of sly practices across time and space. The ways around land laws put some money in the pockets of employees and settlers – an imperfect distribution of wealth to be sure. Comparable distribution were not, however, common features of land-consolidation practices in Argentina and Brazil.

When topography and ecology could not direct grazers to indispensable tracts, they worked with surveyors to plot geometrical configurations that might hold the most territory. Grid-ironing (buying land in strips) and spotting, or peacocking (buying in blocks), were contemporary labels for arrangements to protect runs against raiding in

Australia and New Zealand.[70] Oft-told anecdotes of cunning, repeated
in regional and local histories, may paint accounts with colourful
episodes that exaggerate guile, while meticulous local studies may some
day show tenure conversion to be a prosaic activity, linked more
explicitly to regional environmental circumstances. However, the fact
that numerous incidents in several jurisdictions look alike does suggest
a pattern, and one that accents shiftiness. Grid-ironing and related
practices seem widspread. Grid-ironing left open acreage between the
freehold strips. Rumours were planted that these open bands were in
freehold too. The risk was that surveyors in the know might sell
information to hostile grazers, who could acquire the open sections,
spoiling the runs and forcing a payout.[71]

   In a classic example of spotting or peacocking, William Fannin near
Napier, New Zealand, attempted a scattered purchase in 1857. He
wanted to select fifty scattered blocks of forty acres each.[72] American
ranchers also deemed forty acres a handy block, cheap yet adequate
for obstructing adversaries. Years later, probably in the late 1860s,
William Davidson threatened to spot a New Zealand station to thwart
a surveyor working for outside buyers. Selection laws required drawing
lots for tracts if, on the day when a region was opened for sale, other
parties applied for the same land. His rival picked blocks of several
thousand acres each and then, to multiply chances at a draw, lined up
proxies from dummy selectors. To defend his employer's paddocks,
Davidson diced the contested area into 150 parcels and insisted on
balloting for each. Odds favoured his winning a few draws, thus
spoiling the rival's bid for large blocks. By this dog-in-the-manger trick,
Davidson forced a compromise.[73] On this occasion, as well as on
others, buyers lined up accomplices. In Queensland in 1878, a grazer
and several associates employed thirteen dummies to select land in
non-contiguous packages so as to render good agricultural sections
inaccessible to farmers.[74] In 1888–89, Oregon rancher Peter French
marshalled scrip to ring a rival's ranch with forty-acre farms and hired
men to spot homesteads on the other rancher's operation, buying them
out if their farms failed.[75]

   Homesteading and selecting occurred on such huge scales as to defy
summary evaluation, but almost every assessment agrees that, where
arid territory was involved, farmers secured too little land to prosper
on crops alone. Raised on a Queensland selection, humorist Arthur
Davis witnessed the struggles to scratch a living. "Sandy's selection
was on Sleepy Creek, a hundred and sixty acre one. All beautiful too.
Three acres of it were cleared. Sandy was struggling to clear one more.
The remaining hundred and fifty-five were under scrub, prickly-pear,
wallaby-bush and Bathurst-burr." Fences failed to ward off kangaroos,

rats, and death adders, and there was not a blade of grass on the selection, because "it had been overstocked for fifty years."[76] Joseph Powell appraised selections as "gigantic folk experiments with the environment" where selectors – as well as grazers – advanced and retreated for sundry reasons.[77]

Like selectors, many North American homesteaders lacked the resources and knowledge to farm an entire quarter-section. A few, as Paul Voisey reveals in his study of Vulcan, Alberta, earned wages away from their homesteads and anticipated capital gains from selling to late arrivals. Four out of ten homestead entries in the Vulcan area were cancelled – a rate close to that for western Canada in general. In Nebraska, Kansas, and Minnesota two homesteaders abandoned their entries for every one that succeeded. "In the majority of cases," notes Donald Worster with respect to homesteaders on the southern plains of the United States, "they came wanting not a place to stay forever, but simply cash – a stake to take with them someplace else."[78] Just over one million acres was applied for in 1865 under the terms of the Homestead Act, and five years later, when applicants would have been eligible to claim title, only half the acreage went to patent.[79] Citing the high plains and southern Saskatchewan and Alberta, Walter Nugent concludes that the chimera of frontier farming "carried many would-be settlers farther than they should have gone."[80] He could claim the same for parts of Australia and southern Africa. A different state of affairs emerged in Argentina. At the turn of the century, heavily capitalized sheep grazers secured huge tracts directly, without prospect of challenge by small operators. Even so-called small establishments in Patagonia Austral typically covered 10,000 hectares. Over a third of the large-scale *latifundia* in that newly opened region – *estancias* of more than 75,000 hectares – were owned by grazers of British origin.[81]

Enthralled by the yeomen ideal, champions of small spreads in British Colonial and American jurisdictions failed to appreciate that people from all backgrounds – including putative yeomen – would, as we have just seen, turn to quick gains and upset the purpose of laws supposedly designed to launch smallholders. In Australia, New Zealand, the United States, and Canada, as we have just witnessed, grazers supplied employment and speculative opportunities to smallholders; they spread money when they enlisted dummies, or paid homesteaders to cancel entries, or bought strategic tracts. Often they paid with borrowed funds. Banks were more inclined to allow pastoralists rather than farmers to overdraw accounts. Commission agents propped up clients with advances, and wealthy opportunists came to the rescue. In pastoral regions on the North Island, New Zealand, English investor

Algernon Grey Tollemache preserved a few grazers from local rivals and invading Australians. In the early 1870s, his mere appearance at an auction silenced bidders.[82] Debt accumulation forced grazers into dependent relationships with the likes of Tollemache – reviled as a "son of a whore" by some – or into the hands of institutions.[83] Many stockmen failed, surrendering immense areas, so that the real holders of a number of stations and ranches were financiers, shareholders, or lending institutions.[84] Corporate consolidation in the American west also progressed when promoters incorporated cattle companies and floated the stock in the east or in England and Scotland. Whether by direct corporate takeovers or via supervision from lending institutions, ranchers and grazers in large numbers were subjected to managerial scrutiny from afar. In Australia, banks and other companies held only 37 grazing leases in 1866, while partnerships and individuals accounted for 3,484; in 1890, the numbers were 611 and 1,001, respectively.[85] After takeovers and consolidations, managers and investors wondered who was in charge, because, once mired in the game, they could neither sidestep lobbying and litigation nor evade additional investment. After making strategic purchases and building fences, a good number of grazers and financiers sank money into irrigation measures to underpin prior investments. It was not just grazers who assembled land and invested in improvements with bank support. On the south U.S. plains, "the quarter-section farm eventually disappeared," writes Donald Worster. "The big farmers bought out the small ones, and land moved to oligarchy."[86]

BREAKING UP THE BIGGEST ESTATES: RENEWED SEIZURES OF INDIGENOUS PEOPLES' LANDS

In New Zealand, the United States, and southern Africa, the largest estates to attract notice from landhunters and legislators, when the idea of scarcity stirred, were unalienated territories belonging to indigenous peoples. The same was true in Argentina in the 1870s. Well-capitalized pastoralists convinced the government there to restrict the Indians on the southern *pampas* and through northern Patagonia to reservations. General Julio Roca orchestrated a series of campaigns that slaughtered thousands of indigenous people and expanded the country's public domain. During a wool boom in the first years of the twentieth century, pastoralists took over a number of Indian reserves in Patagonia.[87] British colonial and American authorities meanwhile wished to appear to be upholding the niceties of legal processes. Therefore procurement of country still under Maori and Indian collective title required the guise of lawful mechanisms. When preparing the requisite extractive apparatus, settler politicians discussed how to transform customary collective interests into private ownership. They summoned arguments about the readiness of first peoples for a drastic shift in social relations and debated the desirability of accelerating an upheaval even if some first peoples resented being thrust into an environment of private property. When they set out to dismember tribal land holdings, colonizers knew that they were assailing customary authority within indigenous communities and understood that they caused dissension. In fact, official policy in New Zealand and the United States leaned towards privatized title both to free land and to promote assimilation. Those first peoples who preferred custom lacked the financial backers and astute agents to help them, while those who signed up for changes in tenure found settler allies or were enticed and sponsored by accomplished speculators.

In southern Africa in the late nineteenth century, settler governments generally denied private title to land for blacks, and so white colonizers, instead of founding and manipulating privatization processes like those established in New Zealand and the United States, used coarse land-grabbing practices, taking land through war against the southern Sotho (1866), the Zulus (1879), and the N'debele (1893) and receiving land in return for mercenary service to the chiefs of the Thlaping and Rolong (1882). White trusteeship over tribal territory offered another path – one where racial prejudice affected land distribution. Settler societies in the United States, New Zealand, and southern Africa shared at least one feature in native land legislation. With little or no consultation between first peoples and themselves, legislators devised laws on land conversion and trustee arrangements that benefited mainly colonizers. Australia witnessed no comparable legislative onslaughts on first peoples' unalienated lands, because initial takings had been ample. Australian colonies escaped dealing with the issue thanks to a persistent application of the doctrine of *terra nullius* by their judges. I now look in detail at the treatment of indigenous lands in New Zealand, the United States, southern Africa, Australia, and Canada.

New Zealand inaugurated land courts in 1862 for converting the customary land rights of indigenous peoples into titles that they held from the crown, thereby allowing the Maori to sell or lease directly to settlers. Until this innovation, land-acquisition practices in the colony required public negotiations between agents of the sovereign and Maori chiefs. This process allowed tribal control over land, and that power, by the late 1850s, inhibited sales to the crown on the North Island. Unless tribal cohesion was intrinsically strong, the new provisions splintered Maori communities, because, wherever individuals or groups of Maori wished to deal with colonists with respect to land, they upset tribal control by working with a settler agency. Furthermore, Maori wishing to secure a crown title often took this step with the encouragement and backing of settler allies who subsequently acquired the property. Therefore a number of transactions that put land in colonists' hands amounted to conspiracies. The land-court setup led to grazers and speculators acquiring Maori land piecemeal.

New Zealand's first Native Land Act (1862) repeated conventional legal thinking about native title in New Zealand. It reaffirmed that Maori were the proprietors of customary interests in the land, including uncultivated land; however, it reaffirmed a point expressed in several previous acts and judicial rulings to the effect that these interests were not cognizable in a court of law. They could not, for example, be transferred; settlers who used these lands could not prosecute rivals for trespass. Only a government act could confer a crown title, which extended the protection of full property rights. That now could be accomplished by a special court – a panel of local chiefs chaired by a crown official – that would determine, on application, the rights of communities or individuals to particular estates. On hearing a request to bring a parcel of land under a crown title, the court could issue certificates of title to an individual or individuals, and these in turn were exchangeable for crown titles. To secure a certificate, applicants had to have a survey made, and they had to convince the court of their rightful occupation. Other groups or individuals could challenge the petition. The certificates did not exactly individualize title, because they could list the names of a number of people. That was a complication. But the certificates created transferable paper; lessees or buyers could now deal with legally defined groups for specific tracts.[88]

Francis Dart Fenton, appointed chief judge of the Native Land Court in 1865, drafted a new act that further weakened Maoris' customary land practices. Judges replaced the chiefs on the bench, and the judges were to hear evidence only in courtrooms, not to investigate matters by visits to the sites in question. Attempts by politicians sympathetic to the plight of the Maori to reform the courts failed. During a series of parliamentary attacks on his legislation in 1871, Fenton wrote, "it is beyond the power of man to transfer the land of a Country from one race to another without suffering to the weaker race ... It is contrary to the truth of history and human nature."[89] Had that been his attitude in 1865, it might have served as a chilling coda for the new court. In the estimation of historian Alan Ward, "many Maori willingly used the court to define their interests for dealing in the land or perhaps developing it," but many others struggled against "false or exaggerated

claims."⁹⁰ Among additional changes harmful to Maori but useful to
land agents, the 1865 act enabled the court to grant absolute title to
a limited number of applicants rather than to a host of people who
might have had interests in the area. The practice developed of restricting collective title to no more than ten people. In combination, these
attributes meant that, although many Maori believed that the ten were
trustees, they were owners "who could and did dispose of huge
amounts of land without reference to the rest of the tribe."⁹¹ The land-
court acts were just the beginning of manipulations to wrest more land
from Maori. They lasted into the 1920s and included renewed crown
buying and the creation of more opportunities to undermine collective
Maori interests.⁹²

In 1881, Indian land in the United States under federal protection
amounted to more than 156 million acres, most of it west of the
Mississippi. The self-governing Indian Territory (Oklahoma) comprised the largest block. Scattered smaller parcels – Indian reservations
– consisted of land assigned to tribes by the federal government. The
amount left in tribal hands depended on the location of the tribe and
on its relative size and strength. Some treaties negotiated in the 1850s
included provisions for an eventual allotment of lands to individual
Indians; however, the status of most Indian lands resembled that of
Maori territory and reserves. Without titles, Indians could not lease
land to grazers; neither could they sell, because courts would not
enforce the putative rights of lessees or buyers. As we saw in the last
chapter, that disability did not deter leasing by grazers, but it left
tenants vulnerable. During the 1870s, the concept of allotment to
individual Indians gained acceptance in Congress for several reasons.
Some white Indian agents reported the willingness of people on their
reservations to accept an allocation of land. Influential philanthropic
reformers endorsed allotment as part of a sweeping program of assimilation. Western land interests supported an allocation system and
warmed to details in the General Allotment Act (Dawes Act) passed
by Congress in 1887.

The Dawes Act empowered the U.S. president to initiate a compul-
sory allotment of a reservation. It exempted some reservations and the
Indian Territory (now Oklahoma) because of special rights granted
when they were created, although most Indians living on reservations
came under the jurisdiction of the act, and they could not opt out of
an allotment exercise once the president decreed it. The process
assigned acreage on the basis of household size and the type of land.
Initially, these allotments were held in trust for twenty-five years, to
thwart land agents and to constrain allotment holders to secure a living

by working the land, not by selling it. Later amendments permitted this trust period to be altered on an individual basis, enabling some parties to sell or lease earlier. Even more helpful to land agents, speculators, grazers, and settlers, the act provided that unallotted land constituted a surplus to be opened for settlement. Indian land could be acquired by leasing allotments, by purchasing allotments once the trusteeship was lifted, and by buying or homesteading the surplus. The General Land Office of the United States organized the reallocation of reservation surpluses by allowing standard entry claims, organizing entry by competitive land runs, or distributing by lottery. Some unsold lands were leased out for grazing, logging, mining, and oil-drilling; the federal government was supposed to distribute the royalties to Indians but misappropriated a portion.[93]

By the late 1880s, white settlers were swamping the Indian population in the Indian Territory, and several immense livestock organizations based there operated in a legal limbo. Under immense federal pressure, the tribes divided the terrain among their members. Unlike the tribes on federally supervised and supported reservations, those on the self-governing Indian Territory possessed in law the entire acreage. Consequently no surplus reverted to federal authorities; however, enrolled Indians often took their allotments in two types of land: homestead blocks around their homes and tracts elsewhere, which were quickly sold to non-Indians. The Dawes Act and the break-up of the Indian Territory expedited the transfer of an immense amount of land out of Indian hands. It is striking how little legislation, in comparison to New Zealand, was required to reduce reserves. This contrast expressed the fact that the settler society of mid- and late-nineteenth-century New Zealand operated from a somewhat less confident position with respect to Maori than did whites vis-à-vis Indians in the United States during the same years.

There also were legal differences. American Indian reservations were creations of government, but unalienated Maori land was recognized by treaty. The occupation of land by first peoples frustrated private ambitions and, in the eyes of white governments, defied improvement. Canadian governments, beginning in the late 1850s, likewise equated individualized title and surveyed plots with a coinciding improvement of land and indigenous people. This assimilationist dogma influenced the Indian Department's policies respecting reservations in the western territories commencing in the 1880s. Unlike the severance schemes of New Zealand and the United States, the objects of Canadian "severalty" did not initially include a ferocious ambition to extract surplus land but aimed mainly to speed assimilation. As the last huge land reserve, the Canadian west in the 1880s and 1890s still held seemingly abundant unalienated territory. In the early twentieth century, that perception changed, and the Indian Department took the view that reserves did obstruct settlement. American speculators and Canadian Indian department officials were among the buyers of land detached from reserves.[94]

Nowhere was land taking from first peoples in the late nineteenth and early twentieth centuries more complicated than in southern Africa – a circumstance that we can ascribe in part to the diversity of powers – African tribes, Afrikaner republics, and British authorities at the Cape and in London – claiming authority. Although episodes of disputed or deficient authority often allowed landhunters to make their own rules, there was more to the story than multi-sided struggles for sovereignty.[95] Racial discrimination affected land policy in Natal, the Orange Free State, and the Transvaal. The republics granted inadequate reserves to Africans and obstructed their owning land outside the reserves. Substantial new land taking by whites in the late nineteenth century occurred in Zululand, as well as between the Limpopo and Zambezi rivers in Matabeleland and Mashonaland. In response to petitions from farmers in Natal and the Transvaal, Natal annexed Zululand in 1897, and in 1902 it opened about 40 per cent of it – 2,613,000 acres – for sale. Restrictions on blacks securing land titles were applied, despite initial promises to permit them to buy. Like the republics, Natal also reserved some land for black Africans. White trustees could dispose of territory, although the real problem was that, relative to the population, the areas under trusteeship were small. In the assessment of Shula Marks, the reserves were also "barren, rugged, arid, and cold."[96]

The invasion of Matabeleland and Mashonaland in 1890 was the culmination of encroachments begun by ivory hunters and gold prospectors (1850s–70s). In the 1880s, the British declared the area a sphere of interest, and soon afterwards Cecil Rhodes formed the British South African Company (BSA), and set about acquiring mining and land-granting rights through concessions acquired from chiefs in Mashonaland. With a modicum of legal cover, the BSA sent a column of pioneers into Mashonaland in 1890 to establish Fort Salisbury. The colony was not a great success. As a consequence of frontier clashes between N'debeles and white colonists, the company set out in 1893 to conquer Matabeleland and throw it too open for farming and mining.[97] The attack succeeded. Rhodes claimed the territory as a conquest, and the BSA allocated land to members of its invading force; however, the N'debeles were not broken. In 1896, they renewed their resistance, and some Shonas also rose up against the company.

In victory, the BSA seized – and distributed – more land and cattle. During the 1890s, it granted land lavishly to its troops, friends, and applicants. Speculators accumulated large holdings by purchasing these entitlements. The company also promoted treks from Cape Colony and the Orange Free State and granted farms of 3,000 morgen (6,000 acres) – a size that had been traditional among Afrikaners for two centuries. By 1895, a new generation of trekkers had pegged out 1,070 of these farms; however, it would be decades before cash crops flourished in Rhodesia. In the judgment of Arthur Keppel-Jones, the marginal quality of the land ordained that "white Rhodesia, considered in isolation, did not have an economic leg to stand on."[98] Still, the colonial encroachment had consequences, for the immense size of individual holdings and the Afrikaner origins of some farmers promoted the exploitation of black labour on terms long established in southern Africa.[99] Small late steps in the northward migration of Afrikaner grazers occurred in 1902 and 1905, when a few *bittereinders*, die-hards who despised the English, left South Africa for the highlands of German East Africa. They were not the land improvers that the Germans wanted, and many moved to Kenya, where most lived by hunting and as carriers on the wagon routes.[100]

Australia contained no large territories where nineteenth-century authorities acknowledged the legal interests of indigenous peoples, but the elites of Western Australia believed that the United Kingdom treated their colony – the continent's largest – as an imperial reserve, not for indigenous people but for future emigrants. London withheld responsible government, decades after it had granted this form of self-government to other settlement colonies, and it often intervened in land matters from the 1840s to the 1880s. There were several rationales for supervision. For most of the period when London meddled, the colony's population was small, and the home government wanted it to nurse its land revenues. In the 1870s and 1880s, other reasons developed. The colony's political leaders routinely attempted to liberalize land regulations, and the colonial office detected self-interested profligacy on the part of a local establishment stacked with adept landhunters. For example, the influential Forrest brothers, Alexander and John, were deeply involved in pastoral enterprise and distrusted in London because of a perception that they hatched unduly-generous allocation practices. Furthermore, in the desirable grazing lands of the northern Kimberley districts – drenched by the "big wet" of monsoons – the murders of Aboriginal people by grazers disturbed enough English parliamentarians to complicate a complete, prompt transfer of the crown's responsibility for land.

Confrontations with London came to a head in 1887–89 when
Surveyor General John Forrest proposed the introduction of assorted
land-allocation schemes to stimulate investment. Forrest had been a
field surveyor and traverse explorer who openly exploited his official
travels to accumulate property. Understandably, the parliamentary and
press reaction in England to the idea of full self-government focused
on the idea that members of a Perth clique would shortly divide a
British patrimony among themselves.[101] The bitterness caused by British
resistance to Forrest's plans furthered an insistence on self-government,
which was granted in 1891. Along with Canada's prairies, Rhodesia,
and Kenya, the better-watered parts of Western Australia, in the extreme
south and extreme north, were among the last regions to feature in
the great land rush.

THE AMERICAN MARX:
HENRY GEORGE AND THE SINGLE TAX

In British colonies and the United States, schemes to reduce the lands
of indigenous people or to split up pastoral estates usually recognized
a principle of compensation for individual occupants. Concurrently, a
more aggressive land reform arose from an urge to banish poverty and
fed on the belief that unreasonably large amounts of land were locked
up. In the 1880s, the writings of Henry George, an American icono-
clastic sensation who urged a drastic course – confiscation through
taxation – swept through reform and labour movements in the English-
speaking world, nowhere more so than in the United Kingdom. Com-
municating in robust Sunday-school language, pilgrim George more
than economist Marx "was the true catalyst of Britain's insurgent proletariat."[102] It is very difficult to imagine someone with George's rhetoric and social cure emerging and thriving in Argentina and Brazil or
anywhere in the empires of Portugal, the Netherlands, Russia, or
Germany. The disappointments that he collected, interpreted, and
sought to remedy were comprehensible only where smallholders had
been assured participation in the great land rush. No tables of data or
intricate discussion of political economy backed George's tax cure. He
connected contemporary events to literature, history, and religious
texts, and he excelled at striking fiery poses. Although he wrote incon-
sistently about his ultimate plans for private property, he insisted that
"if chattel slavery be unjust, then is private property in land unjust."[103]

Had he been obsessive about consistency, George would have qualified that remark and, in so doing, blunted its message. What he meant
was that private property, accumulated so that it could not reach the
masses, was unjust. A special tax on land alone could remedy that evil

and address the flaws in contemporaneous methods of reallocating land, since it could make accumulation too costly for speculators or large estate holders – specifically railway companies, grazers, and aristocrats. In the language of the single taxers, the levy would effect a *restoration* of land to labouring families. The vocabulary of single-tax reformers drew on anxieties and hopes that accompanied the conclusion of the land rush. Restoration implied a return to a finer age and the achievement of social justice. From the perspective of Georgite believers in the single-tax cure, these good things should occur because land hoarders transgressed the moral code of improvement.

In late 1869, during a stint in Philadelphia and New York, George, then a young newspaper reporter, encountered extreme urban poverty and its inescapable contrast with metropolitan wealth. The incongruity of poverty amid plenty troubled him. Offered an editorship in Oakland, George returned to California, where his newspaper career had begun in 1866. One day, while riding in the hills outside the city, he stopped to rest his horse. A teamster passed by, and they struck up a conversation, in the course of which George asked the fellow what the surrounding *vacant* land was worth. "'I don't know exactly,' said the teamster. And pointing in the direction of some grazing cows, small in the distance, he added, 'But there is a man over there who will sell some land for a thousand dollars an acre.'" He had his answer to the riddle of poverty amid plenty.[104] Market value derived from something other than toil. It seemed that the growth of the city – a collective effort – elevated the land's market value, if speculators withheld the land from use long enough. George uncovered no new principle but stumbled onto issues that had arisen in controversies between Malthus and Ricardo on how a country could extract maximum benefit from its land. George's full-blown theory, adorned in orotund rhetoric with illustrations from the world's literatures and religions, contained two hard-hitting conclusions and a seemingly uncomplicated remedy. First, the removal of land from useful production cut people off from that which was essential for life itself – namely, the soil. Second, he insisted that the private gains of speculation should be treated, in a moral sense, as an unearned increment, because land value had social roots. Accepting physiocratic conceptions of economic life, George sprinkled his speeches, essays, and books with intimations that low urban wages and overcrowding in the cities would vanish if people could just get on the land, where, he assumed, they would be happier.[105]

In the United States, the chimera of land as a safety-valve for urban distress stretched back to at least the late 1830s. However, George attached urgency to this familiar prescription, since in his estimation – made as early as 1870 – the worthwhile parts of the American public domain, while not all used, were all owned, either by railways or by speculators. When looked at closely – he warned, in a declaration unusually pessimistic for the time – the land office's awe–inspiring summary of the unalienated public domain "begins to melt away," leaving mountain ranges, the dry, elevated plains of the eastern slopes of the Rocky Mountains, and the alkali-cursed terrain of the great interior basin. Stock raising, he correctly forecast, would flourish, but the proportion of good agricultural land in the west was small. In the 1880s, the surrender of some railway lands and the opening of Indian reserves gave relief, although George saw only more evidence of trouble in the way in which people raced for each release of land. "Go west, find people filing along, crowding around every Indian reservation that is about to be opened; travelling through unused and half-used land in order to get an opportunity to settle – like men swimming in a river in order to get a drink."[106]

George could not afford initially to devote himself to works of political economy. Journalism and partisan writing for the Democratic Party in the early 1870s helped pay for food and rent. Even so, in this period his tracts criticized American land policies, and some articles advocated a land tax in lieu of other levies. He began to write his first and most influential book, *Progress and Poverty*, in September 1877 and completed it eighteen months later.[107] In it he argued that wealth originated in land and that poverty derived from its monopolization by a few. This situation was more than unfortunate – it was, as I noted above, doubly unjust, denying people a natural right and allowing hoarders to profit from social progress. A tax on land could correct the wrongs, because the revenue would fund social improvements and smash estates for redistribution. Parties who forfeited property interests by failure to pay confiscatory taxes were ineligible for compensation for a simple reason. Since property was theft, was there any "reason that I should conclude that the robber has acquired a vested right to rob me?"[108]

George's love of aphorisms and metaphors blurred his message, as did his almost-unintelligible position on the state of landownership that would prevail after the single tax pulled terrain out from under speculators. Different radical sects could deduce almost whatever they wished from the wrath and hope of *Progress and Poverty*. Additionally, George accepted speaking invitations from various radical groups to hawk his message. In the early 1880s, when his work first achieved popularity, leaders of several reform movements in the United Kingdom recruited him as an ally. It is probable that he might never have achieved international fame had the Irish Land League not begun looking for American supporters. The messianic Irish home-rule leader,

Charles Stewart Parnell, visited the United States in 1879, shortly after endorsing the Irish Land League's aggressive tactics against rural landlords. George was willing to assist the Land League. In return it promised support for *Progress and Poverty*. However, George soon broke with Parnell over the Irish leader's willingness to compensate landlords if they surrendered their land to tenants. Tensions in Ireland in 1880–81 and an agrarian depression in Scotland and England prepared the way for George to have an impact in the United Kingdom. He began his first visit in late 1881 and gained invaluable publicity when police detained him in Ireland a year later. Although he was sent abroad to write articles on Ireland for the New York *Irish World*, he also spoke on behalf of his reform ideas in late 1882. Socialists could be forgiven for thinking that George shared with them something more substantial than a vague longing for social justice, because he seemingly attacked private property and dismissed compensation for land expropriation. Yet he was antagonistic towards state socialism for land – "the needless extension of government machinery which is to be avoided."[109] He wriggled out of an absolute rejection of private ownership of land. Landowners could still possess what they called their land. "Let them buy and sell, and bequeath and devise it. We may safely leave them the shell, if we take the kernel. *It is not necessary to confiscate land; it is only necessary to confiscate rent.*"[110]

George thought that the single tax would abolish the exchange value of land and spur the migration of capital from investment in land into equipment, alleviating underemployment in the cities. The collapse in land prices would incidentally free millions of acres "from which settlers are now shut out by high prices."[111] The small, productive landowner, reasoned George, should not be disturbed by the fall in land prices, for "he is a loser only as a man who has bought himself a pair of boots may be said to be loser by a subsequent fall in the price of boots. His boots will be just as useful to him, and the next pair of boots he can get cheaper."[112] He failed to see that land speculation in British and American jurisdictions had not been confined to plutocrats. Landhunters and speculators came from many walks of life. After the tax had worked its magic, according to George, the new social and spatial equilibrium would tend towards an even distribution of wealth and, importantly, population. People would move from overcrowded cities – an unnatural distribution – into the country, to the ultimate benefit of both the unhappy city dwellers and existing rural residents, who would no longer be cut off by the sparseness of population from culture, amusements, and education.[113] George understood that perfect social and spatial evenness could never be realized because of personal variations in skill, knowledge, industry, and prudence, but at least the non-producers would "no longer roll in luxury while the producer got the barest necessities of animal existence." George subscribed whole-heartedly to justification by improvement. "No one was allowed to play the dog in the manger with the bounty of the Creator."[114] George felt that his single tax guaranteed that creative workers would put God's munificence to work, for he exempted improvements from taxation.

From 1882 until his death in 1897, Henry George campaigned for the single tax in the United States, and made two further visits to the United Kingdom; he also lectured in Canada, Australia, and New Zealand. After his death, land leagues dedicated to the single tax lobbied in a number of European countries as well as across the English-speaking world. In the land-rush countries, a few jurisdictions – notably Manitoba, Saskatchewan, Alberta, New Zealand, South Australia, New South Wales, and towns and cities there and in the United States – adopted parts of the single-tax cure, but never the whole package, never with a passionate intention to reform society. Many municipal politicians, for example, thought a single tax that exempted buildings a splendid way to attract investment. The passage of a single tax through legislative bodies required compromises on one or more of three points. First, as with the valuation of land for purposes of original alienation, assessment of intrinsic value for taxa-tion was an intimidating prospect, and the colonial, state, provincial, or municipal governments that toyed with the single tax backed away from annual assessments. Second, assessments filled in only half the equation; setting the tax rate was a touchy issue, because how much a government collected for each dollar or pound of value determined whether the tax was intended just to gather revenue or to pry land loose from speculators. True believers disparaged the generally low rates. Third and finally, legislators often inserted a tax schedule for improvements, thus violating the single tax's purity.

The movement lost momentum during the First World War, but George had accomplished two things. First, *Progress and Poverty* – a book inspired partly by the closing phases of the land rush – contrib-uted mightily, if briefly, to radical causes in several countries. Second, the single tax itself came into its own as a measure for stimulating improvement. American single-tax enclaves included California's irri-gation districts, where bonds to raise funds for dams and aqueducts were paid off by a single tax.[115]

BIDDING THE DESERTS TO DRINK: IRRIGATION

By the mid-nineteenth century, before speculative irrigation colonies appeared in semi-arid regions, pastoralists in the United States and

Australia experimented with shallow wells, dams, and ponds.[116] Meanwhile, the Mormons, who sought a refuge near the Great Salt Lake (1847), commenced conquering semi-arid and arid lands. "They were frightfully innocent of the first principles of water application," observes Donald Worster, "and they had no vernacular or folk tradition to guide them in the enterprise."[117] Yet before the end of the century, they had not only planted irrigation colonies within Utah, but the way they conceived their fabricated oases represented a model for cultivating dry lands elsewhere. Engineering lessons from Utah were useful, although many could have been acquired by a study of the enormous projects in the Ganges and Jumna valleys of India that the British Raj undertook in the 1870s.[118] Apart from engineering and management practices, what made early American experiments eye–catching to later land developers across the semi-arid west, as well as in Australia and southern Alberta, were court decisions and legislation touching on rights to water. Water had to be secured for use by a colony's members, and in the second half of the nineteenth century legal models for achieving this goal proliferated in the United States, because of state jurisdictions.

There was a legal obstacle – *riparian rights* - to garnering water for irrigation schemes. This common law principle maintained that only people living on the banks of a channel of water could claim access to its natural flow, and they could not divert it to the detriment of parties holding the same right downstream. Originated in England, where there was ample rainfall, and at a time prior to industrial uses of water-power, the doctrine was thought to be "biased against economic development."[119] Consequently, in the 1820s and 1830s, before landhunters had reached the semi-arid U.S. west, the doctrine became riddled with exceptions in New England, where water-powered mills forced clashes between riparian rights and the urge to develop for business purposes.[120] If not by riparian rights, then by what doctrines could jurists and legislators guide water allocations? The political battle over preemption for land on the U.S. public domain pointed towards a principle of *prior appropriation*. California gold miners adapted this idea to take water for their sluice boxes, and the territory of Colorado recognized it for irrigation. This so-called Colorado doctrine, eventually adopted by seven states, recognized rights of exploitation for any party who established a prior claim, but the stakes were so high that counterclaims generated rounds of litigation. Prior appropriation had another flaw. It favoured a concentration of rights unsuited to densely occupied irrigation colonies, "where justice demanded that the water supply provide the greatest good to the greatest number."[121]

Seldom do common law jurisdictions immediately overthrow one rule for another. Across the U.S. west, therefore, courts and legislatures debated the merits of riparian rights and prior appropriation for some time.[122] In a landmark decision in 1886, the California Supreme Court reaffirmed riparian rights while holding that irrigation companies or groups of farmers could acquire water rights by purchase or adverse use. Subsequent legislation facilitated acquisition.[123] In essence, the California doctrine, ultimately followed in nine states, balanced rival principles. Interpretations of sovereignty affected the choice of the Colorado or California doctrine. Riparian rights persisted in states where federal ownership of water – along with the public domain – was unchallenged. States that followed the Colorado doctrine presumed that water rights, unlike the public domain, came under the authority of territories and states, a position strengthened in Colorado and Wyoming because their constitutions – ratified by Congress – specified state ownership of water. In Australia and Canada, governments influenced by U.S. litigation and by a tradition of crown title to resources legislated away riparian rights and asserted crown ownership of water rights, in order to arrange their sale to companies or to farmers' co-operatives. Canada accomplished this by adapting Victoria's legislation.[124]

In addition to needing management of water rights, irrigation colonies required large blocks of contiguous land. Irrigation developments frequently emerged on grazing lands – not only were these tracts often semi-arid and sometimes locales for modest water-collection efforts, but they seemed extensive enough for the recovery of investments in dams and canals. In California, the land consolidation necessary for irrigation colonies occurred in an unusual way. The great drought of 1864 weakened the local cattle industry – open range to the northeast meant that grazers were not compelled to invest in irrigation but could resume landhunting. This decline of California ranching prepared the way for a wheat boom that exploited huge farms. These operations withered during a drought that persisted into the early 1870s. In the estimation of Donald Pisani, this crisis fostered initial enthusiasm for major irrigation projects, which, though limited in number and posing as an ally of wheat farms, prepared the state for later, ambitious schemes for fruit production. In the 1880s and 1890s, "California boosters touted irrigation as a tool to break up large estates, promote the family farm, diversify crops, and increase the state's population."[125] Some of the state's first experiments originated as reactions to an immediate problem, but the next ones followed the doctrine of improvement.

By the late 1880s, with doctrines for water rights sorted out in U.S., Australian, and Canadian jurisdictions and land assembly either in place or contemplated, the stage was being set for a profusion of

irrigation colonies watered by companies, co-operatives, or governments. At the same time, there was a related sign of attention to
marginal land. Deep-well drilling in the semi-arid and arid American
west started in the 1870s and caught on in the 1880s and 1890s in
the higher valleys of Arizona and in eight western states, from Texas
to North Dakota, which sat atop the Ogallala aquifer system.[126]
Illustrating the belief that technology could liberate marginal land in
an era when easy plucking was at an end, Governor F.A. Tritle of
Arizona wrote in 1884 that while the bottom lands of his territory
were now occupied, there were "millions of acres among the hills and
on the plains which could be made very productive if there was
sufficient water for irrigation." Arizona had offered a reward in 1875
for anyone who could find artesian water; a successful claimant in
1883 inspired optimism.[127]

Just when drought roused initial experiments with irrigation in
California, a prolonged dry spell led to desperate searches for artesian
water on Australia's stations during the mid-1880s. The crisis coincided with the end of exploration on North America's first major
oilfield at Petrolia, Ontario. Despondent station owners discovered
what turned out to be the Great Artesian Basin in Queensland and
parts of neighbouring colonies.[128] Migrant Canadian drillers, cast up
by the collapse of the Petrolia boom, helped in the basin's initial
exploitation. Ironically, a country abounding in fresh water had the
expertise to assist agriculture on the world's driest continent: a Canadian was hired to develop bores for the government of Queensland in
1887. The reputation of Canadian drillers rose further when, in 1889,
the Ontario Boring Company struck water at 1,000 feet on a Salisbury
Downs station. It bubbled six feet above the surface.[129] Pastoral management companies encouraged their squatters to drill. The Australian
Mortgage, Loan, and Finance Company (AMLF), for example, contracted with "an expert from Canada" to assist clients. Between 1889
and 1891, over sixty productive bores in New South Wales and
Queensland had been drilled on behalf of AMLF grazers – most at
depths of over 750 feet. The average yields were 100,000 gallons per
day in New South Wales, and 200,000 in Queensland, and one well
produced 4 million gallons per day. Successful wells transformed stations. In 1895, on Tinnenburra, a huge Queensland station with nine
bores, 300 bullocks hauled the construction equipment to build a
system of dams and canals that supplied water for 500,000–600,000
sheep.[130] Comparable relief on other stations inspired general optimism. The chairman of the board of Goldsbrough, Mort & Co., a
pastoral commission house and consolidator of stations, reported in
1893 that productive bores rendered their fortunate possessors "to

some extent independent of the seasons, but enormously increasing the carrying capacity of their country."[131]

The massive American Ogallala aquifer was probably first tapped by deep-well drilling rigs in the 1870s. Groundwater did not always jet to the surface from Australian and American aquifers; many wells required mechanical lift. Self-directing and self-governing windmills therefore proliferated across the great plains in the 1870s, spread soon to Australia, and were introduced in South Africa in the 1890s.[132] Helpful to stockmen, they could not lift sufficient water for irrigation farming. Desperate farmers had rushed to an inadequate technology and thus began their race between sinking water tables and technological innovations, between farm production and rising energy costs. While significant details of this ongoing history lie after 1900, several of this book's themes relate to the Sisyphean struggle to pull water from non-renewable aquifers. The idea of an end to bounty could not be easily accommodated within cultures that placed great faith in improvement, had grown accustomed to engrossing new resources, and had developed many clever technological innovations for acquiring, allocating, and defining land. Groundwater in the nineteenth century led to individualistic irrigation efforts, in part because the scale of the resource flowed stealthily. Surface water, however, elicited grandiose schemes, since it was not simply manifest but – in the eyes of improvers – unco-operative and unreliable in its natural state and therefore required dams or pumping stations, canals and aqueducts. If outlays on these structures were to repay investors or society, large tracts of watered land were needed.

There were international connections among the irrigation visionaries and engineers who effected the necessary land assemblies and supply systems – most notably through the Chaffey brothers. The founding of an early irrigation colony in California's San Bernadino valley influenced Australia's premier irrigation community on the Murray River near Victoria's border with South Australia, and a Utah Mormon founded an irrigation colony in southern Alberta. Among the links between irrigation in California and in Australia, there were the Chaffey brothers, George, William, and Charles, originally from Brockville, Ontario. Members of the Chaffey clan, who emigrated to California in the late 1870s and early 1880s, founded the California community of Ontario, where they broke up a cattle ranch into irrigated citrus farms, defeating waste by implanting "a new irrigation colony on land given over to cactus, sage brush, and manzanita."[133] Ontario's developers had found a way to provide water with every lot. The critical technology derived not from engineering, but from law. To avoid litigation over who had access, the promoters organized a mutual water-supply company. When they bought the ranch, the Chaffeys secured the water rights, which they then sold to the water company. Each buyer of a ten-acre lot received ten shares. The company assumed responsibility for water distribution proportionate to shares held. Thus the land developers neatly evaded an ongoing responsibility.[134]

Contacts with Australians in 1885 alerted the Chaffeys to the potential for irrigation farming on the driest continent.[135] At this time the voices of Australia's own prophets of irrigation brushed aside criticism, because drought's immediate misery overwhelmed political debate. Despite differences between Australia and the American west – notably, the former's erratic extremes of flood and drought – U.S. achievements could not be shrugged off in desperate times.[136] Thus in 1885 a young member of the government of Victoria, Arthur Deakin, established a royal commission to visit the western United States and report on irrigation.[137] Deakin's report increased Victoria's receptivity to a proposition from the Chaffeys to form an irrigation colony on the Murray. Victoria resumed land from pastoral lessees and sold it to the Chaffeys, who planned to set up an irrigation plant, sell the improved land, and pass on the expense of running the system to farmers through water fees. At Mildura, the bench level of the land above the river forced the company to pump water. The overhead charged to farmers – some of whom expected that the water right sold with the land conveyed a right to free water – contributed to resentment and defaults, as did difficulties with establishing profitable crops. Uncertain revenues and a collapse in Australian real estate and banking left the Chaffeys without a line of credit, and so they declared insolvency in 1895. The governments of Victoria and South Australia rescued the twin colonies at Mildura and Renmark with loans for improvements.[138]

The Chaffeys were not finished waving the water wand over marginal land. William stayed in Australia and was knighted in 1924 for his services to the dried-fruit industry. Charles went to British Columbia and became a land assessor in the fruit-growing irrigation district of the Okanagan valley. George returned to California in 1897, went into banking, and in the delta country of the lower Colorado River beheld his third opportunity to coax fortune from waste. The river's wandering left behind a silt-filled depression known as the Salton Sink. George found a way to divert some of the Colorado to an old channel, thence into the depression, which he renamed the Imperial Valley. The consortium that organized this venture typically underestimated the investment and organization required to turn the valley into a rich agricultural domain, but in time – as with Mildura – government assistance created valuable land.[139]

During the same years that Canadian drillers worked for drought-stricken Australian stations and the Chaffey brothers launched their Australian colony, a handful of Canadians contemplated irrigation for southern Alberta. The nucleus was an enterprise originally assembled to cash in on coal mining and the sale of grazing land. Thanks to Canada's grants for the support of railways, the venture acquired substantial acreage. Promoter Alexander Galt and son Elliott developed coal-fields and connected them by rail with the mainline of the Canadian Pacific Railway (CPR). From 1883 to 1890, they secured subsidies amounting to 1 million acres for their Alberta Railway and Coal Company (AR&CCo). Friends in government assisted Galt with his western land grants, and later with their help he arranged an adjustment to national land policy. Alexander Galt asked in 1885 that his company be permitted to select alternate townships rather than alternate sections, because to market semi-arid land for ranches he needed large, contiguous tracts. As it turned out, the federal government's grazing leases undercut the market for land sales, but the change in the basic unit of corporate land grants initiated a trend in land assembly in the semi-arid parts of Alberta.[140]

Fortunately for the Galts, Charles Ora Card, a Mormon leader arrested in Utah for cohabitation with three wives, fled for southern Alberta in 1886. Looking for opportunities, Card bought nearly 10,000 acres from AR&CCo and interested the company's manager, Charles A. Magrath, in large-scale irrigation. In 1893, the Galts and the Mormons entered into "a partnership which completely altered the natural character of southern Alberta."[141] It took several years to clear obstacles before work began. A shortage of funds had to be overcome, and the way in which the AR&CCo held its grants created problems. Township blocks were suitable for ranchers, but to maximize profits from land sales along the line of its canals – to eliminate free riders – an irrigation company needed to monopolize the territory that stood to benefit from its water. The CPR already had been granted a right to consolidate its grants. Ottawa conceded that right to AR&CCo as well, professing by its actions that improvement in semi-arid regions required huge tracts, which were also a salient feature of irrigation colonies in the United States and Australia. The Galt venture benefited from assorted government subsidies and in 1902 acquired an additional block of 500,000 acres of crown land on generous terms. Thanks to Mormon labour and experience, and British financing, the Galt interests grew and increased in value until in 1912 their administration was transferred to the CPR. The corporate giant planned to open its own irrigation colony just to the north, across a 3-million-acre block on an open prairie plateau. With control of two major

irrigation regions, the CPR boasted in 1914 that it was constructing
the largest such project on the continent, capable of servicing more
land than was currently irrigated in California or Colorado.[142]

The history of major irrigation projects encompassed more than technology, law, private enterprise, land assembly, and state aid. Advocacy
of irrigation at the turn of the century effloresced into an international
crusade, whose travelling evangelists hailed the latest successes and
filed feasibility studies with firms and governments. The engineer and
trained horticulturalist supplanted the yeoman farmer – not to mention
the grazer – in campaigns to defeat natural limitations by using capital,
technology, and education. The irrigation crusade led to brilliant engineering feats in a quest for climate-free agriculture. But it bequeathed
a host of problems. In the short term, system maintenance thrust
unexpectedly high fees on the backs of shocked small farmers. With
unintended irony, the (U.S.) Western Irrigation Association espoused
the motto "Wise men not only pray for rain – they pay for it."[143]
Indeed they did, again and again, and then, lacking faith, they complained. To sustain optimism and sales, the former director of the
United States Reclamation Service, Frederick Newell, advised the
Canada Land and Irrigation Company in 1917 to avoid selling to
trouble-making "knockers."[144] Irrigation's contributions to the long
land rush thinned out into costly subsidies, engineering studies, and
even recommendations about the character of would-be purchasers.
Silting behind dams and soil salinization were eventually recognized
as costly long-term challenges. Companies and governments tackled
irrigation's predicaments through ever-greater investments. To succeed,
irrigation farmers eventually had to follow disciplined consumption
and marketing conventions, which were the antithesis of the free-
wheeling practices of squatters and landhunters. The rush was over.

Irrigation's promise as a technological wonder was crowded by
others, which achieved deeper popular penetration in wealthy urban-
izing societies. Electric power, the internal combustion engine, and
wireless communications assailed the limits of plodding steam or
animal power and the inconveniences of distance. But the panoply of
improvements to land – individualizing title, surveying, registration,
reallocation, irrigation – had arrived to stay. Throughout the twentieth
century, missionaries of improvement – this time not landhunters or
irrigation engineers but economists, bankers, and the governments of
developed countries – promoted it in other regions of the world.

The Modern World Surveyed

Traces of the great land rush – a faith in increase, a pursuit of bounty justified by improvement, allusions to new frontiers, refinements of legal instruments governing new forms of property, the abstracted representation of places on documents, a free-enterprise distrust of government combined with a reliance on government – depict a *modern* temperament. The great land rush was integrated with advances in the market economy. The formation of landed property rights grew in scale and refinement in tandem with European commerce, the formulation of capital-raising instruments such as stocks and bonds, and the grading of staples – flour, grain, meat, fleece, and lumber – which facilitated commodity trading. The pursuit of land also shared with the evolving market economy and with the emergence of classical economics a disregard for moral, customary, or judicious restraints on dreams of unlimited material possibilities. This was modern. So too was the idea, often implied in taking land from indigenous peoples, that they would benefit, that they would be improved. This notion was connected to the Lockean moral caveat which implied that, after a shift in control of resources, the parties ceding them should be no worse off than before. When colonizers engaged the language of betterment with respect to land, they frequently claimed that first peoples would also be improved. By entering the world of the colonizers, it was proposed, they would be no worse off, and surely better. That gave land taking an ideological boost and linked it to the many strategies and implements (armies, reservations, schools) of order and control that colonizers applied to first peoples. The presumed reformation of people was modern.

Studying the modern world rising in five constellations of settlement frontiers has involved more than checking off a list of similarities and observing the migration of ideas, more than seeing consequential links between the market economy's evolution and specific land-market institutions. This book's exploration should also have succeeded in keeping in sight the variety – the diversity of actions and experiences on many frontiers. The official plans for the organization and distribution of landed property rights, and their actual dispersal, disclosed a number of expressly local practices. Further, government strategies to control frontiers precipitated separate storms; as well, various hues of settlers' defiance launched distinctive regional and national political legacies. This book has been concerned with these and other differences, in addition to deep parallels. Ecologies varied, and colonizers adapted old-country ideas after acquiring experience with local flora, soil, and climates.[1] Land-taking practices often centred around the scarcity of water, to such an extent that, for southern Africa, Australia, and the United States west of the 100th meridian, control of water amounted to the possession of land. It was surely important for world history, not simply for American history, that land from the eastern seaboard to the Mississippi was not arid and could consequently sustain smallholder farms. That particularity, in conjunction with democracy, promoted the idea that land distribution should be open to all improvers. This aspiration had currency in regions outside temperate ecological zones, because it had thrived in the mainly congenial territories of eastern North America.

Any list of variations among the frontiers is bound to be a long one. European diseases and changes to indigenous habitat harmed first peoples in distinct ways. In southern Africa, the relative immunity of cattle-herding black Africans to European diseases meant that white landhunters on the eastern frontiers of the Cape encountered large, well-organized populations. The Indians of North America and Aboriginal people of Australia were far more susceptible to introduced microbes. If a particular indigenous people survived the dislocations of disease and destruction of habitat in sufficient number to resist, their conventions respecting strangers, enemies, and warfare played a part in the tempo and direction of colonization. For example, between two indigenous peoples with warrior traditions at the time of colonization – the Zulus and Maori – there were important differences, with consequences for colonizing newcomers. The Zulus demonstrated the bravery of infantry attack; the Maori eventually devised defensive traps and, shortly thereafter, guerrilla raids. Zulu practices led to punishing losses of young Zulu men and seizures of Zulu land; the struggle of some Maori induced colonists to turn from war and to execute economic and legal manipulations to wrest land from reluctant vendors.

The great land rush played out differently in its various locales. Land-grabbing practices in southern Africa and New Zealand, for example, occurred in unique ecological circumstances and were implicated in the foundation of dissimilar national political cultures. The legalism applied in New Zealand from the Treaty of Waitangi on – although it could be distorted – at least upheld a myth of fair play, which could have progressive consequences. By contrast, the *boer* military conquest later became the centrepiece of a nationalist legend that presented mastery on the highveld as an act of providence. That story does not itself completely explain racist practices by a succession of governments in South Africa, because white – boer and English – addiction to cheap labour incited racial discrimination in wages, summary punishment, and land tenure. Still, although there were many sources for racism in southern Africa, at the heart of the entangled affairs of race, poverty, and wealth in the region lay crucial episodes of landhunting.

Variety is apparent in the great land rush because of changes in government plans. Land pricing and sale techniques, as we saw, invited experimentation. In many places at many times, however, rough-and-ready procedures amounted to admissions by authorities that they could not superintend frontiers. The free selection of land without reference to a mapped scheme, for example, was a concession practiced extensively in southern Africa, Virginia, Australia, and New Zealand. Within the family of free-selection colonies, the circular loan farms of southern Africa – first in the Cape Colony and then in the boer states – showed in a conspicuous form how colonists adjusted to an arid climate. Free selection was not formally allowed in Upper Canada, the American public domain, or the Canadian prairies. In Upper Canada and on U.S. public domain, the grid surveys could not preclude illegal occupation, but geography and environment could make it difficult. The mid-continental location of the Canadian prairies contributed to the long, hard winter and assured its lengthy seclusion; geography and climate slowed occupation, enabling authorities to maintain orderly settlement on a declared grid. Most of this region could not support pastoralism. Notwithstanding this study's chronicling of abundant and deep differences, it proposes a core of universal traits for the great land rush. These traits mentioned at the start of this epilogue were modern.

THE ENDURING QUALITIES OF THE MODERN

What is the modern world, and how did the extended land rush described in this book contribute to its shaping? Conventional Western historical writing offers several schemes of periodization leading to a modern world. An early-modern era began in the mid-seventeenth century, a period that witnessed the emergence of France and England as nation-states capable of supporting standing armies, the formation of market economies operating over long distances, and the growth, beginning with the Treaty of Westphalia (1648), of both a system of international order negotiated by treaties and political acceptance of religious toleration. Many historians see a modern era commencing with the French Revolution, which by imperfect steps advanced individual rights. The British industrial revolution of the late eighteenth and early nineteenth centuries reinforces the idea that the modern world began about 1800, although Jan de Vries and Ad van der Woude argue that the Dutch republic launched the first modern economy in the late seventeenth century.[2] These competing scales of history are Eurocentric representations of the modern world. "Modern," can be a qualitative as well as a chronological notion. The qualitative countenance of modern, as I am about to describe it, has problems too, because its features originate in Western social science. A Western understanding of modern, influenced by Max Weber's sociology, proposes concepts rather than dramatic events, and this approach complements the treatment of history presented in the chapters above. Moreover, the great land rush originated in ideas and ambitions fostered in western Europe.

Modern has been associated – thanks to Weber – with a transition from traditional, customary, and affective practices to rationalized, utilitarian, and calculated forms of action that have been self-consciously refined to achieve specific objectives. Technology (including law) and science (including the social science of economics) displace belief; calculation replaces commitment and allegiance; institutions become less symbolic and more instrumentally adept.[3] A modern world is one in which material gains can be effectively extracted, but at the risk of harming those people who resist professionalized functional processes or who are denigrated as unimproving. The great land rush teemed with rationalizing projects, including the acquisition of land from indigenous peoples and the associated individualization of title, the allocation of land by sale rather than by royal grants, innovations in land surveying, refinements in property descriptions, facilities for document registration, experiments in land valuation, and – more generally – the abstraction of land into ciphers readily traded at a distance. Through these episodes, modern states augmented their culture of legality. The idea of material improvement provided an instrument to extend the boundaries of legality while maintaining "the centrality of a culture of legality."[4] Improvement added elasticity to the legality of property rights.

Some essentials of this modern world still thrive and in recent decades have enlarged their scope, because landed property rights are being extended into new territories, including the world's rain forests, mineral-rich corners of tundra and deserts, and ocean floors. Property rights also are being applied to an assortment of things, from ancestral designs by indigenous people to images developed by entertainment corporations, from music to genetic material, from telecommunication broadcast privileges to warrants to pollute. Not only has the range of property rights multiplied, but parties with claims to rights have increasingly been disposed to define, hold, and enforce them. Through litigation as well as by lobbying for statutes and treaties, rights seekers have laboured to squelch evasion. Property rights have exploded into a global obsession. The creation of new property rights has been beset with challenges of allocation, boundary enforcement, and initial pricing comparable to the troubles experienced during the great land rush. This outline of the growth of property rights leaves out details about alternatives, resistance, and violations; illegal copying and unauthorized use of intellectual property, for example, are prevalent. This comes as no surprise, because the chapters above have shown that subversion of rules accompanied an earlier scramble for property rights. Studies of episodes in the spread of property rights since 1900, and especially since 1990, will unearth intricacies similar to those of the great land rush. The enlargement of property rights in a number of so-called Third World countries and, beginning in the 1990s, in the republics of the former Soviet Union, plus the establishment of international bureaucracies to support rights to intellectual property, are linked to the formation of landed property rights on settlement frontiers. Additionally, in the United States there have been experiments with trading limited property rights to zoning restrictions and to the authority to pollute air.[5] Even these new property rights cannot exist without governments, because they are the creations of governments and require enforcement. By definition and practice, property rights are political. That is a lesson of the great land rush.

During the great land rush, methods for framing rights to an enormous quantity of new properties were pioneered and were enforced by government authority. Individualized property rights – defined by government surveyors, secured by government-managed registration systems, and supported by legislation – figured as prime assets in the economies of newly colonized places. Individualized property rights mingled too with ideas about improvement. In subsequent phases in the spread of property rights, comparable traits – the idea of individualization, support from governments, and forecasts of improvement – can be seen. Landed property rights of the kind that emerged during the rush were studied and debated in the twentieth century by colonial powers, newly independent countries, and international organizations, including the United Nations and the World Bank. The model of property rights provided by the rush did not quickly displace customary practices or collectivist experiments by socialist and communist states. There was, moreover, a brief period during the last century when the United States and the United Kingdom had slightly different positions on the global expansion of individualized property rights. American forays into international leadership by 1950 included assertions about property rights that were narrower and more resolute than those heard from London during the empire's sunset years.

Historically, British authorities tended to recognize indigenous peoples' interests to land and preferred to introduce individual title slowly. This official outlook persisted into the twentieth century, when imperial authorities dealt with land questions in African colonies, although there were as many land-management procedures as colonies, and there was abundant land grabbing. The thrusting land-acquisition designs of colonists in the last potential Neo-Europes in Africa often made the Colonial Office's promises of protection for indigenous peoples look hypocritical. Formally, however, the British retained a paternalistic doctrine.[6] At a 1951 symposium on land tenure in African and East Indian colonies, a summary of British policy echoed a rationale for the Royal Proclamation of 1763. "The grant of land in freehold has not usually been favoured where it has been considered important to protect the interests of indigenous peoples."[7] In debates at the United Nations about land reform in the 1950s, the United Kingdom maintained that the collective rights of indigenous peoples should be respected. During the Cold War, the Soviet Union and the United States squared off to dispute the meaning of land reform. American officials insisted that private property rights presented the true path to reform, leaving behind the nuanced British position. In international arenas by the 1970s, land reform as individualization faded as a topic of debate, replaced by environmental concerns. But the break-up of the Soviet empire cleared the way for a new round of American-led initiatives to implant or revive private property rights in land.

An influential expression of modernism – Weberian modernism – has bloomed in recent years, having been refreshed by the influence of the world's superpower and by waves of invention that have inspired efforts to protect intellectual property rights. Therefore, if historical periodization makes room for a postmodern age, it must be an era packed with hardy specimens of quite modern propensities. If postmodern has a claim to an age, it began in the 1960s, when some creative people in architecture, literature, and cinema in the West rejected trends that they felt expressed an outmoded modernism – more specifically, the overly confident systems of thought that implied movement along one ideological path or another towards a prescribed better world. Postmodernists attacked and disavowed master narratives. The idea of the modern in this restricted sense was not comprised of Weberian characteristics but, according to one description, included "abstract expressionism in painting, existentialism in philosophy, the final forms of representation in the novel, the films of the great *auteurs*, or the modernist school of poetry."[8] Among practices contested by postmodern artists and academics were functional design, linear and didactic story-telling in fiction and film, and lists of indispensable literary classics. Favoured practices included mixing historical styles in architecture; while in literature and criticism, irony, word-play, and an emphasis on multiple viewpoints were esteemed. Postmodern trends can be detected in entertainment, advertising, retailing, and tourism, which have constructed images and places devoid of historical reference points, all the better – it is claimed – to achieve manipulation through disorientation. Postmodernist intellectuals distrust heroic grand projects and posturing, the manipulation of images and language, and the single-minded pursuit of utopias of capital or labour.

A loose sheaf of critical attitudes distrustful of master narratives, postmodern discourses have rarely appraised the language of property rights and the connected doctrines of justification, including the powerful idea of improvement. By wrapping essays around particular books, films, or buildings, rather than exploring the actual workings of society and of the economy, some postmodernist commentators have understandably missed the persistence of Weberian modern trends, the persistence of capitalism, and the evolution of property rights. At its start, the great land rush exhibited conflicts and blurred distinctions, qualities that could lend themselves to postmodern and postcolonial scholarship; however, in later stages the rush became a rationalized, modern project. During the 1990s a few reports on land reform recommended that governments and non-government agencies ought to understand traditional land uses and incorporate them into law codes. This seemingly postmodern prescription still does not slip the Weberian net, since the exercise of preserving what may already be an altered "tradition" involves surveys, title registries, and codification.[9] The great land rush may have been postmodern at its start and modern thereafter.

Distrustful of claims to truth, postmodernists have eschewed the inductive probes favoured in historical writing, although Fredric Jameson once insisted that historical inquiry could contribute profoundly to human self-awareness. "The retrospective dimension" was "indispensable to any vital reorientation of our collective future."[10] Jameson proposed in 1984 that there were several striking new things, historically speaking, in the postmodern world – the world of multinational capital – including the "penetration and colonization of Nature and the Unconscious: that is, the destruction of precapitalist third world agriculture by the Green Revolution, and the rise of the media and the advertising industry."[11] With respect to the media, he had a case for something novel. The colonization of nature, however, was not new; the green revolution originated in the idea of improvement. Moreover, areas of economic development, which he could not have foreseen, have produced a bumper crop of exceedingly profitable innovations, whose exploitation requires the tested props of a Weberian modern world. Major innovations have propounded new property rights, typically intellectual property rights. The bull market that drove stock exchanges during the late 1990s drew strength from investors' conjectures that patents and copyrights were pregnant with future earnings. Knowing something about how landed property rights developed should assist with appraisals of the ongoing penetration and colonization of nature and with appraisal of the not-so-new new economy of the 1990s. In part, that economy involved scrambles to invest in the latest, hottest property rights. *The Great Land Rush* does not include descriptions of any rural or urban land bubbles; however, these common episodes would have provided cautionary tales for all investment enthusiasms.

A postmodern age may be a problematic construction. Some leading indicators can be adduced, but they may not represent a *Zeitgeist*. However, the postmodernists' way of deconstructing language and representation, of remarking on ambiguity and unresolved tensions, could help with an understanding of property rights. Like the term "modern," "postmodern" is both chronological and conceptual.[12] Both senses of the term have been worn nebulous through frequent application, although Steven Connor, in his review of postmodern culture, worries that postmodernism is in danger of becoming "overcoherent." He means that, by trying to formulate approved systems, some writers could blunt postmodernism's capacity to puncture orthodoxy.[13] In a similar vein, Stanley Fish writes that the critical legal studies movement, if it tries to formulate positive reform schemes, runs the risk of veering "back in the direction of rationalism and universalism that the critical/ deconstructive project sets out to demystify."[14] In the eyes of these two writers, pure postmodernists should expose intentions by breaking down images and words, and they should hold to the belief that it is essential to understand who prepares or controls representation.[15]

This study shares ground with these postmodern critical theorists, because it considers the intentions of those who articulated and applied doctrines of improvement and waste, developed legal doctrines about extinguishing native title, drafted laws for resource allocation, and advocated reformation of property laws and of the concentration of landholding. The social construction of property rights – the ways in which they have been justified, installed, changed, spread, and modified

– is a matter of language representing a particularly influential trend in Western culture.[16] This volume supposes that guiding trends flourished first in England and then acquired refinements amid tense, troubled, creative relationships between government officials and landhunters on environmentally conducive settlement frontiers. While property rights invite appraisal by philosophers, economists, and postmodern critics, history bursts with pertinent insights, because it is nothing less than the study of real opportunities seized, changes forced, justifications contrived, paths ignored, dilemmas encountered, damages inflicted, and problems produced for later generations. The great land rush, for example, helped initiate several profound human difficulties, including environmental ones, and it had a leading role in harming first peoples. Vital matters deferred during the great land rush are far from being resolved today.

THE LEGACY OF PENDING QUESTIONS

Patricia Nelson Limerick once wrote that "in the second half of the twentieth century, every major issue from 'frontier' history reappeared in the courts or in Congress."[17] She was right, although her remark has wider applications. The great land rush shaped more than original frameworks and justifications for property rights and affected more than the evolution of the United States. In their hasty manœuvres, landhunters and the governments that tried to manage them invariably left predicaments for future generations. Land claims by indigenous peoples, for example, affected late-twentieth-century national politics in New Zealand, Australia, Canada, and southern Africa.They have been relatively less visible in national politics in the United States. New Zealand inaugurated a process for resolving land claims in the wake of Maori demonstrations in the 1970s intended to awaken white New Zealanders to an acceptance of Maori rights and identity presumably guaranteed by the Treaty of Waitangi. Indians in Canada and the United States "were influential in sharpening awareness of rights that might be conceded, and in demonstrating methods of protest that might strike at the weak points of the dominant culture."[18] The clamour led New Zealand's Parliament in 1975 to create the first Waitangi Tribunal. This body had no authority to consider matters arising before the 1975 legislation. However, after a revised act in 1985, a second Waitangi Tribunal was allowed to investigate claims back to 1840, permitting a searching review of the entire colonial period, tract by tract, act by act. While the tribunals have not had the authority to force settlements, their exhaustive findings have squeezed out agreements and extracted evidence for reconsidering the historical record.

Across the Tasman Sea, the politics of Aboriginal claims burst into the mainstream of Australian politics during the 1990s as at no other time, principally because a High Court decision that overturned after 150 years the doctrine of *terra nullius*. Several Torres Islanders challenged Queensland's right to have granted a fish-packing company land on an island in the straits between Australia and Papua–New Guinea. The appellants successfully maintained that indigenous rights had not been previously extinguished. The court rejected Queensland's assertion that *terra nullius* enabled it to turn over the land without having to clear native interests. With this decision, the court opened the door to comparable land claims on the continent. Although the federal government promptly established procedures for land claims, the country was riven over the *Mabo* decision and the subsequent *Wik* decision. Mining companies, states with mineral deposits, and a bloc of conservative voters believed that litigation would delay resource development. Nervous pastoralists worried about their leaseholds, should the crown land that they used be included in settlements. A change in government put the country under leadership hostile to land claims, and in 1998 legislation enabled development to proceed on lands even if Aboriginal claims were still being processed. Whether or not this move violates human rights – as some Australians insist – it directed a coarse blow to race relations.[19]

Land seizures have prompted difficult, urgent, political negotiations in former settlement colonies in southern Africa. White-operated farms in Zimbabwe since independence have been an object of land reform and, beginning in early 2000, a pretext for violence manipulated to intimidate opposition to President Robert Mugabe. Reform was mismanaged and even perverted in Zimbabwe, but that does not diminish the authenticity of problems originating from the South African Company's land distributions in Southern Rhodesia. Meanwhile, in parts of South Africa, the land seizures that attract attention are the forced uprootings executed during the Apartheid decades. Earlier land acquisitions may be subjected to critical review in due course, because they were as crude as anywhere during the great land rush and debilitating for those black Africans who lost prime territory. Land reform or compensation for losses promises to be an immense and necessary task for the governments of southern Africa, requiring enormous sensitivity.

Generalizing about native land claims in Canada is a challenge, since the scale of the country, the diversity of environments, the multiplicity of distinctive first peoples, and a protracted period of multiple colonizations contribute to a fragmented history. The political history of the federation adds a complication. Policy initiatives in the field of relations between first peoples and governments have been drawn into federal–

provincial quarrels. It is clear, however, that land disputes have never been more significant in Canadian public affairs than during the last thirty years; unlike the United States, where the subject receded from view after an initial flash in the 1970s and early 1980s, in Canada it remained prominent. When they organized in the 1970s to influence the way in which resource development occurred in regions that they considered theirs, Canadian natives met with some success. Courts started to rule that where there had been evidence of first peoples' occupation and no treaties of cession – for example, in the Northwest Territories and most of British Columbia – native title applied. Negotiated settlements have followed precedent-setting claims. There have also been a few suits alleging that the federal government has not lived up to the promises that its predecessors made when clearing native title. Canada's first peoples have barely started to escape the shadows of the great land rush.[20] The consequences of the rush need to be considered in conjunction with evaluations of social justice, considerations of restitution, and attention to environmental assessment.

In the United States, a series of lawsuits, known collectively as the Eastern Indian land claims, covering an estimated 35 million acres, began in the early 1970s. In several key cases, claims hinged on technicalities about whether states that purchased Indian land in the 1780s and 1790s enjoyed adequate constitutional authority. The U.S. government negotiated a few settlements, and then a major decision in 1988 upheld the legality of several substantial New York acquisitions. In the 1970s and early 1980s, the federal government began to negotiate the clearing of native title issues with the first peoples of Alaska. Land disputes between first peoples and state and federal governments then disappeared from headlines, and Indian land claims have not again been featured in national politics.[21] The most persistent American land controversies arose not from first peoples seeking government restitution, but from critics of the federal government's control over the huge sections of public domain in the west. For over one hundred years, the management of large, unalienated regions of the west has excited debate. For decades, the inconsistent enforcement of the 1885 anti-fencing legislation showed a major unresolved legacy of the rush. Enforcement of the prohibition against fencing on the open range fluctuated until the passage of the Taylor Grazing Act (1934), which aimed to put the immense unsold portions of the public domain under bureaucratic management by the Department of the Interior.

The act repackaged the sharply opposing objectives of ranchers and federal administrators. The former still wanted greater security for their informal landholdings at low cost, while the latter planned management with land-use controls and tried to restrict grazers' legal interests.[22] In practice, the property rights of the ranchers were at first built up (1930s–50s) because of their political leverage and then weakened (1960s–70s). A "sagebrush rebellion" by traditional resource users in the west (late 1970s) prompted a privatization debate that peaked in the early 1980s. In part, this protest "was simply a recurrence of range wars that had flared up periodically for the past century between the grazers on the public lands and the federal authorities."[23] Some so-called rebels also pushed for the transfer of public land to the western states, and they ignited unusually extensive discussions over the future of the public domain, because environmentalists joined the fray. Instead of leading to decisive shifts in authority and property rights, the controversies of the 1980s fragmented into multisided deliberations, much as had those of a century earlier. The advocates of fundamental change failed. They had a weak sense of history and failed to notice that the public domain was privatized to a greater degree than they realized. "There already existed a wide range of de facto private rights – or so the people who used the public lands tended to regard their past privileges – that were grounded in long historical experience."[24] Ranchers in the 1980s still looked for the greatest security at the lowest price, and privatization schemes, as they saw matters, simply threatened to turn the clock back to the days when pastoralists defended their turf against homesteaders and speculators. The debate about western land in the 1980s turned on who should own western public land. However, at the end of the millennium, for reasons of their own, environmentalists joined in a condemnation of the status quo in western land management, for they exposed ranching as an incomparable threat to native plants and ecosystems.

Starting about 1900, U.S. state and federal research documented degradation caused by overstocking. Abundant by 1940, these studies sought to guide ranchers towards better practices, not to condemn their industry. In contrast, Debra Donahue's *The Western Range Revisited* (1999) argued for livestock's removal from public land to preserve biodiversity. The public domain is again contested territory.[25] Reliant on irrigation reservoirs and pumping down the Ogallala aquifer, the small family farms on the arid Great Plains are vanishing, replaced by large-scale operations. The history of rural settlement and depopulation of the plains – the latter a trend also on the Canadian prairies – has led a few observers to conclude that parts of this region should revert to grassland with buffalo herds, a perspective that contests the doctrine of improvement. In all dry farming regions of the great land rush, depopulation indicates that certain experiments with marginal land have seen their day.

On the American public domain, as in many other parts of the world, the essence of property rights – politically constructed relationships among people concerning who gets access to something valuable – is as discernible today as it was during the land grabs executed by British adventurers in early-twentieth-century Kenya, the late-nineteenth-century conflicts on the U.S. open range, the New Zealand wars, the pastoralists' sweeps through New South Wales, the *voortrekkers'* expeditions across the Orange River, and the many competitions for land in the Ohio valley during the mid- and late eighteenth century. Contests over property rights form one of the more central tales in the modern world – a story that integrates a considerable amount of history and whose future seems limitless. Property rights can never escape intense debate. The world faces constraints, and experts proffer solutions that often incorporate the creation of individual property rights. The proprietors of commercially promoted remedies for food shortages and plagues – the laboratories and corporations – expect the protection of intellectual property rights to guarantee them material rewards. If rigidly maintained, the position that most of them take – property rights secure the revenues that support and inspire more research – clashes with need among the world's poor.

We ought to keep ethics and global perspectives in sight as new property rights are fashioned and enforced. If we asked of actions in the great land rush, were they ethically right?, the answer would often be an unwavering "no." Are indigenous peoples, subject to the acquisitions of colonizers, better off than they were before? The answer from many of them would be "no." It will be tragic if writers in the decades ahead reach the same conclusion when they assess how property rights developed in our time. "The conquest of the earth," writes Robert Williams concerning native title, "is not a pretty thing when you look into it too much."[26] There is no reason to believe that new frontiers of discovery will turn out better. The doctrine of improvement, which had been so powerful in the great land rush, must be exposed to scepticism and moral scrutiny. The recent relentless expansion of intellectual property rights displays the same irrepressible momentum, haste, and global scope as the great land rush. In common with that older frenzy to engross property, the current mad scramble may also shrink the public domain, placing amazing riches in private hands in the name of improvement.[27]

Notes

INTRODUCTION

1 Alfred W. Crosby, *Ecological Imperialism: The Biological Expansion of Europe, 900-1900* (Cambridge: Cambridge University Press, 1986), 4. The book recounts the sequence of accidental developments that led Europeans to excel in long-distance sailing and then indicates how readily European biota spread through the regions where Europeans landed.

2 Alfred W. Crosby, *Germs, Seeds, and Animals: Studies in Ecological History* (New York: M.E. Sharpe, 1994), 75.

3 James C. Scott, *Seeing Like a State: How Certain Schemes to Improve the Human Condition Have Failed* (New Haven, Conn.: Yale University Press, 1998), 1-50.

4 A stimulating and well-illustrated study of land surveys aiding the state in Europe and its colonies is provided by J.P. Cain and Elizabeth Baigent, *The Cadastral Map in the Service of the State* (Chicago: University of Chicago Press, 1992).

5 Michael Adas, *Machines as the Measure of Men: Science, Technology, and Ideologies of Western Dominance* (Ithaca, NY: Cornell University Press, 1989), 210-221.

6 An example is Hernando De Soto, *The Mystery of Capital: Why Capitalism Triumphs in the West and Fails Everywhere Else* (New York: Basic Books, 2000). De Soto uses squatting on the American public domain to argue that people who have extra-legal interests in property in Third World countries will progress if their interests can be converted into property rights. That may be an admirable end, but he employs the American example to suggest that this conversion was not too difficult there and by extension should be possible elsewhere. That is doubly optimistic. First, he does not mention native title issues and

sloughs off as side issues the violence and cheating of white squatters. Second, what could make conversion of squatting into property rights more problematic in Third World settings than in the United States (and British settlements colonies) is the fact that future contests for rights will not be as simple as those on frontiers, where indigenous peoples without political power were displaced, but could involve clashes with the powerful who already claim rights. The great land rush cannot be repeated. The remaining path to distributing property rights therefore supposes reform struggles.

CHAPTER ONE

1 Richard Grassby, *The Business Community of Seventeenth-Century England* (Cambridge: Cambridge University Press, 1995), 386.
2 Roy M. Robbins, *Our Landed Heritage: The Public Domain, 1776–1936* (Lincoln: University of Nebraska Press, 1962; first printed in 1942), 277.
3 Herbert Gibson, *The History and Present State of the Sheep-Breeding Industry in the Argentine Republic* ((Buenos Aires: Ravenscroft and Mills, 1893), 5. For British interests in the era of Rosas, see John Lynch, *Argentine Dictator: Juan Manuel de Rosas, 1829–1852* (Oxford: Clarendon Press, 1981), 247–94. The influence of British capital is a recurrent topic in Laura Randall, *A Comparative Economic History of Latin America, Vol. 2, Argentina* (Ann Arbor, Mich.: University Microfilms International, 1977).
4 Gibson provides a first-hand account in *The Sheep-Breeding Industry*, 15–37.
5 Miguel Ángel Cárcano, *Evolución del régimen de la tierra pública, 1810–1916* (Buenos Aires: Eudeba, 1972; first pub. 1917), 181. During most of the first half of the nineteenth century, the provinces exercised considerable authority over public land; there usually was no single policy for the whole country.
6 Juan Carlos Rubenstein covers the background ideas, the political debates, the aims, and the implementation of *enfiteusis* in *Filiacion historica y sociopolitica de la enfiteusis Rivadaviana* (Buenos Aires, 1984). He mentions (142–3) Rividiavia's interest in Sismondi, who maintained that governments had a legitimate role in economic life. Sismondi distinguished between, on one hand, agricultural income derived from the quality of the land and, on the other hand, labour and capital and was an early critic of industrial capitalism.
7 Lynch, *Argentine Dictator*, 25. For a summary see Lynch, "From Independence to National Organization," in Leslie Bethell, ed., *Argentina*

since Independence (Cambridge: Cambridge University Press, 1993), 22–34. All subsequent references to Lynch relate to the 1981 biography.

8 Cárcano, *Evolución del régimen*, 113.

9 Lynch, *Argentine Dictator*, 89. H.S. Ferns suggests that landed interests obstructed industrial development; *The Argentine Republic, 1516–1971* (New York: Barnes and Noble, 1973), 52. In Santa Fe, although there were agricultural colonies founded between 1856 and 1895, estancieros dominated politics. Ezequiel Gallo, *Farmers in Revolt: The Revolutions of 1893 in the Province of Santa Fe, Argentina* (London: Athlone Press, 1976), 5–7, 87–9. Andres M. Carretero studied land consolidation during the Rosas era and concludes that the general allowed elites to increase their control of land; *La propriedad de la tierra en la epoca de Rosas* (Buenos Aires: Editorial El Coloquio, 1972), 29–30, 37–9. A similar concentration occurred in Paraguay, whose war with Argentina led to the sale of large parts of the public lands at low prices, which benefited estancieros. Harris Gaylord Warren, with the assistance of Katherine F. Warren, *Rebirth of the Paraguayan Republic Era, 1878–1904* (Pittsburgh: University of Pittsburgh Press, 1985), 168–73.

10 Jeremy Adelman, *Republic of Capital: Buenos Aires and the Legal Transformation of the Atlantic World* (Stanford, Calif.: Stanford University Press, 1999), 12, 127–8.

11 Cárcano, *Evolución del régimen*, 120–1.

12 Hilda Sabato, *Agrarian Capitalism and the World Market: Buenos Aires in the Pastoral Age, 1840–1890* (Albuquerque: University of New Mexico Press, 1990), 41–2.

13 Sabato, *Agrarian Capitalism*, 48–53.

14 Adelman, *Republic of Capital*, 129–30.

15 On the army and land allocation, see Cárcano, *Evolución del régimen*, 247–52. The army, the conquest of the "wilderness," and the militarization of Argentina's politics is also discussed in Néstor Tomás Auza, "La ocupacion del espacio vacio: de la frontera interior a la frontera exterior, 1876–1919," in Gustavo Ferrari and Ezequiel Gallo, eds., *La Argentina del ochenta al centenario* (Buenos Aires: Editorial Sudamericana, 1980), 61–86. No one has hazarded a guess as to the numbers of indigenous people killed during the century. However, the vicious attitude of some soldiers towards natives was reported by Charles Darwin in *The Voyage of the Beagle* (New York: Collier and Sons, 1909), 114.

16 Rubenstein, *Filiacion Historica*, 47.

17 Quoted in Patricia Nelson Limerick, "Turnerians All: Dreams of a Helpful History in an Intelligible World," *American Historical Review* 100 (June 1995), 698.

18 Jeremy Adelman and Stephen Aron, "From Borderlands to Borders: Empires, Nation States, and the Peoples of North American History," *American Historical Review* 104 (June 1999), 817.

19 A good review of the controversy appears in Michael Kammen, "The Problem of American Exceptionalism: A Reconsideration," *American Quarterly* 45 (March 1993), 1–33; quote at 15. Ian Tyrrell tackles the origins of a narrowness to American national history in "Making Nations/Making States: American Historians in the Context of Empire," *Journal of American History* 86 (Dec. 1999), 1015–44.

20 Donald Worster, *Dust Bowl: The Southern Plains in the 1930s* (New York: Oxford University Press, 1979), 87.

21 J.A. Hobson, *Imperialism: A Study*, intro. by Philip Siegelman (Ann Arbor: University of Michigan Press, 1967), 81.

22 C.A. Bayly, "The First Age of Global Imperialism, c. 1760–1830," *Journal of Imperial and Commonwealth History* 26 (1998), 43.

23 Selected works and commentaries are well represented in William Roger Louis, ed., *Imperialism: The Robinson and Gallagher Controversy* (New York: New Viewpoints, 1976).

24 Strong support for this feature of their thesis comes from Deryck M. Schreuder, *The Scramble for Southern Africa, 1877–1895: The Politics of Partition Reappraised* (Cambridge: Cambridge University Press, 1980). Robinson and Gallagher famously propose an informal empire of trade and financial influence. Their claim was subject to rebuttals by Oliver Macdonagh and D.C.M. Platt; see Louis, ed., *Imperialism*.

25 P.J. Cain and A.G. Hopkins, *British Imperialism: Innovation and Expansion, 1688–1914* (London: Longman, 1993). Winfried Baumgart places a comparable emphasis on the late nineteenth century and argues that economic motives were secondary or absent; *Imperialism: The Idea and Reality of British and French Colonial Expansion* (Oxford: Oxford University Press, 1982). I share Bayly's critique of the stress placed on later imperialism in "The First Age of Global Imperialism," 28–9. Economic motives need to be understood from the periphery as well as from the core. A good case for examining the impact on colonial-development policies of commodity demands from the core industrialized nations appears in Allen Isaacman and Richard Roberts, "Cotton, Colonialism, and Social History in Sub-Saharan Africa," in Isaacman and Roberts, eds., *Cotton, Colonialism, and Social History in Sub-Saharan Africa* (Portsmouth: Heinemann, 1995), 5–11.

26 William Cronon, *Nature's Metropolis: Chicago and the Great West* (New York: W.W. Norton, 1991). Cronon argues that human ambitions and ingenuity embody a "second Nature," which changes countryside and city alike.

27 A fine discussion of the importance of being first on the land is found
in Rusty Bitterman, "The Hierarchy of the Soil: Land and Labour in a
Nineteenth Century Cape Breton Community," *Acadiensis* 18 (autumn
1988), 39. As well, note Sean Gouglas, "The Influences of Local Environmental Factors on Settlement and Agriculture in Saltfleet Township,
Ontario, 1790–1890" (unpublished PhD thesis, McMaster University,
2001), 64–154.

28 Richard Lachmann, *From Manor to Market: Structural Change in
England, 1536–1640* (Madison: University of Wisconsin Press, 1987),
120.

29 G.E. Mingay, *A Social History of the English Countryside* (London: Routledge, 1990), 51. Mingay and J.D. Chambers stress the complexity of
land use and the survival of small farmers amid the enclosures; *The Agricultural Revolution, 1750–1880* (London: B.T. Batsford, 1966), 93–7.

30 Ann Bermingham, *Landscape and Ideology: The English Rustic Tradition, 1740–1860* (Berkeley: University of California Press, 1986), 1.

31 Ibid., 10.

32 Timothy Parson, *The British Imperial Century: A World History
Perspective* (Lanham: Rowman & Littlefield Publishers, 1999), 122
(emphasis added).

33 Lillian F. Gates, *Land Policies of Upper Canada* (Toronto: University
of Toronto Press, 1968), 93; Eric Jarvis, "Military Land Granting in
Upper Canada following the War of 1812," *Ontario History* 67
(1975), 121–34.

34 Stephen Nicholas and Peter R. Shergold, "Transportation as Global
Migration," in Nicholas and Shergold, eds., *Convict Workers: Reinter-
preting Australia's Past* (Melbourne: Cambridge University Press,
1988), 28–38. J.B. Hirst discusses the freedom that convicts could
negotiate in their daily routines in *The Convict Society and Its Enemies*
(Sydney: George Allen & Unwin, 1983), 78–188.

35 Emilia Viotti da Costa, *The Brazilian Empire: Myths and Histories*
(Chicago: University of Chicago Press, 1985), 78–93.

36 Robinson early recognized that indigenous peoples used Europeans for
strategic purposes. "Non-European Foundations of European Imperialism: Sketch for a Theory of Collaboration," in William Roger Lewis,
ed., *The Robinson and Gallagher Controversy* (New York: New Viewpoints, 1976), 134. The shorter original article appeared in 1953.

37 Terms for Land Grants in New Colonies reproduced in *Royal Instructions to British Governors, 1670–1776*, vol. II (New York: American
Historical Association, 1936; reprinted Octagon Books, 1967), 528.

38 Gilbert Rist, *The History of Development: From Western Origins to
Global Faith* (London: Zed Books, 1996), 38.

39 Walter Eltis, *The Classical Theory of Economic Growth* (London, 1984), 8. The basis for the argument that Quesnay wished to see French agriculture exposed to bourgeois energy appears in S. Malle, "Marx on Physiocracy," in Mark Blaug, ed., *François Quesnay (1694–1774), Volume II* (Aldershot: Edward Elgar, 1991), 185–95.

40 For the idea of "agricultural patriotism," see C.A. Bayly, *Imperial Meridian: The British Empire and the World, 1780–1830* (London, 1989), 121.

41 Donald Winch, *Riches and Poverty: An Intellectual History of Political Economy in Britain, 1750–1834* (Cambridge: Cambridge University Press, 1996), 33–123, 223–388; Biancamaria Fontana, *Rethinking the Politics of Commercial Society: The Edinburgh Review, 1802–1832* (Cambridge: Cambridge University Press, 1985), 46–111.

42 Bayly, *Imperial Meridian*, 8.

43 Eric Stokes, *The English Utilitarians and India* (Oxford: At the Clarendon Press, 1963), 81–139.

44 John R. Nelson, *Liberty and Property: Political Economy and Policy-making in the New Nation* (Baltimore: Johns Hopkins University Press, 1987), 162–75.

45 There is a small library of these studies published by the World Bank in Washington, DC. For examples that express this perspective, note Henry Bruton, *Sri Lanka and Malayasia: The Political Economy of Poverty, Equity and Growth* (1992); Zvi Lerman et al., *Land Reform and Farm Restructuring in Ukraine* (1994); Karen Brooks et al., *Agricultural Reform in Russia: A View from the Farm Level* (1996); and World Bank Country Study, *El Salvador: Rural Development Study* (1998). I am indebted to Michelle Vosburgh for her review of this literature.

46 J.M. Powell, *Plains of Promise, Rivers of Destiny: Water Management and the Development of Queensland, 1824–1990* (Brisbane: Boolarong, 1991), 52. Mary Durack's celebrated book about her family – *Kings in Grass Castles* (1959) – reproaches some of its deeds. A movie, faithful to the book, was made in 1999. The epic includes the family's participation in the murder of Aborigines in the Kimberleys.

47 See the discussion of culture in Liah Greenfeld, *Nationalism: Five Roads to Modernity* (Cambridge, Mass.: Harvard University Press, 1992), 17–21. The application of culture – especially of images – to new-world lands is the subject of Joseph M. Powell's stimulating book, *Mirrors of the New World: Images and Image-Makers in the Settlement Process* (Folkestone: Dawson-Archon Books, 1977).

48 Bernard Bailyn, *Context in History* (Melbourne: La Trobe University, North American Studies, 1995), 27.

49 Lauren Benton, "From the World-Systems Perspective to Institutional World History: Culture and Economy in Global Theory," *Journal of World History* 7 (1996), 283.

50 Peter Bakewell, "Conquest after Conquest: The Rise of Spanish Domination in America," in Richard Kagan and Geoffrey Parker, eds., *Spain, Europe and the Atlantic World: Essays in Honour of John H. Elliott* (Cambridge: Cambridge University Press, 1995), 305.

51 See Peter Bakewell's rounded account of rural labour and the colonists' contribution and the problem of native depopulation. Ibid., 311–12.

52 J.H. Elliott, *Spain and Its World, 1500–1700* (New Haven, Conn.: Yale University Press, 1989), 14–15.

53 Nicholas P. Cushner, *Lords of the Land: Sugar, Wine, and Jesuit Estates of Coastal Peru, 1600–1767* (Albany: State University of New York Press, 1980), 27–57; Maurice Zeaitlin, *The Civil Wars in Chile* (Princeton, NJ: Princeton University Press, 1984), 13, 24–30; Warren Dean, *Rio Claro: A Brazilian Plantation System, 1820–1920* (Stanford, Calif.: Stanford University Press, 1976), 10–23.

54 Dennis Morrow Roth, *The Friar Estates of the Philippines* (Albuquerque: University of New Mexico Press, 1977), 31.

55 Ibid., 15–62. Ronald G. Edgerton, "Americans, Cowboys, and the Cattlemen of the Mindanoa Frontier," in Peter W. Stanley, ed., *Reappraising an Empire: New Perspectives on Philippine–American History* (Cambridge, Mass.: Harvard University Press, 1984), 171–97.

56 Douglass C. North, "Institutions, Transactions Costs, and the Rise of Merchant Empires," in James D. Tracy, ed., *The Political Economy of Merchant Empires: State Power and World Trade, 1350–1750* (Cambridge: Cambridge University Press, 1991), 26–7.

57 Mancur Olson, *Power and Prosperity: Outgrowing Communist and Capitalist Dictatorships* (New York: Basic Books, 2000), 39.

58 Until the mid-eighteenth century, estate laws in New Spain favoured the accumulation of land in a few hands. Encomiendas could not be divided, and entails preserved the estates of the aristocracy and clergy. The quote is from John H. Coatsworth, "Economic and Institutional Trajectories in Nineteenth-Century Latin America," in Coatsworth and Alan M. Taylor, eds., *Latin American and the World Economy since 1800* (Cambridge, Mass.: Harvard University, David Rockefeller Center for Latin American Studies, 1998), 41. A summary of Argentina's late-nineteenth-century land laws is found in Jeremy Adelman, *Frontier Development: Land, Labour, and Capital on the Wheatlands of Argentina and Canada* (Oxford: Clarendon Press, 1994), 63–70. Thomas H. Holloway discusses land reforms in southern Brazil in *Immigrants on the Land: Coffee and Society in São Paulo, 1886–1934* (Chapel Hill: University of North Carolina Press, 1980), 113–38.

59 Adelman, *Frontier Development*, 66; Warren Dean, *Rio Caro: A Brazilian Plantation System, 1820–1920* (Stanford, Calif.: Stanford University Press, 1976), 17.
60 E. Bradford Burns, *A History of Brazil* (New York: Columbia University Press, 1980), 31.
61 Dean, *Rio Caro*, 12–13.
62 Costa, *The Brazilian Empire*, 91. See Stanley Stein, *Vassouras: A Brazilian Coffee County, 1850–1900* (Cambridge, Mass.: Harvard University Press, 1970), 10–17.
63 Dean, *Rio Caro*, 16–17.
64 Holloway, *Immigrants on the Land*, 123.
65 Ronald M. Schneider, *"Order and Progress": A Political History of Brazil* (Boulder, Col.: Westview Press, 1991), 26–7; Leslie Bethell, *Brazil: Empire and Republic, 1822–1930* (Cambridge: Cambridge University Press, 1989), 233–4.
66 Pierre Monbeig, *Pionniers et planteurs de São Paulo* (Paris: Librairie Armand Colin, 1952), 125–48. Though older, this work remains a superb contribution to the study of human ecology and historical geography. Holloway, *Immigrants on the Land*, 116–19, 131–8.
67 James Duffy, *The Portuguese in Africa* (Cambridge, Mass.: Harvard University Press, 1959), 1–102; Allen Isaacman, *The Tradition of Resistance in Mozambique: Anti-colonial Activity in the Zambesi Valley, 1850–1921* (London: Heinemann, 1976), 1–39, 76–9; Malyn Newitt, *Portugal in Africa: The Last Hundred Years* (London: C. Hurst & Co., 1981), 1–93; Gervase Clarence-Smith, *The Third Portuguese Empire, 1825–1975: A Study in Economic Imperialism* (Manchester: Manchester University Press, 1985), 23, 34–5, 100–12.
68 Brian Young, *The Politics of Codification: The Lower Canadian Civil Code of 1866* (Montreal: McGill-Queen's University Press, 1994), 54–60.
69 Gianni Vaggi, "The Limits of Physiocracy and Smith's Fortune," in *La diffusion internationale de la physiocratie (XVIIIe–XIXe)* (Grenoble: Presses Universitaires de Grenoble, 1995), 59–75; Francis Démier, "Néo-physiocratie et première industrialisation français," in ibid., 231–63; Louis Argemi, José-Luis Cardoso, and Ernest Lluch, "Postface: la diffusion internationale de la physiocratie: quelques problèmes ouverts," in ibid., 473–80. For a discussion of the particular advanced ideas of François Quesnay, see Elizabeth Fox-Genovese, *The Origins of Physiocracy: Economic Revolution and Social Order in Eighteenth-Century France* (Ithaca, NY: Cornell University Press, 1976), 246–314.
70 Jean-Claude Vatin, *L'Algérie politique, histoire et société* (Paris: Fondation nationale des sciences politique, 1974), 121–6; Robert Aldrich, *The French Presence in the South Pacific, 1842–1940* (Honolulu: University of Hawaii Press, 1990), 139–40.

71 J. Ruedy, *Land Policy in Colonial Algeria: The Origins of the Rural Public Domain* (Los Angeles: University of California Press, 1967), 1.

72 Ibid., 13–105.

73 Aldrich, *The French Presence*, 114; Aldrich, *Greater France: A History of French Overseas Expansion* (New York: St Martin's Press, 1996), 206–8.

74 Ingrid Moses, "The Extension of Colonial Rule in Kaiser Wilhelmsland," in John A. Moses and Paul M. Kennedy, eds., *Germany in the Pacific and the Far East, 1870–1914* (Brisbane: University of Queensland Press, 1977), 288–309; L.H. Gann, "Economic Development in Germany's African Empire, 1884–1914," in *Colonialism in Africa, 1870–1960; Volume 4, The Economics of Colonialism* (Cambridge: Cambridge University Press, 1975), 219, 223–43.

75 Adam Hochschild has written an intelligent popular description of the Belgian Congo. *King Leopold's Ghost: A Story of Greed, Terror, and Heroism in Colonial Africa* (Boston: Houghton Mufflin Company, 1998). A thorough analysis of how a coercive concessionary economy operated is given in L.H. Gann and Peter Duignan, *The Rulers of Belgian Africa, 1884–1914* (Princeton, NJ: Princeton University Press, 1979).

76 Helmut Bley, *South-West Africa under German Rule, 1894–1914* (Evanston, Ill.: Northwestern University Press, 1971), 100–3, 113–19. Accounts of land-acquisition practices in South-West Africa appear in Mark Cocker's indictment of colonialism, *Rivers of Blood, Rivers of Gold: Europe's Conquest of Indigenous Peoples* (New York: Grove Press, 1998), 302–13; John H. Wellington, *South West Africa and Its Human Issues* (Oxford: Clarendon Press, 1967), 174–254.

77 John Iliffe, *Tanganyika under German Rule, 1905–1912* (Cambridge: Cambridge University Press, 1969), 56–63, 126–41, and *A Modern History of Tanganyika* (Cambridge: Cambridge University Press, 1979), 126–7.

78 Illife, *Tanganyika*, 126.

79 Illife, *A Modern History of Tanganyika*, 262, 450–1, 499–500.

80 J.M. Pieters, "Netherlands East Indies before the Second World War," in Afrika Instituut, Leiden, *Land Tenure Symposium: Tropical Africa – Netherlands East Indies before the Second World War* (Leiden: Universitaire Pers Leiden, 1951), 120–6; M.C. Ricklefs, *A History of Modern Indonesia since c. 1300* (Stanford, Calif.: Stanford University Press, 1993), 119–25; Daniel Headrick, *The Tentacles of Progress: Technology Transfer in the Age of Imperialism, 1850–1940* (New York: Oxford University Press, 1988), 219–50.

81 Geoffrey Hosking, *Russia: People and Empire, 1552–1917* (Cambridge, Mass.: Harvard University Press, 1997), 13–15.

82 Richard A. Pierce, *Russian Central Asia, 1867–1917: A Study in Colonial Rule* (Berkeley: University of California Press, 1960), 17–18.
83 Ibid., 122–3; Dominic Lieven, *Empire: The Russian Empire and its Rivals* (New Haven, Conn.: Yale University Press, 2000), 210.
84 Lieven, *Empire*, 217.
85 Steven L. Hoch, "The Serf Economy, the Peasant Family, and the Social Order," in Jane Burbank and David L. Ransel, eds., *Imperial Russia: New Histories for the Empire* (Bloomington: University of Indiana Press, 1998), 199–208; Jane Burbank, "Thinking Like an Empire: Estate and Reform in Imperial Russia" (unpublished paper), 2–9; Priscilla Roosevelt, *Life on the Russian Country Estate: A Social and Cultural History* (New Haven, NJ: Yale University Press, 1995), 220–38.
86 Christine D. Worobec, *Peasant Russia: Family and Community in the Post-Emancipation Period* (Princeton, NJ: Princeton University Press, 1991), 17–29; Boris Mironov, "The Peasant Commune after the Reforms of the 1860s," in Ben Eklof and Stephen Frank, eds., *The World of the Russian Peasant: Post-Emancipation Culture and Society* (Boston: Unwin Hyman, 1990), 32–3; Donald W. Treadgold, *The Great Siberian Migration: Government and Peasant in Resettlement from Emancipation to the First World War* (Princeton, NJ: Princeton University Press, 1957), 41–51.
87 John Warkentin, "Mennonite Agricultural Settlements of Southern Manitoba," *Geographical Review* 49 (1959), 344. Cultural adaptation is the subject of Royden Loewen, *Hidden Worlds: Revisiting the Mennonites of the 1870s* (Winnipeg: University of Manitoba Press, 2001).

CHAPTER TWO

1 Eric Stokes, *The English Utilitarians and India* (Oxford: Clarendon Press, 1959), 110–39; Ainslie T. Embree, "Landholding in India and British Institutions," in Robert Eric Frykenberg, ed., *Land Control and Social Structure in Indian History* (Madison: University of Wisconsin Press, 1969), 40–51; Nilmani Mukherjee and Frykenberg, "The Ryotwari System and Social Organization in the Madras Presidency," in Frykenberg, *Land Control*, 217–25.
2 There are differences between A.B. Guthrie's screenplay and Jack Schaefer's short novel. Guthrie, who wrote American historical-adventure novels, extended the dialogue and changed the names of the rancher and farmer to Richer and Stark (the spellings may differ), respectively. The German root words for these names happen to fit the character development in the movie. For an example of dialogue about property rights in the novel, see Jack Schaefer, *The Short Novels of*

Jack Schaefer (Boston: Houghton Mifflin Company, 1967), 90–1. For a modern recitation of Richer's view of history, see Robert H. Fletcher, *Free Grass to Fences: The Montana Cattle Range Story* (New York: University Publishers, 1960), 27–83.

3 "First peoples" or "indigenous peoples" are terms in current usage. Many people refer to themselves by their tribal name; however, a generic term – such as first peoples – is helpful in summary statements.

4 This book maintains that a history of property rights on frontiers around the globe exposes common themes in terms of ideas, actions, and dilemmas. An emphasis on similarities among frontiers has been disputed. Donald Denoon went down the path of comparison when he looked at settler societies in the Southern Hemisphere. His hemispheric focus was deliberate, for his aim was to discredit the American model of economic development and to point out local social and political factors. See Denoon, *Settler Capitalism: The Dynamics of Dependent Development in the Southern Hemisphere* (Oxford: Oxford University Press, 1983), 220–30. British imperial historians who write about land policy mention comparisons between British colonies and the United States; however, their attention to administrators was bound to accent peculiarities and variety. Although they wrote carefully documented accounts of individual colonies, they only added comparative conclusions. See, for example, the conclusions in Leslie Clement Duly, *British Land Policy at the Cape, 1795–1844: A Study of Administrative Procedures in the Empire* (Durham, NC: Duke University Press, 1968), 187–91.

5 Attracta Ingram, *A Political Theory of Rights* (Oxford: Clarendon Press, 1994), 27.

6 C.B. Macpherson, *Property: Mainstream and Critical Positions* (Toronto: University of Toronto Press, 1978), 202. A different conception of property, which stresses the rights of owners, is J.W. Harris, *Property and Justice* (Oxford: Clarendon Press, 1996).

7 Ingram, *Political Theory of Rights*, 30. On the complexity of the legal usage of the term "ownership," see also Tony Honoré, *Making Law Bind: Essays Legal and Philosophical* (Oxford: Clarendon Press, 1987), 161–92.

8 J.T. Kempe to Sir William Johnson, 12 Aug. 1765, in Milton W. Hamilton, ed., *The Papers of Sir William Johnson*, vol. 11 (Albany: University of the State of New York, 1953), 889. Hereafter *Johnson Papers*.

9 For some background, see William Johnson to Robert Leake, 9 March 1764, in *Johnson Papers*, vol. 4, 360.

10 For the early Cape practice, see Johannes Petrus van der Merwe, *The Migrant Farmer in the History of the Cape Colony*, trans. Roger B. Beck (Athens: Ohio University Press, 1995), 19–100.

11 Ibid., 99.

12 John C. Weaver, "'Beyond the Fatal Shore': Pastoral Squatting and the Occupation of Australia, 1826–1852," *American Historical Review* 101 (Oct. 1996), 1004–5.

13 Sabato, *Agrarian Capitalism*, 43.

14 United States Public Lands Commission, *Report of the Public Land Commission Created by Act of March 3, 1879, Relating to Public Lands in the Western Portion of the United States and to the Operation of Existing Land Laws* (Washington, DC: Government Printing Office, 1890), 511. Mary E. Young, "Congress Looks West: Liberal Ideology and Public Land Policy in the Nineteenth Century," in David M. Ellis, ed., *The Frontier and American Development: Essays in Honor of Paul Wallace Gates* (Ithaca, NY: Cornell University Press, 1969), 90–1.

15 Ernest Staples Osgood, *The Day of the Cattleman* (Minneapolis: University of Minnesota Press, 1929), 56–7; Joseph Nimmo, *Report in Regard to the Range and Ranch Cattle Business of the United States* (New York: Arno Press, 1972, reprint of 1885), 43–4.

16 M.P.K. Sorrenson, *Origins of the European Settlement in Kenya* (Nairobi: Oxford University Press, 1968), 140–1. Mwangi Wa-Githumo provides an account of land taking in *Land and Nationalism: The Impact of Land Expropriation and Land Grievances upon the Rise and Development of Nationalist Movements in Kenya, 1885–1939* (Washington, DC: University Press of America, 1981). On the contrasts between Kenya and Southern Rhodesia, see Dane Kennedy, *Islands of White: Settler Society and Culture in Kenya and Southern Rhodesia, 1890–1939* (Durham, NC: Duke University Press, 1987), 97. Robert M. Maxon concludes that the Colonial Office prevented the colony from becoming a white settler state. *Struggle for Kenya: The Loss and Reassertion of Imperial Initiative* (Rutherford, NJ: Fairleigh Dickinson University Press, 1993), 280–5. A narrow victory by black Africans against white settlers is recounted in C.J. Duer and G.L. Simpson, "Land and Murder in Colonial Kenya: The Leroghi Land Dispute and the Powys 'Murder' Case," *Journal of Imperial and Commonwealth History* 25 (Sept. 1997), 459–62.

17 Catherine Anne Wilson, *A New Lease on Life: Landlords, Tenants, and Immigrants in Ireland and Canada* (Montreal: McGill-Queen's University Press, 1994), 67–8.

18 Lieutenant Governor Sorell to Governor Lachlan Maquarie, 10 Aug. 1818, *Historical Records of Australia* series 3 (Library Committee of the Commonwealth Parliament, 1921), vol. 2, 345–7. Hereafter citations will refer to HRA and the volume.

19 Osgood, *Day of the Cattleman*, 185.

20 Oliver Gillespie, *South Canterbury: A Record of Settlement* (Timaru: Timaru Herald Company, 1971), 105–6.

21 Robert C. Ellickson, *Order without Law: How Neighbors Settle Disputes* (Cambridge, Mass.: Harvard University Press, 1991), 141–3, 191–206. This chapter owes much to the definitions and the stimulation of this thesis. Ellickson studies a ranching community to demonstrate how norms can provide order; however, he does not consider the initial sorting out of boundaries and access. He notes, with respect to the whalers, that norms that enrich one group's members may impoverish those outside the group.

22 Douglass North, *Institutions, Institutional Change and Economic Performance* (Cambridge: Cambridge University Press, 1990), 13–16, 69.

23 Ellickson, *Order without Law*, 249. For a study of the replacement of informal understandings when stakes were low and their replacement by legislation when the stakes increased, see Gary Libecap, "Economic Variables and the Development of the Law: The Case of Western Mineral Rights," in Lee Alston, Thráinn Eggertsson, and Douglass C. North, eds., *Empirical Studies in Institutional Change* (Cambridge: Cambridge University Press, 1996), 34–58.

24 North, *Institutions*, 36–45.

25 Bernard W. Sheehan, *Savagism and Civility: Indians and Englishmen in Colonial Virginia* (Cambridge: Cambridge University Press, 1980), 144–76.

26 On the question of how American historians have treated the question of similarities among frontiers, see Edward Countryman, "Indians, the Colonial Order, and the Social Significance of the American Revolution," *William and Mary Quarterly* 53(April 1996), 342–66. He challenges U.S. exceptionalism by focusing on Americans who were not free – namely, Indians and slaves.

27 Leonard Guelke and Robert Shell, "Landscape of Conquest: Frontier Water Alienation and Khoikhoi Strategies of Survival, 1652–1780," *Journal of Southern African Studies* 18 (Dec. 1992), 804–24. For relations between the Dutch and the Khoikhois from 1652 to 1720, see Richard Elphick, *Khoikhoi and the Founding of South Africa* (Johannesburg: Ravan Press, 1985). When explaining the collapse of Khoikhoi society near the Cape, he stresses a smallpox epidemic in 1713, while Guelke and Shell accent an assault on the ecology. The difference is one of emphasis. Elphick, *Khoikhoi*, 217–34.

28 Petrus Johannes van der Merwe, *Die noordwaartse beweging van die boere voor die groot trek (1770–1842)* (The Hague: W.P. Van Stockum & Zoon, 1937), 25–58; M.F. Katzen, "White Settlers and the Origins of a New Society," in Monica Wilson and Leonard Thompson, eds.,

The Oxford History of South Africa (Oxford: At the Clarendon Press, 1969), 212–13.

29 Van der Merwe, *The Migrant Farmer*, 209–48; Leonard Thompson, *Survival in Two Worlds: Moshoeshoe of Lesotho, 1786–1870* (Oxford: Clarendon Press, 1975), 219, 281–5; Noël Mostert, *Frontiers: The Epic of South Africa's Creation and the Tragedy of the Xhosa People* (New York: Alfred A. Knopf, 1992), 726–60. The best overall account of the first half of the nineteenth century is Timothy Keegan's *Colonial South Africa and the Origins of the Racial Order* (London: Leicester University Press, 1996). Of interest is William W. Collins, *Free Statia: Reminiscences of a Lifetime in the Orange Free State* (Cape Town: C. Struik, 1965; reprint of 1907 edition), 124–51, 153–6, 189–90, 220–37. See the important discussion of conflicts over land, water, and stock in Leonard Guelke and Robert Shell, "Landscape of Conquest: Frontier Water Alienation and Khoikhoi Strategies of Survival, 1652–1780," *Journal of Southern African Studies* 18, no. 4 (Dec. 1992), 803–24. For a book that stresses the state power of the colonizers, see Clifton C. Crais, *White Supremacy and Black Resistance in Pre-Industrial South Africa: The Making of the Colonial Order in the Eastern Cape, 1770–1865* (Cambridge: Cambridge University Press, 1992).

30 Richard White, *The Middle Ground: Indians, Empires, and Republics in the Great Lakes Region, 1650–1815* (Cambridge: Cambridge University Press, 1991), 489. For a parallel in South Africa, see Crais, *White Supremacy*, 96–121.

31 Edward M. Curr, *Recollections of Squatting in Victoria, then Called the Port Phillip District (From 1841 to 1851)* (Melbourne: George Robertson, 1851), 167.

32 On the murder of Aboriginals, see Don Watson, *Caledonia Australis: Scottish Highlanders on the Frontiers of Australia* (Sydney: Collins, 1984), 161–83; Jan Critchett, *A Distant Field of Murder: Western District Frontiers, 1834–1848* (Melbourne: Melbourne University Press, 1990), passim; Maurice French, *A Pastoral Romance: The Tribulation and Triumph of Squatterdom* (Toowoomba: University of Southern Queensland, 1990), passim; Noel Loos, *Invasion and Resistance: Aboriginal–European Relations on the North-Queensland Frontier, 1861–1897* (Canberra: Australian National University, 1979), 47–51. Mary Durack, *Kings in Grass Castles* (Condell: Corgi Books, 1985), 329–333. Durack is candid and critical about her father's raids; the quote is on 291.

33 *Government Gazette Hawke's Bay*, vol. 2, no. 37, 13 March 1861, 1–3; John Yule to the Superintendent of the Southern District, 26 Oct. 1846, Colonial Secretary, Incoming Letters, IA 1/46, National Archives of New Zealand.

34 Olson, *Power and Prosperity*, 60.

35 For Cape Colony, see van der Merwe, *The Migrant Farmer*, 59–100. For Australia and New Zealand, see Weaver, "Beyond the 'Fatal Shore,'" 995–1000; "Frontiers into Assets," *Journal of Imperial and Commonwealth History* 27 (Sept. 1999), 42–8. There are many accounts of using sheep with "scab" to scare off rivals. See Douglas Cresswell, *Squatter and Settler in the Wairarapa Country* (Wairarapa County Council, 1952), 31.

36 Charles Wayland Towne and Edward Norris Wentworth, *The Shepherd's Empire* (Norman: University of Oklahoma Press, 1945), 138.

37 Lemont K. Richardson, "Private Land Claims in Missouri," *Missouri Historical Review* 50 (1956), 285.

38 Bill O'Neal, *Cattlemen vs. Sheepherders: Five Decades of Violence in the West, 1880–1920* (Austin: Eakin Press, 1989), 16–20. Testimony of Dr M. Beshoar, Trinidad, Colorado, United States, Public Lands Commission, *Report of the Public Land Commission Created by Act of March 3, 1879, Relating to Public Lands in the Western Portion of the United States and to the Operation of Existing Land Laws* (Washington, DC: Government Printing Office, 1880), Testimony of Cornelius Downing Hendren, Walsenburg, Colorado, in ibid., 273.

39 Giles French, *Cattle Country of Peter French* (Portland, Ore.: Binfords & Mort, 1964), 151–2.

40 In a comparison of conflict and property allocation in the United States and Brazil, Lee J. Alston, Gary D. Libecap, and Bernardo Mueller find little serious conflict among emigrants over land east of the 100th meridian and little violent conflict between ranchers and homesteaders in the west. These dubious assertions misdirect their comparisons, but they do identify a low level of American government backing for homesteaders. The authors conclude, however, that American smooth settlement derived from little government intervention and that Brazil has too much government intervention. They failed to investigate American frontier violence rigorously. Alston, Libecap, and Mueller, "Property Rights and Conflict: A Comparison of Settlement of the U.S. Western and Brazilian Amazon Frontiers," in John H. Coatsworth and Alan M. Taylor, eds., *Latin America and the World Economy since 1800* (Cambridge, Mass.: David Rockefeller Center for Latin American Studies, 1998), 55–75.

41 Peter Burroughs, *Britain and Australia: A Study in Imperial Relations and Crown Lands Administration* (Oxford: Clarendon Press, 1967), 162.

42 The Royal Proclamation of 1763 is the best-known example; however, British authorities applied the same policy in southern Africa, Australia, and New Zealand. See van der Merew, *Die Noordwaarts*

beweging, 209–19; Weaver, "Beyond the 'Fatal Shore,'", 989; Weaver, "Frontiers into Assets," 19–29.

43 It is possible that the doctrine had its greatest initial trials on the frontiers of New York. There the Dutch established a policy of fair dealing with the Iroquois (Five Nations); the British believed in the strategic necessity of preventing direct dealings, because fraud with respect to these contracts might turn the Iroquois towards an alliance with the French. New York frontier land did in fact involve significant direct dealing and fraud. See Georgiana C. Nammack, *Fraud, Politics, and the Dispossession of the Indians: The Iroquois Land Frontier in the Colonial Period* (Norman: University of Oklahoma Press, 1969), 3–21.

44 Douglass C. North, *Structure and Change in Economic History* (New York: W.W. Norton, 1981), 36.

45 For Europeans who wanted enforceable rights, the challenge was how to individualize native title, to move from tribal collective interests to private plots. Governments could undertake acquisition and division. Another path was for indigenous peoples to break collective holding into plots and sell to individuals. This was supported at times by government measures: land courts (New Zealand after 1865) or executive acts (southern African republics and the United States by 1870s). There was ample room for falsehood and betrayal in these systems, and destitution also came to play a significant part in land alienation. A discussion of alternatives to breaking up collective ownership appears in Leonard A. Carlson, *Indians, Bureaucrats, and Land: The Dawes Act and the Decline of Indian Farming* (Westport, Conn.: Greenwood Press, 1981), 176–9.

46 Louis Pelzer, "A Cattleman's Commonwealth on the Western Range," *Mississippi Valley Historical Review* 13, no. 1 (June 1926), 30. See the New Zealand example of a combine cited in Weaver, "Frontiers into Assets," 40–1.

47 Kermit Hall, "The Legal Culture of the Great Plains," reprinted in John R. Wunder, ed., *Law and the Great Plains: Essays on the Legal History of the Heartland* (Westport, Conn.: Greenwood Press, 1996), 14.

48 Granville Stuart, "The End of the Cattle Range," in Ted Stone, ed., *The Cowboy Reader: Remembering the Open Range* (Red Deer, Alta.: Red Deer College Press, 1997), 244.

49 Rodman W. Paul, *The Far West and the Great Plains in Transition, 1859–1900* (New York: Harper and Row, 1988), 202. The opposite and dubious claim appears in Pelzer, "A Cattleman's Commonwealth," 36, and in Hazel Adele Pulling, "History of the Cattle Industry of Dakota," *South Dakota Historical Collections* 20 (1940), 520. H.L. Bentley, *Cattle Ranges of the Southwest* (Washington, DC: Government Printing Office, 1898), 6–9.

50 For example, Harold Hedges, *A Survey of the Cattle Industry in the Nebraska Sand Hills* (Lincoln: University of Nebraska, 1926), 15; R.T. Burdick, Martin Reinholt, and G.S. Klemmendson, *Cattle-Ranch Organization in the Mountains of Colorado* (Fort Collins: Colorado Experimental Station, 1928), 16; M.B. Johnson, *Cattle Ranch Organization and Management in Western South Dakota* (Brookings: South Dakota State College, 1930), 49–50; A.F. Voss and Harry Pearson, *Cattle Production on Wyoming's Mountain Valley Ranches* (Laramie: University of Wyoming, 1933), 35; C.A. Brennen, *The Public Range and the Livestock Industry of Nevada* (Reno: University of Nevada, 1935), 13.

51 Edward Everett Dale, "The Cherokee Strip Live Stock Association," *Chronicles of Oklahoma* 5 (1927), 71. Dale called this association the greatest livestock organization in the world. Stock associations did more than manage the range for members. They also worked to suppress rustling, secure advantageous freight rates, and enforce quarantines. Dale had been a small Oklahoma rancher before turning to history. Michael Malone, ed., *Historians and the American West* (Lincoln: University of Nebraska Press, 1983), 221.

52 Hall, "The Legal Culture," 14.

53 Many American historical assessments of vigilantism have sanctioned actions outside the law. For example, the histories of stockmen's associations stress their struggles against cattle rustling and say little about their function in controlling access to the range and the labour of cowboys. Biased writing, particularly by local historians, has promoted a regrettable romantic jocularity about lynching in the wild west. For an old but valuable discussion, see Richard Maxwell Brown, "The American Vigilante Tradition," in Hugh Davis Graham and Ted Robert Gurr, eds., *Violence in America: Historical and Comparative Perspectives* (Beverly Hills, Calif.: Sage Publications, revised edition, 1979), 153–78. Kermit Hall got around the question of violence on the plains by pointing to higher recent homicide rates that showed the southern states as more violent and by alleging that areas influenced by southern traditions were more prone to violence than areas with Scandinavian immigrants. Even if this is true, it does not address the question of range violence historically.

54 For blacklisting and blackballing, see Bob Lee and Dick Williams, *Last Grass Frontier: The South Dakota Stock Grower Heritage* (Sturgis, SD: Black Hills Publishers, 1964), 174; W. Turrentine Jackson, "The Wyoming Stock Growers' Association: Its Years of Temporary Decline, 1886–1890," *Agricultural History* 22 (1948), 261. For the critique of the claim of rights by first occupation, see Ingram, *Political Theory of Rights*, 56–8.

55 Helene Sara Zahler, *Eastern Workingmen and National Land Policy,*
    1829–1862 (New York: Columbia University Press, 1941), 193; Leslie
    E. Decker, "The Great Speculation: An Interpretation of Mid-
    Continent Pioneering," in Ellis, ed., *The Frontier in American Devel-*
    opment, 373; Allan Bogue, "The Iowa Claims Clubs: Symbol and Sub-
    stance," *Mississippi Valley Historical Review* 45 (Sept. 1958), 231–53.
    Squatters could file for a pre-emption right to hold the land until it
    came up for sale, but by the 1830s few bothered; they assumed that
    occupation would suffice. Donald Pisani provides a well-rounded
    account of squatters in California. He argues, perhaps too hopefully,
    that the squatter story involved a vision of equal access to the land.
    See Pisani, "Squatter Law in California, 1850–1858," *Western Histori-*
    cal Quarterly 25 (autumn 1994), 277–310. His reference to California
    claims clubs is at 281.
56 James E. Davis, *Frontier Illinois* (Bloomington: University of Indiana
    Press, 1998), 215.
57 Alfred Brunson, "A Methodist Circuit Rider's Horseback Tour from
    Pennsylvania to Wisconsin, 1835," in Reuben Gold Thwaites, ed., *Col-*
    lections of the State Historical Society of Wisconsin 15 (1900), 277–8.
58 W. Aitkin, *Journey up the Mississippi River from its Mouth to*
    Nauvoo, the City of the Latter Day Saints (Ashton-under-Lyne: John
    Williams, 1845), 15.
59 Bogue, "The Iowa Claims Clubs," 253.
60 Stephen C. LeSueur, *The 1838 Mormon War in Missouri* (Columbia:
    University of Missouri Press, 1987), 110.
61 Alan Taylor, "'To Man Their Rights': The Frontier Revolution," in
    Ronald Hoffman and Peter Albert, eds., *The Transforming Hand of*
    Revolution: Reconsidering the American Revolution as a Social Move-
    ment (Charlottesville: University Press of Virginia, 1995), 231–57.
62 A fine short account of some of these dealings appears in Thomas M.
    Doerflinger, *A Vigorous Spirit of Enterprise: Merchants and Economic*
    Development in Revolutionary Philadelphia (New York: W.W. Norton
    and Company, 1987), 314–29. For a detailed description of the opera-
    tions of one of the era's greatest speculators, see Barbara Ann
    Chernow, *Robert Morris: Land Speculator, 1790–1801* (New York:
    Arno Press, 1974).
63 There is a strain of admiration for the squatters among a number of
    American historians of the early republic. For an older, brilliant his-
    tory of the period that treats squatters sympathetically, see Merrill
    Jensen, *The New Nation: A History of the United States during the*
    Confederation, 1781–1789 (New York: Alfred A. Knopf, 1958), 357;
    for another sympathetic, but fuller account, see Taylor, "'To Man
    Their Rights'"; and "'A Kind of Warr': The Contest for Land on the

Northeastern Frontier, 1750–1820," *William and Mary Quarterly* 46 (Jan. 1989), 3–26. Also Pisani, "Squatter Law," 278, 310.

64 Historians have contributed to debates on the sources of American violence. See Edward Ayers, *Vengeance and Justice in the American South*; Richard Maxwell Brown, "Violence," in Clyde A. Milner, Carol A. O'Connor, and Martha A. Sandweiss eds., *The Oxford History of the American West* (New York: Oxford University Press, 1994), 393–423. Ayers argued that the U.S. record of violence originated partly from a southern code of direct action, exemplified by duelling. Southern traditions, including this one, spread westward. Brown draws attention to a bitter western struggle between labour and industrial corporations and describes it as the Western Civil War of Incorporation.

65 Van der Merwe, *Die noordwaartse beweging*, 32–110. This well-documented history provides information about the company's policies, its weakness, the land-occupation practices of the *trekboers*, the confrontation over habitat, and the slaughter of the Khoikhois. It attempts to defend the actions of the white settlers and argues that the company bears responsibility for allowing matters to get out of control on the frontiers. Van der Merwe draws many parallels between American and South African frontiers. Also see M.F. Katzen, "White Settlers and the Origins of a New Society, 1652–1778," in Monica Wilson and Leonard Thompson, eds., *The Oxford History of South Africa* (Oxford: At the Clarendon Press, 1969), 226–7.

66 For contemporary ideas on direct action and defiance of governments before the Great Trek, see André du Toit and Hermann Giliomee, *Afrikaner Political Thought: Analysis and Documents, Volume One: 1780–1850* (Berkeley: University of California Press, 1983), 127–63. For the continuity of settler practices in southern Africa, see van der Merwe, *The Migrant Farmer*. Afrikaner nationalists have argued that the Great Trek arose from a series of grievances against British authorities. They do not deny hunger for land as a motive. See, for example, Johannes Meintjes, *The Voortrekkers: The Story of the Great Trek and the Making of South Africa* (London: Cassell, 1973), 23. The grazing system was intrinsic to the frontier, and even Meintjes notes (39–40) that land regulations were a source of *boer* resentment and that land was a factor in the Great Trek.

67 Jorge Gelman, *Un funcionario en busca del estado: Pedro Andrés Garcia y la cuestión agraria bonaerense, 1810–1822* (Buenos Aires: Universidad Nacional de Quilmes, 1997), 11–14; Documento 7, 115–20.

68 Carl Abbott, "The Federal Presence," in *The Oxford History of the American West*, 470.

69 Weaver, "Beyond the 'Fatal Shore,'" 987; Mostert, *Frontiers*, 573.

70 In 1851, the Métis of Red River had a pitched battle with the Sioux on the Grand Coteau of the Missouri, on American territory. Margaret Arnett MacLeod and W.L. Morton, *Cuthbert Grant of Grantown: Warden of the Plains of the Red River* (Toronto: McClelland and Stewart, 1974), 143–151. The rebellions of 1870 and 1885 were closer to political uprisings than to violent encounters between indigenous people and invading settlers, although in 1885 the Metis rebels made some Indian allies.

71 This goes to the heart of a contradiction noted by Patricia Limerick, who observed how disrespectful landhunters were with respect to the public domain, but how jealous they were of individual, exclusive property rights. Patricia Nelson Limerick, *The Legacy of Conquest: The Unbroken Past of the American West* (New York: W.W. Norton, 1987), 62.

72 Evidence taken from Henry Dangar, 5 June 1844, New South Wales, *Report of the Select Committee on Crown Land Grievances, Minutes with Appendix, Minutes of Evidence, and Replies to Circular Letters* (Sydney: William John Row, 1844), 23.

73 Gene M. Gressley, *Bankers and Cattlemen* (Lincoln: University of Nebraska Press, 1966), 148–9. Gressley observes that once grazers had to make strategic purchases of land to defend their access to the range, they needed large dollops of eastern capital.

74 Pent-up demand was evident even in the least commercially sensitive frontier, Cape Colony. Leslie Clement Duly, *British Land Policy at the Cape: A Study of Administrative Procedures in the Empire* (Durham, NC: Duke University Press, 1968), 75–7; A.J. Christopher, *The Crown Lands of British South Africa, 1853–1914* (Kingston: Limestone Press, 1984), 22.

75 These contrasting "needs" are recognized by economists, who see them in terms of a search for universal principles of economic behaviour, and by historians, who take sides in a social debate about the legitimacy of elite positions backed by law versus the claims of people who justify their possession by labour.

76 For a convincing study that argues that Locke's theory of property was based mainly on the idea of a maker's right, see Gopal Sreenivasan, *The Limits of Lockean Rights in Property* (New York: Oxford University Press, 1995), 59–92. In the early modern period, the European empires each developed distinctive rituals for asserting sovereignty. English practices accented the application of labour to land. Patricia Seed, *Ceremonies of Possession in Europe's Conquest of the New World, 1492–1640* (Cambridge: Cambridge University Press, 1995), 31–40.

77 Ellickson, *Order without Law*, 138.

78 For example, because Locke stressed a justification by labour, his theory is critical of acquisition by gift and inheritance. See Sreenivasan, *The Limits of Lockean Rights*, 95–119.

79 North, *Institutions*, 17.

80 See, for example, John Roamer, *Theories of Distributive Justice* (Cambridge, Mass.: Harvard University Press, 1996), passim.

81 Paul W. Gates, *Landlords and Tenants on the Prairie Frontier: Studies in American Land Policy* (Ithaca, NY: Cornell University Press, 1974), 12.

82 Thomas Perkins Abernethy, *Western Lands and the American Revolution* (New York: Russell and Russell, 1959), 368–9.

83 For a favourable analysis of rural land dealing, see Allan Bogue, *From Prairie to Corn Belt: Framing on the Illinois and Iowa Prairies in the Nineteenth Century* (Chicago: University of Chicago Press, 1963); Robert P. Swierenga, *Pioneers and Profits: Land Speculation on the Iowa Frontier* (Ames: Iowa University Press, 1968): for the general argument in support of North, see 59–60.

84 John H. Haeger, "Economic Development of the American West," in Roger L. Nichols, ed., *American Frontier and Western Issues: A Historiographical Review* (Westport, Conn.: Greenwood Press, 1986), 36.

85 For Gates's progressivism, see Lawrence B. Lee, "Introduction," in Paul Gates, *Land and Law in California: Essays on Land Policies* (Ames: Iowa: Iowa State University Press, 1991), xiv–xviii; Frederick Merck, "Forward," in Ellis, *The Frontier in American Development*, x–xxx. A first-hand account of dispossession is provided in the diary of Omar H. Morse, which appears in James M. Marshall, *Land Fever: Dispossession and the Frontier Myth* (Lexington: University of Kentucky Press, 1986).

86 The Colonial Office in the 1830s, for example, was pulled by a number of conflicting interests. Confusion is depicted in John S. Galbraith, *Reluctant Empire: British Policy on the South African Frontier, 1834–1854* (Berkeley: University of California Press, 1963), passim; Claudia Orange, *The Treaty of Waitangi* (Wellington: Bridget Williams Books, 1987), 19–31. I do not look at the plan for colonization promoted by Edward Gibbon Wakefield, because when archival material on actual settlement is reviewed it quickly collapses, even in the two colonies that were assumed to be Wakefieldian: South Australia and Canterbury.

87 Galbraith, *Reluctant Empire*, 61.

88 Duly, *British Land Policy*, 190; Weaver, "Beyond the 'Fatal Shore,'" 985–88.

89 Robbins, *Our Landed Heritage*, 290

90 Ernest Sinclair MacDermott, *Manual of the Practice of the Land Title Office Sydney* (Sydney: Websdale, Shoesmith and Company, 1904). For

an excellent history of land titles in a single jurisdiction, see Robert
Crundwell, Hilary Golder, and Robert Wood, *From Parchment to
Passwords: A History of the Lands Titles Office of New South Wales*
(Sydney: Hale & Iremonger, 1995).

91 13 Victoriae, No.1. An Ordinance to regulate the Occupation of Waste
Lands of the Crown in the Province of New Ulster. [23rd August
1849]; 41 Victoriae, No.29. An act to regulate the Sale or other
Disposal of the Land of the Crown in New Zealand [10th December
1877].

92 Peter Charles Hoffer, *Law and People in Colonial America* (Baltimore,
Md: Johns Hopkins University Press, 1992), 70.

93 Gordon Wood, *The Radicalism of the American Revolution* (New
York: Alfred Knopf, 1992), 116–7, 181. Wood provides an argument
against his own thesis of the revolution as a radical departure when he
notes that a tenantry and rent-producing estates could not be secure
investments in a part of the world where land was plentiful and cheap.
That condition was common to non-American frontiers as well. Ibid.,
113–4.

94 Allan Kulikoff, *From British Peasants to Colonial American Farmers*
(Chapel Hill: University of North Carolina Press, 2000), 285; Robert
A. East, *Business Enterprise in the American Revolutionary Era* (New
York: Columbia University Press, 1938), 224–6.

95 Helene Sara Zahler, *Eastern Workingmen and National Land Policy,
1829–1862* (New York: Columbia University Press, 1941), 19–98.

96 Avner Offer, *Property and Politics, 1870–1914: Landownership, Law,
Ideology, and Urban Development in England* (Cambridge: Cambridge
University Press, 1981), 1–104; A.W.B. Simpson, *A History of the
Land Law* (Oxford: Clarendon Press, 1986), 270–91; J. Stuart
Anderson, *Lawyers and the Making of English Land Law* (Oxford:
Clarendon Press, 1992), 85–136.

97 Thomas D. Clark and John W. Guice, *Frontiers in Conflict: The Old
Southwest, 1795–1830* (Albuquerque: University of New Mexico Press,
1989), 81.

98 Edward Curr, *Recollections of Squatting in Victoria, then Called the
Port Philip District (From 1841 to 1851)*, 165.

99 North, *Institutions*, 31.

100 For the idea of a bundle of rights and a discussion of the persistence of
communal rights, see Robert W. Gordon, "Paradoxical Property," in
John Brewer and Susan Staves, eds., *Early Modern Conceptions of
Property* (London: Routledge, 1996), 95–108.

101 Even before land was sold in Maryland and Virginia, ship's captains
received rights to land for transporting indentured servants, and these
servants were entitled to acreage on their freedom. Land jobbers

bought the captains' warrants and the servants' head rights and used them to patent the best land on river valleys. Abbot Emerson Smith, "The Indentured Servant and Land Speculation in Seventeenth Century Maryland," *American Historical Review* 40 (April 1935), 467–72.

102 Sir Thomas Brisbane to Lord Bathurst, 10 April 1823, *HRA* (see note 18, above), series 1, vol. 10, 834. By custom, the public may have accepted these promises, but they could not be enforced in the courts. Enid Campbell, "Promises of Land from the Crown: Some Questions of Equity in Colonial Australia," *University of Tasmania Law Review* 13 (1994), 1–42.

103 Richardson, "Private Land Claims," 285; Chernow, *Robert Morris*, 126–7, 144–69, 175; Beverley W. Bond, "Introduction: John Cleve Symmes, Pioneer," in Bond, ed., *The Correspondence of John Cleve Symmes: Founder of the Miami Purchase* (New York: Macmillan, 1926), 16–22. On the hazards of land speculation on a large scale in the mid-nineteenth century, see Henry Cohen, "Vicissitudes of an Absentee Landlord: A Case Study," in Ellis, ed., *The Frontier in American Development*, 192–208. In regions where Spanish or Mexican grants had been made, squatters and holders of alleged grants clashed in the courts for years. See Gordon Morris Bakken, *Practicing Law in Frontier California* (Lincoln: University of Nebraska Press, 1991), 75–6.

104 Burroughs, *Britain and Australia*, 44, 77.

105 George Washington to Presley Neville, 16 June 1794, in C.W. Butterfield, ed., *Washington–Crawford Letters. Being the Correspondence between George Washington and William Crawford, from 1767 to 1781, Concerning Western Lands* (Cincinnati: Robert Clarke and Company, 1877), 79.

106 Joseph Weller to Jackson Barwise (?), 26 April 1841, Weller Brothers Papers (copies of originals in Dixon Library of the Mitchell Library, Sydney), folder 1, MS 0872, Alexander Turnbull Library, National Library of New Zealand.

107 John Clarke, *Land, Power, and Economics on the Frontier of Upper Canada* (Montreal: McGill-Queen's University Press, 2001), 375.

108 Gates, *Landlords and Tenants*, 83–4.

109 Ingram, *A Political Theory of Rights*, 47.

110 Nozick, *Anarchy, State, and Utopia* (New York: Basic Books, 1974), 150.

111 John Locke, *Two Treatises of Government*, critical edition with intro. by Peter Laslett (Cambridge: At the University Press, 1967), The Second Treatise, section 28, 306.

112 Sreenivasan contends that Nozick's modernized Lockean theory leaves the landless worse off than they would have been under the terms of Locke's theory of property rights because it had included a place for

charity and the right of people to labour. Sreenivasan, *The Limits of Lockean Rights*, 120–39.

113 Nozick, *Anarchy*, 177. Harris sees the idea of an untainted original acquisition – creation-without-wrong – as implausible or utopian. *Property and Justice*, 200–4.

114 Richard H. Bartlett, *Native Title in Australia* (Sydney: Butterworths, 2000), 531–64; *Economist* (23–29 March 2002), 33.

115 Nozick, *Anarchy*, 231. In 1977, Tony Honoré published a critique of Nozick's idea of just transactions legitimizing property rights. He pointed out that such a system would have to provide for a redistribution arrangement "when the moral basis on which they originally rested has been eroded." The article was reprinted in Honoré, *Making Law Bind*, 215–26, quote at 219.

116 In the United States, treaty disputes have been dealt with through a federal commission. David Wishart, "Belated Justice: A Comparison of the Indian Claims Commission and the Waitangi Tribunal," unpublished conference paper, Land and Law Conference, Newcastle, New South Wales, July 1999.

117 An excellent review of the many issues involved in a restitution exercise appears in Urban Foundation, *A Land Claims Court for South Africa? Exploring the Issues* (Johannesburg: Urban Foundation, 1993), 2–33.

118 Roemer, *Theories of Distributive Justice* (Cambridge, Mass.: Harvard University Press, 1996), 91.

119 For a logical dissection of legal and political questions surrounding the crown's fiduciary responsibilities in Canada, see Leonard Ian Rotman, *Parallel Paths: Fiduciary Doctrine and the Crown–Native Relationship in Canada* (Toronto: University of Toronto Press, 1996).

120 H.C. Shepstone, quoted in W.A. Stals, "Die kwessie van naturelle-eiendomsreg op Grond in Transvaal, 1838–1884," *Argiefjaarboek vir Suid-Afrikaanse geskiedenis* 35, no. 2 (1972), 33. From its foundation, the South African Republic prohibited non-whites from holding land titles. There were individual exceptions. T.R.H. Davenport and K.S. Hunt, eds., *The Right to the Land* (Cape Town: David Philip, 1974), 31–61. For the importance of landownership as an economic springboard in South Africa, see Colin Murray, *Black Mountain: Land, Class and Power in the Eastern Orange Free State, 1880s to 1980s* (Edinburgh: Edinburgh University Press, 1992).

121 For a useful introduction, see Leonard Thompson and Howard Lamar, "Comparative Frontier History," in Lamar and Thompson, eds., *The Frontier in History: North America and South Africa Compared* (New Haven, Conn.: Yale University Press, 1981), 3–13. Also see Donna J. Guy and Thomas E. Sheridan, "On Frontiers: The Northern and

Southern Edges of the Spanish Empire in the Americas," in Guy and Sheridan, eds., *Contested Ground: Comparative Frontiers on the Northern and Southern Edges of the Spanish Empire* (Tucson: University of Arizona Press, 1998), 3–15.

122 Leonard Thompson, *Survival in Two Worlds: Moshoeshoe of Lesotho, 1786–1870* (Oxford: At the Clarendon Press, 1975), 106.

123 For an extended discussion of the evolving forms of contact between Europeans and first peoples, and of the impact of political organization and the weight of numbers, see Richard White, *The Middle Ground: Indians, Empires, and Republics in the Great Lakes Region, 1650–1815* (Cambridge: Cambridge University Press, 1991), passim.

124 Silvio Barretta and John Markoff, quoted in Guy and Sheridan, "On Frontiers," 10. Terry G. Jordan and Matti Kaups, *The American Backwoods Frontier: An Ecological Interpretation* (Baltimore, Md.: Johns Hopkins University Press, 1989), 31.

125 Duly, *British Land Policy*, 81–4; Galbraith, *Reluctant Empire*, 181.

126 Thompson and Lamar, *The Frontier in History*, 11; Walter Nugent, "Frontiers and Empires in the Late Nineteenth Century," in Patricia Nelson Limerick, Clyde A. Milner, and Charles E. Rankin, ed., *Trails: Toward a New Western History* (Lawrence: University of Kansas Press, 1991), 170–81.

127 *Andrew Smith's Journal of His Expedition into the Interior of South Africa, 1834–36*, ed. William F. Lyle (Cape Town: A.A. Balkema, 1975), 47.

128 Appendix B, *Lord Durham's Report on the Affairs of British North America*, ed. Sir Charles Lucas (Oxford: Clarendon Press, 1912; reprinted 1970), vol. III, 63.

129 Galbraith, *Reluctant Empire*, 227–9, 242–76. In 1835, Governor Benjamin D'Urban had annexed a region on the eastern frontier and was immediately forced by the Colonial Office to renounce it, but this was a relatively small region.

130 Martin Legassick, "The Northern Frontier to 1820: The Emergence of the Griqua People," in Richard Elphick and Hermann Giliomee, *The Shaping of South African Society, 1652–1820* (Cape Town: Longman Penguin, 1979), 278.

131 Douglas W. Allen, "What Are Transactions Costs?" *Research in Law and Economics* 14 (1991), 1–18.

132 A fine, brief description of this phenomenon appears in Byron Farwell, *Queen Victoria's Little Wars* (New York: W.W. Norton, 1972), 220–3.

133 Daniel Feller, *The Public Lands of Jacksonian Politics* (Madison: University of Wisconsin Press, 1984), 16–17.

134 Richard B. Morris, *The Forging of the Union, 1781–1789* (New York: Harper and Row, 1987), 229; R. Douglas Hurt, *The Ohio Frontier:*

Crucible of the Old Northwest, 1720–1830 (Bloomington: University of Indiana Press, 1996), 144–8; John K. Mahon, "Indian–United States Military Situation, 1775–1848," in Wilcomb Washburn, ed., *History of Indian-White Relations,* vol. 4 (Washington, DC: Smithsonian Institution, 1988), 162.

135 William W. Savage, *The Cherokee Strip Live Stock Association* (Columbia: University of Missouri Press, 1973), 72–3, 79–83.

136 Report of Lieutenant-Colonel Joseph Foveaux to ———, 10 Sept. 1808, in *HRA,* series 1, vol. 6, 663. Tim Bonyhady interprets Bligh's conduct as I do; *The Colonial Earth* (Melbourne: Miegunyah Press, 2000), 49–65.

137 Quoted in van der Merwe, *Die noordwaartse bewging,* 212.

138 New South Wales, 4 William IV, No. 10. An Act for protecting the Crown Lands of this Colony from encroachment, intrusion, and trespass. [28th August 1833].

139 Elliott West, "American Frontier," in Clyde A. Milner, Carol A. O'Connor, and Martha A. Sandweiss, eds., *The Oxford History of the American West* (New York: Oxford University Press, 1994), 144–5.

140 Robert D. Mitchell, *Commercialism and Frontier: Perspectives on the Early Shenandoah Valley* (Charlottesville: University of Virginia Press, 1977), 78–81.

141 Canadian historical geographers working on Ontario have made clever use of records to distinguish among speculators. Randy Widdis, "Motivation and Scale: A Method of Identifying Land Speculators in Upper Canada," *Canadian Geographer* 23 (1979), 337–51. John Clarke discusses the question of who was a speculator in conjunction with a study of power; *Land, Power, and Economics,* 295–335.

142 Governor William Bligh to William Windham, 31 Oct. 1807, Commonwealth of Australia, *Historical Records of Australia: Series I: Governor's Despatches to and from England,* vol. 1 (Library Committee of the Commonwealth Parliament, 1916), 149.

143 Bogue, "The Iowa Claims Clubs," 236.

144 Edward McConnell, quoted in Davis, *Frontier Illinois,* 214.

145 Clarke, *Land, Power, and Economics,* 155–83, 331–5. J.K. Johnson, *Becoming Prominent: Regional Leadership in Upper Canada, 1791–1841* (Kingston: McGill-Queen's University Press, 1989), 51–9.

146 Clarke, *Land, Power, and Economics,* 301.

147 David Ward, *The Autobiography of David Ward* (New York: Private Printing, 1912), 26. Ward looked for timber lands and in payment received a quarter of what he found for clients.

148 John Mack Faragher, *Sugar Creek: Life on the Illinois Prairie* (New Haven, Conn.: Yale University Press, 1986), 184–5.

149 Clarke, *Land, Power, and Economics*, 161. The Canada Company encountered squatters on the crown land that it bought. Roger D. Hall, "The Canada Company, 1826–1843" (PhD dissertation, Cambridge University, 1973), 199–202.

150 Van der Merwe, *Die noordwaartse beweging*, 176–240.

151 Ibid., 256–78, 307–21, 342–53.

152 Edward Everett Dale, *The Range Cattle Industry: Ranching on the Great Plains from 1865 to 1925* (Norman: University of Oklahoma, 1960), 125–45. Written in 1925 and first published in 1930, this book remains useful as a source for certain details. In recent years, there has been a revived interest in western history that accents the corporate interests and government collaborations that so often determined resource allocations. See, for example, Limerick, *The Legacy of Conquest*.

153 Chernow, *Robert Morris*, 54.

154 C. Peter Magrath, *Yazoo: The Case of Fletcher v. Peck* (New York: W.W. Norton, 1967), 14.

155 Gates, *Landlords and Tenants*, 176.

156 Joseph M. Powell, *The Public Lands of Australia Felix: Settlement and Land Appraisal in Victoria with Special Reference to the Western Plains* (Melbourne: Oxford University Press, 1970), 144–5; W. Keith Hancock, *Discovering Monaro: A Study of Man's Impact on His Environment* (Cambridge: At the University Press, 1972), 90–1.

157 Charles Sellers, *The Market Economy: Jacksonian America, 1815–1846* (New York: Oxford University Press, 1991), 290–2, 312–14.

158 There were as many as ten, but the major ones included Otago and Canterbury, which had public land. W.P. Morrell, *The Provincial System in New Zealand* (Christchurch: Whitcombe and Tory, 1964), 69–104, 278–9; Keith Sinclair, *A History of New Zealand* (Auckland: Penguin Books, revised edition, 1984), 108–11; Weaver, "The Social Construction of Property," 44–6.

159 Robin Fisher, *Contact and Conflict: Indian–European Relations in British Columbia, 1774–1890* (Vancouver: University of British Columbia Press, 1977), 160.

160 Locke, *Two Treaties of Government*, II, section 27. For a discussion and critique of this theory, see Matthew H. Kramer, *John Locke and the Origins of Private Property: Philosophical Explorations of Individualism, Community, and Equality* (Cambridge: Cambridge University Press, 1997), 93–150.

161 See the argument in Michael Adas, *Machines as the Measure of Men: Science, Technology, and Ideologies of Western Dominance* (Ithaca, NY: Cornell University Press, 1989), 210–18.

162 Nicholas Canny, *Kingdom and Colony: Ireland and the Atlantic World* (Baltimore, Md.: The Johns Hopkins University Press, 1988), 24.

163 Adams, quoted in Cyrus Thomas, "Introduction," in Charles C. Royce and Cyrus Thomas, *Indian Land Cessions in the United States; Eighteenth Annual Report of the Bureau of American Ethnology* (Washington, DC: Government Printing Office, 1899), 536.

164 Henry Jones, *The New Valuations; or, the Case of the South Australian Squatter Fairly Treated* (Melbourne: Henry Tolman Dwight, 1864), 10.

165 William Cronon, *Changes in the Land: Indians, Colonists, and the Ecology of New England* (New York: Hill and Wang, 1983), 19–33.

166 Donald Worster, *Nature's Economy: A History of Ecological Ideas* (Cambridge: Cambridge University Press, second edition, 1994), 27. While many adherents of popular Christianity believe that humans have been given the earth to do with as they wish, Judaeo–Christian ideas of creation are more subtle. See Robert R. Gottfried, *Economics, Ecology, and the Roots of Western Faith: Perspectives from the Garden* (London: Rowman & Littlefield, 1995), 29–62.

167 Worster, *Nature's Economy*, 55.

168 Rist, *The History of Development*, 37.

169 Boyd Hilton, *The Age of Atonement: The Influence of Evangelicalism on Social and Economic Thought, 1795–1865* (Oxford: Clarendon, 1988), 32–5; *Corn, Cash, Commerce: The Economics of the Tory Governments, 1815–1830* (Oxford: Oxford University Press, 1977), 314.

170 Kramer, *John Locke*, 239.

171 Sreenivasan, *The Limits of Lockean Rights*, 143.

172 Joan Thirsk, "Agricultural Policy: Public Debate and Legislation," in Thirsk, ed., *Agricultural Change: Policy and Practice, 1500–1750* (Cambridge: Cambridge University Press, 1990), 214.

173 J.M. Neeson, "Parliamentary Enclosure and the Disappearance of the English Peasantry, Revisited," *Research in Economic History*, Supplement 5, Part A (London: JAI Press, 1989), 114. Marx argued that the historical basis for industry was to be found in what he considered the classic mode of English agriculture, which he thought began in the sixteenth century with enclosures. A complex account of English agricultural capitalism is found in Keith Tribe, *Genealogies of Capitalism* (London: Macmillan, 1981), 35–100. Tribe points out that English agriculture afforded a variety of opportunities for capitalism.

174 John G. Gazley, *The Life of Arthur Young, 1741–1820* (Philadelphia: American Philosophical Society, 1973), 322.

175 Ibid., 77–80, 161–9, 306–59, 436–9.

176 C.A. Bayly, *Imperial Meridian: The British Empire and the World, 1780–1830* (London, 1989), 121.

177 Arthur Young, *General Report on Enclosures* (New York: Augustus M. Kelley, 1971; Reprints of Economic Classics), 37–8.

178 Roger E. Backhouse, *Economists and the Economy: The Evolution of Economic Ideas* (London, 1994), 35. For a more complete discussion, see Donald Winch, *Riches and Poverty: An Intellectual History of Political Economy in Britain, 1750–1834* (Cambridge, 1996), 349–88.

179 Winch, *Riches and Poverty,* 351–3.

180 Robert Gourlay, *Statistical Account of Upper Canada,* abridged and with intro. by S.R. Mealing (Toronto: McClelland and Stewart, 1974), 308.

181 Edward Gibbon Wakefield is presumed to have influenced Buller's recommendation of a fixed and sufficient price for land, but the notion of using prices and taxes to discourage passive speculators was not unusual. Buller's account formed an appendix to Lord Durham's report on the troubles in the Canadas. Appendix B, *Lord Durham's Report,* vol. 3, 81–113.

182 In 1805, the reform-minded Batavian government at the Cape established a Commission for Stock Raising and Agriculture in hopes of beginning to eliminate grazing and build up intensive agriculture. Van der Merwe, *The Migrant Farmer,* 141. Donald Moodie, quoted in van der Merwe, *Die noordwaatrse beweging,* 324–5.

183 Osler, Hammond, Nanton to Arthur Cox, 12 Nov. 1912, file 11, box 11, Arthur Cox Papers, M281, Glenbow Institute.

184 Europeans were also assisted in their colonization efforts by the biota that they imported from home and their resistance to assorted diseases that accompanied them. See Alfred Crosby, *Ecological Imperialism: The Biological Expansion of Europe, 900–1900* (Cambridge: Cambridge University Press, 1986), 146–308; Jared Diamond, *Guns, Germs, and Steel: The Fates of Human Societies* (New York: W.W. Norton, 1999), 85–214.

185 On the decline of biodiversity, see Edward O. Wilson, *The Diversity of Life* (Cambridge, Mass.: Belknap Press of Harvard University Press, 1992), 215–80.

CHAPTER THREE

1 Washington to William Crawford, 17 Sept. 1767, quoted in John Alexander Williams, *West Virginia: A Bicentennial History* (New York: W.W. Norton and Company, 1976), 14. Williams has written a splendid, concise account of land speculation in western Virginia, ibid., 3–27. The letter was cited too in Thomas Perkins Abernethy, *Western Lands and the American Revolution* (New York: Russell and Russell, 1959), 69.

2 James Grindell to Alex McLean, 24 Feb. 1865, Donald McLean Papers, ms. 32, folder 954, Alexander Turnbull Library, National Library of New Zealand.

3 John B. Thomas to Joseph Ames, 12 July 1885, letterbook, 1881–1889, box 3, John B. Thomas Papers, accession 141, American Heritage Center (henceforth AHC), University of Wyoming.

4 C.A. Allison to S.A. Guthrie, 2 Nov. 1902, folder 1902, box 2, accession 923, AHC.

5 This estimate attempts to exclude mountainous land or desserts.

6 Paul Hirst and Grahame Thompson, *Globalization in Question: The International Economy and the Possibilities of Governance* (Cambridge, Mass.: Polity Press, 1996), 31.

7 Charles Durand, *Reminiscences of Charles Durand of Toronto, Barrister* (Toronto: Hunter, Rose Co., 1897), 31.

8 William W. Collins, *Free Statia: Reminiscences of a Lifetime in the Orange Free State* (Cape Town: C. Struik, 1965; reprint of 1907 edition), 17.

9 Edward M. Curr, *Recollections of Squatting in Victoria, then Called the Port Phillip District (From 1841 to 1851)* (Melbourne: George Robertson, 1851), 179.

10 *Autobiography of E.D. Swan*, 20 and 64–6, folder 6, box 1, accession 371, AHC.

11 Alfred W. Crosby, *Ecological Imperialism: The Biological Expansion of Europe, 900–1900* (Cambridge: Cambridge University Press, 1986), 172–94, 270–308; Jared Diamond, *Guns, Germs, and Steel: The Fate of Human Societies* (London: W.W. Norton, 1997), 157–75.

12 Rev. Henry William Haygarth, *Recollections of Bush Life in Australia, during a Residence of Eight Years in the Interior* (London: John Murray, 1864), 121. Thomas R. Dunlap suggests that, among the new societies of the English-speaking world, attitudes towards Nature in the British dominions were more closely linked to those in England than was the case in the United States. As well, Dunlap claims that the United States alone saw the emergence of a spiritual movement identified with Nature and wilderness. *Nature and the English Diaspora: Environment and History in the United States, Canada, Australia, and New Zealand* (New York: Cambridge University Press, 1999). For an account of Australian attitudes towards Nature that depicts independence and tensions between the spiritual and the exploitative, see Tim Bonyhady, *The Colonial Earth* (Melbourne: Miegunyah Press, 2000).

13 Terms for Land Grant in New Colonies, reproduced in *Royal Instructions to British Governors, 1670–1776*, vol. II (New York: American Historical Association, 1936; reprinted Octagon Books, 1967), 528.

These instructions went to the governors of Georgia, East Florida, West Florida, Quebec, and Nova Scotia.

14 Quoted in James Lemon, *The Best Poor Man's Country: A Geographical Study of Early Southeastern Pennsylvania* (Baltimore, Md.: Johns Hopkins Press, 1972), 57.

15 Peter Burroughs, *Britain and Australia, 1831–1855: A Study in Imperial Relations and Crown Lands Administration* (Oxford: Clarendon Press, 1967), 121; Pamela Stratham, ed., *The Tanner Letters: A Pioneer Saga of Swan River and Tasmania, 1831–1845* (Nedlands: University of Western Australia Press, 1981), xv–xviii.

16 Alan Taylor, *Liberty Men and Great Proprietors: The Revolutionary Settlement on the Maine Frontier, 1769–1820* (Chapel Hill: University of North Carolina Press, 1990), 231.

17 Donald Worster, *Under Western Skies: Nature and History in the American West* (New York: Oxford University Press, 1992), 27–8.

18 Joseph M. Powell, *The Public Lands of Australia Felix: Settlement and Land Appraisal in Victoria with Special Reference to the Western Lands* (Melbourne: Oxford University Press, 1970), 119.

19 Daniel Feller, *The Public Lands in Jacksonian Politics* (Madison: University of Wisconsin Press, 1984), passim.

20 Donald Pisani, *From the Family Farm to Agribusiness: The Irrigation Crusade in California and the West* (Berkeley: University of California Press, 1984); Donald Worster, *Rivers of Empire: Water, Aridity, and the Growth of the American West* (New York: Oxford University Press, 1985).

21 For a study on the persistence of concepts of property and property law on a frontier without institutionalized law and order, see John Philip Reid, *Law for the Elephant: Property and Social Behavior on the Overland Trail* (San Marino, Calif.: Huntington Library), 335–64. Reid argues that migrants on the overland trails took with them a firm sense of private property.

22 Paul W. Gates, *Landlords and Tenants on the Prairie Frontier: Studies in American Land Policy* (Ithaca, NY: Cornell University Press, 1973), 53.

23 R. Wright, *The Bureaucrats' Domain* (Melbourne: Oxford University Press, 1989), 41.

24 There has been a question as to whether the Royal Proclamation of 1763 was a strong and enduring feature of British policy or merely, as Philip Deloria expresses it, "a blip on the wide screen of history." It appears from British frontier policy in Australia, Cape Colony, and New Zealand that it was more than a blip. See Deloria, "Revolution, Religion, and Culture in Multicultural History," *William and Mary Quarterly* 53 (April 1996), 369.

25 See, for example, the activities of Thomas Jefferson's father and Patrick Henry's father. Robert Douthat Meade, *Patrick Henry: Patriot in the Making* (Philadelphia: J.B. Lippincott, 1957), 32–3.

26 Virginius Dabney, *Virginia: The New Dominion* (New York: Doubleday and Company, 1971), 93; Lewis A. Thomas, *For King and Country: The Maturing of George Washington, 1748–1760* (New York: HarperCollins, 1993), 12–20. On the origins and development of the Fairfax claim, see Fairfax Harrison, *The Proprietors of the Northern Neck: Chapters of Culpepper Genealogy* (Richmond: Old Dominion Press, 1926), 74–88, 125–31.

27 Kenneth Bailey, *The Ohio Company of Virginia and the Westward Movement, 1748–1792: A Chapter in the History of the Colonial Frontier* (Glendale: Arthur H. Clark Company, 1939), 17–60. Grant of Land in Ohio Country, in Leonard Woods Larabee, *Royal Instructions to British Colonial Governors, 1670–1776* (New York: Octagon, 1967), vol. II, 682.

28 Gordon Wood, *The Radicalism of the American Revolution* (New York: Alfred Knopf, 1992), 47, 127. For a discussion of land prices, see Richard Lyman Bushman, "Markets and Composite Farms in Early America," *William and Mary Quarterly* 55 (July 1998), 371–2. The quote is from Robert D. Mitchell and Warren R. Hofstra, "How Do Settlement Systems Evolve? The Virginia Backcountry during the Eighteenth Century," *Journal of Historical Geography* 21 (1995), 141.

29 Jordan and Kaups, *The American Backwoods Frontier,* 31. They muster persuasive evidence that the backwoods pioneer drew from the experience of Finnish colonists in New Sweden.

30 For background on this movement, see Lemon, *The Best Poor Man's Country,* 61.

31 Also known as the Five Nations and later the Six Nations; the affiliated tribes acknowledged a constitutional confederation.

32 Parke Rouse, *The Great Wagon Road from Philadelphia to the South* (New York: McGraw-Hill, 1973). For a discussion on the role of tidewater agricultural practices in fostering landhunting, see David O. Percy, "Ax or Plow?: Significant Landscape Alteration Rates in the Maryland and Virginia Tidewater," *Agricultural History* 66 (spring 1992), 66–74.

33 Bailey, *The Ohio Company,* 106–12; Anthony F.C. Wallace, *King of the Delawares: Teedyuscung, 1700–1763* (Salem, NH: Ayer Company, 1984, reprint of 1949 edition), 141.

34 Albert T. Volwiler, *George Croghan and the Westward Movement, 1741–1782* (Cleveland: Arthur Clark Company, 1926), 209–77.

35 On the migration of Pennsylvania tenant farmers out of that colony, see Lucy Simler, "Tenancy in Colonial Pennsylvania: The Case of Chester County," *William and Mary Quarterly* 53 (Oct. 1986), 542–69.

36 A similar selection process had emerged on the Penn lands in Pennsylvania, despite the family's reluctance to accept what technically amounted to squatting. See Lemon, *The Best Poor Man's Country*, 55–7.

37 Sara Hughes, *Surveyors and Statesmen: Land Measurement in Colonial Virginia* (Richmond: Virginia Surveyors Foundation, and Virginia Association of Surveyors, 1979), 4–5.

38 Thomas Perkins Abernethy, *Western Lands and the American Revolution* (New York: Russell and Russell, 1959), 369.

39 Gates, *Landlords and Tenants*, 21–6.

40 Bailey, *The Ohio Company*, 64–7.

41 Washington to Lord Botetourt, 8 Dec. 1769, quoted in Williams, *West Virginia*, 12.

42 Dorothy V. Jones, *License for Empire: Colonialism by Treaty in Early America* (Chicago: University of Chicago Press, 1982), 87–119.

43 Williams, *West Virginia*, 3.

44 Samuel M. Wilson, *The Ohio Company of Virginia, 1748–1798* (Lexington: Offprint from the Kentucky Law Journal, 1926), 17–53. The importance of this antiquarian pamphlet is its documentation of the company's surveying and selecting efforts in Kentucky in the 1770s and 1780s.

45 Quoted in Andrew R.L. Cayton, *Frontier Indiana* (Bloomington: University of Indiana Press, 1996), 81.

46 This judgment is shared by ibid., 97.

47 Thomas Donaldson, *The Public Domain. Its History with Statistics* (Washington, DC: Government Printing Office, 1884), 233.

48 Crawford to Washington, 2 August 1771, quoted in Williams, *West Virginia*, 11.

49 William Crawford to James Tilgman, 9 Aug. 1771, in Butterfield, *The Washington–Crawford Letters*, 22.

50 Abernethy, *Western Lands*, 69.

51 Weaver, "Frontiers into Assets," 17–48.

52 The term refers to those farmers of Dutch descent in the western Cape who, from 1836 to 1840, participated in a large-scale migration across the Orange River frontier.

53 John M. MacKenzie, *The Empire of Nature: Hunting, Conservation, and British Imperialism* (Manchester: University of Manchester Press, 1988), quote at 88; examples on 89–91, 109, 115. An example of game hunting turning into a mineral-prospecting expedition on the Mashonaland plateau is given in Stephen Taylor, *The Mighty Nimrod: A Life of Frederick Courteney Selous, African Hunter and Adventurer, 1851–1917* (London: Collins, 1989), 123–5.

54 John B. Thomas to Henry Rogers, 9 July 1886, letterbook, 1881–1889, box 3, John B. Thomas Papers, accession 141, AHC.

55 John Mack Faragher, *Daniel Boone: The Life and Legend of an American Pioneer* (New York: Henry Holt and Company, 1992), 240–1.
56 The Cherokees seemed to be willing vendors who wanted trade goods. Jones, *License for Empire*, 111–16.
57 Willard Rouse Jillson, *The Kentucky Land Grants: A Systematic Index of All the Land Grants Recorded in the State Land Office at Frankfort, Kentucky, 1782–1924* (Baltimore, Md.: Genealogical Publishing Co., 1971: reprint of 1925 edition), vol. 1, 3.
58 Faragher, *Daniel Boone*, 129.
59 Ibid., 101.
60 Ibid., 238.
61 Abernethy, *Western Lands*, 304.
62 Frederick Merk, "Foreword," in David M. Ellis, ed., *The Frontier in American Development: Essays in Honor of Paul Wallace Gates* (Ithaca, NY: Cornell University Press, 1969), xxiv.
63 Faragher, *Daniel Boone*, 247.
64 William Crawford to George Washington, 15 March 1772, in Butterfield, *The Washington–Crawford Letters*, 24.
65 Donald Kerr, *The Principles of the Australian Land Titles (Torrens) System* (Sydney: Law Book Company of Australasia Limited, 1927); Blair C. Shick and Irving Plotkin, *Torrens in the United States: A Legal and Economic History and Analysis of American Land-Registration Systems* (Lexington, Ky.: Lexington Books, 1978).
66 James Flint, *Letter from America* (Edinburgh: W. & C. Tait, 1822), in Reuben Gold Thwaites, *Early Western Travels, 1748–1846* (New York: AMS Press, 1966), vol. 9, 184.
67 F.A. Michaux, *Travels to the West of the Allegheny Mountains* (London: B. Crosby, 1805), in Reuben Gold Thwaites, *Early Western Travels* (New York: AMS Press, 1966), vol. 3, 247.
68 Some of his grants were entered with this title. Compared to some other frontier landhunters, he appears to have retained relatively small grants. See Jillson, *The Kentucky Land Grants*, 13–255.
69 Michael Lofaro, *The Life and Adventures of Daniel Boone* (Lexington: University of Kentucky Press, 1986), 113–14.
70 William E. Foley, *The Genesis of Missouri: From Wilderness Outpost to Statehood* (Columbia: University of Missouri Press, 1989), 77; Richardson, "Private Land Claims in Missouri, Part 1 and Part 2," 132–44, 271–86.
71 Ogden's Letters, in Reuben Gold Thwaites, *Early Western Travels, 1748–1846* (New York:AMS Press, 1966), vol. 19, 64. Grazers comprised a second wave of frontiersmen, following trappers and traders. Between the late 1780s and the 1820s, they were moving up several tributaries of the Mississippi. For their presence on the Red River, see

Dan L. Flores, *Jefferson and Southwestern Exploration: The Freeman and Custis Accounts of the Red River Expedition of 1806* (Norman: University of Oklahoma Press, 1984), 140, note 24.

72 A gazetteer quoted in Richardson, "Private Land Claims in Missouri," part 3, 397.

73 Thomas Nuttall, *Travels into the Arkansas Territory* (Philadelphia: Thomas Palmer, 1821), in Thwaites, *Western Travels*, vol. 13, 103.

74 William H. Goetzmann, *Exploration and Empire: The Explorer and the Scientist in the Winning of the American West* (New York: Alfred A. Knopf, 1966), xiii.

75 Dan Flores, "Editor's Epilogue: The Last Jeffersonian Exploration," in Flores, ed., *Jefferson and Southwestern Exploration: The Freeman and Custis Accounts of the Red River Expedition of 1806* (Norman: University of Oklahoma Press, 1894), 308.

76 Nuttall, *Travels*, in Thwaites, *Western Travels*, vol. 13, 207–22.

77 Frederick Law Olmsted, *A Journey through Texas, or a Saddle-Trip on the Southwestern Frontier* (Austin: University of Texas, 1978; reprint of 1857 edition), 369.

78 Andy Adams, *The Log of a Cowboy* (Boston: Houghton Mifflin Company, 1927), 114. First published in 1903 about a cattle drive in 1882, this memoir is among the best of the genre.

79 Crosby, *Ecological Imperialism*, 171–94.

80 George R. Wilson, *Early Indiana Trails and Surveys* (Indianapolis: C.E. Pauley, 1919), 349–50. On range and demise, see Ted Franklin Belue, *The Long Hunt: Death of the Buffalo East of the Mississippi* (Mechanicsburg, Penn.: Stackpole Books, 1996).

81 Terry G. Jordan, *North American Cattle-Ranching Frontiers: Origins, Diffusion, and Differentiation* (Albuquerque: University of New Mexico Press, 1993), 307. Jordan argues persuasively that southern Ohio and Missouri were as much founding regions of western cattle ranching as Texas and California.

82 Paul Henlein, "Cattle Kingdom in the Ohio Valley: The Beef Industry in the Ohio Valley, 1783–1860" (unpublished Phd thesis, University of Wisconsin, 1957), 112–25; Carl O. Sauer, *The Geography of the Ozark Highland of Missouri* (Chicago: University of Chicago Press, 1920), 121–2, 157–61; also see the "Cattle Industry" in Howard R. Lamar, ed., *The New Encyclopedia of the American West* (New Haven, Conn.: Yale University Press, 1998), 175–7.

83 Quoted in Galbraith, *Reluctant Empire*, 186.

84 David Breen, *The Canadian Prairie West and the Ranching Frontier, 1874–1924* (Toronto: University of Toronto Press, 1983).

85 John R. Stilgoe, *Common Landscape of America, 1580 to 1845* (New Haven, Conn.: Yale University Press, 1982), 55. For a discussion of the

dispersal of farms in Pennsylvania in a North Atlantic context, see Lemon, *The Best Poor Man's Country*, 106–9. When did the market idea with respect to land arise in New England, and when did dispersal begin to undermine the attempts of local governments to control settlement patterns? Lemon argues that these tendencies began early, certainly by the mid-seventeenth century. "The drive for independent ownership, control, and autonomy thus underlay the organization of space in the Anglo–American spatial process." Lemon, "Spatial Order: Households in Local Communities and Regions," in Jack P. Greene and J.R. Poole, eds., *Colonial British America: Essays in the New History of the Early Modern Era* (Baltimore, Md.: Johns Hopkins University Press, 1984), 94.

86 Alan Taylor, *Liberty Men and Great Proprietors: The Revolutionary Settlement on the Maine Frontier, 1760–1820* (Chapel Hill: University of North Carolina Press, 1990), 11–121.

87 Barbara Ann Chernow, *Robert Morris: Land Speculator, 1791–1801* (New York: Arno Press, 1978), 35–128, 170–98.

88 For an outsider's assessment of the land boom and bust in the early United States, see Isaac Weld, *Travels through the United States of North America*, vol. 1 (New York: Johnson Reprint Corporation, 1986; original published in 1807), 403–6.

89 Taylor, *Liberty Men*, 209–35.

90 Morton J. Horwitz, *The Transformation of American Law, 1780–1860* (Cambridge, Mass.: Harvard University Press, 1977), 61.

91 See, for example, *The Squatters Manual: A Complete Compendium of the Acts of the Imperial and Colonial Legislatures, Orders in Council, and Local regulations Relating to the Occupation of Lands in New South Wales* (Melbourne: William Kerr, 1848), 17. On the operation of compensation for improvements in New Zealand, see B.R. Paterson, "Whatever Happened to Poor Waring Taylor? Insights from the Business Manuscripts," *Turnbull Library Record* 24 (Oct. 1991), 125. Noeline Baker, ed., *A Surveyor in New Zealand, 1857–1896: The Recollections of John Holland Baker* (Auckland: Whitcombe & Tombs, 1932), 217.

92 Taylor, "The Frontier Revolution," 256. He argues that the ordinance was intended to restore the primacy of monied gentlemen in profiting from frontier lands. The ordinance and other measures pursued this social objective, and that insight properly affirms class and property struggles as topics in the history of the early republic. But a celebration of defiance is disquieting, because avoidance of state and national laws regarding property rights contributed to a contempt for law and government and perhaps to a weakening of respect for public lands unless immediately exploited.

93 Thomas Lloyd Miller, *The Public Lands of Texas, 1591–1970*
    (Norman: University of Oklahoma Press, 1972), 51–3.
94 Andrew R.L. Clayton, "'A Quiet Independence': The Western Vision of
    the Ohio Company," in Peter Onuf, ed., *The New American Nation,
    1775–1820: State and Local Politics in the New Nation* (New York:
    Garland Publishing, 1991), 553–80.
95 R. Douglas Hurt, *The Ohio Frontier: Crucible of the Old Northwest,
    1720–1830* (Bloomington: University of Indiana Press, 1996), 164–5.
96 Norman J.W. Thrower, *Original Survey and Land Subdivision:
    A Comparative Study of the Form and Effect of Contrasting Cadastral
    Surveys* (Chicago: Rand and McNally, 1966), 15.
97 Richardson, "Private Land Claims in Missouri," part 3, 399. There is
    a description of a Missouri squatter family that had lived in Virginia,
    Kentucky, and Tennessee in John Mason Peck, *Pioneer Life: Memoir of
    John Mason Peck D.D.* (Philadelphia: American Baptist Publication
    Society, 1864), 149.
98 Robert D. Mitchell, "The Formation of Early American Cultural
    Regions: An Interpretation," in James R. Gibson, ed., *European Settle-
    ment and Development in North America: Essays on Geographical
    Change in Honour and Memory of Andrew Hill Clark* (Toronto:
    University of Toronto press, 1978), 66–90.
99 Milton B. Newton quoted in ibid., 78.
100 Solomon Alexander Wright, *My Rambles as East Texas Cowboy,
    Hunter, Fisherman, Tie-Cutter* (Austin: Texas Folklore Society, 1942),
    1–2. One of California's largest landowners and ranchers was Hugh
    Glenn. He was born in Virginia and often took stock west from Mis-
    souri. Giles French, *Cattle Country of Peter French*, 17–18. Terry G.
    Jordan has written extensively on characteristics and diffusion of the
    midwestern system of cattle ranching with its southern connections.
    A summary that includes Canada appears in "Does the Border Matter?
    Cattle Ranching and the 49th Parallel," in Simon M. Evans, Sarah
    Carter, and Bill Yeo, eds., *Cowboys, Ranchers and the Cattle Business:
    Cross-Border Perspectives on Ranching History* (Calgary: University of
    Calgary Press, 2000), 1–10.
101 The settlers of Kentucky used the laws of Virginia – "the legal code
    familiar to the largest number." Malcolm Rohrbough, *The Trans-
    Appalachian Frontier: People, Societies, and Institutions, 1775–1850*
    (New York: Oxford University Press, 1978), 45. For an example of
    cultural geography, see Jordan and Kaups, *The American Backwoods
    Frontier*.
102 Rules for Sale of Land, 1774, Larabee, Vol. II, 533–7.
103 There are many descriptions of this system. There is a sound and
    compact one in Thrower, *Original Survey*, 5.

104 Hildegard Binder Johnson, *Order upon the Land: The U.S. Rectangular Land Survey and the Upper Mississippi Country* (New York: Oxford University Press, 1976), 57.

105 One of the first scholarly discussions of the problem appears in Wallace Stegner, *Beyond the Hundredth Meridian: John Wesley Powell and the Opening of the West* (Boston: Houghton Mifflin Company, 1953), 225–31.

106 See Stilgoe, *Common Landscapes of America*, 193.

107 Gottfried Duden, *Report on a Journey to the Western States of North America and a Stay of Several Years along the Missouri*, gen. ed. James W. Goodrich (Columbia: University of Missouri Press, 1980), 71–2.

108 Flint's Letters from America in Thwaites, *Western Travels*, vol. 9, 179.

109 Gates, *Landlords and Tenants*, 43. He considers the Spanish and Mexican land grants excessive and therefore properly vulnerable to improving squatters. A more sympathetic treatment of California's Hispanic grazers appears in Leonard Pitt, *The Decline of the Californios: A Social History of the Spanish-Speaking Californians, 1846–1890* (Berkeley: University of California Press, 1966).

110 Jürgen Osterhammel, *Colonialism* (Princeton, NJ: Markus Wiener Publishers, 1997), 10–12.

111 The hopes and boasts of English immigrants about Upper Canada land are well represented in the letters collected in Wendy Cameron, Sheila Haines, and Mary McDougall Maude, eds., *English Immigrant Voices: Labourers' Letters from Upper Canada in the 1830s* (Montreal: McGill-Queen's University Press, 2000).

112 Powell, *The Public Lands of Australia Felix*, 32; *The Squatter's Manual: A Complete Compendium of the Acts of the Imperial and Colonial Legislatures, Orders in Council, and Local Regulations Relating to the Occupation of Crown Lands in New South Wales* (Melbourne: William Kerr, 1848), 13; *The Resident and Cultivation Licences* (Melbourne, 1861), 5, pamphlets in the Mitchell Library. Quote in *Government Gazette* (South Australia), 18 April 1844.

113 This explains the origin of many farm names – for example, Lange*fontein*, Groot*fontein*, Sterk*fontein*, Matjes*fontein*.

114 There are many accounts of this system. In sequence of publication, the following are notable. C. Graham Botha, *Early Cape Land Tenure* (Cape Town: Cape Times, 1919); P.J. van der Merwe, trans. by Roger Beck, *The Migrant Farmer in the History of the Cape Colony, 1652–1842* (Athens: Ohio University Press, 1995); Leonard Guelke, "Land Tenure and Settlement at the Cape, 1652–1812," in C.G.C. Martin and K.J. Friedlander, eds., *History of Surveying and Land Tenure in South Africa: Collected Papers*, vol. 1 (Cape Town: University of Cape Town, 1984). Van der Merwe was a pathbreaking historian.

115 J.S. Marais, *The Coloured People of the Cape, 1652–1937* (Johannesburg: Witwatersrand, 1962; first printed in 1938), 53. Beacons were
also used as symbols of sovereignty. See Robert Ross, *Adam Kok's
Griquas: A Study in the Development of Stratification in South Africa*
(Cambridge: Cambridge University Press, 1976), 50.

116 National Archives of South Africa, Cape Town Repository, Colonial
Secretary's Office (CO) 4439, Correspondence on Land Tenure,
Colonel Bird to Johannes Andres Truter, 21 Dec. 1810.

117 *Guide to the Records Relating to Crown Lands* (Sydney: Archives
Authority of New South Wales, 1977), 1.

118 R.G. MacBeth, *The Selkirk Settlers in Real Life* (Toronto: William
Briggs, 1897), 46; Archer Martin, *The Hudson's Bay Company Land
Tenures and the Occupation of Assiniboia by Lord Selkirk's Settlers
with a List of Grantees under the Earl and the Company* (London:
William Clowes and Sons, 1898), 91; Thomas Flanagan, *Metis Lands
in Manitoba* (Calgary: University of Calgary Press, 1991), 199–215.

119 Leonard Thompson, *A History of South Africa* (New Haven, Conn.:
Yale University Press, 1995), 93.

120 James R. Gibson, *Farming the Frontier: The Agricultural Opening of
the Oregon Country, 1786–1846* (Vancouver: University of British
Columbia Press, 1985), 133–4.

121 Ibid.; quote from William Armistead Goulder, *Reminiscences: Incidents
in the Life of a Pioneer in Oregon and Idaho* (Moscow: University of
Idaho Press, 1989; reprint of 1909 edition), 167. An 1850 act of Congress allowed them to claim title to a half-section as individuals and a
section as a married couple. The early occupants were able to tie up the
best lands for speculation, and subsequent entries under the Homestead Act were not numerous. Gilbert Fite, *The Farmers' Frontier,
1865–1900* (New York: Holt, Rinehart and Winston, 1966), 143–5.

122 Walter Nugent, *Into the West: The Story of Its People* (New York:
Alfred A. Knopf, 1999), 80–2.

123 Burroughs, *Britain and Australia*, 143.

124 T.M. Perry, *Australia's First Frontier: The Spread of Settlement in New
South Wales, 1788–1829* (Melbourne: Melbourne University Press in
Association with the Australian National University, 1966), 121.

125 Weaver, "Frontiers into Assets," 46.

126 For a history of these two types of river transport, see Michael Allen,
*Western Rivermen, 1763–1861: Ohio and Mississippi Boatmen and the
Myth of the Alligator Horse* (Baton Rouge: Louisiana State University
Press, 1990). John Cleve Symmes to Jonathan Dayton, 25 Nov. 1788,
in Bond, ed., *The Correspondence of John Cleve Symmes*, 55–8.

127 On the land hunger of the Grahamstown settlers, see Noël Mostert,
Frontiers: The Epic Tragedy of South Africa's Creation and the

Tragedy of the Xhosa People (New York: Alfred A. Knopf, 1992), 860–1; Basil de Cordeur and Christopher Saunders, *The War of the Axe, 1847* (Johannesburg: Brenthusrt Press, 1981), 16. Note especially Crais, *White Supremacy and Black Resistance*, 134–5. The quest for a port is mentioned in Johannes Meintjes, *The Voortrekker: The Story of the Great Trek and the Making of South Africa* (London: Cassell, 1973), 48.

128 See Joseph Hugh Greenwood Diary, entries from 15 Sept. to 8 Dec. 1843, MS 4882, Alexander Turnbull Library, National Library of New Zealand.

129 Richard Elphick, *Khoikhoi and the Founding of White South Africa* (Johannesburg: Ravan Press, 1985), 224.

130 Symmes to Dayton, 17 July 1789, Bond, ed., *Correspondence*, 104.

131 White, *The Middle Ground*, 413–523.

132 Francis Paul Prucha, *The Great Father: The United States and the American Indians*, vol. 1 (Lincoln: University of Nebraska Press, 1984), 179–242.

133 Anthony McGinnis, "Intertribal Conflict on the Northern Great Plains and Its Suppression, 1738–1889," *Journal of the West* 18 (April 1979), 49–60.

134 Richard Elphick, *Khoikhoi and the Founding of White South Africa* (Johannesburg: Ravan, 1985), 222–5.

135 Petrus Johannes van der Merwe, *Die noordwaartse beweging van die boere voor die groot trek (1700–1842)* (The Hague: W.P. van Stockum & Zoon, 1937), 1–24, 24–104.

136 Leonard Thompson, *Survival in Two Worlds: Moshoeshoe of Lesotho, 1786–1870* (Oxford: At the Clarendon Press, 1975), 106; van der Merwe, *Die noordwaartse beweging*, 107–8.

137 Van der Merwe, *Die noordwaartse beweging*, 106–7.

138 James Belich, *The New Zealand Wars and the Victorian Interpretation of Racial Conflict* (New York: Penguin, 1998); Weaver, "Frontiers into Assets," 46.

139 Sharon Morgan, *Land Settlement in Early Tasmania: Creating an Antipodean England* (Cambridge: Cambridge University Press, 1992), 144–51.

140 Jan Critchet, *A Distant Field of Murder: Western District Frontiers, 1837–1848* (Melbourne: University of Melbourne Press, 1990), 86–113; Maurice French, *Conflict on the Condamine: Aborigines and the European Invasion* (Toowoomba, Queensland: Darling Downs Institute Press, 1989), 103–8.

141 Bruce Trigger, *The Children of Aataentsic: A History of the Huron People to 1660* (Montreal: McGill-Queen's University Press, 1987), 499–850; Richard White, *The Middle Ground: Indians, Empires, and*

Republics in the Great Lakes Region, 1650–1815 (Cambridge: Cambridge University Press, 1991), 1–185. On the Mississauga, see P.S. Schmalz, "The Role of the Ojibwa in the Conquest of Southern Ontario," *Ontario History* 56 (1984), 326–52; Donald B. Smith, *Sacred Feathers: The Reverend Peter Jones (Kahkewaquonaby) and the Mississauga Indians* (Toronto: University of Toronto Press, 1989), 16–33.

142 For an early assessment of the *Mfecane*, see T.R.H. Davenport, *South Africa: A Modern History* (London: Macmillan, 1977), 12–21. Debates about the Mfecane raged among scholars from the mid-1980s to the mid-1990s. Attempts to revise history downplayed the seriousness of the disruptions and alleged that they originated in Cape Colony. Major revision has not endured. Notions of violent disruptions and depopulation helped justify white occupation, but there remains substantial evidence that wars, precipitated probably by the emergence of a powerful Zulu kingdom, did have extensive consequences. The highveld was not perhaps depopulated, but refugee groups were on the move and looking for alliances. The Great Trek interacted with a fluid and violent phase in tribal politics; the voortrekkers' pursuit of territory met with resistance; however, the unusual situations created by the Mfecane assisted the colonizing expeditions. See the essays in Carolyn Hamilton, ed., *The Mfecane Aftermath: Reconstructive Debates in Southern African History* (Johannesburg: Witwatersrand University Press and University of Natal Press, 1995) – for our purposes, especially chapters 5, 6, 7, 10, 13, 14.

143 There is abundant evidence for these points. See, for example, Morgan, *Land Settlement in Early Tasmania*, 158–9; Howard Lamar and Leonard Thompson, eds., *The Frontier in History: North America and South Africa Compared* (New Haven, Conn.: Yale University Press, 1981), 9; James Belich, *The New Zealand Wars and the Victorian Interpretation of Racial Conflict* (Auckland: Penguin Books, 1988), 211–15; J.J. Wagoner, "History of the Cattle Industry in Southern Arizona, 1540–1940," *University of Arizona Bulletin*, no. 20 (1952), 35–6.

144 Access to water was essential in earlier incidents of landhunting by colonial peoples at the Cape. See Leonard Guelke and Robert Shell, "Landscape of Conquest: Frontier Water Alienation and Khoikhoi Strategies of Survival, 1652–1780," *Journal of Southern African Studies* 18 (Dec. 1992), 803–24. For water and early nineteenth-century expansion, see van der Merwe, *Die noordwaartse beweging*, 176–240.

145 Malcolm Rohrbough, *The Land Office Business: The Settlement and Administration of American Public Land* (Belmont, Calif.: Wadsworth Publishing Company, 1990), 103.

146 Ibid., 107. For the impact of the cotton boom on Indian land issues, see Prucha, *Great White Father*, 195.
147 Weaver, "Frontiers into Assets," 17–21.
148 Testimony of Samuel Gibson, *United States Public Lands Commission*, 55.
149 Quoted in van der Merwe, *Die noordwaartse beweging*, 220.
150 Charles Sellers, *The Market Revolution: Jacksonian America, 1815–1846* (New York: Oxford University Press, 1991), 46.
151 Robert Morris and his agents had been able to use the same property for multiple loans because of the absence of title registration. A land system that allowed imperfect titles led to distrust of American land speculation in European financial centres. See Chernow, *Robert Morris*, 144–5.

CHAPTER FOUR

1 Geoffrey Parker, "Europe and the Wider World, 1500–1750: The Military Balance," in J.D. Tracey, ed., *The Political Economy of Merchant Empires* (Cambridge: Cambridge University Press, 1991), 163.
2 Groundwork for this argument appears in Patricia Seed, *Ceremonies of Possession in Europe's Conquest of the New World, 1492–1640* (Cambridge: Cambridge University Press, 1995). Seed elaborates on the rituals of acquisition performed by the English, French, Spanish, Portuguese, and Dutch. David Spurr suggests differences in the self-affirmations of various colonizing powers at the end of the nineteenth century; *Rhetoric of Empire: Colonial Discourse in Journalism, Travel Writing, and Imperial Administration* (Durham, NC: Duke University Press, 1993), 114.
3 Robert Aldrich, *The French Presence in the South Pacific, 1842–1940* (Honolulu: University of Hawaii Press, 1990), 178–82; Ingrid Moses, "The Extension of Colonial Rule in Kaiser Wilhelmsland," in John A. Moses and Paul M. Kennedy, eds., *Germany in the Pacific* (Cambridge: University of Cambridge Press, 1975), 294–5, 299–300.
4 Recently jurists have proposed that native title is *sui generis*, alleging that its characteristics cannot be discerned from common law rules. Richard H. Bartlett, *Native Title in Australia* (Sydney: Batterworths, 2000), 79–81. That position seems incorrect. First, normally the British recognized that first peoples had interests that had to be purchased; this suggests that a common law principle informed them. Second, the common law has throughout its history absorbed customs relating to property; recognition of native title in common law courts acknowledges that it is an interest like all others that have been accorded common law status.

5 It is difficult to reconstruct eighteenth- and nineteenth-century thought about these rights. They seem to have been construed as interests arising from occupation and readily extinguished. The commentaries focused on how these rights limited the absolute title of the crown; they were silent or dismissive on the nature of the native rights underlying this limitation. In the late twentieth century, the notion that native title was something unknown to the common law, but worth taking into account, appeared in several important decisions. On native title, see *Mabo and Others and the State of Queensland,* in *Commonwealth Law Reports, High Court* [1991–2], 89 (hereafter cited as *Mabo*). For its development in Canadian law, see Bruce Clark, *Native Liberty, Crown Sovereignty: The Existing Aboriginal Right of Self-Government in Canada* (Montreal: McGill-Queen's University Press, 1990), 31. The French and Spanish in North America did not recognize native title, although by the late eighteenth century fur traders west of the Mississippi sometimes secured documented transfers from first peoples and subsequently petitioned for and received Spanish grants. See William E. Foley and C. David Rice, *The First Chouteaus: River Barons of Early St. Louis* (Urbana: University of Illinois Press, 1983), 51, 179–81. On New France, see Cornelius J. Jaenen, "French Sovereignty and Native Nationhood during the French Régime," in J.R. Miller, ed., *Sweet Promises: A Reader in Indian–White Relations in Canada* (Toronto: University of Toronto Press, 1991), 34–8. Jaenen suggests that the French were uninterested in land, except in the riverine colony along the St Lawrence. They were dedicated to maintaining alliances with first peoples. Also see Olive Dickason, "Concepts of Sovereignty at the Time of the First Contacts," in L.C. Green and Olive P. Dickason, *The Law of Nations and the New World* (Edmonton: University of Alberta Press, 1989), 217–26. For the Spanish legal position, see Cyrus Thomas, "Introduction," in *Indian Land Cessions in the United States: Eighteenth Annual Report of the Bureau of Ethnology* (Washington, DC: Government Printing Office, 1899), 539–45. Early republican American policy towards Indians (1784–86) was dictatorial and aimed at extracting land by forced treaties. In 1787, the British approach of negotiating treaties and providing purchase money was adopted, and it was official policy until 1871. See Reginald Horsman, "United States Indian Policies, 1775–1815," in Wilcomb E. Washburn, ed., *History of Indian–White Relations,* vol. 4 (Washington, DC: Smithsonian Institute, 1988), 29–39; Horsman, *Expansion and American Indian Policy, 1783–1812* (East Lansing: Michigan State University Press, 1967).

6 There is a helpful discussion of land tenure in various settings in R. Gerald Ward and Elizabeth Kingdon, "Some Comparison," in Ward

and Kingdon, eds., *Land, Custom and Practice in the South Pacific* (Cambridge: Cambridge University Press, 1995), 6–36.

7 *Macdonald v. Levy* (1833), quoted in Kent McNeil, *Common Law and Aboriginal Title* (Oxford: Clarendon Press, 1989), 121; also see 290–7. McNeil's excellent discussion of possessory rights as the real basis of native title anticipated both Australian and Canadian judicial reassessments of the concept; 193–243.

8 This insistence on the values of the intruder as the standard for judging rights persists to a degree in white Australia. For an unquestioning defence of it, see Barry Bridges, "The Aborigines and the Land Question in the Period of Imperial Responsibility," *Journal of the Royal Australian Historical Society* 56 (June 1970), 92–107.

9 An erudite critique of the basis for claims of sovereignty by the United States is found in Robert A. Williams, Jr, *The American Indian in Western Legal Thought: The Discourses of Conquest* (New York: Oxford University Press, 1990), 308–17. Williams maintains that the crown's doctrine of exclusive right to patent land derived from a feudal concept requisitioned to colonize Indian territory. He does not mention the practical obstacles to land titles based on direct transfers. Ideologies that denied indigenous peoples the right to direct sales are dangerously at odds with human rights. Yet the history of free exchanges that were carried out does not encourage confidence in the idea that more of the same could have benefited indigenous peoples.

10 For an economist's discussion of crown pre-emption, see Jennifer Roback, "Exchange, Sovereignty, and Indian–Anglo Relations," in Terry L. Anderson, ed., *Property Rights and Indian Economies: The Political Economy Forum* (Lantham, Md.: Rowman & Littlefield, 1992), 11–17. Roback suggests an economic motive for crown pre-emption – namely, achievement of a distribution monopoly; however, the individual colonies that directed land grants or sales on the crown's behalf gave land away generously. Defence of land price was not as important to them as avoiding conflict arising from disputed titles. As well, the policy was applied in order to compel land sales to government agents. Leo A. Johnson, "The Mississauga–Lake Ontario Surrender of 1805," *Ontario History* 83 (Sept. 1990), 244–5.

11 Cyrus Thomas, "Introduction," in Charles C. Royce and Cyrus Thomas, eds., *Indian Land Cessions in the United States: Eighteenth Annual Report of the Bureau of American Ethnology* (Washington, DC: Government Printing Office, 1899), 619–20. Although this essay is filled with statements about colonial benevolence, it also has information on native title and crown pre-emption. Cronon, *Changes*, 57. In his book about Spanish opponents of the exploitation of Indians, Lewis Hanke claimed that Roger Williams was the exception that proved the

rule that the English, unlike the Spanish, were not preoccupied with the legal basis of their rule. As I have stressed, the English were obsessed with property rights. *The Spanish Struggle for Justice in the Conquest of America* (Boston: Little, Brown and Company, 1965, first pub. in 1949), 172. Hanke and others discovered in the writing of the sixteenth-century theologian and jurist Francisco de Vitoria a brave champion of indigenous peoples. However, in a reassessment of Vitoria's famous two lectures, Anthony Anghie claims that Vitoria distinguished between sovereign Spaniards and non-sovereign Indians and thus accepted a doctrine of subordination. "Francisco de Vitoria and the Colonial Origins of International Law," in Eve Darian-Smith and Peter Fitzpatrick, eds., *Laws of the Postcolonial* (Ann Arbor: University of Michigan Press, 1999), 89–104.

12 In the case of New Zealand, a brief for the natural rights of indigenous peoples to sell land without the involvement of the crown was also made by the London-based Aborigines Protection Society. See Louis Alexis Chamerovzow, *The New Zealand Question and the Rights of Aborigines* (London: T.C. Newby, 1848).

13 Williams, *The American Indian*, 227–80; Francis Paul Prucha, *American Indian Policy in the Formative Years: The Indian Trade and Intercourse Acts, 1790–1834* (Cambridge, Mass.: Harvard University Press, 1962), 144–5.

14 Williams, *The American Indian*, 308–17. U.S. Chief Justice John Marshall's decision in *Johnson v. McIntosh* was reached for pragmatic reasons, although it also maintained additional grounds for rejecting direct dealings in land between first peoples and individuals. In rejecting *Camden–Yorke*, Marshall observed that it made reference to "princes and governments," but in treating with North American Indians the crown and the republic spoke of "their sachems, their warriors, and their chiefmen." The implication was that the states of India were on a par with those of Europe and the tribes of North America were not. *Johnson and Graham's Lessee v. M'Intosh* in *The American Indian and the United States: A Documentary History*, vol. 4 (New York: Random House, 1973), 2537–53.

15 Burroughs, *Britain and Australia*, 162; J.H. Wedge to J. Bonwick, 23 Feb. 1856, Port Phillip Company Papers, microfilm reel 1046, Mitchell Library, State Library of New South Wales; Proclamation of Sir Richard Bourke, 26 Aug. 1835, Broadsides Collection, D365/1–20, no. 1/7, Mitchell Library.

16 Speculators adopted resolutions to place before Captain William Hobson before he sailed to establish sovereignty over New Zealand. William Hobson to John Clarke, 11 Jan. 1840, and John Clarke to George Weller, 11 Jan. 1840, in Weller Brothers Papers, 1832–1841

(Copies of Originals in Mitchell Library), M.S. 0872, folder 1, Alexander Turnbull Library, National Library of New Zealand.

17 Minutes of the Legislative Council of New South Wales, 28 May and 9 July 1840, ms. 0842, Turnbull Library. Gipps also cited legal opinions secured by Bourke when he dealt with the Port Phillip Association. New Zealand was soon separated from New South Wales, and the new colony immediately passed its own ordinance – 4 Vic. No. 2: An Ordinance to Repeal within the Said Colony of New Zealand a Certain Act of the Government and Council of New South Wales (June 1841). For Wentworth's land dealings, see Documents of Titles and other Documents from the Office of Minter, Simpson and Company, A4024, Mitchell Library, State Library of New South Wales. For his arguments, see Orange, *The Treaty of Waitangi* (Wellington: Bridget Williams Books, 1987), 94.

18 *New Zealand Government Gazette (Auckland)*, vol. 7, no. 11 (6 July 1847), 63–6.

19 Galbraith stresses the political character of the Great Trek, although he does not elaborate, even though he had mastered the colonial documentation. He seems to think it an overworked topic. *Reluctant Empire: British Policy on the South African Frontier, 1834–1854* (Berkeley: University of California Press, 1963), 171.

20 Williams, *The American Indian*, 326.

21 This is one of the themes in Richard White's indispensable *The Middle Ground: Indians, Empires, and Republics in the Great Lakes Region, 1650–1815* (Cambridge: Cambridge University Press, 1991). See, for example, his assessment of General Jeffrey Amherst and British policy, 257–68.

22 "Pre-emption" was a term used in many contexts on different frontiers. In all settings, it meant the same: a privileged standing, secured usually by occupation, that granted a right of first purchase when a tract was on the market.

23 Robert Venables, "Iroquois Environment and 'We the People of the United States': Gemeinschaft and Gesellschaft in the Apposition of Iroquois, Federal, and New York Sovereignties," in Christopher Vecsey and Robert W. Venables, eds., *American Indian Environments: Ecological Issues in Native American History* (Syracuse: Syracuse University Press, 1980), 124.

24 On the Iroquois (Six Nations) and Cherokee cessions of 1767–69, see Thomas Abernethy, *Western Lands and the American Revolution* (New York: Russell and Russell, 1959), 37–67. The larger story of the failure of enduring pan-Indian opposition to white occupation is covered in Gregory Evans Dowd, *A Spirited Resistance: The North American Indian Struggle for Unity, 1745–1815* (Baltimore, Md.: Johns Hopkins

University, 1992). Dowd traces the divisions between accommodation-
ists and nativists, concluding with the War of 1812, which he sees as
forcing Indians into a civil war that was the nativists' "crushing
failure." Ibid., 183.

25 For Weiser's insights into the manipulation that occurred during negotiations on land cession, particularly about the use of rum, see Robert
L.D. Davidson, *War Comes to Quaker Pennsylvania, 1682–1756* (New
York: Temple University Publications by Columbia University Press,
1957), 73.

26 Anthony F.C. Wallace, *King of the Delawares: Teedyuscung, 1700–
1763* (Salem, NH: Ayer Company, 1984, reprint of 1949 edition),
61–2.

27 Edward Weller to George Weller, 15 Jan. 1840, Weller Brothers Papers,
folder 1, ms. 0872, Alexander Turnbull Library, National Library of
New Zealand.

28 Michael Adas, *Machines as the Measure of Men: Science, Technology,
and Ideologies of Western Dominance* (Ithaca, NY: Cornell University
Press, 1989), 64–5, 273–4.

29 Robert A. Williams, *The American Indian in Western Legal Thought:
The Discourses of Conquest* (New York: Oxford University Press,
1990), 271. His account of the revolutionary era follows that of Jack
M. Sosin, *Whitehall and Wilderness: The Middle West in British
Colonial Policy* (Lincoln: University of Nebraska Press, 1961).

30 Philip J. Deloria, "Revolution, Religion, and Culture in Multicultural
History," *William and Mary Quarterly*, 3rd series, 53, no. 2 (April
1996), 369. For the wider critique of the revolution, see Edward
Countryman, "Indians, the Colonial Order, and the Social Significance
of the American Revolution," *William and Mary Quarterly* 53
(April 1996), 343–62.

31 This argument follows John S. Galbraith; see his *Reluctant Empire*,
1–9, 123–50. For a discussion of "the limits of occupation" in
Australia, see Weaver, "'Beyond the Fatal Shore': Pastoral Squatting
and the Occupation of Australia, 1828–1852," *American Historical
Review* 101 (Oct. 1996), 986.

32 Report on Instructions to the *Landdrost* for Graaff-Reinet, 6 Jan. 1786,
in H.C.V. Leibrandt, ed., *Precis of the Archives of the Cape of Good
Hope: Requesten (Memorials, 1715–1806)* (Cape Town: Government
Printers, 1906), vol. 2, 486.

33 Where pressure from Dutch settlements impinged on Indian fields and
villages there was conflict. Allen W. Trelease, *Indian Affairs in Colonial New York: The Seventeenth Century* (Lincoln: University of
Nebraska Press, 1997; reprint of 1960), 40–1. At the end of the second
Esopus War (1663–4), several tribes were required to cede "most of

their tribal lands around the European settlements." Oliver A. Rink, *Holland on the Hudson: An Economic and Social History of Dutch New York* (Ithaca, NY: Cornell University Press, 1986), 260.

34 Georgiana C. Nammack, *Fraud, Politics, and the Dispossession of the Indians* (Norman: University of Oklahoma Press, 1969), 3–38; Wallace, *King of the Delawares*, 139–45.

35 P.G. Brink to F.G, Farewell, 5 May 1824, in John Bird, ed., *The Annals of Natal*, vol. 1 (Cape Town: C. Struik, 1965; facsimile reprint), 73; Chaka's Grant, 8 Aug. 1824, in ibid., 193–5. Farewell's widow and creditors tried unsuccessfully as late as 1843 to claim land under this deed.

36 T.R.H. Davenport, *South Africa: A Modern History* (London: Macmillan, 1987), 81, 144, 149, 156, 165; Johannes Meintjes, *The Voortrekkers: The Story of the Great Trek and the Making of South Africa* (London: Cassell, 1973), 45, 75, 98–9, 106. Meintjes is at pains to emphasize cessions of land to voortrekkers.

37 "The heroic and honorific nomenclature" – the Great Trek – was not used at the time. Neither was voortrekker – those who travel ahead. The participants thought of themselves as *uitgewekenen* emigrants. For a discussion of the importance of these terms, see André du Toit and Hermann Giliomee, *Afrikaner Political Thought: Analysis and Documents, Volume One: 1780–1850* (Berkeley: University of California Press, 1983), 200.

38 Meintjes, *The Voortrekkers*, 141–2.

39 Major Mathew Richmond to Robinson, 11 April 1845, Colonial Secretary of New Munster, Despatches to Local Officials, NM 10/3, NZ.

40 Commissioners of crown lands commanded the police and could refuse grazing licences to squatters of bad character and deny licences for dangerous regions. But the small police detachments had to cover impossibly large areas. The commissioners thought that frontiers would become stabilized as more Aborigines were employed on stations. G.J. Macdonald to Colonial Secretary, 18 April and 11 June 1840, 4/2438.2; Henry Bingham to Colonial Secretary, 13 Oct. 1840, 4/2486.1; —— Mayne to Colonial Secretary, 16 May 1842, 4/2564.1; —— Hunter to Colonial Secretary, 8 Jan. 1844, 4/2640; Colonial Secretary, Letters Received from Crown Land Commissioners, Archives of New South Wales.

41 R. Wright, *The Bureaucrats' Domain* (Melbourne: Oxford University Press, 1989), 25; Vivienne Rae-Ellis, *Black Robinson: Protector of Aborigines* (Melbourne: University of Melbourne Press, 1988), 178–9.

42 *The South Australian Government Gazette*, 26 May 1842, Mortlock Library, State Library of South Australia.

43 Claudia Orange, *The Treaty of Waitangi* (Wellington: Bridget Williams Books Limited, 1992), 93.
44 Galbraith, *Reluctant Empire*, 78.
45 Ronald Hyam, *Britain's Imperial Century, 1815–1914* (London: B.T. Batsford, 1976), 45–6. Humanitarian impulses in British public life were fading, and assertions of racial inequalities were strengthening during the 1860s. The Indian Mutiny (1857), a rebellion in Jamaica (1865), and the New Zealand Wars (1860–70) had adverse effects on reform societies. Christine Bolt, *Victorian Attitudes to Race* (London: Routledge & Kegan Paul, 1971).
46 From 1776 to 1880, the United States spent $322,049,595 on acquiring and surveying Indian land and realized $200,702,849 from the public domain. In effect, it was subsidizing land-based enterprise. Thomas Donaldson, *The Public Domain: Its History with Statistics* (Washington, DC: Government Printing Office, 1884), 20–1.
47 Francis Paul Prucha, *The Great Father: The United States and the American Indians* (Lincoln: University of Nebraska Press, 1984), 350.
48 The report on army engagements with Indians is taken from a copy of United States Army, Adjutant General's Office, *Engagements of Indians with US Troops, January 1, 1666 to January 1, 1891* (n.p., n.d.), found in folder 4, box 15, L.R.A. Condit Papers, accession 4, American Heritage Center University of Wyoming (AHC).
49 Robert M. Utley, "Indian–United States Military Situation, 1848–1891," in Wilcomb E. Washburn, *History of Indian–White Relations*, vol. 4 (Washington, DC: Smithsonian Institution, 1988), 183. See Prucha on the Black Hawk War, *Great White Father*, 253–64, and, for other conflicts, 339–483.
50 *Autobiography of E.D. Swan*, 40, accession 371, AHC.
51 Ibid., 115–16.
52 Clifton C. Crais, *White Supremacy and Black Resistance in Pre-Industrial South Africa: The Making of the Colonial Order in the Eastern Cape, 1770–1865* (Cambridge: Cambridge University Press, 1992), 143.
53 James Belich, *I Shall Not Die: Titokowaru's War, New Zealand, 1868–1869* (Wellington: Bridget Williams Book, 1999; first pub. 1989), 218.
54 Recognition of this was the basis for the High Court's decision, in *Mabo*, that the principle of "native title" found in the Torres Islands could also apply to the continent. See Brennan, J., in *Mabo and others vs. The State of Queensland* [1991–1992], 40. For an elaboration of the revived status of indigenous rights in international law and how these may apply to Canada, see Michel Morin, *L'usurpation de la souveraineté autochtone* (Montreal: Boréal, 1997), 164–268.

55 Cuthbert Fetherstonhaugh, *After Many Days* (Melbourne: E.W. Cole, 1883), 293–4.

56 David Spurr, *The Rhetoric of Empire: Colonial Discourse in Journalism, Travel Writing, and Imperial Administration* (Durham, NC: Duke University Press, 1993), 32.

57 William Cronon, *Changes in the Land: Indians, Colonists, and the Ecology of New England* (New York: Hill and Wang, 1983), 56–7.

58 Pat Maloney, "Colonisation and Cultivation: Early Victorians and the Extension of Their World," paper presented at the Land and Freedom Conference, July 1999, Newcastle, Australia. I am indebted to Professor Maloney for his insight. For Adam Smith's lecture, see "Private Law," in R.L. Meek, D.D. Raphael, and P.G. Stein, eds., *Adam Smith: Lectures on Jurisprudence* (Oxford: Clarendon Press, 1978), 459–60. Andrew Skinner provides an account of Smith's ideas about the stages of history in "Adam Smith: An Economic Interpretation of History," in Skinner and Thomas Wilson, eds., *Essays of Adam Smith* (Oxford: Clarendon Press, 1975), 155–78.

59 Jared Diamond, *Guns, Germs, and Steel: The Fates of Human Societies* (New York: W.W. Norton, 1999).

60 Spurr discusses the uses of classification by late-nineteenth-century British imperial administrators; *The Rhetoric of Empire*, 68–9.

61 The injustices to first peoples continued, "not from having to settle on poor lands, but from the ultimate lack of secure and permanent enjoyment of the lands they received." Francis Paul Prucha, *The Great Father: The United States Government and the American Indians* (Lincoln: University of Nebraska Press, 1984), 229. See his account of removal, 183–292.

62 James Sean McKeown, "Return J. Meigs: United States Agent in the Cherokee Nation, 1801–1823" (unpublished PhD dissertation, Pennsylvania State University, 1985).

63 On the prosperity and assets of the Cherokees, see Douglas C. Wilms, "Cherokee Land Use in Georgia before Removal," in William L. Anderson, ed., *Cherokee Removal: Before and After* (Athens: University of Georgia Press, 1991), 1–24. On the shaping of the policy of removal, see Ronald Satz, *American Indian Policy in the Jacksonian Era* (Lincoln: University of Nebraska Press, 1975), 19.

64 Walter Mantell, Report on the Demand of Resident Natives of Waikonaiti that their Reserve be extended … , 4 Sept. 1852, Walter Mantell, Letterbook, November 1851–January 1855, Micro ms. 661, Alexander Turnbull Library, National Library of New Zealand. Mantell later regretted some of his views and actions. See Joanne Wilkes, "Walter Mantell, Geraldine Jewsbury, and Race Relations in New Zealand," *New Zealand Journal of History* 22 (Oct. 1988), 107.

William Cronon suggests that perhaps English colonial leaders criticized Indians because their lives were "too close to certain English
pastoral and aristocratic fantasies for Calvinists to tolerate." Cronon,
Changes, 56.

65 Cock was a Swedish trader. A Swedish trading company established
a colony on the Delaware River in 1638 and surrendered to the Dutch
in 1655. C.A. Weslager, *The Delaware Indians: A History* (New
Brunswick, NJ: Rutgers University Press, 1972), 113–52.

66 Weslager, *The Delaware Indians*, 161–71; Urs Bitterli, *Cultures in
Conflict: Encounters between European and Non-European Cultures,
1492–1800* (Cambridge: Polity Press, 1989), 121–32.

67 Wallace, *King of the Delawares*, 18–30.

68 Nammack, *Fraud, Politics, and the Dispossession of the Indians*, 27.

69 Ibid., 92–3.

70 Paul W. Gates, "A Fragment of Kansas Land History: The Disposal of
the Christian Indian Tract," *Kansas Historical Quarterly* 6 (1937),
227–40.

71 Washington to Crawford, 21 Sept. 1767; in C.W. Butterfield, ed.,
*Washington–Crawford Letters. Being the Correspondence between
George Washington and William Crawford, from 1767 to 1781,
Concerning Western Lands* (Cincinnati: Robert Clarke and Company,
1877), 3.

72 Abernethy, *Western Lands*, 68.

73 Thomas Gage to William Johnson, 16 May 1764, in *Johnson Papers*,
vol. 4, 425. See White, *The Middle Ground*, 308.

74 Albert Volwiler, *George Crogan and the Westward Movement, 1741–
1782* (Cleveland: Arthur H. Clark, 1926), 212–13; William Crawford
to George Washington, 29 Sept. 1767, in Butterfield, *Washington–
Crawford Letters*, 6.

75 Volwiler, *George Crogan*, 27.

76 Abernethy, *Western Lands*, 11–12. He provides no background on the
theory of indigenous interests and leaves the impression that the proclamation may have been more of a departure than it was. The clear
recognition of indigenous interests, specifically in western lands, though
new, was an extension of theory and practice, not a policy innovation.

77 Volwiler, *George Crogan*, 70–1.

78 Alan Taylor, *William Cooper's Town: Power and Persuasion on the
Frontier of the Early American Republic* (New York: Vintage Books,
1995), 45.

79 Abernethy, *Western Lands*, 69.

80 Ibid., 16.

81 "Some Wisconsin Indian Conveyances, 1793–1836," in Reuben Gold
Thwaites, ed., *Collections of the State Historical Society of Wisconsin,*

vol. 15, 2–20; Lela Barnes, "Journal of Isaac McCoy for the Exploring Expedition of 1830," *Kansas Historical Quarterly* 5 (1936), 350.
82 Woody Holton, *Forced Founders: Indians, Debtors, Slaves, and the
Making of the American Revolution in Virginia* (Chapel Hill:
University of North Carolina Press, 1999), 10.
83 Volwiler, *George Crogan*, 222–5.
84 Jones, 115–19. Woody Holton discusses the land speculation failures
that frustrated a handful of leading Virginians. Holton, *Forced
Founders*, 28–36. George D. Wolf, *The Fair Play Settlers of the West
Branch Valley, 1769–1784: A Study of Frontier Ethnography* (Harris-
burg: Pennsylvania Historical and Museum Commission, 1969), 3–15,
32–46.
85 Robert F. Berkhofer, "Barrier to Settlement: British Indian Policy in the
Old Northwest, 1783–1794," in David M. Ellis, *The Frontier and
American Development: Essays in Honour of Paul Wallace Gates*
(Ithaca, NY: Cornell University Press, 1969), 266–76; Abernethy,
Western Lands, 316–18.
86 Jones, 156. See also R.S. Cotrell, "Federal Indian Management in the
South, 1789–1825," *Mississippi Valley Historical Review* 20 (March
1934), 333–52. Cotrell suggests that memories of how the United
States treated the Five Civilized Tribes may have influenced their
support for the Confederacy during the Civil War.
87 Robert Utley sees parallels between the western American and prairie
Canadian experience with native title; *The Indian Frontier of the
American West, 1846–1890* (Albuquerque: University of New Mexico
Press, 1984), 270–1. Leo A. Johnson, "The Mississauga–Lake Ontario
Surrender of 1805," *Ontario History* 83 (Sept. 1990), 233–50. The
sequence of treaties of cession in Upper Canada and the west can be
found in Pierrette Désy and Frédéric Castel, "Native Reserves of
Eastern Canada to 1900," Plate 32, "Native Reserves: Names and
Descriptions," Plate 33, Native Reserves of Western Canada to 1900,"
in R. Louis Gentilcore, ed., *Historical Atlas of Canada, Volume II, The
Land Transformed, 1800–1891* (Toronto: University of Toronto Press,
1993).
88 Manfred Nathan, *The Voortrekkers of South Africa* (London: Gordon
and Gotch, 1937), 81. A ninety-nine-year lease is mentioned in
"Herinneringen van Karl Trichardt," Gustavus Preller, *Voortrekkermense II* (Kaapstad: de Nationale Pers, 1920), 5. The lease may have
started a rumour that Louis Trichardt had supported the Xhosa paramount Hintsa in the frontier war of 1834. See J.L. Dracopoli, *Sir
Andries Stockenstrom, 1792–1864: The Origins of Racial Conflict in
South Africa* (Cape Town: A.A. Balkema, 1969), 136. Other grazers
used Xhosa lands or left cattle under Xhosa care. See *Copy of Minutes*

of Proceedings of the Court of Inquiry ... to Investigate and Report upon the Circumstances Attendant on the Fate of the Caffer Chief Hintza (Cape Town: Brand's, 1837), 29.

89 Ross, *Adam Kok's Griquas: A Study in the Development of Stratification in South Africa* (Cambridge: Cambridge University Press, 1976), 135. J.S. Marais was the first historian to tell the story of the Griquas' demise with sympathy and fairness in *The Cape Coloured People* (Johannesburg: Witwatersrang University Press, 1957), 32–73.

90 Van der Merwe, *Die noordwaartse beweging*, 316–21. Dealings with the Khoikhoi are discussed in David Arnot and Francis H.S. Orpen, *The Land Question of Griqualand West* (Cape Town: Saul Solomon, 1875), 21.

91 Nathan, *The Voortrekkers*, 141. See the negotiations mentioned by Trigardt in his diary, T.H. Le Roux, ed., *Die Dagboek van Louis Trigardt* (Pretoria: J.L. van Schaik, 1964), 19 Aug. 1837, 82–3.

92 Johannes Meintjes, *The Voortrekkers: The Story of the Great Trek and the Making of South Africa* (London: Castells, 1973), 47.

93 Edgar H. Brookes and Colin de B. Webb, *A History of Natal* (Pietermaritzburg: University of Natal Press, 1965), 16–21.

94 Robert C.-H. Shell, *Children of Bondage: A Social History of the Slave Society at the Cape of Good Hope, 1652–1838* (Hanover, NH: Wesleyan University Press, 1994), 171.

95 Galbraith, *Reluctant Empire*, 178; Meintjes, *The Voortrekkers*, 44.

96 Daniel Neumark, *Economic Influences on the South African Frontier, 1652–1836* (Stanford, Calif.: Stanford University Press, 1957), 169. The idea that trekboers had commercial ties to the coast – the so-called Neumark thesis – has been criticized. Critics propose that family increase and partible inheritance were the main causes of frontier expansion. But the trade links did exist, and the grazers traded for gunpowder and other commodities. See van der Merwe, *The Migrant Farmer in the History of the Cape Colony* (Athens: University of Ohio Press), 159–64.

97 Petrus Johannes van der Merwe, *Nog verder noord: Die Potgieter-kommissie se besoek aan die gebied van die teenwoodige Suid-Rhodesïe, 1836* (Johannesburg: Nasionale Boekhandel, 1962), 17–20; L. Tregardt (sic) to the Portuguese authorities at Delagoa Bay, 11 May 1837, in Le Roux, *Die Dagboek*, 42; Meintjes, *The Voortrekkers*, 61.

98 The quote is from Gert Maritz in 1837 and appears in Meintjes, *The Voortrekkers*, 75. For land sales in Natal, see Volksraad of Natal to Commissioner Cloete, 4 Sept. 1843, in André du Toit and Hermann Giliomee, *Afrikaner Political Thought: Analysis and Documents, Volume One, 1780–1850* (Berkeley: University of California Press, 1983), 221–2.

Notes to pages 163–5

On the Caledon valley, see Timothy Keegan, *Colonial South Africa*, 251–2; on the Orange River Sovereignty, see Galbraith, *Reluctant Empire*, 271; on the Transvaal, see Davenport, *South Africa*, 85.

100 Extensive *voortrekker* dealings in land rights in Natal were reported in 1842–43. See remarks about Commandant Gert Rudolph in Captain J.C. Smith to Sir George Napier, 14 Aug. 1842; H. Cloete to Napier, 20 June 1843; in John Bird, ed., *The Annals of Natal* (Cape Town: C. Struik, 1965; facsimile reprint), vol. 2, 72, 191. Smith forwarded examples of deeds issued by the Natal Volksraad, Smith to Napier, 14 Oct. 1842, in ibid., 107–9.

101 "Attorney Cleote," quoted in "The Cape Town Merchants' Memorial of 1834," in Percival Kirby, *Andrew Smith and Natal: Documents Relating to the Early History of That Province* (Cape Town: Van Riebeeck Society, 1955), 147–8. Other proponents of annexation insisted on the idea of an uninhabited region, and it was a claim accepted by the colonial land commissioners in London in 1841. See their report in ibid., 227–38.

102 "Narrative of Willem Jurgen Pretorius," in Bird, *The Annals of Natal*, vol. 1, 234–5.

103 The claim was that much of the veld was unoccupied. The tribes whom white settlers encountered were alleged to be migrants. From this belief, it was a simple step to *terra nullius*. W.A. Stals, *Die kwessie van naturelle-eigendomsreg op grond in Transvaal, 1838–1884* (Pretoria: Argiefjaarboek vir Suid-Afrikaanse Geskiedenis, 1977), 1–7. For the white-settler assertion of sovereignty respecting Mpande, see "Pretorius," in Bird, *The Annals of Natal*, vol. 1, 237. A good account of the relations between voortrekkers and Zulus appears in Stephen Taylor, *Shaka's Children: A History of the Zulu People* (London: HarperCollins, 1994), 77–158. For Mpande's approach to the voortrekkers, see Minutes of the Volksraad, 15 Oct. 1839; Report of the Landdrost of Tugela [Embassy to Mpande], Oct. 1839, in Bird, *The Annals of Natal*, vol. 1, 536–44.

104 "Declaration and Protest of the Assembly of the Emigrants [11 November 1839]"; Proclamation of Andries Wilhelmus Jacobus Pretorius [14 Feb. 1840], both in Bird, *The Annals of Natal*, vol. 1, 544–6, 595.

105 Davenport, *South Africa*, 165–70.

106 "Journal of the Late Charl Celliers," in Bird, *The Annals of Natal*, vol. 1, 240.

107 Nathan, *The Voortrekkers*, 154–9.

108 A.H. Potgieter, Sand River, to Governor D'Urban, 3 Dec. 1838, in du Toit and Giliomee, *Afrikaner Political Thought*, 216.

109 For two summaries of land appropriations, see Davenport, 136–183; Leonard Thompson, *A History of South Africa* (New Haven, Conn.: Yale University Press, 1995), 122–32. There are detailed accounts in J.M.S. Matsebula, *A History of Swaziland* (Cape Town: Longman, 1988), 50–2; Peter Delius, *The Land Belongs to Us: The Pedi Polity, the Boers and the British in the Nineteenth-Century Transvaal* (Berkeley: University of California Press, 1984), 30–3.

110 Davenport, *South Africa*, 24.

111 P. Stigger, *The Land Commission of 1894 and the Land* (Salisbury: Historical Association of Zimbabwe, 1980), 1–34. For a definitive account, see Arthur Keppel-Jones, *Rhodes and Rhodesia: The White Conquest of Zimbabwe, 1884–1902* (Montreal: McGill-Queen's University Press, 1983).

112 When Piet Retief allowed his command to be overwhelmed by Dingane, it was because of the latter's ruse of a meeting to close a treaty.

113 This summary of Maori genius and British errors is elaborated on throughout James Belich, *The New Zealand Wars and the Victorian Interpretation of Racial Conflict* (Auckland: Penguin, 1988).

114 White, *The Middle Ground*, 257–9.

115 T.R.H. Davenport and K.S. Hunt, eds., *The Right to the Land* (Cape Town: David Philip, 1974), 20–30, 40–6. For the destruction of the Zulu kingdom and land seizures by the South African Republic (Transvaal), see Jeff Guy, *The Destruction of the Zulu Kingdom: The Civil War in Zululand* (Johannesburg: Ravan Press, 1982), 222–7, 232–5.

116 The evidence is presented in Orange, *The Treaty of Waitangi*, 17–31.

117 Orange is correct in identifying the Colonial Office's dilemmas. Ibid., 30.

118 Monica Wilson and Leonard Thompson, eds., *The Oxford History of South Africa* (Oxford: Clarendon Press, 1969), 354.

119 George Weller to Edward Weller, 16 March 1835; George Weller to Alexander Macleay, Colonial Secretary, 27 July 1835, Weller Brothers Papers, microfilm, CY reel 117, A 1609, Dixson Library, Mitchell Library.

120 Alan Ward, "The Treaty and the Purchase of Maori Land," *New Zealand Journal of History* 22 (Oct. 1988), 170.

121 Orange, *The Treaty of Waitangi*, 91.

122 On FitzRoy's removal of crown pre-emption, see Paul Moon, *FitzRoy: Governor in Crisis, 1843–1845* (Auckland: David Ling, 2000), 200–5.

123 Prucha, *The Great Father*, I, 91–3.

124 Weaver, "Frontiers into Assets," 37–44.

125 John Munro to Donald McLean, 3 March 1857, 9 June 1857, 1 February 1858, ms. 32, folder 470, Alexander Turnbull Library, National Library of New Zealand.

126 Council of Policy, 13 April 1672, 24 June 1677, 5 Aug. 1679, in
     Theal, *Abstract of the Debates and Resolutions*, 127, 155, 181.
127 Jonkvrouw Augusta Uitenhage de Mist, *Diary of a Journey to the Cape
     of Good Hope and the Interior of Africa in 1802 and 1803* (Cape
     Town: A.A. Balkema, 1954), 30.
128 Stals, *Die Kwessie*, 1–7; J.W.N. Tempelhoff, *Die okkupasiestelsel in die
     Distrik Soupansberg, 1886–1899* (Pretoria: Die Staatsdrukker, 1997),
     1–3.
129 Stals, *Die Kwessie*, 4.
130 Government Notices, 29 May 1846, 27 Aug. 1846, in W.J. Dunbar
     Moodie, ed., *Ordinances, Proclamations, etc., Relating to the Colony
     of Natal* (Pietermaritzburg: May and Davis, 1856), 230. The taking of
     Zulu land, including events in the twentieth century, is covered in
     Taylor, *Shaka's Children*, 193–281.
131 Government Notice, 5 May 1847, in Moodie, ed., *Ordinances*, 258.
132 Richard H. Bartlett, *Native Title in Australia* (Sydney: Butterworths,
     2000), 4.
133 Alexander Berry was one pioneer who elected to make gifts to local
     chiefs. "Passages in the Life of a Nonagenarian," mss. 315/112, Dixson
     Library, Mitchell Library.
134 John Stieglitz to Sir Richard Bourke, 18 Oct. 1836, in Michael Cannon
     and Ian MacFarlane, eds., *The Crown, the Land and the Squatter,
     1835–1840: Historical Records of Victoria, Foundation Series,
     Volume 6* (Melbourne: Melbourne University Press, 1991), 21–2.
135 William Wiseman to Chief Commissioner of Crown Lands, 28 Aug.
     1855, microfilm 0110, Letters of William Wiseman, 1855–1860, Oxley
     Library, State Library of Queensland.
136 Wiseman to Chief Commissioner, 5 Jan. 1856, ibid. For similar atti-
     tudes on the same frontier, see Cuthbert Fetherstonaugh, *After Many
     Days* (Melbourne: E.W. Cole, 1917), 293–6.
137 Anne Allingham, *Taming the Wilderness* (Townsville: Department of
     History, James Cook University, 1977), 154–67.
138 Bartlett, *Native Title in Australia*, 544–5.
139 Paul Tennant, "The Historical and Legal Dimensions," in Frank Cassidy,
     ed., *Reaching Just Settlements: Land Claims in British Columbia*
     (Lantzville, BC: Oolichan Books and the Institute for Research on Public
     Policy, 1991), 27–31. There is an excellent discussion in Sidney L.
     Herring, *White Man's Law: Native People in Nineteenth-Century
     Canadian Jurisprudence* (Toronto: Published for the Osgoode Society for
     Canadian Legal History by University of Toronto Press, 1998), 186–216.
140 Robin Fisher, *Contact and Conflict: Indian–European Relations in
     British Columbia* (Vancouver: University of British Columbia Press,
     1977), 195–6.

141 W.D. Hamilton, "Indian Lands in New Brunswick: The Case of the Little South West Reserve," *Acadiensis* 13 (spring 1984), 3–28, quote at 28.

142 Prucha, *The Great Father*, 530–33.

143 For a history of the administration of the Dawes Act and an assessment of the failure of allotment to help Indians, see Janet A. McDonnell, *The Dispossession of the American Indian, 1887–1934* (Bloomington: Indiana University Press, 1991). McDonnell points out that allotment was not accompanied by any educational programs and broke up Indian social and economic life.

144 Bryan D. Gilling, "Engine of Destruction? An Introduction to the History of the Maori Land Court," *Victoria University Law Review* 24 (July 1994), 115–39; "The Queen's Sovereignty Must be Vindicated: The 1840 Rule in the Maori Land Court," *New Zealand Universities Law Review* 16 (Dec. 1994), 136–74; Tom Brooking, "'Busting Up' the Greatest Estate of All," *New Zealand Journal of History* 26 (April 1992), 78–89. Brookings points out that purchasing of crown land thrived at the turn of the century. For an overview of southern Africa, see Davenport and Hunt, eds., *The Right to the Land*, 31; for a detailed, tragic account of land grabbing in one region, see Colin Murray, *Black Mountain: Land, Class and Power in the Eastern Orange Free State* (Edinburgh: University of Edinburgh Press, 1992), 21–51. Consequences of discrimination in land policy and reform possibilities are discussed in Hans P. Binswanger and Klaus Deininger, "South African Land Policy: The Legacy of History and Current Options," *World Development* 21, no. 9 (1993), 1451–75.

CHAPTER FIVE

1 Eric R. Wolf, "Facing Power – Old Insights, New Questions," *American Anthropologist* 92, no. 3 (1990), 586.

2 Donna Merwick, *Possessing Albany, 1630–1710: The Dutch and English Experiences* (Cambridge: Cambridge University Press, 1990), 294.

3 Leonard Thompson, *A History of South Africa* (New Haven, Conn.: Yale University Press, 1990), 33.

4 Viola Florence Barnes, "Land Tenure in English Colonial Charters of the Seventeenth Century," in *Essays in Colonial History Presented to Charles McLean Andrews by His Students* (New Haven, Conn.: Yale University Press, 1931), 14–16.

5 Jack P. Greene summarizes the course of this development for Virginia in *Pursuit of Happiness: The Social Development of Early Modern British Colonies and the Formation of American Culture* (Chapel Hill: University of North Carolina Press, 1988), 8–13.

6 Barnes mentions Ulster; ibid., 23–4. However, its colonization is best
reviewed in T.W. Freeman, *Pre-Famine Ireland: A Study in Historical
Geography* (Manchester: Manchester University Press, 1957), and
T.W. Moody, *The Londonderry Planation, 1609–41* (Belfast: William
Mullen, 1939). The quote is from Nicholas Canny, *Kingdom and
Colony: Ireland in the Atlantic World* (Baltimore: Johns Hopkins
University Press, 1988), 7.

7 Charles M. Andrews, *The Colonial Period of American History: The
Settlements*, vol. 1 (New Haven, Conn.: Yale University Press, 1964,
first pub. 1934), 321–2. Andrews's emphasis on political and constitutional history, grounded in documentation, makes his works a suitable
source for this section of my study. For an appraisal of his legacy, see
Richard R. Johnson, "Charles McLean Andrews and the Invention
of American Colonial History," *William and Mary Quarterly* 43
(Oct. 1986).

8 Andrews, *Colonial Period*, vol. 1, 281–2.

9 Ibid., 279–99, 344–74.

10 William Cronon, *Changes in the Land: Indians, Colonists, and the
Ecology of New England* (New York: Hill and Wang, 1983), 74.

11 Theodore K. Rabb, *Enterprise and Empire: Merchant and Gentry
Investment in the Expansion of England, 1575–1630* (Cambridge,
Mass.: Harvard University Press, 1967), 19–101. Rabb notes that
importance of a combination of merchants and gentry to imperial
expansion. Members of the gentry were prominent in terms of numbers and capital in the Massachusetts Bay, New England, Providence
Island, and Virginia companies, but less so in the great trading venture,
the East India Company. See 30, 66.

12 For a survey history that includes accounts of the Penn family's
involvement in government and land developments, see Joseph J.
Kelley, Jr, *Pennsylvania: The Colonial Years, 1681–1776* (New York:
Doubleday, 1980).

13 D.K. Fieldhouse, *The Colonial Empires: A Comparative Survey from
the Eighteenth Century*, 2nd ed. (London: Macmillian, 1982), 52;
C.R. Boxer, *The Dutch Seaborne Empire, 1600–1800* (London:
Penguin, 1990; first pub. 1965), 26–50. This idea is sustained by
Jonathan I. Israel, *Dutch Primacy in World Trade, 1585–1740*
(Oxford: Clarendon Press, 1989), 69–70, 103.

14 For an account of the West Indies Company and land policies, see
Clarence White Rife, "Land Tenure in New Netherland," in *Essays in
Colonial History Presented to Charles McLean Andrews*, 41–73. The
state of settlement at New Netherland is discussed in Oliver A. Rink,
*Holland on the Hudson: An Economic and Social History of Dutch
New York* (Ithaca, NY: Cornell University Press, 1986), 139–71, 259.

15 Some in the company believed that the fur trade could be lucrative if it could eliminate competition from colonists. See Rink, *Holland on the Hudson*, 94–138.

16 Ibid., 65.

17 There are several studies of the Hudson manors and their demise: David Maldwyn Ellis, *Landlords and Farmers in the Hudson-Mohawk Region, 1790–1850* (New York: Octagon Books, 1967), and Charles W. McCurdy, *The Anti-Rent Era in New York Law and Politics, 1839–1865* (Chapel Hill: University of North Carolina Press, 2000); Reeve Huston provides an excellent account of the decline of the landlords, in *Land and Freedom: Rural Society, Popular Protest, and Party Politics in Antebellum New York* (Oxford: Oxford University Press, 2000).

18 For an illuminating discussion of settlement at Cape Colony under the Dutch, see Leonard Guelke, "The White Settlers, 1652–1780," in Richard Elphick and Hermann Giliomee, eds., *The Shaping of South African Society, 1652–1820* (Cape Town: Longman Penguin, 1979), 41–74. Much of my argument is indebted to this well-researched and stimulating article. Also see Richard Elphick, *Khoikhoi and Founding of White South Africa* (Johannesburg: Ravan Press, 1985), 90–174, quote, 110.

19 Elphick, *Khoikhoi and the Founding of White South Africa*, 221; Leslie Clement Duly, *British Land Policy at the Cape, 1795–1844: A Study of Administrative Procedures in the Empire* (Durham, NC: Duke University Press, 1968), 14–20.

20 Leonard Guelke and Robert Shell, "Landscape of Conquest: Frontier Water Alienation and Khoikoi Strategies of Survival, 1652–1780," *Journal of Southern African Studies* 18 (Dec. 1985), 813.

21 Ibid., 222–3.

22 African fat-tailed sheep – good for mutton, but not for wool – were long favoured by the Dutch-speaking farmers because of their durability in southern African conditions. Moreover, producing wool required more labour and capital than producing mutton. See S. Daniel Neumark, *Economic Influences on the South African Frontier, 1652–1836* (Stanford, Calif.: Stanford University Press, 1957), 165–70. On the demand for proper titles to frontier lands, see Duly, *British Land Policy*, 113–6. On consolidation of grazing estates, see Clifton C. Crais, *White Supremacy and Black Resistance in Pre-Industrial South Africa: The Making of the Colonial Order in the Eastern Cape, 1770–1865* (Cambridge: Cambridge University Press, 1992), 134–5; on speculation, see A.J. Christopher, *The Crown Lands of South Africa, 1853–1914* (Kingston: Limestone Press, 1984), 21–3.

23 Guelke, "The White Settlers, 1652–1780," 64–5.

24 Van der Merwe, *Die noordwaartse beweging van die boere voor die groot trek (1770–1842)* (The Hague: W.P. Van Stockum & Zoon, 1937), 109, 128.

25 Christopher, *The Crown Lands*, 193–200.

26 For a discussion of climate see John S. Galbraith, *Reluctant Empire: British Policy on the South African Frontier, 1834–1854* (Berkeley: University of California Press, 1963), 31.

27 Duly, *British Land Policy*, 21–158.

28 For a good defence of the company's accomplishments along the St Lawrence, see Marcel Trudel, *Histoire de la Nouvelle-France: La seigneurie des Cents-Associés, 1627–1663: Tome 1, Les événements* (Montreal: Fides, 1979), 387–409.

29 William J. Eccles, *France in America* (New York: Harper & Row, 1972), 1–89.

30 Richard Colebrook Harris, *The Seigneurial System in Early Canada: A Geographical Study* (Montreal: McGill-Queen's University Press, 1984), 25.

31 Ibid., 26–7.

32 Tradition credited the Carignan–Salières Regiment with a nearly providential role in New France. Subsequently, one of the most influential interpreters of the history of New France, William Eccles, accepted these earlier claims, because his work accented the importance of the military to New France. A thorough history of the regiment by Jack Verney established that its soldiers were like those found throughout the French army. Moreover, this account argues that the Richelieu River seigneuries were not as strategically important as had been maintained. See Jack Verney, *The Good Regiment: The Carignan–Salières Regiment in Canada, 1665–1668* (Montreal: McGill-Queen's University Press, 1991), 118–19. For Eccles's views, see his *France in America*, rev. ed. (Markham, Ont.: Fitzhenry and Whiteside, 1990), 125–56.

33 Eccles, *France in America*, 67.

34 Allan Greer, *Peasant, Lord, and Merchant: Rural Society in Three Quebec Parishes, 1740–1840* (Toronto: University of Toronto Press, 1985), 139.

35 Carl Ekberg, *French Roots in the Illinois Country: The Mississippi Frontier in Colonial Times* (Urbana: University of Illinois, 1998), 5–137. On the strategies behind transfers of portions of estates, see Laurent Marien, "Les arrière-fiefs au Canada sous le régime français; des expressions d'enjeux socio-économiques," in David Bussieret, ed., *France in the New World: Proceedings of the 22nd Annual Meeting of the French Colonial History Society* (East Lansing: Michigan State University Press, 1998), 151–9.

36 Louise Dechêne, "La rente du faubourg Saint-Roch à Québec, 1750–
   1850," *Revue d'histoire de l'amérique française* 34 (March 1981),
   569–96. See also Dechêne, "The Seigneuries," Plate 51, R. Cole Harris,
   ed., *Historical Atlas of Canada, Volume 1, From the Beginning to
   1800* (Toronto: University of Toronto Press, 1987).

37 The Dutch and English empires were unequal, and to some extent the
   Dutch employed place names and cartography to assert their territorial claims. See Benjamin Schmidt, "Mapping an Empire: Cartographic
   and Colonial Rivalry in Seventeenth-Century Dutch and English North
   America," *William and Mary Quarterly* 54 (July 1997), 435–58. Also
   see Thomas J. Condon, *New York Beginnings: The Commercial Origins of the New Netherlands* (New York: New York University Press,
   1968), 144–79. For the character of government at the Cape, see
   Gerrit Schutte, "Company and Colonists at the Cape," in Richard
   Elphick and Hermann Giliomee, eds., *The Shaping of South African
   Society, 1652–1820* (Cape Town: Longman, 1979), 173–87.

38 For a discussion of how the fur trade and rural Quebec society inter-
   acted see Alan Greer, *Peasant, Land, and Merchant: Rural Society in
   Three Quebec Parishes, 1740–1840* (Toronto: University of Toronto
   Press, 1985), 177–93.

39 Geoffrey V. Scammell, *The First Imperial Age: European Overseas
   Expansion c. 1400–1715* (London: Unwin Hyman, 1989), 159.

40 Barnes, "Land Tenure," 40. This older work in legal history remains
   reliable. For the crown's effort to assert its prerogatives in colonial
   affairs, particularly by establishing the Board of Trade, see Ian K.
   Steele, *Politics of Colonial Policy: The Board of Trade in Colonial
   Administration, 1696–1720* (Oxford: Clarendon Press, 1968), 15–18.
   Steele proposes that improved communications in the eighteenth cen-
   tury allowed for a greater centralization of colonial politics. See Steele,
   *The English Atlantic: An Exploration of Communication and
   Community* (New York: Oxford University Press, 1986), 247–50.

41 A good account of these events is spread throughout Thomas
   Abernethy, *Western Lands*, which should be read with Richard White,
   The Middle Ground.

42 The expression was popularized, if not coined, by David M. Potter. See
   Potter, *People of Plenty: Economic Abundance and the American Character* (Chicago: University of Chicago Press, 1954). Potter argues that
   it was not the frontier that made the American character, but abundance. He never asks what the source of abundance might have been.

43 Douglas Hurt, *The Ohio Frontier: Crucible of the Old Northwest,
   1720–1830* (Bloomington: University of Indiana Press, 1996), 128–42.

44 Merrill Jensen, *The New Nation: A History of the United States during
   the Confederation* (New York: Alfred A. Knopf, 1958), 384–5.

45 Ibid., 382–98.
46 Thomas M. Doerflinger, *A Vigorous Spirit of Enterprise: Merchants and Economic Development in Revolutionary Philadelphia* (New York: W.W. Norton and Company, 1986), 310.
47 See, for example, William Graham Sumner, *The Financier and the American Revolution*, 2 vols. (New York: Burt Franklin, 1970, reprint of 1891 edition), and Clarence L. Ver Steg, *Robert Morris: Revolutionary Financier with an Analysis of His Earlier Career* (New York: Octagon Books, 1972).
48 Ver Steg, *Robert Morris*, 1–12; Sumner, *The Financier*, vol. I, 1–4.
49 Forrest McDonald, *Alexander Hamilton: A Biography* (New York: W.W. Norton & Company, 1979), 183.
50 Ver Steg, *Robert Morris*, 20–42.
51 Ibid., 193.
52 Sumner, *The Financier*, vol. II, 278.
53 Henry Laurens quoted in Ver Steg, *Robert Morris*, 27.
54 Sumner, *The Financier*, vol. II, 173.
55 Rules for Sale of Land, 1774, in Larabee, ed., *Royal Instructions*, vol. II, 533–7.
56 Daniel Friedenberg, *Life, Liberty, and the Pursuit of Land: The Plunder of Early America* (Buffalo: Prometheus Books, 1992), 346. This book extracts information from many studies to make the point that many early American leaders were heavily involved in land dealings. The style is breezy, and the approach is censorious.
57 Miami Lands for Sale, advertisement in *Brunswick Gazette and Weekly Monitor*, 8 Jan. 1788, in Beverley W. Bond, *The Correspondence of John Cleve Symmes: Founder of the Miami Purchase* (New York: Macmillan, 1926), 281–2.
58 Agreement between John Cleve Symmes and Zachariah Hole and Associates, 21 May 1795, Bond, *Correspondence*, 286.
59 van der Merwe, 24.
60 Symmes to Dayton, 18, 19, 20 May 1789, in Bond, *Correspondence*, 54.
61 Jonathan Dayton to Symmes, 12 September 1788, in ibid., 202.
62 McDonald, *Hamilton*, 174–88. From his vantage point in Congress, Dayton reported on the fluctuations in the value of securities and the likely impact of Hamilton's report on the public debt. Dayton to Symmes, 16 Feb. 1790, in Bond, *Correspondence*, 240.
63 Symmes to Jonathan Dayton, 6 Aug. 1795, in ibid., 174–5.
64 Ibid., 22–3.
65 Dayton to Symmes, 15 Aug. 1789, in ibid., 224–5.
66 Ibid., 302, note 23.
67 Huston, *Land and Freedom*, 45.

68 J.M. Bumsted, *Land, Settlement, and Politics on Eighteenth-Century Prince Edward Island* (Montreal: Queen's-McGill University Press, 1987), 15.

69 Ibid., 12–26. Bumsted concentrates on the Egmont schemes. For an account of the lottery and subsequent resale, see F.W.P. Bolger, "The Beginnings of Independence, 1767–1787," in Bolger, ed., *Canada's Smallest Province* (Charlottetown: Prince Edward Island Centennial Commission, 1973), 37–42.

70 Monica Wilson, "Co-operation and Conflict: The Eastern Cape Frontier," in *The Oxford History of South Africa*, 248; Crais, *White Supremacy*, 76–82.

71 Sharon Morgan, *Land Settlement in Early Tasmania: Creating an Antipodean England* (Cambridge: Cambridge University Press, 1992), 32.

72 Appendix B, *Lord Durham's Report on the Affairs of British North America*, ed. Charles Lucas (Oxford: Clarendon Press, 1912), 42–4, 74.

73 On the controversial "Oatlands" grant to Captain Henry Somerset, see G.E. Cory, *The Rise of South Africa* (Cape Town: Struik, 1965; reprint of 1913 edition), vol. II, 323–4. For additional evidence of favouritism and the value of powerful contacts at home, see Arthur Keppel-Jones, ed., *Philipps, 1820 Settler: His Letters* (Pietermaritzburg: Shuter and Shooter, 1960), 111, 236–7, 243, 327. On the conditions of grants, see Duly, *British Land Policy*, 61–2.

74 Catharine Anne Wilson, *A New Lease on Life: Landlords, Tenants, and Immigrants in Ireland and Canada* (Montreal: McGill-Queen's University Press, 1994), 50–3.

75 Ibid., 47.

76 Paul W. Gates, *Landlords and Tenants on the Prairie Frontier: Studies in American Land Policy* (Ithaca, NY: Cornell University Press, 1974), 108–39.

77 John Morgan Gray, *Lord Selkirk of Red River* (Toronto: Macmillan, 1964), 1–36.

78 J.M. Bumsted, "Editorial Introduction," in Bumsted, ed., *The Collected Writings of Lord Selkirk, 1799–1809* (Winnipeg: Manitoba Record Society, 1984), 49–54.

79 Gray, *Selkirk*, 56–62; Bumsted, "Editorial Introduction," in Bumsted, ed., *The Collected Writings of Lord Selkirk, 1810–1820* (Winnipeg: Manitoba Record Society, 1987), xvii–xix.

80 Bumsted, *Selkirk, 1810–1820*, xxxvii, 9–39. Selkirk proposed a pastoral colony.

81 Gerald Freisen, *The Canadian Prairies: A History* (Toronto: University of Toronto Press, 1984), 66–83; Thomas Flanagan, *Metis Lands in Manitoba* (Calgary: University of Calgary Press, 1991), 13–15.

82 Lilian Gates, *Land Policies of Upper Canada* (Toronto: University of Toronto Press, 1968), 20.

83 On Upper Canada, see Alan Wilson, *The Clergy Reserves in Upper Canada* (Ottawa: Canadian Historical Association, 1969), 5. The clergy and crown lands of Upper Canada were arranged as regular plots on a surveyed grid. Similar lands were to be set aside in Australia, but there, because the grid was not used widely, the commissioners of crown lands had opportunities to select sites in the public interest. See Wright, 93, 109–16, 122, 126–7, 148–154. In Cape Colony, the governors set aside the clergy reserve policy; Duly, *British Land Policy*, 88–9.

84 Fred Hamil Coyne, *Lake Erie Baron: The History of Colonel Thomas Talbot* (Toronto: Macmillan, 1955); Alan G. Brunger, "Thomas Talbot," *Dictionary of Canadian Biography*, vol. 8 (Toronto: University of Toronto Press, 1985).

85 Seymour V. Connor, *Kentucky Colonization in Texas: A History of the Peters Colony* (Baltimore, Md.: Genealogical Publishing, 1983), 9.

86 Wilson, *A New Lease on Life*, 118–35.

87 For an apologetic biography, see Anthony Kendal Millar, *Plantagenet in South Africa: Lord Charles Somerset* (Cape Town: Oxford University Press, 1965). The connections are well described in Noël Mostert, *Frontiers: The Epic of South Africa's Creation and the Tragedy of the Xhosa People* (New York: Alfred A. Knopf, 1992), 410–11. A critical assessment appears in T.R.H. Davenport, "The Consolidation of a New Society: The Cape Colony," in Monica Wilson and Leonard Thompson, *The Oxford History of South Africa*, 314–18. For a liberal settler's opinion, see Keppel-Jones, *Phillips, 1820 Settler*, 207–8, 228–30.

88 Thompson gives Cuyler a scathing assessment in *A History of South Africa*, 58. For details on his land dealings, see John Thomas Bigge and William Colebrooke to Somerset, 17 Jan. 1825, Government House (GH) 19/1; [illegible name] Surveyor to Col. Cuyler, 6 Sept. 1819, Inspector of Lands and Woods (ILW) 5, Uitenhage file, National Archives of South Africa, Cape Town Repository.

89 Keppel-Jones, *Philipps, 1820 Settler*, 9.

90 Mostert, *Frontiers*, 480; Thompson, *A History of South Africa*, 55.

91 Mostert, *Frontiers*, 442–90.

92 Crais, *White Supremacy*, 87–95; Keppel-Jones, *Philipps, 1820 Settler*, passim.

93 Crais, *White Supremacy*, 125–72. This summary is part of Crais's argument. The counterpart consists of his description of how black resistance, particularly ideological resistance, developed. Also Thompson, *A History of South Africa*, 67.

94 J.W.N. Tempelhoff, *Die okkupasiestelsel in die Distrik Soutpansberg, 1886–1899* (Pretoria: Die Staatsdrukker, 1997), 14–17.

95 Alexander Berry, "Passages of Life of a Nonagenarian (newspaper clippings of articles written by Berry)," mss. 315/112, Alexander Berry Papers, Dixson Library, Mitchell Library. Jan Kociumbas, *The Oxford History of Australia: Possessions, 1770–1860* (Melbourne: Oxford University Press, 1992), 109–11, 167–8.

96 Kociumbas, *Oxford History*, 127.

97 James Busby, *Authentic Information Relative to New South Wales, and New Zealand* (London: Simpkin and Marshall, 1832), 34–9. *The Return of the Alienation of Crown Lands, in New South Wales and Van Dieman's Land Respectively, during the Last Ten Years* (London: House of Commons, 1832), 2–14.

98 Charles J. King, "An Outline of Closer Settlement in New South Wales, Part I: The Sequence of Land Laws," *Review of Marketing and Agricultural Economics* 25 (Sept.–Oct. 1957), 17–32. For insight into how the government had judged character in the 1820s, see George Gipps to Lord Glenelg, 3 Aug. 1838, Governor's Despatches to the Secretary of State for the Colonies, vol. 30, microfilm A1220 CY reel, Mitchell Library.

99 Berry, "Passages of Life."

100 Alexander Macleay to Messrs Berry and Wollstonecraft, 29 April 1829, A5375/2, no. 60, Alexander Berry Papers, Norton Smith Papers, Dixon Library, Mitchell Library.

101 Alexander Berry to Acting Colonial Treasurer, 15 April 1840, A5375/1, no.1, Alexander Berry Estate Papers, Norton Smith Papers, Dixon Library, Mitchell Library.

102 T.N. Bradshaw, *Coolangatta*, brochure, 1972, 5–12.

103 Pamela Stratham, ed., *The Tanner Letters: A Pioneer Saga of Swan River and Tasmania* (Nedlands: University of Western Australia Press, 1981), xv–xxi; Kociumbas, *The Oxford History of Australia: Possessions, 1770–1860* (Melbourne: Oxford University Press, 1992), 120–3.

104 Wood, *The Radicalism of the American Revolution*, 113–14.

105 For the origins of the Prince Edward Island estates, see J.M. Bumsted, *Land, Settlement, and Politics on Eighteenth-Century Prince Edward Island* (Montreal: McGill-Queen's University Press, 1987). For the long struggle against the landlords and the demise of the estates, see F.W.P. Bolger, "Land and Politics, 1787–1824," "The Demise of the Quit Rents and Escheat, 1824–1842," and "Long Courted, Won at Last," in F.W.P. Bolger, ed., *Canada's Smallest Province* (Charlottetown: Prince Edward Island Centennial Commission, 1973).

106 Gates, *Land Policies of Upper Canada*, 170.

107 The quote is taken from a report of the Executive Council to Sir Peregrine Maitland, William Campbell to Maitland, 29 Oct. 1825, RG 1, C-III-4, vol. 10 (available as ms. 693, reel 194), Archives of

Ontario. Copies of the following pertinent documents are in the same volume: John B. Robinson to R. Wilmot Horton, 7 July 1825; Lord Bathurst to Maitland, 28 July 1825; William Campbell to Maitland, 21 Nov. 1825; and Campbell to Thomas Ridout, Surveyor General, 9 June 1826.

108 Gates, *Land Policies of Upper Canada*, 304.
109 Ibid., 282–3.
110 Ibid., 190–5.
111 Duly, *British Land Policy*, 150–9.

CHAPTER SIX

1 F.M.L. Thompson, *Chartered Surveyors: The Growth of a Profession* (London: Routledge & Kegan Paul, 1968), 1–63.
2 Deputy Attorney General, Manitoba, to Attorney General, Queensland, 25 Aug. 1884, Torrens Title, 1884, Attorney General, JUS/A33, Queensland State Archives; Louis William Coutleé, *A Manual of the Law of Registration of Titles of Real Estate in Manitoba and the North-West Territories* (Toronto: Carswell, 1890), iv–vii; William C. Niblack, *An Analysis of the Torrens System* (Chicago: Callaghan, 1903), passim.
3 Carl J. Dahlman, *The Open Field System and Beyond* (Cambridge: Cambridge University Press, 1980), 221.
4 Evidence of G.S. Wright in South Australia, *Report of the Commission on the Land Laws of South Australia; Together with Minutes of Proceedings, Evidence, and Appendices* (Adelaide: H.F. Leader, 1888), 10.
5 Paul W. Gates, "Adjudication of Spanish Land Claims in California," in Gates, *Land and Law in California: Essays on Land Policies* (Ames: Iowa State University Press, 1991), 3–5.
6 In Upper Canada, many recipients of location certificates who had not patented their land used the certificates as collateral. They and their creditors possessed interests in the land. A special commission determined who had rightful claims. Lilian Gates, "The Heir and Devisee Commission of Upper Canada, 1797–1805," *Canadian Historical Review* 38 (March 1957), 21–36; H. Pearson Gundy, "The Family Compact at Work: The Second Heir and Devisee Commission of Upper Canada," *Ontario History* 67 (1975), 129–43. Something similar was established in New South Wales: 4 William IV, no. 9 (Aug. 1833). For New Zealand, see 19 & 20 Victoria, no. 21 (Aug. 1856).
7 S. Newlands, *Our Waste Lands and our Productions* (Adelaide: Burden and Bonython, 1888), 1–15, quote at 2.
8 British Columbia retained control of crown lands when it joined Canada. See Robert F. Cail, *Land, Men, and the Law* (Vancouver:

University of British Columbia Press, 1974), 28. For Texas, see Alden Socrates Lang, *Financial History of the Public Lands of Texas* (New York: Arno Press, 1979, reprint of 1932 edition), 47–56.

9 J.L. Little, "Contested Land: Squatters and Agents in the Eastern Townships of Lower Canada," *Canadian Historical Review* 80 (Sept. 1999), 383–4.

10 South Australia, *Report on the Disposal of Crown Lands in South Australia; Parliamentary Paper No. 60* (Adelaide: Government Printer, 1890), Appendix A, n.p. Pastoral estates built on these holdings. The myth that South Australia was a land of smallholders, free of large pastoral estates, is criticized in Eleanore Williams, *A Way of Life: The Pastoral Families of the Central Hill Country of South Australia* (Adelaide: Adelaide University Union Press, 1980), 39–41, 61–8.

11 Thomas Donaldson, *The Public Domain. Its History with Statistics* (Washington, DC: Government Printing Office, 1884), 198; Malcolm Rohrbough, *The Land Office Business: The Settlement and Administration of American Public Land* (Belmont, Calif.: Wadsworth Publishing Company, 1990), 13.

12 Broadsides concerning the preliminary land orders in South Australia, D 365/1–20, nos. 4/7, 4/44, and 4/56, Mitchell Library; Special Memorandum, Plymouth Company, ms. 2443, Alexander Turnbull Library, National Library of New Zealand.

13 James Larmer, Commissioner of Crown Lands, Braidwood, to Colonial Secretary, 28 June 1844, Colonial Secretary's Papers, Letters Received, 4/2640.0, Archives of New South Wales.

14 Rohrbough, *The Land Office Business*; 36; John Mack Faragher, *Daniel Boone: The Life and Legend of an American Pioneer* (New York: Henry Holt and Company, 1992), 81; Richard White, *The Middle Ground: Indians, Empires, and Republics in the Great Lakes Region, 1650–1815* (Cambridge: Cambridge University Press, 1991), 388, 392.

15 Rohrbough, *The Land Office Business*, 38–64.

16 Ibid., 171.

17 Bogue, "The Iowa Claims Clubs: Symbol and Substance," *Mississippi Valley Historical Review* 45 (Sept. 1958), 238.

18 William Faux, *Memorable Days in America*, in Reuben Gold Thwaites, ed., *Early Western Travels* (New York: AMS Press, 1966), vol. 11, 189.

19 For descriptions of the auction system and its initial problems see Donaldson, *The Public Domain*, 201–5; Daniel Feller, *The Public Lands in Jacksonian Politics* (Madison: University of Wisconsin Press, 1984), 10–11; Roy M. Robbins, *Our Landed Heritage: The Public Domain, 1776–1936* (Princeton, NJ: Princeton University Press, 1942), 31; Rohrbough, *The Land Office Business*, 93–9.

20 Appendix B, *Lord Durham's Report*, vol. 3, 93.
21 Zahler, *Eastern Workingmen and the National Land Policy, 1829–1862* (New York: Columbia University Press, 1941), 113.
22 Pre-emption was the right to hold land before payment, on a promise to buy the land at a stipulated time. It was initiated by settlement and by filing a declaratory statement. This clear definition appears in George Hesselman, *Digest of Decisions of the Department of the Interior in Cases Relating to the Public Lands* (Washington, DC: Government Printing Office, 1913), 466.
23 Zahler, *Eastern Working Men and the National Land Policy*, 25–35; Feller, *The Public Lands*, 170.
24 Burroughs, *Britain and Australia*, 242–329.
25 Buller, Appendix B, *Lord Durham's Report*, vol. 3, 107.
26 Zahler, *Eastern Working Men and the National Land Policy*, 130.
27 *Australian Almanack, 1827* (Sydney: Robert Howe, 1827), 120–1, Mitchell Library.
28 Governor Sir Charles Fitzroy to Earl Grey, 6 Dec. 1847, in United Kingdom, *Papers Relative to the Occupation of Crown Lands, New South Wales* (London: W. Clowes & Son, 1848; Irish University Press reprint), 25.
29 For a discussion of the origins of the Ripon regulations (named after the secretary of state for the colonies, the Earl of Ripon), see Burroughs, *Britain and Australia*, 35–75, quote at 14.
30 This understanding of the provincial system of land sales is based on archives – for example, Alfred Domett to Major Mathew Richmond, 18 March 1853; Public Notice 29 July 1853, Superintendent of the Southern District, Nelson, Incoming Letters, SSD 1/6; Charles Clifford to Major Mathew Richmond, 24 Sept. 1853, Lands and Survey Department, Nelson, LS-N, 1/3, National Archives of New Zealand. On Canterbury, see Francis Fuller, *Five Years' Residence in New Zealand; or, Observations on Colonization* (London: Williams and Norgate, 1859), 63–5.
31 T.L. Mitchell to Sir George Murray, 28 Jan. 1831, Despatches of the Governor of New South Wales to the Secretary of State for the Colonies, CY reel 1541, A1208, Mitchell Library.
32 Hilda Sabato, *Agrarian Capitalism and the World Market: Buenos Aires in the Pastoral Age, 1840–1890* (Albuquerque: University of New Mexico Press, 1990), 53.
33 John L. Tyman, "The Appraisal of Farm Lands in Western Canada, 1870–1930," in Brian Blouet and Merlin P. Lawson, eds., *Images of the Plains* (Lincoln: University of Nebraska Press, 1975), 77–83.
34 William Campbell to Thomas Ridout, Surveyor General, 9 June 1826, RG 1-CIII-4, vol. 10, Archives of Ontario (available as ms. 693, reel

194). The results of the valuation exercise have been studied to determine what factors affected property values in Upper Canada. See John Clarke and John Buffone, "Manifestations of Imperial Policy: The New South Wales System and Land Prices in Upper Canada," *Canadian Geographer* 40 (summer 1996), 121–36.

35 W.R. Lawson, *Our Wool Staple; or A History of Squatting in South Australia* (Adelaide: John Howell, 1865), iv, 28, Mortlock Library, State Library of South Australia.

36 Eric Stokes, *The English Utilitarians and India* (Oxford: At the Clarendon Press, 1959), 88.

37 For a full account, see John C. Weaver, "Exploitation by Design: The Dismal Science, Land Reform, and the Cape *Boers*, 1805–1822," *Journal of Imperial and Commonwealth History* 29 (Sept. 2001), 1–32.

38 Juan Carlos Rubenstein, *Filiacion historica y sociopolitica de la enfiteusis Rivadaviana* (Buenos Aires, 1984), 178–81.

39 A.W. Richeson, *English Land Measuring to 1800: Instruments and Practice* (Cambridge, Mass.: MIT Press, 1966), 30–89.

40 Richardson, *English Land Measuring*, 108–9; Robert Rich, "Land Surveying and Levelling," in C.F. Dowsett, ed., *Land: Its Attractions and Riches by Seventy-five Writers* (London: Land Roll Office, 1892), 619–28.

41 Reginald E. Middleton and Osbert Chadwick, *A Treatise on Surveying* (London: E.&F.N. Spon, 1899), vol. 1, 237–51.

42 Michael Cannon and Ian Macfarlane, eds., *Historical Records of Victoria, Volume 5: Surveyors' Problems and Achievements, 1836–1839* (Melbourne: Victorian Government Printing Office, 1988), xv–xvii, 46–7.

43 Governor Sir George Gipps to Lord Glenelg, 1 July 1839, *Historical Records of Australia* (HRA), series 1, vol. 20, 210.

44 George Carrington, *Colonial Adventures and Experiences of a University Man* (London: Bell and Daldy, 1871), 49; Lela Barnes, "Journal of Isaac McCoy," *Kansas Historical Quarterly* 5 (Dec. 1936), 354–5; Charles Aeneas Shaw, *Tales of a Pioneer Surveyor*, ed. by Raymond Hull (Toronto: Longman Canada Limited, 1970), 131.

45 Barnes, "Journal of Isaac McCoy," 341.

46 Carrington, *Colonial Adventures*, 49.

47 Donald McLean, memo, LS NA, 1/1a, 53/3, NA.

48 Gustav Baumann and Elfrieda Bright, *The Lost Republic: The Biography of a Land Surveyor* (London: Faber and Faber, 1940), 76.

49 Symmes to Dayton, 18, 19, 20, May 1789, in Beverley W. Bond, *The Correspondence of John Cleve Symmes: Founder of the Miami Purchase* (New York: Macmillan, 1926), 73.

50 Nancy M. Taylor, *Early Travellers in New Zealand* (Oxford: At the Clarendon Press, 1959), 347.

51 F.A. Michaux, *Travels to the West of the Allegheny Mountains* (London: B. Crosby and Co., 1805), reprinted in Thwaites, ed., *Early Western Travels*, vol. 3, 227.

52 George R. Wilson, *Early Indian Trails and Surveys* (Indianapolis: C.E. Pauley, 1919), 421.

53 Rohrbough, *The Land Office Business*, 48, 80.

54 James McCoy, "Survey of Kansas Indian Lands," *Transactions of the Kansas State Historical Society, Sixth Biennial Report*, (1889), 308.

55 Robert A. Sauder, "Sod Land versus Sagebrush: Early Land Appraisal and Pioneer Settlement in an Arid Intermountain Frontier," *Journal of Historical Geography* 15 (1989), 407.

56 Matthew Edney, *Mapping an Empire: The Geographical Construction of British India, 1765–1843* (Chicago: University of Chicago Press, 1997), 326.

57 Thongchai Winichakul, *Siam Mapped: A History of the Geo-Body of a Nation* (Honolulu: University of Hawaii Press, 1994), 118.

58 Circular Letter to Contract Surveyors from the Surveyor General's Office, 24 Aug. 1840, Commissioner of Crown Lands, Murray District, Record Group 94, Unit 1, Victoria Public Record Office.

59 Keith Sinclair, *A History of New Zealand* (New York: Penguin, 1991), 77; James Belich, *The New Zealand Wars and the Victorian Interpretation of Racial Conflict* (New York: Penguin, 1998), 21; Mathew Richmond to William Wakefield, 2 May 1844, 44/30, NM 10/5, National Archives of New Zealand.

60 Harold J. Jenks, *Forgotten Men: The Survey of Tauranga and District, 1864–1869* (Tauranga, n.d.), 28–32; Nola Easdale, *Kairuri: The Measure of the Land* (Petone: Highgate, Price, Milburn, 1988), 149.

61 James Belich, *I Shall Not Die: Titokowaru's War, New Zealand, 1868–1869* (Wellington: Bridget Williams Books, 1999), 14.

62 Jenks, *Forgotten Men*, 28–32; Easdale, *Kairuri*, 149.

63 W.L. Morton, *Manitoba: A History* (Toronto: University of Toronto Press, 1957), 119–20. For an account of the acquisition of Rupert's Land that contends that the government of Canada had authority to dispose of unoccupied lands, see Thomas Flanagan, *Metis Lands in Manitoba* (Calgary: University of Calgary Press, 1991), 1–25.

64 Shaw, *Tales of a Pioneer Surveyor*, 105.

65 D.N. Jeans, "The Breakdown of Australia's First Grid Rectangular Grid Survey," *Australian Geographical Studies* 4 (Oct. 1966), 119–28.

66 Letter from the Court of Justice Relative to the Manner by which Lands are to be Surveyed, Circulated to Landdrosts and Land Surveyors by Order of the Governor, 14 Jan. 1814; Evidence of Henry Dangar, 5 June 1844, *Report of the Select Committee on Crown Grievances, Minutes of Evidence Taken*, 23.

67 Thomas F. McIlwraith, *Looking for Old Ontario* (Toronto: University of Toronto Press, 1998), 50–8; Wilbur E. Garrett et al., *Historical Atlas of the United States* (Washington, DC: National Geographic Society, 1988), 105; Courtney C.J. Bond, *Surveyors of Canada, 1867–1967* (Ottawa: Canadian Institute of Surveying, 1966), 22.

68 This favourable view of the grid was held by some Australian land commissioners. Sharon Morgan, *Land Settlement in Early Tasmania: Creating an Antipodean England* (Cambridge: Cambridge University Press, 1992), 50.

69 Rohrbough, *The Land Office Business*, 79.

70 John Clarke, "Mahon Burwell," *Dictionary of Canadian Biography*, vol. 7 (Toronto: University of Toronto Press, 1988), 126. On the authority of surveyors to select good lands, see Lillian Gates, *Land Policies of Upper Canada* (Toronto: University of Toronto Press, 1968), 158. Randy Widdis describes some of their speculative activities in "Speculation and the Surveyor: An Analysis of the Role Played by Surveyors in the Settlement of Upper Canada," *Histoire sociale/Social History* 15 (Nov. 1982), 443–58.

71 Gates, *Land Policies of Upper Canada*, 291–4. New Zealand, House of Representatives, "Correspondence Relating to a Royal Commission to Inquire into the Administration of the Canterbury Waste Lands and Survey Department," *Appendix to the Journals of the House of Representatives*, Report C-11 (Wellington, 1876), 1–17.

72 See surveying contracts in folder 9, box 11, and folder 5, box 12, John B. Thomas Papers, accession 141, American Heritage Center, University of Wyoming (AHC); for advice to clients, see reports enclosed with John B. Thomas to Thomas Sturgis, 10 Nov. 1881, letterbook, 1881–1889, box 3; for the start of their own grazing activities, see Converse and Warren to John B. Thomas, 12 Aug. 1873, letterbook, 1871–1873, box 221 (microfilm reel 286), Frances E. Warren Papers, accession 13, AHC.

73 G.B. Goodell to Andrew J. Robertson, 16 May 1884, folder 5, box 2, Andrew J. Robertson Papers, accession 1306, AHC.

74 M.P. Mayo, *The Life and Letters of Colonel William Light* (Adelaide: F.W. Preece and Sons, 1937), 128; J.L. Burton Jackson, *Not an Idle man: A Biography of John Septimus Roe: Western Australia's First Surveyor General (1797–1878)* (Freemantle: Freemantle Arts Centre Press, 1982), 75.

75 *Lord Durham's Report*, vol. 2, 232.

76 Testimony of Sherman Day, former Surveyor General of California, testimony of T. Hermann, surveyor at San Jose, in United States Public Lands Commission, *Report of the Public Lands Commission* (Washington, DC: Government Printing Office, 1880), 49, 70–3.

77 Z.A. Enos, *The Early Surveyors and Surveying in Illinois* (Springfield, Ill.: Springfield Printing Company, 1891), 1–4; J.W. Hawes, *Manual of United States Surveying* (Philadelphia: J.B. Lippincott, 1868), 120–1.

78 For example, see reference to New Zealand in Theodore B.F. Ruoff, *An Englishman Looks at the Torrens System* (Sydney: Law Book Company of Australasia, 1957), 54.

79 A.E. Baker, *Historical Notes on Land Surveyors and the Surveyor-General's Office* (Cape Town: Surveyor-General's Office, 1958), 18.

80 Hildegard Binder Johnson, *Order upon the Land: The U.S. Rectangular Land Survey and the Upper Mississippi Country* (New York: Oxford University Press, 1976), 121–30; *United States Public Lands Commission*, xvii; *Government Gazette* (South Australia), 22 Aug. 1839, n.p.

81 Baumann, *The Lost Republic*, 82–3; McCoy, "Survey of Kansas Indian Lands,L 304; Shaw, *Tales of a Pioneer Surveyor*, 41.

82 Baumann, *The Lost Republic*, 76.

83 Cape of Good Hope, *Topographical Survey of Southern Africa; Proceedings of a Conference Held at Cape Town* (Cape Town: Government Printers, 1904), 1–8.

84 John C. Weaver, "Beyond the Fatal Shore: Pastoral Squatting and the Occupation of Australia," *American Historical Review* 101 (Oct. 1996), 995.

85 *The Residence and Cultivation Licenses* (Melbourne, 1861), 5, pamphlet collection, Mitchell Library; John Forrest, *Report on the Land Policy of Western Australia from 1829 to 1888* (Perth: Government Printer, 1889), 6.

86 Alan Jones, *Backsight: A History of Surveying in Tasmania* (Hobart: Institution of Surveyors, 1989), 74–5.

87 Oxley Library, *Dixon–Stapleyton–Warner: Queensland's First Surveyors* (Brisbane, 1989), 7–9.

88 M.P. Mayo, *The Life and Letters of Col. William Light* (Adelaide: F.W. Preece & Sons, 1937), 167–8, 247.

89 J.A. McRae, *New Zealand Institute of Surveyors, 1888–1988* (Otago: New Zealand Institute of Surveyors, 1989), 14–19.

90 Brian Warner, ed., *The Cape Diaries and Letters of William Mann, Astronomer and Mountaineer, 1839–1843* (Cape Town: Friends of the South African Library, 1989), 15; *Topographical Survey of Southern Africa*, 1–16.

91 Bond, *Surveyors of Canada*, 22.

92 *Report on the Survey of New Zealand, 1883–4*, ii–iv; Bond, *Surveyors of Canada*, 78.

93 Edney, *Mapping an Empire*, 332–40.

94 Good discussions of the use of maps appear in Winichakul, *Siam Mapped*; Edney, *Mapping an Empire*; and Roger J.P. Cain and Elizabeth Baigent, *The Cadastral Map in the Service of the State* (Chicago: University of Chicago Press, 1992). The power of representation in the process of colonization is discussed in Timothy Mitchell, *Colonizing Egypt* (Berkeley: University of California Press, 1991).

95 Robert Devlin, *A Treatise on the Law of Deeds* (San Francisco: Bancroft-Whitney, 1897; Gaunt Reprint, 1999), vol. 2, 1398–9.

96 *Catalogue of Lands for Sale with Torrens Titles and on Easy Terms* (Winnipeg, 1890), file 6, box 20, MG14 C66, Edmund Baker Papers, Provincial Archives of Manitoba (PAM).

97 For grain and lumber, see William Cronon, *Nature's Metropolis: Chicago and the Great West* (New York: W.W. Norton & Company, 1991), 116–23, 177–8.

98 I found printed grids with spaces left for the number of the township, range, and meridian west in a number of ranchers papers. Examples are in folder 9, box 11, John B. Thomas Papers, accession 141, and folder 1, box 89 (microfilm reel 194), Frances E. Warren Papers, accession 13, AHC.

99 State regulation of these companies seems to have begun in the 1890s. By 1942 there were specific statutes for them in thirty-six states. Kansas Revisor of Statutes, "Title Insurance Laws of the States: A Brief Digest of Important Features with Statutory Citations," Tokepa, typescript, 1942.

100 Peter Roebuck, "The Irish Registry of Deeds: A Comparative Study," *Irish Historical Studies* 18 (March 1972), 61–71.

101 Plymouth Colony required registration in 1636, and Massachusetts in 1641. Leonard A. Jones, *A Treatise on the Law of Real Property* (Boston: Houghton, Mifflin and Company, 1896), 263. Cronon, *Changes*, 74.

102 State laws as they stood in the 1890s were summarized with some chronology in Devlin, *Law of Deeds*, vol. 2, 566–625. He reviewed the case law on the protection afforded by registration, at 626–724. Legal commentaries are helpful to historians, but since they are concerned with the current state of the law they rarely chronicle, let alone explain, changes.

103 Brian Young, *The Politics of Codification: The Lower Canadian Civil Code of 1866* (Montreal: McGill-Queen's University Press, 1994), 6–98.

104 Little, "Contested Land," 409.

105 T.J. Scott and Susan Scott, *Willie's Law of Mortgage and Pledge in South Africa* (Cape Town: Juta and Company, 1987), 7–157; Joseph Foster, *The Practice of the Deeds Registry Office of the Cape Colony*

(Cape Town: J.C. Juta, 1892), 38–44; Cape of Good Hope, *Report of the Committee to Inquire into the Law of the Debtor and Creditor* (Cape Town, 1843), pamplet collection, National Library of South Africa.

106 K.R. Bowes, *Land Settlement in South Australia, 1857–1890* (Adelaide: Libraries Board of South Australia, 1968), 177.

107 Douglas Whalan, "The Origins of the Torrens System and Its Introduction into New Zealand," in G.W. Hinde, *The New Zealand Torrens System Centennial Essays: Written to Commemorate the Hundredth Anniversary of the Passing of the Land Transfer Act of 1870* (Wellington: Butterworths, 1971), 13.

108 Lionel Robbins, *Robert Torrens and the Evolution of Classical Economics* (London: Macmillan, 1958), 3–5, 250–8.

109 For a profile, see the entry on Robert Torrens in *The Dictionary of Australian Biography*. For the contributions of others to the idea of indefeasible land titles, see Douglas J. Whalan, "The Origins of the Torrens System and Its Introduction into New Zealand," in G.W. Hinde, ed., *The New Zealand Torrens System Centennial Essays: Written to Commemorate the Hundredth Anniversary of the Passing of the Land Transfer Act 1870* (Wellington: Butterworths, 1971), 2–7

110 Sir Robert Torrens, *An Essay of the Transfer of Land by Registration under the Duplicate Method Operative in British Colonies* (London: Cassell & Company, 1882), 18–20.

111 A. Angladette, "Le regime foncier des territoires français d'Afrique," *Land Tenure Symposium*, 90–1; Norman G. Owen, *Prosperity without Progress: Manila Hemp and Material Life in the Colonial Philippines* (Berkeley: University of California Press, 1984), 85.

112 Henry Sewell, Attorney General, Memorandum on the Secretary of State's Despatch on the Land Registry Act, 1860, in New Zealand, A-2A, Papers Relative to the Land Registry Act, 1860, in New Zealand, *Appendix to the Journals of the House of Representatives of New Zealand ... 1862* (Wellington: Government Printer, 1862), n.p.

113 For a note about amendments and variations, see William Niblack, *An Analysis of the Torrens System of Conveyancing Land* (Chicago: Callaghan Company, 1912), 8–14, 245–76.

114 The major legal treatise on the subject within the British empire records each variation and lists the associated jurisdictions without comment on the particular social and political interests that might have caused deviations from the model. James Edward Hogg, *Registration of Title to Land throughout the Empire* (Toronto: Carswell, 1920), 1–399.

115 Blair C. Shick and Irving H. Plotkin, *Torrens in the United States: A Legal and Economic History and Analysis of American Land-Registration Systems* (Lexington, Ky.: Lexington Books, 1978), 2–3,

147. Explanations for the limited scope of Torrens title are outlined in Edward Lawrence McKenna, *State Insurance of Land Titles in the United States* (Philadelphia: University of Pennsylvania, 1923), 14–100. Title insurance is unlike ordinary insurance because it avoids some risk by allocating some of the premium's cost to title search and examination. See James L. Gosdin, *Title Insurance: A Comprehensive Overview* (Chicago: American Bar Association, 1996), 1.

116 Donald Kerr, *The Principles of the Australian Land Title (Torrens) System* (Sydney: Law Book Company of Australiasia Limited, 1927), 26.

117 For an account of the attempts of the English aristocracy to consolidate and protect landholdings as the foundation of family power, see Charles Reid, "The Seventeenth-Century Revolution in the English Land Law," *Cleveland State Law Review* 43 (1995), 221–302. Reid notes the struggles of the common law lawyers to develop a balance between conserving the estate and employing assets for economic development. For the reformation of land law that enabled the aristocracy to adapt to capitalism, see Andrew Buck, "Property, Aristocracy and the Reform of the Land Law in Early Nineteenth Century England," *Legal History* 16 (1995), 63–95.

118 A.W.B Simpson, *A History of the Land Law* (Oxford: Clarendon Press, 1989), 244–6.

119 Deputy Judge-Advocate Bent to Earl Liverpool, 19 Oct. 1811; Letters Patent to Establish Courts of Civil Judicature in New South Wales, 4 Feb. 1814, Letters *HRA*, series 4 (legal series), sec. A, vol. 1, 65, 77–94.

120 John C. Weaver, "While Equity Slumbered: Creditor Advantage, a Capitalist Land Market, and Upper Canada's Missing Court," *Osgoode Hall Law Journal* 28 (winter 1990), 881–914.

121 Morton J. Horwitz, *The Transformation of American Law, 1780–1860* (Cambridge, Mass.: Harvard University Press, 1977), 265.

122 New Zealand, 5 Victoria No. 10, An Ordinance to Facilitate the transfer of Real Property and to Simplify the Law Relating Thereto [18 Jan. 1842].

123 Michael Doucet and John C. Weaver, *Housing the North American City* (Montreal: McGill-Queen's University Press, 1991), 249–52.

124 New Zealand, *Statutes of the General Assembly of New Zealand Passed during the First and Second Parliaments, 1854–1860* (Wellington: Government Printer, 1871), 448–50; E.A. Frances, *Mortgages and Securities for the Payment of Money* (Sydney: Butterworths, 1975), 98–9; Kerr, *The Principles*, 417.

125 James Buchanan, ed., *Cases Decided in the Supreme Court of the Cape of Good Hope, as reported by the Late Hon. William Menzies, Esquire*, 2 vols. (Cape Town: J.C. Juta, 1881), vol. 1, 5–10.

126 Cape of Good Hope, *Report of the Committee to Inquire into the Law of the Debtor and Creditor* (Cape Town, 1843), 4, National Library of South Africa (Cape Town).

127 T.J. Scott and Susan Scott, *Willie's Law of Mortgage and Pledge in South Africa* (Cape Town: Jutta & Co., 1987), 2–129.

128 Paul Gates, *Landlords and Tenants on the Prairie Frontier; Studies in American Land Policy* (Ithaca, NY: Cornell University Press, 1973), 84.

129 Philip Girard, "Land Law in British North American Legal Culture: A Reconnaissance, 1750–1920," (unpublished paper, Feb. 2001).

130 Hugh L. Bellot, *The Law Relating to Unconscionable Bargains with Money Lenders, Including the History of Usury to the Repeal of Usury Laws* (London: Stevens and Haynes, 1897), 14–24.

131 *Macdonald v. Levy* in J. Gordon Legge, *Selection of Supreme Court Cases in New South Wales* (Sydney: Charles Potter, 1862), vol. 1, 39–64, quote at 59.

132 Harry Nunn, ed., *Select Documents of the Nineteenth Century: Volume One, 1834–1872* (Melbourne: National Australia Bank, 1988), 37–52.

133 Richard Risk, "The Golden Age: The Law about the Market in Nineteenth Century Ontario," *University of Toronto Law Journal* 26 (1977), 319–23; Michael J. Doucet and John C. Weaver, *Housing the North American City* (Montreal: McGill-Queen's University Press, 1991), 256–7.

134 Memorandum by Deputy Secretary Ellis, 16 July 1821; Report of the Commissioners of Enquiry to Lord Bathurst, Upon Colonial Law and Jurisprudence, 18 Aug. 1827, in George McCall Theal, ed., *Records of the Cape Colony* (Cape Town: Printed for the Government of the Cape Colony), vol. 14, 49–52; vol. 33, 28–9. Sutherland Brothers v. Elliott Brother [12 July 1841] in James Buchanan, ed., *Cases Decided in the Supreme Court of the Cape of Good Hope, as Reported by the Late Hon. William Menzies, Esquire* (Cape Town: J.C. Juta, 1888), vol. 1, 99–101.

135 Horwitz, *The Transformation of American Law,* 219–20.

136 Ibid., 243. The diversity of usury laws was captured in the fact that the printers of American pocket diaries summarized them along with other helpful information such as weights and measures.

137 Gregory S. Alexander, *Commodity and Propriety: Competing Visions of Property in American Legal Thought, 1776–1970* (Chicago: University of Chicago Press, 1998), 99. In this important book, Alexander argues that in American property law there has not been a single Lockean tradition. Consequently, he maintains, the claim that every government action that interferes with the ability of property owners to use their property exclusively to satisfy a private desire offends a solid tradition are wrong.

138 List of Rights, 4 Dec. 1869, Meeting of French and English Representatives Meeting at Fort Garry, MG3, A1–5, Red River Disturbances,
PAM.

139 It has been suggested that cattle introduced brucellosis to buffalo
herds. See Lee Whittlesey, "Cows All over the Place: The Historical
Setting for the Transmission of Brucellosis to Yellowstone Bison by
Domestic Cattle," *Annals of Wyoming* 66 (1994–5), 42–57. William
Dobak discounts the disease theory in "The Killing of the Canadian
Buffalo," *Western Historical Quarterly* 27 (1996), 33–52. He notes a
rise in the Indian population and its participation in commercial hunts.
The U.S. army is assigned some blame by David Smits, who suggests
that it wanted to reduce the Indians' commissary on the hoof and thus
assisted buffalo hunters. See Smits, "The Frontier Army and the
Destruction of the Buffalo, 1865–1883," *Western Historical Quarterly*
25 (1994), 312–36. Smits acknowledges the commercial drive behind
the hunts and points out that after 1871 buffalo leather was sought
after for machine belting. For an overview that argues that from 1750
to 1880 the Great Plains Indians were involved in ecological changes
that they could not control, see Andrew C. Isenberg, "Indians, Whites,
and the Buffalo: An Ecological History of the Great Plains, 1750–
1900" (PhD dissertation, Northwestern University, 1993). William
Cronon relates the history of the destruction of the buffalo to the rise
of cattle ranching and of Chicago in *Nature's Metropolis*, 213–18.

140 Gerald Friesen, *The Canadian Prairies: A History* (Toronto: University
of Toronto Press, 1984), 131–5. Friesen mentions that the Cypress
Hills were also the scene in 1873 of a murderous attack of white wolf
hunters on a camp of Assiniboines, but the attack was significant
because of its uniqueness.

141 W.F. Wesley Fitz Gerald to John Schultz, 28 Dec. 1876, Schultz Papers,
MG 12 E1, PAM.

142 Glen Grismer, "Early Squatter Holdings in Saskatchewan, 1878–1886,"
Regina Geographical Studies (1980), 22–30.

143 Chester Martin, *"Dominion Lands" Policy*, ed. with intro. by Lewis H.
Thomas (Toronto: McClelland and Stewart, 1973), 17.

144 J.R. Miller, *Skyscrapers Hide the Heavens: A History of Indian–White
Relations in Canada* (Toronto: University of Toronto Press, 1989), 161.

145 Minnesota's ties with the Red River are featured in Alvin C. Glueck, Jr,
*Minnesota and the Manifest Destiny of the Canadian Northwest:
A Study in Canadian–American Relations* (Toronto: University of
Toronto Press, 1965), 119–219.

146 Hudson's Bay Company (HBC), *Report of the Governor and the
Committee of the Hudson's Bay Company, July 5th, 1866* (London:
Henry Kent Causton & Son, 1866), 1–11; *Report of the Governor and*

Committee of the Hudson's Bay Company, November 20th, 1866 (London: Henry Kent Causton & Son, 1867), 6–13, HBC Archives, PAM. The negotiations leading to the annexation are described in John S. Galbraith, *The Hudson's Bay Company as an Imperial Factor, 1821–1869* (Berkeley: University of California Press, 1957), 391–428.

147 Archer Martin, *The Hudson Bay Company's Land Tenures and the Occupation of Assiniboia by Lord Selkirk's Settlers with a List of Grantees under the Earl and the Company* (London: William Clowes & Sons, 1898), 14–33.

148 W.L. Morton, "Introduction," in E.E. Rich, ed., *London Correspondence Inward from Eden Colville, 1849–1852* (London: Hudson's Bay Record Society, 1956), xiv–xxvi, quote at xxv.

149 Martin, *"Dominion Lands" Policy*, 131; Gerhard J. Ens, *Homeland to Hinterland: The Changing Worlds of the Red River Metis in the Nineteenth Century* (Toronto: University of Toronto Press, 1996), 31–5.

150 Adam Thom's response to the Report of the Select Committee Inquiry into the Hudson's Bay Company, 1857 (n.d.), HBC Archives, E.18/8, PAM. "Adam Thom," in *Dictionary of Canadian Biography*, vol. 11 (Toronto: University of Toronto, 1982), 874–6.

151 *McKenny v. Spence*, cited in E. Douglas Armour, ed., *Reports of Cases Argued and Determined in the Court of Queen's Bench in Manitoba both at Law and in Equity* (Toronto: Carswell, 1885), 12–13.

152 Louis William Coutleé, *A Manual of the Law of registration of Titles of Real Estate in Manitoba and the North-West Territories* (Toronto: Carswell, 1890), 1–52.

153 John Forrest, *Report on the Land Policy of Western Australia from 1829 to 1888* (Perth: Government Printer, 1889), iii–viii. The railways were slow to build lines and "locked up" 6 million acres. See Francis Keble Crowley, *Forrest, 1847–1918, vol. 1, 1847–91: Apprenticeship to Premiership* (St. Lucia: University of Queensland Press, 1971), 189.

154 Courtney C.J. Bond, *Surveyors of Canada, 1867–1967* (Ottawa: Canadian Institute of Surveying, 1967), 26.

155 "Charles John Brydges," in *Dictionary of Canadian Biography*, vol. 11, 121–5.

156 Brydges to Armit, 29 Jan. 1880, HBC, RG 1, series 3A/1, PAM.

157 Brydges to Armit, 10 May 1880, HBC, RG 1, series 3A/1, PAM.

158 H. John Selwood and Evelyn Baril, "The Hudson's Bay Company and Prairie Town Development," in Alan F.J. Artibise, ed., *Town and City: Aspects of Western Canadian Development* (Regina: Canadian Plains Research Center, 1981), 83–91.

159 There is an extensive literature on the North West Mounted Police. See Roderick C. Macleod, *The NWMP and Law Enforcement, 1873–1905* (Toronto: University of Toronto Press, 1976), and the articles collected in William M. Baker, ed., *The Mounted Police and Prairie*

Society, 1873–1919 (Regina: Canadian Plains Research Centre, 1998).
Most pertinent are contributions by Morton, Bayfield, and Betke.
A comparison of the American and Canadian frontiers appears in
"Canadian Frontier," in Howard R. Lamar, ed., *The New Encyclopedia of the American West* (New Haven, Conn.: Yale University Press,
1998), 410.

CHAPTER SEVEN

1 Little, "Contested Land: Squatters and Agents in the Eastern Townships of Lower Canada," *Canadian Historical Review* 80 (Sept. 1999),
385–96.
2 Memorial from the Settlers in the District of Albany, Cape of Good
Hope, to Earl Bathurst, 10 March 1823, in George McCall Theal, ed.,
Records of the Cape Colony, vol. 15 (London: Printed for the
Government of the Cape of Good Hope, 1903), 305–11.
3 Malcolm Rohrbough, *The Land Office Business: The Settlement and
Administration of American Public Land* (Belmont, Calif.: Wadsworth
Publihing Company, 1990), 110.
4 Charles D'Escury, Inspector of Government Lands and Woods,
"General View of Land Tenure at the Cape of Good Hope [1823], in
George M. Theal, ed., *Records of the Cape Colony*, vol. 15, 335.
5 James ——— to Colonial Secretary, 23 July 1837, Letters and Reports
from the Crown Land Commissioners, 4/2348.2/1837, Archives of
New South Wales.
6 20 March 1840, Niel Black's Journal Commencing 30 September 1839,
ms. 6053 (box 99/1), 71, LaTrobe Library.
7 *Nelson Examiner*, 2 March 1859.
8 L.G.D. Acland, *The Early Canterbury Runs* (Christchurch: Whitcoulls,
1975), 272.
9 R.D. Hill, "Pastoralism in the Wairarapa, 1844–53," in R.F. Watters,
ed., *Land and Society in New Zealand* (Wellington: A.H. & A.W.
Reed, 1965), 31.
10 Giles French, *Cattle Country of Peter French* (Portland, Ore.: Binfords
& Mort, 1964), 21–4.
11 D.W. Meinig, *On the Margins of the Good Earth: The South
Australian Wheat Frontier, 1869–1884* (Adelaide: South Australian
Government Printer, 1988; reprint of 1962 edition).
12 Rohrbough, *The Land Office Business*, 50–85; Paul W. Gates and Paul
W. Swenson, *History of Public Land Law Development* (Washington,
DC: Government Printing Office, 1968), 234–46.
13 Hildegard Binder Johnson, *Order upon the Land: The U.S. Rectangular Land Survey and the Upper Mississippi Country* (New York:
Oxford University Press, 1976), 64–5.

14 Paul Gates suggests that claims clubs may not always have been managed by "impecunious frontiersmen." See *Landlords and Tenants on the Prairie Frontier: Studies in American Land Law* (Ithaca, NY: Cornell University Press, 1973), 111.

15 Cattle also appear as a factor in the economy of western Virginia in the 1740s–50s. Robert D. Mitchell, *Commercialism and Frontier: Perspectives on the Early Shenandoah Valley* (Charlottesville: University of Virginia Press, 1977), 147–9.

16 Terry G. Jordan, *North American Cattle-Ranching Frontiers: Origins, Diffusion, and Differentiation* (Albuquerque: University of New Mexico, 1992), 241–307; J. Orin Oliphant, *On the Cattle Ranges of the Oregon Country* (Seattle: University of Washington Press, 1968), 30–147. For accounts of Oregon's role in supplying stock for ranching in Wyoming, see John K. Rollison, *Wyoming Cattle Trails* (Caldwell, Idaho: Caxton Printers, 1948).

17 There is a first-hand account of this recognition in the Journal of the Voyage of Charles Johnson Pharazyn from London to New Zealand and in the Journal of Watarangi Station, 1840–1850, 19–25, ms. 1774, Alexander Turnbull Library, National Library of New Zealand. For a transition in thinking among the Albany colonists in Cape Colony, see Clifton C. Crais, *White Supremacy and Black Resistance in Pre-Industrial South Africa: The Making of the Colonial Order in the Eastern Cape, 1770–1865* (Cambridge: Cambridge University Press, 1992), 87–121; John Moodie, *Ten Years in South Africa, Including a Particular Description of the Wild Sports of that Country* (London: Richard Bentley, 1835), vol. II, 231.

18 Undated entries for 1871, entries for 7 Feb. 1871 and 1 May 1872, transcript of diaries of Andrew J. Robertson, folder 2, box 2, Andrew J. Robinson Papers, Accession 1306, American Heritage Center (AHC), University of Wyoming.

19 Shorty to Robertson, 27 Dec. [1874], folder 7, box 7, Andrew J. Robertson Papers, Accession 1306, AHC.

20 Dr. H. Latham, *Trans-Missouri Stock Raising: The Pasture lands of North America* (Omaha: Daily Herald, 1871), 55–6. On his raid, see Charles L. Kenner, "The Great New Mexico Cattle Raid – 1872," *New Mexico Historical Review* 37 (Oct. 1962), 243–59. The mayhem of punitive action without due process is described in this study. People were killed without proof of criminal conduct.

21 King, quoted in Tom Lea, Holland McCombs, and Francis L. Fulgate, *The King Ranch*, vol. 1 (Boston: Little, Brown and Company, 1957), 100.

22 Frederick L. Olmsted, *A Journey through Texas; or A Saddle-trip on the Southwestern Frontier* (Austin: University of Texas Press, 1978, reprint of 1857 edition), 370.

23 Johannes Van der Merwe, *The Migrant Farmer in the History of the Cape Colony*, trans. Roger B. Beck (Athens: Ohio University Press, 1995), 39–41.

24 German traveller O.F. Mentzel (1785–87), quoted in T.R.H. Davenport and K.S. Hunt, eds., *The Right to the Land* (Cape Town: D. Philip, 1974), 6.

25 Robert Ross, *Beyond the Pale: Essays on the History of Colonial South Africa* (Johannesburg: Witwatersrand University Press, 1994), 151.

26 Report by Lt. Col. C.J. Moysey on Claims to Land in the Keate Award Territory (1882), quoted in Davenport and Hunt, eds., *The Right to the Land*, 24.

27 Donald Gollan to Donald McLean, 2 Feb. 1857, microfilm, ms. 535, reel 55, Donald McLean Papers, Alexander Turnbull Library. On Gollan, see Miriam Macgregor, *Early Stations of Hawke's Bay* (Wellington: A.H. & A.W. Reed, 1970), 115.

28 Rodman Paul, *The Far West and the Great Plains in Transition, 1859–1900* (New York: Harper and Row, 1988), 212.

29 Christopher Pemberton Hodgson, *Reminiscences of Australia, with Hints on the Squatter's Life* (London: W.N. Wright, 1846), 50.

30 Donald Harman Akenson, *God's People: Covenant and Land in South Africa, Israel, and Ulster* (Montreal: McGill-Queen's University Press, 1991), 64–72.

31 Thomas Southey, *The Rise, Progress and Present State of Colonial Wools* (London: Smith, Elder, and Co., 1848), 41–3.

32 Acland, *The Early Canterbury Runs*, 185.

33 Hilda Sabato, *Agricultural Capitalism and the World Market: Buenos Aires in the Pastoral Age, 1840–1890* (Albuqueque: University of New Mexico Press, 1990), 28–9; Herbert Gibson, *The History and Present State of the Sheep-Breeding Industry in the Argentine Republic* (Buenos Aires: Ravenscroft and Mills, 1893), 30–1.

34 Iris Higbie Wilson, *William Wolfskill, 1798–1866: Frontier Trapper to California Ranchero* (Glendale, Calif.: Arthur H. Clark, 1965), 200; Jordan, *North American Cattle-Ranching Frontiers*, 248.

35 Terry L. Anderson and P.J. Hill, "The Evolution of Property Rights: A Study of the American West," *Journal of Law and Economics* 18 (April 1975), 171.

36 H.M. Robertson, "Distance and Diminishing Returns in Relation to Land Tenure Policy at the Cape in the 18th Century," in C.G.C. Martin and K.J. Friedlaender, eds., *History of Surveying and Land Tenure in South Africa: Collected Papers, Vol. I: Surveying and Land Tenure in the Cape, 1652–1812* (Cape Town: University of Cape Town, 1984), 112.

37 Harold E, Briggs, "Ranching and Stock-Raising in the Dakota Territory," *South Dakota Historical Collections* 14 (1928), 421–3;

Hazel Adele Pulling, *History of the Range Cattle Industry of Dakota* (MA thesis, University of Chicago, 1931), 470–2; Bob Lee and Dick Williams, *Last Grass Frontier: The South Dakota Stock Grower Heritage* (Sturgis, SD: Black Hills Publishers, 1964), 36–80.

38 Edward M. Curr, *Recollections of Squatting in Victoria, then Called the Port Phillip District (From 1841 to 1851)* (Melbourne: George Robertson, 1883), 48.

39 J.O. Randell, *Pastoral Settlement in Northern Victoria, Volume 1, The Cloiban Distrtict* (Melbourne: Queensbury Hill Press, 1979), 40.

40 John Campbell, *The Early Settlement of Queensland and other Articles* (Ipswich: Ipswich Observer, 1875), 27.

41 Anne Allingham, *Taming the Wilderness* (Townsville: Department of History, James Cook University, 1977) ,19.

42 Paul, *The Far West and the Great Plains*, 213–18.

43 J.M. Powell, *The Public Lands of Australia Felix: Settlement and Land Appraisal with Special Reference to the Western Plains* (Melbourne: Oxford University Press, 1970), 18–19. For contemporary advice on the management of sheep and the keeping of reserve lands for special purposes, see Thomas Southey, *Treatise on Sheep Addressed to Flock-Masters of Australia, Tasmania, and South Africa* (London: Smith and Elder, 1840), 15–6, 28, 34–7, 199.

44 On securing extra acres, see John Dunmore Lang, *Cooksland in North-Eastern Australia; the Future Cotton-Field of Great Britain: Its Charac-teristics and Capabilities for European Colonization. With a Disquisi-tion on the Origins, Manners, and Customs of the Aborigines* (London: Longmans, 1847), 293; 346; Charles H. Eden, *My Wife and I in Queensland: An Eight Years' Experience in the Above Colony with Some Accounts of Polynesian Labour* (London: Longmans, 1872), 58. For droughts in Cape Colony, see van der Merwe, *The Migrant Farmer*, 128. On Natal, note the evaluation in James Alexander, Private Secretary to the Late Governor of the Cape of Good Hope to Lord John Russell, 1 April 1840, in Percival Kirby, ed., *Andrew Smith and Natal: Documents Relating to the Early History of that Province* (Cape Town: Van Riebeek Society, 1955), 219. New South Wales's droughts are mentioned in Eric Rolls, *A Million Wild Acres* (Ringwood: Penguin, 1984), 84; for California, see Jordan, *North American Cattle-Ranching Frontiers*, 249–51. Selfishness was height-ened during droughts; see W.A. Brodribb, *Recollections of an Austra-lian Squatter, or Leaves from My Journal since 1835* (Sydney: John Wood & Co., 1883), 97–8, and Christopher Penberton Hodgson, *Reminiscences of Australia with Hints on the Squatter's Life* (London: W.N. Wright, 1846), 53.

45 Bill Gammage, *Narrandera Shire* (Narrandera Shire Council, 1986), 32; Brodribb, *Recollections*, 14. The colonial land commissioners made an astute assessment of voortrekker ways in their 1841 evaluation of Natal as a potential colony. Kirby, *Andrew Smith*, 234.

46 Edward Parry to Colonial Secretary, 22 Dec. 1832, Australian Agricultural Company, General Despatches, Archives of Business and Labour, Noel Butlin Archives Centre, Australian National University. For a summary history of the AAC, see P.A. Pemberton, *Pure Merino and Others: The Shipping Lists of the Australian Agricultural Company* (Canberra: Archives of Business and Labour, 1986).

47 Lady Alice Lovat, *The Life of Sir Frederick Weld: A Pioneer of Empire* (London: John Murray, 1914), 50–72; *New Zealand Gazette (Province of New Munster)* 4 no. 5 (21 Feb. 1851), 30–4.

48 Arthur Keppel-Jones, ed., *Philipps, 1820 Settler: His Letters* (Pietermaritzburg: Shuter and Shooter, 1960), 12–13, 236–7, 327.

49 W.K. Hancock, *Discovering Monaro: A Study of Man's Impact on His Environment* (Cambridge: At the University Press, 1972), 46; Jan Kociumbas, *The Oxford History of Australia: Possessions, 1770–1860* (Melbourne: Oxford University Press, 1992), 198–9; Resolutions Moved by Benjamin Boyd at a Public Meeting in Sydney, 9 April 1844, in New South Wales, *Land Grievances, Report of the Select Committee on Crown Land Grievances with Appendix, Minutes of Evidence, and Rellies to Circular Letters*, Appendix (Sydney: William John Row, Government Printer, 1844), n.p.

50 Colonial Secretary to Andrew Sinclair, 29 Feb. 1856 [enclosure from Colonial Land and Emigration Office], 56/47, LS-N 1/6, George Duppa to C.A. Dillon, 22 Aug. 1851, 51/14, LS-N, 1/1, Lands Department Office at Nelson, National Archives of New Zealand. W.J. Gardner, *The Amuri: A County History* (Culverden: Amuri County Council, 1956), 96.

51 Andrew Smith, *Andrew Smith's Journal of His Expedition into the Interior of South Africa, 1834–36* ed. William Lyle (Cape Town: A.A. Balkema, 1975), 27.

52 J.W.N. Tempelhoff, *Die okkupasiestelsel in die Distrik Soutpansberg* (Pretoria: Die Staatsdrukker, 1997), 8–9.

53 Leonard Guelke, "Land Tenure and Settlement at the Cape, 1652–1812," in C.G.C. Martin and K.J. Freidlaender, eds., *History of Surveying and Land Tenure in South Africa: Collected Papers, Vol. I; Surveying and Land Tenure in the Cape, 1652–1812* (Cape Town: University of Cape Town, 1984), 18–19. Guelke, engaging in a debate about the degree to which *veeboeren* were integrated into a market economy, accents the poverty and non-commercial nature of stock

raisers. A recent study proposes a compromise that documents considerable exchange between stock raisers and merchants but alleges that this activity was not a tightly managed business. Susan Newton-King, *Masters and Servants on the Cape Eastern Frontier, 1760–1803* (Cambridge: Cambridge University Press, 1999), 150–209.

54 Scrip was issued on all frontiers covered in this book. Typically, the certificates, redeemable in land, were granted to people to compensate for public service or for losses of land in particular places. Land orders were purchased. Both were accumulated by land speculators at discounts that reflected the illiquidity of land, the current market for land, and the poverty and need of certificate holders. Rare inside perspectives on the traffic in scrip abound in the David MacArthur Papers, MG 14 C21, Provincial Archives of Manitoba (PAM). MacArthur employed a Métis to find eligible claimants, assist with their claim, and purchased their scrip for resale.

55 Wilson, *William Wolfskill*, 116–19.

56 For the quote, see Charles H. Eden, *My Wife and I in Queensland: An Eight Years' Experience in the Above Colony with Some Account of the Polynesian Labour* (London: Longuans, Green & Company, 1872), 178. For remission tickets, see C.J. LaTrobe to Bells & Buchanan, 26 Oct. 1841, in P.L. Brown, ed., *Clyde Company Papers, vol. 3, 1841–45* (Oxford: Oxford University Press, 1958), 112–3.

57 Moodie, *Ten Years in South Africa*, vol. 2, 219.

58 James Cowan, *Sir Donald Maclean: The Story of a New Zealand Statesman* (Wellington: A.H. and A.W. Reed, 1940), 44–57. Cowan used Sir Donald's son's spelling of the family name. For an example of his frontier reports, see McLean to Colonial Secretary, 10 April 1849, Despatches from the Lieutenant Governor of New Munster to Governor in Chief of New Zealand, G 7/5, National Archives of New Zealand.

59 Oscar de Satgé, *Pages from the Life of a Queensland Squatter* (London: Hurst and Blackett, 1901), 3–10, 145–69.

60 Hancock, *Discovering Monaro*, 68.

61 de Satgé, *Pages from the Life of a Queensland Squatter*, 147.

62 For the trek, see Manfred Nathan, *The Voortrekkers of South Africa* (London: Gordon and Gotch, 1937), 76–85; also Sir George Napier to Lord Glenelg, 18 May 1838, in Bird, *Annals of Natal*, vol. 1, 394–5. Napier's account mentions the interdependence of Dutch grazers. For Australian squatters' co-operation during landhunts, see 30 Nov. 1839, in Log Book of Alexander Hunter of Stromness, in A.M. Hunter Diaries, 1840–2, ms. 10300, LaTrobe Library, State Library of Victoria.

63 *An Overlanding Diary by Alexander Fullerton Mollison*, ed. J.O. Randell (Melbourne: Mast Gully Press, 1980), 47, 81; Randell,

Pastoral Settlement in Northern Victoria, Volume I, 46; 25 and
30 Nov. 1839, in A.M. Hunter Diaries, ms. 10300, LaTrobe Library.

64 30 Nov. 1839, in A.M. Hunter Diaries, ms. 10300, La Trobe Library.
65 Andy Adams, *A Log of a Cowboy, a Narrative of the Old Trail Days* (Lincoln: University of Nebraska Press, 1964), 57.
66 Brodribb, *Recollections*, 9–12.
67 Acland, *The Early Canterbury Runs*, 298–9.
68 John Mack Faragher, *Daniel Boone: The Life and Legend of an American Pioneer* (New York: Henry Holt and Company, 1992), 92–105.
69 Richard White, *The Middle Ground: Indians, Empires, and Republics in the Great Lakes Region, 1650–1815* (Cambridge: Cambridge University Press, 1991), 356–65.
70 John Bird, ed., *The Annals of Natal* (Cape Town: C. Struk, 1965; facsimile reprint), vol. 2, 395.
71 Patrick Henry to Captain William Fleming, 10 June 1767, quoted in Thomas Perkins Abernethy, *Western Lands and the American Revolution* (New York: Russell and Russell, 1959), 61–2.
72 Washington to Crawford, 21 Sept. 1767, in C.W. Butterfield, ed., *Washington–Crawford Letters* (Cincinnati: Robert Clarke and Company, 1877), 2.
73 "Narrative of Willem Jurgen Pretorius, [1834–1839]," in Bird, *Annals of Natal*, vol. 1, 230.
74 Ebden to James Donnithorne, 28 Oct. 1836, quoted in Randell, *Pastoral Settlement in Northern Victoria*, vol. 1, 42.
75 6 March 1840, Niel Black Journal, LaTrobe Library.
76 Noeline Baker, ed., *A Surveyor of New Zealand, 1857–1896: The Recollections of John Holland Baker* (Auckland: Whitcombe & Tombs, 1932), 27–8.
77 Rev. Henry William Haygarth, *Recollections of Bush Life in Australia during a Residence of Eight Years in the Interior* (London: John Murray, 1864), 17–18.
78 5 Dec. 1841, in A.M. Hunter Diaries, 1841–2, ms. 10300, LaTrobe Library.
79 Brodribb, *Recollections*, 44–51.
80 James Flint, *Letters from America* (Edinburgh: W.&C. Tait, 1822), reprinted in Thwaites, ed., *Early Western Travels, 1748–1846* (New York: AMS, 1966), vol. 9, 180.
81 Ibid., 129–30.
82 Moodie, *Ten Years in South Africa*, vol. 2, 142.
83 John Campbell, *The Early Settlement of Queensland and Other Articles* (Ipswich: Ipswich Observer, 1875), 6. For New Zealand, see John Wilson, *Reminiscences of the Early Settlement of Dunedin and South Otago* (Dunedin: J. Wilkie & Co., 1912), 64.

84 Wilson, *Reminiscences*, 64.

85 Flint, *Letters from America*, in Thwaites, ed., *Early Western Travels*, vol. 9, 180.

86 Patrick Leslie's sister-in-law, quoted in Maurice French, *Conflict on the Condamine: Aborigines and the European Invasion* (Toowoomba: Darling Downs Institute, 1989), 63.

87 Quoted in Kirby, ed., *Andrew Smith and Natal*, 5. Smith published the itinerary of his trip in the *Graham's Town Journal*, 13 Aug. 1832; Kirby, *Smith*, 9–36.

88 This was written in 1834. See "Historical Précis by Dr. Andrew Smith," in Bird, *Annals of Natal*, vol. 1, 266.

89 "Herinerringe van Ferdinand Paulus van Gass," in Gustav S. Preller, *Voortrekkermense I* (Kapstaad: Nationale Pers, 1918), 10–11; "Verhaal van Dirk Uijs," in ibid., 273–9; Nathan, *The Voortrekkers*, 16–20.

90 Alfred Duncan, *The Wakatipians: or Early Days in New Zealand* (London: Simkins, Marshall and Company, 1888), 4–21; Alexander Mollison to Jane, 10 June 1838, Alexander Mollison Papers, ms. 1465; 25 Nov. 1839, Log Book of Alexander Hunter from Stromness, in A.M. Hunter Diaries, 1840–2, ms. 10300, LaTrobe Library.

91 P.L. Brown, *Clyde Company Papers, Volume I, 1836–40* (Oxford: Oxford University Press, 1952), 3–4, 53, 127–8; Thomas Francis Bride, *Letters from Victoria Pioneers, Being a Series of Papers on the Early Occupation of the Colony, the Aborigines, etc.* (Melbourne: William Heineman, 1969; reprint of the 1898 edition), 137–8.

92 Charles Hazelwood to Colonial Secretary, 30 Aug. 1851, 51/1212; 1 Sept. 1851, 51/1213, New Munster 8/49, National Archives of New Zealand.

93 Soloman Alexander Wright, *My Rambles as East Texas Cowboy, Hunter, Fisherman, Tie-cutter* (Austin: Texas Folklore Society, 1942), 52; Ernest Staples Osgood, *The Day of the Cattleman* (Minneapolis: University of Minnesota Press, 1929), 182–3: Giles French, *Cattle Country of Peter French* (Portland, Ore.: Binfords & Mort, 1964), 42.

94 I found over thirty letterhead descriptions in the incoming correspondence of the Wyoming Stock Growers' Association from 1881 to 1886; boxes 16 to 22, WSGA, accession 14, AHC.

95 Unidentified report on the advantages of fencing to ranchers, 25 Jan. 1883, collection of newspaper items, file 18, box 227, Wyoming Stock Growers' Association, accession 14, AHC.

96 Agreement between Jonathan Brown and Thomas and Page, 6 Aug. 1883, folder 4, box 9, John B. Thomas Papers, accession 141; M.L. Patrick to Thomas Sturgis, 8 Aug. 1883, folder 2, box 17, Wyoming Stock Growers's Association, Accession 14, AHC.

97 Entry on Pete Kitchen in the Arizona volume of ranch histories complied by Lamar Moore, box 9, Lamar Moore Collection, accession 675, AHC.

98 Bert Haskett, "History of the Sheep Industry in Arizona," *Arizona Historical Review* 7 (1936), 18.

99 Evidence of E.V. Smalley, editor of the *Northwest* (St Paul), in Joseph Nimmo, *Report in Regard to the Range and Ranch Cattle Business of the United States* (New York: Arno Press, 1972; reprint of 1885 edition), 77–9; John Clay, *My Life on the Range* (New York: Antiquarian Press, 1961), 67–251; Eden, *My Wife and I in Queensland*, 65–71; Will Barnes, *Western Grazing Grounds and Forest Ranges* (Chicago: Breeder's Gazette, 1913), 27–8.

100 Entry on Aztec Cattle Company in the New Mexico volume of ranch histories complied by Lamar Moore, box 9, Lamar Moore Collection, accession 675, AHC. D.J. Smythe, *My Experience in Wyoming* [1947], 16–17, accession 1335, AHC; John F. Goodly, *Early Day History of the Little Snake River Valley* [1962], 7, 17–18, accession 1067, AHC.

101 Quoted in van der Merwe, *The Migrant Farmers*, 19.

102 Ibid., 20–37.

103 Ibid., 54–5.

104 There are several accounts of these developments. Ibid., 83–92; Guelke, "Land Tenure," 18–24; Theal, *Records of the Cape Colony*, vol. 15, 328–36. For an example of a dispute over pasturage and water, see Memorial of P. Retief, early 1787, in H.C.V. Leibrandt, *Precis of the Cape of Good Hope: Letters and Documents Received* (Cape Town: W.A. Richards & Sons, 1898), vol. 2, 719.

105 Augusta Uitenhage de Mist, *Diary of a Journey to the Cape of Good Hope and the Interior of Africa in 1802 and 1803* (Capetown: A.A. Balkema, 1954), 33.

106 Ibid., 32.

107 Ibid., 20–61.

108 It threatened to use this power when it wanted to collect delinquent rents from loan farms. See Report on the *landdrost* at Graaff-Reinet, 19 July 1786, Leibrandt, *Precis*, vol. 2, 498.

109 Van der Merwe, *Migrant Farmers*, 62–77; Duly, *British Land Policy*, 39–40.

110 Duly, *British and Policy*, 77–8.

111 On the urge to hold land cheaply, see *Andrew Smith's Journal of His Expedition into the Interior of South Africa, 1834–36*, ed. William F. Lyle (Cape Town: A.A. Balkena, 1975), 47; 108.

112 The classic study remains useful. Walter Prescott Webb, *The Great Plains* (New York: Grosett & Dunlap, 1971; first pub. 1931), 280–318.

113 Wilbur E. Garrett et al., *Historical Atlas of the United States* (Washington, DC: National Geographic Society, 1988), 103.

114 Mexican land grants were the basis of some large patents and some companies that leased land to cattlemen. See Miguel Antonio Otero, *My Life on the Frontier, 1864–1882: Incidents and Characters of the Period when Kansas, Colorado, and New Mexico were Passing through the Last of their Wild and Romantic Years* (New York: Press of the Pioneers, 1935), 109–15. On sheepmen and leasing of railway lands, see Will C. Barnes, *Western Grazing Grounds and Forest Ranges* (Chicago: Greeders' Gazette, 1913), 143.

115 John B. Rae, "Commissioner Sparks and the Railroad Land Grants," *Mississippi Valley Historical Review* 25 (March 1939), 212–15; "Land Reform," in Lamar, ed., *The New Encyclopedia of the American West*, 615.

116 Peter Burroughs, *Britain and Australia: A Study in Imperial Relations and Crown Lands Administration* (Oxford: Clarendon Press, 1967), 147.

117 Randell, *Pastoral Settlement in Northern Victoria*, 40. Hancock sees a connection between the Cape and New South Wales; Hancock, *Discovering Monaro*, 47.

118 Burroughs, *Britain and Australia*, 122; *Guide to the Records Relating to Crown Lands* (Sydney: Archives of New South Wales, 1977), 1.

119 Colonial Secretary's Minute on Henry Bingham to Colonial Secretary, 21 Jan. 1838, Colonial Secretary, Letters and Reports Received, Commissioners of Crown Lands (1838), Archives of New South Wales.

120 Ebden to James Donnithorne, 28 No. 1836, quoted in Randell, *Pastoral Settlement*, 43.

121 See the discussion of commissioners in Weaver, "Frontiers into Assets," 39–43.

122 Minutes of Evidence Taken, Oliver Fry, Commissioner of Crown Lands for the Clarence River District since 1841, United Kingdom, House of Lords, *Papers Relative to the Occupation of Crown Lands, New South Wales; Papers Relating to Australia, 1847–48* (Dublin: Irish University Press, reprint of 1848 edition), 88.

123 9 Dec. 1839, in Niel Black's Journal, ms. 6053, LaTrobe Library.

124 Randell, ed., *An Overland Diary*, 63.

125 Testimony of George Leslie, Minutes of Evidence Taken, *Papers Relative to the Occupation of Crown Lands*, 87. On high ranges as early boundaries, see Cuthbert Fetherstonhaugh, *After Many Days* (Melbourne: E.W. Cole, 1917), 74.

126 Tempelhoff, *Die okkipasiestelsel in die Distrik Soutpansberg*, 5–7.

127 Olmsted, *A Journey through Texas*, 375.

128 Entry on John Chisum (his spelling) in the New Mexico volume of ranch histories compiled by Lamar Moore, box 9, Lamar Moore Collection, accession 675, AHC.

129 Paul, *The Far West and the Great Plains*, 199–201. Lee and Williams, *Last Grass Frontier*, 102–3.

130 Archer Butler Gilfillan, *Sheep: Life on the South Dakota Range* (Minneapolis: University of Minnesota Press, 1958; first pub. 1928), 159.

131 *Autobiography of E.D. Swan*, 87, 118, accession 371, AHC.

132 William Lonsdale to Colonial Secretary, 9 June 1837, in Cannon and Macfarlane, eds., *The Crown and the Squatter*, 179; Randell, *Pastoral Settlement in Northern Victoria*, vol. 1, 149.

133 29 Feb. 1840, in Niel Black's Journal, ms. 6053, LaTrobe Library. Oscar de Satgé describes a similar process of spreading stock to hold more land than regulations allowed. See de Satgé, *Pages from the Life of a Queenland Squatter*, 170.

134 James ——— (from Queanbeyan) to the Colonial Secretary, 23 July 1837, Colonial Secretary, Letters and Reports from the Crown Land Commissioners, 4/2348.2 (1837); Bill Gammage, *Narrandera Shire*, 41; Randell, *Pastoral Squatters*, vol. 1, 97, 221–3.

135 Maurice French, *Conflict on the Condamine: Aborigines and the European Invasion* (Toowoomba: Darling Downs Institute Press, 1989), 60.

136 Donald Welsh, "Pierre Wibaux, Cattle King," *North Dakota History* 20 (1953), 18; Osgood, *The Day of the Cattleman*, 56–7.

137 Testimony of W.C. Gillette, Dearborn, Montana, in United States, *Report of the Public Land Commission*, 363.

138 Colonial governments in Australia shifted to a leasing system in the late 1840s, and the regulations for these often stipulated straight lines. However, a map of squatters' runs on the rich Darling Downs of Queensland in 1864 still depicted curved boundaries. J.W. Buxton, *Squatting Map of the Darling Downs* (Brisbane: J.W. Buxton, 1864), one sheet, 100 cm by 60 cm, Mitchell Library.

139 Sabato, *Agrarian Capitalism*, 42.

140 Curr, *Recollections of Squatting*, 123.

141 Samuel Butler, *A First Year in Canterbury Settlement with Other Early Essays*, ed. R.A. Streatfield (London: Jonathan Cape, 1923), 96. Butler arrived in 1860 and sold out in 1864, doubling his capital.

142 Wilson, *William Wolfskill*, 165.

143 Macgregor, *Early Stations of Hawke's Bay*, 48.

144 Robert Gilkison, *Early Days in Central Otago: Being Tales of Days Gone By* (Auckland: Whitcombe and Toombs, 1936), 15.

145 Anne Allingham, *Taming the Wilderness* (Townsville, Queensland: Department of History, James Cook University, 1977), 58.

146 For boundary with Brock, see 22–3 Oct. 1845; for arbitration, see 13–16 Feb. 1844, in Station Journal of John Carre Riddell, 1843–1847, ms. 10766, LaTrobe Library.

147 Entries in the Diary of the Commissioner for Crown Lands, Darling Downs, 1 July 1845–21 Sept. 1852, State Archives of Queensland.

148 Macgregor, *Early Stations of Hawke's Bay*, 262.

149 George E. Loyau, *The History of Maryborough and the Wide Bay and Burnett District from the Year 1850 to 1895* (Brisbane: Pole, Outridge & Co., 1897), 64.

150 William Wiseman to Chief Commissioner of Crown Lands, 16 Jan. 1856, microfilm 0110, Letters of William Wiseman, 1855–1860, Oxley Library.

151 Hodgson, *Reminiscences*, 50.

152 Most examples appear in previous chapters, but, for others, see Ion L. Idriess, *Forty Fathoms Deep: Pearl Divers and Sea Rovers in Australian Seas* (Sydney: Angus and Robertson, 1937), 82; Malcolm Rohrbough, *The Land Office Business: The Settlement and Administration of American Public Lands* (Belmont, Calif.: Wadsworth Publishing Company, 1990), 184.

153 David M. Delo, *Peddlers and Post Traders: The Army Sutler on the Frontier* (Helena, Mont.: Kingfisher Books, 1998), 172–93. See "Articles of co-partnership entered into the 27th day of June 1878, between E. Tillotson of Fort Fetterman, Wyoming, and John V.R. Hoff of the US Army," folder 4, box 1, Ephraim Tillotson Papers, accession 401, AHC.

154 Pulling, *History of the Range Cattle Industry of Dakota*, 470; J.J. Waggoner, "History of the Cattle Industry in Southern Arizona," *University of Southern Arizona Bulletin* 23 (April 1952), 37; Lee and Williams, *Last Grass Frontier*, 53, 57, 60.

155 R. Douglas Hurd maintains that natives "taught white farmers the importance of protecting the corn crop from rodents and from weather by storing it in cribs." *Indian Agriculture in America* (Lawrence: University of Oklahoma Press, 1987), 41.

156 Moodie, *Annals of Natal*, vol. 2, 149. Also see the discussion about the collaboration of individuals in Robert Ross, *Beyond the Pale: Essays on the History of Colonial South Africa* (Middletown, Conn.: Wesleyan University Press, 1993), 87–9.

157 Robert Shell, *Children of Bondage: A Social History of the Slave Society at the Cape of Good Hope, 1652–1838* (Hanover, NH: University Press of New England, 1994), 171.

158 4 July 1837, in Randell, ed., *An Overlanding Diary*, 17.

159 4 Dec. 1840, in Niel Black's Journal, ms. 6053, LaTrobe Library.

160 French, *Conflict on the Condamine*, 71.

161 *New Zealand Government Gazette (Province of New Munster)* vol. 4, no. 5 (21 Feb. 1851), 31.

162 John Wilson, *Reminiscences of the Early Settlement of Dunedin and South Otago* (Dunedin: J. Wilkie & Co., 1912), 64–5; John Campbell, *The Early Settlement of Queensland and Other Articles* (Ipswich: Ipswich Observer, 1875), 9.

163 Jeanine Graham, *Frederick Weld* (Auckland: University of Auckland Press, 1983), 7.

164 Tempelhoff, *Die okkupasiestelsel in die Distrik Soutpansberg*, 7; Report of the Commissioners (Native Locations), 27 Nov. 1846, in W.J. Dunbar Moodie, *Ordinances, Proclamations ... of Natal* (Pietermaritzburg: May and David, 1856), 239.

165 Comando General del Ejécito, Dirección de Estudios Históricos, *Politica seguida con el aborigen, 1820–1852* (Buenos Aires: Circulo Militar, 1974), 71–2; Gibson, *The History and Present State of the Sheep-Breeding Industry*, 28; John Lynch, *Argentine Dictator: Juan Manuel de Rosas, 1829–1852* (Oxford: Clarendon Press, 1981), 54–5.

166 One of the better accounts of the political and legal status of white grazers on Indian reservations covers this topic. See Donald J. Berthrong, "Cattlemen on the Cheyenne–Arapaho Reservation, 1883–1885," *Arizona and the West* 13 (1971), 7, 17.

167 David Arnet and Francis H.S. Orpen, *The Land Question of Griqualand West: An Inquiry into the Various Claims to Land* (Cape Town: Saul Soloman, 1875), 29.

168 *Government Gazette* (South Australia), 31 Oct. 1839, Mortlock Library, State Library of South Australia. On the problems of using European names, see George Duppa to Commissioner of Crown Lands, 22 Sept. 1852, 52/45, LS-N, 1/2 (Land Department, Nelson), National Archives of New Zealand.

169 T.L. Mitchell, Circular Letter to Surveyors, 5 Sept. 1829, in Michael Cannon and Ian Macfarlane, eds., *The Crown, the Land and the Squatter, 1835–1840: Historical Records of Victoria* (Melbourne: University of Melbourne Press, 1991), xviii.

170 Ora Brooks Peake, *The Colorado Range Cattle Industry* (Glendale, Calif.: Arthur Clarke Company, 1937), 80–97.

171 Testimony of Sherman Day, former Surveyor General of California, in United States Public Lands Commission, *Report of the Public Lands Commission* (Washington, DC: Government Printing Office, 1880), 49.

172 Minutes of the Laramie County Stock Association for 18–19 November 1879, Minute Book, 29 November 1873 to 9 November 1883, box 43, Wyoming Stock Grower's Association (WSGA), accession 14, AHC. The WSGA instructed the territorial congressman to do all that he could to defeat legislation aiming at the sale of large blocks of land

in Wyoming and adjoining territories (minutes for 16 Feb. 1880). The records of the WSGA have been helpful in indicating how ranchers in northern Colorado, the Dakotas, Montana, western Nebraska, and Wyoming thought about land issues. Its members had interests in these areas, and it was probably the most powerful of several score western ranchers' associations. The commission and its lack of impact are discussed in Donald Worster, *A River Running West: The Life of John Wesley Powell* (New York: Oxford University Press, 2001), 373–9.

173 Boone McClure, "The Laws and Customs of the Open Ranch," *Panhandle-Plains Historical Review*, no. 10 (1937), 64.

174 Harrel, "Oklahoma's Million Acre Ranch," 73; McClure, "The Laws and Customs," 77; Charles M. Russell, *Free Grass to Fences: The Montana Cattle Range Story* (New York: University Publishers, 1960), 75.

175 William W. Savage, Jr, *The Cherokee Strip Live Stock Association* (Columbia: University of Missouri Press, 1973), 34–5.

176 Fetherstonhaugh, *After Many Days*, 74, 317–18.

177 The "prickly pear" became a serious nuisance in the 1920s. See John H. Meeks, *Bench Marks and Boundaries* (Brisbane: Hallett Brier, 1991), 70–1; Webb, *The Great Plains*, 285–95. Information on the *bois d'arc* comes from interview with H.D. Stine, 29 Aug. 1938, Life History Project, WPA, Library of Congress (LC); interview with George Marlin, no date, WPA, LC. Marlin worked for a bois d'arc contractor. For a brief account of fencing, see the entry on "Barbed Wire" in Lamar, ed., *The New Encyclopedia of the American West*, 79–80. Leslie Hewes and Christian L. Jung, "Early Fencing on the Middle Western Prairie," *Annals of the Association of American Geographers* 71 (June 1981), 177–201. For southern Africa, see *Statutes of Natal*, vol. 1, section on fences, n.p.

178 Peake, *The Colorado Range Cattle Industry*, 69.

179 Paul, *The Far West and the Great Plains*, 202–5; Warren Elofson, *Cowboys, Gentlemen and Cattle Thieves: Ranching on the Western Frontier* (Montreal: McGill-Queen's University Press, 2000), 137.

180 Kermit Hall, "The Legal Culture of the Great Plains," reprinted in John R. Wunder, ed., *Law and the Great Plains: Essays on the Legal History of the Heartland* (Westport, Conn.: Greenwood Press, 1996), 14.

181 Allan Ward, *A Show of Justice: Racial "Amalgamation" in Nineteenth Century New Zealand* (Auckland: University of Auckland Press, 1973), 79; see too 104, 148.

182 Earl W. Hayter, "Barbed Wire Fencing – A Prairie Invention," *Heritage of Kansas*, vol. 4 (Sept. 1960), 9–26; James C. Olson and Ronald C. Naugle, *History of Nebraska* (Lincoln: University of Nebraska Press, 1997), 193–5.

183 Major W. Shephard, *Prairie Experience in Handling Cattle and Sheep* (London: Chapman and Hall, 1884), 125.

184 See, for example, the situation in southern Texas described in David Montejano, *Anglos and Mexicanos in the Making of Texas* (Austin: University of Texas, 1987), 56. For Oregon see Oliphant, *On the Cattle Ranges of the Oregon Country*, 210.

185 Nimmo, *Report in Regard to the Range*, 15; Barnes, *Western Grazing*, 143; Don D. Walker, "The Carlisles: Cattle Barons of the Upper Basin," *Utah Historical Quarterly Society* 32 (1964), 275–6; Harrel, "Oklahoma's Million Acre Ranch," 70–8; Maurice Frink, W. Turrentine Jackson, and Agnes Wright Spring, *When Grass Was King: Contributions to the Western Range Cattle Industry Study* (Boulder: University of Colorado Press, 1956), 386. The public lands of Texas, never part of the American public domain, could be leased under terms specified in laws passed in 1879 and 1883. Waggoner, "History of the Cattle Industry in Southern Arizona," 44.

186 Circular of W.C. Hill, 26 Aug. 1885, folder 6, box 1, John B. Thomas Papers, accession 141, AHC.

187 John B. Rae, "Commissioner Sparks and the Railroad Land Grants," *Mississippi Valley Historical Review* 25 (March 1939), 212–14. For an example of squatting on and then renting grazing rights on Indian lands, see Savage, *The Cherokee Strip Live Stock Association*, 70–111.

188 Peake, *The Colorado Range Cattle Industry*, 75; Osgood, *The Day of the Cattlemen*, 182, 190–1. For an instance of the use of swamp-development legislation that helped ranchers in the far west, although it was designed for the south, see French, *Cattle Country of Peter French*, 62–5, 144–50.

189 For Dorsey's ranch, see the entry on him in the New Mexico volume of ranch histories complied by Lamar Moore, box 9, Lamar Moore Collection, accession 675, AHC. The letter outlining his strategy was written to government beef contractor J.W. Bosler, 12 May 1883, folder 2, box 61, Bosler Family papers, accession 5850, AHC.

CHAPTER EIGHT

1 Irene M. Spry and Bennett McCardle, *The Records of the Department of the Interior and Research Concerning Canada's Western Frontier of Settlement* (Regina: Canada Plains Research Center, 1993), figures 22–3. In his book on Canadian efforts to attract Americans to the prairies, Harold Troper observes that there were large open tracts on the American public domain; however, the millions of acres remaining was inferior. While extensive areas were legally open for homesteading, they included range controlled by ranchers. Harold Martin Troper, "*Only*

Farmers Need Apply": Official Canadian Government Encouragement of Immigration form the United States, 1896–1911 (Toronto: Griffin House, 1972), 102–7.

2 D.W. Meinig, *On the Margins of the Good Earth: The South Australian Wheat Frontier, 1869–1884* (Adelaide: South Australian Government Printer, 1982), 70; Worster, *Dust Bowl*, 82; John Opie, "100 Years of Climate Risk Assessment on the High Plains: Which Farm Paradigm Does Irrigation Serve?" *Agricultural History* 63 (spring 1989), 248; David C. Jones, *Empire of Dust: Settling and Abandoning the Prairie Dry Belt* (Edmonton: University of Alberta Press, 1987), 14–15. The editor of a recent collection, describing the degradation of marginal land in arid parts of the world when subjected to farming, believes that the myth still had a following; Michael H. Glantz, *Drought Follows the Plow* (Cambridge: Cambridge University Press, 1994), 3.

3 On the interest in Argentina, see the entry "George Dean Greenwood" in S.G. Scholefield, ed., *A Dictionary of New Zealand Biography: Volume I* (Wellington: Department of Internal Affairs, 1940); Walt Coburn, *Pioneer Cattleman in Montana: The Story of the Circle C Ranch* (Norman: University of Oklahoma Press, 1968), 222–7. Wool production in Patagonia is covered in Elsa Mabel Barbería, *Los dueños del la tierra en la Patagonia Austral, 1880–1920* (Rio Gallego: Universidad Federal de la Patagonia Austral, 1993), 17–237.

4 Extracted from incoming letters to Arthur Cox, boxes 1–12, M281, Arthur Cox Papers, Glenbow-Alberta Institute and Archives (hereafter Glenbow).

5 Henry George, *Our Land and Land Policy: Speeches, Lectures and Miscellaneous Writings* (New York: Doubleday and McClure Company, 1901), 318.

6 Details about the introduction of leasing are explained in *The Squatter's Manual: A Complete Compendium of the Acts of the Imperial and Colonial Legislatures, Orders in Council, and Local Regulations Relating to the Occupation of Crown Lands in New South Wales* (Melbourne: William Kerr, 1848), Mitchell Library. While there was no leasing on the U.S. public domain, Texas entered the republic with its own public lands and began to lease land in 1883. See Edward Everett Dale, *The Range Cattle Industry: Ranching on the Great Plains from 1869 to 1925* (Norman: University of Oklahoma, 1960), 113.

7 Francis Fuller, *Five Years' Residence in New Zealand; or, Observations on Colonization* (London: Williams and Norgate, 1859), 152.

8 John Dunmore Lang, *Repeal or Revolution: A Glimpse of the Irish Future: In a Letter to the Right Honourable Lord John Russell* (London: Effingham Wilson, 1848), 8, Mitchell Library.

9 David Breen, *The Canadian Prairie West and the Ranching Frontier 1874–1924* (Toronto: University of Toronto Press, 1983), 47.

10 *Opinions of Counsel as to the Rights of the Pastoral Tenants of the Crown* (Melbourne: Wilson, Mackinnon and Fairfax, 1856), 2–36, Mitchell Library. This pamphlet was produced and circulated by the Pastoral Protective Association.

11 Edward M. Curr, *Recollections of Squatting in Victoria, then Called the Port Phillip District (From 1841 to 1851)* (Melbourne: George Robertson, 1851), 3–4.

12 Eleanore Williams, *A Way of Life: The Pastoral Families of the Central Country of South Australia* (Adelaide: University Union Press, 1980), 55–63.

13 Bede Nairn, "Sir John Robertson," in Geoffrey Searle and Russel Ward, eds., *Australian Dictionary of Biography, 1851–1890* (Melbourne: Melbourne University Press, 1976), 40.

14 Victoria Convention, *Resolutions, Proceedings, and Documents of the Victorian Convention, Assembled in Melbourne, July 15 to August 6, 1857* (Melbourne: J.J. Walsh, 1857), 1–31, quote at 13, Mitchell Library.

15 Reformers throughout Australia faced conservative upper legislative chambers that sent bills back to the elected assemblies with amendments. Thus most land acts embodied compromises.

16 For the conservative assessment of the convention and free selection, see Henry Gyles Turner, *A History of Victoria from its Discovery to its Absorption into the Commonwealth of Australia*, 2 vols. (London: Longman, Green, and Co., 1904), vol. 2, 82–5.

17 Gavan Duffy, *Guide to the Land Law of Victoria* (Melbourne: Government Printer, 1862), 4–5.

18 J.M. Powell, *The Public Lands of Australia Felix: Settlement and Land Appraisal in Victoria with Special Reference to the Western Plains* (Melbourne: Oxford University Press, 1970), 89.

19 Duffy, *Guide to the Land Law of Victoria*, 19.

20 Powell, *Australia Felix*, 36, 99.

21 Simon Ville, *The Rural Entrepreneurs: A History of the Stock and Station Agency Industry in Australia and New Zealand* (Cambridge: Cambridge University Press, 2000), 75–6.

22 H.B.T. Strangeways, quoted in South Australia, *Proceedings ... 1865; No.73. Report of the Select Committee of the House of Assembly Appointed to Inquire into the Workings of the System of Selling the Crown Lands together with Minutes of Evidence and Appendix* (Adelaide: W.C. Cox, 1865), 95, Mortlock Library, State Library of South Australia.

23 Steele Rudd, *Sandy's Selection* (Sydney: New South Wales Bookstall Co., 1904), 174–5.

24 W.R. Lawson, *Our Wool Staple; or A History of Squatting in South Australia* (Adelaide: John Howell, 1865), 43, Mortlock Library.

25 *Guide to the Records Relating to Crown Lands* (Sydney: Archives Authority of New South Wales, 1977), 9; Charles J. King, "An Outline of Closer Settlement in New South Wales, Part 1: The Sequence of the Land Laws," *Review of Marketing and Agricultural Economics* 25 (Sept.–Dec. 1957), 60–80.

26 Raymond Wright, *The Bureaucrats' Domain: Space and the Public Interest in Victoria, 1836–84* (Melbourne: Oxford University Press, 1989), 103.

27 Powell, *Australia Felix*, 123.

28 Wright, *The Bureaucrats' Domain*, 103–4.

29 Margaret Birrell, *The Political Influence of the Squatters* (Brisbane: Bound Typescript, 1950), 10–26, Oxley Library, Queensland State Library. See the discussion of South Australia's Waste Lands Alienation Act of 1872 in *Crown Lands and Immigration: Past and Present Land Systems* (Adelaide: E. Spiller, 1881), 9, Land Pamphlets, Mortlock Library.

30 The Dad and Dave articles and books by Arthur H. Davis (also known as Steele Rudd) are notable. His collection of stories *On Our Selection* provided material for a silent film of 1920 and for several other films during the 1930s. *On Our Selection* was remade in 1995. For Davis's life, see Eric Drayton Davis, *The Life and Time of Steele Rudd: Creator of On Our Selection, Dad and Dave* (Melbourne: Landsdowne Press, 1979).

31 Williams, *A Way of Life*, 61–5.

32 S. Newlands, *Our Waste Lands and Our Productions* (Adelaide: Burden and Bonython, 1888), 18.

33 Roger B. Joyce, *Samuel Walker Griffith* (St Lucia: University of Queensland Press, 1984), 93. Strictly speaking, this measure did not resemble George's single tax. Because his writings were critical of large landholdings, they were enlisted in campaigns for land nationalization, which the Queensland measure resembled.

34 "Crown Lands Act of 1884," 48 Victoria no. 26 [23 Dec. 1884], in Queensland, *Acts and Regulations Relating to the Leasing and Alienation of Crown Lands* (Brisbane: Government Printer, 1895); Queensland, *Manual for the Guidance of Land Commissioners and Land Agents in the Practical Working of "The Crown Lands Acts, 1884 to 1894"* (Brisbane: Government Printer, 1895). Also see Margaret Birrell, *The Political Influence of the Squatters* (Brisbane: Bound Typescript, 1950), 54–62. These three items are in the Oxley Library, State Library of Queensland.

35 Queensland, "Special Sales of Land Act of 1891" and "Crown Land Act of 1894," in *Acts and Regulations*.

36 "Crown Land Act of 1884," in ibid.

37 New Zealand, *Evidence taken by the Joint Waste Lands Bill Committee on the Petition of Settlers of Clutha District: Session Paper F. No. 3* (Wellington: Government Printer, 1868), 3–6.

38 Breen, *The Canadian Prairie West and the Ranching Frontier*, 70.

39 Ibid., 70–98; Barry Potyondi, *Where the Rivers Meet: A History of the Upper Oldman River Basin* (Lethbridge: Robins Southern Printing, 1992), 85–9. Joy Oetelaar, "George Lane: From Cowboy to Cattle King," in Simon M. Evans, Sarah Carter, and W.B. Yeo, eds., *Cowboys, Ranchers and the Cattle Business: Cross-Border Perspectives on Ranching History* (Calgary: University of Calgary Press, 1999), 54. Insights into the conduct of settlers and ranchers in southern Alberta may be found in the letters of a regional land agent: Arthur Cox to W.H. Collingham, 11 May 1898, box 3, letterbook I; Cox to Osler, Hammond, Nanton, 16 April 1901, box 3, letterbook III, M281, Arthur Cox Papers, Glenbow.

40 Wright, *The Bureaucrats' Domain*, 259–62. For New Zealand, see 27 Victoria No. 39, An Act to Regulate the Sale, Letting, Disposal, and Occupation of the Waste Land of the Crown within the Province of Otago [14 Dec. 1863].

41 Roy Robbins, *Our Landed Heritage: The Public Domain, 1776–1936* (Princeton, NJ: Princeton University Press, 1942), 207.

42 David M. Ellis, "The Homestead Clause in the Railroad Grants," in Ellis, ed., *The Frontier in American Development: Essays in Honor of Paul Wallace Gates* (Ithaca, NY: Cornell University Press, 1969), 47–72.

43 John B. Rae, "Commissioner Sparks and the Railroad Land Grants," *Mississippi Valley Historical Review* 25 (March 1939), 213–14.

44 Ellis, "The Homestead Clause," 61.

45 Rae, "Commissioner Sparks and the Railroad Land Grants," 229.

46 See the map of the United States in Robbins, *Our Landed Heritage*, facing 224. Regarding Henry George note *Our Land and Land Policy: Speeches, Lectures, and Miscellaneous Writings* (New York: Doubleday and McClure, 1902), 2.

47 Jeremy Adelman, *Frontier Development: Land, Labour, and Capital on the Wheatlands of Argentina and Canada, 1890–1914* (Oxford: Clarendon Press, 1994), 66.

48 There is a description of this activity in "The Land in New Zealand: How it Was Settled and Acquired," chapter in an unidentified pamphlet published about 1880 in conjunction with single-tax reform,

37–40, call number 308 Pa 22, Mitchell Library, State Library of New South Wales.

49 See the entry "cockatoo" in W.S. Ramon, *The Australian National Dictionary* (Melbourne: Oxford University Press, 1988).

50 Burroughs, *Britain and Australia*, 125; Williams, *The Bureaucrats' Domain*, 61. Niel Black of Victoria was buying protectively in 1854–55. See Statistical Report of All the Land Bought by Niel Black & Company in the Australian Colonies down to 1st July 1861, Niel Black Papers, ms. 8996, LaTrobe Library. "Land Disposal: The Land Gets New Owners, 1840 to 1880s," Plate 50, in Malcolm McKinnon, ed., *New Zealand Historical Atlas* (Wellington: David Bateman in Association with Historical Branch, Department of Internal Affairs, 1997).

51 For creditors in Australia, see D.B. Waterson, *Squatter, Selector, and Storekeeper: A History of the Darling Downs, 1859–93* (Sydney: University of Sydney Press, 1968), 25. For the speculation in cattle companies, see John Clay, *My Life on the Range* (New York: Antiquarian Press, 1961), ix–xiii, 13, 139.

52 Wright, *The Bureaucrats' Domain*, 103.

53 Heather B. Ronald, *Wool before the Wind: A History of the Ronald Family and the Australian Mercantile Land and Finance Company* (Pakenham: Landvale Enterprises, 1987), 75.

54 Bill Gammage, *Narrandera Shine* (Narrandera Shire Council, 1986), 64.

55 Breen, *The Canadian Prairie West and the Ranching Frontier*, 77; J.W. Martin to Cox, 26 Oct. 1904, box 10, file 2a, M281, Arthur Cox Papers, Glenbow.

56 Gammage, *Narrandera Shire*, 64; Henry Gyles Turner, *A History of the Colony of Victoria* (London: Longmans, Green and Co., 1904), vol. 2, 85.

57 Hancock, *Discovering Monaro*, 90–1.

58 Quoted in ibid., 98.

59 Helena Huntington Smith's history of the Johnson County War covers well the maverick and small-rancher issues for Wyoming; *The War on the Powder River* (New York: McGraw-Hill, 1966), 51–120. A first-hand account of these matters, as factors precipitating the Johnson County conflict, was prepared at the time by O.H. Flagg: "A Review of the Cattle Business in Johnson County, Wyoming," folder 8, J. Elmer Brock Collection, accession 102, AHC.

60 William Scarfe, *Re: The Proposed Extension of the Pastoral Leases of Queensland* (Rockhampton: Record Printing Company, 1900), 19.

61 Smith, *The War on the Powder River*, 96.

62 John B. Thomas to Thomas Sturgis, 10 Nov. 1881, Report of Ranch owned by Thurlow and McIntyre, letterbook, 1881–1889, box 3, John B. Thomas Papers, accession 141, AHC.

63 Robbins, *Our Landed Heritage*, 154–5, 218–20; Granville Stuart, "The End of the Cattle Range," in Ted Stone, ed., *The Complete Cowboy Reader: Remember in the Open Range* (Red Deer, Alta.: Red Deer College Press, 1997), 35. On women filing homestead entries for speculative gain as well as for securing property, see H. Elaine Lindgren's well-researched *Land in Her Own Name: Women as Homesteaders in North Dakota* (Fargo: North Dakota Institute for Regional Studies, 1991),

64 Breen, *The Canadian Prairie West and the Ranching Frontier*, 117–35.

65 In some instances, it has been argued, land prices were low enough that "there was no need for elaborate schemes for spotting and gridironing. Large blocks could be purchased without excessive capital outlay." See P.R. Stevens, "The Age of the Great Sheep Runs, 1856–80," in R.F. Watters, ed., *Land and Society in New Zealand* (Wellington: A.H. & A.W. Reed, 1965), 53. This claim may slight the struggles faced by undercapitalized New Zealand squatters when they sought to protect their runs against better-capitalized outsiders. Moreover, low land prices still involved outlays that grazers would rather have invested in other ways.

66 William Soltau Davidson, *William Soltau Davidson, 1846–1924, A Sketch of His Life Covering a Period of Fifty-Two Years, 1864–1916, in the Employment of the New Zealand and Australian Land Company* (Edinburgh: Oliver and Boyd, 1930), 79–82; New Zealand, *Parliamentary Debates: Second Session of the Sixth Parliament, Legislative Council and House of Representatives* (Wellington: Government Printer, 1877), 688; Thomas Condie to Alex McLean, 3 Sept. 1862, Donald McLean Papers, ms. 32, folder 945, Turnbull Library, National Library of New Zealand. For ecology and Montana ranchers, see Ernest Staples Osgood, *The Day of the Cattleman* (Mineappolis: University of Minnesota Press, 1929), 56–7.

67 Gammage, *Narrandera Shire*, 63–4; J.J. Waggoner, "History of the Cattle Industry in Southern Arizona," *University of Southern Arizona Bulletin* 23 (April 1952), 63.

68 Maurice Frink et al., *When Grass Was King: Contributions to the Western Range Cattle Industry Study* (Boulder: University of Colorado Press, 1956), 383–6.

69 Walt Coburn, *Pioneer Cattleman in Montana: The Story of the Circle C Ranch* (Norman: University of Oklahoma Press, 1968), 32.

70 Francis Fuller, *Five Years' Residence in New Zealand*, 73–8.

71 Unidentified pamphlet (308 Pa 22), 38, Mitchell Library.

72 William Fox to Henry Tiffen, 2 July 1857, LS-NA (Lands and Surveys, Napier, Incoming Letters), 1/2, 57/68, National Archives of New Zealand.

73 Davidson, *A Sketch of his Life*, 77.

74 Joyce, *Samuel Walker Griffith*, 48.

75 Peter K. Simpson, *The Community of Cattlemen: A Social History of the Cattle Industry in Southeast Oregon, 1869–1912* (Moscow: University of Idaho Press, 1987), 34.

76 Davis, *Sandy's Selection*, 2–3.

77 J.M. Powell, *An Historical Geography of Modern Australia: The Restive Fringe* (Cambridge: Cambridge University Press, 1988), 11–12.

78 Donald Worster, *Dust Bowl: The Southern Plains in the 1930s* (New York: Oxford University Press, 1979), 84.

79 Paul Voisey, *Vulcan: The Making of a Prairie Community* (Toronto: University of Toronto Press, 1988), 43–4. A model local study, this book describes the diverse adaptations of people to their environment. James Richtik and Don Measner, "Homesteading and Agriculture in the West, 1872–1891," Plate 42, *Historical Atlas of Canada*, vol. II (Toronto: University of Toronto Press, 1993). Phillip O. Foss, *Politics and Grass: The Administration of Grazing on the Public Domain* (Seattle: University of Washington Press, 1960), 22.

80 Walter Nugent, "Frontiers and Empires in the Late Nineteenth Century," in Patricia Nelson Limerick, Clyde A. Milner, and Charles E. Rankin, eds., *Trails: Toward a New Western History* (Lawrence: University Press of Kansas, 1991), 180.

81 Barbería, *Los dueños de la tierra en la Patagonia Austral*, 186–237.

82 Tollemache to John Harding, 29 May 1873, folder 1, ms. 662, John Harding, Mount Vernon Papers, Alexander Turnbull Library, National Library of New Zealand.

83 J.W. Carlisle to Donald McLean, 28 July 1876, Donald McLean Papers, micro ms. 535, Turnbull Library.

84 The involvement of eastern bankers, financiers, and commission agents in organizing and defending western cattle companies is analysed in Gene M. Gressley, *Bankers and Gentlemen* (Lincoln: University of Nebraska Press, 1966); British investment is the subject of Lawrence Wood, *British Gentlemen in the Wild West: The Era of the Intensely English Cowboy* (New York: Free Press, 1989).

85 The records of the Australian Mortgage, Loan, and Finance Company (AMLF), which sold debentures in the United Kingdom and used the capital to buy and improve numerous estates in New South Wales and Queensland, describe detailed control. The company felt that squatters were "very tightly held by their Bankers and Agents." Sydney Office, Special Letters for London, 30 Sept. 1879, 162/3116, AMLF Papers, Noel Butlin Archives Centre, Australian National University (hereafter ANU). Noel Butlin discusses the consolidation; he points out that even in the 1880s many pastoral enterprises remained partnerships, although

financiers were indirectly guiding them. Butlin, *Investment in Australian Economic Development, 1861–1900* (Cambridge: Cambridge University Press, 1964), 135–47.

86 Worster, *Dust Bowl*, 87.

87 Adelman, *Frontier Development*, 64; Barbería, *Los dueños del la tierra en la Patagonia Austral*, 294–7.

88 For a summary of the 1862 and 1865 acts, see Alan Ward's indispensable book, *An Unsettled History: Treaty Claims in New Zealand Today* (Wellington: Bridget Williams Books, 1999). Although this book benefits from recent scholarship, Ward's older study of settler–Maori relations remains essential reading for the politics of justice and land; *A Show of Justice: Racial "Amalgamation" in Nineteenth Century New Zealand* (Toronto: University of Toronto Press, 1973). Note "Land and Sovereignty: Crown, Colonists, and Maori, 1840–1860," Plate 31, *New Zealand Historical Atlas* (Auckland: David Bateman, 1997).

89 Francis Dart Fenton to Donald McLean, 12 Aug. 1871, micro ms. 535, reel 52, Donald McLean Papers, Alexander Turnbull Library.

90 Ward, *An Unsettled History*, 133.

91 Bryan Gilling, "'The Queen's Sovereignty Must be Vindicated': The 1840 Rule in the Maori Land Court," *New Zealand Universities Law Review* 16 (Dec. 1994), 148.

92 Tom Brooking, "'Busting Up' the Greatest Estate of All: Liberal Maori Land Policy, 1891–1911," *New Zealand Journal of History* 26 (April 1992), 78–98; Ward, *An Unsettled History*, 149–61.

93 Leonard A. Carlson, *Indians, Bureaucrats, and the Land: The Dawes Act and the Decline of Indian Farming* (Westport, Conn.: Greenwood Press, 1981), 3–20. The ideas and influence of philanthropic assimilationists have been described in several places by Francis Paul Prucha. See, for example, *Indian Policy and the United States: Historical Essays* (Lincoln: University of Nebraska Press, 1981), 229–51. Gordon Moore, "Registers, Receivers, and Entrymen: U.S. Land Office Administration in Oklahoma Territory, 1889–1907," *Chronicles of Oklahoma* 67 (spring 1989), 56–69; *Economist* (23–29 March 2002), 33.

94 Sarah Carter, *Lost Harvests: Prairie Indian Reserve Farmers and Government Policy* (Montreal: McGill-Queen's University Press, 1990), 194–6, 200–1, 244–53.

95 Davenport provides the best concise account of the land-taking incidents in T.H.R. Davidson, *South Africa: A Modern History* (London: Macmillan, 1978), 123–83.

96 Shula Marks, *Reluctant Rebellion: The 1906–8 Disturbances in Natal* (Oxford: Clarendon Press, 1970), 120–8, quote at 122.

97 It was long thought that the company initiated the war to provide triumphs that would drive up its stock value. The more convincing

explanation relates to the bellicose spirit of whites who wished to punish the N'debele for their raids. Arthur Keppel-Jones, *Rhodes and Rhodesia: The White Conquest of Zimbabwe, 1884–1902* (Montreal: McGill-Queen's University Press, 1983), 225–61, 289–313.

98 Ibid., 367–79. The wider triumph of settler expansion in southern Africa is recounted in Deryck M. Schreuder, *The Scramble for Southern Africa, 1877–1895: The Politics of Partition Reappraised* (Cambridge: Cambridge University Press, 1980), 256–318.

99 Boers also took up land in Kenya in the first decade of the twentieth century. M.P.K. Sorrenson, *Origins of European Settlement in Kenya* (Nairobi: Oxford University Press, 1968), 229–30.

100 John Iliffe, *A Modern History of Tanganyika* (Cambridge: Cambridge University Press, 1979), 59–61.

101 F.K. Crowley, *Forrest, 1847–1918; Volume 1, 1847–91; Apprentice to the Premiership* (St Lucia: University of Queensland Press, 1971), 51–144; John Forrest, *Report on the Land Policy of Western Australia from 1829 to 1888* (Perth: Government Printer, 1889), iii–ix, Battye Library.

102 Elwood P. Lawrence, *Henry George in the British Isles* (East Lansing: Michigan State University Press, 1957), 3.

103 Henry George, *Progress and Poverty* (New York: Robert Schalkenback Foundation, 1940; Fiftieth Anniversary Edition), 347.

104 Anna George de Mille, *Henry George: Citizen of the World* (Westport, Conn.: Greenwood Press, 1972), 58–9.

105 George developed his ideas in isolation but later came to admire the Physiocrats. George, *The Science of Political Economy* (New York: Doubleday and McClure, 1898; first pub. 1897), 148–59.

106 George, "Taxation the Means," in *Our Land and Policy,* 317.

107 de Mille, *Henry George,* 65–84.

108 George, *Progress and Poverty,* 365.

109 Ibid., 404–5.

110 Ibid., 405.

111 Ibid., 436.

112 Ibid., 448.

113 Ibid., 451. For his views on city and country, see the chapter of that name in his *Social Problems* (New York: Doubleday and McClure, 1898; first pub. 1883), 234–40.

114 George, *Progress and Poverty,* 386.

115 Joseph Dana Miller, *Single Tax Year Book* (New York: Single Tax Review Publishing Company, 1917), 19–305; Lawrence, 111–83. For George's impact on the Australian Labor Party and on land tenure in the Australian Capital Territory, see Rae Else-Mitchell, *Legacies of the Nineteenth Century: Land Reformers from Melville to George* (St Lucia: University of Queensland Press, 1975), 16–22.

116 On small projects for South Australia, see Williams, *A Way of Life*, 53; for southern Alberta, see "Efforts of the Department of the Interior to Instigate the Development of Irrigation in Alberta, 1885–1919," M3743, O.S. Langman Papers, Glenbow.

117 Donald Worster, *Rivers of Empire: Water, Aridity, and the Growth of the American West* (New York: Oxford University Press, 1985), 76.

118 For an economist's history, see Ian Stone, *Canal Irrigation in British India: Perspectives on Technological Change in a Peasant Economy* (Cambridge: Cambridge University Press, 1984). On hydraulic technology in India, see Daniel R. Headrick, *The Tentacles of Progress: Technology Transfer in the Age of Imperialism, 1850–1940* (New York: Oxford University Press, 1988), 196.

119 Worster, *Rivers of Empire*, 89.

120 Horwitz, *The Transformation of American Law, 1780–1860* (Cambridge, Mass.: Harvard University Press, 1977), 34–42. Although he does not address this doctrine or several others that seemingly clogged conveyancing, Peter Karsten has written a book that indicates much more complexity in judges' decisions over issues pertaining to the evolution of a capitalist economy. In particular, he notes the importance of biblical references in decisions. *Heart versus Head: Judge-Made Law in Nineteenth Century America* (Chapel Hill: University of North Carolina Press, 1997).

121 Donald Pisani, *From the Family Farm to Agribusiness: The Irrigation Crusade in California and the West, 1850–1931* (Berkeley: University of California Press, 1984), 247.

122 Early western water law is discussed in ibid., 3–53, 191–249. Pisani attributes prior appropriation to California goldminers but notes that Mormons published water claims in newspapers. This practice resembles grazers publishing warnings about a range being closed. There is probably continuity in resource-appropriation practices. Also see Horwitz, *The Transformation of American Law*, 42–4; Worster, *Rivers of Empire*, 91–2.

123 Pisani, *From the Family Farm to Agribusiness*, 229.

124 Geoffrey Searle, *The Rush to Be Rich: A History of the Colony of Victoria, 1883–1889* (Melbourne: Melbourne University Press, 1974), 55; United States, Department of Agriculture, *Irrigation Laws of the Northwest Territories of Canada and of Wyoming* (Washington, DC: Government Printing Office, 1901), 13. "Excerpts from Commons Debates of Canada on the Subject of Irrigation in Western Canada, 1890–1935," compiled by R.E. English, M3743, O.S. Langman Papers, Glenbow.

125 Donald Pisani, "The Origins of Reclamation in the Arid West: William Ralson's Canal and the Federal Irrigation Commission of 1873," *Journal of the West* 22 (April 1983), 10.

126 Worster, *Dust Bowl*, 234–5.

127 Extracts from a Report of Hon. F.A. Tritle, in Joseph Nimmo, *Report in Regard to the Range and Ranch Cattle Business of the United States* (New York: Arno Press, 1972, reprint of 1885), Appendix No. 27, 152–3.

128 J.B. Condliffe, *The Development of Australia* (London: Free Press of Glencoe, 1964), 286–7; Noel Butlin, *Investment in Australian Economic Development, 1861–1900* (Cambridge: At the University Press, 1964), 79–80.

129 J.M. Powell, *Plains of Promise, Rivers of Destiny: Water Management and the Development of Queensland, 1824–1990* (Brisbane: Boolarong Publications, 1991), 65–78. The ALMF events were reported in Special Letters, London, 16 Jan. and 17 July 1889, 163/3117, ALMF, ANU.

130 Special Letters, London, 17 July 1889, 163/3118, 15 July 1891, 163/3118; 17 Jan. 1895, 162/3118, AMLF, ANU.

131 Butlin, *Investment in Australian Economic Development*, 80.

132 Walter Prescott Webb, *The Great Plains* (New York: Grossett & Dunlap, 1971; first pub. 1931), 334–41; Daniel Jacobus Jacobs, *Landbou en veeteelt in die Orangje-Vrystaat* (Johannesburg: Argiefjaarboek vir Suid-Afrikaanse Geskiedenis, 1969), 176. On pumping and distribution technology on the Ogallala, see John Opie, *Ogallala: Water for a Dry Land* (Lincoln: University of Nebraska Press, 1993), 70–1, 122–60. Information about the application of well-drilling and pumping technologies in the late nineteenth century is disappointingly fragmentary.

133 J.A. Alexander, *The Life of George Chaffey: A Story of Irrigation Beginnings in California and Australia* (Melbourne: Macmillan & Co., 1928), 32.

134 Ibid., 35–6.

135 Sydney Wells, *Paddle Steamers to Cornucopia: The Renmark–Mildura Experiment* (Renmark: Murray Pioneer, 1986), 35–6: unidentified clippings, Renmark Newspaper Slips, 1886–1889, 17, 25, Mitchell Library.

136 The differences are well discussed in Ian Tyrrell, *True Gardens of the Gods: Californian–Australian Environmental Reform, 1860–1930* (Berkeley: University of California Press, 1999), 126–7.

137 Deakin had been watching developments in California. Borrowing from a California bill, he drafted an act (1883) for Victoria that enabled communities to organize irrigation trusts (districts). The California legislature succeeded in passing a measure for the formation of irrigation districts only in 1887. Ibid., 123.

138 Wells, *Paddle Steamers to Cornucopia*, 175–7.

139 Jones, *Empire of Dust*, 201–2; Worster, *Rivers of Empire*, 194–7; Tyrrell, *True Gardens of the Gods*, 148–50. For the history of

irrigation in the American west, the books by Pisani, Worster, and Tyrrell are indispensable, for different reasons. Pisani offers a careful reconstruction of the law and politics of irrigation in California. Worster covers the west and weaves firm lines of analysis and argument into his narrative, suggesting that irrigation embodied a cultural urge to subdue nature and required dictatorial administration. Tyrrell puts the west in an international setting. The hazards and deferred costs of irrigation are reported by Marc Reisner, *Cadillac Desert: The American West and Its Disappearing Water* (New York: Viking, 1986).

140 A.A. den Otter, *Civilizing the West: The Galts and the Development of Western Canada* (Edmonton: University of Alberta Press, 1982), 200–1.

141 A.A. den Otter, "The Galts and Irrigation in Alberta: An Examination of the Entrepreneurial Role in Frontier Development" (paper presented to the Canadian Historical Association, June 1975), 15.

142 den Otter, *Civilizing the West*, 228–31, 305–8; *Canadian Pacific Railway Company's Irrigation Project* (Alberta, 1906), n.p., and *Canadian Pacific Railway Company's Irrigation System in Alberta* (Calgary, 1914), 7, both in Glenbow.

143 Letterhead of the Western Irrigation Association, file 97, box 2, Canada Land and Irrigation Company Papers, Glenbow.

144 Frederick Haynes Newell, *A Report on the Management of the Property of the Canada Land and Irrigation Co., Ltd.* (1917), file 269, box 25, M2389, Canada Land and Irrigation Company Papers, Glenbow.

EPILOGUE

1 The borrowing of home-country ideas and the adaptation to new locales is the subject of Thomas R. Dunlap, *Nature and the English Diaspora: Environment and History in the United States, Canada, Australia, and New Zealand* (New York: Cambridge University Press, 1999).

2 On the significance of the standing army, note David B. Ralston, *Importing the European Army: The Introduction of European Military Techniques and Institutions into the Extra-European World, 1600–1914* (Chicago: University of Chicago Press, 1990), 9–12. For the argument about the Dutch economy, see Jan de Vries and Ad van der Woude, *The First Modern Economy: Success, Failure, and Perseverance of the Dutch Economy, 1500–1815* (Cambridge: Cambridge University Press, 1997), 665–722.

3 Max Weber, *The Theory of Social and Economic Organization* trans. A.M. Henderson and Talcott Parsons (New York: Oxford University Press, 1947), 158–358; "The Rational State" in *General Economic History* trans. Frank H. Knight (New York: Greenberg, 1927), 338–51.

4 John L. Comaroff, "Foreword," in Mindie Lazarus-Black and Susan Hirsch, eds., *Contested States: Law, Hegemony, and Resistance* (New York: Routledge, 1994), xi.

5 Robert Nelson, *Public Lands and Private Rights: The Failure of Scientific Management* (Lanham: Rowman & Littlefield, 1995), 346–7. Nelson presents the economist's case for increased privatization of property rights.

6 A good discussion of how legal opinion, official policy, and settler pressure affected land allocation is found in M.P.K. Sorrenson, *Origins of European Settlement in Kenya* (Nairobi: Oxford University Press, 1968), 44–156.

7 L.P. Mair, "British Territories in Africa: Agrarian Policy in the British African Colonies," *Land Tenure Symposium: Tropical Africa – Netherlands East Indies before the Second World War* (Leiden: Universitaire Pers Leiden, 1951), 45.

8 Fredric Jameson, "Postmodernism, or the Cultural Logic of Late Capitalism," *New Left Review* no. 146 (July–Aug. 1984), 53. An update on the scope of postmodernism is offered in Hans Bertens, "The Debate on Postmodernism," in Bertens, ed., *International Postmodernism: Theory and Literary Practice* (Amsterdam: John Benjamins Publishing Company, 1997), 3–13.

9 To sample the arguments in favour of traditional tenure, see Claire Whitemore, *Land for People: Land Tenure and the Very Poor* (Oxford: Oxfam, 1981); Frank M. Mifsud, *Customary Land Law in Africa with Reference to Legislation Aimed at Adjusting Customary Tenures to the Needs of Development* (Rome: Food and Agricultural Organization of the United Nations, 1967); World Bank, *Knowledge for Development: World Development Report, 1998/9* (Oxford: World Bank, 1999), 124; James M. Broughton and K. Sarwar Lateef, "Introduction and Overview," in Broughton and Lateef, eds., *Fifty Years after Breton Woods: The Future of the IMF and the World Bank* (Washington, DC: World Bank, 1995). I am indebted to Michelle Vosburgh for her review of this literature.

10 Jameson, "Postmodernism," 66. Also note his remarks in *The Cultural Turn: Selected Writings on the Postmodern* (London: Verso, 1998), 20. Some observers place Jameson on the margins of postmodernism because of his interest in Marxism. Stanley Fish suggests that judges make a mistake if they believed that they could act freely without regard to the past. Fish, *Doing What Comes Naturally: Change, Rhetoric, and the Practice of Theory in Literary and Legal Studies* (Oxford: Clarendon Press, 1989), 361. What worries some historians about postmodernism is that its acolytes, despite their occasional remarks about the importance of context, are disinclined to delve into

archives and thus seem willing to fabricate context from fragmentary information.

11 Jameson, "Postmodernism," 78.

12 Peter Osborne, "Modernity Is a Qualitative, Not a Chronological, Category: Notes on the Dialectics of Differential Historical Time," in Francis Baker, Peter Hulme, and Margaret Iversen, eds., *Postmodernism and the Re-Reading of Modernity* (Manchester: University of Manchester Press, 1992), 23–40.

13 Steven Connor, *Postmodernist Culture: An Introduction to Theories of the Contemporary* (Cambridge: Blackwell, 1997), ix. Connor offers a good one-volume guide to the subject, while indicating where he thinks postmodernism is in danger of losing its critical acuity by overcoherence and where he believes it sustains its capacity to confound authority.

14 Fish, *Doing What Comes Naturally*, 497.

15 It would be difficult to execute such a project without historical inquiry, although Keith Jenkins alleges that epistemological predicaments prevent historical inquiry from serving any liberating movement. Historical inquiry will mount no better critique than other methods. One problem with his intimation that there can be morality without ethics or history is that his interpretation of morality would be subject to the same epistemological doubts that he levels at history and ethics. For introductions to the controversy, see Jenkins, *Why History? Ethics and Postmodernity* (London: Routledge, 1999); Keith Windschuttle, *The Killing of History: How Literary Critics and Social Theorists are Murdering our Past* (New York: Free Press, 1997). Michael Hardt and Antonio Negri in *Empire* (Cambridge, Mass.: Harvard University Press, 2000) are critical of postmodernism for a different reason. They propose that a new form of empire that insists on global modernization in all regions and all forms of human activity requires new critical skills. However, postmodernism's discourses are directed at old forms of power. *Empire*, 146.

16 Gregory Alexander's *Commodity and Propriety* is a postmodern examination of American legal thinking about property rights and society. He sees the transformation of property into a commodity occurring within a long constitutional debate. A dialectic moved property rights towards narrowing the public interest; however, his hope is that awareness of dissenting views will stimulate renewed respect for diverse ideas about property rights. Michael Hardt and Antonio Negri argue that postmodernism's playfulness deprives it of the rigour needed to criticize a new, pervasive and amorphous, world order; *Empire* (Cambridge, Mass.: Harvard University Press, 2000), 137–56. Their complex speculative discussion cannot be summarized here, but they propose that a new phase in capitalism, one lacking an imperial centre, represents a

paradigm shift. They are vague about particulars, and that makes it difficult to determine if they have overstated their case.

17 Patricia Nelson Limerick, *The Legacy of Conquest: The Unbroken Past of the American West* (New York, 1987), 31.

18 Claudia Orange, *The Treaty of Waitangi* (Wellington: Bridget Williams Books, 1987), 244.

19 Richard Bartlett, *Native Title in Australia* (Sydney: Butterworths, 2000), 16–62.

20 J.R. Miller, *Skyscrapers Hide the Heavens: A History of Indian–White Relations in Canada* (Toronto: University of Toronto Press, 2000), 249–66.

21 George C. Shattuck, *The Oneida Land Claims: A Legal History* (Syracuse, NY: Syracuse University Press, 1991); Alan van Gestel, "When Fictions Take Hostages," in James A. Clifton, ed., *The Invented Indian: Cultural Fictions and Government Policies* (New Brunswick, NJ: Transaction Publishers, 1990), 309; Francis Paul Prucha, *The Great Father: The United States and the American Indian* (Lincoln: University of Nebraska Press, 1984), 1172–9.

22 Gary D. Libecap, *Locking up the Range: Federal Land Controls and Grazing* (Cambridge, Mass.: Ballinger Publishing Company, 1981), 31–61.

23 John G. Francis and Richard Ganzel, "Introduction," in Francis and Ganzel, eds., *Western Public Lands: The Management of Natural Resources in a Time of Declining Federalism* (Totowa, NJ: Rowman & Allanheld, 1984), 20.

24 Nelson, *Public Lands and Private Rights*, 197. The history of the "sagebrush rebellion" and an estimation of its impact are covered in R. McGreggor Cawley, *Federal Land, Western Anger: The Sagebrush Rebellion and Environmental Politics* (Lawrence: University of Kansas Press, 1993). Scott Lehman presents the case against privatization in *Privatizing Public Lands* (New York: Oxford University Press, 1995), as does Gary C. Bryner in *U.S. Land and Natural Resources Policy* (Westport, Conn.: Greenwood Press, 1998), although his preference in all things is caution.

25 Debra L. Donahue, *The Western Range Revisited: Removing Livestock from Public Lands to Conserve Native Biodiversity* (Norman: University of Oklahoma Press, 1999).

26 Williams, *The American Indian*, 325.

27 Richard A. Posner, "The Law and Economics of Intellectual Property," *Daedalus* 131 (spring 2002), 5–12; James Boyle, "Fencing Off Ideas: The Enclosure and the Disappearance of the Public Domain," ibid., 13–25; Carla Hesse, "The Rise of Intellectual Property, 700 B.C.–A.D. 2000: An Idea in the Balance," ibid., 26–45.

Index

Fort Salisbury (South Africa), not
a success, 334
Fort Stanwix, Treaty of, 158–9, 190
Fort Wayne, Treaty of, 229
France, 6, 30, 37–9, 44; aristocracy and estate supervision, 22;
bureaucratic colonization, 33,
41, 44, 117, 174, 186, 403n5,
420nn28–34
freebooting, 21–2
freedom of movement, importance
of, 12, 23
freehold tenure, 4; needed to protect range land, 322
free homestead grants, 14, 17, 47,
48, 77, 94, 219, 324, 327,
453n1, 457n42, 459n63
free selection, 316, 350; abandoned, 112; Australia, 318,
455n16; versus survey/settle-
ment, 317
Free Soil Party, 66
Freidenberg, Daniel, 105
French, Peter, 271, 327, 397n100,
439n10, 446n93, 453n188
Frewen, Moreton, 325
frontiers: defined, 73; exceptional
places, 62; North America and
South Africa compared,
401n143; property rights, 18,
371; rationalized property, 72–6
frontier thesis, 17, 72–3
fur trade, 41, 44, 114, 173, 188–9,
195, 205–6, 251, 253,
437nn146–7, 419nn15–16

Gage, General Thomas, 155,
411n73
Galbraith, John S., 64, 381nn86–7,
385nn125, 129, 395n83,
406n19, 407n31, 409n44,
413n96, 414n99, 420n26,
438n146

Gallagher, John, 19–20, 25,
364nn22–3, 365n36
Gallatin, Albert, 220
Galt, Alexander, 346, 465n140
Galt, Elliott, 346, and irrigating
Canadian west, 465nn140–2
Garcia, Pedro Andrés, 60, 379n67
Gates, Paul W., 63, 64, 95, 115–16,
205, 381nn81, 83, 85, 383n108,
387n155, 391n22, 393n39,
394n62, 398n109, 411n70,
412n85, 423n76, 426n5,
436n128, 439n12, 440n14,
457n42
General Allotment Act (Dawes Act),
176, 332, 333, 417n143, 461n93
gentry, role in imperial expansion,
418n11
George, Henry, 15, 313, 319, 322,
336–40, 454n5, 456n33,
457n46, 462nn102–15; broke
with Parnell, 339; message
blurred, 338; newspaper career,
337; Progress and Poverty
(book), 338, 339, 340,
462nn103, 108–14; restoration
of land to proletariat, 337; speculation as unearned increment,
337
Georgia, sale of land, 17, 80
Germany, 6, 30, 39–40, 369n74,
402n3; German East Africa, 39–
40, 45, 335
Gibson, Arrell M., 175
Gibson, Samuel, 123
Gilfillan, Archer Butler, 295,
449n130
Gill, S.T., 127
Gipps, George, 138, 406n17,
425n98
Goa, India, 37
Goetzmann, William H., 109,
395n74